inside out

WASHINGTON

A BEST PLACES® GUIDE TO THE OUTDOORS

2ND EDITION

RON C. JUDD

SASQUATCH
BOOKS
SEATTLE

Acknowledgments

The author thanks his parents, Ron and Gloria Judd, for pushing him outside in the first place, and friend and colleague Seabury Blair Jr. for helping to keep him there. Thanks also to Sasquatch editors Kate Rogers and Justine Matthies for making it all work, and a special thanks to Jackie, for cutting through the clutter.

Second Edition
07 06 05 04 03 02 01   5 4 3 2 1

ISBN: 1-57061-274-9
ISSN: 1095-9750

Cover photo: Daphne Hougard/oi2.com
Cover design: Karen Schober
Interior design: Lynne Faulk
Composition: Patrick David Barber and Holly McGuire
Maps: GreenEye Design
Photographs on pages 29, 38, 47, 230, and 261 by Mike Siegel. Photograph on page 473 by Dan A. Nelson. All other photographs taken by the author.

Important Note: Please use common sense. No guidebook can act as a substitute for experience, careful planning, and appropriate training. There is inherent danger in all the outdoor activities described in this book, and readers must assume responsibility for their own actions and safety. Changing or unfavorable conditions in weather, roads, trails, waterways, etc. cannot be anticipated by the author or publisher, but should be considered by any outdoor participants. The author and the publisher will not be responsible for the safety of users of this guide.

The information in this edition is based on facts available at press time and is subject to change. The author and publisher welcome information conveyed by users of this book, as long as they have no financial connection with the area, guide, outfitter, organization, or establishment concerned. A report form is provided at the end of the book.

Sasquatch Books
615 Second Avenue,
Seattle, Washington 98104
(206)467-4300
www.SasquatchBooks.com
books@SasquatchBooks.com

Contents

Introduction
and How to Use
This Book

You might want to rope up for this.

Not that anything in these introductory pages is inherently dangerous; it's the stuff that follows that's cause for concern. The Washington outdoor world is a vortex: If you linger long on the edges, you'll invariably get sucked in. Given the addictive nature of jaw-dropping alpine views, miraculous ocean sunsets, and picture-perfect campsites, nobody ever really pulls himself all the way back out. You get lured by the lush greenery of the Olympic Peninsula; seduced by the stone faces, snowy heads, and flower-specked shoulders of the Cascade Mountains; or awed by the sprawling geographic wonders of the Columbia River drainage and Okanogan Highlands. The diversity of the state—really three distinct topographic regions in a single political package—surprises most newcomers and leaves even longtime residents befuddled about where to go, when, and how.

That's where *Inside Out: Washington* comes in. It's designed to be a road map, a trail-tested guide from an experienced, outdoorsy friend. Think of it as the portable, collective knowledge of an Evergreen State native who has spent a lifetime exploring the state's special nooks and outrageous crannies.

Unlike most single-sport guidebooks out there, this one was designed to offer something for *everyone*. A love of, and respect for, Washington's outdoor world is the only prerequisite. The information here is detailed enough to please specialists, but diverse enough to appeal to dabblers. It's an outdoors guide for real outdoors people: People whose choice of activities changes from season to season and decade to decade; people who love to hike and cycle, but also think they'd love to kayak; people who are equally comfortable on a sailboat and in a saddle; people young enough at heart to endure three days of remote backcountry skiing, but old enough to appreciate capping it off with a hot bath and a hot fire at a comfortable inn; and most of all, people who want to do all those things without lugging along a bookmobile full of outdoor and travel guides.

You should know up front that *Inside Out: Washington* is a guide written by a discriminating—and fickle—outdoor traveler. The structure is simple: The state is broken into nine separate geographic regions, which are then sub-divided into a total of 52 specific destinations (or chapters). Each chapter begins with an **introductory essay** about the area, its people, and its unique place in the world of Washington outdoor recreation. Next, in **Getting There,** you'll learn the best way to get to your destination and how long it will take. Then comes the meat and potatoes: The **Inside Out** section in every chapter offers detailed descriptions of the very best outdoor activities, ranked in order of prominence and appeal in that area. These activities vary across the state, but some are universal. Every Inside Out section, for example, describes campgrounds, hiking trails, picnic areas, fishing venues, cycling routes, and some form of aquatic recreation, be it boating, kayaking, rafting, or canoeing. Many sections have tips on where to view wildlife and where and when to take scenic photos. Chapters covering mountainous regions add cross-country and downhill skiing to the Inside Out activities. Dozens of specialized sports creep into the mix, from competitive kite-flying to clam-digging to long-distance horsepacking. New to the guide for this Second Edition is an "Accessible Outdoors" listing, detailing recreation sites in each area fully or partially accessible to wheelchair users—and parents pushing strollers.

All of this is complemented by an **Outside In** section, which lists Best Places reviews of local restaurants and lodgings. Every chapter then concludes with **More Information,** a list of helpful phone numbers and web pages relevant to that area. It's meant to be the best of both worlds, inside and out: the wilderness experience and advice of a Washington native and veteran outdoors writer/photographer for *The Seattle Times,* coupled with the indoor expertise of the editors of the acclaimed Best Places series.

Research for this book has dominated more than one lifetime, and would have been an onerous chore if it wasn't so much fun. In the first edition of this book, I noted that compiling this evaluation of Washington's outdoor world had been exhausting and exhilarating all at once: exhausting because there's just so much of it, and exhilarating because it introduced me to a new world of truly special wilderness places, and reacquainted me with others. The same can be said of my travels in the three years since—time I've spent following my own road map, rediscovering places I'd discovered in the past, and catching on to entirely new ones. That—along with passing it all along to you—is the fun part.

More than anything else, I hope reading this guide will do for you what creating it has done for me: reaffirmed a faith that Washington's outdoor world not only is where I want to be, but where I belong. Ropes or no ropes, I'm in too deep to turn back.

See you out there.

—*Ron C. Judd*

Washington Outdoors Primer

Most advice in this guide on what to do and where to do it is fairly self-explanatory. But it's important to keep some general tenets in mind before setting out into Washington's wild lands. Following is a general activity-by-activity overview, sprinkled with do's and don'ts and better-think-twice's. Reading it before hooking up the trailer, packing away the kids, and heading for Chewelah could save you a lot of wasted time and energy.

Camping

Washington campers are blessed and cursed all at once. They're fortunate to have a healthier-than-average number of campgrounds from which to choose. Problem is, their next door neighbors are likely to be fighting them for that last open site. Available summertime campsites are at a premium in the Evergreen State, particularly in many popular Washington State Parks. Translation: He who sets out on a Saturday in August for a weekend at Deception Pass State Park is liable to end up spending the night in the parking lot of the Oak Harbor Safeway. With Washington's population bursting at its Puget Sound seams—and camping venues not even close to keeping pace (since the first edition of this book in 1997, one new state park has opened, but countless others have cut back their hours)—only two things can leave you reasonably certain of finding a spot. One is camping off-season, a particularly attractive alternative for many RV owners, who laugh in the face of the cold and tune their satellite dishes from the Kalaloch parking lot. The other is a reservation.

Campsite reservations

Reservations are a four-letter word in Olympia, where Washington State Parks officials have struggled for years to develop a fair, efficient, cost-effective way to ensure that campers who drive from Seabeck to Spokane aren't left out in the cold, staring at a CAMPGROUND FULL sign. For many years, a select dozen of Washington's 82 state parks campgrounds operated on a mail-in reservation system. In 1996, the state took a giant step forward by joining forces with **Reservations Northwest,** a toll-free, computer-operated reservation center that books campground reservations for Washington and Oregon state parks. By calling (800) 452-5687, campers can reserve a space as far as 11 months in advance at any of 50 Washington State Parks (they're designated in this guide).

After some initial glitches (inadequate staffing and phone lines to handle the crush), Reservations Northwest has proven to be a fairly effective tool for state campers. Campsites can be reserved and paid for by credit card (a reservation fee is added; at this writing it is $6), and if the campground you seek is full for the requested dates, you'll know so immediately. Telephone operators also can steer you toward alternative campsites. Remember three things:

The **11-month advance window** is crucial. If you're looking to get a site in, say, Fort Flagler on the Fourth of July, you'd better be punching up "redial" on the preceding fourth of August.

The reservation system is in effect only from **April 1 through September 30.** All reservation campgrounds revert to first-come, first-served in the off-season. One exception is Fort Canby State Park, which takes reservations all year. (Contact the park directly in the winter months.)

Don't overlook the fact that many Washington State Parks are not on the reservation system. Sites there can still be nabbed the old-fashioned way: Show up early. Call the **State Parks information** line, (800) 233-0321, for information on campgrounds that are not part of the Reservations Northwest planning system.

An alternative is a national booking agency that handles reservations for many **U.S. Forest Service campgrounds.** A large number of Washington's 500 Forest Service campgrounds (they're designated throughout this book) can be reserved up to 240 days in advance at (877) 444-6777, or online at www.reserveusa.com. Since most of these campgrounds are smaller than state parks, they tend to book up faster. But keep in mind that most Forest Service campgrounds retain a number of non-reservable sites in each campground for first-come, first-served campers.

Just to confuse you, a completely separate reservation system is needed for summertime camping at Mount Rainier National Park. There, reservations at the park's two most popular campgrounds, Ohanapecosh and Cougar Rock, are *required* from late June through the end of Labor Day weekend. Call (800) 365-CAMP, or visit the web site at www.reservations.nps.gov.

Prices

Because campground prices change yearly, individual campsite prices are not listed with campground descriptions in this guide. Generally, however, the following rules apply.

In **Washington State Parks,** primitive campsites (no tables or fire pits) cost $5 per night; standard sites (tables and fire pits but no hookups) are $10 per night; and utility sites (tables, fire pits, sewer and water

hookups) are $15 per night. A summer surcharge is added at some popu-
lar parks.

Most **national park, state Department of Natural Resources, and
county park** campgrounds charge $6 to $14 per night for standard sites.
Add about $5 more per night for hookup sites. **Forest Service** campsites
also charge between $6 and $10 per night, but many, especially those
without piped water, are free.

Observant campers, particularly those in RVs, will notice that—with
a few exceptions—private campgrounds are not listed in this guide. The
reasoning is simple: There are far too many of them to make listings practical, and these campgrounds often change ownership, so it's difficult to
vouch for their quality or level of service. Frequent campers can supplement the campground information in this book with this author's other
campground guide, *Camping! Washington,* which gives fuller descriptions
and ratings for all Washington public campgrounds.

Hiking/Backpacking

Every hike listed in this guide includes both the distance, listed as **round-
trip mileage,** and a difficulty rating, which ranges from easy to difficult.
Easy trails are mostly level, sometimes paved grades that should be
accessible to all family members. **Difficult trails** typically have a vertical
climb ranging from 500 to 1,000 feet per mile. **Moderate trails** fall somewhere in between. Any hikes listed as **extremely difficult** typically
involve extraordinary obstacles, such as snow fields or hazardous rock or
stream crossings. The range included should please everyone, from the
most gung-ho to the most aerobically challenged. If you're new to hiking,
there's plenty of easy stuff here to gradually build up your stamina and
escort you to more difficult hikes. If you're a seasoned veteran, you'll find
an equal number of off-the-beaten track routes and long-distance backpack routes. Most of you average hikers in the middle will enjoy dabbling
in both.

Time estimates aren't included with the hikes, largely because round-
trip times vary dramatically depending on the hiker. A good way to estimate your travel time in advance is to apply the "average-hiker" rule: An
average hiker covers 2 to 2.5 miles per hour on moderate terrain. Add time
if you think you're slower than average, subtract if you know you're faster.

Gear

It's not necessary to spend hundreds of dollars to become a properly
equipped hiker. But there are some essentials. **Boots** are critical, particularly if you're venturing anywhere off the easiest, level trails. Consult with
your local outdoor-shop experts on how much boot you'll need, but do

invest in a sturdy pair of waterproof boots. We're constantly amazed at the numbers of people we see in high places clad only in tennis shoes. This is like begging for a broken bone or a sprained ankle. And with the wealth of reliable but relatively inexpensive boots on the market today, there's no excuse for not having decent footwear. Your feet will thank you for decades. **Clothing** is largely a personal choice, with necessary items fitting into the "10 essentials" category.

The **10 Essentials** list was developed long ago by The Mountaineers, a Seattle-based mountaineering group, and other frequent mountain visitors, but it still stands as the definitive list of must-have survival gear for hikers. No matter where you go—and, if you're hiking in mountainous terrain, no matter when—it's important to carry this stuff. (It needn't weigh you down nor break the bank. Most of the gear is small enough to fit in a compact stuff sack, and much of it can be picked up for low cost at variety stores or used-gear shops.) These items, essentially the minimal equipment you need to survive a night in the woods or to find your way out if you lose the trail, have saved many a life in the Washington backcountry. While they're not necessary for some of the trails designated as "easy" in this guide, they should be carried—always—on longer hikes rated "moderate" or "difficult." Most experienced canoeists, kayakers, backcountry skiers, and other recreationalists carry similar supply caches. The list:

- **Map.** Get a good topographic map, and learn how to use it. For hiking, the 7.5- or 15-minute series USGS topographic maps are good, but hiker-designed specialty maps, such as those from Green Trails, Inc., are easier to follow.

- **Compass.** Use one preferably with a navigational sight.

- **Flashlight** or **headlamp.** Always carry spare batteries and a bulb. Headlamps are more versatile, because they allow hands-free walking or climbing, and many headlamps come with an extra bulb already inside the casing.

- **Extra food.** Energy bars or other compact, high-energy snacks are good.

- **Extra clothing.** A warm fleece or wool pullover, rain- and windshell and pants, fleece or wool gloves, and a warm hat are all Northwest essentials, any time of the year.

- **Sunglasses.** Not just for looks, but to avoid snowblindness in high altitudes.

- **First-aid kit.** Commercially pre-packaged kits from manufacturers such as Outdoor Research are excellent, but be sure to check medicine expiration dates annually and add any specific drugs you might need, for instance bee-sting medication if you're allergic.

- **Pocket knife.** Your basic Swiss Army knife is an indispensable tool.
- **Matches.** Put them in a waterproof cylinder, and/or carry a cigarette lighter, which weighs practically nothing and lights even when wet.
- **Fire starter.** Commercially packaged fire pellets are good. A candle can be even better.

I usually suggest carrying a couple additional items. One obvious one is a **water bottle,** filled before you leave to avoid risking giardiasis from drinking stream water. **Sunscreen** and **bug repellent** are also "must haves" in our packs.

Other items that come in handy include a reflective **space blanket,** which can make long nights in exposed places far more comfortable. Get a sturdy one, and in a pinch it can be rigged with **parachute cord** (another essential!) into a decent weather shelter. A collapsible **walking stick** can be indispensable: It takes the load off on steep downhill stretches, makes impossible stream crossings possible, and even can be used to self-arrest on unplanned snow field slides. (Note, however, that it's no substitute for an **ice ax,** which is a necessary item for trips involving snow field crossings.) The walking stick also makes a grand center post for that emergency space-blanket tent condo. But if you pack only one additional "essential," make it a **candle.** Ounce for ounce, it's one of the best survival tools you can carry.

Permits

When the first edition of this guide went to press in 1997, very few Washington hiking trails required prior planning for permits and reservations. Not true today. The vast majority of hikes in this book that begin on U.S. Forest Service land now require a parking pass, called the Northwest Forest Pass, at trailhead parking areas. The pass, which at this writing costs $5 per day or $30 annually, is available from ranger stations, many private vendors, online at www.naturenw.org, or by calling (800) 270-7504. National Parks and the Mount St. Helens National Volcanic Monument also require trail passes. See those chapters for details.

Call first

A final word to the hiking wise: Do yourself a favor and call the nearest ranger district or national park office before leaving for your hike. Washed-out roads, wildfires, rogue animals, and other acts of nature often make trails inaccessible. Increasingly, too, limited-number permit systems are creeping into the Washington hiking equation, especially in areas such as the Alpine Lakes Wilderness. The only way to be sure you'll get where you want to go is to call first. Ranger district phone numbers are listed along with all the hikes in this guide. Use them.

A good source for general trail information is the Washington Trails Association's *Signpost* magazine and the organization's web site, www.wta.org. Another good general information source is the **Outdoor Recreation Information Center** in Seattle, (206) 470-4060, which dispenses information about all Washington national forests and national parks. It's located upstairs in the Seattle REI store.

Biking

Biking in this guide is divided fairly equally between **road cycling** routes and **mountain biking,** largely based on the physical character of each particular region. In most cases, only a few possible cycle routes are suggested. Most of these have multiple variations and can be made either shorter or longer by adding or subtracting some road-legs. A good map guide showing small, rural roads, such as the *Washington State Atlas & Gazeteer* (or a regional U.S. Forest Service map, if you're on a mountain bike), can be an indispensable tool for cyclists.

Specific mountain-bike roads and trails are also suggested for many destinations. But they rarely represent the net total of routes available to the creative mountain biker. Because **restrictions** vary dramatically according to jurisdiction, it's important to call the information numbers listed in each chapter to inquire about paths. Many new trails and roads are opening—and closing—to mountain bikers every year as land managers seek a balance between foot and wheeled use of wild areas.

It's important to note that mountain bikes remain illegal on the vast majority of hiking trails in Washington state. Bicycles are forbidden on nearly all national park trails, in all federal wilderness areas, and on many non-wilderness Forest Service trails. Heed these restrictions: Failure to do so will only fan the fire of the handful of hikers who'd like to see mountain bikers banned from *all* trails. On the other hand, fat-tire cyclists will find a wealth of opportunities on designated dual-use trails, as well as on roads managed by the Forest Service, the state Department of Natural Resources, and the federal Bureau of Land Management. East-slope Cascade areas—such as the Wenatchee National Forest, where many trails are open to motorcycles, offer the greatest percentage of trails open to mountain bikes.

In many sections of this guide, cycle rental and repair shops are listed for visitors who didn't bring a bike, but are itching to see the countryside from the saddle. Cycling can be an amazingly productive way to tour many of the regions in this guide. You'll see much more from a bicycle than the car, and wildlife sightings increase immeasurably for cyclists. Whichever cycling speed and style you choose, **wear a helmet.**

Kayaking/Canoeing

Paddle venues in this book are listed for nearly every locale, with an eye toward difficulty and scenery. You're the best judge of your own paddling experience and ability, so it's up to you to decide if a particular waterway is within your means. **Canoe routes** listed here are almost exclusively in lakes or other flat water; all, of course, should be equally enjoyable to the sea kayaker. **Sea kayaking** routes and destinations are described in general terms only, based on the experiences of local kayakers and frequent visitors.

That's not the only information you'll need before setting out on a trek, particularly in an open saltwater area. Wise kayakers will consult maps, tide charts, and other resources before putting paddle to untested waters. Another option is to make an initial visit to a new area with an experienced guide, many of whom are listed in this book.

Beginning kayakers, of course, should seek expert advice and take a lesson or two before setting out on their own. Western Washington is blessed with a large number of kayak guide services and schools, many of which, again, are listed in this book. (See particularly the Greater Seattle chapter for information on beginning kayaking courses and rentals.) Unlike many water sports, however, sea kayaking is one that should not scare away the interested newcomer. With the proper training, it's a safe, relaxing sport—one any beginner can pick up in a day.

Once you're ready to head out on your own, it's hard to imagine a sea-kayak playground as rich as the one in our backyard. Puget Sound is packed with quiet coves, protected bays, and scenic islands—all the ingredients for a memorable waterborne single- or multi-day trip. Prime day-trip waters are identified in the Kayaking sections of this guide. Stronger paddlers can link one or more (or all) of the Puget Sound sections by embarking on the **Cascadia Marine Trail,** a unique kayaking and camping circuit stretching 150 miles from Olympia to the San Juan Islands, the second-longest marine trail in the country. Cascadia began with 20 official stopover points, most of them at existing state parks or undeveloped state Department of Natural Resources beaches. The list since has grown to more than 50 campsites, and trail backers, led by the Washington Water Trails Association, hope to boost the number to 200 by the year 2000. That would leave paddlers with a campsite every 5 to 8 miles, running the gamut from swampy mudflats to cozy B&Bs. Most of the current Cascadia stopover points are noted in either the Beaches or Kayaking sections of this guide. For Cascadia maps, annual permits, and volunteer information, contact Washington State Parks, (800) 233-0321, or the Washington Water Trails Association, (206) 545-9161; www.wwta.org.

Fast-action **whitewater kayakers** already know their favorite spots, but we've included a full range of them in this guide, all across the state. Many "runnable" sections of Washington rivers are described in this guide, with general whitewater ratings (Class I to Class V) for notable river obstacles. In many cases, these descriptions are also applicable to whitewater rafting (see below). Whitewater kayakers should never attempt new waters, particularly those rated Class III or higher, without expert help.

Rafting

Rafting is a very popular sport in Washington, drawing some 40,000 customers a year to commercial rafting guide services. This guide contains descriptions of dozens of whitewater venues visited each year by rafters, including advice on when the rivers are best run. It does not contain specific guide service recommendations, for a variety of reasons. The primary reason is that commercial whitewater rafting is *not* regulated by the State of Washington. Any raft guide with proof of insurance and a raft can become a licensed guide, so vouching for the quality of any given raft service can be risky business. However, Washington's rafting industry in general has an excellent safety record, and the vast majority of raft outfitters are staffed by well-trained professionals. Still, it's important for the customer to ask specific questions before booking a trip: How long has the guide been in business? Do all guides escorting the float have a similar level of experience? Does the company keep log books to prove it? Are all rafters issued protective helmets and wetsuits? Use your judgment. The best advice is to seek referrals from the Forest Service Ranger District or other managing agency under whose jurisdiction the river falls. In many cases, Forest Service officials work directly with outfitters in setting individual standards and safety requirements for specific rivers. We've included phone numbers specifically for that purpose throughout this guide.

Fishing

Perhaps nowhere is Washington's outdoor-recreation diversity better illustrated than in its fisheries, which are literally all over the map. You can catch anything from a 250-pound white sturgeon to a thumb-sized bullhead in Washington waters, although figuring out which waterways are open, when, and to whom, can be downright befuddling. In these pages we've offered hundreds of suggestions for local fishing venues, including what you'll catch there, how to pursue it, and generally when. Note the "generally." State fishing regulations change—and in the case of salt water fishing, seemingly become more Byzantine—every year. Many special regulations are placed on fisheries, particularly in the Pacific Ocean and Puget Sound, where fish managers are struggling to save near-extinct salmon and steelhead stocks while protecting traditional sport fisheries.

Given all that upheaval, what we offer in this guide is primarily the "where" and "how" of Washington fishing. To get the only reliable word on "when," it's crucial to pick up a copy of the state Department of Fish and Wildlife's annual **Sport Fishing Rules** pamphlet, which lays out seasons for all species and all waterways in the state. The guide, available free in local outdoor shops each spring, has full details on seasons, catch limits, species identification, special fisheries, and—of utmost importance—licensing. Get the pamphlet and use it. Most of the same information can be found on the State Fish and Wildlife Department's Web site, www.wa.gov/wdfw. Of course, if you're like many people and can't make heads or tails of the constantly expanding regulations, you can always call a local expert and ask. Wherever possible, we've listed such contact numbers in the Fishing section for each area.

Wildlife Watching

One feature of this guidebook we think will appeal to almost everyone is the Wildlife Watching listings, which give tips on what sorts of creatures roam each area of the state and how best to find and view them. In spite of its rapid suburbanization, Washington is home to an astonishing array of creatures, from the banana slug to the moose. Most listings include the best seasons for viewing. What they don't include is this common-sense admonition: For your sake and theirs, **don't approach wild animals** you might encounter in a wildlife-watching zone or elsewhere. Large mammals—such as elk, moose and, of course, bear—can be dangerous. And you can be dangerous to them. Animals that become habituated to humans, whether through feeding or just frequent contact, often develop into "problem wildlife" cases in Washington state. Admire them, but respect them. Keep your distance.

Boating/Sailing

We didn't become one of the most boat-happy states in the nation by sitting around on dry land and watching the dust blow by. When it comes to boating, we are where we live, and for most of us that's somewhere near a major waterway. Included in nearly every section of this guide are descriptions and locations of boat launches, marine-supply outlets, marinas, beachside moorage floats, and other boating facilities. These are most heavily concentrated in the Puget Sound section. Water lovers who don't have their own craft (yet) are far from out of luck. On many state waterways described in this guide, small boats (or big, huge boats, if you're looking to cruise the San Juans) are available for charter, either on your own or with a complimentary skipper. This information occasionally is combined with descriptions of fishing or kayaking venues.

Climbing

Individual approaches to rock pitches in the Cascades are best left to experts, but general descriptions of the state's most popular rock-climbing venues are included in this guide, particularly in the Leavenworth and the Icicle Valley and Snoqualmie Pass Corridor chapters. You'll also find general mountaineering information in many of the Cascade Mountain sections, as well as specific details for those interested in summit attempts on major peaks, such as Mounts Rainier, St. Helens, Baker, Adams, and Olympus. Consult those sections of this guide for more information.

Skiing/Snowplay

I've often said that the best way to survive a wet, dark Washington winter is to get out in it and participate in the weather. Toward that end, this guidebook contains descriptions of every organized downhill and cross-country skiing venue in the state, and a fair number of unorganized ones. All 10 of the state's downhill ski areas—Mount Baker, Crystal Mountain, the Summit at Snoqualmie, Stevens Pass, White Pass, 49 Degrees North, Loup Loup, Mount Spokane and Ski Bluewood—are profiled, as are all of the state's 50-plus Sno-Parks for cross-country skiers, snowshoers, and snowmobilers.

Seasons

Washington's downhill ski season typically begins in late November or early December and continues through the first week of April. Cross-country and backcountry telemark skiers begin earlier (often October, at high elevations) and stay longer (through May, in the high country). And intrepid skiers and snowshoers can get a taste of their addiction literally all year long on Mount Rainier and other high Cascade peaks.

Downhill

The greater Seattle area is home to the second highest number of skiers-per-capita in the nation (behind only Denver). The smarter ones get their start by taking lessons, which can save years of wasted effort and painful bruises. Washington is blessed with dozens of quality ski schools; every major ski area has at least one. Call the mountain information numbers listed in each section for ski-school referrals. The four singly owned ski areas at The Summit at Snoqualmite are home to the bulk of the state's ski schools, largely because the mountain is only 45 minutes east of Seattle on Interstate 90. Intermediate skiers can find more than enough challenging terrain in Washington, particularly at the big, wide-open ski areas such as White Pass, Crystal Mountain, Stevens Pass, and Mount Baker. And even the gutsiest experts can test their mettle on black-diamond pitches at Baker, Alpental (The Summit), and the backcountry areas of Crystal Mountain.

Cross-Country

If downhill skiing disagrees with your knees or sensibilities, don't overlook cross-country skiing, which is a great way to exercise and shake the winter blahs during the cold months. Nordic skiing is easy to learn (beginners can pick up skiing on groomed, flat tracks in about an hour), relatively inexpensive, and very easy to access. **Washington Sno-Parks,** plowed parking lots, and (sometimes) groomed trails maintained by Washington State Parks, are one of the best recreation values in the Northwest. A season pass to all 50 costs only $20 per vehicle—about half the cost of a single day's lift ticket at many major downhill resorts. Surcharges are added at some areas with grooming. Cross-country skiing is one of the best ways to visit alpine backcountry areas in the wintertime, when many take on a peaceful, silent, almost heavenly presence. Beginners can rent gear at any Seattle-area ski shop, pick out a groomed trail with an "easy" rating, and have at it.

It's safe, fun, and an uncommonly fresh breath of air in our long, often insufferably wet winter months. State Sno-Park information is found throughout the guide, but concentrated most heavily in the Snoqualmie Pass Corridor, Stevens Pass Corridor, Leavenworth and the Icicle Valley, Okanogan Highlands and Sherman Pass, Mount Rainier National Park, and Mount St. Helens chapters.

More advanced levels of cross-country skiing can be dangerous, however, particularly for expert Nordic skiers who venture out-of-bounds into the unpatrolled Cascade or Olympic mountain areas. **Avalanche danger** is a constant companion in Washington's winter backcountry. Skiers should check avalanche conditions by calling a local ranger district or the Northwest Avalanche Hotline, (206) 526-6677.

Snowshoeing

Snowshoeing is making a strong comeback in Washington, mostly because it is, bar none, the easiest winter sport to learn, and a grand way for families to enjoy the wonders of the winter outdoors. This edition of *Inside Out: Washington* includes greatly expanded snowshoe-trail descriptions, ranging from pancake-flat beginner tracks at Snoqualmie Summit to serious backcountry routes in Mount Rainier National Park. Also, while tromping across ski trails in snowshoes is a certified no-no, most of the Sno-Parks listed herein are good starting points for backcountry jaunts near ski trails.

Inner-tubing/Snowplay

Lest we forget, entire generations of Washingtonians have received their first taste of winter seat-first, riding an inner-tube at obscene speeds down an icy hill. We've tried to identify the state's maintained, safe-and-sane tubing courses throughout the guide. See particularly the Mount Rainier National Park, Snoqualmie Pass Corridor, and Port Angeles and Hurricane Ridge chapters.

Mountain passes

A final word to winter-sport revelers: Traveling to most of these venues can be risky business when snowstorms blanket mountain passes, as they do more often than not in the winter. Roads can be very hazardous, as can other drivers, many of whom, no matter how long they live in Washington, never seem to really catch on to the art of snow driving. Always carry tire chains, chain tighteners, warm boots, gloves and a hat, and other snow gear when you're headed over a mountain pass. A collapsible snow shovel is a good idea, too. It can make installing chains much easier when the snow is really dumping and there's no such thing as bare ground, anywhere. Mountain-pass road information can be obtained by calling toll-free **(888) SNO-INFO;** www.wsdot.wa.gov/sno-info. Go slow, and for heaven's sake, ease off the brakes.

Windsurfing/Surfing

These two sports are picking up speed fast in Washington, and we've sought to identify reliable venues for both. Washington's coast, believe it or not, is increasingly dotted by wet-suited surfboard riders who congregate in the greatest numbers at Westport on the Southwest ocean coast. See the Grays Harbor: Westport and Ocean Shores chapter for details.

Windsurfing is popular statewide (any place equipped with long stretches of reasonably flat water and semi-reliable winds will do). But the Columbia River Gorge continues to lead the Northwest—indeed the world—in boardsailers per capita. The Gorge windsurfing culture is centered in Hood River, Oregon—a short ride as the board sails from Washington's south coast. Many of the hottest windsurfing sites, though, are actually on the Washington side. See the Bridge of the Gods, White Salmon and Bingen, and Goldendale and Maryhill chapters for full details.

Accessible Outdoors

New to every chapter of this second edition is a listing of outdoor-recreation sites accessible to **wheelchairs.** These listings, drawn largely from a State of Washington database of outdoor sites meeting accessibility criteria established by the Americans with Disabilities Act, are popular not only among outdoor lovers with disabilities, but families with small children, who often travel with **strollers** or other wheeled vehicles. A couple definitions: The terms "accessible" and "barrier-free" mean the facility is connected with barrier-free routes of travel to a parking area. Note that these sites might not be accessible to all people with disabilities; if in doubt, call the contact numbers listed under More Information. Other sites are described as "useable," which means the facility allows significant access, but some people might need assistance entering or exiting.

Disclaimer

These pages are filled with the best, most reliable, most up-to-date information on Washington outdoor-recreation sites available at press time. But we can't be everywhere at all times (or even part of the time, for that matter). Washington's road, river, trail, campground, and water conditions can change in the blink of an eye or the spark of a lightning storm. That means any trail, paddle route, road, or other site described as safe and passable in this guide could turn miserable and deadly under the wrong set of circumstances. Risk is inherent in each and every activity described herein. Much of it can be minimized by knowledge and preparation. But risk can never be eliminated, and you assume it every time you head outdoors.

That is by no means an admonition to stay in. To the contrary. Go out, but go prepared. We've done our best to arm you with basic information in this guide, but it should be a starting point, not an end. Excellent books, classes, and seminars on wilderness safety, first aid, mountaineering, water safety, boating rules, and other outdoor-oriented topics are widely available (and sometimes free) in most communities in Washington State. Take advantage of them.

Finally, a plea for kindness to the lands that are the focus of all this activity. Washington is richly blessed, one of the most scenic places in the world. Its outdoor-recreation sites also are among the most heavily used and abused in the United States, thanks to burgeoning population growth and a flood of interest in outdoor lifestyles. We cannot, in good conscience, send you out the door without asking you to remember to be a good steward. Don't trash campgrounds or backcountry camps. Keep streams clean. Pack out all your litter and a little of someone else's. Play by the rules—and don't hesitate to impose them on someone else. A lot of people love the land you're hiking through, skiing over, paddling across, and sailing into. Treat it well, and it'll do the same for you.

About Best Places® Guidebooks

The restaurant and lodging reviews in this book are condensed from Best Places guidebooks. The Best Places series is unique in the sense that each guide is written by and for locals, and is therefore coveted by travelers. The best places in the region are the ones that denizens favor: establishments of good value, often independently owned, touched with local history, run by lively individuals, and graced with natural beauty. Best Places reviews are completely independent: no advertisers, no sponsors, no favors.

All evaluations are based on numerous reports from local and traveling inspectors. Best Places writers do not identify themselves when they review an establishment, and they accept no free meals, accommodations, or any other services. Every place featured in this book is recommended.

Stars

Restaurants and lodgings are rated on a scale of zero to four stars, based on uniqueness, loyalty of local clientele, performance measured against goals, excellence of cooking, value, and professionalism of service. Reviews are listed alphabetically.

★★★★	The very best in the region
★★★	Distinguished; many outstanding features
★★	Excellent; some wonderful qualities
★	A good place
no stars	Worth knowing about, if nearby

Price Range

Prices are subject to change. Contact the establishment directly to verify.

$$$$	Very expensive (more than $100 for dinner for two; more than $200 for one night's lodgings for two)
$$$	Expensive (between $65 and $100 for dinner for two; between $120 and $200 for one night's lodgings for two)
$$	Moderate (between $35 and $65 for dinner for two; between $75 and $120 for one night's lodgings for two)
$	Inexpensive (less than $35 for dinner for two; less than $75 for one night's lodgings for two)

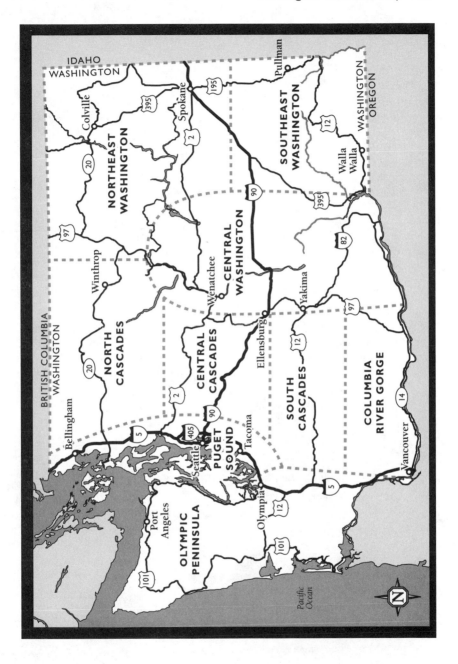

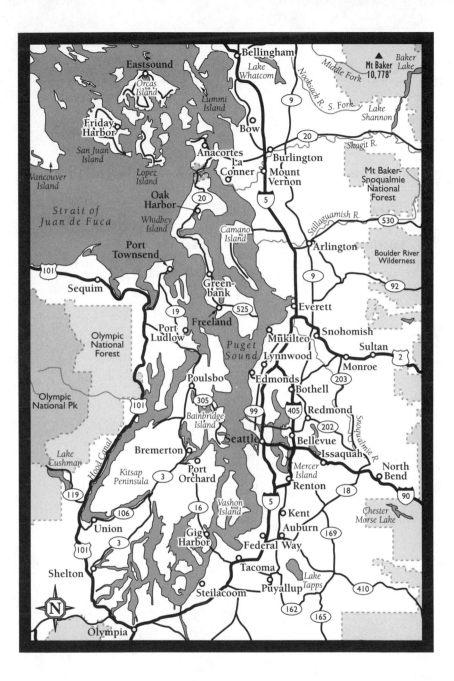

Puget Sound

Puget Sound

Bellingham
and Lummi Island

From Blaine south to Clayton Beach on Chuckanut Drive, west to Lummi Island, and east to Lake Whatcom, including Larrabee and Birch Bay State Parks, Semiahmoo Bay, Bellingham Bay, Lake Whatcom, the lower Nooksack River, and the Interurban Trail.

The moose had good taste. Not too long ago, a full-grown Bullwinkle wandered down from the Canadian north, following Interstate 5 to Bellingham, where it took up residence in the woods of Sehome Hill, in the heart of town. It's easy to see why the beast was confused. Around Bellingham, everything is a lot more like it used to be. Or ought to be, if a passion for outdoor frolicking in clean, uncrowded air, water, and forests happens to be chugging through your veins. From Interstate 5, the Bellingham area may look (and occasionally even smell) like another Everett. But not far off the freeway, the city resting on the banks of the Nooksack River in the shadow of Mount Baker is an undiscovered outdoor treasure trove. This region is well stocked with every conceivable ingredient for outdoor nirvana soup: abundant fresh and salt water, world-class alpine peaks, sprawling forestlands.

So how are Bellingham's parks, trails, shorelines, and rivers better than others around Puget Sound? For starters, you can still get to them. And once there, your chances for sunset solitude are much higher here than in most Puget Sound areas farther south. Bellingham, a progressive city of 52,000 heavy industrial (pulp mill, oil refinery) workers, university students and teachers, artists, farmers, retired draft dodgers, and high-tech workers, still hasn't spilled too far over its own edges. And locals have an unusual, refreshing attitude about what's inside them. This is a community very much in touch with its natural beauty. Support for parks, natural areas, and outdoor recreation is a core value.

It's no wonder. The region's sheer physical beauty—notwithstanding the occasional refinery explosion or pipeline blowout—is perhaps unmatched among the Northwest's smaller cities: secluded saltwater coves and islands on one side, glacier-draped mountains on the other, forest all around. A healthy slate of public facilities takes full advantage of that. Waterfront parks developed and maintained here by Bellingham, Whatcom County, and Washington State Parks are among the best in the Northwest, providing unrivaled boating, kayaking, hiking, picnicking, and wildlife-watching access.

The moose, which ultimately met an untimely death in an encounter with a car, wasn't the only soul to take a quick sniff around Bellingham and decide to set up camp. Many people venture to Bellingham for a day of kayaking Lummi Island (the most northeasterly island in the San Juan Archipelago) or hiking at Larrabee State Park, and just flat out disappear. They leave behind Metro bus passes, cellular phones, therapist's appointments, and a familiar, six-word epitaph: "Went to Bellingham. Never came back."

Getting There

Bellingham is an easy 90-minute freeway commute from the Seattle area. Take Interstate 5 north to exit 250 (Fairhaven area/Chuckanut Drive) or exit 253 (Downtown/Lake Whatcom). To reach Lummi Island, continue north on I-5 to exit 260, following Slater Road about 3 miles west. Turn left (southwest) on Haxton Way, and follow it about 7 miles south to the Lummi Island ferry, (360) 758-2190; www.lummi-island.com/ferry.htm. The Whatcom Chief *sails from Gooseberry Point at least every hour (more often on weekdays), and the crossing takes about 6 minutes.*

inside out

Beaches/Parks

Fresh- and saltwater shorelines make the Bellingham area shine, literally and figuratively. A slew of city, county, and state parks offer excellent access to waterfront areas that provide grand picnicking, strolling, swimming, windsurfing, class-skipping, and dog- or Frisbee-chasing all year long. Some favorites:

Larrabee State Park, 7 miles south of town on Chuckanut Drive, is the oldest and among the most diverse in Washington's well-stocked parks arsenal. From the park's main day-use area, a trail (short, easy enough for

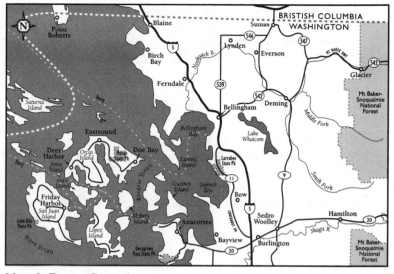

North Puget Sound

kids) leads to 3,600 feet of mostly flat, sandy saltwater beaches on Samish Bay. A half mile farther south on Chuckanut Drive, a newish Department of Natural Resources parking area provides access to another gentle (kid-friendly, mountain-bike accessible) trail, which leads about a half mile downhill to equally nice (and usually less crowded) **Clayton Beach.**

Nearby, just outside city limits, scenic, steep-walled **Teddy Bear Cove** is reached by lurching down a quite steep trail from Chuckanut Drive. The secluded cove has 300 yards of pleasant saltwater beach, more often than not sprawled upon by sun worshippers. At this beach, clothing is optional, gaping frowned upon.

In town, **Boulevard Park,** at State Street and Bayview Drive, is a delightful 14-acre spread on Bellingham Bay in the heart of the city. It's close enough to the unsightly Georgia Pacific operation to smell the plant's warm-tuna breath, but even that tends to fade into obscurity in this peaceful spot. The park has a half mile of beachfront trail (paved, in-line-skate friendly), a boat dock, and picnic shelters, and has become a local windsurfer hangout. Likewise at small-but-memorable **Marine Park,** tucked behind an industrial area at the foot of Harris Street near the Alaska Ferry terminal in the Fairhaven district. Windsurfers will find the beach riprap a bit harsh on the neoprene, but it's a grand place to sit on a bench under the picnic shelter and down a quad-jammer from Tony's Coffee, just up the street.

East of town, 1,000-acre **Lake Padden Park** on Samish Way is a noted swimming, sunbathing, and windsurfing venue (also Fishing, see below), with a nice trail all the way around the lake. Also on the eastside, **Bloedel Donovan Park** (follow Lake Whatcom Boulevard east from exit 253) has a nice Lake Whatcom swimming area that's supervised from June through September.

South of the city, Whatcom County's 39-acre **Samish Park** on Lake Samish Drive (take I-5 exit 246) has a beautiful terraced picnic area, hiking trails, a playground, and 1,500 feet of beach for swimming. Rowboats and canoes are rented in the summer.

On steep-banked Lummi Island, many of the best beaches are accessible only by boat or kayak. Most are Department of Natural Resources sites on the island's east side. One beach accessible by trail (staircase, actually) is **DNR Beach 224,** which extends north about 100 yards from the ferry landing. Park at the landing and walk north along the road to a viewing platform, where stairs lead down.

Farther north, **Birch Bay State Park,** near the Canadian border on Helweg Road (about a 30-minute drive from Bellingham), offers good waterfront access to the saltwater beaches of the Strait of Georgia. Clamming and general beach-combing are popular here. Cinch down your hood: the beach area is gusty enough to be a hot kite-flying venue. Amid the many resort trappings at Semiahmoo is **Semiahmoo Park,** a 300-acre county facility with a mile and a half of gorgeous, flat beach and a mile-long sand spit (see Wildlife Watching, below). It's built on the former site of one of the massive salmon canneries once located here. An interpretive center detailing the once-thriving salmon canning business, a gift shop, and a museum are all that's left of Alaska Packer's Cannery today. Take I-5 exit 270, head west, and follow signs about 7 miles.

Boating/Sailing

The choices are rich in Bellingham, which has been a port longer than it's been a city. The main attraction is the downtown Squalicum Marina (central waterfront; (360) 676-2542), a lovely, recently revamped area with **public moorage** (free for the first 24 hours) and a full range of **marine services.** The complex has a four-lane boat launch, a mall with public rest rooms, showers, shopping, and restaurants, plus a nice public park.

From here, landlubbers can take to sea on numerous daylong **wildlife sight-seeing tours** of the nearby San Juan Islands. Several charter services are open here year-round. The San Juan Islands Shuttle Express, (888) 373-8522; www.orcawhales.com, offers similar daily services (from late May to late September) from the Bellingham Cruise Center in Old Fairhaven. It departs daily at 9:15am and puts you in Friday Harbor at

A family enjoys a sunny day at Clayton Beach, off Chuckanut Drive

11:30, where you can choose between a 4.5-hour shore visit or lunch and a 3-hour whale-watching cruise. The boat leaves Friday Harbor at 4pm and returns to Bellingham by 6:15. Rates: $33 round-trip for adults (summer 2000), more for the added whale cruise. A similar service is offered by Victoria–San Juan Cruises; (800) 443-4552; www.whales.com. And, of course, you can steam your way all the way **up to Alaska** from the same dock, via the Alaska Marine Highway System: (800) 642-0066; www.state.ak.us/ferry.

Boat owners who'd rather do it on their own can put in at Squalicum's grand boat launch, which has ample parking. But other **public boat ramps** are found at Harris Avenue, near the Bellingham Cruise Center in Old Fairhaven, at Larrabee State Park (see Beaches/Parks, above), and at Legoe Bay, on the northwest side of Lummi Island. Avoid the latter one in bad weather; it's rather exposed. In addition, a **launch hoist** is available at Gooseberry Point, near the Lummi Island ferry landing.

Shorelines, secluded coves, and islands around Bellingham Bay are ripe for boat exploration. Favorites include **Inati Bay** on the southeast side of Lummi Island (two mooring buoys, picnic facilities) and nearby **DNR Beaches 223, 223A,** and **223B,** all of which have sandy landings. Most other DNR beaches on Lummi Island are rocky, some of them very hazardous for all but kayakers.

Many sailors use Squalicum Marina as a launching point for ventures into the heavily touristed San Juan Islands, but other small, lesser-known islands in that chain are just offshore from Bellingham and make nice day trips by boat. **Eliza, Vendovi,** and **Sinclair Islands** ring the southern end of Lummi. The largest and westernmost, Sinclair, has a public dock and beach access on the south end. Tiny Vendovi has public tidelands access all the way around, below the high-tide line. Uplands are private, but some nice coves await boaters in small craft. Eliza, the closest to town, isn't well suited for beach landings and is mostly private land.

Sea Kayaking/Canoeing

Most of the waterfront parks listed above under Beaches/Parks make fine small-craft launching points in both fresh and salt water, but there are some standouts. **Larrabee State Park**'s boat launch area in Wildcat Cove is a very secluded, all-weather launch site for kayaks, canoes, and small craft. The smooth, vertical rock walls stretching into the waters of Chuckanut and Samish Bays make for great half-day kayak trips.

Lummi Island's many secluded DNR beaches also make fine kayak destinations. One of them, **Lummi Island Recreation Site,** near Reil Harbor on the southeast side of the island, is a designated beachside campsite for the state's **Cascadia Marine Trail** (a state-managed water trail including campsites from Olympia to Vancouver, British Columbia; (206) 545-9161). Note: No running water.

If you're looking for a guided sea kayak tour in the area, contact Moondance Sea Kayaking Adventures, (360) 738-7664; Pacific Water

Sports in Sea-Tac also leads guided tours of the Chuckanut Bay area, departing from Larrabee; (800) 934-6216; www.pswkayaks.com. For canoe and kayak rentals, see Bellingham Boat Rental at Bloedel Donovan Park, (360) 676-1363, or The Great Adventure at the Cruise Terminal in Fairhaven; (360) 733-5888. Renaissance Adventure Guides on Lummi Island runs summertime San Juan kayak tours, (360) 758-2145; www.raguides.com. For windsurfing, water skis, and the like, contact Washington Wind Sports, 501 Harris; (360) 676-1146.

Inland, **Lake Padden** and **Lake Whatcom** are good year-round paddle venues, and the usually calm waters of **Lake Samish** south of town are plied very, very early every day by Western Washington University's crews.

Camping

The primary camping venue here is the aforementioned **Larrabee State Park,** which has 87 campsites (26 with full hookups; RVs to 60 feet). Campsites, renovated in 1997, are situated in tall (some old-growth) fir, madrona, and maple trees, and don't have water views. The tent sites offer decent privacy, and 8 walk-in sites are favored by cyclists. All sites are pleasantly cool in the summer, but can be dark and dreary in bad weather. Larrabee is open all year. Campsites can be reserved up to 11 months in advance by calling Reservations Northwest, (800) 452-5687. *7 miles south of Bellingham on Chuckanut Dr; (360) 676-2093 or (800) 233-0321.*

Equally popular, although a 30-minute drive north, is **Birch Bay State Park** (see Beaches/Parks, above), which has 167 sites (20 with water/electrical hookups; RVs of any length) and a trailer dump facility. This camping area was in use for centuries by local Semiahmoo, Lummi, and Nooksack tribal members, who came here for the same reasons you might: a wealth of open saltwater shoreline. Clamming, sunbathing, general beach-combing, and kite-flying are the chief activities here. This is an extremely popular park in the summer, drawing large crowds from both sides of the border. Reservations are recommended. Birch Bay is open all year. Sites can be reserved up to 11 months in advance by calling Reservations Northwest, (800) 452-5687. *Follow signs west from I-5 exit 270; (360) 664-8112 or (800) 233-0321.*

A couple more-remote options: Department of Natural Resources sites at **Lily** and **Lizard Lakes** (9 total sites, no piped water) are hike-in campgrounds reached by a 3.5-mile hike from the Blanchard Hill trailhead on Samish Lake Road south of Bellingham. A DNR camp off scenic Hwy 9 is **Hutchinson Creek** (14 sites, no piped water), 2.5 miles east of Acme, off Mosquito Lake Road. Call DNR, (360) 856-3500 for directions and information.

Walking/Hiking

Some of the best trails in the area can be sampled right from the city. Boulevard Park (see Beaches/Parks, above) is the best place to set foot on the **South Bay Trail** (easy; 4 miles round trip), a pleasant stroll along Bellingham Bay. Other access points are at Maple Street at Railroad Avenue, Wharf Street at N State Street and Boulevard Drive, and 10th Street and Mill Avenue. Also in the city proper, **Whatcom Falls Park** has, or had, a very popular trail system along Whatcom Creek. Much of this was literally destroyed by the massive Olympic Pipeline gasoline explosion here in 1999. City crews and volunteers are already rebuilding it, though. A walk through recently reopened trails here might be an instructive lesson (1401 Electric Avenue).

For a longer jaunt, park at Fairhaven Park or on Fairhaven Parkway near 24th Street and follow the **Interurban Trail** (easy; 7 miles one way), a fine rails-to-trails conversion, south to Larrabee State Park. The route, former path of the old interurban electric trolley from Bellingham to Mount Vernon, parallels Chuckanut Drive. It's mostly flat (good for kids) and open to mountain bikes and horses. There's one steep section heading south through Arroyo Park; cyclists hoping to bypass it can take Old Samish Road and Chuckanut Drive to the North Chuckanut Mountain trailhead at California Street, to the south. An offshoot is the **Larrabee/Post Point Trail,** a half-mile path that connects the Interurban at 10th and Donovan to the Padden Lagoon and the south shore of Marine Park. One popular Interurban option: mountain-bike down the Interurban Trail to Larrabee, then lock up the bikes and climb on the popular trail from Chuckanut Drive to **Fragrance Lake** (moderate; 4 miles round trip) in the highlands above the park's shoreline area.

The steep climb up Chuckanut Mountain to **Pine and Cedar Lakes** (difficult; 5.6 miles round trip), an undeveloped Whatcom County Park, yields excellent Mount Baker and San Juan Island views. The trailhead is on the Old Samish Road between Chuckanut Drive and I-5 exit 246. **Lake Padden Park** has a delightful 2.6-mile (mostly flat) loop trail all the way around the lake, as well as 5 miles of segregated bridle trails. Some of the nicer trails in the region are hidden inside **Whatcom Falls Park,** a beautiful, forested refuge with 5.5 miles of trails of varying difficulty.

Another little-known favorite, the **Sehome Hill Arboretum** (moderate; various lengths possible) is used primarily by students at abutting Western Washington University, thanks (or no thanks) to the lack of a single developed trailhead with good parking, except for one at the very top of the hill. More than 5 miles of unmarked trails and abandoned roads (mostly up and down moderate hills) skirt the mountain. At the mountaintop is one of our favorite spots in Bellingham—a tall observation platform with awe-inspiring views of Bellingham Bay, Mount Baker, and the far northern Cascades. Sehome Hill is where the moose came to live. You'll see why. If you're here when school is out of session, park at WWU behind the Environmental Science Building/Miller Hall (take your first right at the campus visitor center) and look for the trail in the woods behind you.

On Lummi Island, a popular hike leads from a Seacrest Drive trailhead to the top of **Lummi Peak** (moderate; 7 miles round trip), which has grand views of the San Juans and the North Sound. Warning: The trail is hard to follow at the top. Careful along the cliffs.

If you're up for a longer day trip, the Mount Baker Highway between Bellingham and the mountain is your pathway to some of the finest day-hiking in the Northwest. (See the Mount Baker Highway chapter.) For hiking maps and supplies, visit Base Camp, Inc., (360) 733-5461.

Biking

The road is narrow and shoulders nonexistent, but cyclists still are drawn to the 11-mile cliff-side stretch of **Chuckanut Drive** south from Fairhaven to the northern fringe of the Skagit Valley. The views over northern Puget Sound to the San Juan Islands, provided you ever take your eyes off traffic, are stupendous. The trip often is made as a 40-mile round trip by continuing south all the way to Bay View State Park on Padilla Bay (see the Skagit Valley chapter). Road riders also love the 7-mile triangular loop around the north end of **Lummi Island,** made by crossing on the Lummi ferry and following Nugent Road, West Shore Drive, and Legoe Bay Road. It's moderately hilly. (Stronger riders can turn this into a 30-mile round trip by starting and finishing in Ferndale, off I-5 at exit 262.) Bicycle rentals are available at the store next to The Islander, a few yards from the ferry landing.

Mountain bikers love riding the **Interurban Trail** (see Walking/Hiking, above), as well as a number of closed roads in the highland area of **Larrabee State Park** and **Lake Padden Park** (see Walking/Hiking, above). The **Pine and Cedar Lakes Trail** is another option for mountain bikers with monster thighs.

For supplies and rentals, see Fairhaven Bike & Mountain Sports, 1103 11th Street; (360) 733-4433.

Skiing

Mount Baker Ski Area, a nationally known deep-powder heaven for skiers and snowboarders, is 56 miles east on Hwy 542. For details, call (360) 734-6771, see www.mtbakerskiarea.com, or see the Mount Baker Highway chapter.

Fishing

The mix is excellent here. Bellingham is a good home port for summer and fall **coho, chinook, sockeye, chum**, and, during odd-numbered years only, **pink salmon** fishing in northern Puget Sound and the San Juan Islands, as well as **blackmouth** (immature chinook) fishing all winter long. Salmon charters are available from Jim's Salmon Charters in Blaine; (360) 332-6724.

Trout anglers are in luck around here. State-stocked local lakes, such as Padden, Silver, Toad, and Cain, typically are among the strongest trout producers in Western Washington, especially in the early season of April and May. Of these, Padden has by far the best bank access, and it's stocked with some 18,000 legal-size trout every spring. State fishing access sites also are found on the east side of Samish Lake and the south end of Lake Whatcom.

Largemouth bass fans will be pleased with Lake Terrell west of Ferndale (see Wildlife Watching, below). **Kokanee** anglers usually troll the broader, deeper waters of Lake Whatcom or Baker Lake. Local **steelheaders** catch winter-run fish on the main stem of the Nooksack in the Lynden/Everson area, but catch rates are down substantially in recent years. The river does have decent fall **coho** and winter **chum salmon** runs, however (see also the Mount Baker Highway chapter in the North Cascades section). The Washington Department of Fish and Wildlife has information; (206) 775-1311; www.wa.gov/wdfw.

Wildlife Watching

Not many Puget Sound cities offer as many chances to rub binocular lenses with wild animals as the Bellingham area. **Whale** watchers and **seabird** lovers can book boat trips from Bellingham to North Sound islands (see Boating/Sailing, above). Downtown, the Maritime Heritage Center, 1600 C Street; (360) 676-6806, provides great viewing of **spawning salmon** in the fall and winter—a good chance to enlighten and educate the kids, who'll learn something important without feeling a thing. Shoreside marine wildlife lovers are hardly left out up here, however. Good **marine mammal** haunts are the rocks and small islands off the west side of Lummi Island. Most are protected portions of the San Juan Island National Wildlife Refuge.

Semiahmoo Park, near Blaine, provides access to the 1.5-mile-long Semiahmoo Spit, where **shorebirds** often congregate. To the west, Lighthouse Marine Park at Point Roberts, operated by Whatcom County, has a viewing tower that makes a great **orca**- and **bird**-watching post, as well as a long beachfront boardwalk. The 22-acre park, reached by driving about an hour north through British Columbia, makes an interesting full-day excursion from Bellingham. Winter trips are best for spotting migratory birds such as **loons** and **numerous duck species.**

The **Terrell Marsh Nature Trail** at Birch Bay State Park (see Camping, above) is a good bird-watching trail. It's short and easy enough for children. Keep them quiet long enough, and you might spot beautiful **harlequin ducks,** which look like they were painted by the same guy who did the Partridge Family bus. To the north, the 11,000-acre Lake Terrell Habitat Management Area near Ferndale (I-5 exit 260) is a major stopover point for **migratory ducks.** Note: Hunting occurs here in season.

Just south of Ferndale near the mainstem Nooksack River, **Tennant Lake Interpretive Center,** operated by Whatcom County Parks, has an observation tower and mile-long boardwalk offering frequent sightings of ducks, bald eagles, and hawks, particularly in winter. The Interpretive Center, part of Hovander Homestead Park, a pioneer farm, is at 5299 Nielsen Road. Take I-5 exit 262, go west to the railroad underpass, immediately turn left and follow signs; (360) 384-3444. A sometimes overlooked local wildlife hot spot is the North Fork Nooksack River along Hwy 542, where winter visitors see hundreds of wintering **bald eagles** and **elk,** with a tiny fraction of the crowds attracted to the better-known Skagit River eagle habitat to the south. (See the Mount Baker Highway chapter in the North Cascades section.)

Photography

The observation tower atop **Sehome Hill** (see Walking/Hiking, above) is a grand sunset spot. But this area's grand-champion tripod spot is farther south: summer sunsets from the pullouts along **Chuckanut Drive** are among the most spectacular you'll ever see.

Accessible Outdoors

Nature lovers shouldn't miss the award-winning **Fragrance Garden** adjacent to the Tennant Lake Interpretive Center (see Wildlife Watching, above). The garden, more than 3,000 square feet of raised beds, was built to provide a special garden for the sightless. The barrier-free facility has a Braille identification system for plants. Visitors are encouraged to touch, feel, and smell the garden's 200-plus plant species. A mile-long **interpretive trail** through the nearby Tennant Lake marsh also is barrier-free; open daily June through Labor Day weekend; (360) 733-2900. **Larrabee State Park** has barrier-free rest rooms and camp and picnic sites, as does **Birch Bay State Park** (see Camping, above).

Restaurants

Cafe Toulouse ★ The Cafe's claim to fame continues to be huge, well-orchestrated breakfasts. $; *114 W Magnolia St, Bellingham; (360) 733-8996.* &

Colophon Cafe / Colophon Cafe Downtown Both Colophon Cafes serve soups, sandwiches, and delicious quiches. $; *1208 11th St, Bellingham; (360) 647-0092; $; 308 W Champion St, Bellingham; (360) 676-6257; www.colophoncafe.com.*

India Grill ★ Delicious Northern Indian cuisine, including an inexpensive lunch buffet. $; *1215½ Cornwall Ave, Bellingham; (360) 714-0314.* &

The Oyster Bar on Chuckanut Drive ★★★ Enjoy a spectacular view of Samish Bay and gourmet fare, mostly seafood. $$$; *2578 Chuckanut Dr, Bow; (360) 766-6185; www.chuckanutdrive.com.*

The Oyster Creek Inn ★ This well-loved restaurant has the same stellar offerings, in new digs. $$; *190 Chuckanut Dr, Bow; (360) 766-6179.* &

Pacific Cafe ★★ A sophisticated mix of cuisines from Europe, India, China, Malaysia, and Hawaii. $$; *100 N Commercial, Bellingham; (360) 647-0800.* &

Pepper Sisters ★★ Cheerful service at this Bellingham institution known for its Southwestern fare. $; *1055 N State St, Bellingham; (360) 671-3414.* &

The Rhododendron Cafe ★ The perfect starting or ending point for a scenic trek on Chuckanut Drive. $$; *5521 Chuckanut Dr, Bow; (360) 766-6667.*

Lodgings

Benson Farmstead Bed & Breakfast Once part of a dairy farm, this B&B is packed with Scandinavian memorabilia. $$; *10113 Avon-Allen Rd, Bow; (360) 757-0578 or (800) 441-9814; www.bbhosts.com/bensonbnb.*

Best Western Heritage Inn ★★ Rooms have a classic elegance at this professionally run hotel. $$; *151 E McLeod Rd, Bellingham; (360) 647-1912 or (800) 528-1234; www.bestwestern.com/heritageinnbellingham.*

North Garden Inn ★ This historic Victorian house is especially popular with visitors to nearby WWU. $$; *1014 N Garden St, Bellingham; (360) 671-7828 or (800) 922-6414; www.northgardeninn.com/ngi.*

Resort Semiahmoo ★★★ Nestled on a wildlife preserve, Resort Semiahmoo offers golf and walking trails. *$$$; 9565 Semiahmoo Pkwy, Blaine; (360) 371-2000 or (800) 770-7992; www.semiahmoo.com.* ♿

Samish Point by the Bay ★★ Beach access and miles of wooded trails at this estatelike property. *$$$; 4465 Samish Point Rd, Bow; (360) 766-6610 or (800) 916-6161; www.samishpoint.com.*

Schnauzer Crossing ★★★ This sophisticated B&B attracts everyone from newlyweds to businesspeople. *$$$; 4421 Lakeway Dr, Bellingham; (360) 734-2808 or (800) 562-2808; www.schnauzercrossing.com.*

South Bay B&B ★★ Privacy, views, forest—all offer a real eagle's-nest getaway. *$$$; 4095 South Bay Dr, Bellingham; (360) 595-2086 or (877) 595-2086; www.southbaybb.com.*

Stratford Manor ★ Set amid farmland, this rambling English Tudor-style home overlooks a pond. *$$$; 4566 Anderson Wy, Bellingham; (360) 715-8441 or (800) 240-6779; www.stratfordmanor.com.*

More Information

Alaska Marine Highway System: *(800) 642-0066; www.state.ak.us/ferry.*
Bellingham Parks and Recreation: *(360) 676-6985.*
Bellingham/Whatcom County Visitors and Convention Bureau:
 (360) 671-3990 or (800) 387-2032; www.bellingham.org.
Cascadia Marine Trail: *(206) 545-9161.*
Chuckanut Drive/South Bellingham web resource: *www.chuckanut-drive.com.*
City of Bellingham on the web: *www.cob.org.*
DNR: *(360) 856-3500.*
Lummi Island Ferry: *(360) 758-2190.*
Lummi Island web site: *www.lummi-island.com.*
Mount Baker Ski Report: *(360) 671-0211; www.mtbakerskiarea.com.*
Reservations Northwest: *(800) 452-5687.*
Washington Department of Fish and Wildlife: *(206) 775-1311; www.wa.gov/wdfw.*
Whatcom Parks and Recreation: *(360) 733-2900.*

San Juan Islands
and Anacortes

From Anacortes west to Haro Strait, north to Patos Island, and east to Rosario Strait, including Lime Kiln Point, Spencer Spit, and Moran State Parks, Mount Constitution, the San Juan Islands National Wildlife Refuge, and the northern stretch of the Cascadia Marine Trail.

Welcome to paradise. Please don't block the ferry lane. To many Evergreen State natives, the San Juan Islands are the perfect bite-size example of everything that's always been right—but keeps going wrong—with Washington's premier outdoor treasures. As a just-far-enough-away retreat from the Seattle metro mess, the placid shorelines, quiet coves, and cool forests of the San Juans are the ultimate outdoor retreat. But as an increasingly desirable national tourist destination—and a year-round residence for the rich, super-rich, and pseudo-rich—they also have all the trappings of paradise lost.

For those of us who love the islands the way they always used to be, summertime San Juan visits have been abandoned, mostly for mental-health and sagging-spirit reasons. Summertime in the San Juans is frenetic, with thousands of condo-dwellers, kayakers, camping cyclists, and yacht skippers clogging local parks, roadways, ferry lines, and latte stands. Just getting to the idyllic archipelago can be a trying experience in June, July, or August, when Washington State ferries built to handle early 1970s loads creak, groan, and shudder under the crushing weight of tourism. And once you're in the islands, even a little noise seems like a lot, because, well, it just shouldn't be this way.

Not everyone agrees with this assessment, proving once again that many people are just plain wrong. Some summertime San Juan adventurers say the islands' soothing qualities and great weather (the islands, in the Olympic rain shadow, are drier and sunnier than Seattle, but contain one-third more fat per serving) more than make up for the trouble of getting there and back. That's a valid assessment. But we can't help believe the truly savvy Washington outdoor lover tends to avoid the islands during the peak California migration season.

Smarter island hoppers don't start jumping until mid-September. Then, after all those Midwestern kids are back in school and East Coasters are back in therapy, the islands reopen to the rest of us. And what a grand reunion it is. The islands in the off-season are the islands of old. The air is crisp enough to fold into origami sailboats. The deafening silence keeps you awake all night in the tent at Moran State Park. The porpoises look up at the bow of the boat and sigh in relief that it's only you. All is right with the world of water, and there's no better place to recharge the spiritual batteries than the islands called San Juan.

Perhaps we overestimate the seasonal difference. The islands—743 when the tide goes out, 428 when it comes back in—are, after all, a world-class marine getaway even in the summer, particularly to those who explore their myriad coastlines by boat or sea kayak. Few Washington summer experiences can top a week at Moran State Park or a day on the water capped by a surprise brush—and by that, we mean actual fin-to-stern contact—with an orca whale.

But you old-timers know what we mean. We love the San Juan Islands not so much for what they are as for what they were. For many of us, they're the plush winter reward for spartan summer toils. The San Juans are the cheesecake dessert on our outdoors menu. Palatable in any form. But best served cold.

Getting There

Two primary options: Go off-season, or wait in line.

The most obvious and cost-effective way of getting to the San Juans is via Washington State ferries, which run year-round from Anacortes, about 90 minutes north of Seattle (west of Interstate 5 on Highway 20). For ferry rates, schedules, and information: (206) 464-6400; (800) 84-FERRY or www.wsdot.wa.gov/ferries. Expect the ferries to be packed to the gills—and beyond—in the summer. Getting a ferry out of Anacortes can be a long, dull 3-hours-and-up wait. Bring a good book—or park the car and board with a bike. Money-saving tip: Cars only pay westbound. If you plan to visit more than one island, arrange to go to the farthest first (San Juan) and work your way east.

There are a few ways to cheat if you don't need your car (and if you work at it hard enough, you probably won't). The Victoria Clipper makes a once-a-

day trip from downtown Seattle to Friday Harbor from mid-May through mid-September. The summer-only ferry departs Pier 69 at 7:30am and arrives in Friday Harbor at 11:30am; it makes a trip to Victoria, British Columbia, and back, then departs Friday Harbor at 4pm, hitting Seattle by 7 pm. Round-trip fares are $49, $32 one way (summer 2000). For Clipper information, call (206) 448-5000 or (800) 888-2535, or book on-line at www.victoriaclipper. com. Another summertime option is via Bellingham; the Island Shuttle Express provides passenger-only ferry service to the San Juan Islands, May through September. Call for reservations: (360) 671-1137.

For the total-express experience, fly. Kenmore Air schedules four flights a day during peak season. Round-trip flights start at about $150 per person (summer 2000). Prices are higher for weekends. Call (206) 486-1257 or (800) 543-9595, or book on-line at www.kenmoreair.com.

inside out

Parks/Camping

The islands have one of the highest mind-boggling-picnic-spot-per-square-mile ratios in the Northwest. Camping facilities, conversely, are somewhat limited in relation to the crush of summer visitors. But what's there is first-rate. We'll take it island by island.

Fidalgo Island

One of the San Juans' best beachfront parks isn't even technically in the San Juans. **Washington Park** in Anacortes is an island park, nonetheless. The 220-acre park on Fidalgo Head, just beyond the Anacortes ferry terminal, is one of the loveliest waterfront getaways in the Northwest. The campground, with 70 sites (46 full or water/electrical hookups; RVs to 70 feet) is rather cramped and pedestrian, and better suited to RVs than tents (not a lot of privacy in most sites). But the camp does have some pleasant amenities, including coin-op showers and an RV dump station. Campsites can be reserved in summer months by city of Anacortes residents only. The rest of the park is a gem, however. The day-use area has a pleasant beach, picnic area, and boat launch, but the highlight is a 3.5-mile loop road that skirts the shoreline all the way around the park. The narrow road can be driven one way—or, better yet, walked or cycled—to grand waterfront picnic spots with views of Guemes Channel, the San Juans, and all the pleasure craft headed toward them. It's a wonderful place to spend a few hours if you're stuck in a day-long ferry line. The park is about a 20-minute walk or 5-minute bike ride from the ferry terminal. It's open all year. *From Commercial Avenue (Hwy 20) in downtown Anacortes, turn left on 12th Street and proceed about 2 miles west, staying left at the Washington State Ferry terminal; (360) 293-1927.*

Orcas Island

The largest of the San Juan Islands is home to the chain's most diverse outdoor-recreation site, **Moran State Park.** The sprawling 4,800-acre park is one of the jewels of the state park system, with a rich mix of old-growth forests, freshwater lakes, pleasant campsites, and a 2,400-foot mountaintop where the view is as gorgeous as any in the Northwest. The park, named for shipbuilder and former resident Robert Moran (who donated the park land and whose mansion now is the focus of nearby Rosario Resort), often surprises first-time visitors who expect a marine environment. Even though it's the largest park in the San Juan Islands, most of the park is wooded, mountainous terrain. Waterborne activities at Moran are on freshwater, not salt. Four small, picturesque lakes are found in the park, two of them ringed by scenic campsites.

Campers pack the park's 166 campsites (no hookups; RVs to 45 feet) all summer. In fact, you're likely to be out of luck unless you reserve a site well in advance. Those who land a site are rarely disappointed. This is a big, diverse park, with two main camping areas, pleasant picnic grounds, two boat launches, bathhouses, swimming beaches, and moorage docks with rental boats. Also on site is a large Environmental Learning Center, which offers cabins for rent to large groups. Park activities include fishing, kayaking, canoeing, or boating in Mountain or Cascade Lake and hiking on the park's 30-mile trail system (see also the Boating/Sailing, Fishing, and Hiking sections, below).

One of those trails leads from the park's lowland camping areas to Moran's highlight—2,400-foot Mount Constitution, the highest spot in the San Juans. At the summit (which also can be driven to during daylight hours), the view in all directions is spectacular. Climb up the stairway in the 12th-century-replica stone observation tower, and you can see as far south as Mount Rainier and the Olympics, west to Vancouver Island, north to Vancouver, British Columbia, and east into the North Cascades. It's an airplane-style view—not to be missed.

Moran State Park is open all year. Campsites can be reserved up to 11 months in advance by calling Reservations Northwest; (800) 452-5687. *Follow signs 13 miles northeast from the Orcas Island ferry landing; (360) 376-2326 or (800) 233-0321.*

Also on Orcas are Doe Bay Village Resort, (360) 376-2291, which offers 50 campsites (8 have hookups), clothing-optional hot tubs, and other services; the primitive **Obstruction Pass** DNR campsite (near the mouth of East Sound south of Olga), which has 9 campsites accessible via the beach or a half-mile trail (no piped water); and West Beach Resort west of Eastsound, (360) 376-2240 or (877) 937-8224, a **private facility** with 72 campsites (36 with hookups).

Lopez Island

The favorite island of cyclists has plenty of parks providing great day-trip or overnight stopovers. Two popular westside day-use parks, **Otis Perkins** (at the south end of Fisherman Bay spit, past Lopez Village) and **Upright Channel** (a DNR picnic area northeast of Flat Point, off Military Rd), are great for exploring, with good beach access. **Agate Beach County Park,** on Outer Bay at the southwest tip of the island near Mackaye Harbor, has a pleasant rocky beach for the tired cyclist, with views of the lighthouse at Iceberg Point. A great place for a sunset. Nearby **Hughes Bay County Park** is another pleasant beach, accessible by stairs from a wooded upland (off Huggins Rd, reached by following Aleck Bay Rd east and Watmough Head Rd south). Seals and bald eagles can often be seen from the rocky promontory of **Shark Reef Recreation Area,** a long stone's throw away from the southernmost tip of San Juan Island. A rare stand of old-growth timber remains in this park.

Two good campgrounds are found a short distance from the Lopez ferry terminal. **Odlin County Park** on Upright Channel is an 80-acre spread with 30 campsites (no hookups), a boat launch, and low-bank waterfront access. Sites here can be reserved (two-night minimum). This is a perfect first-night stopover for cyclists bound for a tour of Lopez. The camp is a short roll (just over a mile) from the ferry, so getting there even late in the evening doesn't pose too much of a challenge. *Odlin is 1.3 miles south of the Washington State Ferry terminal on Ferry Rd; 360) 468-2496.*

On the northeast side of the island a short ride or drive away is a Lopez highlight, **Spencer Spit State Park,** a 130-acre park with 39 water-front sites (no hookups; RVs to 20 feet) and a 10-person group camp that can be reserved. Campsites can be reserved up to 11 months in advance by calling (800) 452-5687. The park, one of the most pleasant in the islands, is a designated Cascadia Marine Trail campsite (see Sea Kayaking, below), and its 16 moorage buoys make it a popular boat-in campground for mariners of all sorts. No matter how many visitors arrive to explore the sandy beach, however, there's still twice as many rabbits here as people. Special close-quarters alert: The park has an RV dump station, but unlike most state parks, this one has no hot showers! Open March through October. *5 miles southeast of the ferry terminal on Baker View Rd; (360) 378-2044 or (800) 233-0321.*

San Juan Island

Popular day-use parks on the San Juans' most populous island include **American** and **English Camps**, **San Juan County Park** on West Side Road (see below), and **Lime Kiln Point State Park** (see Accessible Outdoors, below).

The best campground is **Lakedale,** a private resort with 117 campsites (19 with hookups), cabin tent rentals, and three small lakes for fishing and swimming. Rental cycles, boats, and camping gear are available here. As the primary campground on the island, it's often overcrowded, and the pricing is a bit rich ($38 a night for a family of five in summer 2000, for example). But sites can be reserved in advance at (800) 617-CAMP. The park is open March 15 to October 15. *On Roche Harbor Rd 4.5 miles north of ferry terminal; www.lakedale.com.*

San Juan County Park, near Smallpox Bay, has 20 campsites (8 full hookups; RVs to 25 feet), a boat ramp, and beach access, plus a lush green lawn. Campsites here are overcrowded, but can be reserved by calling (360) 378-2992. The offshore area of this park is a favorite of island scuba divers. It's open summers only. *10 miles west of ferry terminal on West Side Rd.*

Private camping alternatives include the Pedal Inn on the island's southwest end (25 hiker/biker sites; 1300 False Bay Dr; (360) 378-3048) and Snug Harbor Marina Resort near the island's northwest end (12 sites, 4 with hookups; 1997 Mitchell Bay Rd; (360) 378-4762). In Friday Harbor proper is Town and Country Trailer Park, which has 40 sites (some with hookups), showers and laundry facilities; (360) 378-4717.

Shaw Island

The sole choice for campers on the quiet island of Shaw is **South Beach County Park,** where the beach is the main draw. The 3,200 feet of splendid sand, in fact, makes this one of the finer picnic spots in the San Juans, and campers lucky enough to snare one of the 12 pleasant, upland campsites here are in for plenty of rest and relaxation. South Beach also serves as a popular boat launch site for canoeists and kayakers, who can paddle a short distance across Indian Cove to Canoe Island, home of a summer camp for teens. On shore, a short walk on a local road leads to another quiet beach on Squaw Bay, just to the west. The park is a popular boat-in destination for powerboaters and paddlers based in Friday Harbor, less than 4 nautical miles away. *From the ferry terminal, follow Blind Bay Rd southwest to Squaw Bay Rd, turn left, and follow signs a short distance to the park; (360) 378-8420.*

Boat-in San Juan/North Sound campgrounds

Private boaters will find an almost overwhelming array of quality public moorages with access to primitive beachfront or upland campsites, managed by Washington State Parks or the Department of Natural Resources. Many of these also serve as campsites for the Cascadia Marine Trail, a state-managed water trail with campsites from Olympia to British Columbia; (206) 545-9161. (See the Washington Outdoors Primer on page vii for details.) Most have moorage floats or docks. Fees (usually $5) are charged at most during the summer, and fresh water usually is limited. Avid boaters say these parks offer some of the best boat camping (or boat-in camping) in the country. Most marine state parks have picnic tables, pit or composting toilets, and moorage floats for pleasure boaters, whereas most DNR-maintained sites are more primitive.

Popular boat-in spots include state marine parks at **Stuart Island** (NW of San Juan Island, 19 primitive sites on the north side of the island, with moorage in Reid and Prevost harbors); **Sucia Island** (55 primitive sites and ample moorage floats on the north side of the island, 2.5 miles north of Orcas); **Patos Island** (7 sites and no piped water on the east side of the island, 4 mi NW of Sucia Island); **Clark Island** (8 sites, moorage floats and no piped water, NE of Orcas Island); **Matia Island** (6 sites on the island's northeast side, 2 mi N of Orcas); **Posey Island** (1 or 2 primitive sites and not much else, just off San Juan Island's Roche Harbor); **Blind Island** (4 sites and no piped water, north of Shaw Island); **Turn Island** (12 primitive campsites and no piped water, a short float east from Friday Harbor); **James Island** (13 primitive sites and a moorage dock on the island's east shore, just east of Decatur Island on Rosario Strait); **Doe Island** (5 sites southeast of Orcas Island); **Saddlebag Island** (5 sites, no piped water, east of Guemes Island and north of Anacortes); and **Skagit Island** and **Hope Island** (both in Skagit Bay, off the northeast shores of Whidbey Island).

Of these, the Northern Boundary islands—Sucia, Patos, Matia, Clark, and Barnes (just west of Clark)—are the most scenic, best developed, and most heavily used. Sucia Island, with moorage for some 700 boats, is a splendid spot, but can look more like a small city than a wild refuge on summer weekends. Patos and Stuart Islands also receive fairly heavy use. For information, call Washington State Parks, (800) 233-0321.

North Sound and San Juan Islands DNR sites include **Lummi Island** (4 sites with no piped water, 1 mile south of Reil Harbor on the SE tip of Lummi Island); **Obstruction Pass,** a (half-mile) hike- or boat-in camp (9 sites on Orcas Island's East Sound near Olga, no piped water); **Point Doughty** (4 sites with no piped water 3 mi NW of Eastsound on the NW side of Orcas); **Cypress Head** (10 sites, no piped water, moorage floats, on the E side of Cypress Island near Anacortes); **Pelican Beach** (4 sites, group camp shelter, no piped water, moorage buoys, 4 mi N of Cypress Head on the east side of Cypress Island); **Strawberry Island** (4 sites, no piped water, a half mile west of Cypress); and **Griffin Bay** (several sites on the southeast side of San Juan Island). For information, call the DNR's Northwest Region (Sedro Woolley) office, (360) 856-3500.

Cycling

All four of the San Juan Islands served by ferry—Lopez, Shaw, Orcas, and San Juan—are great places to explore by bicycle. Many visitors, particularly those returning after an initial visit, prefer to come by bicycle, for several reasons. One is that each of the islands is small enough to cross by bicycle in a couple of hours, although some are quite hilly. A larger advantage to a cycle visit, however, is ease of access. Cyclists get first shake in the ferry line at Anacortes. In midsummer, commuting to the islands by bicycle could shave half a day off the ferry-line wait. Don't expect to be the only one savvy enough to figure this out. The San Juans are one of the few destinations in the country where cyclists occasionally overwhelm available facilities. As many as 150,000 cyclists are believed to invade the islands every year. In midsummer you're likely to find a line even for cycles at the ferry landings, and popular cycling roads on Lopez and San Juan Islands have actual bike jams (or "gaper jams," if you're a local). That makes it even more important than usual to observe smart riding etiquette. Stay single file, ride in groups of five or less, and get clear of the road whenever you stop. An excellent pocket-size cycle map of the islands, the "Bicyclists Touring Companion," is published by Cycle San Juans. The map, which lists point-to-point mileages and other helpful information, is available at outdoor stores and cycle shops.

Lopez is by far the most popular cycling venue, largely because it's almost exclusively flat. A 30-mile loop, easy enough for most riders to make in a day, circles the island, with good saltwater views and park stopovers all along the route. Or devise your own route by following a map and meandering along the island's 70 miles of county roads. You can bring your own bike on the ferry for a small fee, or rent one from several sources on the island. Vendors such as the Bike Shop at Lopez Village, (360) 468-3497, will deliver rented bikes to the ferry or wherever you're staying. Lopez Bicycle Works, 2847 Fisherman Bay Road, (360) 468-2847, has been renting cycles, selling supplies, and dispensing tour advice for more than 20 years. From the ferry terminal, overnighters can pedal an easy mile to Odlin County Park, or 4.5 miles to Spencer Spit State Park. See Parks/Camping, above, for details and a list of other stopover points along the Lopez cycling route.

Almost as popular among cyclists is **San Juan Island,** laced with 95 miles of mostly flat roads, many with good views. The scenic West Side

Road is a water-view standout. Lakedale Resort (see Parks/Camping, above) is a popular cycle-in overnight spot 4.5 miles from the ferry terminal. The 10-mile ride to San Juan County Park has great local marine views; nearby Lime Kiln Park is specifically designed for shore-based whale watching. Cycle rentals are available two blocks from the ferry terminal at Island Bicycles, 380 Argyle Avenue, (360) 378-4941; www.island-bicycles.com. Reservations are recommended.

Strong riders will get a good workout on hilly **Orcas Island,** where some local hills are torturous (i.e., "The Wall," a 16.5-degree grade on Enchanted Forest Rd west of Eastsound, or the lung-busting 2,000-vertical-foot jaunt up Mount Constitution). But it's not all that way. Many riders come specifically to wheel their way to Moran State Park (see Parks/Camping, above), 14 miles from the ferry terminal. Rentals are conveniently located near the ferry terminal at Dolphin Bay Bicycles, (360) 376-4157, and in Eastsound at Wildlife Cycles, (360) 376-4708. Hint: Wait until the ferry traffic clears before you head out!

While it lacks amenities such as cycle rental shops, **Shaw Island,** the least cluttered in the chain, is another grand two-wheel destination because of expansive views, truly rural landscapes, and roads virtually devoid of auto traffic.

Sea Kayaking

First-time visitors to the San Juans often go home disappointed that they've just spent a week in a chain of islands with very little access to a beach. The sad fact is that most waterfront property in the islands is privately owned (probably by your boss), and except for a handful of state and county parks, it's mostly off-limits. Not so for paddlers, however. A healthy string of public beaches and take-outs ring the San Juans, including the many islands in the archipelago that are accessible only by water. The islands—which form a long string of protected waterways rife with hidden coves, quiet waters, and abundant wildlife—are as close to a sea-kayaking paradise as you'll find in the Northwest.

Some paddlers spend entire waterborne lifetimes exploring the chain, and we won't begin to attempt to list all the possible destinations here. (For some small-island destinations, see Camping, above.) If you're serious about exploring the San Juans in depth from a sea kayak, we suggest picking up a San Juan-specific marine guidebook. *The San Juan Islands Afoot & Afloat,* by Marge and Ted Mueller (The Mountaineers Books) lists nearly all the publicly accessible beach sites on the major islands, with an eye toward the mariner. Or consult with one of the many top-notch kayak outfitters offering rental boats and gear, maps, and even guided tours. Paddlers with even a minimal degree of sea-kayaking experience can rent a boat for about $30 a day and set off on their own, get a 2- or 3-hour guided tour for $30 to $50, or splurge for a full-blown $300-to-$500 weekend trip where the guide leads the way, points out the wildlife, pitches the tents, and cooks the meals. These can be an unforgettable experience, one you're not likely to find anywhere else in the Lower 48 states.

Experienced paddlers setting out on their own multi-day trip should keep in mind the growing number of campsites along the **Cascadia Marine Trail**—a state-managed water trail from Olympia to British Columbia recently established in the islands. At this writing, 14 Cascadia-designated sites dot the island chain, all available for waterborne travelers. More will likely be added in coming years. Some are state parks sites; others are state Department of Natural Resources sites (see Parks/Camping, above). For Cascadia Marine Trail permit information, maps, and a brochure, contact Washington State Parks, (800) 233-0321, or Washington Water Trails Association, (206) 545-9161; www.wwta.org.

Many a Washington paddler has received an introduction to sea kayaking in East Sound, the large bay dividing the halves of saddlebag-shaped **Orcas Island.** Rentals are available here at Crescent Beach Kayaks, (360) 376-2464. Lessons and guided tours are available from Orcas Outdoors, (360) 376-4611, on the boardwalk near the ferry terminal, or Shearwater Adventures in Eastsound, (360) 376-4699; www.shearwaterkayaks.com. The latter, an Orcas fixture since 1982, also offers orca whale-watching expeditions in conjunction with the Whale Museum at Friday Harbor, (800) 946-7227.

An outfitter on **Lopez Island,** Lopez Kayaks, (360) 468-2847, is open summers only (May to October). On **San Juan Island,** kayaks can be rented from any of a slew of Friday Harbor vendors. Contact the San Juan Islands Chamber (see More Information, below) for a full list of kayak guides in Friday Harbor. At last count, 10 outfitters here offered single- and multi-day wildlife-watching adventures—all fun, educational tours through fantastic surroundings. Whale and other wildlife sightings are common, and there's no more thrilling way to see an orca than from water level. Beginners shouldn't shy away from an overnight tour; most trips are led by patient, skilled guides quite accustomed to leading paddlers with virtually no experience.

Newcomers, in fact, can test the waters before they ever get to them. On the way to the islands, stop by Eddyline Watersports in Anacortes (1019 Q Ave, Cap Sante Marina; (360) 299-2300; www.seakayakshop.com) to test-paddle a kayak from this longtime local manufacturer, or rent one for a weekend. The company also recently began offering an innovative Island Sherpa Water Taxi service, dropping paddlers and their boats off at popular starting points for island trips. Rates begin at $200 for near-side islands, but the custom-built, 30-foot taxi boat can handle six paddlers and gear, cutting the price to just over $30 each. This service offers a huge time savings over ferry commuting, although kayaks can be carried on Washington State Ferries for a small charge in addition to the walk-on fee.

Wildlife Watching

The San Juan Islands are an indescribably rich wildlife habitat, boasting healthy populations of marine and land creatures, some found in greater numbers here than anywhere else in the contiguous United States. But one species, the **orca** or "killer" whale, draws the bulk of attention from visitors. The San Juans are the permanent home to three sizable pods of orcas (80 to 90 in all), which are commonly spotted from boats, kayaks, the state ferries, and even occasionally from island streets. A literal armada of whale-watching tourist boats descends on the islands every summer, hauling binocular-armed tourists out for a brush with the friendly, fascinating mammals.

Whale watching has grown into a science here. An organized network of whale spotters throughout the island chain keeps close tab on the pods. The orcas rarely venture anywhere near the major islands without being spotted, then followed by the radio-equipped armada. Estimates indicate as many as 100,000 visitors a year engage in Washington/British Columbia whale-watching, which has become a $10 million annual industry. So far, whales and tour boats have coexisted fairly well, although government studies are under way to determine if the whales are bothered by all the commotion. However you choose to pursue the whales, start your quest with a stop at Friday Harbor's Whale Museum, (800) 946-7227; www.whale-museum.org. It's free, and open daily.

The best time to see orcas is in the summer, when pods from the Southern Resident Community follow migrating salmon in close to shore. But sightings occur throughout the year. It's not hard to find a commercial whale-watching ride in the summer. Dozens of vendors offer whale-watching trips, and airplane whale tours also are available. Most are based in Friday Harbor, but some tours depart from Bellingham, Anacortes, or even downtown Seattle (via the *Victoria Clipper*; see Getting There, above). Daylong whale tours cost between $40 and $60, and most vendors belong to an industry group, the Whale Watch Operators Association Northwest, which heeds whale-engagement rules. A leading service is Western Prince Cruises, (360) 378-5315 or (800) 757-ORCA(6722). The Seattle Aquarium, (206) 386-4300, www.seattleaquarium.org, also has summer whale tours, some of which include transportation to the departure point in Everett. For a full list of operators, call the San Juan Islands Visitor Information Center, (360) 468-3663, or click the "whale watching" link on the Whale Museum web site, www.whale-museum.org.

Kayak tour guides also offer whale-watching trips, with opportunities for a truly memorable encounter for those fortunate enough to come (literally) eye-to-eye with the orcas. See Sea Kayaking, above, for outfitter information. And the whales occasionally are spotted from land. San Juan Island's Lime Kiln Point State Park on whale-rich Haro Strait (see Parks/Camping, above) was designed specifically for land-based whale watching. From a vantage point near the picturesque Lime Kiln Lighthouse, you can gaze across the Strait with binoculars and sometimes spot pods of whales as close as three-quarters of a mile from shore. Knowledgeable volunteer spotters from the Whale Museum are on hand daily in the summer, weekends in the fall.

Other fascinating wildlife species, largely overlooked in the orca frenzy, include **California sea lions, harbor seals, river otters, minke whales,** and **Dall's porpoises**, which are commonly seen in local waterways. The islands also are a particularly important bird habitat; 84 islands in the archipelago, in fact, are designated as the San Juan Islands National Wildlife Refuge. All these islands except Matia and Turn are off-limits to the public, but they can be viewed easily from boats, including the Washington State ferries. A walk on ferry ride through the San Juans, in fact, is about as productive (and inexpensive) a wildlife tour as you're likely to find anywhere in the Northwest. Bring the binoculars and bird guide, and you're not likely to be disappointed. Common species are **bald eagles** (which nest here in greater numbers than anywhere else in the Lower 48), **golden eagles, great blue herons, belted kingfishers,** various **owls** and **hawks, turkey vultures,** and marine birds such as **tufted puffins, cormorants, scoters, rhinoceros auklets,** and **glaucous-winged gulls.**

Bring your bicycle along (see Cycling, above), and you can combine your boat tour with a land-based wildlife venture on San Juan Island, which is particularly productive for bird- and whale-watching. Lime Kiln Point State Park (see above) is a grand whale-watching post, and Cattle Point, at the extreme south end of San Juan Island, is home to nesting bald eagles all year-round.

Most of the common land mammals found throughout Western Washington also are present in the islands. Don't be surprised if a **black-tailed deer** pads through your campsite at Moran State Park—or if a **raccoon** burgles your cooler at Spencer Spit State Park.

Boating/Sailing

Choose your pleasure. During the dry, sunny summer months, the San Juans are the indisputable boating capital of the Northwest—a place where 8-foot Livingstons are happily at home among 60-foot yachts. A full range of boat rentals, facilities, and services is available, both in the islands themselves and nearby Anacortes, which serves as a staging area for many island excursions. All the major islands have moorage facilities and basic services, but the primary boating havens here are found at Anacortes and Friday Harbor.

Marina facilities

In Anacortes, Cap Sante Boat Haven, (360) 293-0694, a great facility managed by the Port of Anacortes, has extensive moorage, fuels, rest rooms, showers, laundry facilities, and nearby marine-supply stores. It's a primary starting point for many San Juan guided excursions, and boats and yachts often are turned over to renters here. Cap Sante is just east of downtown Anacortes.

In the islands, the Port of Friday Harbor, (360) 378-2688, is the largest moorage and full-service marina facility, with ample guest moorage and full boater services on San Juan Island. Roche Harbor Resort, (360) 378-2155, on the northwest tip of San Juan, is another popular boater destination. On Lopez, Islands Marine Center, (360) 468-3377, is a full-service marina near Lopez Village. On the west side of Orcas, Deer Harbor Resort & Marina, (360) 376-4420, is a popular spot with guest moorage (call ahead) and other services. Other popular Orcas boater stop-ins are West Sound Marina, (360) 376-2314, and West Beach Resort, (360) 376-2240, also on the west side, and Rosario Resort, (800) 562-8820, on the east side of the island.

Rentals and tours

If you're looking for a small-to-medium powerboat for fishing or island exploration, most of the marinas listed above can put you in the driver's seat. **San Juan Boat Rentals** in Friday Harbor, (360) 378-3499, also offers a wide range of boats.

If a skippered cruise, either on a power- or sailboat, is more to your liking, there's no shortage of opportunities here. More than a dozen **skippered charter services** operate in the San Juans, with home bases at Friday Harbor, Deer Harbor, Eastsound, and Anacortes. Bare-boat rentals also are available from a number of yacht brokers. A small, basic sailboat costs about $100 a day, while fully skippered cruises can run several thousand dollars per person per week. Rentals are available all year, but they're substantially cheaper outside the peak tourist season. Two leading charter ser-

San Juan visitors spot an Orca whale on a day trip from Friday Harbor

vices with both bare-boat and skippered tours are Charters Northwest, (360) 378-7196, and Trophy Charters, (360) 378-2110. On Orcas, try Deer Harbor Charters, (800) 544-5758. The San Juan Islands Visitors Information Center, (360) 468-3663; www.guidetosanjuans.com, can help you match your desires with a suitable skipper. (Note: Guided San Juan boat tours also are available from Bellingham. See the Bellingham and Lummi Island chapter.)

Boat camping

Private boaters will find an almost overwhelming array of quality **public moorages** with access to **primitive beachfront** or **upland campsites**, managed by Washington State Parks, (800) 233-0321, or the Department of Natural Resources. (Many of these also serve as Cascadia Marine Trail campsites; see Parks/Camping, above.) Most have moorage floats or docks. Fees are charged at some during the summer, and fresh water usually is limited. Avid boaters say these parks offer some of the best boat camping (or boat-in camping) in the country.

Fishing

Freshwater and saltwater anglers can get their licks in on the islands—or around the islands, if salmon is the prey of choice. The rocky shoals and kelp beds around the San Juans have been among the most productive **king salmon** fishing grounds in the state during the 1990s. Catch rates have remained consistent here and, more important, the islands have been spared most of the summer-long closures plaguing the nearby Strait of Juan de Fuca and North Puget Sound. Trophy kings upward of 40 pounds (most bound for British Columbia's Fraser River system) are not uncommon here, although finding where, when, and how to pursue them can be tricky. First-timers should strongly consider a guided charter trip, available through Trophy Charters in Friday Harbor, (360) 378-2110, and a half-dozen other vendors.

Waters around the islands are open all year for salmon fishing. Prime time for kings is July and August, and hot spots include Cattle Point and Eagle Point on the south end of San Juan Island. But the islands also boast productive summer **coho, winter blackmouth** (resident coho), and, during late summer weeks in odd-numbered years, **pink salmon** fisheries. **Lingcod** and **halibut** fishing also can be fair, particularly in the spring.

Trout and **bass** anglers keep themselves busy with above-average fishing in Mountain and Cascade Lakes in Moran State Park (see Parks/Camping, above), Egg Lake and Sportsman's Lake on San Juan Island, and Hummel Lake on Lopez. Hummel, Egg, Sportsman's, and Mountain Lakes are open all year. Fishing also is available all year on the three small private lakes at Lakedale Resort on San Juan Island, where no license is required (see Parks/Camping, above). Heart Lake and Lake Erie outside Anacortes are perennial **rainbow trout** producers, especially early in the spring.

Hiking

Moran State Park on Orcas Island is the best—and really only—hiking venue in the San Juans, where most of the land is privately owned and inaccessible to long-distance strollers. Moran State Park on Orcas Island makes up for the lack of quantity in the island chain, however. The park has more than 30 miles of trails, most of which skirt the sides of 2,400-foot Mount Constitution. Many of these are steep, forested routes. But the access road to the top of Mount Constitution allows a cheater's option: hitch a ride to the top and walk back down, passing some fabulous scenery on the way to a pickup—or your campsite—in the lower portion of the park. A popular route is the **Mount Constitution/Twin Lakes Trail** (difficult; 1.5 miles one way), which drops more than 1,000 feet in a mile down from the lookout tower to Twin Lakes, where a side trail can be caught back to Mountain Lake and the main Moran camping area. Again, this is a good one to walk downhill. Uphill striders will struggle, but it's a grand workout.

Not all trails in the park are this extreme. The most popular route, no doubt, is the **Cascade Falls Trail** (easy; 1 mile round trip), which can be hiked either from a signed roadside pullout along the Mount Constitution Road or as part of a 3-mile (one way) hike between the Mountain Lake and Cascade Lake camping areas.

Other popular routes in the park include the **Mountain Lake Loop** (easy; 3.5 miles round trip), **Little Summit Trail** (moderate; 4.5 miles round trip), and **North Side Trail** (moderate; 9.5 miles round trip). For more hiking information, contact the state park at (360) 376-2326.

A very pleasant hike that offers a sense of what the San Juans would be like if they were public land completely open to recreation is the **Washington Park Loop** (easy; 3.5 miles round trip), a combination one-way road/walking path at Washington Park in Anacortes (see Parks/Camping, above). The loop is open to auto traffic, but cars are relatively rare, and in some places the single-track trail leaves the road and skirts the highly scenic cliffs and rocky beaches of Fidalgo Head. Throw a loaf of bread and a bottle of wine in a day pack and give it a try. It's a walk that rarely disappoints. And don't overlook the scramble to the top of **Mount Erie.**

Scuba Diving

Many Washington divers swear the deep coves, bays, and straits between the San Juan Islands offer the best cold-water (48 to 52°F year-round) diving on the planet. A major center for gear, rentals, and instruction is Emerald Seas Diving Center, 180 First Street, Friday Harbor; (360) 378-2772 or (800) 942-2547; www.emeraldseas.com. Gear also is available at Island Dive & Water Sports at Rosario, (360) 378-7615 or (800) 303-8386, www.divesanjuan.com; and Snug Harbor Marina Resort, (360) 378-4762, www.snugresort.com.

Accessible Outdoors

Lime Kiln Point State Park, on the west side of San Juan Island, has excellent barrier-free amenities, including rest rooms, drinking water, interpretive boardwalks, and shoreline viewing of orca whales (see Wildlife Watching, above). Also on San Juan, the **Cattle Point Viewpoint** on Cattle Point Rd has barrier-free rest rooms and saltwater-view access. On Orcas Island, **Moran State Park** (see Parks/Camping, above) has barrier-free rest rooms and drinking water. On Lopez Island, the **Upright Channel Picnic Area,** a state DNR site, offers barrier-free picnicking and rest rooms. From Lopez ferry terminal, proceed south 3 miles to Military Rd and turn right.

outside in

Restaurants

The Bay Cafe ★★★   The twinkling Bay Cafe is a come-as-you-are kind of place—and people do. $$; *90 Post Rd, Lopez Island; (360) 468-3700.*

Bilbo's Festivo ★   A cozy little place where the fare includes Mexican and New Mexican influences. $; *North Beach Rd, Eastsound; (360) 376-4728.*

Cafe Olga ★   A popular midday stop serving wholesome international home-style entrees. $; *Olga Junction, Olga; (360) 376-5098.* &

Christina's ★★★   A bewitching blend of pastoral locale and urban sophistication. $$$; *310 Main St, Eastsound; (360) 376-4904; www.christinas.net.*

Duck Soup Inn ★★   Duck Soup's owners are committed to local seafoods and seasonal ingredients. $$; *3090 Roche Harbor Rd, Friday Harbor; (360) 378-4878.* &

Julianne's Grill ★★   The most elegant dining room in Anacortes. $$; *419 Commercial Ave (Majestic Hotel), Anacortes; (360) 299-9666.* &

Katrina's ★   Look for a changing menu of simple sensations in this airy Victorian. $; *135 2nd St, Friday Harbor; (360) 378-7290.* &

La Petite ★★   French-inspired food with a touch of Dutch. Selection is small; quality is high. $$; *3401 Commercial Ave, Anacortes; (360) 293-4644; www.islandsinn.com.*

The Place Next to the San Juan Ferry Cafe ★   A rotating world of cuisines (lots of fish and shellfish) garners local praise. $$; *1 Spring St, Friday Harbor; (360) 378-8707.* &

Ship Bay Oyster House ★★   A great spot for fresh fish and local oysters in an Atlantic Coast ambience. $$; *326 Olga Rd, Eastsound; (360) 376-5886.* &

Springtree Cafe ★★   With an emphasis on local produce, the flavors here lean toward the Pacific Rim. $$; *310 Spring St, Friday Harbor; (360) 378-4848.* &

Lodgings

Cascade Harbor Inn ★★   Forty-eight modern units—some studios, some two-queen rooms—all with decks. $$$; *1800 Rosario Rd, Eastsound; (360) 376-6350 or (800) 201-2120; www.cascadeharborinn.com.*

Chestnut Hill Inn Bed & Breakfast ★★★   An elegant, renovated farmhouse, perched atop a pastoral rise near the ferry. *$$$; 414 John Jones Rd, Orcas; (360) 376-5157; www.chestnuthillinn.com.*

Deer Harbor Inn and Restaurant ★★ Rooms in the 1915 lodge are small, but new cabins have a nice beachy feeling. *$$; 33 Inn Ln, Deer Harbor; (360) 376-4110; www.deerharborinn.com.* &

Duffy House ★ This 1920s farmhouse offers five comfy guest rooms, all with private baths. *$$; 760 Pear Point Rd, Friday Harbor; (360) 378-5604 or (800) 972-2089; www.san-juan.net/duffyhouse.*

Edenwild Inn ★★ This majestic Victorian B&B features eight individually decorated rooms. *$$$; 132 Lopez Rd, Lopez Island; (360) 468-3238; www.edenwildinn.com.* &

Friday Harbor House ★★★ Some consider this stylish urban outpost a welcome relief from Victorian B&Bs. *$$$; 130 West St, Friday Harbor; (360) 378-8455; www.fridayharborhouse.com.* &

Harrison House Suites ★★★ This crisply renovated Craftsman inn features five impressive suites. *$$; 235 C St, Friday Harbor; (360) 378-3587 or (800) 407-7933; www.san-juan-lodging.com.* &

Highland Inn ★★★ Just two lovely suites are offered here, both with views of the Olympics. *$$$; west side of San Juan Island; (360) 378-9450 or (888) 400-9850; www.highlandinn.com.*

Lonesome Cove Resort ★ Six immaculate cabins at the water's edge: a lighthearted honeymooner favorite. *$$; 416 Lonesome Cove Rd, Friday Harbor; (360) 378-4477.* &

MacKaye Harbor Inn ★ This powder-blue house sits above a beach, perfect for sunset strolls. *$$$; 949 MacKaye Harbor Rd, Lopez Island; (360) 468-2253.*

The Majestic Hotel ★★ Every one of the 23 rooms is unique at this renovated landmark, built in 1889. *$$$; 419 Commercial Ave, Anacortes; (360) 293-3355 or (800) 588-4780; www.majesticinn.com.* &

Orcas Hotel ★ Originally a boardinghouse, this pretty 1904 Victorian has period pieces inside. *$$$; Orcas ferry landing, Eastsound; (360) 376-4300; www.orcashotel.com.*

Outlook Inn ★ The old part of the inn is affordable; newer, swanky suites have bang-up views. *$$–$$$; 171 Main St, Eastsound; (360) 376-2200 or (888) 688-5665; www.outlook-inn.com.* &

Roche Harbor Resort This stately old hotel boasts a terrific view and pretty gardens. *$$$; Roche Harbor; (360) 378-2155 or (800) 451-8910; www.rocheharbor.com.* &

Rosario Resort & Spa ★★★   This historic, waterfront estate has seen expensive room-redecorating efforts. *$$$–$$$$; 1400 Rosario Rd, Rosario; 360-376-2222 or 800-562-8820; www.rosarioresort.com.* &

Spring Bay Inn ★★★   The handsome Spring Bay Inn is stylishly appointed inside and scenic without. *$$$; 464 Spring Bay Trail, Olga; (360) 376-5531.*

Turtleback Farm Inn ★★   Amid tall trees and rolling pastures, Turtleback offers seven spotless rooms. *$$$; 1981 Crow Valley Rd, Eastsound; (360) 376-4914 or (800) 376-4914; www.turtlebackinn.com.* &

Wharfside Bed & Breakfast ★   Two guest rooms aboard a 60-foot sailboat are nicely finished. *$$; K dock, Friday Harbor; (360) 378-5661; www.slowseason.com.*

More Information

Cascadia Marine Trail: *(206) 545-9161.*
DNR Northwest Region office: *(360) 856-3500 (Sedro Woolley).*
Island Shuttle Express: *(360) 671-1137.*
Kenmore Air: *(206) 486-1257 or (800) 543-9595; www.kenmoreair.com.*
Lopez Island Chamber of Commerce: *(360) 468-4664; www.lopez island.com.*
Orcas Island Chamber of Commerce: *(360) 376-2273; www.orcas.org.*
San Juan Island Chamber of Commerce: *(360) 378-5240; www.san-juanisland.org.*
San Juan Islands Visitors Information Center: *P.O. Box 65, Lopez, WA 98261; (360) 468-3663; www.guidetosanjuans.com.*
Victoria Clipper: *(206) 448-5000 or (800) 888-2535; www.victoria clipper.com.*
Washington Department of Fish and Wildlife: *(206) 775-1311; www.wa.gov/wdfw.*
Washington State Ferries: *(800) 84-FERRY; www.wsdot.wa.gov/ferries.*
Washington State Parks: *(800) 233-0321; Reservations Northwest, (800) 452-5687.*
Washington Water Trails Association: *(206) 545-9161; www.wwta.org.*
Whale-Spotting Hotline: *(800) 562-8832.*

Skagit Valley

From Samish Island south to La Conner and east to Big Lake, including Bay View State Park, the Skagit River Delta, and the Padilla Bay National Estuarine Research Reserve.

For an area that's mostly flat, Skagit Valley offers plenty of depth when it comes to outdoor action. Physically, it's unique. The valley, a sprawling, farm-studded floodplain, looks a lot like many other lowland valleys around Puget Sound: a large river (the Skagit) running through it floods several times a year, sending dairy cows and stubborn lowland homeowners scurrying. But there the comparisons end.

What makes Skagit Valley special is its location. The combination of flat, sandy farmlands and wide, quiet, saltwater bays is a delightful mix made more fascinating by looming mountains to the northeast (Mount Baker and the North Cascades) and west (Orcas Island's Mount Constitution). Climb on a bicycle and head west through the valley on a lonesome country road, and the flat pasturelands abruptly end, spilling out into the open salt water, giving the area a farmlands-to-the-sea feeling reminiscent of Holland. Stroll along one of the valley's many placid saltwater beaches, and you can watch migratory snow geese riding a saltwater breeze to a splash landing in a field already occupied by cows.

Seaweed mingling with silage can be downright confusing, but it all comes together in rather splendorous fashion during the spring bloom season. Then, the valley floor looks like it's been carpet-bombed by paint balls as daffodils, tulips, and irises jump to colorful attention in sprawling bulb-farm fields. The bloom season, mid-March to early May, is prime time in the valley, drawing thousands of motorists and, increasingly, cyclists to otherwise-deserted roads. A spring ride through the bulb fields can't be underrated. It's a uniquely Northwest experience, one of those dozen or so every Washingtonian must undertake to earn his or her veteran's stripes.

But don't make the mistake of overlooking the valley during the rest of the year, especially during the winter, our favorite time to visit. Whatever you do here, the pace is slow, deliberate, relaxed. The Skagit Valley will unwind you—even if you didn't know you were wound.

Getting There

The Skagit Valley is approximately 60 miles north of Seattle on Interstate 5. Most attractions discussed below are accessible by taking I-5 exit 226 (Mount Vernon) or exit 231 (Sedro Woolley/Hwy 20).

inside out

Cycling

Here's where the valley really shines. The Skagit flats have become one of the Northwest's premier cycling destinations, thanks to hundreds of miles of flat country roads that roll through thousands of acres of unbelievably colorful bulb fields during the spring tulip/daffodil bloomathon. The options are so numerous that describing particular routes is almost superfluous. A good strategy is to pick a safe, reliable parking spot, consult the free daffodil-fields map available from one of the local Chambers of Commerce (see More Information, below), and design a loop with a length to your liking. Most of the largest bulb fields lie south of Hwy 536, between Mount Vernon and La Conner.

One popular **daylong loop** takes you through the best of the valley: beaches, bird-watching estuaries, tulip fields, Mount Baker viewpoints, the Skagit River, and downtown Mount Vernon. It's mostly flat, and traffic is generally very light except during the peak bloom season of mid-March to mid-May. We highly recommend it as a full valley tour; it's one of the more scenic rural routes around Puget Sound. The full tour: Park at Bay View State Park (see Camping, below) and travel north on Bay View-Edison Road, turning east to go through the small towns of Edison and Bow on Hwy 237, then south along Worline Road, Ershig/Avon-Allen Roads, and McClean Road to Mount Vernon. From the city, follow Riverbend Road south along the Skagit to Penn Road, then cut back west across the valley on Calhoun Road, returning north to Bay View via Best Road or La Conner-Whitney Road, then Bay View-Edison Road. It's a 40- to 50-mile loop, depending on your particular route.

For a shorter, **2-hour loop** circling the peaceful, less-traveled north end of the valley, follow the route above, but turn west off Avon-Allen Road onto Wilson Road and return to Bay View, rather than proceeding south across Hwy 20 and into Mount Vernon. Similarly, cyclists who want to proceed straight to the bloom fields can make a nice half-day trip from Bay View by riding the general full-circle route in the reverse direction and eliminating the northern portion.

Camping

Bay View State Park on Padilla Bay is the primary public camping venue. The park, 3 miles north of Hwy 20 on Bay View-Edison Road, has 79 campsites (9 with hookups; RVs to 40 feet). It's a pleasant, sunny park, with plenty of flat grasslands for baseball and/or Frisbee use. Many RV-equipped birders flock here in the winter, parking in Bay View's grassy, somewhat closely packed sites. But the real attraction is the 1,320 feet of saltwater shoreline on Padilla Bay, much of which is protected as a National Wildlife Refuge (see Wildlife Watching, below). The beach area, separated from the campground by the highway, is a great day-use area—the best beach spot in the valley. Picnickers or cyclists can use the beach parking lot as a base for a day's exploring. Bay View is open all year. Campsites can be reserved up to 11 months in advance by calling Reservations Northwest; (800) 452-5687. *From the I-5/Hwy 20 interchange, drive 7 miles west on Hwy 20 to Bay View-Edison Rd, turn north, and continue 3 miles;* (360) 757-0227 or (800) 233-0321.

River Bend Park, a private campground along the Skagit River in Mount Vernon, is an alternative, but it's primarily an I-5 motorhome stopover, with 25 tent sites and 95 RV pull-throughs with hookups. Take the College Wy exit from I-5 to 305 W Stewart Road; (360) 428-4044. Another private campground, **Burlington KOA,** has 120 sites, many with hookups, plus 6 cabins and the usual KOA camper amenities. On North Green Road, Burlington, via I-5 exit 232, Cook Rd, and Hwy 9; (360) 724-5511.

Some valley recreators prefer to camp at Larrabee State Park, a 20-minute drive north on Chuckanut Drive (see the Bellingham and Lummi Island chapter).

Wildlife Watching

The lower Skagit Valley is one of Washington's best—and least-utilized — wild bird-watching venues, particularly during the winter. While wintering bald eagles are feasting on spawning salmon and attracting (too) much attention on the middle Skagit River (see the North Cascades Scenic

Tulips during the annual spring bloom near Mount Vernon

Highway chapter), far greater numbers of migratory birds, many of them quite rare, are quietly biding their time lower down the valley.

One of the best ways to see the valley's rich winged wildlife is from the saddle of a bicycle, which will put you up close to birds without scaring them away. Cyclists find a full range of migratory fowl in local fields during the cold season: **ducks** of all stripes, **mergansers, cormorants, great blue herons,** and even **snow geese** stop over or stay in swampy fields throughout the winter. The north-end valley loop described in Cycling, above, is one of the most wildlife-rich road routes we've ever found. In the winter, birds along the way will outnumber cars 10 to 1.

Most day visitors, however, are content to get their two binocular-lenses worth at the Padilla Bay National Estuarine Research Reserve, which has a full interpretive center, an interpretive trail, an observation deck (across the street), and a handicapped-accessible trail (see Hiking, below). Start the tour at the Breazeale–Padilla Bay Interpretive Center, just north of Bay View State Park (see Camping, above). From a viewing blind here, winter visitors are likely to see **canvasbacks, harlequin ducks,** and **black brant.** Other common visitors are numerous small **shorebirds, great blue herons, dunlins, black-bellied plovers, bald eagles,** and an occasional **peregrine falcon. Harbor seals** also are sometimes spotted in the bay. The center is open 10am to 5pm, Wednesday through Sunday. On Bay View-Edison Road, about 3 miles north of Hwy 20; (360) 428-1558.

The long peninsula known as Samish Island, part of a former delta of the Skagit River, has a small but nice picnic spot and public beach on its north shore. To the north, views of Samish Bay, Mount Baker, and Chuckanut Mountain are excellent, and the sprawling Samish Bay mudflats are a prime landing zone for migratory birds. Bird-watchers often find a day spent here every bit as rewarding as one at the Padilla Bay area to the south. **Black brant, canvasbacks, widgeons,** and the occasional **pere-grine falcon** and **snowy owl** are seen here. Follow Samish Island Rd west to Wharf Rd, turn north, and proceed to Samish Picnic Site. The beach is accessible by stairs.

Another good birding venue, also lesser known, is the Skagit Wildlife Area, at the river's mouth in Puget Sound. This is the place to see **snow geese,** which migrate here each winter from Wrangell Island in the Arctic. As many as 27,000 are believed to winter on this 12,000-acre river delta, a triangle of private farms and grasslands maintained as wildlife habitat. Several hundred **tundra swans** also have made a winter home here, and more than 20 **duck** species have been observed. Viewing is good all win-ter, provided local roads aren't flooded. Stop at the Wildlife Area head-quarters near Conway for viewing advice on several nearby unmaintained dike trails. (Note: The area is open for hunting during duck and goose seasons.) From the Conway exit on I-5, drive west and follow the binocu-lar signs; (206) 775-1311.

Hiking

Generally, hiking trails are few in the valley flatlands. A couple of good ones, however, are the three-fourth-mile meadow/forest **interpretive trail** and the nicely maintained 2.25-mile **Shore Trail** along a dike at the south end of Padilla Bay's wildlife viewing area (see Wildlife Watching, above). Weekenders should consider stretching their wings (or wheels) a bit and partaking in excellent day hikes around Bellingham (see the Bellingham and Lummi Island chapter) or one of several wonderful and little-known trails around nearby Anacortes (see the San Juan Islands and Anacortes chapter).

Picnics

The beach area at **Bay View State Park** (see Camping, above) has nice picnic facilities (windy on occasion). Another good picnicking/beach-combing site is the lightly used **Samish Island beach area** (see Wildlife Watching, above). In Mount Vernon, tables can be found at **Lion's Park** on the Skagit River and **Hillcrest Park** at 13th and Blackburn. Southeast of the city on Blackburn Rd, **Little Mountain Park** is a good picnic spot with a sweeping view of the valley, the San Juan Islands, and the northern Olympics. Squint hard enough, and you might spot migratory trumpeter swans in January and February. Bring the camera.

Canoeing/Kayaking

Padilla Bay is fully explorable by canoe or kayak. In fact, except for a single deep channel through the center, most of its shallow, muddy waters are open only to flat-hulled craft. Good launching spots can be found at Bay View State Park and the Skagit County launch ramp below the Swinomish Channel Bridge along Hwy 20. **Samish Bay,** just to the north of the peninsula forming Samish Island, is another good paddling venue at high tide. But consider that it's less sheltered than Padilla Bay itself and more prone to strong northerly or westerly winds.

Fishing

The Lower Skagit River, low and milky green in the summer and often brown and powerful in the winter, is a major steelhead and salmon freeway. Well, not as major as it used to be. The Skagit used to hold the most prolific stocks of winter steelhead and summer chinook in the Puget Sound area. Not so anymore. Steelhead numbers are down, and the chinook stocks are so troubled you can't fish for them here anymore. (Two major reasons: wasteful fishing and incredibly destructive clearcutting on the upper river, not necessarily in that order.) But decent **steelheading** and good bank and boat fishing for **chum** and **pink salmon** are available in season. The chums roll in around October; look for pinks in late August and September of odd-numbered years only.

Fishing for warm-water species such as **largemouth bass, crappie,** and **perch** can be good in Big Lake, just east of Mount Vernon. And several local Cascade foothills lakes—Cavanaugh, Sixteen, and McMurray—usually are excellent **rainbow trout** producers in the spring. Note: You'll need a boat. Bank-fishing access is poor at all three.

Sailing/Boating

Saltwater pleasure boaters often tie up in La Conner, on the riverlike **Swinomish Channel.** (Caution: tricky tides.) Two Port of Skagit County **marinas** are found just north of town, with guest moorage and full services. The private La Conner Marina, (360) 466-3118, not far away, offers full services year-round, and nearby La Conner Yacht Sales, (360) 466-3300, will rent you a boat.

Three small islands in Padilla Bay, Huckleberry, Saddlebag, and Dot, are undeveloped state parks sites popular with boaters and kayakers. Saddlebag is a designated campsite on the state's Cascadia Marine Trail, a state-managed water trail with campsites from Olympia to British Columbia; (206) 545-9161. (See the Washington Outdoors Primer for details.)

A **public boat ramp** is located at Bay View State Park, but it's a single-lane job usable at high tide only. A newer, more reliable launch is the Skagit County ramp beneath the Swinomish Channel Bridge, just off Hwy 20. This is also a decent picnic spot. Plenty of **public launch spots** are found on the lower Skagit, including at Hamilton, Sedro Woolley, and Burlington, and at Edgewater and Riverbend RV Parks in Mount Vernon.

Accessible Outdoors

Bay View State Park (see Camping, above) has barrier-free campsites, water, and rest rooms. The **Padilla Bay National Estuarine Research Reserve** (see Wildlife Watching, above) has barrier-free interpretive trails, including the 2.25-mile Shore Trail. The **Brezeale Interpretive Center** at Reserve headquarters has an accessible observation deck, and the entire center is barrier-free. Call (360) 428-1558.

outside in

Restaurants

Calico Cupboard ★   It's awfully cute (think Laura Ashley), but most folks come for the pastries. $; *720 S 1st, La Conner (and branches); (360) 466-4451.*

Kerstin's ★★   Kerstin's is likely to stay a while—especially considering the local raves. $$; *505 S 1st, La Conner; (360) 466-9111.*

La Conner Seafood & Prime Rib House ★   Get on the waiting list and go window shopping: the reward is excellent seafood. $$; *614 1st St, La Conner; (360) 466-4014; www.laconnerseafood.com.* &

Pacioni's Pizzeria ★   Pizza is why you come here. (And to watch the owners hand-toss the pizza dough.) $; *606 S 1st St, Mount Vernon; (360) 336-3314.* &

Palmers Restaurant and Pub ★★   La Conner's favorite restaurant serves reliable traditional dinners. $$; *205 Washington, La Conner; (360) 466-4261; $$; 416 Myrtle St, Mount Vernon; (360) 336-9699.*

Lodgings

The Heron in La Conner ★★   The Heron is one of the prettiest hostelries in town, with 12 jewel-box rooms. $$; *117 Maple St, La Conner; (360) 466-4626 or (877) 883-8899; heroninn@ncia.com.*

Hotel Planter ★   Opened in 1907, this Victorian-style hotel is part of La Conner's colorful past. *$$; 715 S 1st St, La Conner; (360) 466-4710 or (800) 488-5409.*

La Conner Channel Lodge ★★   The Lodge is an urban version of its casual cousin, the La Conner Country Inn. *$$$; 205 N 1st St, La Conner; (360) 466-1500 or (888) 466-4113; www.laconnerlodging.com.* &

La Conner Country Inn ★   Despite its name, the La Conner Country Inn is more of a classy motel. *$$; 107 S 2nd St, La Conner; (360) 466-3101 or (888) 466-4113; www.laconnerlodging.com.* &

Skagit Bay Hideaway ★★   A romantic spot, this waterfront hideaway offers privacy and luxury. *$$–$$$; 17430 Goldenview Ave, La Conner; (360) 466-2262 or (888) 466-2262; www.skagitbay.com.*

White Swan Guest House ★★   This classic B&B has been a popular fixture for over 14 years on Fir Island. *$$; 15872 Moore Rd (Fir Island), La Conner; (360) 445-6805; www.thewhiteswan.com.*

The Wild Iris Inn ★★   This 19-room inn is geared toward romance, with Jacuzzis and Cascades views. *$$$; 121 Maple Ave, La Conner; (360) 466-1400 or (800) 477-1400; www.wildiris.com.* &

More Information

La Conner Chamber of Commerce: *(360) 466-4778.*
Mount Vernon Chamber of Commerce: *(360) 428-8547;*
   www.mvcofc.org.

Whidbey and Camano Islands

From Clinton north to Rosario Bay at Deception Pass, including Camano Island, South Whidbey, Fort Ebey, Ebey's Landing, Keystone Spit, Fort Casey, Joseph Whidbey, and Deception Pass State Parks.

Just call them San Juan Lite. In many ways, Whidbey and Camano Islands are like the San Juans without the ferry hassle—or the pretense. Reaching them requires only a fraction of the commitment; both are but a 45-minute commute from the Seattle area. Both are separated from the mainland only by bridged channels. And each offers the great views, beautiful countryside, and stunning parks found in its neighboring islands farther north.

It's amazing how often Whidbey becomes a weekend destination for those of us who haven't planned far enough in advance to arrange transportation, lodging, and other essentials for trips to the mountains, the Olympic Peninsula, or the San Juans. Whidbey and Camano are welcome—and oft-underappreciated—alternatives.

They're also relatively blue-collar outdoor venues. Both Whidbey and Camano have far fewer quaint B&Bs, restaurants, guide services, and other cheesy touristy amenities per square mile than the neighboring northern islands. But that's a large part of their charm to longtime Seattleites, who appreciate the islands as places where change, thankfully, hasn't kept pace with the rest of Puget Sound. Although the hillsides are bursting with Microsoft Millionaire weekend getaways, Camano's beaches look the same today as they did when we were children. And Whidbey has managed to come through the Puget Sound money explosion more or less intact. The island's magnificent public places, particularly the classic Fort Casey and Deception Pass State Parks, just seem to get better with age. Indeed, the rolling farmlands around Ebey's Landing National Historical Reserve look much the same as they did 150 years ago, when some of Puget Sound's first white settlements were founded there.

Early homesteaders in Coupeville, one of Washington's first towns, no doubt were drawn by Whidbey Island's unique topography: high, sandy cliffs on the wind-buffeted west side, several miles of rolling, farmable plateau in the middle, and gentle beaches and curving coves on the protected eastern (leeward) side. They found firm, fertile ground underfoot. Mountains all around. And a watercolor saltwater view in every direction. What more could a settler ask?

Not much. And today, neither do we. The island's unique beauty continues to draw Puget Sound cyclists, sight-seers, campers, beach walkers, kayakers, boaters, and wildlife watchers, many of whom consider Whidbey their own island playground. Poking around here for even a short time prompts admiration for Whidbey's hearty early settlers. And it makes one wonder: did Whidbey sport the first rooflines in Puget Sound because it was a convenient site, or simply because it was the best?

Getting There

The south Whidbey Island port of Clinton is a mere 20-minute ferry ride from Mukilteo, which is a 30-mile drive north of downtown Seattle. From Clinton, Highway 525—the main south Whidbey corridor—runs north, merging with Hwy 20 at mid-island. Northern Whidbey destinations such as Oak Harbor and Deception Pass often are reached by skipping the ferry and driving Interstate 5 to Mount Vernon—60 miles north of Seattle—then following Hwy 20 west across Fidalgo Island to Whidbey. For the best of both worlds, make it a loop, commuting by ferry one way, I-5 the other.

Camano Island is about a 45-minute drive north of Seattle. Travel I-5 to about 18 miles north of Everett, take exit 212 (Camano Island/Stanwood), and follow Hwy 532 about 10 miles west.

inside out

Parks/Camping/Beaches

On Whidbey—45 miles long, but never more than 5 across—you're never more than about a 5-minute drive—or 500 strong pedals—away from a saltwater shoreline. Some of Washington's most pleasant, scenic saltwater beaches are found here. And public access is uncommonly good, thanks to a string of four state parks, beginning with South Whidbey at the

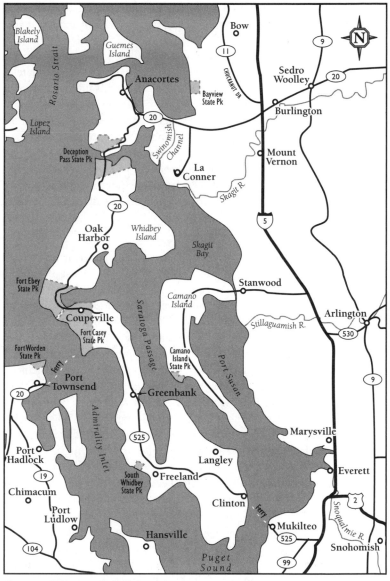

Central Puget Sound

island's far south end and culminating in drop-dead-gorgeous fashion with Deception Pass at the north end. Three of the four Whidbey parks have campgrounds; all have magnificent saltwater access, with views of the Cascades and the entire north Puget Sound marine environment. Just to the south, Camano Island State Park, the recreational focal point of that oft-overlooked island, is a longtime favorite of many Puget Sound area residents.

All the parks are excellent, close-to-home getaways, whether for the day or overnight. But a cautionary note on camping: unfortunately, being very popular and very close to Seattle usually adds up to very crowded, so landing a space on Whidbey can be a challenge in the summer. Thankfully, three of Whidbey's state parks—Deception Pass, Fort Ebey, and South Whidbey—have joined Washington's telephone campsite reservation system. Make the call. Even if you don't, it's still well worth the effort to head this way off-season or midweek, or to play weekend campground roulette by staying in one of the island's less popular venues and scouting for an open site at your favorite. Here's the list of goods for each park, roughly from south to north:

Camano Island State Park

Multiple generations of Puget Sound area folks got their first exposure to outdoor life at Camano, a sprawling park with 6,700 feet of waterfront on sparkling Saratoga Passage. The park's unusually good weather (it's at the far end of the same Olympic Mountain "rain shadow" that keeps the Dungeness Valley dry), exceptional beaches, and plentiful wildlife make it a grand family spot. And spectacular sunsets over the Olympics have spurred many a late-night snuggle on Camano's flat, gravelly beach. Camano begs for large-scale, family-reunion blowout-style picnics, and it gets them. All told, the park has 113 designated picnic sites, plus a full-blown kitchen shelter. Picnic sites are in two groups, with many on the beach and others on a bluff at the park's north end. Wherever you pop open the picnic basket, be warned: scavenging crows have been known to fly right down and scarf sandwiches out of unsuspecting children's hands here. They like the view too.

Camano's unusually wide, flat beach has a grassy area that's great for kite flying and Frisbee tossing. Those more inclined to be sand spuds will find grand sunbathing spots on the upper beach, which has a soft, sandy surface and plenty of driftwood upon which to rest one's head and watch sailboats drift past. A three-lane boat launch makes the beach area a high-traffic boating venue, particularly during summer salmon-fishing season. (Parking your Yugo in one of the boat-trailer spots is not couth, and could lead to accidental fish-sliming of your windshield.) Surf fishing for bottomfish (perch, flounder) can be productive here, and if you're lucky, some steamer clams can be had at very low tide.

About 3 miles of hiking trails run through the park's upper, woodsy area, connecting the picnic area, the beach, and the three main camp-

Deception Pass Bridge looms from the beach at Deception Pass State Park

ground loops. Campers have their choice of 87 sites (no hookups; RVs to 45 feet). The sites are wooded, and for the most part nicely separated by trees. Show up early; you can't reserve sites here. The park also has a group camp for 200 people; call the park for information. Camano Island State Park is open all year. *Take I-5 north to exit 212, 18 miles north of Everett; turn west and follow signs on Hwy 532 west to the park, about 13 miles; (360) 387-3031 or (800) 233-0321.*

South Whidbey State Park

This secluded site on Whidbey's southwest shore is one of our favorite get-out-of-town-for-an-afternoon escapes, particularly on cold, clear winter weekend days. South Whidbey has 4,500 feet of narrow, gravelly beach on Admiralty Inlet—reached via a short, steep trail from the upland day-use area. There's not much room to frolic at high tide, but plenty of space to take a seat on a log, watch the sun go down, and reflect on how lucky you are to be here. The park's real attraction is upland: a stand of old-growth forest, mostly Douglas fir and some grand western red cedars, that's unique in this area. The trees are best seen by following the **Wilbert Trail** (easy; 1.5-mile loop) on the east side of Smuggler's Cove Road, opposite the developed park area. Two other trails, each about a half mile, lead from the day-use area to the beach, and a mile-long **Forest Discovery Trail** is a pleasant, mostly flat nature path. The wooded camping area, on a heavily forested bluff, offers no views, but good privacy. Choose from 54

standard and 6 "primitive" sites (no hookups; RVs to 45 feet). A dump station is available. Day users will find the wooded picnic area a relaxing,
though shady, retreat with a shelter to flee to in bad weather. South Whidbey is open daily in summer and on weekends and holidays only from
November 15 to February 14. Campsites can be reserved up to 11 months
in advance through Reservations Northwest; (800) 452-5687. *From Clinton, follow Hwy 525 north 9 miles, turn west on Bush Point Rd, and follow
signs to the park, on Smugglers Cove Rd; (360) 321-4559 or (800) 233-0321.*

Fort Casey State Park

Old Fort Casey, perched on a prominent point on Whidbey's west shore
across Admiralty Inlet from Port Townsend, truly is one of the most picturesque spots in the Northwest. Choose your highlight: 137 sunny acres,
much of which are wide-open, grassy uplands with stunning views of the
North Sound and Mount Baker. More than 4,000 feet of saltwater shoreline, for uninterrupted beach strolling, surf fishing, or lounging. Gun
emplacements with restored cannons—always a hit with the kids. And a
beachfront campground that's highly sought all year-round, particularly
by RV owners.

The park's focal point is the day-use area, high on a bluff near the old
gun mounts. Sprawling grass fields make a wonderful softball/Frisbee/
kite-flying playground. Trails lead along the bluff to several grassy
(unfenced, be careful with kids) overlooks that are as grand a place to
watch a summer sunset as we've found in the Northwest. Interpretive
signs describe the fort's history as a World War I–era gun emplacement
and World War II–era training facility. A large picnic area is nearby.

At the north end of the day-use area is the stately **Admiralty Head
Lighthouse,** built in the 1860s and moved inland when the area became a
military base. The lovingly restored building now contains an interpretive
center filled with park history. It's one of the most-photographed buildings in the state (aside from Bill Gates's house).

Unfortunately, Fort Casey, one of the state's more popular parks, also
has one of its smaller camping areas. The park has only 35 campsites (no
hookups; RVs to 40 feet). All are almost literally on the water, on a sand
spit below the bluff-top gun emplacements. The setting is idyllic: Puget
Sound just outside your tent flap or doorstep, with two of the state's most
lovingly restored Washington State ferries plying the water from Port
Townsend to a landing right next to the campground. Needless to say, it's a
popular spot—particularly among RVers, who are less troubled by the persistent winds on the mostly exposed beach.

The park also has a boat launch, a couple miles of hiking trails, and
an underwater park for scuba divers (see Scuba Diving, below). The beach

is a popular spot for surf fishing (see Fishing, below). Fort Casey is open all year. Campsites cannot be reserved. *Turn west off Hwy 20 on Engle Rd at Coupeville, follow signs 3 miles southwest to the park, near Keystone ferry terminal; (800) 233-0321.*

Immediately south of Fort Casey State Park, on the far side of the Keystone ferry terminal, is **Keystone Spit,** an undeveloped state park site. Its 6,800 feet of saltwater shoreline are great for strolling, and the equally long freshwater beach on Lake Crockett is a good bird-watching venue.

Fort Ebey State Park

Fort Ebey, another abandoned military base, is smaller, more secluded, and less popular than nearby Deception Pass State Park. But it offers a similar saltwater-beach experience, and its camping area is actually nicer. The main day-use area, perched on a high bluff above Point Partridge, is the northern starting point for a clifftop trail offering great views of Admiralty Inlet, plus a chance to explore gun bunkers abandoned after World War II. Unlike nearby Forts Casey, Worden, and Flagler—all built early in the 20th century—Fort Ebey was a "second-generation" Puget Sound fortress, part of a triad of 16-inch cannon emplacements built during World War II. Ebey's sister installations were built at Cape Flattery and at Striped Peak west of Port Angeles. The remains of Ebey's never-used gun battery are at the park's south end, near the campground. Also from the north (day-use) parking lot, a trail leads down to the beach (almost 3 miles of it is public property here) and the Point Partridge Lighthouse.

The nicely laid-out, lightly treed camping area has two loops with 50 standard sites (no hookups; RVs to 70 feet). It's a particularly nice place to visit in the spring, when wild rhododendrons are out in pale pink splendor. Cyclists, take note: Fort Ebey has 3 very nice primitive campsites at the end of a short trail to Lake Pondilla, a swampy wetland at the park's north end. Fort Ebey is open all year, although some facilities and campsites may be closed in winter months. Campsites can be reserved up to 11 months in advance through Reservations Northwest, (800) 452-5687. *Follow signs from Libbey Rd, which turns west off Hwy 20 just under 6 miles south of Oak Harbor; (360) 678-4636 or (800) 233-0321.*

Joseph Whidbey State Park

This is a day-use spot, with no campground. But the park named in honor of Capt. George Vancouver's fellow 1792 North Sound explorer is one of the best picnic places on Whidbey. The park has 3,100 feet of saltwater shoreline, with good views across the Strait of Juan de Fuca, and 20 picnic sites upland. (Note: No water, not much shade on hot days.) Joseph

Whidbey State Park is open daily in summer, and closed September 30 to March 30. *At Swantown Rd and West Beach Rd, 3 miles west of Oak Harbor; (800) 233-0321.*

Deception Pass State Park

Washington's most popular state park is a showcase for all that is magnetic about the Northwest: clean, sprawling saltwater beaches, jutting cliffs, deep forest, freshwater lakes, and great views. Plus, they threw in a magnificent bridge that might be the most artful assemblage of steel in the country. All told, it's a magnificent package—one that every Washington nature lover must unwrap at least once in his/her career outdoors. This is a park that can't be fully explored in a single day. Deception has an impressive 3,600 acres of wooded uplands, a remarkable 77,000 feet of saltwater shoreline, two campgrounds, multiple day-use areas, and four freshwater lakes.

If you only have time for the highlights, park in one of the Hwy 20 pullouts and walk out on Deception Pass Bridge. After you catch your breath, get back in the car and follow the winding road from the park's main entrance (south of the bridge) downhill to the beach day-use area. From here, trails lead along North Beach to viewpoints of the impressive bridge—actually two steel spans linking Whidbey and Fidalgo Islands—over the turbulent, swift current coursing through Deception Pass. The southern end of the main day-use area fronts on both Rosario Strait and Cranberry Lake, offering fine salt- and freshwater swimming in the summer. A separate picnic area on the opposite shore of Cranberry Lake has a splendid picnic area, a boat launch, and a dock where trout fishing is often good. More of the park is found on the opposite (north) side of the bridge. Pass Lake, a productive fly-fishing lake, is right off Hwy 20. Nearby, a road leads steeply downhill to Bowman Bay, where a saltwater fishing pier, small (16-site) campground, and boat launch are found.

Compared with the park's overall grandeur, the main campground is nothing special. Its location, however, is. Most of the 246 campsites (no hookups; RVs to 30 feet) are within a short walk of the park's memorable North Beach day-use area. If you have a choice (which you probably won't), go low and get one of the more open-air sites closest to the water, thus farthest away from busy Hwy 20. If you're a light sleeper, you might consider packing earplugs. Whidbey Island Naval Air Station is close by, even though the "Please pardon our noise: It's the sound of freedom" sign isn't. And the local vocals—an early morning crow population—are quite healthy. Deception Pass also has a 60-person group camp near North Beach and a separate, fully equipped group camp/Environmental Learning

Center (for parties of 25 or more) and a fully developed boat launch/moorage on Cornet Bay, east of Hwy 20.

All of this is tied together by some 30 miles of trails (see Hiking, below). Deception Pass State Park is open all year, although the North Beach and Rosario day-use areas are closed from early October to late March. Campsites can be reserved up to 11 months in advance through Reservations Northwest; (800) 452-5687. *From I-5 at Mount Vernon, follow Hwy 20 east to Whidbey Island and Deception Pass Bridge, 9 miles northeast of Oak Harbor; (360) 675-2417 or (800) 233-0321.*

A nearby alternative is **Oak Harbor City Beach Park,** an RV-only venue with 56 sites, all with water/electrical hookups; (360) 679-5551. In the Coupeville area, **Rhododendron,** a state DNR camp, has 6 primitive tent sites; 1 mile east of Coupeville on Hwy 20.

Just north of Fort Casey, **Ebey's Landing State Park,** named after the first white settler on Whidbey Island, has a mile-long trail to the grave site of the park's namesake, as well as a path along the top of Perego's Bluff. Worth the walk on a nice day. **Double Bluff Beach,** southwest of Langley, is a sandy waterfront spot, good for walking or kite flying.

Hiking

All the Washington State Parks listed above have hiking trails worthy of the average day hiker. Most are either beach walks or up-and-down hikes along Whidbey's steep, sandy bluffs, with good views of Puget Sound, the Olympic Mountains, and Mount Baker. Lovers of pure, flat **beach walking** might try the 5 miles of wild but public sand between Fort Casey and Fort Ebey State Parks. Fort Ebey's excellent **bluff-top trails** and the old-growth forest loop at South Whidbey State Park also are Whidbey highlights (see above for both). In the center of the island near Fort Casey, a **loop trail** at Ebey's Landing (easy/moderate; 3.5 miles) makes for a grand getaway anytime of the year, but seems especially peaceful in the fall and winter. Worth the walk on a nice day. The trail, part of Ebey's Landing National Historic Preserve, skirts Admiralty Inlet bluffs and passes by a historic cemetery before dropping steeply down to Perego's Lagoon, a good bird-watching area. The area was named for Isaac Ebey, a home-steader who was killed by natives in 1857. The trailhead is on Ebey Rd, just north of Fort Casey.

Especially worth noting is the 27-mile trail network at Deception Pass State Park. Hikes range from short nature trails to long, steep, alarm-ing cliff-top scrambles. From the main (West Point) parking lot on the south side of Deception Pass Bridge, spring-fed Cranberry Lake has a **short trail** (easy) along its sandy west side, with a viewpoint over a marshy area that makes for good bird-watching. On the other side of the lake, kids will like the short (half-mile) **nature trail** that loops through the woods near the Ranger Station. Nearby, at the north end of the day-use area at West Point, a slew of trails head east toward the bridge. You can walk nearly all the way to the bridge on North Beach during low tide, but stick to the upper, **forested trail** during high tides. Keep heading east, and you'll catch a path running right under the bridge and on to awesome views from 500-foot-high Goose Rock (moderate; round trip from West Point is about 3 miles, depending on your route).

A **loop** of the same Goose Rock area can be made from the park's Environmental Learning Center on Cornet Bay, as can a pleasant nature walk, the **Discovery Trail** (easy; 1 mile round trip). Another nice walk on Deception's east side is the **long beach stroll** and **upland loop trail** in the Hoypus Hill Natural Forest (easy; 3.5 miles round trip) at the end of Cornet Bay Rd. The state preserve contains a rare stand of virgin old-growth timber.

On the north side of Deception Bridge, Bowman Bay is the departure point for the park's more challenging—and most alluring—hiking destinations (difficult; various lengths possible). One trail leads south, up a steep rock face and around the top of **Reservation Head** to Lighthouse Point and down to Lottie Bay. Another trail leads from the Bowman Bay parking area west to picturesque Sharp Cove and **Rosario Head.** Both are good half-day hikes, with some tricky spots on the rocks.

Whidbey Island weekenders, particularly those at Deception Pass, also shouldn't overlook the excellent trails in the Anacortes area, such as the scramble to the top of Mount Erie (see the San Juan Islands and Anacortes chapter).

Cycling

Whidbey is a patchwork of glacier-smoothed rolling hills, many of which will challenge beginning cyclists, but none big enough to suck the life from more experienced ones. The island's main drag, Hwy 525, is narrow in places, with so-so shoulder space, and traffic tends to move fast over the long straightaways. But a number of Whidbey side roads make fantastic day trips, many through scenic, rolling farmland with a saltwater beach picnic for a reward at the destination.

On south Whidbey, a number of good routes can be devised to bypass busy Hwy 525. The most popular method: leave your car at Mukilteo, ride the ferry to Clinton, turn west on Deer Lake Road, south on Humphrey Road, or north on Galbreath/Wilkenson Rds. Then just follow the island's east or west shores. It's a good idea to have a map, but you really don't even need one. You can navigate by shoreline. Whichever bank you choose, all south-end roads tend to lead to **Freeland**, at one of the island's many tiny-waist narrow spots. Lunch up at Freeland County Park, rest, ride back. Round-trip mileage, depending on your route, will be from 25 to 40 miles. A good day trip to **South Whidbey State Park** begins at Mukilteo, where you can park in the Mukilteo State Park lot and cycle onto the ferry, disembarking at Clinton and climbing the long hill up Hwy 525. Proceed 9 miles, turn west on Bush Point Road for 3 miles, then follow signs 1.5 miles on Smugglers Cove Road to the park. It's a round trip of about 27 miles.

At mid-island, Fort Casey presents a range of opportunities. Cycling onto the Keystone ferry to tour **Port Townsend** makes a fun day trip for Fort Casey campers. In Port Townsend, cycle up the hill to Fort Worden, where you can have lunch on the bluff and stare back across Admiralty Inlet at Mount Baker, not to mention your own campsite below. Also from Fort Casey, a ride north to **Ebey's Landing State Park** or south to South Whidbey State Park via Keystone Road and Hwy 525 makes a fine day outing. And many visitors get a good taste of Whidbey cycling by parking in Coupeville and following Engle Road—which does have a cycle lane—about 3.5 miles to **Fort Casey.**

Another good day-trip starting point is **Joseph Whidbey State Park.** Rural roads in this gently rolling farmland-turned-residential-area are easy on the knees, easier on the eyes. On the island's north end, **Deception Pass State Park** has more than 16 miles of bike trails that rise and fall over 1,000 feet of elevation. Trails climb to high rocky bluffs with views of the San Juan Islands, then descend to sandy beaches. The trails are single-track, and not all of the park is open to mountain bikes.Cycling from Deception Pass State Park is more limited, but many riders enjoy the 7.5-mile backroad journey (on Rosario and Heart Lake or Havekost Rds) to **Heart Lake** and **Anacortes.** True adrenaline junkies can veer off this course and try the steep climb up **Mount Erie.**

A fairly hilly, but popular, route that takes in long stretches of both sides of central Whidbey begins at Fort Casey and proceeds east on Wanamaker Rd to the island's east shore. From here, you can follow an obvious series of shoreside roads north to Coupeville, around Penn Cove, and all the way to **Oak Harbor** (about 24 miles). The route home is west on Fort Nugent or Swantown Road, south on West Beach Road past Fort Ebey, and south to Fort Casey via Hwy 20 and Engle Road. Round-trip mileage is 40 to 45 miles, depending on your specific route.

Bikes can be rented at Velocity Bicycles in Langley; (360) 321-5040.

Kayaking/Canoeing

Deception Pass State Park (see Parks/Camping/Beaches, above) offers Whidbey's best paddling venue. Canoeists will love sprawling, shallow (maximum depth, 20 feet) **Cranberry Lake,** which has a forest ecosystem on the east side, a marine environment on the west. Sea kayakers will find calm, beautiful water in **Bowman** and **Cornet Bays,** both of which have boat launches and flat beaches with easy launch access and good parking. Both areas offer beautiful scenery and rate as excellent beginner-to-intermediate areas. Deception Pass is a designated stopover on the **Cascadia Marine Trail,** a state-managed water trail including campsites from Olympia to Vancouver, BC; (206) 545-9161.

Conversely, only very experienced paddlers should venture into treacherous, 500-foot-wide **Deception Pass** or the equally nasty 50-foot-wide **Canoe Pass,** the two channels that flow on either side of Pass Island beneath the Deception Pass Bridge. Currents are wicked here, sometimes approaching 10 knots. Even powerboaters wait for slack tide to run this channel.

Many experienced kayakers also use Bowman Bay as a base to cross short open-water stretches to the park's string of offshore islands: **Deception Island**—half a mile west of Deception Pass—is rocky, with a tricky eastside beach landing possible. **Northwest Island,** half a mile northwest of Rosario Beach, is an acre of rock and grass, with not much to see. Three-acre **Strawberry Island,** on the east side of Deception Pass, has decent landing spots on the south and east sides (easiest with higher tides), and offers a jaw-dropping view into Deception Pass. Stronger paddlers can use Cornet Bay as a base for exploring farther east, to **Skagit** or **Hope Island** in the mouth of Skagit Bay just south of Fidalgo Island. The latter, a forested rock of 166 acres, has established campsites on its north side, and a sketchy trail network.

The rest of Whidbey Island is equally kayak-friendly, particularly bays and coves on the eastern (leeward) shores. Kayaks can be rented for day trips on Penn Cove near Coupeville at Whidbey Water Works, located near Captain Whidbey Inn; (800) 505-3800. For 3-hour guided tours on various island waterways, contact Adventurous Spirits Tours, (360) 341-4828.

Boating/Sailing

Whidbey's sheltered coves, deep harbors, and plentiful launch ramps make it a boater's paradise. While boating facilities are found all around the island, most marine activity takes place on the island's east side, which is protected from the raucous weather buffeting the higher-cliffed west banks.

Oak Harbor, several notches below most other Whidbey towns on the schmaltz scale, shines brightly when it comes to boating. The Oak Harbor Marina, (360) 679-2628, is a full-scale, full-service **marina,** with amenities as good as any in the North Sound, including a four-lane launch ramp and transient moorage. This is the site of the famed Whidbey Island Race Week, the Northwest's largest summer yacht race, which draws dozens of top racing yachts in mid-July.

Also on north Whidbey, Deception Pass Marina, (360) 675-5411—on Cornet Bay Road, east of Deception Pass State Park—offers moorage and good boater services near the popular park. It's a good place to wait for slack tide to run through the pass. On the other side of Deception Pass, **Bowman Bay** has mooring floats for waiting out the tide on the Rosario Strait end. Use caution in the bay's rock-studded mouth.

On the south end, Coupeville has its own **boater services,** fuel, and (shallow) moorage maintained by the Port of Coupeville; (360) 678-5020. Nearby **Captain Coupe Park** has some moorage of its own, plus a boat launch. Langley Marina, (360) 221-1771, offers moorage, full supplies, launch ramps, showers, and the like.

If you're not getting your boat in the water from Whidbey, you're not trying hard enough. **Public launch ramps** can be found at Keystone, Coupeville, Oak Harbor, Fort Casey, Point Partridge, Strawberry Point, Possession Beach County Park, Dave Mackie County Park, Penn Cove's Monroe Landing County Park, Langley, Freeland, Mutiny Bay, Bush Point, Deception Pass State Park's Bowman Bay, Cornet Bay, and Cranberry Lake—and probably a few other places we haven't found yet.

Scuba Diving/Snorkeling

Whidbey's many rocky shores offer a plethora of good exploring spots for divers. But two established sites are Puget Sound standouts. **Rosario Bay** at Deception Pass (northwest of the bridge off Rosario Rd) has a locally famous underwater park with a rich, varied display of Puget Sound sea life. It's particularly noted for its brightly colored sea urchins, anemones, and sea pens. Very experienced divers sometimes boat out to the rocky shoals around **Northwest Island** for more of the same. Underwater treasures are equally rich in **Keystone Bay,** a protected cove near Fort Casey State Park where old pilings and jetty riprap attract large numbers of sea creatures, bottomfish, and the occasional octopus. This is also a popular snorkeling spot in the summer. Just watch out for the ferries.

Fishing

One of North Puget Sound's perennial salmon-fishing hot spots, Midchannel Bank, lies off the north end of Marrowstone Island near Port

Townsend, and is an easy boat trip across Admiralty Inlet from Whidbey's west shore. The big underwater shelf is at its best for **chinook** and **coho** during midsummer. Unfortunately, in recent years it's been closed to fishing from July to October to allow passage of wild chinook and coho to Puget Sound spawning streams. When the fishing here is on, it's hot. Same story a short run down at Possession Bar, a Puget Sound hot spot off the island's south end. Most boaters launch at Bush Point or Fort Casey State Park. The deep, tricky waters around Deception Pass are a known lurking spot for big **chinook salmon,** which are present from midsummer to fall. Many a 50-pounder has been hauled into a boat below the south side of the bridge.

The island's western shores also are home to a rather unique shore fishery for passing steelhead. Surf anglers at Bush Point, Lagoon Point, Fort Casey (**bottomfish, salmon,** and **steelhead),** and other western beach locations do surprisingly well at snatching winter steelhead bound for lower-Sound streams from December through February. Most use a long leader with a Spin-N-Glo bobber on top of a "Hoochy squid" salmon lure. Tip: The fish run very close in to shore. Make frequent, short casts.

In the winter, most Whidbey salmon-fishing action shifts to the east side of the island, with boats funneling out of Oak Harbor to fish for **blackmouth (immature chinook) salmon** in the protected leeward waters. All year long, fishing from piers at Deception Pass, Langley, and Coupeville can be a relaxing, though not entirely productive, pursuit.

Trout fishing can be very good on several Whidbey lakes. Near Deception Pass, Cranberry and Pass Lakes are noted trout producers (Pass is fly-fishing only). On the south end of the island, try Goss Lake or Lone Lake, both near Freeland.

For island fishing tips, seasons, and reports, call Ted's Sport Center in Lynnwood, (425) 743-9505.

Wildlife Watching

Whidbey is a delight for birders and marine mammal fans. **Seabirds, bald eagles, seals, otter, whales,** and **deer** are common sights. The island's Audubon Society Chapter recommends the following viewing areas: Deception Pass State Park (see Parks/Camping/Beaches, above) for loons, murrelets, eagles, kingfishers, warblers, and the like; Dugualla Bay and Lake (from Hwy 20 north of Oak Harbor, east on Frostad Rd, north on Dike Rd) for kingfishers, trumpeter swans, peregrine falcons, ospreys, and various ducks; Oak Harbor City Beach (from Hwy 20, south on 30th St) for abundant waterfowl; Joseph Whidbey State Park (see Parks/Camping/Beaches, above) for seals, otters, gray whales, bald eagles, shorebirds, and various waterfowl; Partridge Point near Fort Ebey (from Hwy 20, west on Libbey Rd) for seals, grebes, harlequin ducks, guillemots, scoters, mergansers, and other waterfowl; Fort Ebey State Park (see Parks/Camping/Beaches, above) for deer, otters, marbled murrelets, mergansers, kingfishers, woodpeckers, and kinglets; Kennedy's Lagoon on Penn Cove (from Hwy 20, south on Madrona Wy) for seals, sea lions, waterbirds, goldeneyes, and cormorants; Perego Lagoon and Bluff Trail at Ebey's Landing (see Hiking, above) for porpoises, orcas, mourning doves, great horned owls, warblers, finches, cormorants, yellowlegs, and killdeer; Coupeville Wharf for seals, otters, cormorants, loons, goldeneyes, kingfishers, scaups, and buffleheads; Fort Casey State Park (see Parks/Camping/Beaches, above) for gray whales, seals, grebes, auklets, murrelets, gulls, oystercatchers, and other waterfowl; South Whidbey State Park (see Parks/Camping/Beaches, above) for deer, raccoons, squirrels, ospreys, thrushes, western tanagers, woodpeckers, violet-green swallows, and small perching birds; Double Bluff and Bayview Beaches (from Hwy 525, south on Double Bluff Rd) for seals, gulls, waterfowl, and eagles; and Langley City Beach and Marina for orcas, seals, cormorants, grebes, mergansers, loons, and other waterfowl, as well as jellyfish, crabs, and sea stars visible from the pier.

Accessible Outdoors

Deception Pass State Park (see Parks/Camping/Beaches, above) is home to a fine barrier-free path, the Sand Dune Trail. The 0.8-mile trail offers views of Cranberry Lake, the Olympics, and the San Juans, as well as interpretive information. Deception Pass also offers accessible rest rooms, picnic sites, and campsites. **South Whidbey State Park** has some wheelchair-accessible campsites. **Fort Casey State Park** has barrier-free campsites and a boat ramp. **Rhododendron** campground offers barrier-free campsites, rest rooms, drinking water, and picnicking. **Camano Island State Park** has barrier-free rest rooms. See Parks/Camping/Beaches, above, for more information on all these sites.

outside in

Restaurants

Cafe Langley ★★ The town's best bet offers a fine Mediterranean/Greek dining experience. *$$; 113 1st St, Langley; (360) 221-3090; www.langley-wa.com/cl.* &

Kasteel Franssen ★   Kasteel Franssen has a regal, European feel and a solid reputation among locals. $$; *33575 Hwy 20 (Auld Holland Inn), Oak Harbor; (360) 675-0724; www.kasteel.franssen.*

Lucy's Mi Casita   Locals keep coming back for the homemade Mexican food and lively atmosphere. $; *31359 Hwy 20, Oak Harbor; (360) 675-4800.*

Star Bistro ★   A favorite eatery, the Star hops on weekends and serves luscious vacation food. $$; *201½ 1st St, Langley; (360) 221-2627; www.whidbeynet.net/starbistro.*

Trattoria Giuseppe ★   Locals rave about the Italian food at Trattoria Giuseppe. $$; *4141 E Hwy 525, Langley; (360) 341-3454.*

Lodgings

Anchorage Inn ★   Another "new Victorian" inn, the Anchorage offers moderately priced lodgings. $$; *807 N Main St, Coupeville; (360) 376-828; www.anchorageinn.com.*

Boatyard Inn ★★   Pine accents and Northwest furnishings characterize the Inn's 10 breezy suites. $$$; *200 Wharf St, Langley; (360) 221-5120; www.boatyardinn.com.* ♿

Camano Island Inn ★★   A luxurious waterfront inn with spectacular water views and six rooms. $$; *1054 W Camano Dr, Camano Island; (360) 387-0783 or (888) 718-0783.*

Captain Whidbey Inn ★   History sometimes outranks comfort in these 12 original, almost shiplike rooms. $$; *2072 W Captain Whidbey Inn Rd, Coupeville; (360) 678-4097; www.captainwhidbey.com.*

Chauntecleer House, Dove House, and Potting Shed Cottages ★★   Gorgeous cottages on a quiet bluff just north of downtown Langley. $$$; *5081 Saratoga Rd, Langley; (360) 221-5494 or (800) 637-4436; www.dovehouse.com.*

Cliff House ★★★   For a staggering $425 a night, this dramatic house is an extraordinary getaway. $$$$; *727 Windmill Rd, Freeland; (360) 331-1566; www.cliffhouse.net.*

Country Cottage of Langley ★   A collection of five cottages on 2 acres overlooking downtown Langley. $$$; *215 6th St, Langley; (360) 221-8709 or (800) 713-3860; www.acountrycottage.com.*

Fort Casey Inn ★   Tidy, no-frills accommodation with a historical bent in this neat row of houses. $$; *1124 S Engle Rd, Coupeville; (360) 678-8792.*

Guest House Log Cottages ★★   Fulfill storybook dreams playing house in these varied, pastoral dwellings. *$$$; 24371 Hwy 525, Greenbank; (360) 678-3115; www.whidbey.net/logcottages.*

Inn at Langley ★★★   Hard to imagine an idyllic getaway more evocative of the Pacific Northwest. *$$$–$$$$; 400 1st St, Langley; (360) 221-3033; www.innatlangley.com.* &

Island Tyme ★   Rooms are geared toward romance at this Victorian-style inn on a quiet 10 acres. *$$; 4940 S Bayview, Langley; (360) 221-5078 or (800) 898-8963; www.moriah.com/islandtyme/.* &

Lone Lake Cottages and Breakfast ★   Still one of the most interesting and eccentrically charming B&Bs around. *$$$; 5260 S Bayview Rd, Langley; (360) 321-5325; www.lonelake.com.*

The Old Morris Farm ★   An elegant countryside B&B in a 1909 farmhouse. *$$; 105 W Morris Rd, Coupeville; (360) 678-6586 or (800) 936-6586; www.oldmorrisfarm.com.*

Saratoga Inn ★   Fifteen distinctive rooms, each furnished with a fireplace and warm plaids and prints. *$$$; 201 Cascade Ave, Langley; (360) 221-5801; www.foursisters.com.*

Villa Isola ★★★   Recreate the slow, sweet life of the Old Country in these six sumptuous suites. *$$$; 5489 S Coles Rd, Langley; (360) 221-5052 or (800) 246-7323; www.villaisola.com.*

More Information

Camano Island Chamber of Commerce: *(360) 629-9193; www.whidbey.net/camano.*

Cascadia Marine Trail: *(206) 545-9161.*

Central Whidbey Chamber of Commerce, Coupeville: *(360) 678-5434; www.whidbey.net/coup.*

Langley Chamber of Commerce: *(360) 221-6765; www.whidbey.com/langley.*

Oak Harbor Chamber of Commerce: *(360) 675-3535; www.whidbey.net/oakchamber.*

Reservations Northwest: *(800) 452-5687.*

Welcome to Island County web page: *www.whidbey.net/islandco.*

Greater
Seattle

From Saltwater State Park north to Edmonds, east to Issaquah, and west to West Point, including Mukilteo, St. Edwards, Bridle Trails, Lake Sammamish, and Squak Mountain State Parks.

In Seattle, our inside most assuredly is out. Out as in "green." Out as in "wild." Out as in "unconfined." When it comes to urban areas with faraway places packed right inside city limits, Seattle may have no equal. It's true: we can look out the office window and see rowing crews swishing across Lake Union, anglers pulling salmon over the rail at Seacrest Boathouse, cyclists on the Burke-Gilman Trail, or picnickers at Myrtle Edwards Park, and sigh a smug sigh. It's all here.

If you look hard enough, most of it surely is. Seattle is blessed with a wealth of rich outdoor experiences, thanks largely to the very thing that can otherwise make it a painful place to live and conduct business: water, water, and more water. We're surrounded by it here, whether it's salt water in Elliott Bay, fresh water in Lake Washington, or that salty-fresh hybrid mix floating all those big boats out in Lake Union. We curse it, but we love it. The water gives us scenic vistas in a city park system that clearly ranks among the best on the continent, a county park system that's not far behind, and a dozen suburban city park systems that would beg to differ. Water keeps the Emerald City green, its inhabitants lean. When we're not exercising around water on miles of cycle and hiking trails, we're often lying beside it on grassy beaches—or relaxing upon it, on deck, among one of the nation's most imposing privately held pleasure-craft armadas.

The Seattle area—for all its hundreds of square miles of

The city skyline from the Port of Seattle's new day-use park in West Seattle

(expanding) concrete and longer-than-January traffic jams—still manages to wring a smile from even the biggest urban pessimist among us. Why? Because it really is all here. Without driving more than 20 minutes from home, Seattle recreators can swim, boat, bike, hike, camp, kayak, climb, fly, fish, run, dive, ride, row, pedal, or raft. Ours is the choice, the opportunity, the challenge.

Of course, it could be argued that not many Seattle-area residents spend all their waking hours—or even a small slice of them—actually doing those things. Mostly, a critic would say, Seattleites watch a few other people do them, then plot to get out of town to do them better, somewhere else, some other time.

Little matter. For Seattle's hundreds of thousands of mental REI cardholders—scurrying around between business meetings in hiking boots, Gore-Tex, and Capilene, too busy to recreate—getting out and doing it isn't always the most important thing. Somehow, just knowing we could is enough.

Getting There

Locate Seattle by looking for the center of the big, constant traffic snarl at the junction of Interstate 5 with I-90 and Highway 520. Seattle-Tacoma International Airport, the way most people get here, is 30 minutes south of the city. Shuttle Express is a reliable airport-to-front-door service, reservations required; (206) 622-1424 or (800) 942-0711. Metro buses 174 and 194 make the trip from downtown (the latter is the express route). Metro buses are free *in downtown's commercial core; otherwise the fare is $1 within the city ($1.25 during peak hours) and $1.75 if you cross the city line; (206) 553-3000; http://transit.metrokc.gov.*

Another common commute is on Washington State ferries, which cross Puget Sound frequently to various destinations. Riding the ferries also happens to be one of the most enjoyable ways to view the city's skyline. For ferry rates, schedules, and information: (206) 464-6400 or (800) 84-FERRY; www.wsdot. wa.gov/ferries.

Most of the recreation areas described in this chapter are either inside the city limits, to the north in north King or south Snohomish Counties via I-5, to the south via I-5, or on the Eastside via the Hwy 520 or I-90 floating bridges over Lake Washington.

inside out

Parks/Beaches

In 1884, Seattle pioneers David and Louisa Denny donated to the city a 5-acre plot of land at what is now the corner of Denny Wy and Dexter Avenue N, and Seattle had its first park—**Denny Park.** Since then, the park system has grown to more than 5,000 acres, many of them designed by visionary park planners John Charles Olmsted and Frederick Olmsted Jr. (sons of New York's Central Park mastermind, Frederick Law Olmsted). Seattle's parks range from the classical (Volunteer Park) to the recreational (Green Lake) to the wild (Discovery Park) to the ingenious (Gas Works Park). At last count there were 397 parks and playgrounds in the city of Seattle alone.

Surrounding suburban cities are no slouches in the parks department, either. Many of the area's most popular regional parks are run either by local cities or King County, and lie outside Seattle city limits—a short and (formerly) quick drive from downtown. A compilation of the best parks in the region follows, in the only fair way possible—alphabetical order. To find out more about any of them, call the appropriate parks agency. Washington State Parks: general information (800) 233-0321; Parks Department headquarters in Olympia (360) 902-8500; camping reservations (800) 452-5687. King County parks: (206) 296-4232. Seattle Parks and Recreation Department: (206) 684-4075. Bellevue parks: (425) 452-6885. Issaquah parks: (425) 837-3300. Kirkland parks: (425) 828-1218. Mercer Island parks: (206) 236-3545. Redmond parks: (425) 556-2300.

Alki Beach Park: This 2.5-mile strip of beach marks the spot where the original white Seattle settlers first established homesteads. (The Native American word *alki* meant "by and by," their wry comment on the pioneers' eager hopes of turning their settlement into the New York of the West.) Now the beach has many faces, depending on the season: cool and peaceful in the fall, stormy in winter, and jammed with cyclists and roller skaters in the summer. It also draws throngs of teenagers, who hang out along the Alki Avenue strip, which is lined with beachy eateries on one side, sandy beach on the other. Duwamish Head, at the north end of the strand, offers spectacular views, as does the Coast Guard–maintained Alki Point and Light Station, 3201 Alki Avenue SW, at the tip of the point. The scenic extension of Alki Beach continues southward along Beach Drive past windswept Me-Kwa-Mooks Park and on to Lincoln Park (see below). *Along Alki Ave SW in West Seattle.*

Bellevue Downtown Central Park: You can almost feel the magnetic pull of a billion credit-card strips at Bellevue Square from this 20-acre downtown park, which reflects Bellevue's desire for an oasis in a busy urban area. Tired mall shoppers cross the street to sit by the fountain, enjoy the large formal garden, or stroll by the 240-foot-wide waterfall, which empties into a 1,200-foot reflecting canal. Teak benches placed throughout recall the park benches of London. *1201 NE Fourth St, Bellevue.*

Blake Island State Park: Once an ancestral camping ground of the Suquamish tribe, this tiny island in Puget Sound is now a densely wooded wilderness state park. There are 54 campsites, plus boat moorage. Bring your own boat. There is no ferry service to the island, except for commercial runs to the privately operated Tillicum Village, a staged-for-tourists glimpse of North Coast Indian heritage. But many private boaters overnight on the island, and kayakers paddle from South Kitsap County (see the Kitsap Peninsula chapter) or north Vashon Island (see the Bainbridge and Vashon Islands chapter) launching points to Blake Island's designated Cascadia Marine Trail campsites (the Cascadia Marine Trail is a state-managed water trail including campsites from Olympia to Vancouver, BC; (206) 545-9161; www.wwta.org). Plenty of on-island recreation awaits: 15 miles of hiking trails access about 5 miles of beaches. *(206) 443-1244 (Tillicum Village).*

Bothell Landing: This quaint little community park across the Sammamish River from the Sammamish River Trail offers rolling green lawns for family picnics and Frisbee throwing, an amphitheater (with Friday-evening concerts in the summer), a historical museum housed in a turn-of-the-century frame building, and an adult day center. Canoes and small boats can tie up at the public pier, where ducks await bread crumbs. There is limited parking at the site itself; a parking lot at 17995 102nd Avenue

NE, Bothell, on the south side of the river, has additional spaces. *9919 NE 180th St, Bothell; 425/486-3256, ext 4377.*

Bridle Trails State Park: As its name suggests, this 480-acre park is a densely wooded equestrian paradise laced with horse trails (one links up with Marymoor Park) and even sports an exercise ring complete with grandstand. Though you may feel like an alien if you come to do anything but ride (even the private homes in the area all seem to have stables), the park also has picnic sites. Watch where you step. *116th Ave NE and NE 53rd St, Kirkland; 425/455-7010.*

Camp Long: Run by the Seattle Parks and Recreation Department, Camp Long serves as a meeting/conference facility (a lodge holds 75 people in its upper room and 35 in the basement), an in-city outdoor experience for family or group use (10 rustic bunk-bed-equipped cabins sleep up to 12 people at $30 a cabin), and simply as a 68-acre nature preserve. The park also offers interpretive programs, perfect for school or Scout groups, and family-oriented nature programs on weekends. Climbers seeking practice can hang from a climbing rock or a simulated glacier face. *5200 35th Ave SW in West Seattle; (206) 684-7434.*

Carkeek Park: Here's one of the city's most under-appreciated treats: 198 acres of wilderness in the far northwest corner of the city. Forest paths wind from the parking lots and two reservable picnic areas, (206) 684-4081, to the footbridge spanning the railroad tracks, and then down a staircase to the broad beach. (Use caution around the tracks; trains speed frequently through the park, and the acoustics can be misleading.) Grassy meadows (great for kite flying), picnic shelters, and pretty, meandering Piper's Creek are other good reasons to relax here. Visit in October to witness one of the Northwest's classic cycles of life: chum salmon return from the Pacific ocean via Puget Sound to spawn in Piper's Creek. Trails will take you close enough to get splashed. Keep dogs and kids out of the creek, please! *NW Carkeek Rd and Ninth Ave NW, in North Seattle's Broadview neighborhood.*

Chism Beach Park: One of Bellevue's largest and oldest waterfront parks, Chism sits along the handsome residential stretch south of Meydenbauer Bay. There are docks and diving boards for swimmers, picnic areas, a playground, and a large parking area above the beach. *1175 96th Ave SE, Bellevue.*

Coulon Park: This arboreal park on the shore of Lake Washington is the prize of Renton's park system. It has won national awards for the arresting architecture of its pavilion and restaurant concession (an Ivar's Fish Bar), but is best loved for the beach. Log booms around the swimming area serve as protective barriers for windsurfers. *1201 Lake Washington Blvd N, Renton; 425/235-2560.*

Discovery Park: Formerly the site of Seattle's Fort Lawton army base, this densely foliated Magnolia wilderness has been allowed to revert to its premetropolitan natural order. It is full of variety and even a little mystery—in 1982 a cougar was discovered in the park, and no one knew how it got there or how long it roamed free in the 534 acres. Self-guided interpretive nature loops and short trails wind through thick forests, along dramatic sea cliffs (where powerful updrafts make for excellent kite flying), and across meadows of waving grasses. The old barracks, houses, and training field are the few remaining vestiges of the Army's presence. Discover the park's flora and fauna yourself or take advantage of the scheduled walks and nature workshops conducted by park naturalists. On weekends, the park offers free guided walks and, in spring and fall, bird tours—call ahead to check the schedule, or stop by the visitors center; east parking lot, near the Government Wy entrance; 206/386-4236. Groups can also arrange their own guided walks. Check the tall trees frequently; there's often a bald eagle in residence. Two well-equipped kids' playgrounds are here, along with picnic areas, playfields, tennis and basketball courts, and a rigorous fitness trail. The network of trails is a favorite among joggers; the 2.8-mile Loop Trail circles the park, passing through forests, meadows, and sand dunes. **Daybreak Star Cultural Arts Center,** (206) 285-4425, sponsors Native American activities and gallery exhibits of contemporary Indian art in the **Sacred Circle Gallery.** West Point Lighthouse, built in 1881, is the oldest lighthouse in the Seattle area. *3801 W Government Wy in Seattle's Magnolia area; (206) 386-4236.*

Freeway Park: One of Seattle's most original outdoor spaces, this extraordinary park forms a lid over thundering I-5—a feat of urban park innovation when it was constructed in 1976. Here, amid grassy plateaus and rushing waterfall canyons, the roar of traffic seems to disappear, and brown baggers find rejuvenating solace. *Sixth Ave and Seneca St, downtown Seattle.*

Gas Works Park: What do you do when the piece of property with the grandest skyline and lakeside view in the city is dominated by a greasy old coal-gas-processing plant? In Seattle, you turn it into a park. Gas Works is urban reclamation at its finest. It's one of the city's most delightful parks, and the attractions are diverse. A high, grassy mound topped by a unique sundial/viewpoint offers a killer view of downtown Seattle and Lake Union, and makes a great launch pad for kite flyers. You'll also find a large picnic shelter, (206) 684-4081 to reserve space, and a wonderful play barn. Against a sky full of dancing kites, even the rusting hulk of the old gas works looks oddly handsome. This park has a beat all its own: most summer days, drummers and other acoustic musicians gather here for impromptu jam sessions, their music reverberating through the old concrete and steel structures. The threat of lurking soil pollutants—which closed the park in 1984—has been ruled out, provided you don't eat the dirt. (Parents with toddlers, take note.) Motorists should keep eyes peeled for cyclists: Gas Works is a primary start/stop point for Burke-Gilman Trail riders (see Cycling, below). *N Northlake Wy and Meridian Ave N, north Seattle; 206/684-4075.*

Golden Gardens: Alki Beach's spiritual counterpart to the north, Golden Gardens teems with tanning humanity on summer weekends. A breezy, sandy beach, nearby boat ramp, beach fire pit, and the pretty waters of Shilshole Bay are the biggest lures, although fully half of the park's 95 acres lie to the east of the railroad tracks along the wooded, trail-laced hillside. Watching the sun settle behind the pink Olympic Mountains from the beach at Golden Gardens reminds us why we live here. *North end of Seaview Ave NW, adjacent to Shilshole Marina, west of Seattle's Ballard neighborhood.*

Green Lake: When the sun shines and the joggers, tanners, and in-line skaters muster en masse, the greenbelt around Green Lake looks like a slice of Southern California that's been beamed to the temperate Northwest. Even on dreary days, the recently refurbished 2.8-mile paved inner circuit around the lake is likely to be crowded. For less competition (but more car exhaust fumes), runners can try the 3.2-mile unpaved outer loop. No less a personage than President Bill Clinton has been known to run here (accompanied by a phalanx of Secret Service agents) when he's in town. On any given day, however, you're much more likely to spot couples circling the water in intense conversation—some of them looking distinctly pained. So many love affairs have broken up during Green Lake strolls that many Seattleites cringe at the very thought of visiting here with their paramours.

What is now the center of Seattle's exercise culture is the remnant of a large glacial lake that was well on its way to becoming a meadow when the pioneers arrived. In the 1880s, land surrounding the lake was promoted to "suburban" home builders. But by 1910, construction here had been curbed under a comprehensive city beautification scheme created by John C. Olmsted, nephew and stepson of the famous American landscape designer Frederick Law Olmsted. The younger Olmsted proposed that Green Lake's water level be lowered by 7 feet, exposing more waterfront property to parkland development. City burghers went along with the plan—only to realize, too late, that by filling in the shoreline and diking off natural streams that had fed Green Lake for centuries, they were inviting the water's stagnation. Despite improvements in drainage since the 1960s, bathers still complain of "swimmer's itch."

The lake offers enjoyable sailing and windsurfing, as well as great people-watching—it draws a microcosm of the city's humanity, much as Central Park does in New York. If you'd rather watch birds, they're around too, from Canada geese to red-winged blackbirds to the occasional bald eagle. Although the tennis courts, soccer field, indoor pool and recreation center, outdoor basketball court, baseball diamond, pitch-and-putt golf course, boat rental, thriving commercial district, and considerable car traffic around the lake make it feel like an urban beach resort, you can usually find one or two grassy patches for a picnic. There's a well-equipped kids' playground on the northeast side.

Limited parking can be found in three lots: the northeast lot (Latona Avenue N and E Green Lake Wy N, the most crowded), the northwest lot (7312 W Green Lake Wy N), and the south lots (5900 W Green Lake Wy N). Be forewarned: they're all notorious car-prowl sites. *Between E Green Lake Dr N and W Green Lake Dr N in North Seattle; 206/684-4075.*

Hing Hay Park: Hing Hay (Chinese for "park for pleasurable gathering") is a meeting and gathering place for the International District's large Asian community. From the adjacent Bush Hotel, an enormous multicolored mural of a dragon presides over the park and the ornate grand pavilion from Taipei. A great place to get a feel for the rhythms of International District life. *S King St and Maynard Ave S, in Seattle's International District.*

Hiram M. Chittenden Locks: Talk of digging a navigable canal between the fresh water of Lakes Washington and Union and the salt water of Puget Sound began shortly after Seattle's pioneers arrived in the 1850s. However, debates over the best location for such a waterway and searches for financing delayed the start of work until 1911. And there were still numerous engineering challenges ahead: the biggest was the design and construction of locks near the canal's western end, which could control the difference in water levels between the Sound and the much higher Lake Washington. (In the end, the latter was lowered by 9 feet, exposing new property and interfering with salmon migrations.) Not until 1917 was the 8-mile-long Lake Washington Ship Canal dedicated, and another 17 years would pass before it was officially declared complete. In 1936, the Corps of Engineers named the Locks in honor of the major who had supervised the canal project.

Today, more than 100,000 pleasure and commercial boats per year go through the canal and what are colloquially known as the "Ballard Locks." Couples and families trot down to watch this informal regatta as it works its way through the "water elevator." The descent (or ascent) takes 10 to 25 minutes, depending on which of the two locks is being used. Particularly good people-watching is available during Seafair in July, when boats filled with carousing men and women crowd the locks, impatient to get through.

Across the waterway, in **Commodore Park,** the falls generated by a fish ladder entice struggling salmon each year, the sleek creatures bound for spawning grounds in Lake Washington and Cascade mountain streams. You can watch the fishes' progress from a viewing area with underwater windows onto the ladder: salmon in summer (peak viewing for sockeye is in early July) and steelhead in winter. With the salmon come the playful but controversial sea lions, who know a prime dining spot when they see one—much to the chagrin of salmon conservationists.

Call the visitors center for times of tours (daily in summer, weekends only during the rest of the year); there's also an interesting exhibit that explains the use and building of the locks. The green lawns and tree-lined waterside promenade of the grounds, along with the impressive rose display at the Carl S. English Jr. Botanical Gardens, make grand backdrops for summer picnics. Free; every day 7am–9pm. *3015 NW 54th St, in Ballard; 206/783-7059.*

Kelsey Creek Park: Kids are in their element at this excellent nature park, which comprises 80 acres northeast of the I-90/I-405 interchange. In addition to a variety of parkland habitats (marshy forests, open grassy glades, wooded hillsides), two barns and a farmyard provide an area where kids can see newborn calves, goats, lambs, and piglets in the spring. Kelsey Creek and numerous footpaths (good for jogging) wind throughout. An original 1888 pioneer log cabin adds a historical dimension. The nature park also has nice picnic areas and a small children's playground. *13204 SE Eighth Pl, east of I-405 in Bellevue.*

Kirkland Waterfront: A string of parks, from Houghton Beach Park, NE 59th Street and Lake Washington Boulevard NE, to Marina Park at Moss Bay, line the shore of Kirkland's beautiful Lake Washington Boulevard. The kids feed the ducks and wade (only Houghton Beach and Waverly Beach have lifeguards); their parents sunbathe and watch the runners lope by. This is as close to Santa Cruz as the Northwest gets. *Along Lake Washington Blvd, Kirkland.*

Lake Sammamish State Park: The sprawling beach is the main attraction of this state park at the south end of Lake Sammamish. Shady picnic areas, grassy playfields, barbecue grills, and volleyball courts are excellent secondary draws. Large groups must reserve day-use areas—the place can be overrun in summer. This is one of the most frequently visited parks in all the Northwest. Issaquah Creek, a major passageway for salmon bound for the Issaquah Hatchery, runs through the park's wooded area. *20606 SE 56th St, Issaquah (follow signs from I-90); 425/455-7010.*

Lake Washington Parks: This string of grassy beachfronts acts as a collective backyard for several of the neighborhoods that slope toward Lake Washington's western shore. **Madison Park,** E Madison Street and

43rd Avenue E, the site of an amusement park and bathing beach early in the century, has shed its vaudeville image and is now a genteel neighborhood park, with a roped-in swimming area and tennis courts. If you head west on E Madison Street and turn left onto Lake Washington Boulevard, you'll wind down to meet the beach again, this time at **Madrona Park,** Lake Washington Boulevard and Madrona Drive, a grassy strip with a swimming beach, picnic tables, a summer-only food concession, and a dance studio. Farther south is **Leschi Park,** Lakeside Avenue S and Leschi Place, a nicely manicured city park that occupies the hillside across the boulevard. The park offers great views of the Leschi Marina and the dazzling spinnakers on the sailboats, as well as a play area for kids. Another greenbelt, **Colman Park,** 36th Avenue S and Lakeside Avenue S, also with a play area, marks the start of the seamless strip that includes **Mount Baker Park,** Lake Park Drive S and Lake Washington Boulevard S, a gently sloping, tree-lined ravine; the hydroplane racing mecca—once a marshy slough, now a manicured park and spectator beach with boat launches—called **Stan Sayres Memorial Park,** 3800 Lake Washington Boulevard S; and the lonely wilderness peninsula of Seward Park (see listing in this section). *From Madison Park at E Madison St and 43rd Ave E to Seward Park at Lake Washington Blvd S and S Juneau St.*

Lincoln Park: Lincoln Park, a 130-acre jewel perched on a pointed bluff in West Seattle, offers a network of walking and biking paths amid grassy forests, picnic shelters—call (206) 684-4081 to reserve—recreational activities from horseshoes to football to tennis, and expansive views of the Olympic Mountains from seawalls or rocky beaches. Tide pools can be inspected at low tide, and plenty of beach is available for roaming. Kids will love the playground equipment. Don't miss the (heated) outdoor saltwater Colman Pool (summer only), which began as a tide-fed swimming hole. When you're finished at the park, walk next door to the Fauntleroy ferry dock and take a pleasant 15-minute ferryboat ride to Vashon Island. *Fauntleroy Ave SW and SW Webster St in West Seattle.*

Luther Burbank Park: This park's undulating fields and endless land-and-lake recreational areas occupy a good chunk of the northern tip of Mercer Island and make it the Eastside's favorite family park. It's well equipped, with picnic areas, barbecues, a swimming area, nicely maintained tennis courts, an outdoor amphitheater for summer concerts, a first-rate playground, several playing fields, docks for boat tie-ups (the haunt of sun-worshipping teens in summer), and green meadows that tumble down to the shore. When the main beach is crowded, head north toward the point to find lonelier picnic spots. Parking is plentiful. *2040 84th Ave SE, Mercer Island.*

Magnuson Park: This 194-acre park fronts Lake Washington just southeast of now-closed Sand Point Naval Station, with a mile of shoreline, a boat launch, a playing field, and six tennis courts. Adjacent to the north is the National Oceanic and Atmospheric Administration (NOAA), where you'll find a series of unique artworks along the beach. One sculpture, *A Sound Garden,* is fitted with flutelike aluminum tubes that create eerie music when the wind blows. The site is open every day from dawn to dusk and is a hauntingly wonderful spot to sit on a blue whale bench, listening to the wailing wind vanes and watching the sun come up over Lake Washington. *Sand Point Wy NE and 65th Ave NE in north Seattle.*

Marymoor County Park: This vast expanse of flat grasslands and playfields in Redmond is a regional treasure. Marymoor is home to the famed Marymoor Velodrome (see Cycling, below) and serves as the starting point of the **Sammamish River Trail** used for biking, jogging, and horseback-riding (see Cycling, below), which connects to the Burke-Gilman Trail in Kenmore. But plenty of open-space fun awaits noncyclists: the **Marymoor Historical Museum,** (206) 885-3684, Clise Mansion, picnic facilities, a popular area for flying remote-control model airplanes, an extremely popular off-leash area for dogs along the Sammamish Slough, and about a zillion playing fields. *6046 W Lake Sammamish Pkwy NE, just south of Hwy 520 in Redmond; (206) 296-2966.*

Myrtle Edwards Park: Myrtle Edwards and adjacent **Elliott Bay Park** provide a front lawn to the downtown Seattle shoreline. This breezy and refreshing strip is a great noontime getaway for jogging (the two parks combined form a 1.25-mile trail—see Cycling, below), picnicking on sea-facing benches, or just strolling. The park is a big-time gathering spot for Fourth of July fireworks, and Michael Heizer's prominent granite-and-concrete park sculpture, *Adjacent, Against, Upon,* has truly grown on us. Parking at the Pier 70 lot just south of Myrtle Edwards is at a premium, but the Waterfront Streetcar stops nearby. *Alaskan Wy between W Bay St and W Thomas St, at north end of Seattle's commercial waterfront strip.*

Newcastle Beach Park: This Bellevue park takes full advantage of its lakefront location with a fishing dock, swimming area, and bathhouse facility (complete with outdoor showers). Walking paths—including a three-quarter-mile loop—weave throughout the 28 acres, and a wildlife habitat area offers the chance to see animals and birds in their natural environment. *4400 Lake Washington Blvd S, Bellevue.*

Ravenna Park: This steep woodland ravine strung between residential districts north of Seattle's University District is a lush sylvan antidote to the city around it. At the west end is **Cowen Park,** University Wy NE and NE Ravenna Boulevard, with tennis courts and play and picnic areas. Trails along burbling Ravenna Creek lead to the eastern end of the park and more picnic areas, a wading pool, and playing fields. The whole expanse is a favorite haunt of joggers, as is Ravenna Boulevard, the gracious, tree-lined thoroughfare that defines its southern flank. *20th Ave NE and NE 58th St in north Seattle.*

Saltwater State Park: Folks use this 88-acre Puget Sound–front park for clamming (January to June only; call ahead for red tide report), picnicking, camping, hiking in the forested uplands, or scuba diving in the underwater reef. The views of Vashon Island and the summer sunsets are spectacular. *25205 Eighth Pl S, Des Moines; (206) 764-4128.*

Schmitz Park: Just south of West Seattle's Alki Beach is this 53-acre virgin nature preserve, full of raw trails through thickly wooded terrain. The largest western red cedars and hemlocks here are likely to be about 800 years old—seedlings when Richard the Lionhearted was leading his troops on the Third Crusade. It's a marvelous place for contemplation and nature study. No playgrounds, picnic areas, or other park amenities. *SW Stevens St and Admiral Wy SW in West Seattle.*

Seward Park: This spectacular wilderness occupies a 277-acre knob of land in southeast Seattle and gives the modern-day Seattleite an idea of what the area must have looked like centuries ago. At times, the park is imbued with a primal sense of permanence, especially on misty winter days when the quiet of a solitary walk through old-growth Douglas fir forest is broken only by the cries of a few birds. But at other times—hot summer Sundays, for instance—Seward turns into a frenzy of music and barbecues. You can drive the short loop road to get acquainted with the park, past the bathhouse and beach facilities; **Seward Park Art Studio,** (206) 722-6342, which offers classes in the arts; some of the six picnic shelters—call (206) 684-4081 for reservations; and some of the trailheads, which lead to the fish hatchery, the outdoor amphitheater, and into the forest preserve. *Lake Washington Blvd S and S Juneau St.*

Victor Steinbrueck Park: Pike Place Market's greatest supporter and friend is the namesake behind this splash of green at the north end of Pike Place Market. With the Alaskan Wy Viaduct right below, the park can be quite noisy during peak traffic hours. It also tends to be a favorite hangout for street people. Despite those caveats, the park's grassy slopes and tables make a fine place for a Market picnic, and the view of blue Elliott Bay and ferry traffic is refreshing. *Western Ave and Virginia St in downtown Seattle.*

Volunteer Park: Mature trees, circling drives, grassy lawns, and lily ponds make this the most elegant of Seattle's parks—as stately as the mansions that surround its 48 acres. Designed by the distinguished Olmsted Brothers firm of Massachusetts and dedicated to Seattleites who fought in the Spanish-American War, Volunteer Park graces the top of Capitol Hill and offers sweeping views of the Space Needle, the Sound, and the

Olympic Mountains.

At the north end of the main concourse lies the elaborate 1912 **Volunteer Park Conservatory,** near 15th Avenue E and E Galer Street; (206) 684-4743, boasting three large greenhouse rooms filled with flowering plants, cacti, and tropical flora. It's open (no charge) to the public; step inside for a quick trip to the tropics, complete with the humidity. At the conservatory's entrance, don't miss the Monument to William H. Seward, the U.S. Secretary of State who purchased Alaska dirt cheap from the Russians in 1867. Created by New York artist Richard Brooks for Seattle's 1909 Alaska-Yukon-Pacific Exposition, the statue was supposed to be installed here only temporarily, awaiting a move to Seward Park. But 90 years later, it still hasn't moved. (Traipse a bit farther north from the conservatory and outside the park you'll hit Lake View Cemetery, containing the graves of numerous Seattle pioneers as well as those of father–son martial-arts stars Bruce and Brandon Lee.) At the other end of Volunteer Park's main concourse is an old 75-foot water tower, whose interior steps the hardy can climb for a splendid view of the city and the Olympics. The **Seattle Asian Art Museum** is also located here. *15th Ave E and E Prospect St on Seattle's Capitol Hill; (206) 684-4075.*

Washington Park Arboretum: Year-round, Washington Park Arboretum is as full of people as it is trees. Naturalists and botanists rub elbows with serious runners and casual walkers, for this 200-acre public park (set aside as urban wilderness in 1904 and developed beginning in the 1930s) doubles as a botanical research facility for the nearby University of Washington. The Arboretum stretches from Foster Island, just off the shore of Lake Washington, through the Montlake and Madison Park neighborhoods, its rambling trails screened from the houses by thick greenbelts. More than 5,000 varieties of woody plants are arranged here by family. (Pick up maps or an illustrated guide at the Graham Visitors Center—see below—if you want to find specific trees.)

From spring through autumn, the Arboretum's **Japanese Garden,** 1502 Lake Washington Boulevard E; (206) 684-4725, is well worth a visit. Just off Lake Washington Boulevard E, which winds north-south through the park, this authentic garden was constructed in 1960 under the direction of Japanese landscape architect Juki Iida. Several hundred tons of rock hauled from the Cascades were incorporated into the design, as were stone lanterns donated by the city of Kobe and a teahouse sent by the governor of Tokyo; here, tea ceremonies were performed even before the surrounding garden was completed. Nowadays visitors stroll winding paths, admiring trees and shrubs pruned as living sculptures. The graceful carp pond, spanned by traditional bridges of wood and stone and lined with water plants, is home to countless ducks, herons, and muskrats. Though the original teahouse was destroyed by vandals years ago, it has since been replaced, and the tea ceremony is still performed on the third Saturday of the month, April through October, at 1:30pm by members of the Seattle branch of the Urasenke Foundation. The Japanese Garden is open daily at 10am, March through November; closing time varies seasonally. Admission charge for adults and children over 5. Guided tours are available by arrangement for a fee. Call for event schedules and operating hours.

Just across the road to the north runs **Azalea Way,** a wide, grassy thoroughfare that winds through the heart of the Arboretum. (No recreational running is permitted on this popular route.) Always pleasant, Azalea Way is magnificent in April and May, when its blossoming shrubs are joined by scores of companion dogwoods and ornamental cherries. Drop in on the **Joseph A. Witt Winter Garden,** especially from November through March. The Winter Garden focuses on plants that show distinctive seasonal bark, winter flowers, or cold-season fruit to attract birds. Side trails lead through the Arboretum's extensive camellia and rhododendron groves (the latter collection is world famous).

Follow Azalea Way to the copper-roofed **Graham Visitors Center,** 2300 Arboretum Drive E; (206) 543-8800, where you can find maps and Arboretum guides as well as horticulture-related books, gifts, and informational displays. On weekends beginning at 1pm, guided Arboretum tours begin at the center, which is open 10am–4pm daily. The Arboretum also hosts an annual spring plant sale each April and a fall bulb sale each October. *E Madison Street and Lake Washington Blvd E in east Seattle; (206) 543-8800.*

Waterfall Gardens: How many city downtowns can boast a park with a 22-foot crashing waterfall, even an artificial one? The waterfall in this tiny Pioneer Square park was built to honor United Parcel Service, which started in this location in 1907. It does crash (this is no place for quiet conversation), and the benches do fill up by noon on weekdays, but the park makes for a marvelous little nature fix in the middle of a busy urban day. *219 Second Ave S in downtown Seattle; (206) 624-6096.*

Waterfront Park: A park that spans three piers between the Aquarium and Pier 57, provides a break from the bustling activity of the rest of the waterfront. The park contains a tree-encircled courtyard, raised platforms with telescopes for a voyeur's view of Elliott Bay and islands, plenty of benches, and—strange for a park in this town—nary a blade of grass. *Pier 57 to Pier 61 on Alaskan Wy on Seattle's waterfront.*

Woodland Park: Guy Phinney was an Englishman who wanted to turn his Seattle-area property into something resembling a proper English country estate. **Woodland Park** retains much of its previous owner's vision; no matter that six-lane Aurora Avenue plows right through the middle of it, dividing the property into two distinct areas. The east side of Aurora is the site of most of the sporting activities (lawn bowling, tennis, playing fields, minigolf, picnic areas, and Green Lake Park—see listing above). The west side has the formal rose garden, the zoo's Education Center Auditorium, and the impressive Woodland Park Zoo. *5201 Green Lake Wy N in North Seattle; (206) 684-4075.*

Cycling

Despite the large amount of rainfall and fairly hilly terrain, cycling—from cruising to commuting to racing—is all the rage in and around Seattle. Many bicycle shops rent bikes, from mountain to tandem to kids' bikes, for the day or week. Some even include helmets for free. Al Young Bike & Ski, 3615 NE 45th Street; (206) 524-2642; Bicycle Center, 4529 Sandpoint Wy NE; (206) 523-8300; and Gregg's Greenlake Cycle, 7007 Woodlawn Avenue NE; (206) 523-1822, are all near major bicycle trails.

Cascade Bicycle Club organizes group rides nearly every day, ranging from a social pace to strenuous workouts. The legendary **Seattle-to-Portland Classic (STP)** is a weekend odyssey in which approximately 10,000 cyclists pedal from the Kingdome to downtown Portland in late June or early July. Late February's **Chilly Hilly,** a 33-mile trek on the rolling terrain of Bainbridge Island, marks the beginning of cycling season. Call Cascade's hot line, (206) 522-BIKE, or check their web site, www.cascade.org, for current listings, information about cycling in the Northwest, and upcoming events.

The Seattle Parks and Recreation Department sponsors monthly **Bicycle Saturdays/Sundays** (generally the second Saturday and third Sunday of each month, May through September) along Lake Washington Boulevard, from Mount Baker Beach to Seward Park, which closes to auto traffic. Anyone with a bike is welcome to participate. This great activity offers a serene look at the boulevard and provides a haven for little cyclers who are not yet street-savvy; (206) 684-4075; www.ci.seattle.wa.us/parks/Bicycle.

Following are some of the area's favored rides. The city Bicycle and Pedestrian program, (206) 684-7583, provides a biker's map of Seattle, available at most bike stores. (See also the trails listed under Running in this chapter.)

Alki Trail: This 8-mile West Seattle route from Seacrest Marina (on Harbor Avenue SW, by Alki Beach) to Lincoln Park is along a road wide enough for both bikes and cars. You'll get great views of downtown and Puget Sound. On sunny weekend days, be wary as you pass the Alki Beach area; it is often crowded with skaters and slow-moving walkers.

Blue Ridge: The view of Puget Sound and the Olympic Mountains is spectacular on this ride of less than 2 miles. From Aurora Avenue N at N 105th Street, go west on 105th, which turns into N Holman Rd. Follow Holman southwest, turn right onto 15th Avenue NW, and follow it north to NW 100th Street, where the Blue Ridge neighborhood begins.

Burke-Gilman Trail: A popular off-the-streets route for Seattle cyclers commuting to downtown or the U District, the 12.5-mile path is also great for the bicyclist who wants great views of the city, waterways, and Lake Washington. The Burke-Gilman, built on an old railway bed, has its western trailhead on the Fremont-Ballard border (Eighth Avenue NW and Leary Wy). The trail then meanders east past Gas Works Park on Lake Union, through the University of Washington campus, and north along Lake Washington's west shore, ending at Kenmore's Logboom Park (Tracy Owen Station Park) at the northern tip of Lake Washington. From here cyclists can continue east to Woodinville on the Sammamish River Trail (see listing below).

Elliott Bay Trail: You get a grand view on this brief ride along the shore of Puget Sound. The trail, 1.5 miles long, begins at Pier 70 and goes north to skirt the waterfront, pass between the grain terminal and its loading dock, wind its way through a parking lot of new cars right off the ship, and continue to the Elliott Bay Marina. It's full of runners and in-line skaters at noontime.

Lake Washington Boulevard: There are great views along this serene 5-mile stretch between Madrona and Seward Parks. The road is narrow in spots, but bicycles have a posted right-of-way. On Bicycle Saturdays/Sundays (see above), the southern portion (from Mount Baker Beach south) is closed to cars. On other days of the year, some riders may feel safer using the separate asphalt path that follows this portion of the road. Riders can continue south, via S Juneau Street, Seward Park Avenue S, and Rainier Avenue, to the Renton Municipal Airport and on around the south end of Lake Washington, then return via the protected bike lane of I-90. This makes for a 35-mile ride. Take a map with you. Madrona Park to Seward Park.

Mercer Island Loop: From Seattle, a bicycles-only tunnel leads to the I-90 bridge on the way to Mercer Island (the entrance is off Martin Luther King Jr. Wy, through a park of concrete monoliths and artwork by Seattle's Dennis Evans). Using E and W Mercer Wy, you'll ride over moderate rolling hills the length of this 14-mile loop. The roads are curving and narrow, so avoid rush hour. The most exhilarating portion of the ride is through the wooded S-curves on the eastern side of the island. This is a great route for perusing the varied residential architecture.

Sammamish River Trail: This very flat, peacefully rural route begins near Bothell Landing, follows the flowing Sammamish River for 9.5 miles, and ends at Marymoor Park in Redmond. Stop for a picnic at parklike Chateau Ste. Michelle Winery, just off the trail at NE 145th Street (bring your own lunch or buy one there). Bike rentals are available at Sammamish Valley Cycle, 8451 164th Avenue NE, Redmond; (425) 881-8442.

Seward Park (see Parks/Beaches, above): Take this paved and traffic-free 2.5-mile road around wooded Bailey Peninsula, which juts out into Lake Washington opposite Mercer Island. The peaceful ride offers a look at what may be the only old-growth forest left on the shores of the lake. Eagles sometimes soar overhead, as a few still nest in the park.

Mountain Biking

The fat-tire revolution is well ensconced in Seattle, but true mountain-biking terrain is fairly tough to find within Seattle or even its suburbs. You don't have to drive far, however. Good mountain-bike routes (usually either on Forest Service roads or trails) are found all around Puget Sound's rural areas and, if riding downhill is more your style, some ski areas, such as Crystal Mountain and The Summit at Snoqualmie, turn their snow trails into bike trails in the summer—complete with lift rides up the mountain (see the Snoqualmie Pass Corridor, Stevens Pass Corridor and Lake Wenatchee, and Mountain Loop Highway and the Glacier Peak Wilderness chapters, and all chapters in the Central Cascades section). Keep in mind that mountain bikes are forbidden on national park trails, and allowed only on certain trails maintained by the state Department of Natural Resources, state parks system, and U.S. Forest Service.

The Outdoor Recreation Information Center provides information on trail closures; (206) 470-4060. The Backcountry Bicycle Trails Club, (206) 283-2995; www. dirtnw.com/bbtc, organizes local rides for cyclists at all levels of experience and is adamant about teaching "soft-riding" techniques that protect trails from the roughing-up that can eventually cause closures. The best local guidebook is *Kissing the Trail: Greater Seattle Mountain Bike Adventures* by John Zilly, available at bookstores and biking and outdoor retail outlets

St. Edward State Park: Up to 12 miles of varied terrain make this park great for all skill levels. Located in the Juanita neighborhood of Kirkland (off Juanita Drive NE), it is the largest undeveloped area on Lake Washington and has 3,000 feet of shoreline. Be wary as you ride among the tall trees and up and down the 700 feet of elevation: the park's trails interweave, and it's easy to get lost if you don't pay attention.

Hiking

Most of the parks and gardens listed in Parks/Beaches, above, have hiking trails that don't require a lot of planning or equipment, through forested or waterfront areas, usually with good views of the Olympics or Cascades. Particularly popular among walkers and joggers are **Discovery Park** in Magnolia, **Green Lake Park** and **Carkeek Park** in north Seattle, **Gas Works Park** (with access to the **Burke-Gilman Trail)** on Lake Union, the **Washington Park Arboretum** (with miles of garden trails and a unique 1-mile floating trail along Lake Washington), **Bridle Trails Park** near Redmond, **Marymoor Park** (with access to the **Sammamish River Trail)** in Redmond, and **St. Edward State Park,** between Kirkland and Bothell.

Also wildly popular in recent years are the extensive trail systems on **Cougar Mountain Park,** along with Mount Si and and Tiger Mountain sometimes known as the Issaquah Alps (see the Snoqualmie Pass Corridor chapter for information on dozens of trails in that area). Some of the more spectacular hiking trails in the country are found in the Alpine Lakes Wilderness (see that chapter in the Central Cascades section), between Stevens and Snoqualmie Passes. Many can be hiked in a day trip from Seattle. Hikers looking for accessible day trips or longer that sample the region's vaunted wild lands can head to Mount Rainier National Park or Mount St. Helens National Volcanic Monument (see those chapters in the South Cascades section), or Olympic National Park (see the Olympic Peninsula and Pacific Coast section), all of which offer both short and long hiking trails.

While most major hiking destinations are out of town, Seattle is a virtual storehouse of hiking information. A valuable reference service is the **Outdoor Recreation Information Center,** located at the downtown REI, (206) 470-4060, which offers trail reports, maps, guidebooks, and weather information. Its staff can also direct you to a ranger station near your destination. The REI flagship store itself, 222 Yale Avenue N; (206) 223-1944, is a treasure trove of outdoor information. It carries a generous supply of guidebooks for all outdoor sports, as well as U.S. Geological Survey maps and a wide range of equipment and outdoor clothing. Members get an annual purchase rebate of about 10 percent. REI also has Northwest outlets in Lynnwood, Redmond, Federal Way, Bellingham, and Spokane.

If you can't find the right advice at REI, guidebooks for virtually every corner of the Northwest are available from the bookstore at **The Mountaineers Clubhouse,** 300 Third Avenue W; (206) 284-6310. Other good resources include the Seattle branch of **The Sierra Club,** 8511 15th Avenue NE; (206) 523-2147, and the nonprofit **Washington Trails Asso-**

ciation, 1305 Fourth Avenue, Suite 512; (206) 625-1367, whose monthly magazine, *Signpost,* and web site, www.wta.org, contain trail reports straight from the hikers' mouths. WTA is a leading organizer of volunteer trail maintenance work parties.

Boating

The same thing that makes Seattle such a lousy place for driving (water, water, everywhere) makes it nirvana for boat owners. A full range of services is available, from marine stores with that hard-to-find fuse, to a full-scale boatyard to build the cabin cruiser of your dreams. A wealth of boater services, suppliers, and repair shops are located in the Ballard/Salmon Bay area. And the city is as friendly as can be when it comes to welcoming visiting boaters. The short list of **marina facilities:**

Shilshole Bay Marina, 7001 Seaview Avenue NW; (206) 728-3385, is huge and always open, with full services, an unbeatable location, and a nearby public boat launch, plus spacious parking. Elliott Bay Marina, 2601 W Marina Place; (206) 285-4817, is a newish, fabulous, and well-equipped (free cable!) site at the foot of Magnolia Bluff. Harbor Island Marina, 1001 SW Klickitat Wy; (206) 624-5711, provides service for southern Elliott Bay. Not far away, Seacrest Boathouse, 1660 Harbor Drive SW; (206) 938-0975, has some guest moorage and boater services. Boaters who pass through the Hiram M. Chittenden Locks (see Parks/Beaches, above), the Lake Washington Ship Canal, and/or Montlake Cut will find many private marinas and moorage spaces on Lake Union and Lake Washington.

Sailing

Seattle has a great deal of water but, in the summer at least, precious little wind. Thus many sailors hereabouts reckon that the real sailing season runs from around Labor Day to the beginning of May (although in summer, late-afternoon winds will sometimes fill the sheets). And given a little wind, looking toward Seattle from its bodies of water will give you perspectives you can't get from your car (a glimpse of Bill Gates's house, for example).

The wannabe sailor can find classes or chartered tours. Sailing in Seattle offers three different staffed cruises on a 33-foot sailboat: past the houseboat communities on Lake Union, through the Hiram M. Chittenden Locks on the Ship Canal, or past Gates's house on Lake Washington. Sit back and enjoy the sights or, even if you've never sailed before, try your hand at sailing with instruction from the on-board crew. For regularly scheduled or chartered tours, reservations are a must. Sailing in Seattle also offers a variety of courses for everyone from the beginner to the salty dog who wants **American Sailing Association** certification (2000 Westlake Avenue N, Suite 46; (206) 298-0094; skipper@sailing-in-seattle.com; www.sailing-in-seattle.com). Discovery Charters and Sailing School, offers cruises for one day or up to several days, as well as instruction, aboard the 40-foot yacht *Dream Catcher*, complete with teak interior ((206) 784-7679; saltydog@aa.net; www.members.aa.net/~saltydog/).

For beginning sailors who want to learn the art in a smaller boat and have a few days to pick up the essentials, the **Seattle Sailing Association,** headquartered at the **Green Lake Small Craft Center,** 5900 W Green Lake Wy N; (206) 684-4074, at the southwest corner of the lake, offers classes. **Green Lake,** no more than a mile across in any direction, is the perfect place to learn: it's free from motor cruisers, floatplanes, and barge traffic. Once you know how to sail, you can rent boats from the center with an annual membership. **Mount Baker Rowing and Sailing Center,** on **Lake Washington,** also offers sailing lessons in small boats (3800 Lake Washington Boulevard S; (206) 386-1913).

Salty dogs who want to be their own skipper should try a classic wooden boat at the **Center for Wooden Boats,** 1010 Valley Street; (206) 382-2628; www.eskimo.com/~cwboats, on **Lake Union.** Call and schedule a checkout to show them you know how to tack, jibe, and dock under sail (takes about 25 minutes), and then access to the fleet of rental boats is yours. Rowboats can be rented by anyone. Checking out the exhibits is free; visitors are encouraged to touch the center's approximately 100 historically significant boats and to ask questions of one of the many volunteers. Heritage maritime skills workshops, such as celestial navigation or boat restoration, are offered throughout the year. And, of course, the center offers sailing classes.

Fishing

Salmon

"Fish from your window." The old motto for Seattle's Edgewater Inn used to be taken quite literally by many guests, who would cast from their rooms and maybe hook up with a bottomfish. It was more gimmick than sales point, of course. But the truth is, one of Seattle's most famous qualities always has been its front-door **salmon** fishery. The city surely is one of the few metropolitan centers in the world where anglers routinely hook up with a healthy salmon from a fishing pier literally within the shadow of a downtown skyscraper. Everyone knows Northwest salmon have been on a disturbing downward spiral for the past two decades. Wild chinook spawning in Puget Sound streams, in fact, finally have received federal

Endangered Species Act protection. But in spite of that, the Elliott Bay salmon fishery off downtown Seattle still can be quite productive. They're probably not tourists, but the fact is many anglers still do hook salmon right off the waterfront. If you don't believe it, get up early and watch boat anglers off the mouth of the Duwamish River or spin-casters on the fishing pier at Seacrest Boathouse in West Seattle.

The city's biggest salmon-hooking trick these days isn't technique—it's opportunity. Struggling wild salmon runs all around Puget Sound have caused a crazy quilt of seasonal closures during peak summer months. The road map you'll need in order to know when and where to fish is the state's fishing regulations pamphlet, available at sporting goods stores (such as Warshal's, downtown). Similar information is available on-line from Washington Fish and Wildlife, www.wa.gov/wdfw. Up-to-date information on seasons, closures, and hot spots also can be found in *The Seattle Times* every Thursday; look for Mark Yuasa's weekly fishing column in the sports section, or on-line at www.seattletimes.com. Another way is to consult an expert at a local boathouse or tackle shop. You'll also need a license to catch just about any Washington game fish, and a separate catch record for steelhead, sturgeon, salmon, and halibut. Ask.

In spite of the closures, salmon fishing in Central Puget Sound has remained fair in recent years. The key to successful Puget Sound salmon fishing is timing. Learn when runs begin and peak. Fish early (the best bite often is at dawn). Concentrate on tide changes, which also tend to bring on stronger bites. And use fresh herring. As is true in the rest of the Central Sound, when fishing is open, resident **coho** are available through the spring and summer (larger migratory coho arrive in midsummer), migratory **chinook** are caught primarily from June to August, **pink salmon** are caught in August and September of odd-numbered years, and **chum salmon** are harvested in autumn months. But it's not a summer-only venture. In recent years, winter **blackmouth** (resident chinook) fishing in the Central Sound has been productive from November to March.

Where to go? For Seattle boat owners, top Central Puget Sound fishing spots are right where they have been for decades: interior Elliott Bay (in season); Jefferson Head, Allen Bank, and Point No Point off Kitsap Peninsula; Midchannel Bank near Port Townsend; Possession Bar south of Whidbey Island; and other local favorites. In recent years, popular Central Sound fisheries, including Jefferson Head and Point No Point, have been closed from July to October, sending many Seattle anglers south to Tacoma-area hot spots such as Point Defiance and the nearby "Clay Banks" (see Fishing in the Tacoma and Gig Harbor chapter). Two City of Seattle boat ramps—Don Armeni Ramp in West Seattle and Shilshole

Ramp at Golden Gardens Park—are the most popular launching spots.

If you don't have your own boat, you're far from out of luck. Rental kicker boats are available at Seacrest Boathouse in West Seattle, 1660 Harbor Drive SW; (206) 938-0975. Several charter companies with expert Puget Sound skippers operate daily from Seattle and its suburbs, including A Spot Tail Salmon Guide, Shilshole Bay, (206) 283-6680, or Ballard Salmon Charters, 1811 N 95th Street, (206) 789-6202.

And even though success rates aren't high, you can catch salmon from Puget Sound fishing piers. Some of the most popular pier-casting spots are found at Seacrest in West Seattle, Shilshole Bay Marina near Golden Gardens Park, Pier 86 (just northwest of the grain terminal), the Edmonds Waterfront Pier, and Redondo and Dash Point in south King County. All of these piers also have become popular **squid**-jigging sites in the winter.

Steelhead

Steelhead, sea-run trout known for their ferocity and unusual (for a fish, at least) smarts, may have surpassed salmon as the most sought-after sports fish in Washington. A number of good steelhead streams flow into Puget Sound on all sides of Seattle. The closest are the Green, Snohomish, Snoqualmie, Tolt, and the justly famous Skykomish. Other rivers, farther north or south or on the Olympic Peninsula, are usually better. Steelhead return to local streams throughout much of the year, but the winter season, which generally begins in November and lasts through early April, is the most productive. If you're a newcomer to the game and/or just visiting, your best bet is to hook up with a guide. They come and go (usually to Alaska . . .), so ask for a referral at one of the tackle shops listed in Contacts, below.

Shellfish

Seattle's public beaches are open for **clamming** year-round (butter clams are the big draw), unless pollution alerts are posted, as is all too often the case these days. If beaches are open and you're confident that clams are safe, bring your own bucket, rake or shovel, mud boots, and tide table. Alki Beach Park, Alki Avenue SW, is the most popular in-city spot, but the digging is good at public beaches in Edmonds, Mukilteo, Everett, and on Whidbey Island as well. Clamming does, however, require a license. (Indeed, everything harvested from or near the water now requires a license—even seaweed.) And be warned: Clamming seasons are sometimes shortened or canceled altogether because of drastic decreases in the clam population, so you should consult the Fish and Wildlife Department before setting off. Also be warned: There is an ongoing—and seemingly increasing—danger of paralytic shellfish poisoning (PSP) caused by a microscopic organism that can turn the ocean water red, thus "red tide." The organism is a tonic for bivalves but highly toxic to humans. Cooking does *not* reduce the toxicity. To learn which beaches are unsafe, always call the Red Tide Hotline, (800) 562-5632, before going shellfishing. Also consult the state Department of Fish and Wildlife web site, www.wa.gov/wdfw.

Trout and bass

State fish hatcheries routinely stock catchable (10- to 12-inch) **rainbow trout** in dozens of suburban lakes inside and all around Seattle. Many of these lakes now are open for fishing all year; others open in late April. Most local streams open in June. For seasons and limits on a lake nearest you, contact the Fish and Wildlife Region 4 Headquarters in Mill Creek, (425) 775-1311, or ask at a local tackle shop. Some favorite local spots for Seattleites include Green Lake in north Seattle (see Parks/Beaches, this chapter) and, of course, Lake Washington, a truly spectacular fishing venue that holds hundreds of species, some of which are available all year long. Most Lake Washington parks have fishable shorelines or piers.

Contacts

For general fishing advice, be it on salmon or otherwise, call Linc's Tackle, 501 Rainier Avenue S, (206) 324-7600; Ballard Bait and Tackle, 5450 Shilshole Avenue NW, (206) 784-3016; Ted's Sport Center, 156th SW and Hwy 99, Lynnwood, (425) 743-9505; Salmon Bay Tackle, 5701 15th Avenue NW, (206) 789-9335; or Warshal's Sporting Goods, First and Madison, (206) 624-7300. Leading fly-fishing shops include the Avid Angler Fly Shoppe, 11714 15th NE, (206) 362-4030; Kauffman's Stream-born, 15015 Main, Bellevue, (425) 643-2246; Orvis, 911 Bellevue Wy NE, (425) 452-9138; the downtown REI, 222 Yale Avenue N, (206) 223-1944; and Creekside Angling Co., 1660 NW Gilman Boulevard, Issaquah, (425) 392-3800. A leading discount fishing gear supplier is Outdoor Emporium, 420 Pontius Avenue N, (206) 624-6550.

Canoeing/Kayaking

Seattle's wealth of saltwater shorelines, calm rivers, urban lakes, and other waterways has made it a national mecca for sea kayakers and canoeists. Outside of town, wild rivers such as the Skagit, Skykomish, Sauk, Nook-sack, Stillaguamish, and others make it an equally notable river kayaking destination.

Kayaking—particularly sea kayaking, which employs stable, flat-bot-tomed boats—is safe and easy to learn by just about anyone. But it still can be dangerous, and isn't a sport you should take on by yourself. Begin-ners usually come out ahead by hooking up with a club, whose members can offer expert advice and instruction. One of the oldest kayaking clubs in the nation is the **Washington Kayak Club,** PO Box 24264, Seattle, WA 98124, (206) 433-1983, a safety- and conservation-oriented club that organizes swimming-pool practices, weekend trips, and sea- and whitewater-kayaking lessons in the spring.

Several locations around town will rent canoes and kayaks for day excursions. See listings below for one near your destination. A good general resource is *Boatless in Seattle: Getting on the Water in Western Washington Without Owning a Boat!* by Sue Hacking. Some popular paddle destinations:

Duwamish River: From Tukwila (where the Green River becomes the Duwamish River) to Boeing Field, this scenic waterway makes for a lovely paddle. North of Boeing, you pass industrial salvage ships, commercial shipping lanes, and industrial Harbor Island, where the river empties into Elliott Bay. Rent a canoe or a kayak at Pacific Water Sports, 16055 Pacific Highway S; (206) 246-9385; pws@pwskayaks.com; www.pwskayaks.com, near Sea-Tac Airport—the staff can direct you to one of several spots along the river where you can launch your craft. The current is strong at times, but not a serious hazard for moderately experienced paddlers.

Green Lake: Green Lake's tame waters are a good place to learn the basics. Green Lake Boat Rentals, 7351 E Green Lake Drive N, (206) 527-0171, a Seattle Parks and Recreation Department concession on the northeast side of the lake, rents kayaks, rowboats, paddleboats, canoes, sailboards, and sailboats. Open daily, except in bad weather, March though October.

Lake Union: If you've always wanted to get an up-close look at houseboats, kayaking or canoeing on Lake Union is a great way to do it. You'll also find great views of the city and, if you are ambitious, you can paddle west from Lake Union down the Ship Canal, past the clanking of boatyards and the aroma of fish-laden boats, to the Hiram M. Chittenden Locks (see Parks/Beaches, above)—which will lift you and your kayak up and down for free. A short distance past the locks, you'll find yourself in the salt water of Puget Sound. Rent sea kayaks at Northwest Outdoor Center, 2100 Westlake Avenue N, (206) 281-9694, kayak@nwoc.com, www.nwoc.com. NWOC also offers classes and tours to the San Juan Islands and the Olympic Peninsula. Aqua Verde Paddle Club, 1303 NE Boat Street, (206) 545-8570, also rents kayaks hourly and will give a quick demonstration on the dock before you paddle away. (Reservations are recommended on summer weekends for both of these Lake Union rental outlets.)

Montlake and Arboretum: On a typical hot August day, drivers sitting in bumper-to-bumper commuter traffic on the Evergreen Point Bridge gaze longingly at canoeists in the marshlands of the Montlake Cut and Arboretum. Rent a canoe or a rowboat at low rates at the University of Washington Waterfront Activities Center, (206) 543-9433, behind Husky Stadium. Here the mirrorlike waters are framed by a mosaic of green lily pads and white flowers. Closer to shore, vibrant yellow irises push through tall marsh grasses, while ducks cavort under weeping willows. Pack a picnic lunch and wander ashore to the marsh walk, a favorite bird-watching stroll that meanders from just below the Museum of History and Industry to the lawn of Foster Island. Those with their own canoes or kayaks can venture farther afield.

Puget Sound: Seattle's proximity to the open waters and scenic island coves of Puget Sound makes for ideal sea kayaking. See chapters in the Puget Sound section for more details. Experienced kayakers can make a trek of a half day or half year on the **Cascadia Marine Trail,** a unique, state-managed water trail including campsites and inns from Olympia to Vancouver, BC. Contact Washington Water Trails Association, (206) 545-9161, wwta@wwta.org, www.wwta.org, for more details and permit information.

Sammamish River: The trip up the gently flowing Sammamish Slough is quiet and scenic. Ambitious canoeists can follow the slough all the way to Lake Sammamish, about 15 miles to the southeast, passing golf courses, the town of Woodinville, the Chateau Ste. Michelle Winery, and Marymoor Park along the way.

Kite Flying

In Seattle, you'll find almost as many good places for kite flying as there are parks (see Parks/Beaches, above). For advice on kite-flying conditions, suggestions on where to find breezy areas, and grand selections of colorful wind vessels, wind socks, and kite parts, visit Gasworks Park Kite Shop, 3333 Wallingford Avenue N, (206) 633-4780; or Great Winds, 402 Occidental Avenue S, (206) 624-6886. Thanks to its windswept location, **Gas Works Park**—and particularly the grassy knoll to the west of the Works (check out the sundial at the top)—is a very popular kite-flying spot, attracting stunt fliers and novices alike. **Magnuson Park** is another popular kite-flying spot.

In-line Skating

Roller skaters—and their ubiquitous subset, the in-line skaters—compose an ever-widening wedge of the urban athletic pie. In fair weather, skaters are found anywhere the people-watching is good and the pavement smooth, including the **Alki Trail,** the tree-shaded **Burke-Gilman Trail,** the **downtown waterfront,** and along **Lake Washington Boulevard.** Farther afield, fine skating is found on the **Interurban Trail** south out of Renton, and north on the **Sammamish River Trail** to Redmond's Marymoor Park. (See Cycling, above, and Running, below.) Note: Skate-rental shops won't let you out the door if the pavement is damp.

Green Lake (see Parks/Beaches, above) is the skate-and-be-seenskating spot in town, where hotdoggers in bright Spandex weave and bob through cyclists, joggers, walkers, and leashed dogs. The 2.8-mile path around the lake is crowded on weekends, but during the week it's a good place to try wheels for the first time. When the wading pool on the north shore of the lake isn't filled for kids or commandeered by roller-skating hockey enthusiasts, it makes a good spot to learn to skate backward or to refine your coolest moves. You can rent or buy skates, as well as elbow and knee pads, at Gregg's Greenlake Cycle, 7007 Woodlawn Avenue NE; (206) 523-1822.

Another urban skating site excellent for practicing is the **NOAA grounds,** 7600 Sand Point Wy NE, next to Magnuson Park. The facility can be reached via the Burke-Gilman Trail, and offers a quiet workout along a smooth 1-kilometer loop, with one low-grade hill and some exciting turns.

Rowing/Crew

In a city graced with two major lakes, many people opt to exercise on the water instead of jogging through exhaust fumes or skating through the crowds. They've discovered an affinity for the sleek, lightweight rowing shells, and relish slicing across the silver-black water of early morning. Lake Union Crew, 11 E Allison Street, (206) 860-4199, offers an introductory weekend as a way to explore the sport. This 8-hour coached program (4 hours on Saturday and 4 on Sunday) on **Lake Union** includes all the basics of safety, boat handling, and technique, plus a video review of your on-the-water rowing sessions. This floating boathouse also offers programs for both scullers (two oars) and sweep rowers (one oar each) from novice to competitive levels. After the row, enjoy a latte in front of the fireplace in the Great Room of the boathouse.

The Seattle Parks and Recreation Department runs two rowing facilities: one on **Green Lake,** out of the Green Lake Small Craft Center, 5900 W Green Lake Wy N, (206) 684-4074; and the other at Sayres Park on **Lake Washington,** through the Mount Baker Rowing and Sailing Center, 3800 Lake Washington Boulevard S; (206) 386-1913. Both operate yearround, offer all levels of instruction, host annual regattas, and send their top boats to the national championships. The Lake Washington Rowing Club, 910 N Northlake Wy, (206) 547-1583; and the Pocock Rowing Center, 3320 Fuhrman Avenue E, (206)328-0778; are two boathouses where you can store your boat, find competitive rowing teams, or sign up for introductory rowing programs. Because Seattle has one of the largest populations of adult rowers in the country, you can find numerous other women-only, men-only, or age-specific clubs in the area. For a full list, contact US Rowing, (800) 314-4ROW; www.usrowing.org. Most clubs allow guest rowers to ride in the launch with the coach; some will allow experienced oarspeople to row once or twice without paying fees. Contact individual boathouses to ask about guest policies.

Running

Step out just about any door in the area and you're on a good running course, especially if you love hills. Flat routes can be found, of course, especially along bike paths (see Cycling, above). The mild climate and numerous parks make solo running appealing, yet the city also has a large, well-organized running community that provides company or competition. Club Northwest's *Northwest Runner* (pick it up in any running-gear store) is a good source for information on organized runs and has a complete road-race schedule. Racers, both casual and serious, can choose from a number of annual races (at least one every weekend in spring and summer). Some of the biggest are the 4-mile **St. Patrick's Day Dash** in March, the **College Inn Stampede** and the 6.7-mile **Seward-to-Madison Shore Run** in July, the 8-kilometer **Seafair Torchlight Run** through the city streets in August, and the **Seattle Marathon** in November. One of the finest running outfitters in town, Super Jock 'N Jill, 7210 E Green Lake Drive N; (206) 522-7711, maintains a racing hot line, (206) 524-RUNS. Listed below are some popular routes for runners (for directions to most of them, see Parks/Beaches, above).

The **Arboretum** is a favorite. You can stay on the winding main drive, Lake Washington Boulevard E, or run along any number of paths that wend through the trees and flowers. (The Arb's main unpaved thoroughfare, Azalea Way, is strictly off-limits to joggers, however.) **Lake Washington Boulevard** connects with scenic E Interlaken Boulevard at the Japanese Garden. It then winds east and south out of the Arboretum and down to the lake itself. The northern lakeside leg, from Madrona Drive south to Leschi, is popular for its wide sidewalks; farther south, from Mount Baker Park to Seward Park, the sweeping views make it one of the most pleasing runs you will ever experience.

The 2.8-mile marked path around **Green Lake** has two lanes: one for wheeled traffic, the other for everybody else. On sunny weekends, Green Lake becomes a recreational Grand Central—great for people-watching, but slow going. Early mornings or early evenings, though, it's a lovely idyll, with ducks, geese, red-winged blackbirds, mountain views, and quick glimpses of rowers and windsurfers on the lake. The path connects with a bikeway along Ravenna Boulevard. A painted line establishes the cycling lane; runners can follow the boulevard's grassy median.

On the Eastside, Pretty **Kelsey Creek Park** has a main jogging trail with paths that branch off into the wooded hills. Along the **Kirkland Waterfront,** the Eastside's high-visibility running path stretches along the water from Houghton Beach Park to Marina Park—a little over a mile each way. A 2.5-mile (one way) scenic run along nicely maintained roads in **Medina and Evergreen Point** offers views of Lake Washington and of some of the area's most stunning homes along Overlake Drive and Evergreen Point Rd, in Bellevue.

Various paths and roads cut through thickly wooded **Lincoln Park** in West Seattle, overlooking Vashon Island and Puget Sound. The shoreline is tucked below a bluff where auto traffic can no longer be heard. A striking run in clear weather, the **Magnolia Bluff and Discovery Park** route offers vistas of the Olympic Mountains across Puget Sound. From the Magnolia Bluff parking lot (at Magnolia Boulevard W and W Galer Street), run north along the boulevard on a paved pedestrian trail. Magnolia Park ends at W Barrett Street; continue north for 4 blocks to Discovery Park, which has numerous paved and unpaved trails.

Formerly part of the Naval Air Station at Sand Point, **Magnuson Park** has many congenial running areas, including wide, paved roads and flat, grassy terrain, all overlooking Lake Washington. On clear days, the view of Mount Rainier is superb.

Follow **Ravenna Boulevard** along the wide, grassy median strip beginning at Green Lake and dip into Ravenna Park's woodsy ravine at 25th Avenue NE, near the boulevard's end (Green Lake Wy N and NE 71st St).

Horseback Riding

Stables and outfitters abound on the Eastside and in the Cascade foothills. For weekend or extended trips (camping, exploration, or cattle roundups) on both sides of the Cascades, call High Country Outfitters, 3020 Issaquah-Pine Lake Rd, Suite 554, Issaquah; (425) 392-0111; www.high-country-outfitters.com. (See the I-90 East: Roslyn to Ellensburg chapter for details on High Country's Central Washington offerings.) Some other day-trip outfitters:

One of the oldest ranches in the area, **Aqua Barn** (you can swim there too—though, we assume, not with the horses) offers easy, guided rides in the evenings and on weekends through 100 acres of pasture and foothills. Anyone over age 8 can ride. For advanced riders, Aqua Barn also offers a 2-hour Ridge Ride; children must be 10 years old. The ranch also has a large campground (see Camping, below). 15227 SE Renton-Maple Valley Hwy, Renton; (425) 255-4618

The neighborhood surrounding Bridle Trails State Park (see Parks/Beaches, above) on the Bellevue-Kirkland border looks like a condensed version of Virginia equestrian country, with backyards of horses and stables abutting the park. The park features miles of riding and hiking trails through vast stands of Douglas fir.

Climbing

Don't have time to travel several hours to learn how to climb a mountain face? You don't have to. In Seattle and its environs, several indoor climbing walls allow you to get vertical for after-work relaxation or for a good rush on the weekend. Some suggestions:

The **Marymoor Climbing Structure:** Otherwise known as Big Pointy, this 45-foot, concrete-brick-and-mortar "house of cards," just south of the Velodrome at Redmond's Marymoor Park, was designed by the godfather of rock climbing, Don Robinson. It features climbing angles up to and over 90 degrees. East end of Marymoor Park, off 520; (206) 296-2964.

REI Pinnacle: Said to be the world's tallest freestanding indoor climbing structure at 65 feet, this looming structure (we think the thing bears an uncanny resemblance to Lyndon Johnson), with more than 1,000 modular climbing holds, is very popular—waits can be as long as an hour, and you get only one ascent. You're given a beeper, however, so you can peruse the store while you wait your turn on the rock, and the climb is free. Or you can pay for a beginning climbing class and, while learning the basics and safety, have more time to clamber; 222 Yale Avenue N; (206) 223-1944.

Schurman Rock and Glacier: These West Seattle structures at Camp Long offer good climbing forays for the beginner. Both are unsupervised. Schurman Rock has separate areas so novices can take on one challenge at a time. The glacier is a child's dream structure with deep foot- and handholds; 5200 35th Avenue SW; (206) 684-7434.

Stone Gardens: One section of the gym consists of low overhangs—allowing climbers to practice one of the most difficult maneuvers of climbing within a few feet of the ground. The rest of the gym offers faces that can be bouldered or top-roped, with climbs for beginners to advanced. Staff members wander around offering helpful advice, or you can take one of several classes ranging from one-on-one beginner instruction to several levels of technical erudition; in Ballard at 2839 NW Market Street; (206) 781-9828.

Vertical World: The Redmond location of this rock gym, 15036-B NE 95th Street, offers 7,000 square feet of textured climbing surface, while the newer, equally striking Seattle club, 2123 W Elmore Street; (206) 283-4497, sports 35-foot-high walls and a whopping 14,000 square feet of climbing area. The walls are fully textured, making the more than 100 routes varied and interesting. Lessons are offered at both gyms; (425) 881-8826.

Once you've attained the highest pinnacles indoors and in controlled outdoor settings, take your hardened hands and clenching toes to the great outdoors, where you'll find many challenging and breathtaking faces. **The Mountaineers,** 300 Third Ave W; (206) 284-6310; www.mountaineers.org, the largest outdoor club in the region, is a superb resource, offering group climbs, climbing courses, and general information on climbs, both in the Northwest and elsewhere. For gear, both to rent and to purchase, and occasional free lectures about climbing, try the REI stores—the flagship store is at 222 Yale Avenue N; (206) 223-1944.

Rafting

The Pacific Northwest is webbed with rivers, so it's no wonder that rafting has become one of the region's premier outdoor adventure sports. Rafting companies are sprouting up all over the state, particularly west of the Cascades, and are ready to give you a taste of wild water for $50 to $80 a day. Trips are tailored differently at each company, though there are two basic types: peaceful float trips, often in protected and scenic wildlife areas, and trips through whitewater rapids, which vary in their degree of difficulty. Spring and early summer are the seasons for whitewater trips. Eagle-watching trips on the Skagit River are scheduled between January and March.

In spite of recent efforts to make all river guides subscribe to standardized training and equipment regimes, the best way to find a qualified guide service remains word of mouth and customer referrals. Rafting is an inherently dangerous activity. Most guide services, however, are very well equipped and extremely safety conscious. One way to select a reputable guide is to contact the land manager in the area of your destination (a Forest Service ranger district office, in most cases) and ask for suggestions; these are the people in charge of monitoring commercial raft activity. For information about specific river floats, consult the appropriate chapter in this guide. Most guide services for those rivers, however, are based in the greater Seattle area. Two of the area's more prominent guide services:

Downstream River Runners: This experienced company leads day trips on 12 Washington and Oregon rivers, including the Green, Grande

Ronde, Methow, and Klickitat. The bald eagle float trips down the scenic Skagit in winter (hot homemade soup included) make a great family expedition. 3130 Hwy 530 NE, Arlington; (800) 234-4644; www.riverpeople. com/rafting/htm.

Orion Expeditions: The veteran guides at Orion Expeditions ("the good guys in the white rafts") give lessons and lead rafting trips in Washington, Oregon, Costa Rica, and on the Rio Grande in Texas. 5111 Latona Ave NE, Seattle; (206) 547-6715 or (800) 553-7466; www.orionexp.com.

Windsurfing

Definitely not for dilettantes, windsurfing takes athleticism, daring, and a lot of practice. The sport is big in this town, partly because the Northwest helped put it on the world map. The Columbia River Gorge (about 200 miles south of Seattle) is the top windsurfing area in the continental United States (second in the United States only to Maui), because of the strong winds that always blow in the direction opposite the river's current—ideal conditions for confident windsurfers. See the Columbia River Gorge section of this guide for detailed information. Closer to home, windsurfing can be decent on virtually any body of water (for most listed here, see Parks/Beaches, above).

Green Lake: This is the best place for beginners; the water is warm, and the winds are usually gentle. Experts may find it too crowded, but novices will probably appreciate the company. You can take lessons and rent equipment at Green Lake Boat Rentals, 7351 E Green Lake Drive N; (206) 527-0171, on the northeast side of the lake. At E Green Lake Dr N and W Green Lake Dr N.

Lake Union: Lake Union has fine winds in the summer, but you'll have to dodge sailboats, commercial boats, and seaplanes. You can rent equipment and catch a lesson from Urban Surf, 2100 N Northlake Wy; (206) 545-9463. To launch, head to Gas Works Park (see Parks/Beaches, above).

Lake Washington: Most windsurfers prefer expansive Lake Washington. Head to any waterfront park (see Parks/Beaches, above)—most have plenty of parking and rigging space. **Magnuson Park** is favored for its great winds. At **Mount Baker Park**, you can take lessons at Mount Baker Rowing and Sailing Center, 3800 Lake Washington Boulevard S; (206) 386-1913. Choice Eastside beaches include **Gene Coulon Beach Park** in Renton, where you can also rent boards and get instruction, and **Houghton Beach Park**, with rentals nearby at **O. O. Denny Park,** NE 124th Street and Holmes Point Drive NE, Juanita.

Puget Sound: On Puget Sound, windsurfers head for Golden Gardens Park or Duwamish Head at Alki Beach Park in West Seattle. For rentals and lessons, try one of America's oldest windsurfing dealers: Alpine Hut, 2215 15th Avenue W; (206) 284-3575.

Camping

Let's face it: few people come to the Emerald City to pitch a dome tent. But a handful of suburban campsites are available to RVers who roll into town. For other surrounding campgrounds, consult the Mountain Loop Highway and Glacier Peak Wilderness, Whidbey and Camano Islands, Tacoma and Gig Harbor, Snoqualmie Pass Corridor, Kitsap Peninsula, and Bainbridge and Vashon Island chapters.

Saltwater State Park near Des Moines, immediately south of Seattle, is a Puget Sound waterfront park that offers 52 campsites (no hookups; RVs to 50 feet). The 88-acre park is most often used by scuba divers, who visit the underwater park just off the 1,445 feet of public shoreline. But the campground is adequate, and 2 miles of seldom-maintained but well-trod hiking trails lead into the uplands, offering nice views of Maury and Vashon Islands and the leeward Olympics. The campground is open from April to September. Campsites cannot be reserved. *Follow signs from Hwy 509, 2 miles south of Des Moines; (800) 233-0321.*

North of Seattle, Lake Pleasant RV Park, 24025 Bothell-Everett Highway, I-405 exit 26; (425) 487-1785 or (800) 742-0386, is the biggest **private campground** (and one of the nicest) in the greater Seattle area, with more than 200 campsites, including a dozen tent spots. Also within driving range are **Ferguson Park** (13 sites), a City of Snohomish campground on the shores of Blackman Lake near Hwy 9; (360) 568-3115; **Kayak Point County Park**, 13 miles west of Marysville; (360) 652-7992; and **Flowing Lake County Park** in Snohomish County; (360) 339-1208.

In the south end, Orchard Trailer Park, 4011 S 146th Street, I-5 exit 154, Burien; (206) 243-1210, has limited overnight **private facilities** for RVs. In Kent is KOA Seattle-Tacoma, 5801 S 212th Street, I-5 exit 152; (206) 872-8652, which has more than 140 sites for tents and RVs. Aqua Barn Ranch, 15227 SE Renton-Maple Valley Highway, Renton; (425) 255-4618, is one of the best local tent areas, with 240 sites, many of them grassy. (See also Horseback Riding, above.)

For **private campgrounds** to the east, Blue Sky RV Park, 9002 302nd Street SE, Issaquah; (425) 222-7910, has 51 RV sites. Not far from Lake Sammamish is Trailer Inns RV Park, 15531 I-90, Issaquah; (425) 747-9181, with 115 pull-through RV sites. Issaquah Village RV Park, 650 First Avenue NE; (425) 392-9233 or (800) 258-9233, has 112 RV sites, no tents allowed. On the west side of Lake Sammamish (take I-90 exit 13) is Vasa Park Resort, 3560 W Lake Sammamish Road; (425) 746-3260, a small park with decent tent sites.

Also within driving range are Wenberg State Park on Hwy 531 (take I-5 exit 206, about 12 miles north of Everett; (800) 233-0321); Kayak Point County Park, 13 miles west of Marysville; (360) 652-7992; and Flowing Lake County Park in Snohomish County; (360) 339-1208.

Photography

Shutterbugs can't go wrong in Seattle. But to capture the city in its natural splendor, a select few sites stand out. For details see Parks/Beaches, above.

Gas Works Park on Lake Union offers a nice view of the city with Lake Union in the foreground. It's also a rare place to shoot shoreline photos of kayakers in a very urban setting. Good sunset spot, too. The **Hiram M. Chittenden Locks** in Ballard are a great place to shoot boat closeups, with the Cascades or Olympics in the background. Chances are you'll also encounter sea lions here. **Washington Park Arboretum** is a sure winner in the spring. City streets along **Magnolia Bluff** are a grand place to shoot Puget Sound sunsets, as is **Golden Gardens Park** at Shilshole. The best straight-on shots of Seattle's waterfront skyline are made from West Seattle's **Harbor Drive, Seacrest Fishing Pier,** the viewing platform at the new **Port of Seattle access** near Salty's Restaurant, or, better yet, the deck of a Seattle-Bremerton or Seattle-Winslow **ferry.**

But if you go nowhere else, Seattle's **Kerry Park** on Queen Anne Hill (take W Highland Drive west from Queen Anne Avenue N) is *the* Seattle photo spot. This tiny park with a big reputation among pro shooters is where all those calendar twilight shots are made. Laid out before you are the Space Needle, Seattle Center's "new" KeyArena, the downtown skyline, Harbor Island, and, most spectacularly, Mount Rainier, which at sunset provides a pink backdrop to the whole thing. In the summer, you might have to line up an hour before dark to get a good tripod spot. Wish we were kidding.

Restaurants

Andaluca ★★☆ A romantic place with a lively Mediterranean-influenced seasonal menu. $$$; *407 Olive Wy (Mayflower Park Hotel), Seattle; (206) 382-6999; www.mayflowerpark.com.* &

Anthony's Pier 66 / Bell Street Diner ★★★ / ★★ A complex offering upscale/midscale, upstairs/downstairs seafood with a view. $$$, $$; *2201 Alaskan Wy (at Pier 66), Seattle; (206) 448-6688; www.anthonys-restaurants.com.* &

Assaggio Ristorante ★★ Assaggio brings Roman trattoria ambience to this downtown hotel space. $$; *2010 4th Ave (Claremont Hotel), Seattle; (206) 441-1399; www.assaggioseattle.com.* &

Brasa ★★★ One of the loveliest and most inviting spaces in town, with imaginative food. $$$; *2107 3rd Ave, Seattle; (206) 728-4220.* &

Cafe Lago ★★★ A warm, bustling gem with consistently wonderful Italian fare. $$; *2305 24th Ave E, Seattle; (206) 329-8005.* &

Campagne / Cafe Campagne ★★★★ / ★★★ This restaurant and bistro duo offers the cuisine of southern France. $$$, *86 Pine St, Seattle; (206) 728-2800; $$; 1600 Post Alley, Seattle; (206) 728-2233.* &

Canlis ★★★ Expect to be treated like royalty and pay accordingly here. $$$$; *2576 Aurora Ave N, Seattle; (206) 283-3313; www.canlis.com.* &

Carmelita ★★☆ This neighborhood favorite offers a sophisticated, seasonal vegetarian menu. $$; *7314 Greenwood Ave N, Seattle; (206) 706-7703; www.carmelita.net.* &

Cascadia ★★★ Innovative and unusual dishes using only Northwest foods and flavors. $$$$; *2328 1st Ave, Seattle; (206) 448-8884.* &

Chez Shea / Shea's Lounge ★★★ / ★★ A romantic prix-fixe restaurant and sexy bistro above Pike Place Market. $$$, $$; *94 Pike St, 3rd floor, Seattle; (206) 467-9990.*

Dahlia Lounge ★★★☆ This Tom Douglas restaurant offers exuberant, edgy, and globally fusing food. $$; *2001 4th Ave, Seattle; (206) 682-4142; www.tomdouglas.com.* &

El Gaucho ★★★ A retro-swank Belltown remake of the '70s-era uptown hangout. $$$; *2505 1st Ave, Seattle; (206) 728-1337; www. elgaucho.com.* &

Elliott's Oyster House ★★☆ Known for its slurpable oysters, outside dining, and fresh seafood. $$$; *1201 Alaskan Wy, Seattle; (206) 623-4340; www.elliotts oysterhouse.com.* &

Etta's Seafood ★★★ Etta's is a buoyant, hip seafood house in a colorful, casual space. $$$; *2020 Western Ave, Seattle; (206) 443-6000; www.tomdouglas.com.* &

Flying Fish ★★★☆ Enjoy great seafood in the noisy rooms of this popular Belltown hangout. $$; *2234 1st Ave, Seattle; (206) 728-8595; www.flyingfishseattle.com.* &

The Georgian Room ★★★☆   A grand space for grand occasions, with a seasonally changing menu. *$$$; 411 University St (Four Seasons Olympic Hotel), Seattle; (206) 621-7889; www.fshr.com.* ᕫ

Harvest Vine ★★☆   In this rustic shoebox of a place, it's standing room only for tapas and paella. *$$; 2701 E Madison St, Seattle; (206) 320-9771.* ᕫ

I Love Sushi ★★☆   A pair of bustling, high-energy sushi bars with immaculately fresh fish. *$$; 1001 Fairview Ave N, Seattle; (206) 625-9604; $$; 11818 NE 8th St, Bellevue; (425) 454-5706; www.ilovesushi.com.* ᕫ

Il Bacio ★★   Enjoy Northern Italian home cooking in a Redmond strip mall. *$$; 16564 Cleveland St, Redmond; (425) 869-8815.*

Il Terrazzo Carmine ★★★   Be prepared to spend an entire evening at this comfortably airy restaurant. *$$$; 411 1st Ave S, Seattle; (206) 467-7797.* ᕫ

Kaspar's ★★☆   Classic international cooking imaginatively coupled with Northwest ingredients. *$$$; 19 W Harrison St, Seattle; (206) 298-0123; www.kaspars.com.* ᕫ

Kingfish Café ★★   A stylish, casual, contemporary space serving sassy Southern soul food. *$$; 602 19th Ave E, Seattle; (206) 320-8757.* ᕫ

Lampreia ★★★★   The spare ocher dining room matches the minimalist menu creations here. *$$$; 2400 1st Ave, Seattle; (206) 443-3301.* ᕫ

Macrina Bakery & Café ★★   Gutsy, exceptional breads, which you'll find at the city's finest restaurants. *$; 2408 1st Ave, Seattle; (206) 448-4032.* ᕫ

Marco's Supperclub ★★☆   This sexy restaurant has a funky atmosphere and trip-around-the-world menu. *$$; 2510 1st Ave, Seattle; (206) 441-7801.* ᕫ

Matt's in the Market ★★★   This seafood bar and restaurant might be one of Seattle's best-kept secrets. *$$; 94 Pike St, 3rd floor, Seattle; (206) 467-7909.*

Monsoon ★★☆   A stylish and tasty Vietnamese addition to the diverse Seattle scene. *$$; 615 19th Ave E, Seattle; (206) 325-2111.* ᕫ

Noble Court ★   The dim sum (between 11am and 3pm on weekends) is the best in the area. *$–$$; 1644 140th St NE, Bellevue; (425) 641-4011.* ᕫ

Pagliacci Pizza ★   All locations offer the same eternal lure: thin and tangy cheese pizzas. *$; 426 Broadway E, Seattle (and branches); (206) 324-0730.* ᕫ

The Painted Table ★★★   Some of the most inspired plates in Seattle can be found here. *$$$; 92 Madison St (Alexis Hotel), Seattle; (206) 624-3646; www.alexishotel.com.* ᕫ

Palace Kitchen ★★★   The food is robust and innovative at this Tom Douglas–owned restaurant. *$$; 2030 5th Ave, Seattle; (206) 448-2001; www.tomdouglas.com.* &

The Pink Door ★★☆   This Italian trattoria at Pike Place Market has a speakeasy ambience. *$$; 1919 Post Alley, Seattle; (206) 443-3241.*

Place Pigalle ★★☆   This pretty little bistro offers ambitious French-Northwest-Italian cooking. *$$$; 81 Pike St, Seattle; (206) 624-1756; www.savvydiner.com.*

Ponti Seafood Grill ★★★   Ponti borrows from an array of ethnic flavors, with more than a nod to Asia. *$$$; 3014 3rd Ave N, Seattle; (206) 284-3000; www.ponti.com.* &

Ray's Boathouse ★★☆   Ray's is favored for waterfront dining by tourists and locals alike. *$$$; 6049 Seaview Ave NW, Seattle; (206) 789-3770; www.rays.com.* &

Rover's ★★★★   Choose from three prix-fixe menus served with gorgeous presentation. *$$$$; 2808 E Madison St, Seattle; (206) 325-7442; www.rovers-seattle.com.* &

Sea Garden / Sea Garden of Bellevue ★★ / ★★   Live tanks at the door are a clue to what's best at this Cantonese eatery. *$, 509 7th Ave S, Seattle; (206) 623-2100; $$; 200 106th Ave NE, Bellevue; (425) 450-8833; www.chinesecuisine.com.* &

Shanghai Garden ★★   One of the only places around that offers authentic Chinese food. *$$; 80 Front St N, Issaquah; (425) 313-3188.* &

Shiro's ★★★★   A small menu offers full-course Japanese entrees in an immaculate dining room. *$$$; 2401 2nd Ave, Seattle; (206) 443-9844.* &

Third Floor Fish Café ★★☆   This upstairs beauty has a drop-dead view and the fish is fresh and tasty. *$$$; 205 Lake St S, Kirkland; (425) 822-3553.* &

22 Fountain Court ★★★   This small converted house is one of the Eastside's most romantic destinations. *$$$; 22 103rd Ave NE, Bellevue; (425) 451-0426.* &

Wild Ginger Asian Restaurant and Satay Bar ★★★   Wild Ginger, a Southeast Asia-inspired restaurant, is wildly popular. *$$; 1401 3rd Ave, Seattle; (206) 623-4450.* &

Yarrow Bay Grill / Yarrow Bay Beach Café ★★★ / ★★   One atop the other, these restaurants boast creative food and great views. *$$–$$$, $$; 1270 Carillon Point, Kirkland; (425) 889-9052 (grill) or (425) 889-0303 (café).* &

Lodgings

Ace Hotel ★★　The clean and spare Ace is possibly the city's coolest hotel. *$$; 2423 1st Ave, Seattle; (206) 448-4721; www.theacehotel.com.*

Alexis Hotel ★★★　This lovely hotel is elegant, hedonistic, and whimsical all at once. *$$$$; 1007 1st Ave, Seattle; (206) 624-4844 or (800) 426-7033; www.alexishotel.com.* &

The Bacon Mansion Bed & Breakfast ★★　Its 1909 Tudor-style architecture gives the Bacon decidedly British airs. *$$; 959 Broadway E, Seattle; (206) 329-1864 or (800) 240-1864; www.baconmansion.com.*

Bellevue Club Hotel ★★★　The Bellevue Club has 67 striking rooms and extensive athletic facilities. *$$$; 11200 SE 6th St, Bellevue; (425) 454-4424 or (800) 579-1110; www.bellevueclub.com.* &

Best Western Pioneer Square Hotel ★★　A comfortable, moderately priced establishment in the heart of historic Seattle. *$$; 77 Yesler Wy, Seattle; (206) 340-1234 or (800) 800-5514; www.pioneersquare.com.* &

Chelsea Station on the Park ★★　The word "charm" can't be avoided when describing this bed and breakfast. *$$; 4915 Linden Ave N, Seattle; (206) 547-6077 or (800) 400-6077; www.bandbseattle.com.*

Claremont Hotel ★☆　This hotel offers 121 guest rooms with understated traditional decor. *$$$; 2000 4th Ave, Seattle; (206) 448-8600 or (800) 448-8601; www.claremonthotel.com.* &

Edmond Meany Hotel ★★　The refurbished 1931 Meany is an eye-catching presence in the U District. *$$; 4507 Brooklyn Ave NE, Seattle; (206) 634-2000 or (800) 899-0251; www.meany.com.* &

Four Seasons Olympic Hotel ★★★★　The prices are steep, but this is Seattle's one world-class contender. *$$$$; 411 University St, Seattle; (206) 621-1700 or (800) 821-8106; www.fshr.com.* &

Hotel Edgewater ★★　The Edgewater is the only Seattle hotel literally over the water. *$$$; 2411 Alaskan Wy, Pier 67, Seattle; (206) 728-7000 or (800) 624-0670; www.noblehousehotels.com.* &

Hotel Monaco ★★★　Sunny rooms are decorated in a blend of eye-popping stripes and florals. *$$$$; 1101 4th Ave, Seattle; (206) 621-1770 or (800) 945-2240; www.monaco-seattle.com.* &

Hotel Vintage Park ★★★　Rooms are named after wineries and fireside wine tasting is complimentary. *$$$; 1100 5th Ave, Seattle; (206) 624-8000 or (800) 624-4433; www.hotelvintagepark.com.* &

Hyatt Regency at Bellevue Place ★★　Part of the splashy Bellevue Place complex, this hotel offers many extras. *$$$$; 900 Bellevue Wy NE, Bellevue; (425) 462-1234 or (800) 233-1234; www.hyatt.com.* &

Inn at Harbor Steps ★★   This urban hideaway is in a swanky high-rise retail-and-residential complex. *$$$; 1221 1st Ave, Seattle; (206) 748-0973 or (888) 728-8910; www.foursisters.com.* &

Inn at the Market ★★★☆ This 70-room brick inn at Pike Place Market remains unhurried and intimate. *$$$; 86 Pine St, Seattle; (206) 443-3600 or (800) 446-4484; www.innatthemarket.com.* &

MV *Challenger* Bunk & Breakfast ★   This perky red-and-white 1944 tug moored on Lake Union offers eight rooms. *$$; 1001 Fairview Ave N, Ste 1600, Seattle; (206) 340-1201 or (877) 340-1201; www.challenger boat.com.*

Paramount Hotel ★★   Ideally located for all sorts of diversions, though rooms are small. *$$$; 724 Pine St, Seattle; (206) 292-9500 or (800) 426-0670; www.westcoasthotels.com/paramount.* &

Pensione Nichols ★   Bohemian atmosphere, superb location, and reasonable prices. *$$; 1923 1st Ave, Seattle; (206) 441-7125 or (800) 440-7125; www.seattle-bed-breakfast.com.*

Seattle Marriott at Sea-Tac ★★   For those who want to get in and out of town with a minimum of stress. *$$$; 3201 S 176th St, SeaTac; (206) 241-2000 or (800) 228-9290; www.marriott.com.* &

Sheraton Seattle Hotel and Towers ★★☆   Near the convention center, the Sheraton goes all out for business travelers. *$$$; 1400 6th Ave, Seattle; (206) 621-9000 or (800) 325-3535; www.sheraton.com.* &

Sorrento Hotel ★★★☆   An Italianate masterpiece grandly holding court east of downtown. *$$$$; 900 Madison St, Seattle; (206) 622-6400 or (800) 426-1265; www.hotelsorrento.com.* &

W Seattle Hotel ★★★   "Warm, witty, and welcoming" is the motto of this chain of boutique hotels. *$$$$; 1112 4th Ave, Seattle; (206) 264-6000 or (877) W-HOTELS; www.whotels.com.* &

Westin Hotel ★★☆   The Westin's twin cylindrical towers enclose big rooms with very big views. *$$$$; 1900 5th Ave, Seattle; (206) 728-1000 or (800) WESTIN-1; www.westin.com.* &

The Woodmark Hotel ★★★   Its plain exterior hides one of the finest hotels in or out of Seattle. *$$$; 1200 Carillon Point, Kirkland; (425) 822-3700 or (800) 822-3700; www.thewoodmark.com.* &

More Information

Amtrak: *(800) 872-2245.*
City of Seattle Public Access Network: *www.ci.seattle.wa.us.*

Downtown Visitors Information Center: *Seattle: (206) 461-5840.*

Greater Seattle Chamber of Commerce: *(206) 389-7200; www.seattlechamber.com.*

Greyhound: *(800) 231-2222; www.greyhound.com.*

King County Parks: *www.metrokc.gov/parks.*

Marmot Mountain Works: *827 Bellevue Wy NE, Bellevue; (425) 453-1515.*

Metro Transit: *(206) 553-3000; http://transit.metrokc.gov.*

The Mountaineers: *(206) 284-6310 or (800) 573-8484; www.mountaineers.org.*

The North Face: *1023 First Avenue, Seattle; (206) 622-4111.*

Outdoor Recreation Information Center: *downtown REI, 222 Yale Avenue N, Seattle; (206) 470-4060; www.nps.gov/ccso/oric.htm.*

REI: *222 Yale Avenue N; (206) 223-1944; (888) 873-1938; www.rei.com; www.rei-outlet.com. Also Redmond, (425) 882-1158; Federal Way, (253) 941-4994); and Lynnwood, (425) 774-1300.*

Seattle Parks and Recreation Department: *(206) 684-4075.*

Seattle-King County Convention and Visitors Bureau: *520 Pike Street; (206) 461-5800; www.seattleinsider.com/partners/seeseattle.*

The Seattle Times: *For weekly features on outdoor activities near and far, including this author's "Trail Mix" column, see Thursday's "Northwest Weekend" section; www.seattletimes.com.*

Warshal's Sporting Goods: *First Avenue at Madison Street, Seattle; (206) 624-7300.*

Washington State Ferries: *(206) 464-6400 or (800) 84-FERRY; www.wsdot.wa.gov/ferries.*

Washington State Parks: *(800) 233-0321, general information; (800) 452-5687, camping reservations.*

Washington Trails Association: *(206) 625-1367; www.wta.org.*

Wilderness Sports: *14340 NW 20th, Bellevue; (206) 746-0500.*

Bainbridge and Vashon Islands

Encompassing the whole of Seattle's nearest two Puget Sound commuter islands, including Eagle Harbor, Dockton County Park, Fay Bainbridge, Fort Ward, and Blake Island State Parks, Maury Island, and Quartermaster Harbor.

For all the hype about quaint, natural island living on upscale-chic Bainbridge and organic-chic Vashon, a day spent on either leaves you with a single burning question: What's the use of an island if you can't get to the water? You would think that dual islands in the heart of Puget Sound would be bursting at the shorelines with good public beaches. You'd be mistaken. The fact is that much of the best beach land on either island, particularly Bainbridge, has already been bought, fenced off, and posted "No Trespassing."

Sadly, lack of good public shoreline—or park space of any kind—is a fact of life on these two suburbanized, bedroom-community islands. But the truth is that the ferry trip to the islands—especially for visitors or those hordes of recently transplanted Right Coasters—really is charming enough in its own fresh-air way to make you buy into the island mystique. And what little public space is available on Bainbridge and Vashon is almost nice enough to ameliorate it for the rest of us.

Actually, we're probably too hard on the islands—especially Vashon, where some prime waterfront parklands have been acquired and hold great promise for the future. Even now, marine explorers can find a number of water-accessible public beaches on Vashon. Both islands provide hundreds of miles of attractive shoreline for sea kayakers, canoeists, and small-boat owners. And each island, thanks to its convenient "walk-on" access from Seattle, has become a noted bicycle destination.

In the grand outdoor-world scheme of things, each of these islands deserves at least one full day of exploration, several times a year. Lucky for the islands—if not the islanders—their stone's-throw-from-Seattle location means that's all the time you'll need to invest.

Getting There

Both islands have a front and back door. Keys to the front way are held by Washington State ferries, (206) 464-6400 or (800) 84-FERRY; www.wsdot.wa.gov/ferries, which operates large auto ferries from Colman Dock in downtown Seattle to Bainbridge; auto ferries from Fauntleroy in West Seattle to Vashon; and passenger-only ferries from Colman Dock to Vashon. Vashon has two alternate access routes: a short ferry crossing from the main Vashon terminal to Southworth on the Kitsap Peninsula, and a ferry from a southern terminal on Tahlequah Rd to Tacoma's Point Defiance Park. From Bainbridge, the back entrance/exit is Hwy 305, which crosses Agate Passage by bridge to the Kitsap Peninsula near Poulsbo.

inside out

Parks/Beaches

Fay Bainbridge State Park, perhaps the very best thing about Bainbridge Island, is a wonderful place to laze away a breezy summer afternoon. The 1,400-foot log-strewn beach at this north-island park is sandy smooth, with pits for fires and just enough driftwood to lean on; very nice picnic facilities are nearby, plus a boat launch, horseshoe pits, and two kitchen shelters. It's a popular stop for cyclists on their way around the hilly isle. But the main draw is the view: you look straight across the Sound into the teeth of the beast—downtown Seattle—whose skyline buildings look a lot less imposing from here than when you're stuck in traffic between them; to the south is Mount Rainier. And since you asked: there is not, and never was, a "Fay Bainbridge." The park's name combines that of the island and the original property owner, Temple S. Fay. The park is open all year; the camping area is closed from mid-October through March. (Also see Camping, below.) From the Winslow ferry terminal, drive west on Hwy 305 for just over 4 miles, turn right on the E Day Rd turnoff, and follow signs northeast to the park, about 15 minutes from the ferry dock, 15446 Sunrise Drive NE; (206) 842-3931.

A lonely sailboat waits for high tide on the east side of Vashon Island

On the island's opposite shore, a largely undeveloped recreation area, **Fort Ward State Park,** provides more-solitary beach walking. The park has 4,300 feet of saltwater shoreline and a Cascadia Marine Trail campsite, but neither is really easy to get to. The shoreline is best seen by walking or cycling Pleasant Beach Road (it's closed to auto traffic), which runs parallel to—but a ways up from—the rocky beach. This is a good shorebird-watching area; bird blinds are found at the north and south ends of the beach. It's also a popular summertime scuba-diving venue. Orchard Rocks, an offshore formation near the park's south end, is a designated marine park. Note that it's probably too far offshore for most divers to swim to from the beach; use a boat. A launch is available at the park's north end, near Battery Thornburgh. Fort Ward—reached by Pleasant Beach Drive NE or Fort Ward Hill Road (you'll need a map to find it from Winslow)— was a turn-of-the-century companion fort to Manchester on the other side of Rich Passage. (See the Kitsap Peninsula chapter.) Together, their mission was to employ cannons, mines, and submarine nets to protect the Puget Sound Naval Shipyard at Bremerton. They succeeded; it's still there.

Once an ancestral camping ground of the Suquamish tribe, tiny Blake Island in Puget Sound between Bainbridge and Vashon Islands is now a densely wooded wilderness state park. There are 54 campsites, plus boat moorage. Bring your own boat. There is no ferry service to **Blake Island State Park,** except for commercial runs to the privately operated Tillicum Village, (206) 443-1244, a staged-for-tourists glimpse of North Coast Indian heritage. But many private boaters overnight on the island, and kayakers paddle from South Kitsap County (see the Kitsap Peninsula chapter) or north Vashon Island launching points to Blake Island's designated Cascadia Marine Trail campsites (the Cascadia Marine Trail is a state-managed water trail including campsites from Olympia to Vancouver, BC; (206) 545-9161; www.wwta.org). Plenty of on-island recreation awaits: 15 miles of hiking trails access about 5 miles of beaches.

Vashon Island has a broader mix of somewhat hard-to-find public beach. There's a decent **beach access** just east of the main Vashon ferry terminal, as well as a 12-acre, undeveloped beachfront campsite, **Winghaven Park,** which is a designated Cascadia Marine Trail site. It's three-quarters of a mile from the ferry terminal, below Vashon Highway SW. If the thought of right-wing-oriented radio waves silently penetrating your brain is palatable, the sandy beach below the KVI radio tower (off SW 204th north of Portage) at **Point Heyer,** near Vashon Center, is a very nice waterfront spot. "KVI Beach" is private property, but the station traditionally has left it open to the public. Caution: Parking is limited.

Many of the best beach sites on Vashon are clustered around Maury Island, connected by an isthmus to Vashon's east side. Perhaps the most scenic beach access on the island is the beach area at **Point Robinson Park,** SW 243rd Place and Skalberg Road, at the far eastern tip of Maury Island, where a trail loops down from the grassy, upland picnic area to a nice beach surrounding the 1915 Point Robinson Light. The beach here is directly across Puget Sound from Saltwater State Park in Des Moines (see the Greater Seattle chapter), which looks close enough to paddle to by kayak. It is, if you know how to handle your craft in open water. Up the beach to the southwest is **Maury Island Marine Park,** a prime 340-acre beachfront property recently acquired—but as yet undeveloped—by King County Parks.

Quartermaster Harbor, the protected water between Maury and Vashon Islands, is accessible through several waterfront parks. **Burton Acres,** a Vashon Island park, is a delightful site on a peninsula inside the harbor, with a boat launch, beach access, and miles of trails through a woodsy upland area. Across the harbor on the inside shoulder of Maury Island is **Dockton County Park,** a nice King County facility at the site of an old boatyard. The park has a boat launch, beach access, and modern moorage for visiting boaters. The upland area has about a mile and a half of hiking trails. Both parks are good places to launch a canoe or kayak to explore the quiet harbor waters.

Hiking/Picnics

Ever wonder what it would have been like to stumble up on an island paradise like Bainbridge, fence off as much of it as you could, and have the money to develop it into the garden of your dreams? You can find out at **Bloedel Reserve,** a lovely, 150-acre living monument to the former property owners, the Bloedels of Northwest timber fame. More than half of this former estate, accessible by a pleasant, meandering loop trail, is second-growth (surprise) forest, the rest man-made ponds, gardens, and meadows. It's a gorgeous site, particularly in the spring, when trees and shrubs are in full bloom and the estate ponds are filled with baby ducklings, swans, frogs, and other friendly creatures. A tour of the Reserve takes at least several hours, and includes time to walk through the stately old mansion overlooking Puget Sound. The one catch: to limit the number of bodies roaming about at one time, self-guided tours are by reservation. Call—well in advance if you plan to visit in spring or summer. It's worth the effort, though. Tour guides are available for groups. Bloedel Reserve is open 10am to 4 pm, Wednesdays through Sundays. Admission as of summer 2000 is $6 per person, $4 for children 5–12 and seniors 65 and over. Leave your rice at home: no weddings! 7571 NE Dolphin Drive; (206) 842-7631; www.bloedelreserve.org.

Cycling

What these two islands lack in good beach access, they make up for in vigorous cycling routes. Both islands are hilly, but the back roads are very scenic. Leaving the car at home and taking the ferry to cycle the islands adds a unique touch of Northwest mystique to a Bainbridge or Vashon tour—transporting a bike costs only 60 cents more than the walk-on fee and allows you to avoid waiting in long car-ferry lines.

On Bainbridge, cyclists exiting at the Winslow ferry terminal have a wealth of choices. Our advice: Map a route that gets you, as quickly as possible, off of the main drag—Hwy 305. Bainbridge back roads are pleasant, with mostly slow-moving Explorers and Range Rovers providing occasional accompaniment. **Fay Bainbridge State Park** (see Parks/Beaches, above) is a popular day-trip destination from Seattle. It's about 7 miles (one way) from the ferry terminal via Hwy 305, E Day Rd, and Sunrise Drive NE.

If you're up for a bigger trip, make a 30-mile loop around the island by following low-traffic roads on the signed, hilly **Bainbridge Island Loop,** the general course of the Chilly Hilly, Cascade Bicycle Club's annual spring cycling-season kickoff (see the Greater Seattle chapter). At the Winslow ferry terminal start on Ferncliff heading north (avoid Hwy 305) and work your way counterclockwise around the island (follow the signs).

Vashon is a great place to explore from a cycle seat. If you survive the first uphill stretch out of the ferry terminal (it's a burner), the rest of the island is all downhill. Sort of. The number of possible routes is endless here. A **25-mile ride** (round trip) south down the island's main drag, 99th Avenue SW, then onto and around Maury Island, makes a solid day trip. **Point Robinson Light** and **Dockton County Park**—a nice, secluded spot above the salt water—are good lunch destinations. Note: Bring your own bike; rentals are not available on Vashon.

Camping

These islands are neither the land of the RVing free nor the home of the tenting brave, but campers do have one decent option. **Fay Bainbridge State Park,** on the north end of Bainbridge (see Parks/Beaches, above) has 36 sites (10 have water hookups; RVs to 30 feet), just a short distance from the beach. They're fairly tightly bunched, and cramped by most standards, in this small (17-acre) park. The tent sites are rather exposed to the crowds—and wind off the water. But hey, it's camping, and this park often fills up in the summer. The park also has a group camp and good picnic facilities with covered kitchen shelters, a boat ramp, and mooring buoys. Fay Bainbridge is open all year, but the campground is closed from mid-October through March. Campsites cannot be reserved. *15446 Sunrise Dr NE; follow signs from Hwy 305; (206) 842-3931 or (800) 233-0321.*

Fishing

Fishing action is relatively dead on both islands, but it's still very much alive all around them. Bainbridge and Vashon both lie at the epicenter of an interior Puget Sound salmon fishery that's often quite productive all year for anglers who can land a trip on a boat. Two areas in particular—the Agate Passage area northwest of Bainbridge and the Dolphin Point area off the northeast tip of Vashon Island—have become well known to anglers in recent years. The reason: both areas have been designated special "bubble fisheries" during peak summer **salmon** seasons—while many other North and Central Sound hot spots have been closed. Check with the state Department of Fish and Wildlife for seasons, limits, and restrictions; the department web site, www.wa.gov/wdfw, is a valuable resource. Consult the Fishing sections in the Greater Seattle and Kitsap Peninsula chapters for Puget Sound hot spots and charter information.

Also, Vashon offers a decent shore-fishing opportunity. The Tramp Harbor Fishing Pier, operated by King County Parks, juts 300 feet out into Tramp Harbor. It's off Dockton Road, between Portage and Point Heyer. **Bottom-fishing** fans should take note of the artificial reef just off Point Heyer.

Kayaking/Canoeing

Saltwater kayakers have adopted the shorelines of interior Puget Sound islands, and these two, being as close as they are to the people centers, are no strangers to the paddle dippers. In many ways, the kayak is the tool of choice for exploring the natural beauty of these two islands. Once you set foot on them, most of their watery charm is hidden from view. Not so from a kayak, where all the water is public, all the views memorable.

Popular kayak destinations include the interior waters of **Eagle Harbor** (launch just south of the ferry terminal at Winslow), where beginners can ply the calm waters inside the bay and more experienced kayakers can depart for a day trip through **Rich Passage** to Bremerton (see the Kitsap Peninsula chapter). Fay Bainbridge is another good launch site for north-island exploration, or a base for exploring the narrow **Agate Passage.** Note that the launch site here is unprotected from the wind. For exploration of the southern shores of Bainbridge, put in at the Fort Ward State Park boat launch (see above); for experienced paddlers, **Blake Island** is a short paddle from here.

On Vashon, a particularly good day trip is the quiet water inside **Quartermaster Harbor** at Maury Island. Good launch sites are available on the harbor side of Portage (the isthmus connecting Maury Island to Vashon) or at nearby Dockton or Burton Acres Parks. Launch at the Portage site, and you can circumnavigate the whole of Maury "Island" and return to the same spot. Many kayakers putting in at Vashon's Dolphin Point do so to make the 1.5-mile exposed crossing to **Blake Island,** the southern half of which is an undeveloped state park site with good, though primitive, campsites.

Four sites in this area—Fay Bainbridge and Fort Ward State Parks on Bainbridge and Winghaven (near the ferry terminal) and Lisabeula (southwestern shore, on Colvos Passage) Parks on Vashon—are designated campsites for the **Cascadia Marine Trail,** which extends from Olympia to Vancouver Island; (206) 545-9161; www.eskimo.com/~wwta. Kayakers also should note several other Vashon public beaches accessible only from the water: Department of Natural Resources **(DNR) Beach 85** near Point Beals; **DNR Beach 83** on Maury Island near Portage; **DNR Beach 79,** northeast of Tahlequah; and **DNR Beaches 77 and 78,** two small beach patches on Colvos Passage on Vashon's west shore.

For kayak rentals, contact Puget Sound Kayak Company, on Vashon (206) 463-9257; on Bainbridge (206) 842-9229; www.pugetsound-kayak.com. They also offer weekly lessons for all levels. For kayak clubs and organizations, see the Greater Seattle chapter.

Boating/Sailing

On Bainbridge, a wide range of **marine services** is available on **Eagle Harbor,** near Winslow. **Eagle Harbor Waterfront Park** has guest moorage and great access to Winslow stores. Harbour Marina, (206) 842-6502, has guest moorage available if scheduled ahead. It's also the site of the Harbour Pub, a favorite local brewhouse. Winslow Wharf Marina, (206) 842-4202, has full boater services, plus a supply store, The Chandlery. Eagle Harbor Marina, (206) 842-4003, has limited moorage on the south side of the harbor.

On Vashon, **Dockton Park** in **Quartermaster Harbor,** (206) 296-4287, has 60 guest slips and other facilities, including a nice park area on the upland portion. Between the two islands, **Blake Island Marine State Park** is a favorite local boater destination, with ample dock space, hiking trails, campsites, and picnic facilities; (800) 233-0321.

Accessible Outdoors

Fort Ward State Park offers wheelchair-accessible rest rooms. **Fay Bainbridge State Park** has barrier-free campsites and rest rooms. See Parks/Beaches, above.

outside in

Restaurants

Cafe Nola ★★☆   A small, sunny corner cafe serving pleasingly eclectic dishes. $$; 101 Winslow Wy W, Bainbridge; (206) 842-3822. &

Chui Ga Pan Asian Cuisine ★   A small and friendly spot that offers a variety of Asian dishes. *$$; 9924 SW Bank Rd, Vashon; (206) 463-2125.* ♿

Express Cuisine ★   Locals line up for gourmet takeout dinners at this unassuming restaurant. *$; 17629 Vashon Hwy SW, Vashon; (206) 463-6626.* ♿

Ruby's on Bainbridge ★☆   Casual French-country style and ruby-colored walls warmed by candles. *$$; 4569 Lynwood Center Rd, Bainbridge; (206) 780-9303.* ♿

Streamliner Diner ★   The island's equivalent of a whistle-stop cafe. Breakfast is served all day. *$; 397 Winslow Wy E, Bainbridge; (206) 842-8595.*

Lodgings

Back Bay Inn ★   Although perched on a busy corner, the antique-filled rooms here are charming. *$$; 24007 Vashon Hwy SW, Vashon; (206) 463-5355; www.amazinggetaways.com.*

The Buchanan Inn ★☆   This beautifully renovated 1912 B&B was formerly an Odd Fellows Hall. *$$; 8494 NE Odd Fellows Rd, Bainbridge; (206) 780-9258 or (800) 598-3926; www.buchananinn.com.*

Harbor Inn ★   Three antiques-accented rooms in this modern Tudor-style home have water views. *$$$; 9118 SW Harbor Dr, Vashon; (206) 463-6794.*

More Information

Bainbridge Chamber of Commerce: *(206) 842-3700;*
   www.bainbridgechamber.org.
Cascadia Marine Trail: *(206) 545-9161; www.eskimo.com/~wwta.*
Kitsap Peninsula Visitors and Convention Bureau: *(360) 416-5615*
   or online at www.visitkitsap.com.
Vashon Island Chamber of Commerce: *(206) 463-6217;*
   wwwvashonchamber.com.
Washington State Ferries: *(206) 464-6400 or (800) 84-FERRY;*
   www.wsdot.wa.gov/ferries.

Tacoma
and Gig Harbor

From Fort Lewis north and west to Key Peninsula, east to Dash Point, and south to Spanaway Lake, including Commencement Bay, Point Defiance Park, and Kopachuck, Penrose Point, Joemma Beach, West Hylebos Wetlands, and Dash Point State Parks.

Tacoma has never quite gotten over the image thing: polluted waterfront, toxic soils, high crime rate—and the ubiquitous aroma of industrial activity. The truth, much to the chagrin of city leaders, is that the image lingers because it is, at least in part, based in fact. In spite of their protestations to the contrary, Tacoma's aroma—both in its figurative and literal senses—persists.

But a larger truth is starting to seep out around the edges of Puget Sound's second most powerful urban base: Tacoma has turned the corner. Granted, the town still can smell like month-old tuna when the wind blows in, and some downtown streets are places where you definitely don't want to run out of gas on Saturday night. But to focus solely on that would be to ignore the amazing amount of good that's sprouted in the past decade along Commencement Bay.

The city is rebuilding itself the only way it can, and the only way it should—from the waterline up. Decaying industries have been blown up, scooped up, and hauled away, and replaced by waterfront parks, walkways, and marinas. Arts, business, and educational institutions are reclaiming downtown. Tourists are returning. Location is the lure: Tacoma occupies the ultimate site for a Puget Sound city—right on the salt water, yet close enough to Mount Rainier for its residents to feel the cold wind rolling off the mountain's glaciers. The city's idyllic setting, in fact, probably has fanned

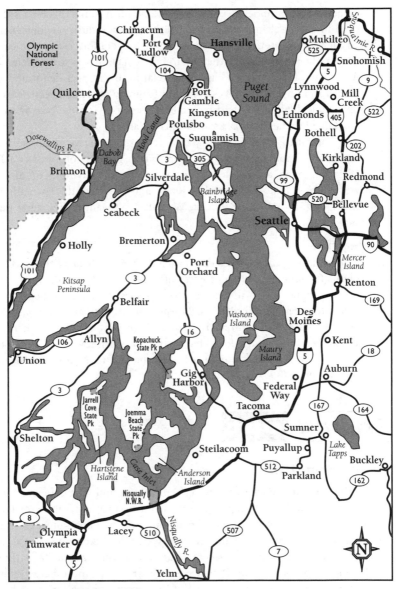

South Puget Sound

much of the regional scorn for its squandered opportunities.

Today, finally, the city is learning to embrace its location, treating it as a drawing card instead of a pleasant sidelight. Walkers, joggers, anglers, and cyclists have proliferated along the waterfront. On the water, garbage barges are outnumbered by kayaks. Make no mistake: Tacoma still is a dyed-in-the-wool industrial center. But its new industry, which includes an aggressive waterfront container-shipping operation, is one that can live with, rather than exploit, the environment. The mix is sort of refreshing. And it's working. Tacoma has come so far in this respect that it now competes for, rather than waves through, Saturday-afternoon recreators who once took their canoes and picnic baskets across Tacoma Narrows to the sparkling beaches and parks around Gig Harbor.

Combined, Tacoma, Gig Harbor, and the rural Key Peninsula are a maritime combination tough to beat. From the seat of a boat off Point Defiance, gazing at Mount Rainier on one side, the Olympics on the other, we're almost tempted to pack a Ryder and move south. Then the wind shifts, and. . . . We'll be honest. We still don't want to live here. But we sure are getting used to visiting.

Getting There

Tacoma, strategically located dead center in the Puget Sound basin, is 32 miles south of Seattle and 30 miles north of Olympia on Interstate 5. Any of the main downtown exits will take you to the city center and to most of the waterfront attractions described below. To reach the Gig Harbor area, from I-5 take exit 132 (Gig Harbor/Bremerton) and drive west on Hwy 16 across the Tacoma Narrows Bridge, following signs to the small town on the east side of the highway. Bus service to Tacoma from the Seattle area is available from Pierce Transit; (800) 562-8109.

inside out

Parks/Beaches

Point Defiance Park is the waterfront sun around which Tacoma's recreation world orbits—fittingly so, since all the best natural features of Tacoma and the South Sound are found here: miles of sparkling saltwater beaches, scenic mountain views, a healthy trail system for hikers and cyclists, some rare old-growth timber, well-kept gardens, and even a zoo and aquarium for the kid in all of us. Point Defiance is truly one of the most magnificent city parks in the country. It's also one of the largest—only New York's Central Park has more acreage; (253) 305-1000; www.pdza.org.

This 700-acre outdoor smorgasbord is best sampled on foot. Many miles of trails interlace in the park. Not all of them are well signed, but they do wander past some impressive old trees—a rarity this close to Puget Sound. From the main parking area just inside the entrance, you can take a

5- to 7-mile stroll around the park's perimeter by using **Five Mile Road** as a navigational aid. Trails generally parallel this popular one-way drive that offers Puget Sound and Olympic Mountain views from pullouts. On Saturday mornings, you can forget the often-confusing trail network and just use the road: it's reserved for bikes and walkers until 1pm.

The **Point Defiance Zoo and Aquarium,** (253) 591-5337, a well-run, progressive facility, is just inside the main entrance off Park Wy. The beluga whale exhibit is particularly good. Watch it, though: belugas spit. A nearby road leads down to the park's northeast shore, then to a boathouse and nearby **Owen Beach,** a very popular sunbather hangout just west of the Vashon ferry terminal. The upper beach is a good picnic area, and (depending on tides) you can walk more than a mile west toward Point Defiance before you run out of beach. This is the only established beach access in the park, which is mostly on a high bluff bordered on one side by Dalco Passage and on the other by the Narrows. The massive boathouse here has launching elevators and a fishing pier (see Fishing, below).

In the park's interior, **Fort Nisqually,** a replica of an 1833 Hudson's Bay outpost, is open for exploration. Some of the buildings are genuine, moved from an actual Hudson's Bay settlement near Du Pont and restored for display. The park also holds a **logging/railroad museum** with a working steam engine, a **kids' playland,** and other things that will make adults cringe if all they're looking for is a quiet picnic table. Be prepared: This park might be huge, but it gets FULL of people in the summertime. From I-5, take exit 132 (Bremerton/Hwy 16) and follow signs to Hwy 16 West/Bremerton/Gig Harbor. Take the Sixth Avenue exit and turn left. Take the next right onto Pearl Street, which dead-ends at Point Defiance Park. Follow signs to parking.

Other Parks

Brown's Point Park on the north side of Commencement Bay, just off Marine View Drive, offers a great view of the city. A lighthouse (complete with caretaker and historical exhibits) marks the point, where massive container ships and other waterborne behemoths traverse the narrow passage between here and the southern tip of Vashon Island. **Dash Point State Park,** north of Brown's Point, has a popular saltwater swimming and scuba beach. **Dash Point City Park,** which has a major saltwater fishing pier, is nearby. **Wright Park,** at Division and I Streets in downtown Tacoma, has nice floral gardens, a fascinating old conservatory—and the highest downtown duck-per-acre concentration. **Thea Foss Waterway,** the Commencement Bay boating channel nearest the downtown area, has its own parklike pedestrian walkway, stretching more than a dozen blocks along the west side of the waterway to **Northwest Point Park,** a grassy picnic spot with nice bay views. You can pick up the walkway just a couple blocks north of the Tacoma Dome and walk the entire waterway.

The best waterfront facilities around Tacoma, however, are a bit farther from downtown. A slew of scenic waterfront parks and public spaces adjoins **Ruston Way,** whose 2-mile-long waterfront sidewalk is Tacoma's version of Seattle's Alki Way. It's the city's leading walking/in-line skating/skateboarding/bike route. To get started, follow Schuster Parkway west from downtown to Ruston Way, and park in one of the streetside lots, preferably one on the east end of Ruston Way. Waterfront highlights along the route are **Commencement Park,** topped by a big sundial; **Old Town Dock,** a public fishing pier/public moorage site; **Les Davis Pier,** one of the more notable public shore-fishing venues in the state (see Fishing, below), and **Marine Park,** which has a grand picnic area, beach access, and a fitness trail, among other charms. A definite be-seen place for the Lycra crowd. In the middle of all this Mount Rainier–view bliss, a fireboat station is an interesting diversion. On foot, skates, or a mountain bike, this stretch can make a great afternoon outing.

Around Point Defiance, on the Tacoma Narrows side of town, several more notable city parks await. **War Memorial Park,** at the south foot of Tacoma Narrows Bridge (Jackson exit off Hwy 16), is the best place to get an up-close look at the bridge—and to argue with your friends about just what holds the thing up. (To start the argument, just suggest "gravity," then stand back and listen.) A trail leading down from this park to the water is a favorite entry point for scuba divers, who've taken up the intriguing (and dangerous, due to ripping-strong currents) sport of diving along the sunken remains of the former Galloping Gertie. One of them tells us he's seen octopuses down there bigger than his car. But then, it's only a VW Bug. Farther south is **Titlow Beach Park,** a 60-acre getaway with picnic facilities, a fitness trail, hiking trails, tennis courts, a pool (Olympian Megan Quann of Puyallup trained here), several bird-inhabited ponds, and grand views of the Narrows Bridge, just up the way. The beach area, reached by following Sixth Avenue past the first entrance, all the way to a dead end, is rocky but very explorable. This is another local scuba hot spot. Mooring buoys float offshore.

In the Steilacoom area, check out **Pioneer Park** on Commercial Street, a good view/picnic spot; **Saltars Point Park**—small, but there's a nice beach down some wooden steps; or **Sunnyside Beach Park,** the best local swimming/sunbathing beach; follow Lafayette Street north from the downtown area.

On the north side of the Narrows, the Gig Harbor area offers visitors a choice of two great waterfront parks on opposite shores of Carr Inlet. One of the closest, **Kopachuck State Park** (follow signs from Hwy 16 near Gig Harbor) has 3,500 feet of prime saltwater shoreline—all flat, shallow areas good for clamming and beachcombing. Kopachuck includes an underwater scuba park, and a short kayak paddle away is tiny **Cutts Island Marine State Park.** On the opposite shore is **Penrose Point State Park** (take the Hwy 302 exit from Hwy 16; follow signs), a spectacular site with nearly 12,000 feet of shoreline on Carr Inlet and Delano Bay. On the other side of Key Peninsula, along Case Inlet, is **Joemma Beach State Park,** the former Robert F. Kennedy State Park. (See Camping, below, for more on all three.)

Boating/Sailing

Perhaps no city of its size in the state can match the Tacoma area's wealth of maritime facilities. Boaters, whether their craft is a 7-foot Livingston or a 60-foot Grand Banks cruiser, probably will find what they're looking for here. Downtown Tacoma, the Narrows, Steilacoom, Gig Harbor, and a dozen other smaller waterfront communities all have marinas with guest moorage, boat launches, and other boater services. In addition, nearly all of the waterfront parks noted above have at least moorage floats, and usually dock space, for visiting boaters.

All serve as departure points for a rich choice of day trips on South Puget Sound. Popular summer boating destinations include **Gig Harbor,** and waterfront parks and islands on Key Peninsula and in nearby Carr or Case Inlet. **Penrose Point State Park** is a particularly popular destination, as are bays and parks along southern Vashon Island, such as Dockton Park in Quartermaster Harbor (see Bainbridge and Vashon Islands chapter).

Point Defiance Boathouse Marina, at the base of Point Defiance Park, offers the full works: extensive **marine services,** restaurants, a tackle shop, fishing charters, boat rentals, launch facilities, and more. It's also salmon-fishing central in Tacoma; (253) 591-5325. **Old Town Dock** on Ruston Way has guest moorage, rest rooms, and access to waterfront parks. The **15th Street Dock**, inside the Thea Foss Waterway, is very close to downtown. You'll find moorage space here, but floatplanes have first priority. Inside Hylebos Waterway is the spiffy new Chinook Landing Marina; (253) 627-7676. In Steilacoom, Steilacoom Marina has guest moorage and other services; (253) 582-2600. The Narrows Marina at the foot of 19th Street (a half mile south of the Narrows Bridge) offers ample moorage and other services; (253) 564-3032. To the north at Day Island is Narrows Marina Bait and Tackle, a noted salmon-fishing tackle shop; (253) 564-4222. This is but a sampling of the major **marine facilities** in the area.

Gig Harbor is a well-known Puget Sound boater's mecca

On the west side of the narrows in Gig Harbor, boat moorage and services are available at **Jerrisch Park City Dock,** (253) 851-8136; Peninsula Yacht Basin, (253) 858-2250; and Arabella's Landing, (253) 851-1793.

Fishing

Boathouses at Point Defiance and Tacoma Narrows are the epicenter of a still-thriving South Sound **salmon** fishery. Success in these waters has been mixed in the past decade, but recent years have seen strong catches of hatchery-produced **coho** and **chinook** from the Nisqually and Puyallup River systems. Those fish usually arrive in late summer and are available through fall. Popular fishing spots include the immediate Point Defiance area, the "Clay Banks," just to the east; Point Dalco, at the south tip of Vashon Island; and inside Commencement Bay, where Puyallup River–bound fish often are intercepted. Farther south, the west side of Tacoma Narrows (north of the bridge) and Gibson Point at the south end of Fox Island are good **blackmouth** (resident chinook) areas. Most of these areas are open all year, and have proven productive for winter blackmouth fishing.

For shore anglers, options include waterfront fishing piers at Old Town Dock and Les Davis Pier, both on Ruston Way; Point Defiance Boathouse; Dash Point City Park; and Redondo in south King County. The Les Davis Pier is particularly well equipped, with rod holders, rest rooms, and other rare niceties. Try casting a Buzz Bomb or other weighted lure, with a slow retrieve. For general salmon-fishing information, including charter bookings and boat rentals, call Point Defiance Boathouse, (253) 591-5325; or Narrows Marina Bait and Tackle, (253) 564-4222.

Good freshwater fishing in the area can be found at Spanaway Lake in Parkland (many planted **trout**, some **bass)**, American Lake (**rainbows,** some big), and Steilacoom Lake (bass), both south of Tacoma near Lakewood. The Puyallup River upstream from Sumner can be good in the fall for migratory salmon, and fair to good in the winter for **steelhead.**

Hiking

Point Defiance Park, of course, is the in-city favorite, with many miles of hiking trails through cool forest. The urban walkway along the **Thea Foss Waterway** makes for a scenic, 23-block stroll for downtown visitors, as does the **Ruston Way** waterfront sidewalk, which stretches about 2 miles west. (See Parks/Beaches, above, for all these.) For the carless, Ruston Way is connected to the downtown area by the 2.5-mile **Bayside Trail,** which stretches from Stadium Way to Commencement Park. Parts of the wooded path seem unkempt and a bit creepy, though. **Snake Lake Nature Center,** on Tyler Street near Hwy 16, has almost 2 miles of interesting nature trails that loop around a wildlife-rich wetland area in the middle of the city; (253) 305-1000.

Other day hikes—long enough to wear out the kids, but short enough to save the parents—can be found at **Titlow Beach Park** on the Narrows or at **Penrose Point, Joemma Beach, Kopachuck,** or **Dash Point State Parks,** all on the outskirts of town (see Parks/Beaches, above). If none of those is enough to scratch your hiking itch (and for serious hoofers, they might not be), remember that Mount Rainier National Park is a mere 90 minutes away via Hwy 7 (see that chapter), and the Nisqually National Wildlife Refuge is about 20 minutes south on I-5 (see Olympia and the Nisqually Delta chapter).

Kayaking/Canoeing

If the shipping traffic and the sense of general toxicity don't bother you, inner **Commencement Bay** is an adventuresome paddle. Actually, the city's inner waterways make for a fascinating day trip, mixing the heavy industry of the inner harbor with the natural feel of the Point Defiance area. Good launch points include Point Defiance Boathouse, Owen Beach at Point Defiance Park, Commencement Park on Ruston Way, Northwest Point Park (downtown), or Brown's Point Park, for cross-bay journeys.

An extensive series of canoe and kayak tours and classes is offered by Tahoma Outdoor Pursuits, located at Backpackers Supply & Outlet, 5206 S Tacoma Wy; (253) 474-8155. They also offer canoe and kayak rentals and supplies.

For a more natural setting, sparkling waters, clean beaches, and a killer Mount Rainier view, cross the Narrows and try the waters inside **Case or Carr Inlet.** Great launching sites are found at Joemma Beach, Kopachuck, and Penrose Point State Parks. From Kopachuck (a great beginner's spot), novices can paddle a short distance to **Cutts Island,** an undeveloped state park site. Likewise, paddlers setting out from Joemma Beach can undertake a longer voyage to primitive campsites at **McMicken Island Marine State Park,** just east of Hartstene Island. Kopachuck and Joemma Beach State Parks are designated **Cascadia Marine Trail** campsites (the Cascadia Marine Trail is a state-managed water trail with campsites from Olympia to British Columbia; (206) 545-9161; www.wwta.org; see Washington Outdoors Primer on page vii).

Cycling

In downtown Tacoma, take the **Ruston Way Waterfront Tour.** Follow Pacific Avenue to Schuster Parkway, heading northwest from downtown to Ruston Way, and proceed along the waterfront 2 miles to Marine Park (see Parks/Beaches, above). Not a long ride, but there's enough to do along the way to make this a good half-day venture. Another Tacoma treat comes once a week only, when **Five Mile Road,** which loops around most of Point Defiance Park, is closed to auto traffic on Saturday mornings. It's a great ride for the whole family. In Gig Harbor, a popular route is the 34-mile **Crescent Lake Loop,** which takes you north on Crescent Valley Road SE to the lake, then back along a waterfront route. The Key Peninsula across Carr Inlet also offers many miles of quiet, backcountry-road cycle touring. For general cycling information, including a Pierce County Parks map of cycle routes, call Tacoma Parks, (253) 305-1000.

Camping

Finding a restful campsite in Tacoma proper is like trying to find a Saturday-morning parking spot at Costco: not likely. Luckily, plenty of beautiful sites await within 30 minutes of downtown.

Kopachuck State Park, a mere 12 miles northwest of town, offers 41 campsites (no hookups; RVs to 35 feet) in a wooded upland area (alas, no views). The park also contains great picnic facilities (Olympic views), a sprawling clamming/beachcombing beach, and an underwater park for scuba fans at Henderson Bay beach. The park is open all year for day use ; the campground is open April through September. Sites cannot be reserved. *From Tacoma, drive 7 miles north on Hwy 16 and follow signs 5 miles west to the park;* (253) 265-3606 or (800) 233-0321.

Penrose Point State Park, tucked inside Carr Inlet's Mayo Cove on the east shore of Key Peninsula, is an idyllic place with 83 campsites (no hookups; RVs to 35 feet), a group camp, picnic facilities, boat moorage, a shallow swimming beach, and miles of hiking trails. It's a local camping hot spot, whether you arrive by car, bicycle, or boat. Penrose Point is open from April through September. Campsites can be reserved up to 11 months in advance by calling Reservations Northwest; (800) 452-5687. *From Tacoma, drive north on Hwy 16 to Hwy 302. Proceed south on Key Peninsula Hwy for about 9 miles. Turn left at Cornwall Rd and follow signs to the park;* (253) 884-2514 or (800) 233-0321.

Joemma Beach State Park, on Key Peninsula's west shore, is the former R. F. Kennedy Multiple Use Area. In 1995, the 22-acre park was transferred from Department of Natural Resources management to the state park system, and the name was changed to honor Joe and Emma Smith, two early residents. The nicely upgraded park now has 22 campsites (no hookups; RVs to 35 feet) in two loops. Also on the premises are a couple of short hiking trails, 1,000 feet of gravelly beach, and a very nice moorage dock for overnighting boaters. Joemma Beach is open all year. Campsites cannot be reserved. *From Hwy 16 near Gig Harbor follow signs along Hwy 302, Longbranch Rd, Whiteman Rd, and Bay Rd to the park, located near Longbranch;* (253) 884-2514 or (800) 233-0321.

North of Tacoma along East Passage, **Dash Point State Park** is a major camper's destination, with 138 sites (28 water/electrical hookups; RVs to 35 feet) on two wooded loops. The park, divided by Hwy 509, also has an extensive hiking trail system, a bluff-top picnic area with good Sound views, and a shallow beach that's a popular late-summer swimming spot. (Just to the west along the shore is Dash Point City Park, with a heavily used salmon fishing pier.) Dash Point State Park is open all year. Campsites can be reserved up to 11 months in advance by calling Reservations Northwest; (800) 452-5687. *Follow signs from Hwy 509, 7 miles north of Tacoma, or from I-5 exit 143, near Federal Way; (253) 593-2206 or (800) 233-0321.*

Wildlife Watching

Minter Creek State Hatchery is one of the best places in the state to learn about the salmon-spawning process. About 15 minutes northwest of downtown Gig Harbor, the recently rebuilt hatchery is open to the public daily or for group visits by special arrangement. Always popular with the kids. Call (253) 857-5077 for directions and information. See Accessible Outdoors, below, for other regional wildlife-viewing venues.

Accessible Outdoors

Three barrier-free fishing piers in and around Tacoma provide some of the best chances in Puget Sound to catch salmon from the bank: **Dash Point Pier,** managed by Tacoma Metropolitan Parks (see Dash Point State Park in Parks/Beaches, above); **Les Davis Pier** on the Tacoma waterfront (from I-5, follow Hwy 705 and Schuster Pkwy to Ruston Way); and the **Fox Island Pier,** reached via a barrier-free, but quite steep switchback trail.

   Joemma Beach State Park has barrier-free campsites, rest rooms, picnic facilities, and a dock on Puget Sound. **Kopachuck State Park** has barrier-free campsites and rest rooms. **Dash Point State Park** has accessible campsites, picnic sites, and rest rooms. See Parks/Beaches, above, for more information.

   The state's **South Puget Sound Wildlife Area,** 7723 Phillips Road SW, a converted pheasant farm, has barrier-free access to an interpretive trail/wildlife viewing area. From Tacoma, take I-5 south to the Bridgeport Wy exit, go west on Bridgeport Wy, and turn left on Steilacoom Blvd. Turn right on Phillips Road to the parking area. The area also contains the state's Lakewood Hatchery, which offers wheelchair access to fish rearing ponds.

outside in

Restaurants

Altezzo ★★   This attractive restaurant at the top of the Sheraton provides a great view of downtown and some of the best Italian cuisine in

Tacoma. *$$; 1320 Broadway Plaza (Sheraton Tacoma Hotel), Tacoma; (253) 572-3200.*

Bimbo's ★   Don't be put off by the slightly disreputable name or location: here's a family Italian restaurant that's attracted regulars for 75 years. *$; 1516 Pacific Ave, Tacoma; (253) 383-5800.*

The Cliff House ★★   Commanding views of Commencement Bay are matched by an equally commanding menu. *$$$; 6300 Marine View Dr, Tacoma; (253) 927-0400.*

East & West Cafe ★   What this haven of Asian goods lacks in location, it makes up for in great food. *$; 5319 Tacoma Mall Blvd, Tacoma; (253) 475-7755.* ⅄

Fujiya ★★   Absolute consistency attracts a loyal clientele to this Japanese restaurant. *$$; 1125 Court C, Tacoma; (253) 627-5319.*

The Green Turtle ★   Panfried wontons are a favorite on a menu that's popular with regulars. *$$; 2905 Harborview Dr, Gig Harbor; (253) 851-3167.* ⅄

Harbor Lights ★   Decor is circa 1950 but this pioneer waterfront restaurant still packs them in. *$$; 2761 Ruston Wy, Tacoma; (253) 752-8600.*

Katie Downs ★   This place is noisy, boisterous, and fun; the deep-dish pizza is a winner. *$; 3211 Ruston Wy, Tacoma; (253) 756-0771.* ⅄

Marco's Ristorante Italiano ★   Everyone in this area loves what Marco's has done for dining in Gig Harbor. *$$; 7707 Pioneer Wy, Gig Harbor; (253) 858-2899.*

Marzano's ★   Lisa Marzano's voluptuous Italian cooking has people arriving from miles away. *$$; 516 Garfield St, Parkland; (253) 537-4191.* ⅄

Stanley and Seaforts Steak, Chop, and Fish House ★★   A panoramic view restaurant that doesn't rest on its sunsetting laurels. *$$; 115 E 34th St, Tacoma; (253) 473-7300.* ⅄

Tides Tavern   This tavern perched over the harbor often has standing room only. *$; 2925 Harborview Dr, Gig Harbor; (253) 858-3982; www. tidestavern.com.*

Lodgings

Anderson House on Oro Bay ★★   Guests have exclusive use of this large house surrounded by woods. *$$; 12024 Eckenstam-Johnson Rd, Anderson Island; (253) 884-4088 or (800) 750-4088; www.non.com/ anderson.*

Chinaberry Hill ★★   This 1889 mansion has been restored and turned into a charming, romantic B&B. $$$; *302 Tacoma Ave N, Tacoma; (253) 272-1282; www.wa.net/chinaberry.*

The Maritime Inn   Fifteen rooms are comfortably appointed here, across from the waterfront. $$; *3212 Harborview Dr, Gig Harbor; (253) 858-1818; www.maritimeinn.com.* &

Sheraton Tacoma Hotel ★   This is the best hotel in town (a recent redecoration has livened up the rooms). $$$; *1320 Broadway Plaza, Tacoma; (253) 572-3200 or (800) 845-9466; www.sheratontacoma.com.*

The Villa Bed & Breakfast ★★   In the heart of the city's historic North End, this gracious B&B stands out from the crowd. $$; *705 N 5th St, Tacoma; (253) 572-1157; www.tribnet.com/bb/villa.htp.*

More Information

Backpackers Supply: *(253) 472-4402.*
Pierce Transit: *(800) 562-8109; www.piercetransit.org.*
Point Defiance Boathouse (fishing gear and licenses): *(253) 591-5325.*
Point Defiance Zoo and Aquarium: *(253) 591-5337; www.pdza.org.*
Tacoma Parks: *(253) 305-1000; www.tacomaparks.com.*
Tacoma/Pierce County Visitors and Convention Bureau: *(360) 627-2836 or (800) 272-2662; www.tpctourism.org.*
Tahoma Outdoor Pursuits (guided trips): *(253) 474-8155.*

Olympia and the Nisqually Delta

From Squaxin Island south to Black Lake, east to Nisqually Delta, and north to Johnson Point, including Budd Inlet, Capitol Lake, the lower Deschutes River, Tumwater Falls, Percival Landing, the Nisqually National Wildlife Refuge, and Squaxin Island Marine, Hartstene Island, Tolmie, and Millersylvania Memorial State Parks.

Two things would happen if large numbers of hikers, kayakers, picnickers, and cyclists began converging en masse on Olympia. Nervous legislators would panic, wondering what they did to offend these usually placid beasts of the forest and field. And large numbers of hikers, kayakers, picnickers, and cyclists would find out they've been missing a great outdoors getaway. In many ways, our state capital typifies Puget Sound–area recreation offerings: it doesn't look like much from the freeway, but once you get in up to your knees ... Whoa: nice place!

This quiet, unassuming city at the southern tip of Puget Sound had big aspirations back in 1846 when it marked the northern end of the Oregon Trail. Its aspirations grew even bigger in the early 1870s, when city fathers banked on Olympia becoming the northern terminus of the approaching Northern Pacific Railroad. Nice try. The railroad went to Tacoma instead (and likely still regrets its choice). Olympia fought tooth and nail for—and won—state government.

The city may have settled for its second choice. But in doing so, residents picked up a lifestyle that's purely first class. Olympia's 30,000 government workers, college students, and other inhabitants gained a permanent job base (indeed, a growth industry)—

government—without sacrificing the area's greatest resource, its pleasant natural setting. (For the opposite, big-industry alternative, see Tacoma, the "winner" in this game, just up the road.) The result: hidden treasure remains stashed all around Olympia. And we don't mean gold coin, or even fine works of art squirreled away from the Capitol Rotunda. Tucked away on the shores of Budd and nearby Eld Inlets are a series of deliciously fresh waterfront parks, quiet cycling paths, and a largely man-made freshwater body, Capitol Lake, that's as rich in history as it is in recreational splendor.

Olympians are a deceptively hip bunch, and they have a good thing going here. It's up to you to find out how good. Plan on spending a long day. That should allow plenty of time to explore Capitol Lake and at least one of the saltwater parks, and perhaps to stroll through a portion of the nearby Nisqually National Wildlife Refuge—one of the last unspoiled estuaries on the West Coast—on the way home.

We have but one plea: when you go, park your rig in a parking lot at the Capitol Campus. The mere sight of all those Yak Racks in one place could do those shut-in legislators—and, ultimately, all of us—a world of good.

Getting There

Olympia is a 60-mile drive south of Seattle on Interstate 5. The Nisqually River Delta is 50 miles south of Seattle on I-5. The best access is through the Nisqually National Wildlife Refuge, exit 114.

inside out

Wildlife Watching

For bird lovers, it doesn't get much better than the Nisqually National Wildlife Refuge, a sprawling 2,818-acre river-bottom wildlife magnet at the Nisqually River Delta. In recent years, the Nisqually has become the proverbial line in the sand for many Puget Sound area conservationists, who seek to prevent suburban and light industrial development here. They have good reason: the Nisqually is the only undeveloped drainage basin left between Mount Rainier and Puget Sound. The lower valley also is a fertile crescent, of sorts, for the Puget Sound basin. Some of the oldest human remains ever discovered in Washington were unearthed here.

The lower Nisqually drainage has been protected since 1974 by the wildlife refuge, which has become an extremely popular outdoor getaway. More than 70,000 visitors a year lug their binoculars and Audubon field guides down here every year. Most head straight for the 5-mile Brown

A visitor scans for wildlife at McAllister Creek in Nisqually Wildlife Refuge

Farm Dike Trail, which follows the top of a berm separating the former Brown Farm from the salt water and the Nisqually. It's a favorite walkway of bird-watchers and hikers, who enjoy the flat, peaceful grade. This truly is a great place to watch birds. The 5-mile loop trail puts you right in their midst: On the outer portions, flocks of **small shorebirds** hop through the mudflats of the river delta or the saltwater shoreline. On the inner side, raptors, **small perching birds,** and thousands of ducks, geese, and other waterfowl are attracted to the flat, marshy terrain. For the serious bird-watcher and photographer, side trails lead inside the refuge to nicely placed photo blinds. The Nisqually Refuge, open all year but most heavily bird-populated in the winter, is a major migratory stop for **mallards, widgeons, teals, Canada geese,** and many other birds. **Red-tailed hawks** and **bald eagles** are year-round residents. Also commonly seen on the grounds are **coyotes, deer, otters,** and other mammals. Much of the wildlife is best viewed by canoe or kayak (see below for launch information).

This is an educational facility, as well. A new visitors center is open Wednesday through Sunday, 9am to 4 pm. The Twin Barns Education Center, a short walk from the parking lot, is filled with interpretive displays and now is open by appointment only for learning groups. Separate 1-mile and half-mile nature loops are available for those who don't want to stroll the entire 5-mile outer loop. Most of the refuge is wheelchair accessible. Note that that local hunting closes the dike trail for short periods. Call refuge headquarters at (360) 753-9467 for seasons and information. The refuge is off I-5 exit 114 about 10 miles north of Olympia, You can pay a voluntary $3-per-family admission fee at the main trailhead, near the parking lot. No pets or bicycles are allowed.

Also: Two fish hatcheries in or near Olympia offer fall viewing of spawning **chinook salmon.** See Accessible Outdoors, below.

Parks

Here's where our capital city really shines. Some extremely nice saltwater shorelines are to be found among Olympia's myriad South Puget Sound rocky points, inlets, and bays. The best day trip is actually a four-in-one: four parks connected by a trail and the Capitol Lake Causeway (about 3 miles), nearly all of it along the saltwater or freshwater shoreline. We'll consider them one at time.

On the downtown waterfront itself is **Percival Landing,** at the foot of W State Street, a waterfront gathering spot with an observation tower to scan the Olympic Mountains, Budd Inlet, and the South Sound. Just to the south, within easy walking distance from Percival Landing on the waterfront boardwalk, lies Capitol Lake, a great day-trip destination for walkers, joggers, in-line skaters, or picnickers. The lake was created nearly 50 years ago, when city leaders got fed up with the pungent Deschutes river-mouth mudflat and built a dam to seal the freshwater in, the salt water out. Today, the lake is a nice scenic area connected by waterfront paths and streets to the downtown waterfront.

The public focus is on the northeast shore, at **Capitol Lake Park,** a good picnic and swimming area. From here, you can catch the Capitol Lake Trail and walk south toward the Capitol, cut across the lake on a small fishing pier/tidal dam to **Marathon Park,** then return on the opposite shore, along Deschutes Parkway. The entire route is along the water, with good views of the Capitol dome. A series of docks and beach accesses make this lake a favorite of canoeists, kayakers, and sailors in training.

Another option from Marathon Park is to continue south up the trail on the west shore of the lake, crossing beneath I-5 and continuing to **Tumwater Historical Park,** one of the area's best grounds for exploring.The park—on a peninsula jutting into Capitol Lake just east of the I-5 overpass—has two boat launches, historical homes open for tours (one of them built by Bing Crosby's grandfather), and nice waterfront trails. You can walk here on the Capitol Lake causeway trail—about 3 miles (one way) from Percival Landing. Keep walking, to another close-by scenic park, **Tumwater Falls,** a short distance up Deschutes Parkway. It's the water: a trail leads down one side of the long, cascading falls on the Deschutes, then crosses the river on a footbridge, and returns on the opposite bank, near the Deschutes Brewery. To reach both parks, take the Brewery exit from I-5 and follow signs to Deschutes Parkway.

Northeast of downtown—a nice bike ride from the downtown waterfront—is **Priest Point Park,** a city park that was Olympia's first, best waterfront recreation area. The park, built on an old mission site, straddles Boston Harbor Road. You'll find miles of upland hiking trails (some through old-growth fir and red cedar), multiple paths to the saltwater beach on Budd Inlet, an extensive floral garden, picnic facilities, and other attractions. To get there, follow Plum Street (it becomes Boston Harbor Rd) north from downtown. A marked cycle route runs all the way to the park, about 2 miles from the city center. North of Priest Point, between downtown and Boston Harbor, is another popular Thurston County getaway, **Burfoot Park.** This park, about 7 miles outside Olympia on Boston Harbor Road, has a great fine-gravel beach area (a major sunbather hangout), good picnic facilities, and a surprisingly interesting trail system that includes a short, family-friendly nature trail.

Northwest of downtown, **Geoduck Beach** at The Evergreen State College is worth exploring. Ask for directions at the parking booth just inside the college's main entrance. Nearby **Fry Cove County Park,** across Eld Inlet, has 2,000 acres of shoreline and a nice wooded upland area. This pleasant picnic spot is at the end of Boardman Road NW. Northeast of town along Nisqually Reach is **Tolmie State Park,** a day-use area with an extensive trail system, picnic facilities, and an offshore underwater park/fishing reef. Follow signs from I-5 exit 111.

Hiking

The **Capitol Lake Causeway** walk described in Parks, above, is a great half-day hiking trip (about 3 miles) for visitors parked either at the waterfront, at the capitol campus, or near Tumwater Falls. Most of the beachfront day-use parks described above also offer **short day-hiking trails.** The **Nisqually National Wildlife Refuge** (see Wildlife Watching, above) is a favorite day-hiking spot for many Olympians.

Farther south down I-5, Millersylvania Memorial State Park (see Camping, below) has more than 7 miles of mostly easy **trails,** plus an exercise track. Also south of town, in the Black Hills area, is a sprawling series of **backcountry trails** in the hills of Capitol State Forest, which lies between the south edge of Olympia and the western leg of US Highway 12 (US 12). The forest, managed by the state Department of Natural Resources, is on the northern edge of a vast sea of heavily logged foothills, stretching from the outskirts of Olympia southwest all the way to Willapa Bay. Many miles of trails are marked here, some connecting to DNR campgrounds (see Camping, below), many leading to stunning mountaintop vistas, such as the summit of Capitol Peak. Alas, most of these trails are open to—and heavily used by—dirt bikes and other annoying smoke-belchers. Trails here are becoming quite popular with mountain bikers, but hikers walk them at their own risk. It should be noted that some trails, such as those emanating from Fall Creek and Margaret McKenny Campgrounds (see Camping, below), are closed to ORV use. Finally, a historical/geologic mystery for centuries, the **Mima Mounds**, make for an interesting walk in a setting you won't soon forget.

Camping

The best public camping venues in the Olympia area are outside the city. **Millersylvania Memorial State Park** once was the 850-acre estate of Johann Mueller, an Austrian general (and bodyguard of Emperor Franz Josef I) exiled to these parts in the late 19th century. Now it's a very pretty, diverse state park with a nice camping area, hiking trails, and swimming (and good trout fishing) in Deep Lake. The park's 187 campsites (52 with hookups; RVs to 45 feet) are nicely set in a stand of stately firs. It's popular with both tenters and RVers. The completing touch is a series of historic Civilian Conservation Corps–era buildings. This is a good family park, with convenient I-5 access. Millersylvania is open all year. Campsites can be reserved up to 11 months in advance by calling Reservations Northwest; (800) 452-5687. *From I-5 take exit 95, go east on Maytown Rd, then north on Tilley Rd; (360) 753-1519 or (800) 233-0321.*

For boaters and paddlers, **Squaxin Island Marine State Park,** a boat-in-only campground at the long, skinny island's south tip, is a nice retreat. Its 20 primitive campsites are well suited for small tents. *At the mouth of Budd Inlet, between Hunter Point and the south end of Hartstene Island; (800) 233-0321.*

The Capitol State Forest has a series of small, primitive campgrounds, all managed by the Department of Natural Resources. They are **North Creek** (5 sites), **Sherman Valley** (7 sites), **Porter Creek** (16 sites), **Middle Waddell** (24 sites), **Fall Creek** (8 sites), and **Margaret McKenny** (25 sites). Only the latter two are off-limits to the noisy dirt bikes and ORVs that frequent this area, so they're more favored by hikers and horseback riders. But even they are too close to all the noise for many campers. Also, most of these campgrounds are used by hunters in the fall. Another DNR-managed campsite popular with horseback riders is **Mima Falls Trailhead** (5 sites), off Hwy 121 near Little Rock. A 5-mile loop trail begins here and runs to Mima Falls. All these campgrounds are free. *All are accessed either from US 12 or Hwy 121, both west of I-5 south of Olympia; (360) 902-1000.*

Boating/Sailing

Olympia is a boater's heaven. On the downtown waterfront along Budd Inlet, three modern **marina facilities** await: private West Bay Marina, (360) 943-2022; the Port of Olympia's East Bay Marina, (360) 786-1400; and Percival Landing Park, (360) 753-8382, home of the Olympia Yacht Club. All have guest moorage, nearby marine services, and good access to downtown shopping, restaurants, and walkways to Capitol Lake parks. (Ask about boat rentals at the marina offices.) A day trip out the inlet and across to **Squaxin Island State Park** is a great summer outing. Another nearby moorage and **marine-services** site is quaint Boston Harbor Marina; (360) 357-5670. Zittel's Marina near Johnson Point is a popular angler's departure point; (360) 459-1950. **Launch ramps** are found at Tumwater Historical Park, Boston Harbor, and Eld Inlet, as well as Luhr Beach, near the mouth of the Nisqually River.

Fishing

Fittingly, **salmon** is king in Washington's capital city. South Sound areas outside the city are byways for many runs of migratory hatchery **coho** and **chinook,** as well as **blackmouth** (resident chinook). Many of the latter are raised in net pens in Capitol Lake, then trucked and released in streams around the state. Unlike many areas in the Central and North Sound, where concern over threatened wild stocks has vastly curtailed summertime fishing, salmon angling is still a year-round activity from the Port of Olympia. The reason: nearly all the fish migrating to and from South Sound streams are hatchery-produced, thus subject to fewer restrictions. Seasons and runs change annually, but in recent years the South Sound has been one of the few Washington saltwater areas open for fishing all year. Typically, blackmouth are taken all year (but fishing is best in the winter); migratory chinook and coho peak in July and August; and some resident coho are available in midsummer and midwinter.

Most of the best salmon action is found to the north, off Johnson Point; off the east side of Hartstene Island; off Devil's Head; and at Tacoma-area hot spots such as the "Clay Banks" and Point Defiance. Tacoma-area boathouses are your best bet for lining up a charter trip to hook a summer chinook bound for the Puyallup or Nisqually River, but anglers with their own boats can find decent fishing close to Olympia. The circle of open water formed by Cooper Point, Hunter Point, Unsal Point on Squaxin Island, and Boston Harbor can be a good blackmouth producer all year long, especially in late winter. Lyle Point, at the south end of Anderson Island, also is a known blackmouth producer. Where the Deschutes River enters Capitol Lake, a fall chinook fishery has been a well-kept secret. For general salmon and boat rental information, call Zittel's Marina at Johnson Point; (360) 459-1950.

Smelt dippers often report success all year round from beaches near Boston Harbor, off the north side of Squaxin Island, and at the inner banks of Totten Inlet. Call the Boston Harbor Marina, (360) 357-5670, to find out when the smelt are running.

Trout fishing can be productive in Black, Ward, Hicks, Long, Patterson, St. Claire, Offut, and Deep Lakes. For fishing tips and licenses, call Tumwater Sports Center; (360) 352-5161. Also, the Deschutes River produces a few winter **steelhead.**

Kayaking/Canoeing

Totten, Eld, Budd, and Henderson Inlets (from west to east) are excellent kayak territory. Their waters are fairly protected, and beach landings at waterfront parks are many (see Parks, above). A good launching spot is Boston Harbor. Experienced paddlers also can begin here and make an overnight trip north across **Dana Passage** to **Squaxin Island State Park.** Currents in the passage can be dangerous for beginners, however.

Beginning kayakers and canoeists will love **Capitol Lake.** Launch at Capitol Lake Park, Marathon Park, or Tumwater Historical Park (see Parks, above), and miles of smooth, scenic waters are at your disposal. You can even paddle up to the frothy waters at the base of Tumwater Falls.

The saltwater estuary around the **Nisqually Delta** is another very popular canoe/kayak destination. A good launch site is Luhr Beach, at the mouth of McAllister Creek. Follow Old Hwy 99 and Meridian Rd from I-5 exit 114. (Note: No launch facilities are found inside the Nisqually National Wildlife Refuge.)

Cycling

The Capitol Campus and downtown Olympia both are good starting points for urban bike ventures. Head south up the shores of Capitol Lake, following **Deschutes Parkway** several miles to Tumwater Falls. Or scoot the other way out of town, following Plum Street to East Bay Road, which becomes Boston Harbor Road, for a great day trip with stops at Priest Point Park, Burfoot County Park, and, finally, the quaint Sound-side village of **Boston Harbor.** Round trip is about 15 miles, and much of the road there has a marked cycle path.

Mountain Biking

Some mountain bikers don't share hikers' disdain for the ORV activity in the Capitol State Forest (see the Hiking and Camping sections, above.) Several routes there, particularly the 20-mile **Capitol Peak Tour** off Hwy 121, as well as numerous routes near the Rock Candy Mountain entrance off Hwy 8, have become popular mountain-bike tours. Call the Department of Natural Resources, (360) 902-1000 or (360) 902-1234, for information about seasonal openings and closings, and other routes in this rugged area.

Accessible Outdoors

Most trails and exhibits at the **Nisqually National Wildlife Refuge** are wheelchair-accessible. One nearby access to the Nisqually River provides barrier-free shore fishing access. Fishing for salmon, steelhead, whitefish, and cutthroat trout is possible in season. Take I-5 exit 113, turn left on Nisqually Cutoff Road, drive 1.2 miles, and turn left on Kuhlman Road SE. Proceed a half mile, then turn left on Old Pacific Hwy. Continue three-tenths of a mile to Sixth Avenue SE, turn right, and proceed a half mile to the parking area.

Two fish hatcheries in the area provide barrier-free fall viewing of spawning chinook salmon. **McAllister Creek** is on Steilacoom Road SE (take I-5 exit 111); **Tumwater Falls** is in Tumwater Falls Park (I-5 exit 103; see Parks and Hiking, above).

The **McClane Creek Trailhead** is a state DNR day-use area with a barrier-free interpretive trail that leads to a beaver pond. From Olympia, follow US 101 west 4 miles, exit at Mud Bay (on Eld Inlet), go south on Delphi Road for 3.3 miles, turn right, and continue a half mile to the site.

The **Mima Mounds Natural Area** on Waddell Creek Road west of Little Rock has an interpretive display and trail through the oddly mounded prairie area. It's a good wildflower viewing venue in the spring. No pets allowed.

In the Capitol State Forest, **Margaret McKenny, Middle Waddell, and Fall Creek Campgrounds** (see Camping, above) offer barrier-free campsites and rest rooms, as does **Mima Falls Trailhead Campground. Millersylvania State Park** also has barrier-free camping facilities and rest rooms.

outside in

Restaurants

Alice's Restaurant ★   Hearty dinners, all including soup, greens, entree, and dessert. $$; *19248 Johnson Creek Rd SE, Tenino;* (360) 264-2887.

Arnold's Country Inn ★   Steaks and meat dishes dominate at Arnold Ball's latest restaurant. $$; *717 Yelm Ave E, Yelm;* (360) 458-3977. ⅃

Budd Bay Cafe ★   The nothing-fancy menu (steaks, sandwiches, pasta, seafood) is made for boaters. $$; *525 N Columbia St, Olympia; (360) 357-6963; www.olywa.net/bbaycafe.*

Gardner's Seafood and Pasta ★★   To loyal fans, Gardner's simple good food is the hands-down favorite in Olympia. $$; *111 W Thurston St, Olympia; (360) 786-8466.* &

La Petite Maison ★★   Imaginative, skillfully prepared Northwest cuisine reigns at this quiet refuge. $$; *101 Division NW, Olympia; (360) 943-8812.* &

Louisa ★★   Louisa continues to generate a buzz with primarily Italian cuisine. $$; *205 Cleveland Ave SE, Tumwater; (360) 352-3732.*

Seven Gables ★★   A most striking restaurant, with a Mount Rainier view and an elegant menu. $$; *1205 West Bay Dr NW, Olympia; (360) 352-2349.* &

Sweet Oasis ★   This informal spot on Capitol Way offers some delicious Mediterranean foods. $; *507 Capitol Wy, Olympia; (360) 956-0470.* &

Lodgings

Cavanaughs at Capitol Lake   One of few urban hotels to take advantage of the Northwest's natural beauty. $$; *2300 Evergreen Park Dr, Olympia; (360) 943-4000 or (800) 325-4000; www.cavanaughs.com.* &

Harbinger Inn ★★   Occupying a restored mansion, this B&B offers a fine outlook over Budd Inlet. $$; *1136 E Bay Dr, Olympia; (360) 754-0389; harbingerinn.uswestdex.com.*

More Information

Greater Olympia Visitors and Convention Bureau: *(360) 704-7544 or (877) 704-7500; www.visitolympia.com.*
Intercity Transit: *(360) 786-1881; www.intercitytransit.com.*
Olympia/Thurston County Chamber of Commerce: *(360) 357-3362; www.olympiachamber.com.*
Pierce Transit: *(253) 581-8000; www.piercetransit.com.*
Tumwater Area Chamber of Commerce: *(360) 357-5153; www.tumwaterchamber.com.*

Olympic
Peninsula
and the **Pacific**
Coast

Olympic Peninsula and the Pacific Coast

Kitsap Peninsula

From Manchester north to Foulweather Bluff, west to Hood Canal, and south to Belfair, including Point No Point; Scenic Beach, Illahee, Manchester, and Kitsap Memorial State Parks; and the Foulweather Bluff Preserve.

Welcome to the great in-between. Kitsap Peninsula, a long thumb of land that's almost an island unto itself, sits smack-dab between the height of civilization (Seattle) and the depths of wilderness (the Olympic Peninsula). That's perfectly fitting, because Kitsap's mix of mild and wild incorporates a bit of each.

For outdoor lovers, the peninsula, which runs from the Gig Harbor area north to Foulweather Bluff at Hansville, is a grab bag of the good and bad qualities of suburban Puget Sound. The good here is the endless shoreline: Kitsap Peninsula has 236 miles of saltwater beach. But only a small fraction of it is publicly accessible, the rest dominated by private home development or military installations, which have held sway over the landscape here for a century. That's the bad.

But whether that defeats the good, or vice versa, largely lies in the eye of the beholder. We know one thing for sure: select portions of the Kitsap Peninsula provide sweet, clean outdoor experiences of a kind you're not likely to find around any other populated areas in the country. And most of them are 60 minutes or less from downtown Seattle.

Secluded pockets of peninsula shoreline—most notably the inner bays near Poulsbo and Suquamish, and the fantastic, relatively unspoiled stretch of Hood Canal to the west—are great same-day outdoor getaways from the Seattle area. And they're often less crowded than similar places much farther away, such as the San Juan Islands or the coast of the Strait of Juan de Fuca.

Those who take the time to discover the beaches along Foulweather Bluff, or take in the Olympics-meet-saltwater view from Scenic Beach State Park, quickly learn that Kitsap County doesn't always have to be a launching point to somewhere else. When Seattle gets too hot, but the coolness of the Olympic Peninsula is simply too far, two options come to mind: stay hot and shut up, or lower your sights and aim for Kitsap County, the happy medium. Sometimes, lukewarm feels just right.

Getting There

If you were a crow, you'd leave Ivar's Acres of Clams and fly 9 miles due west. If you're not, the Kitsap Peninsula, directly across Central Puget Sound from Seattle, is reached by driving 30 miles south on Interstate 5 to Tacoma and 18 miles northwest on Highway 16 to Port Orchard and Bremerton. For the water route, take the Edmonds-Kingston, Seattle-Bainbridge, Seattle-Bremerton, or Fauntleroy-Southworth ferry. For rates and schedules: (206) 464-6400 or (800) 84-FERRY; www.wsdot.wa.gov/ferries.

Locals' advice: In the summer, it's almost always faster (by about an hour) to drive by way of Tacoma, particularly if your destination is in the south or central portion of the Kitsap Peninsula. Possible exceptions: Leaving downtown Seattle on a Friday afternoon. (Why would you do that, anyway?) In this case, win or lose, you lose. If you do choose a ferry, avoid the Edmonds-Kingston run at all costs during summer months. Rule of thumb: Every 2 hours in the Edmonds-Kingston ferry line shaves two years off your life.

inside out

Camping/Parks

Kitsap County isn't widely considered a camping haven, but several choice spots remain favorites among people who know the place. Chief among them is **Scenic Beach State Park,** a wonderful waterfront site on Hood Canal near Seabeck. On clear summer days, this is one of the prettiest state parks in the Northwest. Wild rhododendrons burst into bloom in May, and the view across Hood Canal into the Olympics is stunning; from this angle, you're looking right up east-slope Olympic valleys (namely the Duckabush and Dosewallips), and the mountains appear many times larger than when they're viewed from Seattle. The park also has a nice saltwater beach, some hiking trails, and a beach-bluff picnic area that's truly

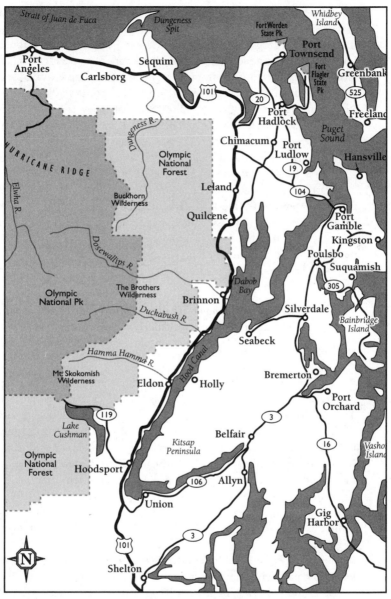

Kitsap Peninsula and the East Olympics

special. Also on the park property is Emel House, the old homestead for this former resort property. The house can be reserved for weddings and other functions.

Also reservable is the park's group camp, which holds 50 campers; (360) 830-5079. The camping area is simple but very pleasant, with 52 nicely spaced campsites (no hookups; RVs to 40 feet) spread through two forested loops in the upland section of the park. The Scenic Beach campground is open from April through September; day-use is available in the winter. Campsites can be reserved up to 11 months advance through Reservations Northwest, (800) 452-5687. *From Hwy 16/3 near Silverdale, take the Newberry Hill Rd exit and drive 3 miles west to Seabeck Hwy NW. Turn right and proceed through Seabeck, turning right on Miami Beach Rd NW (just after Seabeck Elementary School). Proceed about a mile to the park entrance at the end of the road; (360) 830-5079 or (800) 233-0321.*

Farther north, between Poulsbo and the Hood Canal Floating Bridge, is **Kitsap Memorial State Park,** another Hood Canal waterfront site. The park has 1,800 feet of rocky shoreline reached via a wood stairway at the end of a short trail from the camping area, although the views can't compare with those at Scenic Beach. The park has a good day-use site, with acres of open, grassy fields attracting softball players, kite fliers, and dog runners. The campground has 43 campsites (18 with water/electric hookups; RVs to 35 feet), more than half situated in a dark, forested area. A 30-person group camp also is available. Kitsap Memorial is open all year. Campsites cannot be reserved. *On Hwy 3, 4 miles north of Poulsbo, 3 miles south of Hood Canal Floating Bridge; (360) 779-3205 or (800) 233-0321.*

Another interesting park, in an odd location, is **Illahee State Park,** a 74-acre waterfront site tucked below one of Bremerton's suburban neighborhoods. This is another popular day-use park, with extensive picnic facilities. The park is split in two, with a boat launch and small saltwater mooring dock in the lower, waterfront portion, and a picnic area and campground in the wooded upper sector. The 1,785 feet of waterfront are the primary draw. It's a popular shore fishing, picnicking, and sun-worshipping spot. The mooring docks are protected by a breakwater, and often draw anglers and scuba divers. The small camping area has 25 sites (no hookups; RVs to 30 feet), and a group camp can be reserved. Illahee is open all year. Campsites cannot be reserved. *Follow Sylvan Wy west from Hwy 303 in East Bremerton, look for signs; (360) 478-6460 or (800) 233-0321.*

In the south county, **Manchester State Park** is a pleasant Puget Sound waterfront park with an intriguing history. It was built in the early 1900s as a base to mine the waters of Rich Passage to protect Puget Sound Naval Shipyard in the event of war. Remnants of that operation remain, including a giant concrete shell of a torpedo warehouse that's now used as a picnic shelter. (And you thought none of that military spending ever comes home to roost!) A trail leads from the day-use area to the rocky beach and some lingering gun emplacements. You're liable to see scuba divers here in the

The Point No Point Lighthouse near Hansville is an easy drive from Seattle

summer months. The camping area has 50 sites (no hookups; RVs to 45 feet) split into two unremarkable wooded loops. Manchester State Park is open all year. Campsites can be reserved up to 11 months in advance through Reservations Northwest, (800) 452-5687. *From Port Orchard, follow signs from Beach Dr E; from the Southworth ferry terminal, follow Hwy 160 and SE Colchester Dr west to Manchester, proceed a short distance north on Beach Dr E, and follow signs; (360) 871-4065 or (800) 233-0321.*

Beaches/Wildlife Watching

Give one peninsula 236 miles of shoreline, and you ought to be able to find a place to walk on the beach. That's not as easy as you might think in Kitsap County, where the vast majority of saltwater shoreline surrounding the island-like Kitsap Peninsula has been snatched up by private or government landholders, chief among them Uncle Sam and his nuclear Navy. Still, a bit of minor scratching, digging, and map-reading will yield some very worthwhile beach-strolling results, particularly for birders and marine-mammal buffs.

On the north end off Hansville Road NE, the beach area around Foulweather Bluff and **Point No Point** near Hansville is a great spot. In fact, given its close proximity to the Kingston ferry terminal, we've never been able to figure out why it's not more heavily populated. (One possible answer: parking. It's scarce in this residential area/public space. Park in the lot at Point No Point Resort, now owned by the state, or alongside the road if the gate is closed.) In any case, don't tell your neighbors. For a short outing, the beach east of the picturesque Point No Point Lighthouse is a nice stretch, often frequented by surf fishers casting for salmon off the point. Parents like this place, because you can park practically on the beach. Tours of the lighthouse can be arranged; (360) 638-2261. Public beach here extends around the point and about a half mile to the south, on beachfront that's part of a mostly undeveloped 35-acre Kitsap County park.

Historical note: Look for the small plaque near the lighthouse commemorating the signing of the Treaty of Point No Point in 1855. This is where tribes on the west side of Elliott Bay ceded "the land lying from the crest of the Olympic Mountains to Puget Sound" to the United States of America. My, how we've always wanted someone to tally up the current assessed value of that parcel of real estate. Court squabbles continue to this day over what the tribes got in return (fishing rights, and not much else).

In the other direction, 2.8 miles west of Hansville along NE Twin Spits Road, is the Nature Conservancy's **Foulweather Bluff Preserve.** Watch for the easily missed sign on a tree on the left (south) side of the road. A trail leads through a rare stand of (surviving) waterfront alder, fir, and western red cedar woods to a marshy area, separated from 3,700 feet of Hood Canal shoreline by a sandbar. The swampy area, a nesting site, is prime bird-watching habitat. Watch for **bald eagles, ospreys, great blue herons, buffleheads, loons, grebes, scoters,** and other seabirds. Note: No fires, mountain bikes, clam digging, unleashed dogs, or other even mildly destructive activity is allowed in this quiet refuge. Heed the signs near the trailhead, and the Conservancy might let you come back.

For short strolls or sunny summertime picnicking, consider the public beaches at **Kitsap Memorial, Scenic Beach, Illahee, and Manchester State Parks;** the **waterfront park in Silverdale;** or **Salsbury Point County Park,** just north of the Hood Canal Floating Bridge near Port Gamble. The latter is a particularly nice picnic spot that sees surprisingly little use. (Watch for the "County Park" sign just north of the floating bridge.)

Cycling

Kitsap County hasn't gone out of its way to be cycle-friendly, but it's not unfriendly, either. Many of the county's rural roads make good bike-touring thoroughfares.

A **North End tour** (moderate; 31 miles) starts at the west side of the Agate Pass Bridge on Hwy 305 near Bainbridge Island, where ample parking is available. Follow Suquamish Road several miles north to Suquamish, and another 10 miles north (the road becomes Hwy 104) to

Port Gamble, a good lunch stop. Proceed about 5 miles west and south on Hwys 104 and 3 to Kitsap Memorial State Park, then another 6 miles south on Big Valley Road NE and Bond Road NE to Poulsbo. From here, it's about 6.5 miles east on Hwy 305 to your starting point.

A good loop **South End tour** (moderately hilly, 25 miles) begins at the Southworth ferry terminal (leave your car in Seattle and walk your bike on). Follow Hwy 160 and SE Colchester Drive north along the shoreline to Manchester State Park (about 6 miles), then continue another 7 miles on Beach Drive E to Port Orchard. From here, ride south on Bethel Road SE and east on SE Sedgwick Road, about 12 miles, back to the Southworth terminal.

A good scenic route on the **Central Peninsula** (very hilly, about 25 miles) skirting Hood Canal can be ridden from Silverdale. From downtown, follow NW Anderson Hill Road and Seabeck Highway NW 9 very hilly miles to Seabeck. Scenic Beach State Park (see Camping/Parks, above) is a 2-mile side trip from here. Continue 4 miles south on NW Seabeck-Holly Road to Camp Union. Turn left on NW Holly Road and ride 6 miles east, past Wildcat Lake County Park, to Seabeck Highway NW. Turn left and proceed 3 miles to Newberry Hill Road, which dips another 3 miles east back to Silverdale. This is a major up/down ride, with some world-class whoop-de-doos—not for the faint of heart or aerobically challenged. But it's particularly beautiful during the spring, when wild rhododendrons bloom all along the route.

For supplies and **rentals**, consult Mount Constance Mountain Shoppe in Bremerton, (360) 377-0668; or Silverdale Cyclery, (360) 692-5508.

Fishing

Salmon fishing has been a favorite pastime for Kitsap County residents for generations. Nearby Puget Sound waters continue to produce decent results, in spite of slowdowns in Washington's salmon fishery. For boat anglers, the most popular salmon-fishing spots from Kitsap County ports are the same as those fished by Seattle-area anglers: Point No Point, Jefferson Head, Midchannel Bank, Allen Bank off Southworth, and dozens of other Puget Sound spots. Keep in mind that interior Puget Sound fishing is seasonal and, these days, very spotty: some areas close for months at a time during the peak summer season, for example. Fishing for **blackmouth** (immature chinook) is productive all winter long, when weather allows.

When fishing is open, West Sound residents do enjoy one hometown salmon advantage. Point No Point—a deep-water hole near Hansville that's a perennial hefty **chinook** producer, awaits at the north end of the peninsula for boat or shore anglers. Point No Point Resort, (360) 638-

2233, now owned by the state Fish and Wildlife Department, rents kicker boats, which need be driven only a short distance offshore to reach productive waters. One unique thing about Point No Point is that salmon can be—and often are—hooked right from the beach. The rapid drop-off from the point makes it possible to reach deep water fairly easily with a casting lure, such as a Buzz Bomb. Fly casters even occasionally hook into a chinook off the beach here. Remember that you'll want insulated waders to fish here, even in the summer.

A leading local gear shop is Kingston Tackle and Marine, (360) 297-2521. Others include Kitsap Sports Shop in Bremerton, (360) 373-9589, or Silverdale, 10516 Silverdale Wy NW, (360) 698-4808; and Viking Marine in Poulsbo, (360) 779-4656.

Trout fishing in lakes on the peninsula is better than average for the Puget Sound area. Popular fishing spots are Wildcat Lake and Kitsap Lake, both west of Bremerton; Buck Lake near Hansville; and Tiger, Panther, Horseshoe, and Long Lakes farther south. Most lakes are open from the last Saturday in April to October 31. For trout-fishing advice, not to mention fine flies and other supplies, consult the Northwest Angler in downtown Poulsbo, (360) 697-7100.

A rather unique fishing opportunity was born with construction of the new (replacement) Hood Canal Floating Bridge, which includes a finger fishing pier on the north side of the structure. Park in the westside parking lot and follow signs to the pier, which leads far out on Hood Canal. Fishing can be decent for **bottomfish** here, and a rare salmon might happen by. Another little-known, little-used bottom-fishing area is found to the south, off Misery Point near Seabeck, where an underwater fishing reef attracts some bottomfish. The closest launches are at Seabeck or Miami Beach, just around the corner to the southeast. Boat rentals, tackle, and licenses are available at Seabeck Marina; (360) 830-5179. (This is a popular launching spot for boaters going after Hood Canal shrimp. See the Hood Canal chapter).

Canoeing/Kayaking

The protected waters between the Kitsap Peninsula and Bainbridge and Blake Islands are favorite haunts of many Seattle-area sea kayakers. Paddlers often make use of Washington State ferries to Bainbridge Island and Bremerton, carrying their boats on one ferry, **paddling between Bremerton and Winslow,** then packing the boat home on the other. It's a one-way trip of about 10 water miles, and can be expanded into an overnighter by stopping at Manchester, Illahee, or Blake Island State Parks. For experienced paddlers, **Blake Island** is a reasonable hop from Manchester State

Park. Remember to watch your rear-view mirror: ship traffic is heavy in relatively narrow Rich Passage between Manchester and Bainbridge.

For shorter, partial-day trips, **Eagle Harbor** near Winslow and **Sinclair Inlet** between Bremerton and Port Orchard both provide interesting waters with good launch points. For a short, safe, beginner trip, **Liberty Bay** in Poulsbo is a great spot, and a local vendor, Olympic Outdoor Center, 18971 Front Street; (360) 697-6095; www.kayakproshop.com, makes it easy to dip your toes in the water. The center, which gives a 3-hour, introductory lesson and tour of Liberty Bay for $45, also offers short- or long-term rentals, supplies, and expert advice. But it's more than a kayak store. Olympic Outdoor's staff also offers an impressive array of classes, and leads guided tours of nearby kayak getaways (such as the Dungeness National Wildlife Refuge in Sequim; see the Sequim and the Dungeness Valley chapter).

If that's not enough territory, consider that nearly all of **Hood Canal** is a prime waterway, lightly used by boat traffic of any kind. One popular destination is **Salsbury Point County Park,** near the east foot of the Hood Canal Floating Bridge. Paddlers launching here can make a short trip north into the protected waters of **Port Gamble.**

Boating/Sailing

Nearly every town on the Kitsap Peninsula is located on the water, and a full range of **marine services** and moorage is available. In the south end, the highly popular Port Orchard Marina, (360) 876-5535, home of the Port Orchard Yacht Club, offers a full range of marine services, plus extensive guest moorage (no charge for day use). Most Port Orchard sights and services are within walking distance.

In the central county, Bremerton-area visitors have their choice of **marinas.** Bremerton Marina, (360) 373-1035, next to the ferry terminal, is a newer facility with full marine services, ample guest moorages, and walking-distance access to downtown attractions such as the battleship USS *Turner Joy*. In the Port Washington Narrows is Port Washington Marina; (360) 479-3037. Around the corner in Silverdale, the Port of Silverdale Marina, (360) 698-4918, has 60 guest slips and minimal services. Farther west, **Illahee State Park** has some moorage, and the Port of Brownsville Marina, (360) 692-5498, offers full services and is close to the Keyport Undersea Warfare Museum.

To the north, Poulsbo is a booming boating center. The Port of Poulsbo Marina, (360) 779-3505, www.poulsbo.net/portofpoulsbo/, has guest moorage and full services, and it's very conveniently located to downtown Poulsbo attractions, such as Liberty Bay Park and the Marine

Science Center. The Kingston Marina, (360) 297-3545, near the Kingston ferry terminal, is a protected spot with 39 guest slips and basic services.

Boat launches or slings are found at Miami Beach, Seabeck, and Salsbury Point County Park on Hood Canal; Point No Point, Kingston, Miller Bay, Poulsbo, Keyport, Brownsville, Illahee State Park, Port Washington Narrows, Tracyton, Silverdale, Chico, downtown Bremerton, Port Orchard, Retsil, and Manchester.

Hiking

Hiking trails aren't one of Kitsap County's stronger suits. The primary hiking venue here is 1,700-foot **Green Mountain,** a minor, antenna-farmed peak in the center of the county to which you can also drive (and, alas, ride dirt bikes); it's about 2 miles to the top. The trailhead is off NW Holly Rd, west of Bremerton. If you're looking for a good day hike on Kitsap Peninsula, consider a stroll on one of the **saltwater beaches** described in Beaches, above, or partake in one of the nearby leeward Olympics hikes.

Photography

We've shot some fine sunset panoramas of the Olympics from the Seabeck area. **Scenic Beach State Park** is a good place to set up your tripod. Fans of wildflowers should consider a trip to the Seabeck/West Kitsap area in May, when wild pink rhododendrons are in bloom. Nice pictures across Central Puget Sound to downtown Seattle can be captured from the top of **Green Mountain,** a short hike or drive in central Kitsap County (see Hiking, above).

Accessible Outdoors

Kitsap Memorial, Scenic Beach, Illahee, and Manchester State Parks (see Camping, above) all offer wheelchair-accessible picnic areas and rest rooms. Illahee also has wheelchair-accessible camping; (360) 478-6460 or (800) 233-0321.

outside in

Restaurants

Bahn Thai ★★   The same menu and clean, exotic look as the Seattle Bahn Thai. $; *9811 Mickelberry Rd, Silverdale; (360) 698-3663.* &

Benson's Restaurant ★★★   This clean-lined restaurant offers mouth-watering, good-for-you selections. $$; *18820 Front St, Poulsbo; (360) 697-3449.* &

Boat Shed ★   A casual seafood restaurant overhanging the Port Washington Narrows. $; *101 Shore Dr, Bremerton; (360) 377-2600.* &

Yacht Club Broiler ★   Seafood is big at this simple restaurant with a water view and elegant touches. $$; *9226 Bayshore Dr, Silverdale; (360) 698-1601.* &

Lodgings

Manor Farm Inn ★★   Once, a small gentleman's farm in the middle of nowhere; now, a lavish retreat. $$$; *26069 Big Valley Rd NE, Poulsbo; (360) 779-4628; www.manorfarminn.com.*

Reflections Bed and Breakfast Inn ★★   A sprawling four-room B&B set on a hillside overlooking Sinclair Inlet. $$; *3878 Reflection Ln E, Port Orchard; (360) 871-5582; www.portorchard.com/reflections.* &

Silverdale on the Bay ★   A tastefully designed resort hotel, good for a conference or a getaway. $$; *3073 NW Bucklin Hill Rd, Silverdale; (360) 698-1000 or (800) 544-9799; www.westcoasthotels.com/silverdale.*

Willcox House ★★★   A copper-roofed, art-deco manse with five rooms and views of the Olympics. $$$; *2390 Tekiu Rd, Seabeck; (360) 830-4492 or (800) 725-2600; www.willcoxhouse.com.*

More Information

Kitsap County Parks: *(360) 337-4595.*
Kitsap Peninsula Visitors and Convention Bureau: *(360) 416-5615; www.visitkitsap.com.*
Kitsap Transit: *(360) 373-BUSS.*
Mount Constance Mountain Shoppe, *east Bremerton, for supplies and advice: (360) 377-0668.*
Olympic Outdoor Center, *Poulsbo: (360) 697-6095; www.kayakproshop.com.*
The Sun: *For general outdoors information—including fishing columns by local guide Drew Hathorne and columns by Seabury Blair Jr., one of the Northwest's leading outdoor writers, read Kitsap County's daily paper: (360) 377-3711; www.mroutdoors.com.*
Washington State Ferries: *(206) 464-6400 or (800) 84-FERRY; www.wsdot.wa.gov/ferries.*

Olympic National Forest
and the East Slope
Olympics

From Lake Cushman northwest to O'Neil Pass in Olympic National Park, north along the eastern Olympic crest to Gray Wolf Ridge, and east to Hood Canal, including the Lake Cushman/Staircase area; Hoodsport Trail and Lake Cushman State Parks; the Buckhorn, Brothers, Mount Skokomish, and Wonder Mountain Wildernesses; and the Gray Wolf, Dungeness, Quilcene, Dosewallips, Duckabush, Hamma Hamma, and North Fork Skokomish River drainages.

Many of the nation's most scenic wildlands have federal land managers lurking in the corners. It's a bit less subtle than that on the Olympic Peninsula, where the U.S. Forest Service has the Olympic Mountains in nothing short of a headlock. Like it or not, most of the lower-elevation slopes of Washington's most scenic mountain range are controlled by timber-hungry Olympic National Forest, which virtually surrounds the wilderness lands of Olympic National Park. Just as it has been elsewhere around the United States, that federal designation has been both good and bad for wildlands inside the 632,000-acre Olympic National Forest. Okay, mostly bad. But it really depends where you look.

Look at the formerly great lowland rain forest on the peninsula's west side, and you see a picture of devastation: too much old growth cut too fast in too short a time with too little regard for the impact on fisheries and wildlife. Get airborne and see for yourself: virtually all of the west-side Forest Service land is clear-cut, right up to the Olympic National Park border. Surrounded as they are by thousands of acres of shrubby second growth, the national park's preserved highlands loom like an island of life in a rather dead lowland sea. For that reason—and also because better, untrammeled national park lands are available nearby—Olympic National Forest lands on the west side of the peninsula have been largely ignored by recreators.

Not so on Olympic Forest's east-peninsula lands, where the picture is more mixed, and recreation opportunities are many. To be sure, massive clear-cutting also has been undertaken here, often with the same sort of reckless disregard as on the west side. In the hearts and minds of longtime visitors, logging swaths here cut even deeper, because they blazed right through areas already heavily used for recreation—mostly hiking, back-packing, and fishing. A system of long river-drainage trails that stretched from Hood Canal west to the Olympic crest was replaced by a patchwork quilt of shorter trails, abruptly bisected by clear-cuts and their accompanying logging roads. That's why many East Slope Olympic trails now have an "upper" and a "lower" portion, the upper usually running through old growth to the alpine country, the lower winding through second growth, and potholed roads forever dividing the two.

This equation has more than one upside, though. Logging has slowed to a crawl here, and the roads left by decades of clear-cutting have shortened the walking distance to some of the Olympic Mountains' most spectacular alpine country. And on this side of the forest, not all of that splendor lies within national park boundaries. Olympic National Forest's east-peninsula lands contain four high-country wilderness areas. (Don't fool yourself into believing the government set them aside out of guilt for the carnage below. Most of these areas are simply too high and too rugged to be logged.) From north to south, the 44,000-acre Buckhorn Wilderness, the 16,000-acre Brothers Wilderness, the 13,000-acre Mount Skokomish Wilderness, and the 2,300-acre Wonder Mountain Wilderness add a bit of long-term preservation insurance for fans of the eastern Olympics.

In spite of their checkered land-management past, the east slope Olympics remain one of the more diverse outdoor playgrounds in Western Washington. Some second-growth forests here are now unusually large. And the small forest patches spared from logging are magnificent, with massive Douglas fir, hemlock, and western red cedar trees thundering skyward, while clustered groups of bright pink wild rhododendrons explode in the broken sunlight below. Rivers flowing east from the mountains to Hood Canal are uncommonly beautiful and undeveloped. Wild streams of liquid glass such as the Duckabush, Dosewallips, Hamma Hamma, Gray Wolf, Big Quilcene, and Dungeness are spectacular in their own right, but the mountains-meeting-the-sea setting makes them all the more memorable.

Generations of Washingtonians have been drawn to this rich, wild

The author atop Mount Ellinor, above Lake Cushman in the leeward Olympics

mix—much of which is literally within sight of downtown Seattle. Given their close proximity to the city, it's surprising that the east slope Olympics don't draw even more hikers, campers, and anglers. One possible reason: logistical confusion. People can't quite figure out how to navigate these parts. And for good reason. Unlike the west side, where access to the high country is concentrated in a few well-known places, the east side is rife with openings. Credit—or blame, as the case may be—goes to the maze of logging roads. More than 2,500 miles of gravel roads wind through Olympic National Forest, most of them poorly marked and maintained. Staring at a Forest Service map detailing the squirming-wormpile road structure can give you a headache. There's no obvious focal point here: just a series of river drainages stacked end to end from Sequim to Shelton, all flowing toward salt water, and concealing miles of backcountry wonders.

This is a big, diverse area. Don't expect to see it all, or even a fraction of it, in a single visit. Our best advice is to get a Forest Service map and navigate by river drainage. Pick a river, visit for a weekend, hike the trails, camp the campgrounds, drive the roads. Come back and do another drainage. By the time you've worked through all of them, you'll be amazed—and the river you started with probably will have changed dramatically, forcing you to begin anew.

That's the inspiring—and disconcerting—thing about the east slope

Olympics. Like it or not, change—often radical—is a fact of life in the Olympic National Forest. No area in Washington exemplifies the double-edged sword of multiuse better—or worse—than this one.

Getting There

Most eastern slope Olympic National Forest trailheads and campgrounds are reached via US Highway 101 on the west shore of Hood Canal (see the Hood Canal chapter). From that highway, access roads lead west into the forest in the Quilcene, Duckabush, Hamma Hamma, and Skokomish River drainages. A major access route to the interior east slope Olympics is Lake Cushman Rd/Hwy 119, which leads west to the Lake Cushman area from Hoodsport.

inside out

Olympic National Forest Rules and Regulations

Because all Olympic National Forest lands share at least one border with Olympic National Park, many visitors assume rules are the same throughout. Not true. Some key differences:

Dogs, a definite no-no in the national park backcountry, are allowed on trails in the national forest.

Olympic National Park does not require day-hiking permits, but charges fees for mandatory overnight **wilderness permits.** Olympic National Forest—in keeping with the federal government's goal of keeping hikers as confused as possible—uses a completely separate system. Most popular Olympic National Forest trailheads require a **parking pass.** For $5 a day or $30 a year, this "Northwest Forest Pass" allows you to park at trailheads and visitors centers in most Northwest national forest areas. They're available from ranger stations, from many private vendors, on-line at www.naturenw.org, or by calling (800) 270-7504. Note that many longer hiking trails in the east slope Olympics climb through Forest Service land, then enter the national park. In these cases, you'll likely need a Northwest Forest Pass to park, then a national park Wilderness Permit (and possibly a reservation, if you're hiking into Royal Basin or Flapjack Lakes) to spend the night. Don't bother telling them you already gave at the office; it's been done.

Hunting, particularly for black-tailed deer and Roosevelt elk, is allowed in most of the national forest (something to be mindful of when hiking in the fall). It's illegal in the park.

Backcountry **party size** in the national park is limited to 12 people and eight stock animals; there's no restriction in the national forest, except in its designated wilderness areas, where the 12 persons/eight stock rule (or just 12 living beings, which lumps people and stock together) applies. **Campfires** are allowed in national forest backcountry, except in designated wilderness. They're prohibited above 3,500 feet in most areas of the national park. State **fishing licenses** are required in the national forest, and state regulations apply. With the exception of permits for razor-clam digging and catch-record cards for salmon and steelhead, state licenses are not required in the national park. **Firearms** are allowed in the national forest, forbidden in national parks. **Roadside camping** is allowed in the national forest, forbidden in national parks.

An organizational note: Because the bulk of recreation opportunities in Olympic National Forest lie within the Hood Canal Ranger District on the east slopes of the Olympics, we've focused the outdoors listings in this chapter on that geographic area. Details about the recreation offerings in the Olympic Ranger District (the consolidated district comprising the former Sol Duc and Quinault districts) can be found in the Lake Crescent and the Upper Soleduck chapter; the Forks and La Push chapter; and the Lake Quinault and the Quinault River Valley chapter.

Camping

Like most Forest Service campgrounds, Olympic National Forest sites in the leeward Olympics are far from fancy: pit toilets, running water (maybe), and not much else. But you've gotta love the packaging. Most of these campsites are streamside, in old-growth or mature second-growth forest. They're quiet, remote—and usually worth the effort to locate. A popular state park and two Olympic National Park campgrounds round out the picture.

Lake Cushman campers flock to **Lake Cushman State Park,** on the east shore of the Tacoma City Light reservoir. The park straddles the lake's Big Creek Inlet (which used to be a stream canyon before the river was dammed). Tent sites are on the north shore, RV sites and the picnic area on the south. In all, the park has 80 campsites (30 with hookups; RVs to 60 feet). A smooth, fine-gravel beach and a boat ramp make this a popular summer hangout for sunbathers, water skiers, canoeists, and trout anglers. About 4 miles of marked hiking trails wind through the park, although nicer ones are just up the road at Staircase. Lake Cushman is open April through October. Winter camping is allowed in the day-use area only. Campsites can be reserved up to 11 months in advance by calling (800) 452-5687. *On Lake Cushman Rd (Hwy 119) 7.5 miles west of Hoodsport; (360) 877-5491 or (800) 233-0321.*

Nearby, at the head of the lake, is **Staircase Campground,** an Olympic National Park site. Staircase, nicely situated near the North Fork Skokomish trailhead, has 59 sites (no hookups; RVs to 21 feet). It's very popular with hikers and backpackers. The campground is open all year. *17 miles west of Hoodsport via Lake Cushman Rd (Hwy 119); (360) 452-0330 or (360) 877-5569.*

Two smaller alternatives are nearby. **Big Creek Campground,** just up the road from the state park, has 23 sites (no hookups; RVs to 30 feet) in a wooded area. Big Creek is open from May through September. Campsites cannot be reserved. *Near the intersection of Lake Cushman Rd (Hwy 119) and Forest Rd 24, 9 miles west of Hoodsport; (360) 877-5254.*

Lilliwaup Creek, a state Department of Natural Resources site, has 13 campsites for tents or small trailers (no hookups). It's open all year, and campsites cannot be reserved. *On Forest Rd 24, 6.5 miles west of Big Creek Campground (above); (360) 902-1234.*

A more remote site on the South Fork Skokomish is **Brown Creek,** which has 20 sites (no hookups; RVs to 21 feet), a horse camp, and access to hiking trails. It's open all year. Campsites cannot be reserved. The road is rough, and you'll need a Forest Service road map to find this place. *On Forest Rd 2353, 21 miles north of Shelton; (360) 877-5254.*

One river drainage north, **Hamma Hamma** has 15 sites (no hookups; RVs to 21 feet). Nothing fancy, but it's a nice spot, set on one of the region's most gorgeous rivers. Nearby **Lena Creek,** another Forest Service riverfront campground, has 14 sites (no hookups; RVs to 21 feet). It's near the Lena Lakes trailhead. Both campgrounds are open summer months only, and campsites cannot be reserved. *On Forest Rd 25 (Hamma Hamma River Rd) 6.5 and 8 miles, respectively, west of US 101; (360) 877-5254.*

In the Duckabush drainage, the only option is **Collins,** a Forest Service camp with 16 sites (no hookups; RVs to 21 feet). It's open mid-May through September. Sites cannot be reserved. *On Forest Rd 2510 (Duckabush River Rd), 5 miles west of US 101; (360) 877-5254.*

The Dosewallips drainage has two nice campgrounds. **Elkhorn,** a Forest Service camp, offers 20 riverfront sites (no hookups; RVs to 21 feet). It's open mid-May through September (the road up the river closes just beyond here in the winter, because Olympic National Park doesn't maintain the part inside its borders.) *11 miles west of Brinnon via US 101 and Forest Rd 2610 (Dosewallips Rd); (360) 765-2200.*

Dosewallips, a tents-only Olympic National Park campground, is a pretty spot and a bit more centrally located, at least if you're a hiker (the Dosewallips trailhead is right across the parking lot). You'll find 30 tent sites (no hookups; no RVs) near the river, and they're often full on summer nights. Dosewallips is open summer months only. Campsites cannot be reserved. *At the end of Forest Rd 2610 (Dosewallips Rd), 16 miles west of Brinnon; (360) 452-0330.*

Near the confluence of the Dungeness and Gray Wolf Rivers, **Dungeness Forks,** a Forest Service campground, has 10 tent sites (no hookups), near the popular Gray Wolf trailhead. It's open May through September, and isn't recommended for RVs. Campsites cannot be reserved. *On Forest Rd 2880, 11 miles south of Sequim via Palo Alto Rd and Forest Rd 2880; call (360) 765-2200 for directions.*

Just to the south, **East Crossing**'s 10 tent sites (no hookups; no RVs) are set along the Dungeness River. The campground is open summer months only; sites cannot be reserved. *On Forest Rd 2860, 13 miles south of Sequim; call (360) 765-2200 for directions and repair updates (flood damage closed this campground during the winter of 1999–2000).*

Hiking/Backpacking

Simply put, this is one of the best and most diverse places to put foot to trail in Washington. The lower slopes of the leeward Olympics are mostly logged, but the upper hills are fantastic, and—because most are now protected by wilderness or national park designation—likely to stay that way.

Hikers should note that national forests, wilderness areas, and national parks all have different backcountry restrictions (see Olympic National Forest Rules and Regulations, above). That's particularly important in this area, where it's possible to begin hiking in the national forest, stumble into a wilderness area, then pass through to the national park—all on the very same trail. If you have any doubt about the rules, consult one of the ranger stations listed below.

That said, the hiking menu here is like the wine list at a fine restaurant: almost overwhelming, but a joy to sample, sip by sip. Generally, this isn't the best place to come for a short day hike (although plenty are available for the persistent). Most trails here begin in the deep lowland woods and follow a stream drainage west, where they enter wildflower- and view-rich alpine areas in the high Olympics. If you're day hiking, consider that great views or notable destinations often aren't found for a dozen or more miles up the trail—assuming drop-dead gorgeous mountain streams and valleys don't count. Those same features, however, make this a superb backpacking area, whether you're out for an overnighter or a two-week, cross-Olympics jaunt.

A note on seasons: Many of the best trails here begin fairly high in the mountains and end even higher. Most are likely to be snowed in from November through the early summer. High alpine areas in the leeward Olympics generally aren't passable to casual hikers and backpackers until

June or later, although from year to year this can vary by as much as a month. Ask a ranger.

An important note on access: Most trailheads in the Olympic National Forest are reached by traveling a series of often baffling Forest Service roads. They often wash out, and the government is fond of changing road numbers, just to confuse us. For road closure information and detailed driving directions to trailheads, we strongly urge you to call a local ranger district office before setting out. Trail specialists at these offices also can help you pick a specific hike. A comprehensive—though by no means complete—list of favorites follows. They're listed by river drainage, north to south.

Gray Wolf drainage

Quilcene Ranger Station, (360) 765-2200:

The **Gray Wolf River Trail** (moderate; various lengths) is a magnificent walk up one of the least-spoiled river drainages on the Olympic Peninsula. The trail's lower half is great beginner/intermediate backpacking terrain. From a trailhead near Dungeness Forks Campground (see Camping, below), it follows the silvery river about 10 miles upstream to a major trail junction, Three Forks. Good backcountry campsites are located near the river all along the way; go until you run out of gas, then make camp. (Note: Extensive slides closed the lower portion of this trail in the winter of 2000. Call the Quilcene Ranger Station to check on repair status.)

From the trail junction at Three Forks, high-country trails lead north to **Deer Park** (difficult; 4.3 miles one way; see the Port Angeles and Hurricane Ridge chapter); southwest up beautiful **Cameron Creek Trail** to Cameron Pass (difficult; 11 miles one way); and south along the bubbling **upper Gray Wolf** to Gray Wolf Pass (difficult; 9.5 miles one way). Strong backpackers can combine the Lower Gray Wolf, Cameron Creek, Dosewallips, and Upper Gray Wolf Trails for a 6- to 8-day, 50-mile Olympic backcountry loop. But sticking to the Gray Wolf itself is tough to beat. A round-trip hike to **Gray Wolf Pass** is about 39 miles. (Name trivia note: Yes, there used to be gray wolves here. This was one of their last refuges from bounty hunters. They're now extinct in the area.)

Dungeness drainage

Quilcene Ranger Station, (360) 765-2200:

On its route north, the Gray Wolf dumps into the Dungeness River, which has its own pleasant trail system—assuming you can get to it. Hikers headed for Dungeness trails should note that a washout closed a portion of a main arterial, Forest Road 2860, from its junction with Forest Road 28 in 2000, blocking access to trails in this section on the lower

Dungeness. A workaround is possible by taking Forest Road 2880 beyond Dungeness Forks Campground (see Camping, below), then turning left on Forest Road 2870, which leads to Forest Road 2860 above the washout. Call the ranger station for road updates.

Assuming you can get to the trailhead on Forest Road 2860, the **Upper Dungeness Trail** follows the upper river to Camp Handy (moderate; 6.4 miles round trip) and on to Boulder Shelter (difficult; 6.8 miles round trip), near the junction with the Marmot Pass/Big Quilcene Trail. This rain-shadow area is a very good backpack destination, particularly when weather is questionable elsewhere on the peninsula. Note that cougars have been very active in this area in recent years.

A mile up the Dungeness Trail is a junction with a path to one of Olympic National Park's most notable backpacking destinations, **Royal Basin** (moderate; 14 miles round trip). The trail empties into a stunning alpine valley beneath 7,788-foot Mount Deception. Campsites are exceptional in the beautiful, wildflower-enriched basin. If you're lucky, you might see a mountain goat on the upper ridges. If you're looking for a great weekend backpack trip to familiarize yourself with the area, this is it. Note: Royal Basin now has a national park overnight quota system. Call Olympic National Park's Wilderness Information Center, (360) 452-0300, for permit information.

In the lower Dungeness drainage, a good day hike—and an increasingly popular mountain bike route—is the **Gold Creek Trail** (moderate; 12.6 miles round trip), which follows the Dungeness drainage about 2,000 feet up from a lower trailhead on Forest Road 2860 to a trailhead farther up the same road. It can be ridden or walked one way for a fairly easy, 6.4-mile day hike that's especially nice in spring, when wild rhododendrons are in bloom. As long as Forest Road 2860 is washed out (see road-access note, above), only the upper trailhead can be used for this one.

Near the Gold Creek Trail's upper trailhead is the **Tubal Cain Mine Trail** (moderate; various lengths), which follows Copper Creek beneath Iron and Buckhorn Mountains to the stunning alpine terrain of 6,100-foot Marmot Pass (difficult; 17.6 miles). It's a long, tough haul to the pass, 3,300 feet above the trailhead—but worth the climb if you're in shape. (The trail continues south from there into Olympic National Park, over Constance Pass, and down to the Dosewallips Trail.) The Tubal Cain Trail also can be hiked as a nice day hike to abandoned mine sites turned into beautiful alpine meadows, about 4 miles up the trail.

Access note: Most trailheads in the Dungeness drainage are reached by following Palo Alto Road west from US 101 near Sequim Bay State Park to Forest Road 28, then connecting Forest Service roads. Call a ranger for specific directions.

Quilcene drainage

Quilcene Ranger Station, (360) 765-2200:

Much of this area is logged over, but a couple of notable trails stand out. The **Mount Townsend Trail** (difficult; 11 miles round trip) is a popular thigh-burner that gets you to truly stunning views atop a 6,280-foot peak. You can see all the way to Seattle and Mount Rainier, and the wild rhododendron display here in the late spring might be the best in the state. If the 3,400-foot elevation gain sounds like a bit much, make it a 2-day trip. Decent campsites are available at Camp Windy (3.5 miles) and at nearby Silver Lakes (2.5 miles south on a connecting trail). The trailhead is on Forest Road 2760, reached via Penny Creek and Big Quilcene River Roads out of Quilcene.

Another very popular day hike—probably the best short one in the Quilcene area—is the climb to the old fire lookout atop **Mount Zion** (moderate; 3.6 miles round trip). The trail is fairly steep, but short enough to get most people to the top, where views of Hood Canal and Puget Sound are nothing short of awesome. This is another good place to hike among blooming wild rhododendrons in the late spring. Elevation gain is about 1,300 feet. The trailhead is on Forest Road 2810. Take Lords Lake Loop Road and Forest Road 28 north of Quilcene.

Also in this area, the **Upper Big Quilcene Trail** is yet another steep route to Marmot Pass (difficult; 10.5 miles round trip); and the **Lower Big Quilcene Trail** has become a popular mountain-bike route (see Mountain Biking, below).

Dosewallips drainage

Hood Canal Ranger Station, (360) 877-5254:

This is the heart of the leeward Olympics, and some of the best hiking trails are found here. Most trailheads are reached by following Dosewallips Road west from Brinnon.

The **West Fork Dosewallips Trail,** which begins as the Dosewallips River Trail near Dosewallips and Elkhorn Campgrounds (see Camping, below), is a favorite here. It follows the beautiful, clear river to a grand backpacking destination—Honeymoon Meadows (moderate; 17.6 miles round trip), then climbs to 4,400-foot Anderson Pass (difficult; 21 miles round trip). Wiser hikers camp in the meadow and day-hike to Anderson Pass. Cross-Olympic hikers continue west from here, dropping down the East Fork Quinault Trail to Enchanted Valley (see the Lake Quinault and the Quinault River Valley chapter). Hikers should note that, at this writing, the High Dose Bridge—the only safe passage over the West Fork Dosewallips in this area—was closed and awaiting repairs, blocking access to Honeymoon Meadows. Call the national park for updates before backpacking in the area. If the park service continues to drag its feet on the bridge repairs, make it a day hike. Follow the Dosewallips River Trail 1.4 miles to the major trail junction at Dose Forks, then a short distance beyond on the West Fork trail to the east end of the High Dose footbridge.

Backpackers who continue straight at Dose Forks, and follow the main-channel Dosewallips west, have several options. About 2.5 miles from the main trailhead, the **Constance Pass Trail** turns north, climbing steeply over the pass and continuing to Boulder Shelter (difficult; 11.5 miles one way). This is a popular connecting route between the Dosewallips and Dungeness drainages. Or proceed west from Dose Forks up the main-stem Dosewallips, a beautiful, isolated area. Popular destinations include the grand views and wildflower meadows at **Dose Meadows** (moderate; 26 miles round trip) and the alpine terrain of **Hayden Pass** (moderate/difficult; 31 miles round trip). Another trail drops 8.5 miles west of Hayden Pass to a junction with the Elwha River Trail (see the Port Angeles and Hurricane Ridge chapter).

A short, very steep trail that begins on Dosewallips Road near the national park border leads to **Lake Constance** (very difficult; 4 miles round trip), one of this area's most heavily (over)used backcountry campgrounds. Don't let the short distance fool you; the trail is an absolute beast, gaining 3,400 feet in its 2-mile ascent. The lake is nice, but overuse here has led to restrictions of 20 overnighters per day. Permits (free, so far) can be reserved through Staircase Ranger Station; (360) 877-5569. You pick them up at Dosewallips Ranger Station near the trailhead (it has no phone). Day hikers don't need a permit. Just thighs of iron.

Duckabush drainage

Hood Canal Ranger Station, (360) 877-5254:

Two good day-hiking trails are found in the lower Duckabush drainage. **Interrorem Interpretive Trail** (easy; one-third-mile loop), which begins near the Interrorem Guard Station about 4 miles west of US 101 on Duckabush Road, is a cool loop trail through lush second-growth forest (with plenty of massive stumps to remind you of the first). Connecting to this trail is the equally popular **Ranger Hole Trail** (moderate; 1.6 miles round trip; quite steep at the bottom, near the river), which leads from the guard station to a stunningly beautiful fishing hole on the Duckabush (once extremely productive for fishing, now mildly so, on a good day). Nice picnic grounds near the historic 1907 guard station—a former wilderness outpost—make this a good place to spend an afternoon with the kids. Keep 'em away from the river, though. It's very swift at Ranger Hole and elsewhere.

Up the road a bit, the **Duckabush River Trail** (moderate/difficult;

various lengths) is a lovely river walk, snow-free much of the year. The trail climbs 23 miles to the majestic alpine country around Marmot Lake and LaCrosse Basin, which provide access to the O'Neil Pass Trail down into Enchanted Valley in the Quinault drainage. But day hikers and overnighters enjoy the easier, lower sections of the Duckabush, which ventures into fine stands of old-growth timber. Good campsites are found along the route. The first 2.5 miles are easy, then huffing commences. The 8-mile round trip to Big Hump and back is a great day hike.

Hamma Hamma drainage

Hood Canal Ranger Station, (360) 877-5254:

Some of the region's most popular trails are found here. One of them, **Lower Lena Lake** (easy; 6 miles round trip), is so easy (1,200-foot elevation gain) and so scenic that it's been virtually trampled in the past decade. Revegetation work is going on here; use one of the 28 established campsites. Fishing can be good in the lake, and the setting is idyllic. The campground here is a major staging area for climbers headed to the 6,866-foot summit of The Brothers. (The Lower Lake trailhead is on Forest Rd 25, 7.5 miles west of US 101.) A connecting trail leads from the north end of the lake up **East Fork Lena Creek** to a bivouac base camp. Another connecting trail leads from Lower Lena Lake up—2,800 feet up—to **Upper Lena Lake** (difficult; 14 miles round trip). It's worth the effort: views and wildflowers are stunning here, and camping space more plentiful. Note that the upper lake remains frozen well into summer.

Also in the area is a rough, rarely maintained trail to **Mildred Lakes** in the Mount Skokomish Wilderness (difficult; 9 miles round trip). Not highly recommended, but potentially a great source of solitude. If that's not enough discouragement, consider that a bad slide about 4 miles below the trailhead made the access road, Forest Road 25, impassable to all but high-clearance vehicles. Repairs were set for sometime in 2001—or beyond.

North Fork Skokomish drainage

Hood Canal Ranger Station, (360) 877-5254, or Staircase Ranger Station, (360) 877-5569:

Easy access via the paved Lake Cushman Road from Hoodsport to good camping facilities around Lake Cushman makes this area an east-slope Olympics favorite. One of the big draws is the **North Fork Skokomish Trail,** which leads up the river from Staircase Ranger Station to superb alpine backpack campsites at Home Sweet Home (moderate; 27 miles round trip). Here—and in countless other areas along this trail—alpine wildflowers and views of the interior Olympics are sublime. Side trips can be made to Mount Steel or Mount Stone, and through hikers can follow the path all the way to a junction with the Duckabush Trail, O'Neil

Pass, and ultimately Enchanted Valley in the Quinault drainage. Trout fishing in the Skoke is very good.

A popular side trip from the North Fork Skokomish Trail leads to **Flapjack Lakes** (moderate; 16.2 miles round trip from Staircase), where nice campsites await with awesome views of the knife-edged Sawtooth Range of the Olympics—a challenging rock-climbing venue. Side trips to **Black and White Lakes** or **Smith Lakes** are possible, and might be desirable: Flapjack Lakes is so popular that it's now limited to 30 overnighters at a time. Permits can be reserved up to 30 days in advance by calling (360) 452-0300, or by visiting the Staircase Ranger Station. If it's sold out, one backcountry option remains. **Wagonwheel Lake** is only about 3 miles from Staircase—but it's also 3,200 vertical feet, making it one of the steeper Olympic trails you'll find. Brace yourself. Also from Staircase, the **Six Ridge Trail** (difficult; 16.5 miles one way) is a challenging route between the North and South Fork Skokomish drainages. It ultimately leads to Sundown Lake and Sundown Pass, then connects to the Graves Creek and Upper South Fork Skokomish trail system.

Staircase campers looking for a great day hike shouldn't miss the **Staircase Rapids Trail** (easy; 2-mile loop), which begins near the ranger station and follows the cool, clear North Fork Skokomish up one side, then returns down the other. A great walk on a hot day.

A challenging day hike in the same vicinity is the trail to the top of **Mount Ellinor** (difficult; 6.2 miles round trip). For well-equipped hikers with experience in the snow, this is a fun early-spring trip when you can walk 2.5 snow-free miles from the lower trailhead (there are two for this hike; the lower one is on Big Creek Road and melts out earlier) to Chute Flats, then climb the snow chute straight up to the summit, where truly memorable views of Hood Canal and the inner Olympics await. In the summer, it's safer to stay on the trail around the east side of the peak. And the view is just as grand. To reach the lower trailhead from Lake Cushman Road, turn right on Forest Road 24, proceed 1.6 miles, veer right on Forest Road 2419, and proceed 4.9 miles. You can trim nearly half the round-trip distance off this hike by starting at the upper trailhead, off Spur Road 014. But it's not as much fun.

Cross-Country Skiing/Snowshoeing

Many people overlook the East Slope Olympics when considering where to head out in the SUV with the skinny skis or snowshoes. Mistake! Lots of good trampin' and schussing ground can be found here, most of it with a fraction of the customers you'll find in the west-side Cascades. A couple examples: **Mount Townsend** (difficult; 11 miles round trip; see

Hiking/Backpacking, above), a challenging ascent that leads to stunning views and a decent winter campsite. It's usually sufficiently snow-covered by late December. Be sure to consult avalance forecasts before venturing into this area, much of which is open clear-cut terrain. Another popular winter snowshoe trek is **Lena Lakes** (difficult; 6 miles round trip; see Hiking/Backpacking, above).

Fishing

All of the streams flowing into Hood Canal through Olympic National Forest offer outstanding **rainbow trout** fishing during the summer stream-fishing season (June 1 to October 31, unless otherwise posted). Limits typically are two trout a day, minimum size 12 inches. Flies and light spinning tackle do well, but check on local gear restrictions. Access to each river is good, particularly at the many streamside Forest Service campgrounds listed in Camping, above.

Most rivers in this region also have local **sea-run cutthroat** and very fishable, often productive winter and summer **steelhead** runs. Seasons and restrictions change frequently. Check with the state Department of Fish and Wildlife, or pick up a state fishing pamphlet at a tackle or sporting goods store.

Backpacking anglers usually find fair-to-good trout-fishing conditions at alpine lakes listed under Hiking/Backpacking, above. Note that you don't need a state fishing license for streams and lakes inside Olympic National Park, but licenses are required for all waterways in Olympic National Forest. Most of these lakes are frozen until June.

Lake Cushman, a massive, 10-mile-long reservoir, is rife with fish, including **cutthroat, rainbow trout, landlocked salmon,** and some **bass.** But they're fairly stubborn about leaving the water. Cushman is very deep and normally very, very clear. Lightweight leaders are usually necessary, and most of the fish caught here are hooked by boat anglers trolling pop gear along the lake banks.

Mountain Biking

At last count, 30 Olympic National Forest trails were open to mountain bikes, with about 85 total miles of terrain. Check with the ranger district offices listed in More Information at the end of this chapter about local restrictions. Two particular Forest Service trails in this area—**Gold Creek,** with trailheads in two places along Forest Road 2860, and **Lower Big Quilcene,** off Forest Road 2700-080—have emerged as mountain-biking favorites. The latter is only 6 miles one way, but riding local Forest Service roads that connect the upper and lower trailheads creates a very scenic

18.5-mile loop. Beware, however, of dirt bikes. Also popular for cyclists are the **Lower Dungeness** and **Mount Zion** trails (see Hiking/Backpacking, above.)

Actually, trail riding is but a fraction of the lure here. The Olympic National Forest is literally laced with **gravel logging roads,** most of which are rarely traveled by cars. Roadways in the **upper Dungeness area,** near East Crossing and Dungeness Forks Campgrounds, are excellent mountain-biking tracks, as are the many side roads **around Lake Cushman.**

Photography

Many hiking photographers make award-winning photos on east-slope Olympic Mountain trails in the spring (May, typically), when the deep green forests come alive with pink blobs—wild rhododendrons breaking into bloom. Call the Quilcene Ranger Station for a current bloom update before setting out. Note: This is one activity that might be best in a warm spring rain, which adds a silvery sheen to the forest landscape.

Canoeing/Kayaking

Lake Cushman is a great canoe getaway, particularly if you can snare a campsite at Lake Cushman State Park or Staircase (see Camping, above).

Accessible Outdoors

Lilliwaup Creek DNR campground on Forest Road 24 (see Camping, above) has barrier-free rest rooms and campsites rated usable (accessible with assistance). **Lake Cushman** and **Staircase** campgrounds have barrier-free campsites, and the Staircase area has some barrier-free trail access into the rainforest on the North Fork Skykomish River. **Hamma Hamma Campground** has a short, barrier-free interpretive path, the Living Legacy Trail, to the Hamma Hamma River.

More Information

Northwest Avalanche Hot Line: *(206) 526-6677.*
Olympic National Forest Headquarters: *1835 Black Lake Blvd SW,*
  Olympia, WA 98512-5623; (360) 956-2400; www.fs.fed.us/r6/olympic.
  Hood Canal Ranger District, Hood Canal Ranger Station:
    (360) 877-5254.
  Hood Canal Ranger District, Quilcene Ranger Station:
    (360) 765-2200.
  Pacific Ranger District, Quinault Ranger Station: *(360) 288-2525.*
  Pacific Ranger District, Soleduck Ranger Station: *(360) 374-6522.*

Olympic National Park Headquarters: *(360) 452-4501;*
   www.nps.gov/olym.
Staircase Ranger Station (summer only): *(360) 877-5569.*
Port Angeles Visitors Center: *(360) 452-0330.*
Wilderness Information Center: *(360) 452-0300.*
Road updates: *(360) 452-0329.*

Hood
Canal

*The Hood Canal shoreline area from Port Ludlow south to Union and
east to Belfair, including Mount Walker; Potlatch, Twanoh, Belfair, Triton
Cove, Pleasant Harbor, and Dosewallips State Parks; and the lower
Skokomish, Hamma Hamma, Duckabush, Dosewallips, and Quilcene
Rivers.*

If mountain ranges had brakes, giant smokin' skid marks would
still be visible at the mouth of the Dosewallips River. That's how
dramatic the collision between mountain and sea seems along
Hood Canal, 60 miles of saltwater serenity stretching from Admiralty Inlet south toward Shelton. Even in a state known for its thousands of miles of stunning shoreline, Hood Canal (it's really not a
canal at all, but the nation's longest fjord) is a place of uncommon
beauty. The waterway's gentle shores are sheltered (especially along
the north end) from the open-ocean elements by the Olympics,
which tower above the west shore like protective big brothers.
Some of the Olympics' most impressive alpine peaks—The Brothers, Mount Constance, Mount Washington, and others—loom
here, providing a stop-the-car backdrop for one of the state's most
intriguing marine playgrounds.

Hood Canal's eastern shores, in Kitsap and North Mason
Counties, have been heavily mini-malled and home-ownered. But
the west side—marked by the mouths of still-free rivers such as
the Hamma Hamma, Dosewallips, and Duckabush—remains relatively green and blue. Granted, most of the uplands between the
Olympics and the shore have been logged, courtesy of Olympic
National Forest (another "land of many (ab)uses": chief among
them wood production). But except for a string of private summer

Kids enjoy a nature trail at Seal Rock Campground on Hood Canal

homes and residences along the beach, the waterway is comparatively unspoiled.

Recreation is focused on a string of Washington State Parks along US Highway 101 (US 101), which runs the length of the west shore, usually within view of the salt water. They're some of the most relaxing campground getaways in the state. Also some of the most diverse—just about every Hood Canal campground offers a chance to fish, dig clams, gather oysters, hike, swim, bicycle, kayak, or just plain relax—all from the same spot. The canal also is a wildlife-rich area, with many shorebirds, raptors, and marine mammals popping into view.

Whether you're drawn more strongly to the water or to the mountains (see the Olympic National Forest and the East Slope Olympics chapter), Hood Canal is a dependable fresh-air destination. And it's a good year-round draw. Winter months, when shellfish gathering is best, are magnificently quiet, and the shoreside campgrounds rarely receive snow.

Summer months are equally alluring, especially for boaters and swimmers. Unlike deep, murky Puget Sound, Hood Canal is a fairly shallow
waterway—it warms substantially in late summer. The farther south you
drive, the warmer the water gets. This is the best place in the state for a
saltwater swim, and one of the best places to learn saltwater kayaking.

Perhaps best of all, the location is ideal. The canal is just close
enough to Seattle for weekend-getaway convenience, just far enough away
to escape the shadow of the Columbia Tower. Look at it this way: the cell
phone will still work—you'll just lose the desire to use it.

Getting There

*The west side of Hood Canal is accessed by US 101, which stretches along the
shoreline for 53 miles between the Hwy 104 junction north of Quilcene and
south to the Hwy 106 junction on the Skokomish Indian Reservation. (Hwy
106 continues 18 miles east along the canal's "Great Bend," ending in Belfair.)*

*To get there from the north, take the Seattle-Bainbridge, Seattle-Bremer-
ton, or Edmonds-Kingston ferry, (206) 464-6400 or (800) 84-FERRY, to Kitsap County, cross the Hood Canal Floating Bridge, and continue west 16 miles
on Hwy 104 to the US 101 junction. To get there from the south, follow US 101
about 30 miles north from Interstate 5 at Olympia, or follow Hwy 3 from Bremerton south to Belfair and proceed 18 miles west on Hwy 106.*

inside out

Parks/Beaches

Near the east end of the Hood Canal's southern "hook," **Belfair State
Park** has 1,300 feet of saltwater shoreline, much of it at the site of a long-
since-abandoned commercial oyster bed. Commerce has fled, but many
oysters still remain, making this a favorite spot for oyster pickers. In
recent years, however, pollutants have closed the beach here. Check with
the park or the state Department of Fish and Wildlife, (800) 562-5632;
www.wa.gov/wdfw, for information about closures, whether from local
contaminants or red tide.

Even if you can't pick oysters, Belfair's beach is a pleasant spot. The
wild, marshy beach uplands are a favorite tromping place for kids, and the
terrain draws a wealth of birdlife. Just inland from the beach, Belfair has
another unique feature: a tidal "swimming pool" that fills with warm salt
water when the tide comes in. This is the best—and cleanest—place for a
dip in the park. In midsummer, the water actually gets quite warm. The
park's campground is a local favorite (see Camping, below). The park is 3

miles southwest of Belfair on Hwy 300/North Shore Road.

A short distance down Hwy 106 on the south shore, **Twanoh State Park** is best known for its sunny beach area and its unusually clean, warm saltwater swimming on Hood Canal. The park has 3,200 feet of shoreline on the canal, with a large bathhouse, children's wading pool, a boat launch and boat dock, and good picnic facilities. Across the highway is a nice campground. (See Camping, below).

Three miles south of Hoodsport (just north of the Hwy 106/US 101 junction) is another picturesque beach area, **Potlatch State Park.** If you have time for only one rest stop on a tour around Hood Canal, make it this one. At Potlatch you'll find an impressive 10,000 feet of saltwater beach, much of which turns into a sprawling mudflat at low tide. That makes this a favorite park for oyster picking and clam digging, when tides and seasons are right. When the tide's in, the gravelly beach is equally popular with boaters (who can tie up to moorage buoys) and kayakers (who can explore the saltwater estuary at the mouth of the Skokomish River to the south). The area is particularly rich with seals, birds, and other wildlife. On the beach, the grassy picnic facilities are first-rate, and a small campground is located across US 101 (see Camping, below).

Triton Cove State Park, a small, former resort site on US 101 between Lilliwaup and Duckabush, has a waterfront picnic area and boat launch.

Just south of Brinnon on US 101, **Dosewallips State Park,** on the southern banks of its namesake river, is a large, very popular day-use and camping destination. From the campground, a trail leads beneath the highway to the mouth of the Dosewallips River, where plenty of shorebirds and small animals are seen in the marsh grass. Kayaks are common sights in this mini delta. The beach itself isn't a good one for lounging; it's fairly marshy and ripe-smelling. But it always has been a healthy clam and oyster producer. Until recently, that is, when high levels of fecal contamination have turned up in local shellfish. Harbor seals, drawn to the river mouth to feed, have proliferated, and biologists believe their waterborne feces contaminated the clams and oysters. Meanwhile, clamming beaches have been closed here, but might reopen when anti-seal measures—such as fencing—are put in place. Check with the park or the state Department of Fish and Wildlife, (800) 562-5632; www.wa.gov/wdfw, for information about closures, whether from local contaminants or red tide. Dosewallips also has a large, well-developed campground (see Camping, below).

A short distance north on US 101, **Seal Rock Campground,** an Olympic National Forest site, is one of our favorites in this region. This is the only Forest Service campground in the state that offers saltwater shore access. And it's a beauty of a shore. The rocky tidelands here offer excellent oyster gathering, clam digging, and crabbing. Don't be alarmed by the sea monsters: gigantic Trident submarines, each as long as the Space Needle is high, often cruise just offshore, bound for their deep-water testing ground in Dabob Bay. A picnic area has great views across the canal to Mount Rainier. And the campground (see Camping, below) is first-rate.

Shine Tidelands State Park, at the west foot of Hood Canal Floating Bridge, is a pleasant waterfront stopover with picnic sites and primitive camping. Another nice—and lightly used—beach site is **Bywater State Park,** which has a primitive campground, a boat launch, and a day-use area at the north side of the Hood Canal Floating Bridge's west end, just north of Hwy 104. It's a pleasant picnic spot, with views north to Mount Baker.

Finally, several beach stretches along Hood Canal are controlled by Washington State Parks, but have no developed facilities. Most have boat access only. But one, **Lilliwaup Tidelands** just north of Lilliwaup, is accessible from US 101. It's a popular clam-digging site.

Camping

Belfair State Park is a Hood Canal favorite. The southern-canal park has 184 campsites (47 with full hookups; RVs to 75 feet). The sites are divided into two areas: a broad, open, flat area just off the beach, with planted lawn and imported shrubs and trees, and a more natural (though darker) wooded area just to the north. Usually full for much of the summer (reservations are a good idea), Belfair is open all year. Campsites can be reserved up to 11 months in advance by calling Reservations Northwest; (800) 452-5687. *3 miles southwest of Belfair on Hwy 300; follow signs from Hwy 3; (360) 275-0668 or (800) 233-0321.*

Twanoh State Park, best known for its day-use beach area on the north side of Hwy 106 (see Parks/Beaches, above), has a pleasant, secluded camping area on the south side. Among the big second-growth trees, you'll find 47 campsites (13 with full and 9 with partial hookups; RVs to 35 feet) and a 15-site, 40-person group camp. The sites are divided, with smaller tent sites in one loop, RVs in the other. The scenery is nice, with cool shade along Twanoh Creek. Several miles of trails follow the creek through the greenery on the hillside above (bring your bug dope). Also note the old stone buildings here; most were built by CCC crews in the 1930s. Twanoh is open from April through October. Campsites cannot be reserved. *On Hwy 106, 6 miles east of Union; (360) 275-2222 or (800) 233-0321.*

Potlatch State Park's extensive beach area is even more popular (see Parks/Beaches, above), making its smaller campground across US 101 a popular destination. Potlatch has 37 campsites (18 with hookups; RVs to 60 feet). The campground is open from late March through October, although the day-use area is open all year. Campsites cannot be reserved. *On US 101, 3 miles south of Hoodsport; (360) 877-5361 or (800) 233-0321.*

Hoodsport is the turnoff for Lake Cushman, where Lake Cushman State Park and Staircase Campground are popular overnight spots. See the Olympic National Forest and the East Slope Olympics chapter for details. **Pleasant Harbor State Park**, 1.25 miles south of Brinnon, offers a small beach area and boat moorage.

Dosewallips State Park, less than a mile south of Brinnon, is likely the most popular campground on the canal. The park's 130 campsites (40 with hookups; RVs to 60 feet) are situated in flat, grassy loops on the west side of US 101. There's not a huge amount of privacy between sites, but the cushy grass feels mighty nice under the backs of tent campers. (Note: The older sites, numbers 81 to 105, are on the east side of a US 101 underpass that's too short for RVs. Sites here have no hookups, but offer a bit more privacy and shade than those on the other side.) A trail leads down to the beach, and 4 to 5 miles of trails wind through the shady upland area east of the park. For would-be campers lacking gear, this park also offers three frame tents, which can be reserved in advance just like campsites. You'll also find a small cluster of bicycle-camping spots. Dosewallips is open all year. The park often fills up in the summertime; reservations are a good idea. Campsites can be reserved up to 11 months in advance by calling Reservations Northwest; (800) 452-5687. *On US 101, 1 mile south of Brinnon; (360) 796-4415 or (800) 233-0321.*

A short mountain-bike ride north on the highway is **Seal Rock Campground**, one of our favorite Forest Service camps. The park has 42 sites (no hookups; RVs to 21 feet, although we've seen longer ones squeezed into the pullout waterfront sites), nicely spread through a wooded area just off Hood Canal. Sites are very private, and most have beautiful, sand-filled, perfectly level pads for pitching tents. A major bonus for tenters! The spaces down along the beachfront fill first. The rocky beach area (see Parks/Beaches, above) is a particular asset, as is the short boardwalk interpretive trail along the beach bluff. Seal Rock is open from mid-April through September. The park is fully wheelchair–accessible. *On US 101, 2 miles north of Brinnon; (360) 765-2200.*

Near Quilcene, **Falls View Campground**, another Olympic National Forest site, has 35 sites (no hookups; RVs to 21 feet) inland in a nice wooded area, with the rushing Big Quilcene River below to lull you to sleep. A trail leads a short distance to the picturesque falls. The park is open from May to mid-September. *On US 101, 3.5 miles south of Quilcene; (360) 765-2200.*

Not far away is **Rainbow Group Campground**, which has 9 primitive group-camping sites (no hookups; tents only), day-hiking trails, and some picnic facilities. The park is open all year. Individual campsites cannot be reserved, but the entire campground can be reserved for up to 50 people by calling (360) 765-2200. *On US 101, 5 miles south of Quilcene; (360) 765-2200.*

To the north, at the west end of the Hood Canal Floating Bridge, **Shine Tidelands State Park** has 16 primitive campsites, but they're very exposed to wind, as well as Hwy 104 and boat-launch traffic. A nice day-use area, but last-resort-only for camping, unless you're in an RV. *On Hwy 104 west of Hood Canal Bridge; (800) 233-0321.*

Hiking

Although some of them can be downright frustrating to locate, many of Washington's finest mountain hikes are found in the valleys of rivers that drain east into Hood Canal. The North Fork Skokomish, Dosewallips, Hamma Hamma, Quilcene, and Duckabush drainages contain dozens of long trails, most of which begin in Olympic National Forest and continue into—and sometimes all the way through—Olympic National Park. For trip advice in the Hood Canal area, stop by the Hood Canal Ranger District's Hoodsport or Quilcene offices (see phone numbers in More Information, below). Also consult the Olympic National Forest and the East Slope Olympics chapter, which contains extensive hiking information for trails west of Hood Canal.

The Hood Canal lowlands have their own hiking charms, however. Most of the state parks listed above have at least several miles of **wooded hiking trails,** few of which receive heavy use. Twanoh and Dosewallips have particularly well-developed trail systems (see Camping, above).

Want to sample the local forest environment without investing too much time (or logging too many Forest Service road miles)? Try **Hoodsport Trail State Park** (easy/moderate; various distances), 3 miles west of Hoodsport on Lake Cushman Road. The state-protected forest has several miles of trails, open summers only. This is a good short-day-hike opportunity for campers at Potlatch State Park. The park is closed from October 1 to April 30.

Hiking is perhaps more scenic along the canal's north end, however. From US 101 about 5.5 miles south of Quilcene, watch for signs for **Mount Walker Lookout** (difficult; 4 miles round trip) on the east side of the highway. In the summer, when the gated road is open, you can drive 5 miles to the top of this 2,750-foot hill, which offers sweeping views of Hood Canal, the eastern Olympics, and all the way east to Seattle and south to Mount Rainier. But a trail that runs up one side of the mountain is a fun, although lung-busting, hike. The road is a great thigh-burner of a mountain-bike ride, especially when it's gated to traffic. As you wheeze, just keep thinking of the ride down.

Nearby Rainbow Campground (5 miles south of Quilcene on US 101) has a good leg-stretcher hiking trail that drops a half mile to a **waterfall in Rainbow Canyon** on the Big Quilcene River. Falls View Campground (3.5 miles south of Quilcene on US 101) also offers **short day-hiking trails.** And a unique, wheelchair-accessible **boardwalk nature trail** runs along the beach in Seal Rock Campground (2 miles north of Brinnon on US 101).

Canoeing/Kayaking

Hood Canal is a surprisingly underutilized sea kayak playground. **Day-use areas** at the state parks listed in Parks/Beaches, above, all have convenient launch sites. Keep in mind that most of these areas are desirable only during higher tides, particularly in the south end of the canal, where tidal fluctuation is extreme. Show up at low tide, and you're launching into an ocean of mud.

For much of the summer, canoeists will find the near-shore waters of Hood Canal calm enough for safe paddling. But all small-craft users should keep in mind that winds can whip up swiftly—and quite dramatically—in the canal. Don't venture too far from shore in an open craft, particularly if the weather is iffy. On those days, a good destination is **Dabob Bay,** near Seal Rock Campground south of Quilcene. It's usually protected from bad weather. But beware the submarines. This deep-water cove is one of the Navy's primary test areas for Trident ballistic subs. Also, keep in mind that nearly all beach areas inside the bay are private property. A good launch site is Point Whitney Shellfish Lab, which is marked on US 101. Some other popular spots:

Mats Mats Bay, a small, protected waterway just north of Port Ludlow, is a favorite day trip and a good area for beginners. Follow Oak Bay and Verner Roads north from Port Ludlow to the public launch ramp on the bay. Farther south, the **Hood Head area,** just north of the west end of the Hood Canal Floating Bridge, includes a protected lagoon that's fun to explore during high tides. It's easy enough for beginners, as long as you stay in the calm waters south of Hood Head. Access is from Shine Tidelands State Park (see Camping, above).

Quilcene Bay is a pleasant, protected stretch of water off Dabob Bay. Launch at the ramp on Linger Longer Road. Paddlers who launch at Dosewallips or Pleasant Harbor State Park can explore the shoreline between the two, as well as the protected cove inside **Pleasant Harbor.** Stronger paddlers can **cross the canal** (about 1.5 miles) for lunch at Scenic Beach State Park near Seabeck (see the Kitsap Peninsula chapter). At the far south end of the canal, the **Skokomish River delta** is a popular exploring spot, with good launch sites at Potlatch State Park and the boat launch in Union.

Rental kayaks are available at Poulsbo's Olympic Outdoor Center Center (18971 Front Street; (360) 697-6095; www.kayakproshop.com).

Fishing

The clear, relatively clean waters of Hood Canal are rightly famous for producing **oysters** with few equals. Oyster season on Hood Canal generally runs from September through May, but you'll need to check local seasons and restrictions. **Clams** can be dug on Hood Canal public tidelands any time of the year, but diggers should check with the state Department of Fish and Wildlife, (800) 562-5632, www.wa.gov/wdfw, for information about closures, whether from local contaminants or red tide. Good beaches include Potlatch State Park, Lilliwaup Tidelands, Pleasant Harbor State Park, Dosewallips State Park, and Seal Rock Campground.

Waters of the canal have waned significantly as a **salmon**-fishing spot. The recreational season here has become almost nonexistent, because of large-scale shutdowns ordered to protect troubled **wild coho** stocks. Some winter **blackmouth** are caught on early morning tide changes, but not as many as in Puget Sound. **Sea-run cutthroat** also are found here, but in declining numbers.

One exception is the popular beach fishery at the Hoodsport Hatchery, where anglers cast for incoming **chum** and **pink salmon** in the fall. (Pinks are in good supply during August and September of odd-numbered years only. Chum runs arrive every October.) These fish are very finicky, but a determined caster often can coax one to hit on a bright pink or chartreuse lure, spinner, or salmon fly, or just a plain black hook with a Day-Glo bobber and fluorescent yarn. Rules require single barbless hooks only. (Tip: Use lightweight, trout-size tackle in this ultra-clear water.) You're usually allowed to keep two of these fish, but many anglers voluntarily make this a catch-and-release event. The area around the hatchery is best fished with chest waders. And the crowds here can get out of control on weekends. You'll think you're in Alaska.

Another famous Hood Canal sea creature, the **shrimp,** is a prized prey in these waters. Shrimp in the canal's deeper spots—most notably the Dabob Bay area—are unusually large, plump, and tasty, and they've become highly sought-after delicacies. The shrimp season is short and sweet. It's usually in May, for about a week only, or until a state-determined shrimp quota has been met. Consult a local tackle shop such as Seabeck Marina, (360) 830-5179, for gear (a shrimp pot and float), a license (required), and bait (believe it or not, smelly fish-flavored canned cat food is the weapon of choice). Fishing tackle and supplies also are available at Cove RV Park Grocery near Brinnon, (360) 796-4723, and at other marinas along the canal. (See Boating/Sailing, below.)

Boating/Sailing

Hood Canal's broad, generally smooth waters are a grand place for boaters, although a lack of well-developed support facilities seems to limit most marine traffic to locals only. **Pleasant Harbor State Park,** midway up the canal off US 101, is a favorite boater's destination. It offers good, protected moorage, with state park day-use facilities in the upland section. **Marinas** include the following: Pleasant Harbor Marina, (360) 796-4611, has moorage, supplies, and bait and tackle. Across the canal, Seabeck Marina, (360) 830-5179, has rentals (bring your own motor) and fishing gear. Hood Canal Marina near Union, (360) 898-2252, also has a launch ramp and supplies. Hoodsport Marina, (360) 877-9657, has moorage and rest rooms. On the north end, Quilcene Boathaven, (360) 765-3131, has fuel, guest moorage, and supplies.

Other **launch ramps** are found at Potlatch State Park, Twanoh State Park, Belfair State Park, Triton Cove State Park, Union, Quilcene Bay, Bywater Bay State Park, Mats Mats Bay, Hoodsport, and Tahuya, on North Shore Road opposite Union.

Wildlife Watching

Believe it or not, **seals** often are seen off the beach at Seal Rock. Also **bald eagles.** Both species also are usually in good supply at other local beach-front sites, particularly the beach around Potlatch State Park.

A major state fish hatchery at Hoodsport affords a rather rare, up-close encounter with homecoming Hood Canal **salmon.** Runs of **chinook, chum, and pink** often can be seen splashing through a causeway into the hatchery during fall months. Keep your eyes open as you drive by: large numbers of pickups parked along the road usually indicate a run is underway, and fishermen will be lined up in the canal outside the hatchery. The hatchery is right on US 101 in Hoodsport.

Accessible Outdoors

Twanoh State Park has 22 barrier-free campsites and wheelchair-accessible rest rooms. **Belfair State Park** offers three accessible campsites, as well as barrier-free rest rooms, picnicking, a bathhouse, and beach access. **Potlatch State Park** offers barrier-free camping, as does **Seal Rock Campground,** which also offers a short, barrier-free interpretive trail along Hood Canal. **Triton Cove State Park,** 8 miles south of Brinnon, offers barrier-free picnicking, boat launching, and beach access. **Falls View Campground** has barrier-free rest rooms. See Camping, above, for more information on all these sites. In addition, the **Hoodsport Hatchery** on US 101 in Hoodsport has barrier-free fish viewing areas (see Wildlife Watching, above).

Restaurants

Timber House   A hunting lodge gussied up to be comfortable. Local seafood is the main draw. $$; *Hwy 101 S, Quilcene; (360) 765-3339.* &

Victoria's ★★   The stone-and-log structure is one of the area's better eateries. $$; *E 6790 Hwy 106, Union; (360) 898-4400.* &

Xinh's Clam & Oyster House ★★   One of the best (and freshest) little clam and oyster houses on the Peninsula. $$; *221 W Railroad Ave, Ste D, Shelton; (360) 427-8709; www.taylorunited.com/xinhs.* &

Lodgings

Heron Beach Inn ★★   A gorgeous, peaceful retreat in the manner of a New England estate. $$$; *1 Heron Rd, Port Ludlow; (360) 437-0411.* &

Port Ludlow Resort and Conference Center   This popular resort facility caters to groups; tennis, golf, and pool available. $$$; *200 Olympic Pl, Port Ludlow; (360) 437-2222 or (800) 732-1239; www.portludlow-resort.com.*

More Information

Olympic National Forest Headquarters: *(360) 956-2400; www.fs.fed.us/r6/olympic.*
Hood Canal Ranger District, Hoodsport office: *(360) 877-5254.*
Hood Canal Ranger District, Quilcene office: *(360) 765-2200.*
Shelton/Mason County Chamber of Commerce: *(360) 426-2021, (800) 576-2021; www.sheltonchamber.org.*

Port
Townsend

From Oak Bay north to Point Wilson, west to Discovery Bay, and east past Marrowstone Island to Midchannel Bank in Admiralty Inlet, including Fort Flagler, Fort Worden, and Old Fort Townsend and Anderson Lake State Parks.

Port Townsend brings out the pirate in all of us. Also the Victorian-era industrial titan, the rich socialite world traveler, the visiting diplomat, and the freeloading scalawag. No surprise there, given the historical development of the little port town perched like a hangnail on the Quimper Peninsula, a thumb of land jutting into Puget Sound toward Whidbey Island. Port Townsend is, always was, and always will be a port. Its deep-water harbor, strategically located between the head of the Strait of Juan de Fuca and the mouth of Puget Sound, made it a force to be reckoned with in Washington's interior waters well before the little town of Seattle got up and running. This was a swanky place during the Tall Ships era, and most folks expected it to get swankier.

Several tons of money, most of it venture capital, came ashore here between 1851 and 1890, fueling a building boom most people expected to pay dividends when this area became the anticipated far-northern terminus of the Union Pacific Railroad. Victorian mansions, hotels, restaurants, and other fineries sprang up like blackberry vines. Which is exactly what they were covered with by 1900, when most of Port Townsend's people, money, and prospects fled south after the railroad dream went up in smoke.

But the infrastructure remained, much of it essentially mothballed for decades. Nearly a hundred years later, Port Townsend is entering its second boom. A walk into the little port city is a stroll

Kite flyers and sailors enjoy the summer breezes at Fort Flagler State Park

into the past, with most of the old buildings painstakingly restored and maintained as lovingly as the family china by a new generation of merchants—tourist capitalists.

Port Townsend is thriving as a Seattle-area getaway. Its convenient access, countercultural feel, and amazing wealth of bed-and-breakfast, restaurant, and performing arts finery create an irresistible lure to many city dwellers. Once they get here, most of them sweep aside the fine lace curtains, peer out the window, and discover something truly powerful: a stunning natural setting, much of it also effectively mothballed for generations.

Port Townsend's extensive shorelines have been protected in something close to their natural state by a totally different force—the U.S. military. While other Puget Sound locales with abundant waterfront property, sweeping views of snow-clad mountains, and a ready supply of local timber were being swept up in a tide of single-family waterfront estates, Port Townsend's most spectacular beaches, bluffs, and forests were locked behind gates. The government held the keys. Thanks again to the area's strategic location, three major artillery batteries were built here between 1856 and 1902.

The oldest, Old Fort Townsend, burned in 1895 and never was effectively rebuilt. But the other two, mighty Forts Worden and Flagler, lived long lives as keepers of the gates to Puget Sound. Big artillery guns at the two forts, coupled with similar firepower at Whidbey Island's Fort Casey, combined to form a "triangle of fire," guarding the door to the inner waters' thriving population centers. (Another, more modern, layer of artillery defense—guns at Whidbey's Fort Ebey, Striped Peak west of Port Angeles, and Cape Flattery near Neah Bay—was built later to prevent Japanese invasion during World War II. So far, it seems to be working.)

By the early 1950s, the wars were over, big guns were obsolete, and Washington State Parks was fortunate—and far-sighted—enough to latch onto the abandoned gun sites. Today, the two big forts on either side of Port Townsend are reverting to nature—and a splendorous nature it is. In spite of the constant concrete-bunker reminders of the military past, the physical features of this priceless real estate are basically unaltered. The view across Admiralty Inlet hasn't changed much in the past century, adding a pure, natural flavor to the already clean air.

Saltwater shorelines, picturesque lighthouses, and abundant wildlife make these parks favorites among campers, anglers, cyclists, and paddlers—as all-around marine-oriented recreation venues, they might be unequaled in Western Washington. Coupled with the surviving—and thriving—finery of Port Townsend, the parks and waterways make this region an absolute classic, must-visit outdoors venue.

Getting There

Port Townsend and Marrowstone Island lie at the northeast corner of the Olympic Peninsula, 50 miles northwest of Seattle via the Seattle-Bainbridge or Edmonds-Kingston ferries, (206) 464-6400 or (800) 84-FERRY, and Highways 104 and 19 or 20. From Port Townsend, ferries also travel to Keystone on Whidbey Island, and, in the summer, the Puget Sound Express, 431 Water Street, (360) 385-5288, runs a daily ferry to Friday Harbor on San Juan Island.

inside out

Beaches/Picnicking

Port Townsend's heritage grew from the waterline up, and its many miles of shoreline remain its chief drawing card for outdoor lovers. A sampling:

Fort Flagler State Park, at the northern tip of Marrowstone Island across the bay from Port Townsend, is a favorite. The park has more than 19,000 feet of saltwater shoreline on Admiralty Inlet, Port Townsend Bay, and Kilisut Harbor, but the far northern beach is a standout day-use area. It's accessible either from the campground area or a narrow road that drops from the blufftop Environmental Learning Center to the picturesque Marrowstone Point Lighthouse. The entire stretch of fine-graveled beach in between—more than a mile—is open for strolling, and the views across the water to Port Townsend, east to Whidbey Island, and northeast to Mount Baker are sublime. Seals often are seen playing offshore here, and it's a favorite destination of sea kayakers, scuba divers, beachcombers, and salmon anglers. The large, open playfield just off the beach south of the camping area is a highly popular kite-flying venue. See also Camping, Fishing, and Cycling, below.

Closer to town, **Fort Worden State Park,** the epicenter for Port Townsend fresh-air activities, has a fine beach of its own. The historic park has 11,000 feet of shoreline, nearly all of it walkable at low tide. Follow signs to the boat launch, or beyond to the Point Wilson Lighthouse, to get your start. From here, with an occasional upland detour, the beach can be walked west to **North Beach County Park,** or you can head toward town on the beach to **Chetzemoka City Park,** at Jackson and Blaine Streets, a gorgeous spot with waterfront access. Both are good picnicking spots for those who'd rather relax on the beach than stroll upon it; the latter has a nice grassy area that runs right to the waterline. The 10-acre Chetzemoka Park also has a water garden, kids' play equipment and a grand picnic area.

South of town off Hwy 20, **Old Fort Townsend State Park** has a pleasant, less heavily used stretch of saltwater beach marked by tall pilings and other reminders of this 1850s-vintage military outpost.

Camping

Fort Flagler State Park is a winner, which is no secret to Washington campers. The picturesque beachfront campground here is one of the most popular in the state. You'll probably need to get a reservation to land a site here in midsummer, particularly on or anywhere near a holiday. The campground has 102 sites (14 with water and electricity; RVs to 50 feet). RV sites are on a flat, tidal upland with very little privacy between sites. More private are sites 1 through 47, on a wooded hillside in the park's southwest corner. The overall setting is spectacular, and the campground is a great base from which to explore this unique 800-acre park. Fort Flagler has a stunning stretch of beach, its own lighthouse, a fascinating collection of abandoned gun emplacements and other military artifacts, two boat launches, moorage floats, an underwater park, a youth hostel, a bicycle camp, hiking trails, extensive group camping and group cabin facilities in old barracks, and a host of other wonders. Note: The park's large fishing pier has been closed to the public until money can be found to shore it up. We've been going here for years, and probably still haven't seen it all. Because the park is so big and spread out, this is a good place to bring your bicycle. Fort Flagler campground is open March through October. Campsites can be reserved up to 11 months in advance by calling (800) 452-5687. *At the north end of Marrowstone Island, 8 miles northeast of Hadlock on Fort Flagler Rd (follow "Marrowstone Island" signs from Hwy 20); (360) 385-1259 or (800) 233-0321.*

Fort Worden State Park has a full slate of overnight accommodations (see Lodgings, below), but its campground is nothing to sneeze at, either. While it's not as scenic as the one at Fort Flagler, the RV-equipped campground is one of the region's most extensive. The camping loops, on a bluff over the beach on the east side of the park, offer 80 sites (30 with electricity/water; RVs to 50 feet). Views across Admiralty Inlet to Whidbey Island are grand on clear days. The park's wealth of other attractions— abandoned gun emplacements, lighthouse, sprawling saltwater beaches, marked hiking and cycling trails, museum exhibits, and more—make this a great place to camp with children. Fort Worden is open all year. Campsites can be reserved up to 11 months in advance by calling Reservations Northwest; (800) 452-5687. *Follow signs 1 mile north of downtown Port Townsend; 385-4730 or (800) 233-0321.*

Old Fort Townsend State Park, 3 miles south of town, just east of Hwy 20, has 43 sites (no hookups; RVs to 40 feet). The campsites aren't as close to the beach as they are at the other two nearby forts, but beach access is easy, and the campground doesn't fill up quite as fast. The 367-acre park also has a nice picnic area and several miles of good hiking trails through its wooded uplands. Old Fort Townsend is open from April through September. Campsites cannot be reserved. *Follow signs from Hwy 20; 385-3595 or (800) 233-0321.*

Kayaking

Many paddlers consider Port Townsend to be Washington's kayak central. For good reason—nearly everywhere you look on the Quimper Peninsula, an inviting beach or bay beckons. All three Port Townsend-area state parks, **Fort Flagler, Fort Worden,** and **Old Fort Townsend,** are popular day-use areas for paddlers who enjoy skimming along near the beach, with fantastic maritime and North Cascades views all along the route. Fort Flagler, in particular, is a good day-use area. Launching facilities are excellent, with two boat ramps and thousands of feet of flat, sandy beach, usually without significant surf. Also, the camping area is within easy portage distance of the beach and one of the boat ramps, making this a great vacation getaway for kayakers who like to build their camping trips around daily paddle expeditions.

The scenic, placid waters of **Kilisut Harbor** (between Marrowstone and Indian Islands) make a great day trip from Fort Flagler. Or the bay can be reached more directly by launching at **Mystery Bay State Park,** a tiny launch and moorage site halfway up Marrowstone Island on the way to Fort Flagler.

Just to the west, the waters all around **Indian Island,** an off-limits naval facility (it holds one of the Navy's major West Coast ammunition dumps) are a favorite of many adventuresome paddlers. No beach landings are permitted, but a paddle all the way around the island is a unique trip, because it includes passages through the narrow Port Townsend Canal between Indian Island and the mainland, and through the swift-moving Marrowstone–Indian Island Causeway, which barely separates the south ends of the two islands. Good launching points for this daylong trip are **Indian Island or Oak Bay County Parks,** both near the island's south end. Other good launch points are the boat ramps at Mystery Bay and Fort Flagler. A total circumnavigation of the island is a trip of between 11 and 12 water miles. Warning: Tricky currents at the canal and causeway make this a trip recommended for more advanced paddlers only.

Those are just a couple examples of dozens of good day trips in this area. For strong paddlers, it's possible to launch at Fort Worden, run **across Port Townsend Bay,** and explore the entire shorelines of Marrowstone and Indian Islands in one very long day.

For advice, supplies, no-experience-required guided tours, and rentals, see Kayak Port Townsend, 435 Water Street, (360) 385-6240; Sport Townsend, 1044 Water Street, (360) 379-9711; Port Townsend Outdoors, 1017B Water Street, (360) 379-3608, www.ptoutdoors.com; or Olympic Outdoor Center in Poulsbo, (360) 697-6095.

Fishing

Port Townsend Boat Haven is a hot spot for Puget Sound **salmon** fishing action. It's a very short hop from here to known North Sound salmon hot spots, such as Possession Bar, Midchannel Bank, and Bush Point. In recent years, the most productive waters—at the entrance to Puget Sound, between Port Townsend and Whidbey Island—have been closed from July to October—peak summer months—in an effort to protect struggling **wild coho** stocks. But for much of the year, fishing is on up here. If fishing is open, coho are available in August, September, and early October; migratory **chinook** are caught primarily from mid-May through August; **pink salmon** are caught in August and September; and **chum salmon** are harvested in autumn months. In recent years, winter **blackmouth** (immature chinook) fishing in the North Sound has been productive from December through March.

Charter trips are available from mid-April to mid-November at Sea Sport Charters in the Port Townsend Boat Haven; (360) 385-3575. The company also will go fishing for **bottomfish** or chase after whales and shorebirds when the salmon fishing slows or closes. For licenses, supplies, and gear, see The Fish in Hole at the Port Townsend Boat Haven; (360) 385-7031. There's a local salmon derby the first weekend in August, and the annual Discovery Bay Salmon Derby is the third weekend in February.

Decent bottom-fishing can be found off most local beaches, particularly deep-water sites such as Point Wilson and Marrowstone Point. When the salmon season is on, expect to see plenty of hip-wadered anglers in up to their waists at both spots. These are surprisingly productive beach salmon fisheries. Tie on a weighted Buzz Bomb or Point Wilson Dart (the name is no coincidence; the heavy candlefish lure was invented in Port Townsend and named for the local landmark), heave it as far as you can, and hope for some excitement on the retrieve. Catching a salmon off the beach is a rare thrill.

Trout fishing for **planted rainbows** is available in season at Anderson Lake State Park, 8 miles south of Port Townsend via Hwy 20 and Anderson Lake Road.

Boating/Sailing

Port Townsend got its start as a rather extravagant boat dock, and it's still a central passageway and moorage point for most traffic into and out of Puget Sound. The town, with a **deep-water port** strategically located between the Strait of Juan de Fuca and Puget Sound, is well equipped to handle the traffic. The downtown Port Townsend Boat Haven, operated by the Port of Port Townsend, (360) 385-2355, is about as centrally located as a marina can get. Daily, monthly, and permanent moorage is available, as are a full slate of marine services. Boat rentals and guided excursions also are readily available here; call ahead for rates and schedules. The nearby private facility, Point Hudson Resort and Marina, just northeast of the ferry terminal, also has full marine services; (360) 385-2828. To the south of town, moorage and supplies can be found at Port Ludlow Marina; (360) 437-0513.

Day-use boaters and sailors also are well treated in the Port Townsend area. **Launch facilities** are found at Fort Flagler and Fort Worden State Parks, downtown near the Ferry Terminal, and at Oak Bay and Mystery Bay. In addition to the two marinas above, **transient moorage** is available at Mystery Bay (dock space), Fort Flagler (dock and mooring buoys), Fort Worden (dock and buoys), and Old Fort Townsend (buoys).

Scuba Diving

Established marine sanctuaries are located just offshore at **Fort Flagler and Fort Worden State Parks.** Boaters and kayakers should take heed and watch for divers' flags. Supplies are available at Port Townsend Dive Shop; (360) 379-3635.

Cycling

Even though many road cyclists pass through this area on a tour of the Olympic Peninsula, it's frankly not a great place for street riding. Once you get outside Port Townsend city limits, most highways on the Quimper Peninsula are narrow two-laners, with little to no shoulders for quick escapes, and traffic can be quite heavy. But the Port Townsend area still can be a wonderful place to explore from a bicycle seat. A couple of suggestions:

The **"back route"** out of Port Townsend, west on Hastings Street and south on Beckett Point Road, makes a nice half-day tour, with good views down into Discovery Bay and across to the Miller Peninsula. Shoulders are still narrow, but traffic is relatively light. Continue south on Chevy Chase ROad to Discovery Road for a loop back north to town, or continue east to Hwy 20 and parts west or east.

Park and ride at **Fort Flagler or Fort Worden.** Both of these sprawling state parks have many miles of either marked cycle paths or winding park roads where traffic is limited to 25 mph. A day exploring one or both parks from a bicycle saddle is a great way to enjoy them even if you didn't plan ahead far enough to snag a campsite. From Fort Worden, it's a short, downhill ride to downtown Port Townsend.

Another fun Port Townsend ride—a guaranteed hit with the kids—is a daylong tour involving a run across Admiralty Inlet on the Port Townsend–Keystone Ferry. Park downtown near the ferry terminal and walk the bikes onto one of the two nicely restored, classic old ferries, and enjoy the scenery, the Mount Baker view, and perhaps even an orca sighting on the 20-minute ride across. At Keystone, hang a left and pedal up the hill to spectacular **Fort Casey State Park** (see the Whidbey and Camano Islands chapter), where you can spend hours roaming the old gun bunkers, touring the scenic Admiralty Head Lighthouse, or building or flying kites on the grassy fields. If time allows, ride east toward Keystone, along Keystone Spit, with Crockett Lake on one side of the road, Admiralty Bay on the other. This is a good bird-watching area. Hop the ferry back and go to bed early.

Photography

The beaches of **Fort Flagler**—we hate to go on and on about them—make for some highly productive photo sessions, with the deep blue waters of Admiralty Inlet in the foreground, Mount Baker in the back. This is especially true of the park's east side, where the Marrowstone Point Lighthouse can be drawn into your photos. Try it at sunset for some intriguing light. An impressive vista of the entire area is found at **Chetzemoka City Park** (named after a local chief) at the northeast corner of Port Townsend at Jackson and Blaine Streets. This also is a very fine picnic spot.

Accessible Outdoors

Fort Flagler State Park has accessible campsites, rest rooms and an Environmental Learning Center. **Port Townsend City Dock**, a city-managed fishing pier, provides barrier-free fishing access on the downtown waterfront. **Fort Worden State Park** has accessible rest rooms, camping, picnicking, and a fishing pier.

outside in

Restaurants

Ajax Cafe ★   The Ajax Cafe, in a forgotten hardware storefront, is funky and riotous fun. $$; *271 Water St, Port Hadlock;* (360) 385-3450; *www.ajaxcafe.com.* &

Fountain Cafe ★★   Our favorite town place to eat lunch or dinner in unpretentious intimacy. $$; *920 Washington St, Port Townsend;* (360) 385-1364.

Lanza's ★★   No mistaking the Italian here, but some delightful Northwest elements, too. $; *1020 Lawrence St, Port Townsend;* (360) 379-1900; *www.olympus.net/lanzas/.* &

Lonny's ★★★   One of the Olympic Peninsula's best. Low-fat eating? Forget about it. $$; *2330 Washington St, Port Townsend;* (360) 385-0700; *www.lonnys.com.* &

Manresa Castle ★★★   Yes, it's a real castle, now home to a bed-and-breakfast and a fine dining room. $$; *7th and Sheridan, Port Townsend;* (360) 385-5750 or (800) 732-1281; *www.manresacastle.com.*

The Public House ★   A large space with soaring ceilings, the Public House is comfortable and casual. $; *1038 Water St, Port Townsend;* (360) 385-9708; *www.thepublichouse.com.* &

Silverwater Café ★   A warm, lovely gathering place with satisfying food served on handmade plates. $$; 237 Taylor St, Port Townsend; (360) 385-6448. &

Wild Coho ★☆   A favorite place to wake up: endless coffee and breakfast is served all day. $; 1044 Lawrence St, Port Townsend; (360) 379-1030. &

Lodgings

Ann Starrett Mansion ★★   The most opulent Victorian in Port Townsend has rooms furnished with antiques. $$; 744 Clay St, Port Townsend; (360) 385-3205 or (800) 321-0644; www.starrettmansion.com. &

Bay Cottage ★★   These two cottages on the shore of Discovery Bay have a private sandy beach. $$; 4346 S Discovery Rd, Port Townsend; (360) 385-2035; www.olympus.net/biz/getaways/BC/index.htm.

The Ecologic Place ★   Rustic cabins in a natural setting: great for families who enjoy the outdoors. $$; 10 Beach Dr, Nordland; (360) 385-3077 or (800) 871-3077; www.ecologicplace.com.

Fort Worden ★   This happily situated fort is now a state park, conference center, and hostel. $$; 200 Battery Wy, Port Townsend; (360) 344-4400; www.olympus.net/ftworden.

Hastings House/Old Consulate Inn ★★   This red Victorian is one of Port Townsend's much-photographed "Painted Ladies." $$$; 313 Walker St, Port Townsend; (360) 385-6753 or (800) 300-6753; www.oldconsulateinn.com.

The James House ★★★   The first bed-and-breakfast in the Northwest (1889) is still in great shape. $$; 1238 Washington St, Port Townsend; (360) 385-1238 or (800) 385-1238; www.jameshouse.com.

Lizzie's ★   Many of the seven rooms in this model of Victorian excess have views. $$; 731 Pierce St, Port Townsend; (360) 385-4168 or (800) 700-4168; www.kolke.com/lizzies.

Quimper Inn ★★   This 1886 home has big windows and an uncluttered but warm character. $$; 1306 Franklin St, Port Townsend; (360) 385-1060 or (800) 557-1060; www.olympus.net/biz/quimper/quimper.html.

More Information

Centrum: (360) 385-3102 or (800) 733-3608; www.centrum.org.
Port Townsend Chamber of Commerce: (360) 385-2722 or (888) ENJOYPT; www.ptchamber.org.

Sequim
and the Dungeness Valley

From Sequim Bay west and north to Dungeness Spit and south to the Upper Dungeness River Trail in Olympic National Park, including John Wayne Marina, Cline Spit, Dungeness Recreation Area, Sequim Bay State Park, and the Dungeness National Wildlife Refuge.

Sequim is a work in progress. This is true of Sequim, the city—an adolescent town in the awkward stage of transition from farm town to suburban refuge for retirees and telecommuters. It's also true of Sequim, the place—a broad, peaceful plain serving as a sort of demilitarized zone between the warring Olympic Mountains and the Strait of Juan de Fuca.

The continuing change in town and landscape leaves the strong impression that the Sequim (it's pronounced "Skwim") you enjoy today in a car, from a boat, or on the beach isn't necessarily the Sequim your great-grandchildren will know. The exploding business district is in constant flux; so is the Dungeness Valley's greatest single attraction, the Dungeness Spit. Both are sprouting from the ends—one from incoming silt, the other from migratory cash.

For recreators, this flux is a plus. No two days spent in the Dungeness Valley are ever alike. The beaches change with every winter storm, the Dungeness River with every flood, the Olympic Mountain lowlands to the south with every season. And the weather is truly remarkable. Many people are drawn to Sequim by its vaunted sunshine: the valley is tucked directly into the armpit of the Olympic Mountains' rain shadow. Because the Olympics go from sea level to nearly 8,000 feet in less than 30 miles, they suck out most moisture from nasty southwesterly storms that wrack the coast every winter. Sequim, directly opposite the storm path in the

Olympics' northeast corner, just gets the wimpy leftovers—high, poofy clouds that left every ounce of ferocity up on the face of Mount Olympus. The result: Sequim's annual rainfall averages about 16 inches, a fraction of that for the rest of the peninsula, and less than half the average of the greater Seattle area.

But it's not so much the pure sunshine that endears Sequim to outdoor lovers. It's the stark contrast between alpine and marine climates. Seated in a kayak in the quiet, relaxing waters on the leeward side of Dungeness Spit, you often can look directly up the Dungeness Valley and watch the weather wars unfold: clouds dashed apart, lightning flashing in protest, streaks of triumphant sunshine declaring victory—all the while secure in the knowledge that down here, you're untouchable.

This can all be very heady stuff. But don't worry: if you lose yourself in the grandeur, a quick stop at the Sequim Costco can send you homeward with a 2-gallon jar of mayonnaise and a renewed sense of reality. That's the charm of Sequim: a great place to be, whether you can pronounce it or not.

Getting There

Sequim is on US Highway 101 about a 60-mile drive west of Seattle. For the most direct approach, take the Edmonds-Kingston or Seattle-Bainbridge ferry to Kitsap County and follow signs to the Hood Canal Floating Bridge. Cross the bridge into Jefferson County and follow Hwy 104 west to US 101, which leads north and west along the lower west side of Discovery Bay to Sequim and the Dungeness Valley. Travel (in)sanity note: Summer weekend travelers should strongly consider skipping the ferry and instead driving south around Puget Sound, on Interstate 5 to Olympia and US 101 north through Shelton to Hwy 104 west of the Hood Canal Bridge. It adds about 60 miles to the trip, but could save hours of mind-numbing waiting lines at ferry terminals. Call (206) 464-6400 or (800) 84-FERRY for ferry rates and schedules.

inside out

Beaches/Parks

The sandy flats jutting into the Strait of Juan de Fuca north of Sequim just might be the best beach-wandering territory in the Northwest. The beaches are incredibly scenic, and the local weather is far more agreeable than on beaches on the Pacific Coast or even farther west on the Strait. But two special, magical factors draw explorers of all ages to the Dungeness Valley. One is wildlife. You'll find a wealth of shorebirds and marine

The historic Lady Washington *makes a call to John Wayne Marina*

life here. The other is archaeological intrigue. Shores around Sequim have proven to be virtual gold mines of bones, teeth, tusks, and other remains of giant woolly mammoths that frequented these plains as long as 10,000 years ago. Keep your eyes peeled. You might be stubbing your Teva sandals on history.

Much of the area's marine wildlife—and more than a fair share of its awesome views—are found at the **Dungeness National Wildlife Refuge,** Sequim's primary draw. The refuge encompasses **Dungeness Spit,** a 5.5-mile-long sand finger jutting into the Strait of Juan de Fuca. The spit, a low, flat landmass formed by silt from the Dungeness River, is hidden from sight by high bluffs separating the strait from the Dungeness Valley. But it's absolutely worth seeking out.

Walking the length of the **Dungeness Spit** gives you the unique sensation of crossing a land bridge right out into the ocean. On the north (windward) side, surf laps—or pounds, depending on the season—up onto the steep, sandy beach. Ships bound for Puget Sound cruise offshore, as do seals, sea lions, and the occasional orca. On the south (leeward) side, the beach often is alive with shorebirds. The quiet, protected inner waters are prime habitat for more than 250 bird species, including herons, loons, ducks, bald eagles, and cormorants. Bring binoculars. The inner waters also are frequented by windsurfers and kayakers, and the broad spit makes a great kite-launching strip. After the first mile or so of struggle, most walkers will learn how much easier it is to walk the spit near the waterline, on firm sand. Waterproof shoes—or just cold-proof toes—are nice to have along. Hikers with strong legs and good wind shells will want to walk the entire 5 miles (check a tide table; the spit gets pretty skinny at extreme high tides) to the picturesque New Dungeness Lighthouse, built in 1857. Volunteer lightkeepers take turns living in the adjacent 1905 residence, and give tours of the light on weekends, or other times when practical. (To become a keeper, you must join the U.S. Lighthouse Society and put your name on a waiting list, which now stretches about two years ahead. Call (360) 683-9166 for information, or send a self-addressed, stamped envelope to New Dungeness Chapter, U.S. Lighthouse Society, PO Box 1283, Sequim, WA 98382.)

Note where the light stands. It was built at the tip of the spit, which grows some 20 feet a year and now extends a half mile farther east. The beach beyond here is off-limits, as is the adjoining Graveyard Spit, named to commemorate 18 Tshimshians raided and killed by warring Clallams in 1868. The refuge is open from dawn to dusk daily, year-round. A $3-per-family donation is requested at the entrance. A good campground, Dungeness Spit Recreation Area, is adjacent to the refuge. (See Camping, below.) From Sequim, drive 4.5 miles west on US 101 and turn right (north) on Kitchen-Dick Road. Proceed 3.5 miles and follow signs.

On the leeward side of the spit, look closely for a small access road leading to **Cline Spit County Park,** on the site of the original Dungeness settlement. Today, it's really little more than a flat spot, parking lot, and boat ramp (see Sea Kayaking/Windsurfing, below).

Several miles to the east, savvy beach walkers and picnickers enjoy little-known **Marlyn Nelson Park,** on the waterfront at the end of Port Williams Road (an extension of the Old Olympic Highway). Facilities are basic, with picnic sites and rest rooms. The beach is the attraction, with Gibson Spit extending south toward Travis Spit on the Miller Peninsula. From here, it's possible to walk fairly long distances east and west along the strait. This area has yielded an astonishing number of archaeological artifacts, including beautifully preserved, football-size woolly mammoth teeth and bones that land on the beach when high clay bluffs collapse during winter storms. It's a wonderful stroll, and a good foul-weather alternative to Dungeness Spit. Take Sequim-Dungeness Wy north from US 101 at Sequim, turn right (east) on Port Williams Road, and follow it to the water.

Camping

High on a bluff where the northern Olympic Peninsula drops into the sea is **Dungeness Recreation Area,** a nicely maintained, 216-acre Clallam

County park adjacent to the popular Dungeness National Wildlife Refuge. Dungeness has 67 sites (no hookups; RVs of any length), some with good back-window views of the Strait of Juan de Fuca. Campsites ($10) are separated either by head-high shrubbery or short, thick trees, offering good privacy but ample sunlight. Added bonus: Rest rooms have coin-op showers. The campground is open from February 1 to September 30. Campsites cannot be reserved. *From Sequim, drive 4.5 miles west on US 101 and turn right (north) on Kitchen-Dick Rd. Proceed 3.5 miles north and follow signs; (360) 683-5847.*

East of town, easy to miss off busy US 101, is **Sequim Bay State Park,** where you'll find nice picnic and marine facilities, a lot of so-so campsites, and a handful of very nice ones, near the water. Because it's the only state park in this area, it's a popular stopover for RVers and campers making the Olympic Peninsula loop. The 90-acre park has 86 campsites (26 with hookups; RVs to 30 feet). The park also fronts on Sequim Bay, providing boater services, moorage, and launching. (See Boating/Sailing, below.) Sequim Bay is open all year. Campsites can be reserved up to 11 months in advance through Reservations Northwest, (800) 452-5687. *On the north side of US 101, 4 miles southeast of Sequim; (360) 683-4235 or (800) 233-0321.*

For a more rustic, woodsy stay, trek into the hills of nearby Olympic National Forest to **Dungeness Forks Campground,** a nice spot with only 10 sites at the confluence of the Dungeness and Gray Wolf Rivers. The campground, open May through September, is a favorite layover spot for hikers and backpackers (see Hiking/Backpacking, below). *11 miles south of Sequim via Forest Service Roads 28 (Palo Alto Road) and 2880; (360) 765-3368.* (Note: At publication time, Dungeness Forks was closed because of a road washout; call first.)

Hiking/Backpacking

Beach walking gets most of the attention in Sequim (see Beaches/Parks, above), but don't overlook those mountains forming the rain shadow that keeps the valley dry. The upper Dungeness River drainage, in particular, harbors some of the Olympic Peninsula's finest long day hikes and backpack trips. They're typical Olympic ascents, beginning in deep, peaceful forests, climbing along silvery streams, and opening up into spectacular alpine meadows, tarns, and vistas. Most begin in Olympic National Forest and wind up in Olympic National Park (see the Olympic National Forest and the East Slope Olympics chapter). Note that a Northwest Forest Pass, $5 per day or $30 annually, is required to park in many Forest-Service–administered trailheads in this area. They're available from ranger stations, from many private vendors, on-line at www.naturenw.org, or by calling (800) 270-7504. To some degree, trails in this area benefit from the same rain-shadow effect as Sequim. Experienced Olympic hikers head to this region when weather looks iffy elsewhere on the peninsula. For full information and trailhead directions for hikes in the upper Dungeness and nearby Gray Wolf River drainages contact the Olympic National Forest Quilcene Ranger District; (360) 765-3368. Also see the Olympic National Forest and the East Slope Olympics chapter. A sampling:

The first part of the trail isn't among the more spectacular in the Olympics, but the **Deer Ridge to Deer Park Trail** (difficult; 10 miles round trip) will challenge even the most gung-ho hiker. From the trailhead near Slab Camp, off Forest Service Road 2875, this trail climbs fast, gaining about 3,000 feet in the 5 miles to the breathtaking (view-wise and fatigue-wise) panorama from Deer Park, on the shoulder of 6,007-foot Blue Mountain. The vista, taking in Vancouver Island and Mount Baker to the north and much of upper Puget Sound to the east, is one of the best in the state. For a shorter day hike, follow the trail 1.5 miles to a lesser, but still grand, view at View Rock.

Just to the south, Dungeness Forks Campground (see Camping, above) is the takeoff point for the **Lower Gray Wolf River Trail** (moderate; 20 miles round trip). For wild-river lovers the Gray Wolf is as good as it gets in Western Washington. It's one of the best-protected watersheds in the region, with its upper stretches in Olympic National Park, the lower portions in the Buckhorn Wilderness. The Gray Wolf Trail makes a great day hike, short backpack trip (good campsites are found 2, 3, 5, and 7.5 miles up the trail), or first leg of a longer trip to Graywolf or Cameron Passes in Olympic National Park.

Backpackers can hike to the Lower Gray Wolf junction and head due south, following the **Upper Gray Wolf River Trail** (difficult, various lengths) through stunning Gray Wolf Basin to Gray Wolf Pass (9.5 miles from the Lower Gray Wolf junction) and another 3.5 miles south to the **Dosewallips River Trail.** Strong backpackers can combine the Lower Gray Wolf, Cameron Creek, Dosewallips, and Upper Gray Wolf Trails for a fantastic 6- to 8-day, 50-mile climb through some of the Olympics' most memorable wildlands.

Similar to the Lower Gray Wolf Trail is its nearby cousin, the **Upper Dungeness Trail** (moderate; 12.8 miles round trip). The trail attracts backpackers and day hikers alike. It's a good beginner's backpack trip, as good campsites are found at Camp Handy (3.2 miles) and farther up the trail at a major junction, Boulder Shelter (6.4 miles). Longer backpack trails fan out from here, leading south to **Constance Pass** in the Dosewallips drainage and east to **Marmot Pass** on the Big Quilcene Trail.

For an overnight or weekend backpack trip, the nearby **Royal Basin Trail** (moderate; 14 miles round trip) is a Northwest favorite. The trail, which branches off about 1 mile up the Dungeness River Trail (see above), switches back through a church-quiet forest before opening into a stunning alpine valley, with snow-covered peaks (watch for mountain goats) on three sides and a small lake at the valley head. In the early summer, the wildflower explosion makes this a magical spot.

Good medium-length day hikes in the same area include **Gold Creek** (moderate; 12.8 miles round trip and a good mountain-bike venue) and **Tubal Cain Mine** (moderate; 17.6 miles round trip), which leads to good campsites in nice meadows, beyond an abandoned mine site and all the way up to Marmot Pass, 6,100 feet.

Boating/Sailing

A lot of the retired folks living out their golden years around Sequim were into boating long before they arrived here. But even the ones who weren't are now getting started, thanks to top-notch **marine facilities** like the John Wayne Marina on Sequim Bay, on W Sequim Bay Road (follow signs from US 101); (360) 417-3440. The marina, built on land bought and donated for the purpose by the Duke himself, who used to cruise here in his yacht, is one of the finest in the state. Wayne would be proud: the marina has full services year-round, a delightful waterfront park overlooking the bay and Miller Peninsula, 30 guest moorage slips, and good beach access. This is a pleasant spot to spend an afternoon, whether you're a boater, sailor, or just a hapless motorist tired of breathing tour-bus fumes on US 101. The marina also is a great launching point for kayaks or small craft. The marina also has a popular launch ramp, one of only a few in the area.

Other **launch ramps** are found at Sequim Bay State Park (see Camping, above), which offers overnight moorage at a dock and several mooring buoys; and Cline Spit County Park (see Sea Kayaking/Windsurfing, below).

Fishing

The John Wayne Marina is a home port for Strait of Juan de Fuca **salmon** fishing, when the season is open (which is rare of late). It's also within striking distance of North Puget Sound salmon hot spots around Port Townsend, such as Midchannel Bank. Those traditional hot spots have been closed during peak summer months in recent years. But salmon fishing activity in this region has been almost as productive in the winter when anglers pursue **blackmouth** (immature chinook).

A number of Olympic National Forest streams, including the Dungeness and Gray Wolf Rivers, can be productive **trout** fisheries. A state license is required in the national forest; check the state regulations pamphlet for limits and restrictions. No license is required on upper-river portions inside Olympic National Park. Check with park rangers for regulations.

Photography

The **New Dungeness Lighthouse,** described in Beaches/Parks, above, is a wonderful bit of coastal architecture, the perfect anchor for a seascape photo. But you'll have to walk the Dungeness Spit to shoot it. Even with a strong lens, angles from elsewhere in the valley are all wrong. The trick is to shoot it at sunset, but somehow get off the spit before dark. Let us know when you figure it out.

For a unique, airplane-style view of the entire northern Peninsula, drive up Happy Valley Road and take one of the new residential streets to the top of **Bell Hill.** It's truly breathtaking, and even though there's no real public space up here, the wealthy retirees who get to see the view every day probably won't call the cops unless you do something obnoxious.

Sea Kayaking/Windsurfing

The protected waters on the leeward side of Dungeness Spit were long ago discovered by paddlers, and they've increasingly become home port for board sailors. The center of activity here is **Cline Spit County Park**'s boat ramp on the site of the original Dungeness settlement and below view homes on the bluff overlooking Dungeness Spit. For windsurfers, the open water is a hot setup: plenty of wind from the strait sails right over the spit, but the accompanying tidal action does not. Kayakers launching from Cline Spit will love cruising Dungeness Bay's inner shore, rich with bird and marine life attracted to the Dungeness National Wildlife Refuge (see Beaches/Parks, above). A local guide service, Dungeness Bay Touring Company, (360) 681-3884; www.northolympic.com/kayak/, offers guided trips through the refuge, to the lighthouse and other destinations such as Port Williams/Protection Island. Tours range from 2 to 6 hours. To reach Cline Spit from Sequim, drive north on Sequim Avenue (east side of Sequim) toward Dungeness. After crossing the Dungeness River about 5 miles north of US 101, you'll be heading west on Anderson Road. Turn right (toward the water) on Clarke Road. At the stop sign (Marine Drive), turn right and immediately turn left on Cline Road down the hill to the parking area; 360-417-2291.

Sequim Bay, with ample access at John Wayne Marina and Sequim Bay State Park, is the region's next-best kayaking water. Just outside the bay, Marilyn Nelson Park (see Beaches/Parks, above) is a good launch site for exploration of the Port Williams area.

Cycling

The **Dungeness Scenic Loop,** a 12-mile route from one end of Sequim through the Dungeness Valley to the strait and back, was designed for cars. But it's better on a bike. The loop, an ideal regional sampler, begins on Sequim Avenue (east side of Sequim) and proceeds north to Sequim-Dungeness Wy. Signs direct riders out to the strait, across the Dungeness River to the Dungeness National Wildlife Refuge, then back across the valley west of town to Olympic Game Farm, and back to the starting point. Maps are available at the Sequim–Dungeness Valley Visitors Center (US 101 at Washington Street). But the route is easy to follow. The shoulders are good, and traffic's fairly light.

Wildlife Watching

The star of the show most of the year is the Dungeness National Wildlife Refuge. But that's not necessarily true in the winter. Sequim has become one of very few towns in the West (Banff, Alberta, comes to mind) where **wild elk** roam the streets, take up residence in city parks, and generally help themselves to local farmers' hay. The elk, loved by some Sequimites, loathed by others, are a herd of about 50 Roosevelt elk that live in the Dungeness River drainage most of the year. In the winter, encroaching snows—and deer hunters in the Olympic National Forest to the south—chase the elk into the lowlands of Happy Valley, just south of town. And in recent years, rapid residential development here has pushed the elk even farther north, right into town. Watch for the gentle beasts from mid-October to March on either side (and, regretfully, occasionally in the middle) of US 101, on the east side of Sequim. Their frequent presence there has prompted the state Department of Fish and Wildlife to fit some of the elk with radio-transmitter collars that activate highway warning signs. Keep your eyes peeled for the nation's first wired wapiti herd.

Accessible Outdoors

Sequim Bay State Park offers barrier-free campsites, rest rooms, picnic area and an interpretive trail. **Dungeness Forks Campground** has barrier-free rest rooms. (See Camping, above, for both.) The **Dungeness Hatchery** west of Sequim has a barrier-free wildlife-viewing trail, although it's steep and rutted. From US 101 1.5 miles west of Sequim, turn south on Taylor Cutoff Road, proceed 2.5 miles, continue straight on Fish Hatchery Road, and proceed 1.5 miles to the site.

outside in

Restaurants

Khu Larb Thai II ★   This gracious Thai restaurant has quickly become a local favorite. $; *120 W Bell St, Sequim; (360) 681-8550.* &

Oak Table Cafe ★   Breakfast is the thing here, featuring huge omelets, crepes, or puffy apple pancakes. $$; *292 W Bell St, Sequim; (360) 683-2179; www.oaktablecafe.com.* &

Lodgings

Groveland Cottage ★   This place has the comfortable salty-air feel of an old summer house. $$; *4861 Sequim-Dungeness Wy, Sequim; (360) 683-3565 or (800) 879-8859; www.northolympic.com/groveland.*

Juan de Fuca Cottages ★   Five comfortable cottages overlooking Dungeness Spit, or with mountain views. $$; *182 Marine Dr, Sequim; (360) 683-4433; www.dungeness.com/juandefuca.*

More Information

North Olympic Peninsula Visitors and Convention Bureau:
(800) 942-4042; www.northolympic.com.
Sequim-Dungeness Chamber of Commerce: *US 101 and E Washington; (360) 683-6197 or (800) 737-8462; www.cityofsequim.com.*

Olympic National Park: Overview

From Mount Constance west to the Hoh Rain Forest, and from Lake Quinault north to Lake Crescent, including Pacific Coast beach from the Ozette River south to the Hoh River, and nearly one million acres of pristine wilderness in the central Olympic Peninsula.

Choose your adjective. Wild. Unique. Thrilling. Pristine. Awesome. They all fit Olympic National Park, 922,000 acres of protected alpine, rain-forest, and ocean-coast heaven separating the Puget Sound basin from the Pacific Ocean. Olympic National Park, riding bucking-bronco tectonic plates beneath the North American mainland and the Pacific Ocean, literally is an island unto itself: a wildlife-rich wonderland walled off from the rest of the world. In ancient times, the Olympics were isolated by miles-thick glaciers. In more modern times, their deep, impenetrable forests and steep mountain walls have conspired to keep human interlopers out. The mountainous region was so foreboding and daunting that it wasn't fully explored by European settlers until the end of the 19th century. The Olympic Peninsula indeed was, as Olympic history buff Robert Wood has aptly noted, "the land that slept late."

The isolation that kept people out kept plants and animals in. Several species unique on the planet live here. Even some of the park's climatic zones are considered world treasures. Most notable is the park's westside temperate rain forest, where Douglas fir, western red cedar, Sitka spruce, and hemlock, gorged by an average of 14 feet of rain a year, grow to almost ridiculous proportions. The park contains nearly a dozen world-record trees, some believed to be 1,000 years old. The immense forests—the last surviving remnants of a once-great sea of Herculean trees stretching from the Pacific Coast to the Olympic crest—are largely responsible for the park's listing as a World Heritage Park and World Biosphere Site, honors granted to places with unique physical and biological features. The park's magnificent west-side rivers—the Soleduck, Bogachiel, Hoh, Queets, and Quinault—flow through some of the wildest river valleys left on the Pacific West Coast.

Just over the crest of Olympic's westernmost peaks lies an alpine wonderland: hundreds of square miles of snow-filled valleys, soothing tarns, inspiring peaks, and ridgetop meadows. Ninety-five percent of the park is wilderness, and the backcountry, negotiated only by a nearly 600-mile trail system winding through the deep river valleys, is where the park really shines. Here, you'll find large roving herds of Roosevelt elk, a majestic herd of mountain goats (threatened, ironically, by the park itself), plentiful Olympic marmots, black-tailed deer, black bears, coyotes, and cougars.

On the northwestern edge of the Olympic Peninsula, a 57-mile-long coastal strip of the park clings to the Pacific shoreline, separated from the bulk of parklands by heavily logged private and National Forest timberland. The coastal strip is the longest stretch of undeveloped ocean beach in the country, and most of it truly is wild. Very few roads penetrate the forestlands to the ocean here, and access is possible only by long, often wet hikes from the south near La Push, or from the north near Lake Ozette or from scenic Shi Shi Beach. The full length of coastal terrain here recently was designated as the Olympic Coastal Marine Sanctuary, and four separate national wildlife refuges add another layer of protection.

Olympic National Park is a special place, a land held in sacred trust not only by the federal government, but also by the many thousands of Washington recreators who feel a deep emotional connection to its unspoiled interior. Those of us who grew up in its valleys and high meadows, and on its alpine lakes and ocean beaches, guard it with an almost ferocious jealousy—a rare level of devotion, even among notoriously protective conservationists.

People who never visit the Olympics might find this fervent emotional tie to a physical place fairly odd. But the park's regular worshippers believe the connection is as natural as water running downhill. It's a soul-searching link passed down to us from our forebears. For the expanding Lower 48 states, Olympic National Park was the very last frontier. For many of us, it remains so today.

Getting There

Only a few access roads lead into Olympic National Park, but US Highway 101 loops almost completely around it. Most visitors from the Seattle area journey to the park's northern entrances near Port Angeles, a 77-mile trip northwest of Seattle on US 101 (plan on about 2 hours, assuming no ferry backups). For the most direct approach, take the Edmonds-Kingston or Seattle-Bainbridge ferry to Kitsap County and follow signs to the Hood Canal Floating Bridge. Cross the bridge into Jefferson County and follow Hwy 104 to US 101, which leads west through Sequim and the Dungeness Valley to Port Angeles. From there, roads lead to Hurricane Ridge and up the Elwha River. Continue west, then south, on US 101 for roads up the Soleduck (past Lake Crescent), Hoh (south of Forks), Queets, and Quinault Rivers.

Access to the Olympic Coastal Marine Sanctuary is along US 101 in the south near Kalaloch, at La Push on Hwy 110 west of Forks, at Lake Ozette south of Hwy 112 near Clallam Bay, and from Neah Bay at the end of Hwy 112.

Bus service is available from Seattle to Port Angeles on Olympic Van Tours in Port Angeles, (360) 452-3858, which also has daily scheduled sightseeing tours. Arrangements can be made for drop-offs and pickups at trailheads throughout the park. Clallam Transit, (360) 452-4511, offers shuttle service to Lake Crescent, Neah Bay, Forks, and La Push.

inside out

Olympic National Park Rules and Regulations

Trail regulations inside Olympic National Park are substantially more restrictive than those on most national forest trails in Washington: **Campfires** are prohibited in most alpine areas above 3,500 feet and at most other popular backcountry camps at lower elevations. Check with the park visitors center in Port Angeles, (360) 452-0330, for specific rules for the area you plan to visit. Better yet, avoid the problem by carrying a backpacking stove for any overnight trip in the park. Olympic's backcountry is too valuable to mar with fire rings, let alone destroy with a wildfire sparked by a careless camper. A stove is the best investment you can make in your grandchildren's backpacking future.

Pets and mountain bikes are forbidden on all Olympic National Park trails except the Spruce Railroad Trail and Boulder Creek (Olympic Hot Springs) Trail, where bicycles are allowed. If you can't live for a day without your dog or fat tires, pick a trail in the Olympic National Forest, where both are allowed (see Olympic National Forest and East Slope Olympics chapter). Backcountry rangers can—and do—issue citations. Dogs are allowed in campgrounds, on paved roads, and on ocean beaches, providing they're on a leash.

Hiking permits are not required for day hikes—yet. But **backcountry permits** are required for all overnight stays on park trails. Since the summer of 1997, the park charges $5 per party and an additional $2 per person per day for the privilege of walking on its trails. Annual passes can be purchased for $30 per person, $15 for additional household members. The maximum you can be charged is $50 for trips of up to 14 nights with a party of up to 6 people, or $100 for trips of up to 14 nights with groups of 7 to 12 people.

If that's not troublesome enough, consider this: Olympic National Park is now phasing out its "self-registration" process, through which you paid your fees by mail by simply picking up an envelope at the trailhead. Beginning May 2001, all **wilderness permits** must be purchased directly from the park at its Wilderness Information Center (adjacent to the main park visitor center) in Port Angeles, or from the Elwha, Sol Duc, Mora, Ozette, North Quinault, Staircase, Dosewallips, or Hoh Ranger Stations. Assuming someone is there during business hours. Permits also can be purchased by phone, (360) 452-0300, then picked up at the Wilderness Information Center. The park is doing this, it says, "in order to educate visitors how they can better protect the wildlife, plants, and wilderness character of Olympic." Start your education process by contacting the geniuses who devised this scheme, (360) 542-0330; e-mail: olym_wic@nps.gov, and tell them just how user-friendly you find it.

Ah, but there's more: If you're planning a backpack trip to the Ozette coast (Cape Alava/Sand Point); Grand and Badger Valleys out of ObstructionPeak; Royal Basin, Lake Constance, or Flapjack Lakes on the east-slope Olympics; Seven Lakes Basin in the Sol Duc drainage; or Hoh Lake or C.B. Flats in the Hoh drainage, you'll need a **campsite reservation** in addition to the permits discussed above. These are the park's "quota" areas (Royal Basin, Hoh Lake, and C.B. Flats are recent additions). Campsite reservations are obtained at the Wilderness Information Center in Port Angeles or a staffed ranger station. In some areas, such as the Ozette coast, advance reservations are required, and can be made up to 30 days in advance; in others, they're just recommended. Call the WIC, (360) 452-0300, and ask them to explain. You also may request reservations for quota areas on-line; www.nps.gov/olym/reserve.htm.

Got all that? Add this: **Groups** are limited to 12 in the backcountry. Larger groups should divide up, then travel and camp at least a half mile apart. **Pack stock** are allowed on most trails, but forbidden in some sensitive areas. Call the park for a current list of trails open to horses and other pack animals, as well as wilderness guidelines for stock use.

Enough about trail rules and fees. Now for the **road fees.** In Olympic National Park, fee-collection stations have sprung up like warts on many

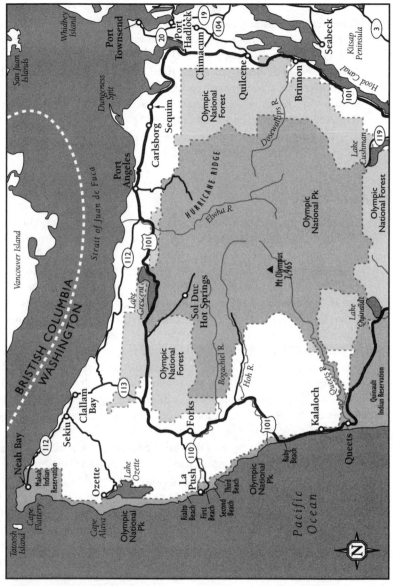

Olympic National Park

roads, notably Hurricane Ridge, Elwha, Sol Duc, and the Hoh River Valley. Fees recently increased to $10 per carload, $5 per person for cyclists and bus passengers. The entrance permit is good for 7 days at all park entrances. Fees generally are collected at all gates from May through September, and on winter weekends at the Heart o' the Hills entrance near Port Angeles. Season passes are $20; Golden Eagle Passes, which permit entrance to all national parks, historic monuments, and wildlife areas, are $65; National Parks passes are $50. The lifetime Golden Age pass costs $10 for people 62 or older and the free Golden Access pass is available to those who can show written proof of permanent disability. If you don't want to pay, try showing up really early and beating the money changers to their squatty little roadside temples.

Campground fees range from $8 to $12 per night; RV dumping costs $3; the daily parking fee at Ozette is $1. All fees listed here are as of summer 2000.

Scenic Drives

Depending on your outdoor persuasion, the best or worst thing about Olympic National Park is that, with a few exceptions, you can't really drive into it. About 95 percent of the park, or about 900,000 acres, is wilderness, with no roads to speak of. The 5 percent of developed parklands are concentrated around Hurricane Ridge, Kalaloch, the Hoh and Soleduck Rivers, Lake Crescent, and Lake Quinault—all places you can drive to, and around, once you get there. Fortunately, US 101 provides a chance to drive around the entire park, providing easy access to its most popular road-accessible attractions. If you're a visitor with only a week to spare, or a newcomer hoping to sample the entire park on one trip, the US 101 loop is a great way to go. Most travelers like to drive only a few hours at a time, then set up camp or check in for lodging at a campground or inn before exploring the area by foot or boat. Follow that schedule, and you ll need about a week to make the entire loop.

Remember, driving the **Olympic Loop** isn't like making a loop trip through Yellowstone. Olympic's natural wonders won't wander up to your car and press their nose against the window. You need to go find them, usually by following a side road 20 to 30 miles into the park's interior. A hasty traveler could, in fact, drive the entire US 101 loop in a day—and see fewer of the park's attractions than someone sitting at home staring at a map.

US 101 is the connector for this trip, not the main attraction. Aside from short stretches along Lake Crescent and the Kalaloch beach strip, in fact, much of the road passes through downright ugliness. Where it travels through the heart of the peninsula, sprawling forestlands on either side of 101 have been devastated by clear-cutting. Logging on state, federal, and even tribal lands here has taken a heavy toll. Most of the western peninsula's great rain forest—lush, unique ecosystems with rapid tree growth unequaled on the planet—was wiped out here between 1910 and the

Strolling some of the 57 miles of pristine ocean beach in Olympic National Park

1970s. Logging practices have improved in recent years, but much of this land was logged early in the century, when environmental restrictions were unheard of. The resulting moonscape surface is a tragic reminder of the long-lasting consequences of industrial greed. So leave yourself enough time to venture into Olympic National Park—the peninsula's only surviving significant rain-forest refuge—for a taste of what this great land once was.

That established, a typical Olympic loop driven counterclockwise from Port Angeles west and then south would include stops at these park highlights: Hurricane Ridge, Lake Crescent, Sol Duc Hot Springs, Rialto Beach, Hoh Rain Forest, Kalaloch, and Lake Quinault. From here, the route exits the park and detours south to US 12 and Hwy 8 east before turning north up the western shore of Hood Canal on US 101 again, through scenic Olympic National Forest terrain (see the Hood Canal, and Olympic National Forest and the East Slope Olympics chapters). From here, you can access popular eastside national park venues such as the North Fork Skokomish, Dosewallips, and Gray Wolf River valleys before heading west through Sequim to close the loop.

Be prepared to poke along. US 101 is two lanes almost all the way, often winding, and frequented by slow traffic. The route used to be plugged with logging trucks. Their numbers have declined of late. But gapers have replaced cutters: it seems as though four Winnebagos have sprung up to replace each dearly departed log hauler. Traveling the peninsula frequently for many years has taught us a lesson, which we'll pass on as locals' advice: if you live in Western Washington and plan to return to Olympic National Park many times over the years, don't kill yourself fighting traffic on the Olympic Loop. Pick one area and get to know it personally by spending several days there, or a week. The rest of it—Congress cooperating—will still be there next time you get a vacation. Further advice: If your Olympic destination is the Kalaloch area or anywhere south, it's probably faster to drive onto the peninsula via I-5 to Olympia, US 12 and Hwy 8 to Aberdeen and Hoquiam, then US 101 north than via the busier northern, Port Angeles route.

Hiking/Backpacking

It may be tough to find any single area in the country with a richer mix of hiking terrain. Because 95 percent of the park's terrain is wilderness that can't be reached by car, foot travel long has been the preferred mode of transport in Olympic. And plenty of people take advantage: about 50,000 hikers a year make tracks in the Olympics—the third-highest total in the national park system. It wasn't always that popular: In the early days, John Huelsdonk, the Iron Man of the Hoh, is said to have carried a cast-iron stove far up a river valley trail, commenting to passersby that the stove was no trouble, but the shifting 50-pound sack of flour inside was giving him fits. In modern days, backpackers whine and bellyache about being forced to carry an extra tent rain fly. But it's safe to say that both parties felt the same satisfaction upon getting where they were going. In Olympic, the carry-your-own-weight-and-then-some tradition lives on. Detailed descriptions of many of Olympic's best short, medium, and long hikes can be found in the chapters for Port Angeles and Hurricane Ridge; Neah Bay, Lake Ozette, and Sekiu; Lake Crescent and the Upper Soleduck; Forks and La Push; Central Coast: Hoh, Kalaloch, and Queets; Lake Quinault and the Quinault River Valley; Hood Canal; and Olympic National Forest and the East Slope Olympics. Also, consult the park's Wilderness Information Center, (360) 452-0300, for permits and reservations (see Regulations, above). But the list below of don't-miss trails might serve as a good starting point.

Short 'n' easy

Even if you're zipping around the Olympic Peninsula by car, with little time to waste on the trail, it's still possible to take a roadside sip of wilderness. Consider a short hike to **Hurricane Hill Summit; Humes Ranch** on the Elwha River; **Marymere Falls** near Lake Crescent; **Spruce Railroad** across Lake Crescent from US 101; **Cape Alava** near Lake Ozette; **Soleduck Falls; Rialto Beach** north of La Push; Hoh River's **Hall of Mosses;** the Queets River 3-mile **nature loop;** Lake Quinault's **Rain Forest Loop, Graves Creek Loop,** or **Maple Glade Rain Forest;** or Kalaloch's **Beach 4** or **Ruby Beach.** The list could go on indefinitely. But if you can hit even a fourth of those, you're guaranteed to be back to discover more on your own.

Weekend backpack routes

Popular 1- to 3-day destinations are too numerous to list here. Hikers should consult a guide such as *Pacific Northwest Hiking* (Foghorn Press), co-written by this author and Dan A. Nelson, or *Olympic Mountains Trail Guide* by Robert S. Wood (The Mountaineers Books). But some personal favorite backpack routes include **Grand Valley and Grand Pass** near Hurricane Ridge; **Appleton Pass** and **Deer Lake** in the Soleduck area; the **Sand Point/Cape Alava Loop** near Lake Ozette; the **Hoh River Trail** to Glacier Meadows; the **East Fork Quinault Trail** to Enchanted Valley; the **North Fork Skokomish Trail;** the **Lower Gray Wolf Trail;** the **West Fork Dosewallips Trail** to Honeymoon Meadows (closed due to a bridge outage in early 2000; call first); and **Royal Basin.**

Long-distance treks

Once the appetite is whetted, many Olympic veterans answer the same call as the legendary Press Expedition heard in the 1890s: "Cross the Olympics." Several routes are possible, ranging from 35 to 46 miles and requiring strong legs, a strong back, and a week of spare time. The **Elwha River/Low Divide/North Fork Quinault traverse,** which follows the Press Expedition route nearly exactly, is the best north-south Olympic traverse. The 45-mile crossing is only moderately difficult, and hikes about the same way in either direction. The high point is Low Divide, 3,650 feet.

The most popular east-west traverse is the **East Fork Quinault/Anderson Pass/Dosewallips River** route (about 30 miles), which can allow stops at two of the park's most spectacular backcountry sites: O'Neil Pass and Enchanted Valley. Other long treks considered park classics include the entire 57-mile **coastal strip** (careful tide planning is required); the 19-mile **High Divide Loop** connecting the Soleduck and Hoh drainages; the **Gray Wolf, Dosewallips, Duckabush,** and **North Fork Skokomish River valleys** in the eastern slope Olympics; and the rugged, isolated **Bailey Range Traverse,** an off-trail journey in the park's northern interior for experienced trekkers only.

Camping

Olympic National Park offers 925 campsites, which range from usually full to usually vacant depending on season and location. The bulk are found in the park's six largest campgrounds: **Heart o' the Hills** on Hurricane Ridge Road (105 sites); **Kalaloch** on US 101 (175 sites); **Mora** near La Push (95 sites); **Hoh Rainforest** (88 sites); **Fairholm** near Lake Crescent (88 sites); and **Sol Duc** (80 sites; closes during snow). Those campgrounds usually are open all year, as are **Staircase, Elwha, Ozette, Queets, North Fork Quinault, July Creek** on Lake Quinault, and **Graves Creek.** The remaining campgrounds—**Altaire** on the Elwha, **Deer Park,** and **Dosewallips**—are open from May to November. In spite of this schedule, if you're camping in winter months, it's always a good idea to call before departing. Wicked weather can and often does close roads.

Campsite fees are $8 to $12 as of summer 2000 and are collected at all campgrounds except North Fork Quinault. Some campgrounds, open during the winter without services such as water, revert to a no-fee status until spring. For heartier campers, particularly those with warm RVs, the colder, off-season months can be a great time to visit Olympic in its natural state, without swarming summer crowds. No sites can be reserved in Olympic, and in the summer, landing a space can be frustrating. That's especially true at the park's most popular destinations: Kalaloch, Hoh, and Mora. See individual chapters on those areas for some tips on getting in—or alternative campgrounds in case you can't. Worth noting are the string of Olympic National Forest campgrounds perched near the park's borders, particularly on the east and west sides. Campsites often are available there even when they're full in national park campgrounds a short distance away.

Olympic's campgrounds have a maximum stay of 14 days. Group campsites are available at Kalaloch (30-person maximum) and Mora (40-person maximum). Group camps can be reserved in advance by calling the park. RVs and multiple vehicles are discouraged.

Fishing

With productive surf fishing on the coast, excellent **salmon** and **steel-head** fishing in its western rivers, and good **trout** fishing in Lake Crescent, Lake Quinault, and dozens of high alpine lakes, Olympic's angling opportunities are uncommonly good, especially for a national park. Consult individual chapters on Olympic destinations for location-specific fishing information. State fishing licenses are not required inside park boundaries, but anglers do need special anadromous fish permits, such as a state steelhead or salmon punch card, to fish for those species. Special state licenses also are required to dig **razor clams** during open seasons at Kalaloch. See the Washington Department of Fish and Wildlife web page, www.wa.gov/wdfw, for seasons and restrictions. Most park waters adhere to general state fishing regulations (pick up a regulations pamphlet at sporting goods stores). But many park lakes and streams also have special restrictions on bait, minimum size, bag limits, and seasons. Some of those rules might differ from the same waters downstream, outside the park. And regulations change frequently. So it's always important to check regulations at local ranger stations.

Canoeing/Kayaking

Surf kayaking is an increasingly popular activity at Olympic's coastal beaches, particularly those with good vehicle access, such as **Kalaloch** and **Rialto Beach** near La Push. Canoeists and sea kayakers love the sprawling waters of **Lake Ozette** (where a boat-in campground is available), **Lake Crescent**, and **Lake Quinault.** River kayakers can be found in most of the park's major rivers, but the **lower Elwha** and **upper and lower Soleduck** are favorites. Remember, Olympic's rivers aren't places for amateurs. Some waterways, such as the Hoh River, have proven particularly dangerous to boaters because of fluctuating water levels and nasty log jams.

Boating/Sailing

Olympic National Park isn't a major destination for boaters, but park visitors can get out on the water in rental craft at **Lake Quinault** and **Lake Crescent.** Many visitors also launch small craft in **Lake Ozette.** See the Neah Bay chapter for more information.

Rafting

Guided raft trips are available on most west side park rivers. Call park headquarters, (360) 452-4501, for a list of outfitters.

Beaches

Sandy shorelines on Olympic's 57-mile coastal strip are among the last remaining undeveloped saltwater beaches in the nation. You can't really go wrong with an Olympic saltwater beach, but enduring favorites remain the beaches around **Kalaloch, Rialto Beach** near La Push, **Cape Alava** and **Sand Point** near Lake Ozette, and **Shi Shi Beach** just south of Neah Bay. All the park's beaches are wilderness, and most offshore islands are protected by Flattery Rocks and Quillayute Needles National Wildlife Refuges. In 1994 the entire coastal area from Cape Flattery south to Copalis and west for 30 miles was designated as the Olympic Coast National Marine Sanctuary, protecting it from heinous threats such as offshore oil drilling. This makes the park's beach strip a favorite destination for wildlife watchers in search of shorebirds, marine mammals, or migratory whales.

Biking

Olympic is not a cyclist's paradise. Far from it, in fact. While some access roads make adequate cycle routes for those determined to turn the pedals, general cycle access is poor. That's due largely to the park's physical layout. The main access route, US 101, is of course open to road cyclists. But it's far from ideal, with heavy truck and RV traffic and inadequate shoulders along many stretches. And the predominantly wilderness designation inside the park leaves almost every backcountry trail off-limits to mountain bikes. As you'll see from the chapters on park destinations, road cycling is possible in most areas of the park. But with minor exceptions such as the **Spruce Railroad Trail,** where mountain biking is allowed, it's simply not what most people come here to do.

Skiing/Snowshoeing

Three small ski lifts are operated by a private ski club at **Hurricane Ridge** during winter months. The vertical drop is tiny compared to other Northwest ski destinations, but Port Angeles locals enjoy the diversion. Hurricane Ridge also is a good cross-country ski destination, with several miles of snow-covered roads—and millions of acres of wide-open backcountry—open to skinny skis. Ski rentals are available in Port Angeles and at the Hurricane Ridge Visitors Center. Guided snowshoe tours also are conducted by park rangers on some winter weekends, and a sliding area usually is maintained for snow tubers. Be aware that strong winds and wet weather often create icy conditions that can make cross-country skiing and snowshoeing a little bit more adventurous than most people prefer. The same weather often wreaks havoc on the park's plowing schedule for

Hurricane Ridge Road. Generally, the road is plowed and open by 9am on Friday, Saturday, and Sunday, but the schedule is always tentative. Call the park's road-conditions recording, (360) 452-0329, before you leave. See the Port Angeles and Hurricane Ridge chapter for more information.

Wildlife Watching

Olympic is rich with animal life, some of it found only here. By most accounts, the park's most majestic creature is the **Roosevelt elk,** which in many respects deserves credit for creation of the park in the first place. President Theodore Roosevelt's passion for big game led in 1909 to protection of much of what now is Olympic National Park. Unlike its cousin, the smaller Rocky Mountain elk, the Roosevelt elk is a shy herd animal that's particularly wary of humans. Most park visitors never see one. That makes happening upon a herd of these gentle beasts an especially rare treat. During summer months, most of the park's herd retreats to high alpine valleys. In the winter and early spring, they're most often seen in westside river valleys. The Queets, North and East Fork Quinault, and Hoh River Trails provide good chances to encounter an elk during off-season months. Watching a herd pass silently across your path is a memory that will stick with you for life. Your best chance to see one from a road is Lake Quinault's North Shore Road. Look for them in the flats on both sides of the road between the Quinault Ranger Station and the Quinault Bridge, which connects North and South Shore Roads.

Conversely, the park's most ubiquitous creatures, friendly **black-tailed deer,** are found throughout the park and often seen in campgrounds and other public places. They're quite bold in the alpine backcountry, where they'll sometimes wander right up to tents filled with sleeping backpackers. Another alpine creature, the **Olympic marmot,** is unique to the park and is a constant friendly companion to backcountry visitors, who are happy to watch them whistle, cavort, and play marmot-tag in alpine meadows. They're commonly seen in the Hurricane Ridge area, as well.

Black bears are common in the park, and are often spotted in the high, treeless alpine terrain. They generally keep to themselves. While basic, common-sense food handling is necessary in the backcountry, human-bear conflicts are exceedingly rare here, though portions of the Elwha River Trail have been closed periodically to reduce bear-human conflict. Most black bears encountered on a trail will do their best to steer clear of human interlopers. But keep in mind that bears should never be approached or provoked, especially a mother with a cub or cubs.

Another park predator, the **cougar,** is thriving, and some menacing encounters with humans have been reported in recent years. Keep a watchful eye for cougars (and **bobcats,** also common in the park), especially when traveling in the backcountry with children. Unlike the continent's other feared predator, the grizzly bear (which you will not find in Olympic), cougars can be intimidated into leaving you alone. If you encounter one, make yourself appear as large, ornery, and formidable as possible. Chances are good you'll go home unscathed—with a great story.

Olympic's backcountry also presents occasional encounters with **coyotes, raccoons, red foxes** (rare), and a rich community of other small mammals. The native Olympic wolf, sadly, was hunted to extinction here in the early 20th century, before the park was protected. Olympic seems a prime candidate for wolf reintroduction, but the park hasn't publicly touched that hot issue yet.

Another warm-blooded Olympic creature, the **mountain goat,** has stirred up a storm of controversy in the past two decades. The park's current goat herd was introduced by hunters in the 1920s (debate continues as to whether goats inhabited the park earlier). After the national park was established in 1938, goat hunting inside the park ceased, and goat numbers grew. Park scientists estimate Olympic's herd grew to more than 1,000 animals in the mid-1980s. Concern about the goats' impact on some rare alpine plants prompted a live-capture-and-removal program in the late 1980s. A 1994 census indicated fewer than 300 goats remain in the park. Unless you trek deep into the park backcountry, you're not likely to ever see one.

In spite of that reduction, park officials continue to maintain that the remaining goats should be shot—probably from helicopters—to protect the park's plants. (Federal policy allows the park to eradicate an "introduced" species if it's doing irreparable harm to an ecosystem. Park scientists say that is true of the Olympic goat, even though they have conceded in studies that none of the park's rare alpine plants are in danger of extinction.)

Surveys have indicated three of four Washington residents oppose killing the gentle beasts. The Washington Department of Fish and Wildlife, which manages mountain goats on Olympic National Forest lands surrounding the park (many goats migrate between jurisdictions) also opposes killing. And animal welfare groups have vowed to sue if a goat-kill policy is approved. But the animals' long-term future in the park is uncertain.

An independent scientific study of the problem, released in summer 2000, did little to solve the controversy. It essentially concluded that there was no evidence the goats are native to the park, but neither has there been credible scientific evidence that the much-ballyhooed destruction of alpine habitat is the fault of goats. So, for the time being, the park's remaining goat herd keeps its head down and hides out in secluded places such as the Bailey Range.

Finally, the park's coastal strip, a fully protected wilderness that surely qualifies as a national treasure, is teeming with marine mammals. **Sea and river otters, bald eagles, harbor seals,** and **sea lions** are common sights on the coast. Special visitors seen only rarely include **elephant seals** and **gray, minke, and humpback whales,** which migrate near the coast in spring and fall months. **Harbor porpoises, orca whales, Dall's porpoises,** and **Pacific dolphins** also have been known to swim through the park's protected coastal waters.

Accessible Outdoors

Many Olympic National Park facilities are wheelchair-accessible. See this listing in the individual chapters of the Olympic Peninsula and Pacific Coast section for more information, or call the park, (360) 452-0330.

More Information

Port Angeles Visitors Center (general information): *(360) 452-0330; www.nps.gov/olym.*

Olympic National Park Headquarters: *Port Angeles; (360) 452-4501.*
   Elwha Ranger Station: *(360) 452-9191.*
   Forks NPS/USFS Information Station: *(360) 374-6522.*
   Heart o' the Hills Ranger Station: *(360) 452-2713.*
   Hoh Rain Forest Ranger Station: *(360) 374-6925.*
   Kalaloch Ranger Station: *(360) 962-2283.*
   Lake Crescent Ranger Station: *(360) 928-3380.*
   Mora Ranger Station: *(360) 374-5460.*
   Ozette Ranger Station: *(360) 963-2725.*
   Queets Ranger Station: *(360) 962-2283.*
   Quinault Ranger Station: *(360) 288-2444.*
   Road and Weather Updates: *(360) 452-0329.*
   Sol Duc Ranger Station: *(360) 928-3380.*
   Staircase Ranger Station: *(360) 877-5569.*
   Wilderness Information Center: *(360) 452-0300.*

Port Angeles
and Hurricane Ridge

From Ediz Hook south to Hurricane Ridge in Olympic National Park, east to Deer Park and west to the Lyre River, including the Elwha River valley, Tongue Point Marine Reserve, and Salt Creek Recreation Area.

Your friends from Boston deliver the fateful news by email: they're coming to Seattle, they want to sample the very essence of Northwest outdoor life, and they're relying solely on you to be their recreational compass. Oh, yeah: they've only got three days. You'd be hard-pressed to send them in a better direction than Port Angeles. The city itself doesn't look like much—a big, belching pulp mill, a lot of Big Timber–era houses that saw their best days back when Lawrence Welk was only ah-one.

The thing about Port Angeles, though, is that this city doesn't need to look like much. The town of 18,000 has the Strait of Juan de Fuca and Vancouver Island on its front porch, the Pacific Coast and Dungeness Valley in side bedrooms, and magnificent Olympic National Park splayed out all over the backyard. Any one of those things would make this a great place to while away a year or 10. The combination of all four makes it a place where many of us would sincerely like to sink roots.

The greatest attraction is the city's immediate proximity to Olympic National Park. The park, 922,000 acres of stunning alpine and coastal wilderness, isn't merely unique in Washington State. In many ways it's unparalleled on the planet. And Port Angeles is the closest thing to a bustling city anywhere near its borders. Its location makes the old port city a natural jumping-off point for the wonders of the northern Olympics, the park's most spectacular terrain. City residents haven't overlooked this bit of good fortune,

Hurricane Ridge Visitors Center is a must-visit Olympic National Park stop

and in the past two decades have shifted to a tourist-driven marketing strategy.

One result is that Port Angeles—once little more than a supply stop on the way to Lake Crescent, Appleton Pass, or the Elwha River Valley—has become a pleasant outdoor-oriented destination unto itself. The city's recent trail and wharf improvements, for example, have turned an ugly waterfront industrial zone into a fairly agreeable place to spend a day on the water. When that gets old, take a drive through the city's upper residential neighborhoods. You just might spot a guidebook author doing very early retirement-property research.

Getting There

Port Angeles is a 77-mile drive west of Seattle on US Highway 101 (plan on about 2 hours, assuming no ferry backups). For the most direct approach, take the Edmonds-Kingston or Seattle-Bainbridge ferry to Kitsap County and follow signs to the Hood Canal Floating Bridge. Cross the bridge into Jefferson County and follow Hwy 104 west to US 101, which leads through Sequim and the Dungeness Valley to Port Angeles. Travel (in)sanity note: Summer weekend travelers should strongly consider skipping the ferry and heading south to cross Puget Sound at the Tacoma Narrows Bridge and driving up Kitsap Peninsula to the Hood Canal Bridge. This route adds about 60 driving miles to the trip, but could save hours of boring waits at ferry terminals.

inside out

Hiking/Backpacking

The interior Olympics contain what many consider to be the cream of the nation's wilderness crop for backpack treks and long day hikes. More than 95 percent of Olympic National Park's wilderness is accessible only by trail, and some of the most magnificent hikes begin within 30 minutes of downtown Port Angeles. For a full range of options, consult with park specialists at the visitors center on Hurricane Ridge Road; (360) 452-0330. Note that Wilderness Permits are required for all overnight stays in the Olympic backcountry, and a per-hiker fee is charged. Contact the park's Wilderness Information Center, (360) 452-0300, for current information. Also, mountain bikes, dogs, and horses are forbidden on most Olympic National Park trails. (See the Olympic National Park: Overview chapter.) Here's a quick guide to the very best of the best trails, divided by area.

Hurricane Ridge

Trails fan out literally in every direction from the ridge, Olympic National Park's high-alpine visitors' heaven 17 miles south of Port Angeles. For a short walk offering a brief sip of the majestic Olympic high country, head out on one of the **Nature Loop trails** (easy; less than 1 mile) from the Hurricane parking lot. They lead north through beautiful alpine meadows (a-bursting with wildflower colors after the snowmelt in June and July), past peaceful black-tailed deer to mile-high views of Port Angeles, the Strait of Juan de Fuca, and much of Vancouver Island. Most loops are short and relatively flat (wheelchair accessible), and take 30 minutes or less. For a slightly more aggressive, much more exhilarating walk, head north on the **Lake Angeles–Klahhane Ridge Trail** (moderate; 7 miles round trip), which leaves from the east end of the parking lot, climbs up along Sunrise Ridge below the stony face of 6,100-foot Mount Angeles, and at 3.5 miles connects with the trail down to Lake Angeles and Heart o' the Hills. Grand views all the way. Warning: Much of the route is wind exposed. Bring water and a good parka. Energy-burst option: If you're liking what you see and want more, follow the path down (way down) to Lake Angeles and arrive, bleeding toes and all, at the Heart o' the Hills trailhead. Total one-way distance: about 10 miles, and 4,000 vertical feet. Wise veterans walk it one way, downhill.

An easy, popular trail that rates as one of the best half-day hikes in the Northwest is the **Hurricane Hill Trail** (moderate; 3 miles round trip), which departs from the end of Hurricane Ridge Road, about a quarter mile beyond the Hurricane Picnic Area. This route, a former road, is a moder-ate uphill climb that starts and ends above treeline in Olympic's amazing alpine country. It's 1.5 miles to the 5,700-foot summit, the site of an old lookout. The 360-degree panorama is awesome, with views north across the Strait of Juan de Fuca to Victoria and south to the alpine peaks of the Olympics. This trail is at its best in early summer, when wildflowers paint the rolling slopes—and just enough snow lingers to whip up a trail margarita at your lunch stop.

If you're looking for an endorphin rush, proceed directly to the notorious **Switchback Trail** (very strenuous; 3 miles round trip), which begins in a pullout several miles below the Hurricane Ridge parking lot. The trail (surprise!) switches back about 17 million times on its steep, torturous, 1.5-mile, 1,600-vertical-foot ascent to Klahhane Ridge. Here, you either (a) drop dead, (b) sit and admire the view, (c) climb Mount Angeles, or (d) continue merrily on your way down the Klahhane Ridge and Lake Angeles or Heather Park Trails.

One of Olympic's premier weekend backpacking trails begins east of Hurricane Ridge, at the end of Obstruction Point Road. The narrow gravel road, which begins at the east end of the ridge parking lot, leads 7.5 miles to a turnaround/trailhead. Here, hikers can embark on the **Grand Ridge Trail** (moderate; 7.5 miles one way), a high-altitude ridgetop walk to Deer Park (see Camping, below). From the same trailhead at Obstruction Point, a separate path leads over Lillian Ridge and down into majestic **Grand Valley** (moderate; various lengths possible), where a string of three lakes—Grand, Moose, and Gladys—await backpackers and strong day hikers. Campsites and wildlife are present at all of the lakes, and hikers will want to walk to the end of the trail at Grand Pass (8 miles from Obstruction Point) for a stupendous all-around Olympic Mountains view. Note: Obstruction Point Road is open during summer months only. The rest of the year, the road makes a fine winter cross-country ski or snowshoe trek, or a spring snow hike.

Heart o' the Hills

A trailhead directly across Hurricane Ridge Road from Heart o' the Hills, Olympic's primary north-end campground, offers two fine day hikes. One is the lower extension of the **Lake Angeles and Klahhane Ridge Trail** (moderate; 7 miles round trip to lake) in the Hurricane Ridge description, above. The first 3.5 miles are a moderate-to-steep uphill walk through deep forest, before the path opens up to beautiful, emerald-green Lake Angeles. The aerobically challenged will want to stop here. But gung-ho hikers can continue on around the lake, up an unsettlingly steep pitch to the top of Klahhane Ridge, and on to Hurricane Ridge parking lot (10 miles) or a junction with the Heather Park Trail (6.2 miles). The other path is the **Heather Park Trail** (difficult; 12.4 miles round trip), which climbs at a similar pace through wooded terrain to a terraced, rocky, park-like area at the base of Mount Angeles, a popular climbing venue. Views from Heather Park are breathtaking, looking mostly north over the Strait of Juan de Fuca. Continue on to a junction, at 6.2 miles, with the Lake Angeles Trail. Strong hikers, you're already ahead of us; you can hike the whole circuit as a 12.4-mile loop—up, over, and back—in a day.

The **Deer Ridge to Deer Park Trail** (difficult; 10 miles round trip), though the first part of the trail isn't among the more spectacular in the Olympics, will challenge even the most gung-ho hiker. From the trailhead near Slab Camp, off Forest Road 2875, this trail climbs fast, gaining about 3,000 feet in the 5 miles to the breathtaking (view-wise and fatigue-wise) panorama from Deer Park, on the shoulder of 6,007-foot Blue Mountain. The vista, taking in Vancouver Island and Mount Baker to the north and much of North Puget Sound to the east, is one of the best in the state. For a shorter day hike, follow the trail 1.5 miles to a lesser, but still grand, view at View Rock.

Elwha River

About 8 miles west of Port Angeles, the Elwha River Road, which leads south up one of the Olympic Peninsula's mightiest waterways, is easy to miss. Don't. Some of the best hiking in the state is just up the way, departing from two major trailheads. The first, Whiskey Bend, is reached by following a gravel road 4.5 miles from the Elwha Ranger Station. This trailhead, the jump-off point for many trans-Olympic backpacking ventures, also was the jump-off point for the famed Press Expedition, which first explored the interior Olympics in 1890. It took the expedition six months (in the winter—go figure) to map a route up the Elwha to Low Divide and down the North Fork Quinault valley. Today, some super-strong hikers follow the same 44-mile route in a single, albeit 15-hour, day. The first 20 miles or so of the **Elwha River Trail** (moderate; various lengths) are a low-elevation walk, snow-free nearly all year. It's not replete with sweeping views, but it's a peaceful path through mostly undisturbed old-growth forest. Most day hikers will be content to wander 2 miles in to Humes Ranch (easy; 4 miles round trip), site of Grant Humes's 1889 homestead cabin, or zip all the way into Elkhorn, a pleasant backcountry camp and seasonal ranger station 11.5 miles up the trail. At 17 miles, a trail leads east to connect with east slope trails such as Cameron Creek, Gray Wolf, and main fork Dosewallips. Many backpackers will follow the Press Expedition route all the way south to Low Divide, and on to the North Fork Quinault Campground, a 44-mile trip of about 4 days. The hike on the same trail into and back out from Low Divide (difficult; 28.5 miles round trip) also is a good, weeklong backpack venture. Note: Some backcountry camps along this route have been closed by the park in the spring in recent years because of black bear encounters. Call before you go.

On the opposite side of this valley, the Elwha River Road climbs past Lake Mills and Glines Canyon Dam, the upper of two Elwha dams built early in the century without fish ladders, thus destroying one of the greatest salmon-spawning habitats in the West. The road eventually turns to gravel, and dead-ends about 10 miles from US 101. Here, on the other side of an automobile gate, a decaying road leads 2.4 miles to (walk-in) Boulder Creek Campground and **Olympic Hot Springs** (easy, 4.8 miles round trip), an always-popular park retreat. The hot springs are at the site of a former hotel and resort, a grand facility that had its own Olympic-size swimming pool. The complex closed after a fire in 1966 and ultimately was bulldozed by its owners. The park then let the hot springs, gurgling from a hillside above Boulder Creek, go natural, prohibiting any new development. (And discouraging most visitation; the hot springs don't even show up on official Olympic maps anymore.) Today, many visitors go natural as well, flagrantly disregarding the park's no-nudity policy in the bathwater-warm hot springs. Don't worry: You won't be excluded if you wear a suit. Helpful tip: The farther up on the hillside it is, the cleaner (and smaller) the hot pool is likely to be.

For strong hikers, however, the hot springs are just a launching point. From here, separate trails lead up the valley to **Boulder Lake** (moderately difficult; 11.6 miles round trip) and **Appleton Pass** (difficult; 15.2 miles round trip). Both are excellent day-hike or weekend backpacking destinations—and can be packed to the gills on sunny summer weekends. Boulder Lake has good campsites, good fishing for brook trout, and a tempting side trip for would-be mountaineers—a steep scramble to the summit of nearby Boulder Peak. Don't do it in the spring without an ice ax. Appleton Pass offers acres of alpine wildflowers, magnificent views of Mount Carrie and the spectacular Bailey Range, and access to the Soleduck River/High Divide/Seven Lakes Basin trail system. Sol Duc Hot Springs Resort is 7.3 miles down and west of the pass; shuttle hikers can make a 15.5-mile one-way hike in either direction. (See the Lake Crescent and the Upper Soleduck chapter.)

Back down on the lower portion of the Elwha River Road, about 2 miles south of US 101, children or those looking for just a short stroll will enjoy the **Madison Falls Trail** (easy; 1.5 miles round trip). It's a nice picnic spot, and the trail to this pretty waterfall is wheelchair accessible.

Outside the park

Another good day-hiking destination in the region is Salt Creek Recreation Area (see Camping, below), where unmaintained trails begin behind the children's playground and lead several miles to a deep-water cove on the Strait of Juan de Fuca and to the top of **Striped Peak,** where a viewpoint offers a pilot's-eye outlook on the strait and Vancouver Island. In Port Angeles itself, the city's new **Waterfront Trail** (easy; optional lengths) is an enjoyable, flat walk along the working waterfront and out onto Ediz Hook. Much of the trail, part of a converted railway, runs along industrial areas, but views of Mount Baker and the North Cascades are very nice, and seals and sea lions sometimes will gaze at you with moonpie eyes from the harbor. The trail, still a work in progress, will be 10 miles long when it's finished. Park and begin at the City Pier, near the foot of Lincoln Street.

For hiking and backpacking supplies and advice, consult Olympic Mountaineering, Front and Oak Streets, Port Angeles; (360) 452-0240.

Camping

Olympic National Park

Heart o' the Hills campground (see Hiking/Backpacking, above) is the primary attraction. The park, perched at Olympic's northern gateway, is an unusually nice campground set in the tall, thin trees. It's quiet, clean, and generally packed with RVs from Nebraska all summer. But you can usually stumble into a site midweek without too much trouble. The campground has 105 sites (no hookups; RVs to 21 feet). The evening campfire talks are usually worth your while, or at least they used to be before the federal government dispensed with such frivolities. Beware the predatory night-stalking raccoons, particularly Old Three Legs, one of our longtime friends. Heart o' the Hills is open all year, weather permitting. Campsites ($10) cannot be reserved. *On Hurricane Ridge Rd 5 miles south of Port Angeles; (360) 452-0330.*

Farther east, **Deer Park,** open during summer months only, is a bit more primitive, a lot more remote, and . . . well, miserably dusty in the dry season. But hey: the view is tough to beat. At 5,400 feet, this is one of the more lofty campgrounds in the state, and the view of the Strait of Juan de Fuca, Dungeness Valley, and most of North Puget Sound is unique. The 18 tent sites are almost an afterthought. Deer Park, the former site of one of Washington's earliest ski lodges, is no place for RVs. The camp recently was changed to tents-only. The campground is open from mid-June to first snows in October. Campsites ($8) cannot be reserved. *From US 101 about 3 miles east of Port Angeles, follow Deer Park Rd 18 miles to the campground at road's end; (360) 452-0330.*

Nine miles west of the city, the Elwha River entrance to Olympic (see Hiking/Backpacking, above) is the gateway to two small but very nice campgrounds on the peaceful Elwha valley floor. The first, **Elwha,** has 41 sites (no hookups; RVs to 21 feet) set in fairly thick forest. A kitchen shelter covers you in extremely bad weather, of which there is much in the winter. Elwha is open all year. Sites ($10) cannot be reserved. *On Elwha River Rd 3 miles south of US 101; (360) 452-0330.*

The location of the second, **Altaire,** makes it more popular. Although it's situated in deep woods that rarely allow the sun to shine through, Altaire is right on the banks of the Elwha, with some sites fronting the clear, cold waters. Snaring a site can be challenging here. There are only 30 to be found (no hookups; RVs to 21 feet). Altaire is open from June to late September. Sites ($8) cannot be reserved. *On Elwha River Rd 4 miles south of US 101; (360) 452-0330.*

Clallam County

About 20 miles west of Port Angeles, **Salt Creek Recreation Area,** one of the state's more scenic (and most-overlooked) campgrounds, sits perched on a bluff above the Strait of Juan de Fuca. Salt Creek, the crown jewel of Clallam County's park system, is the former home of Camp Hayden, a World War II–era 16-inch-gun emplacement. Today, the park's 90 campsites (no hookups; no maximum RV length for half the sites), situated either on a steep bluff above Tongue Point or in a terraced, grassy field in the center of the park, are a wonderful escape any time of the year. Nearly every site offers a gorgeous view of the Strait of Juan de Fuca, where you can watch the parade of cargo and military ships, peer across to Victoria, or scan for orca whales, otters, and sea lions in the salt water. Striped Peak, which looms above the campground to the east, is ringed by hiking trails and old Department of Natural Resources logging roads that make for fine daylong exploration (see Hiking/Backpacking, above). If your eyes are sharp, you might even stumble upon buried ruins of the park's military past. Nearby Tongue Point is one of Washington's best tidal-pool viewing spots (see Beaches, below). Added bonus: coin-op showers. Salt Creek is open all year. Sites ($10) cannot be reserved. *Follow US 101 west from Port Angeles 5 miles to Hwy 112, proceed 8 miles west, then take Camp Hayden Rd 3 miles north to the campground; (360) 928-3441.*

North of Lake Crescent on Hwy 112 is **Lyre River,** a free, semiprimitive Department of Natural Resources campground with 11 sites and piped water. *From the end of East Beach Rd at Piedmont, take Piedmont Rd north to Hwy 112; go west on Hwy 112 to near milepost 46 and turn right, proceeding another half mile north; (360) 902-1000.*

Beaches

Much of the shoreline of the Strait of Juan de Fuca in this area is inaccessible due to steep, hazardous cliffs or off-limits because of private property. But isolated access points are worth the search.

One of the best is right in downtown Port Angeles. **Ediz Hook,** the sand finger formed over the centuries by the surging Elwha River, stretches several miles into the strait, and is accessible by trail and car. The best way to get there: park downtown near the City Pier and follow the 8-mile Waterfront Trail, either on foot or bicycle (see Hiking/Backpacking, above). The paved trail runs from the site of the old Rayonier Mill to the end of Ediz Hook. While you're there, check out the pier and surrounding park, including a steel observation tower offering great views across the strait and into the Olympic foothills. The shoreline along the trail skirts the recently designated Valley Creek Estuary.

West of town, **Freshwater Bay County Park** is a little-known oasis on the shores of the Strait of Juan de Fuca. The 17-acre park has 1,450 feet of shoreline, a nicely landscaped picnic area with a shelter, a boat ramp, and rest rooms. The upper picnic area, rest room, and shelters are open May to September. The lower picnic site, launch ramp, and beach access are open all year. It's 10 miles west of Port Angeles via US 101 and Hwy 112, then 3 miles north on Freshwater Bay Rd; (360) 417-2291.

Farther west, the **Tongue Point Marine Reserve** at Salt Creek Recreation Area is one of the best places in the state to explore tidal pools. The rocky point juts far into the strait, providing acres of exploration at low tide. Remember to leave everything where you found it.

Just to the west, sprawling **Crescent Beach** looks extremely tempting. It's the nicest stretch of sand in this part of the state. Regrettably, it's under private ownership, and you'll have to pay a fee at the nearby campground just to wiggle your toes in the sand. For years, we've been urging Clallam County to buy the beach and add it to Salt Creek Recreation Area. But they keep making some excuse about money.

Skiing/Snowshoeing

Hurricane Ridge is Olympic National Park's primary playground in the winter, and its only established ski venue. The 17-mile road from Port Angeles usually is plowed only Saturday through Monday by park rangers, who reserve the right not to open it at all if weather gets too rough, or if they're shorthanded—or if they don't feel like it. In some years, such as the record-breaking snowfall winter of 1998–99, the road can be closed for weeks at a time. Be sure to call the 24-hour recorded message, (360) 452-0329, before you head out. The Park Service recently began experimenting with a shuttle bus to the summit; ask at the visitors center; (360) 452-0330. Cross-country skiing can be very good on the ridge. It also can be very bad. While the area gets a lot of snow, it's often wind-crusted or just plain glare ice. No fun on skinny skis, to say the least. Most cross-country ski routes begin and end in the Hurricane Ridge parking lot. A popular trail runs west along the (snow-buried) road to the **Hurricane Ridge Picnic Area** and beyond to the Hurricane Hill Trail (see Hiking/Backpacking, above). From here, backcountry telemark skiers and snowshoers fan out along the ridge's deep, windblown snow crust. Venturing very far in this direction is for the experienced only. The terrain is hazardous, particularly on the north side of the ridge, where, unbeknownst to you, the cornice you stand on might be jutting waaay out over sheer cliffs. A much tamer cross-country route runs along the (closed-to-traffic) **Obstruction Point Road,** which winds 8.5 miles through nice alpine scenery to a ski club–maintained cabin at Waterhole. Experienced snow travelers can venture beyond, all the way to storm-blasted Obstruction Point, for winter campouts. This is a particularly good route for snowshoers, for whom crusted snow is much less of a problem than skinny-ski fanatics.

Downhillers and snowboarders get their kicks at the ridge, too. A **poma lift** runs weekends only for skiers and tubers. The vertical isn't much, but hey, it's a lift, and if you're stuck in Port Angeles all winter, it's worth the trip. Lift tickets are $15.

Snowshoers find Hurricane Ridge snow much to their liking, whatever the conditions. Park naturalists lead **guided snowshoe nature walks** on Saturdays, Sundays, Mondays, and holidays through March. Call (360) 452-0330 for details. The walks last about 90 minutes, and snowshoes are provided. Those who bring their own often set off down Obstruction Point Road, or just ply the deep, snowy fields near the Hurricane Ridge Lodge.

For rental skis, snowshoes, supplies, and advice, stop by the Hurricane Ridge Visitors Center on weekends, or consult Olympic Mountaineering, Front and Oak Streets, Port Angeles; (360) 452-0240.

Fishing

Before the big Northwest salmon crash of the 1980s, Port Angeles and nearby Strait of Juan de Fuca hot spots such as Freshwater Bay and even Ediz Hook were among the most choice **king salmon**–fishing waters in Washington. No longer, thanks to tight new restrictions to protect threatened coho runs. Unfortunately, the strait is the funnel through which all Puget Sound salmon stocks run, and it's not practical to fish for hatchery kings without hooking wild coho and other troubled stocks. Result: the strait **coho** and **chinook** fishery has been nearly shut down in recent years. But sporadic fishing for those species, and more frequent fishing for **other salmon** and **bottomfish,** still goes on in the strait. Call the Department of Fish and Wildlife or pick up a state fishing pamphlet, for current seasons and restrictions. The seasonal highlight is Port Angeles Derby Days in late August. It's one of the state's oldest and most prominent derbies. When fishing's open, you can still hop a charter out of Port Angeles and set out after a hefty chinook. Call Port Angeles Charters, (360) 457-6983, for rates and details.

Inland, two dams blocking salmon spawning on the mighty Elwha River haven't prevented **trout** from flourishing there. The lower river inside the park and Lake Mills, behind the Glines Canyon Dam, are noted trout fisheries. The Elwha is open from June 1 to October 31, artificial flies and lures only, 12-inch minimum size. Lake Mills usually is open from the last Saturday in April to October 31, artificial flies and lures only, 12-inch minimum size, two-fish limit. Licenses aren't required inside the national park, but be sure to check seasonal regulations at the Elwha Ranger Station. Someday, you might be able to fish for salmon in the upper Elwha: the two fish-killing lower Elwha Dams now are owned by Olympic National Park. Only a lack of allocated federal demolition/restoration money keeps them standing. West of the city toward Sekiu, the Lyre River is a noted **trout** and **steelhead** stream. And down US 101 to the west, Lake Crescent provides one of the state's most unusual boat fisheries for many trout species (see the Lake Crescent and the Upper Soleduck chapter). A local guide for **salmon, trout,** and **steelhead** fishing on Peninsula Rivers is Dave Rice of Diamond Back Guide Service; (360) 452-9966.

Boating/Sailing

Pleasure boaters can find guest moorage, fuel, and **marine supplies** year-round at the port-operated Port Angeles Boat Haven, (360) 457-4505, at the southwest corner of the main harbor. Just to the east, the City Pier, (360) 457-0411, has guest moorage and more limited facilities, summer only. A **public boat launch** popular with anglers is at Freshwater Bay County Park (see Beaches, above), west of the city off Hwy 112. This also is a good launch point for small craft such as kayaks.

Biking

Port Angeles isn't a noted cycling venue, but the 18-mile **Hurricane Ridge Road** is a challenge many cyclists find irresistible every summer. It's incredibly long, incredibly steep, incredibly torturous. But hey: if you do it, you can pretty much take the rest of your life off. The lower 2.4 miles of the **Olympic Hot Springs Trail** (see Hiking/Backpacking, above) follow an old roadway, and are open to mountain bike use. But wheels are forbidden on all other national park trails in this area, except the Spruce Railroad Trail at Lake Crescent (see the Lake Crescent and the Upper Soleduck chapter). Also, some paths in the Olympic National Forest to the southeast (see the Olympic National Forest and the East Slope Olympics chapter) are fat-tire friendly. Cyclists of all kinds will find the city's long, flat **Waterfront Trail** a pleasant place to ride on a hot day.

For cycle rentals, supplies, and advice, see Pedal 'n' Paddle, 120 E Front Street, (360) 457-1240.

Wildlife Watching/Photography

Bring the wide-angle lenses. Many fantastic mountainscapes can be bagged right from the parking lot at **Hurricane Ridge** (see Hiking/Backpacking, above). Some of the park's most spectacular peaks are visible from here, including portions of 7,965-foot Mount Olympus, the crown jewel of the Olympic chain. Far below, the often fog-draped Elwha River valley provides a stunning contrast to the alpine peaks. Wildlife is plentiful at Hurricane Ridge, too. (So much so that park rangers have taken to shooting paint balls to mark "over-aggressive" deer that beg treats from tourists.) A weekend backpack trip to **Grand Valley** can yield delightful results, whether you're after summer wildflowers, alpine vistas, or **marmots, deer,** and **black bear.** Another good, and easier, wildflower-shooting venue is the **Hurricane Hill Trail.** Try it in June, as soon as the snow melts. In the fall and winter, when shooting on Hurricane Ridge is a tough bet, thanks to the fog, wind, and rain, make a drive to the **Elwha River Valley,** where wildlife often is spotted beneath the valley's big broadleaf trees. Sunset shooters, note: We've seen some prize-winning shots nabbed from the rocky beach at **Salt Creek Recreation Area.**

Kayaking/Rafting

Olympic Raft and Guide Service, 123 Lake Aldwell Rd, (888) 452-1443, www.northolympic.com/olympicraft/; runs float trips on the **Elwha, Hoh,** and **Queets Rivers.** These are primarily placid, nonintimidating tours, with an emphasis on wildlife and natural history. Definitely worth investing a day. The Elwha trip is a short run from Altaire Campground to Elwha Resort, on US 101.

That same route is popular among kayakers. The stretch of river is intermediate (Class II to III). Beware the upper stretch of river between Glines Canyon Dam and Altaire. The Gorge Drop Rapids just above the campground are Class IV to V, and should be attempted only by courageous experts.

Llama Trekking

Some of Olympic National Park's most fabulous trails pass through sensitive meadows that are closed to pack animals, but they're not closed to llamas—agile, strong packers that allow you to get deep into the wilderness without destroying your back on the way. Kit's Llamas, Olalla, Kitsap County, (253) 857-5274, offers guided treks into the park.

Accessible Outdoors

Olympic National Park facilities are well equipped for wheelchair access, including the **Park Visitors Center** in Port Angeles, the **Hurricane Ridge Visitors Center** and two **picnic areas** beyond, and the **Meadow Loop Trails** that begin in the Hurricane Ridge parking lot (see Hiking/Backpacking, above). Also wheelchair accessible is the first half mile of the **Hurricane Hill Trail** (see Hiking/Backpacking, above), which is partially paved, with grades of 2 to 6 percent, and the **Boulder Creek Trail** to Olympic Hot Springs. **Altaire, Elwha, Deer Park, and Heart o' The Hills campgrounds** in Olympic National Park also offer barrier-free camping and rest rooms. In the Elwha area, **Madison Falls Trail** is a barrier-free trail leading to a 100-foot waterfall over basalt cliffs. Note: A 24-hour message on how to receive park information is available to TDD users by calling the park's TDD-dedicated telephone, (360) 452-0306. Non-TDD users can get information at (360) 452-0330.

In the lower Elwha area, the **Elwha Rearing Channel** has a barrier-free wildlife-viewing area. From Port Angeles, drive 4 miles west on US 101 to Laird Road. Turn right and continue a mile to Elwha Road. Proceed to the hatchery, below the Elwha Dam, on Crown Z Water Road. Also, **Salt Creek Recreation Area** (see Camping, above) has barrier-free camping and rest rooms.

To the east, the DNR's **Lyre River** access (see Camping, above) offers barrier-free camping, rest rooms, and bank fishing.

outside in

Restaurants

C'est Si Bon ★★   Yes, it is good—especially if you're yearning for classic French cooking. $$$; 23 Cedar Park Dr, Port Angeles; (360) 452-8888. &

Chestnut Cottage ★   Come here for an exceptional breakfast in Victorian-style surroundings. $$; 929 E Front St, Port Angeles; (360) 452-8344. &

Hacienda del Mar ★   A reincarnation of a longtime favorite Mexican restaurant. $; *408 S Lincoln, Port Angeles; (360) 452-5296.* &

Port Angeles Brewing Company ★★   An upscale but comfortable restaurant with a bar and a sophisticated menu. $$; *134 W Front St, Port Angeles; (360) 417-9152.* &

Thai Peppers ★★   The menu here offers a mix of flavors for both bold and timid taste buds. $; *222 N Lincoln St, Port Angeles; (360) 452-4995.* &

Lodgings

B. J.'s Garden Gate ★★   The newness of this bed-and-breakfast is softened by charming gardens. $$$; *397 Monterra Dr, Port Angeles; (360) 452-2322 or (800) 880-1332; www.bjgarden.com.*

Five SeaSuns ★   A well-kept 1926 Dutch colonial house with sunny, polished rooms. $$–$$$; *1006 S Lincoln, Port Angeles; (360) 452-8248 or (800) 708-0777; www.seasuns.com.*

Tudor Inn ★★   One of the oldest, best looking B&Bs in town, done turn-of-the-century-style. $$; *1108 S Oak St, Port Angeles; (360) 452-3138; www.tudorinn.com.*

More Information

Clallam Parks and Recreation: *(360) 417-2291.*
Clallam Transit System: *(800) 858-3747 or (360) 452-4511.*
North Olympic Peninsula Visitors and Convention Bureau:
    (800) 942-4042; www.northolympic.com.
Olympic Mountaineering: *Front and Oak Streets; (360) 452-0240.*
Olympic National Park Headquarters: *(360) 452-4501;*
    www.nps.gov/olym.
    Road and Weather Updates: *(360) 452-0329.*
    Visitors Center: *(360) 452-0330.*
    Visitors Information: *(360) 452-0330.*
    Wilderness Information Center: (summers only): *(360) 452-0300.*
Port Angeles Visitors Center: *121 Railroad; (360) 452-2363;*
    www.portangeles.org.

Lake Crescent
and the Upper
Soleduck

From the northeast corner of Lake Crescent southeast to High Divide and the Bailey Range in Olympic National Park, including Fairholm Campground, Sol Duc Hot Springs Resort, Sol Duc and Marymere Falls, and the Seven Lakes Basin.

Spirits lurk in every nook and cranny here. You can feel them on the eerily blue waters of Lake Crescent, smell them in the thick bark of 400-year-old fir trees standing guard over the wildlands in the upper Soleduck Valley. The lake and the valley are the passageway to some of the Olympic Mountains' most soul-stirring spots: magnificent waterfalls plunging 100 feet through ancient trees; high mountain passes on obsidian-blade-sharp ridgelines; mountaintop vistas that challenge, combat, and ultimately defeat even the most mulish human ego.

It's no wonder the region's native people, the Quileutes and Clallams, consider much of this area sacred. Their legends live on: Lake Crescent's creation by a vengeful Storm King Mountain, who grew so angry about warring between local tribes that he hurled part of himself into the Lyre River Valley, creating Lake Crescent. The creation of Sol Duc and Olympic Hot Springs by lightning fish who battled endlessly, only to retreat in defeat by burying themselves in the earth, forever to shed steaming tears. Look high up to Storm King's face, or settle deep into the Sol Duc's waters, and it's not so hard to imagine the legends coming to life.

And new legends are created here every year by new inhabitants of the lake and valley: nature lovers who trek here year-round to pursue a rare Lake Crescent trout, stand in awe at the base of a house-size tree, breathe in the soothing mist of a plunging waterfall, or watch powerful salmon and steelhead launch themselves at a wall of whitewater. Many a lifetime memory has been made here by explorers passing through by boot, boat, or bike.

Lake Crescent and the Upper Soleduck Valley are a highlight of Olympic National Park and thus a can't-miss stop on any outdoor lover's tour of Washington State. For us, the region today is exactly what it has been to local inhabitants for eons: a source of fear, mystery, passion, inspiration—and, inevitably, unadulterated awe.

Getting There

From Port Angeles, follow US Highway 101 southwest 22 miles to the east shore of Lake Crescent. Proceed another 13 miles around the lake's south shore to reach the west shore (Fairholm Campground area). Other amenities, such as Lake Crescent Lodge and the Storm King Ranger Station, are located near mid-lakeshore on US 101. To reach the Soleduck area, proceed another 3 miles west of Lake Crescent on US 101 to Soleduck River Road. Turn south and continue 13 miles to Sol Duc Hot Springs Resort, Sol Duc Campground, and the Soleduck Valley trailhead.

inside out

Hiking/Backpacking

Note that Wilderness Permits are required for all overnight stays in the park, and a per-day fee is charged. Quota systems are in effect for some popular backcountry campsites. Permits are not required for day hikes. (See the Olympic National Park: Overview chapter for more permit information.) For a full list of hikes and current trail conditions, contact the Olympic National Park Visitors Center, (360) 452-0330. Call (360) 452-0300 for permit information.

Lake Crescent area

By all means, bring your boots. The northwest corner of Olympic National Park, where Lake Crescent and the upper Soleduck Valley reside, is the takeoff point for some of the most memorable day hikes and backpack treks in the Northwest. Options range from flat, easy trails—such as the Spruce Railroad grade along Lake Crescent's north shore—to the rugged, stunning alpine country of High Divide, between the Hoh and Soleduck River drainages in the interior Olympics.

Here's a list of our best bets:

An easy, popular day hike just off US 101 is the **Marymere Falls Trail** (easy; 2 miles round trip), which begins near Storm King Ranger Station on the lake's south shore (turn where signs indicate Lake Crescent Lodge). Follow the Barnes Creek Trail about a half mile to the Marymere Falls turnoff, where the trail climbs a moderate grade to the 100-foot falls, set against a brilliant green backdrop. The first half mile of this trail is wheelchair accessible. From the same Barnes Creek Trail, you can hang a left after about a third of a mile, and climb up the **Mount Storm King Trail** (difficult; 6.2 miles round trip), which climbs to a fine overlook of Lake Crescent, 4,200 feet. Warning: The top portion of the trail decays into loose, crumbly rock. No place for young ones. Watch your step. Also departing from the Storm King Ranger Station area is the **Moments in Time Nature Trail,** a flat, half-mile loop that winds through old-growth forest and offers nice views of the lake. The trailhead is between Olympic Park Institute and Lake Crescent Lodge.

Almost directly opposite the Storm King area, on the lake's north shore, two other hiking trails depart. The first, **Pyramid Mountain Trail** (moderate; 7 miles round trip), climbs 2,400 feet to Pyramid's 3,100-foot summit, with grand views of the lake and northern Olympics. The trailhead is on North Shore Road, about 3 miles beyond Fairholm Campground (see Camping, below). It's a huffer-puffer in places. Continuing another several miles to the end of North Shore Road brings you to the western trailhead of the **Spruce Railroad Trail** (easy; 8 miles round trip). The Spruce Trail, one of the more underrated hikes in this part of the park, follows Lake Crescent's north shore on the path of a World War I–era railroad, which once hauled Sitka spruce logs to build warplanes. Now it hauls only Vibram soles and mountain bikes. This is one of the few trails in Olympic National Park where mountain biking won't get you a big fat ticket. (Many cyclists choose to circumvent the narrow, windy stretch of US 101 on the opposite shore of Lake Crescent by riding this trail.) The path is a peaceful stroll along a truly unusual lake, with plenty of oddities—abandoned railroad tunnels, bridges, and the like—along the way to keep the whole family engaged. it's also a good trail to consider in the winter, when most Olympic trails are under snow. The eastern trailhead is near Log Cabin Resort (see Camping, and Lodgings, below).

Soleduck River area

From the main trailhead in the Soleduck area, separate trails lead up either side of the river into the stunning Soleduck valley, filled to the brim with ancient fir and hemlock behemoths. For a cool, easy day hike, follow the **Soleduck River Trail** up the north bank to refreshing Sol Duc Falls (easy; 1.5 miles round trip). It's a picturesque, 40-foot silvery free fall—

Backpackers pick their way along a ridge at High Divide in the Upper Soleduck

well worth your valuable vacation time and effort, and easily photographed from the footbridge over the river. Return the way you came, or cross the river here and return on the south bank, thus making the so-called **"Lover's Lane Loop"** of about 6 miles from Sol Duc Campground. Stronger day hikers or overnighters can cross the bridge at Soleduck Falls and follow the **Canyon Creek Trail** another 3 miles up to Deer Lake (moderate/difficult; 7.5 miles round trip). The lake is an ideal overnight backpack spot, with plenty of choice campsites. It's also a perfect first-night stopover for those continuing on to High Divide. And as if you needed to ask: yes, there are deer. Cute to the point of being annoying.

The **High Divide Loop** (difficult; 19 miles round trip) is the granddaddy of all backpacking routes in this area, if not on the entire peninsula. From Deer Lake, the High Divide Trail climbs above the treeline into spectacular **Seven Lakes Basin,** a string of jewel-like tarns on the north side of High Divide. Campsites are excellent, but smooshed to death by overuse. Limits are now in effect for summer overnight visitors. From here, the trail climbs up the spine of the sharp ridge dividing the Hoh and Soleduck River drainages. The walk along the top is nothing short of spectacular, with acres of wildflowers at your feet and unimpeded views of the interior Olympics before your eyes. The loop tops out at the summit of **Bogachiel Peak** (7.8 miles, 5,474 feet), where the view across the Hoh to Mount Olympus will sear itself into your memory. The loop continues to

Heart Lake, then intersects with the **Appleton Pass Trail** (see the Port Angeles and Hurricane Ridge chapter) at about 15 miles, before dropping 5 miles back down the Soleduck River to the trailhead. Note: The High Divide Loop is impassable until midsummer, usually July. Basic mountaineering skills (ice ax and rope-rescue knowledge) are necessary to negotiate the divide anytime snow is present.

Also from the Soleduck area, the **Mink Lake Trail** (easy; 5 miles round trip) is a good day hike from Sol Duc Hot Springs Resort, and the **Ancient Groves Nature Trail** (easy; 1 mile round trip) is a pleasant, kid-friendly walk through a stand of old-growth trees along Soleduck River Road. If getting away from people is high on your list, head 4 miles back down the Soleduck River Road to the **North Fork Soleduck Trail** (moderate; 18 miles round trip). It's a peaceful, up-and-down trail through old-growth forest to the North Fork, a noted trout-fishing stream. The river is reached at about 2.5 miles, but you can continue much farther upstream, leaving tourists and/or annoying family members far behind.

Camping

Choices are somewhat limited, so site-sleuthing is a key skill in summer months. On Lake Crescent, **Fairholm Campground** on the far western shore has 88 sites (no hookups; RVs to 21 feet), all within a short stroll of Lake Crescent. The campground has a nice play area and swimming beach (brrrrr!), and good campfire programs in the summer. It's by far the best local camping area. All the Lake Crescent–area hikes described in Hiking/Backpacking, above, are within a short drive or cycling distance. Fairholm, an Olympic National Park site, is open all year. Sites ($10) cannot be reserved. *On North Shore Rd, just north of US 101 on the west side of Lake Crescent, 26 miles southwest of Port Angeles; (360) 452-0330.*

Sol Duc Campground near Sol Duc Hot Springs has 80 sites, all in the trees (no hookups; RVs to 21 feet). This is the place to stay if you're day hiking in the Soleduck valley. Sol Duc, a national park site, is open all year, but closes when snow is on the ground. Sites ($10) cannot be reserved. *On Soleduck River Rd 13 miles south of US 101; (360) 452-0330.*

A pricey private camping option on Lake Crescent is **Log Cabin Resort,** which has 40 sites (full hookups; unlimited RV length) within a short distance of the lake's east shore. Great access to the Spruce Railroad Trail (see Hiking/Backpacking, above). Check your bank account before you go, however. At this writing, hookup sites were $32 per night, plus an additional $6.64-per-night fee for pets! Log Cabin Resort is open all year, weather permitting. Sites can be reserved. *From US 101 about 18 miles southwest of Port Angeles, turn north on East Beach Rd and proceed 3 miles;*

(360) 928-3325; www.logcabinresort.net.

A bit farther removed is **Klahowya,** an Olympic National Forest campsite farther down US 101. The campground has 25 tent sites and 30 RV sites (no hookups; RVs to 30 feet). Klahowya is open from May to October, with limited winter services. Campsites cannot be reserved. *Just south of US 101, about 8 miles west of Lake Crescent; (360) 374-6522.*

Fishing

Lake Crescent holds some monsters. And we don't mean a Nessie or Ogopogo sea creature. When the region's first settlers built cabins on the shores of Lake Crescent, the deep, icy waters held two trout species not found anywhere else on the planet: the **Beardslee trout** (a sort of oversize rainbow), and the **Crescentii** (a member of the cutthroat family). Sadly, both breeds now have intermingled with other hatchery-produced species. But that doesn't reduce the thrill of trolling the lake's incredible depths for big fish. They're a tricky prey, especially since fishing with bait is illegal in the lake. You'll need a boat, a trolling motor, and the right gear. Inquire about all three at Lake Crescent Lodge, (360) 928-3211, or Log Cabin Resort, (360) 928-3325. The lake is open from the last Saturday in April to October 31, artificial flies and lures only, two-fish limit, 20-inch minimum size.

River fishing also can be fine in this area. The Soleduck River is open below Soleduck Falls from June 1 to October 31, and the minimum-size restriction says something about the size of the **trout:** bag limit is two, minimum length 14 inches. The river is closed between August 1 and October 31 within 100 yards upstream and 250 yards downstream of the Soleduck's Salmon Cascades (see Wildlife Watching, below). Native **steelhead, bull trout,** and **dolly varden** must be released. Licenses are not required for fishing inside the national park.

Biking

Road cycling isn't ideal in this area, thanks—or no thanks—to winding roads and narrow shoulders. Only truly determined US 101 through-riders take the challenge of the long, winding traverse around Lake Crescent. The **Soleduck River Road,** however, makes a nice 13-mile one-way ride for cyclists camped at Fairholm or Sol Duc Campground. Mountain bikers who love Olympic National Park often wind up in the Fairholm area, because the nearby **Spruce Railroad Trail** is one of the few trails in the park accessible to mountain bikes. From the campground, the 5-mile ride on North Shore Road to the Spruce trailhead leads to an 8-mile round-trip ride on the Spruce Trail, along Lake Crescent's north shore. The total trip up the lake and back to Fairholm is about 18 miles—a good day's outing for average riders. Pack a lunch, pick a scenic spot along the lake, and make a day of it. For rentals, see the Port Angeles and Hurricane Ridge chapter.

Boating/Canoeing/Kayaking

Small boats can be launched at Fairholm and Log Cabin Resort on **Lake Crescent.** Both places also rent small boats, as does Lake Crescent Lodge. Beaches at Fairholm and East Beach are good launching points for canoes and sea kayaks.

Experienced river runners can get a workout on the **Upper Soleduck,** a stretch of river rated as advanced, with many Class III rapids. Most floaters put in at the bridge several miles up South Fork Soleduck Road. Klahowya Campground on US 101 (see Camping, above, and in the Neah Bay, Lake Ozette, and Sekiu chapter) has another good river access. Below there, the river is often dotted by anglers' drift boats. But some floaters continue downstream to the Bear Creek fishing access, or all the way to the Sol Duc Hatchery near Sappho. The Soleduck is in best running shape during the spring runoff, generally from April to June.

Wildlife Watching

Deer, black bears, and **marmots** are common sights in the Upper Soleduck River valley, especially at aptly named Deer Lake and along High Divide, where friendly black-tails literally will shove their snouts through the crack in your tent's rain fly. **Bald eagles** and other predatory birds can be seen high in the trees along Lake Crescent's shores.

One of the Olympic peninsula's most engaging wildlife spectacles is the Salmon Cascades, a long, steep rapid on the Soleduck River, 28 miles west of US 101 on Soleduck River Road. A short trail leads to a whitewater overlook, where migrating **steelhead** and **salmon** often are seen launching themselves at the falls. It's mesmerizing, and keeps people coming back year after year. It's possible to see fish jumping here throughout the summer, but fall months are the peak.

Photography

Waterfall shooters can lace up their boots and shoot both **Marymere and Soleduck Falls** in the same day. Bring either a tripod or fairly fast film; light is a precious commodity.

The high vista atop **Bogachiel Peak** on the High Divide Loop (see Hiking/Backpacking, above) is one of the best scenic photo stops in the Northwest. On one side, glacier-capped 7,950-foot Mount Olympus looms above a blanket of old-growth greenery in the Hoh River valley. On the other is an eagle's-eye view straight down to the magnificent Seven Lakes Basin, with Pacific Ocean sunsets serving as a backdrop. An overnight trip to the divide with a lightweight tripod can yield spectacular results. But be warned: Bogachiel Peak's weather gods seem to have their own lens detector. Every time we get here with the right gear, the clouds roll in.

Picnics/Swimming

Fairholm Campground (see Camping, above) has a good swimming/picnicking beach on the west shore of Lake Crescent. Similarly, **East Beach picnic area** on East Beach Road is a sunny spot with an enjoyable flat beach. If you can stand the cold, this is your place. My kid sister Linda ignored all warnings and plunged in here as a kid, and has not been the same since. About halfway up the lake, between Barnes Point and Fairholm, is **La Poel,** a nice lakeside pullout for picnickers.

Accessible Outdoors

Barrier-free Olympic National Park sites in this area include: the first half mile of **Marymere Falls Trail** and the full length of **Moments in Time Nature Trail** (see Hiking/Backpacking, above); in the area near **Lake Cresent Lodge** (the main lodge building and a rest room also are accessible, as is the nearby **Lake Cresent Ranger Station**); pools and several rental cabins at **Sol Duc Hot Spring Resort**; and a wooden view platform above **Salmon Cascades** on the Soleduck River (see Wildlife Watching, above). In addition, **Fairholm** and **Sol Duc Campgrounds** (see Camping, above) offer barrier-free camping, rest rooms, and short interpretive trails. Olympic National Park's **East Beach Access** on Lake Crescent, 17 miles west of US 101 on East Beach Road, has a ramp to the beach, a rest room, and a picnic table. The nearby **West Spruce Railroad trailhead** (see Hiking/Backpacking, above) allows access to the **Spruce Railroad Trail**, one mile of which is accessible, although the first 100 feet are rough and usually require assistance. Note: A 24-hour message on how to receive park information is available to TDD users by calling the park's TDD-dedicated telephone at (360) 452-0306. Non-TDD users can get information at (360) 452-0330.

Elsewhere, **Klahowya Campground** (see Camping, above) offers barrier-free camping, amphitheater, boat launch, rest rooms, and interpretive trail.

outside in

Lodgings

Lake Crescent Lodge ★   Rooms are rustic in the 80-year-old lodge, but the basic cabins can be fun. *$$; 416 Lake Crescent Rd, Port Angeles; (360) 928-3211; www.olypen.com/lakecrescentlodge.* &

Sol Duc Hot Springs Resort   These small cedar-roofed cabins are clustered in a meadow, surrounded by forest. *$$; Sol Duc Rd and Hwy 101, Port Angeles; (360) 327-3583; www.northolympic.com/solduc/index.html.*

More Information

North Olympic Peninsula Visitors and Convention Bureau: *(800) 942-4042; www.northolympic.com.*
Olympic National Forest, Pacific (formerly Soleduck) Ranger District: *Forks; (360) 374-6522.*
Olympic National Park Headquarters: *(360) 452-4501.*
    Road and Weather Updates: *(360) 452-0329.*
    Storm King Ranger Station (summer only): *(360) 928-3380.*
    Visitors Center: *(360) 452-0330.*
    Wilderness Information Center (summer only): *(360) 452-0300.*
Sol Duc Hot Springs Resort: *(360) 327-3583.*

Neah Bay, Lake Ozette, and Sekiu

From Sekiu west to Cape Flattery, south to the south end of Lake Ozette, and east to Lake Crescent, including Cape Alava, Shi Shi Beach, Point of the Arches, Clallam Bay, Pillar Point, and the Flattery Rocks National Wildlife Refuge.

Neah Bay is as close as you can get to Homer, Alaska, without leaving Washington State. Literally. And probably figuratively, too.

It really is the end of the road. Lots of roads. And the farthest northwest point in the United States has all the rustic (emphasis on rust) charm you'd expect, with clean air, mind-boggling scenery, and truly spartan creature comforts. You won't find any four-star resorts out here—or many two-story buildings, for that matter. But the triangle of wild land marked by Neah Bay, Sekiu, and Lake Ozette is a truly grand piece of geometry.

At triangle's top, Neah Bay is a small, struggling fishing village—the longtime home of the Makah Tribe, which has been whaling, fishing, and logging here for at least three millennia. In recent years, the tribe has made global headlines by exercising its treaty right to hunt gray whales; the Makahs harpooned, then shot to death, their first whale in a century in 1999. The future of that endeavor remains unclear. But whaling or no whaling, Neah Bay is likely to continue to hack out a decent living on bottomfishing, sporadic salmon charters, and, increasingly, whale watching, hiking, and camping on its fantastic ocean beaches.

Sekiu—due southeast down the Strait of Juan de Fuca as the cormorant flies—also is a small, struggling fishing village, minus the historical inhabitants. For decades, the town has owed its existence

Taking in the sun on an ocean beach in Olympic National Park

to what until recently was a robust recreational salmon fishery—particularly for hefty chinook salmon—in the strait. That changed radically in the early 1990s, when concerns for troubled Puget Sound salmon stocks led to a near fishing shutdown in the strait. Like many other small Washington coastal communities, the quaint waterfront burg of Sekiu will be forced to adapt or die if fishing fails to recover.

Lake Ozette, the southern end of the triangle, is one of the most popular destinations in Olympic National Park and is the largest natural lake in the state. But the beach strip to its west—including the park's pencil-like, 57-mile coastal strip, the last substantial wilderness ocean beach on the U.S. mainland—is the big show, drawing tens of thousands of visitors each year down a boardwalk trail from the lake to Cape Alava.

The northwest triangle is a must-do for Washington recreators. You'll stand on the very tip of the Lower 48, staring down at the roiling Pacific. And the sunset from Shi Shi Beach makes you wonder how heaven could do it one better.

Getting There

Neah Bay, 75 slow miles west of Port Angeles, is a long haul from Seattle. Plan to spend the bulk of a day getting there, and if you're driving in the summer, pack plenty of slow-traffic patience. Follow directions to Port Angeles (see the Port Angeles and Hurricane Ridge chapter). Proceed west on US Highway 101 to Hwy 112. Follow Hwy 112 west and northwest about 60 miles (the last 20 are winding and narrow) through Clallam Bay and Sekiu to Neah Bay. You can also stay on US 101 to west of Lake Crescent at Sappho, then take Burnt

Mountain Road north to Hwy 112 between Pysht and Sekiu. Lake Ozette is reached from Hwy 112 by turning south on Hoko-Ozette Road, 2 miles west of Sekiu. Drive 18 miles south to the lake and Olympic National Park ranger station.

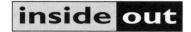

Hiking/Backpacking

Cape Flattery (easy; 1.5 miles round trip), west of Neah Bay, is one of the more memorable day hikes in the Northwest. And it's better than ever now that the old, decaying trail has been rerouted and completely rebuilt by the Makah Tribe, with all new cedar decking over notoriously boggy portions. The area doesn't look like much at first, just a stroll through scrubby forest, across a swamp, and toward a bluff. But the view from the end will brand itself on your memory. The path ends dramatically at a sheer cliff, with the stormy Pacific bashing itself indefatigably on rocks below and against scenic—and eerie—Tatoosh Island, a half mile offshore. The island, a traditional whaling/fishing base and burial ground for the ancient Makahs, holds a Coast Guard lighthouse, built in 1857. Try to imagine being stuck there as the lightkeeper. Not many people could. Some of the earliest keepers reportedly fled in terror of storms, ghosts, and other calamities—real or imagined—before the light was finally automated.

Bring the binoculars: this high bluff is a good spot from which to scan for seals, sea lions, and gray whales, which migrate just offshore in April and May, and again in October and November. Warning: Exercise extreme caution around the cliffs. It's 100 feet down in places. To get there, follow Hwy 112 through Neah Bay, following the road's sharp left bend at the end of town. Turn right at the IHS clinic, drive one block, and, where the road forks in multiple directions, turn left, following signs to the Tribal Center (don't go up the hill). In about 2.5 miles, a quarter mile beyond the Tribal Center, the pavement ends. Proceed another 4 miles to a "Cape Trail" sign, stay left, and find the trailhead in a short distance.

A few miles to the south, **Shi Shi Beach/Point of the Arches** (moderate; 7 miles round trip), the Northwest's most picturesque oceanscape, is officially (wink, wink) off-limits, thanks to a land squabble between Olympic National Park, which owns the beach, and Makah residents, who own the trail through the uplands. Years ago, both parties declared the trail closed until the path could be rerouted and a new trailhead built. But neither party actively discourages hikers from making their way to Shi

Shi. Local Makah residents, in fact, encourage it. They've established a cottage industry here, allowing hikers to park in their yards for a fee. Makah tribal officials say they have no intention of citing hikers for using the trail. So while it's officially closed, Shi Shi remains very much open, and still heavily used. (The Makahs plan a major trail rehab project here, similar to the smaller-scale renovation of the Cape Flattery Trail.)

The current trail wanders about 3.5 miles along the headlands, then down to the spectacular beach area. To the north is Portage Head and a decaying wreck—what's left of the *General M. C. Meigs,* a World War II–era troop ship. A mile to the south is Point of the Arches, a picturesque series of pyramidal sea stacks marching into the Pacific like some half-submerged, stony-spined serpent. Good campsites are found here and there, and fresh stream water is available. This is one of the finest beaches in the country for seascape photography. Many coastal backpackers walk south from here to Cape Alava (see below). From Neah Bay, follow signs to the Air Force base, turning left across the Waatch River after several miles. Follow signs for Sooes Beach and the Makah Fish Hatchery until you see signs for parking near homes on Mukkaw Bay.

The Lake Ozette area is home to another Northwest classic beach hike, the **Cape Alava/Sand Point Loop** (easy/moderate; 6.6 to 9.3 miles round trip). It's actually more of a triangle than a loop. The Cape Alava Trail cuts 3 miles west, mostly on a boardwalk (wear sneakers, not lug soles), through grasslands and forest and past an old homestead, where deer and other wildlife are plentiful. At the ocean, you can wander through what's left (not much) of an archeological dig where Makah long-houses buried in mud 500 to 1,000 years ago were excavated throughout the '70s (the artifacts are in the Makah Tribal Museum in Neah Bay). Many good (and overused; see Important note, below) campsites are found at the Cape Alava beach headland. You can return the way you came, but there's much more to see. Gray whales are often spotted during their spring and fall migrations, and sea lions, seals, otters, and other creatures are seen all year.

About a mile south of Cape Alava are Wedding Rocks, which contain a fascinating series of petroglyphs. Two more miles south, the Sand Point Trail emerges on the beach. This southern leg of the loop leads 3 miles northeast, back to where you started. But keep in mind that in foul, windy weather, it's usually better to hike the loop from south to north, thus keeping the wind at your back on the beach section.

More experienced coastal backpackers (those familiar with tide tables and with skills to cross steep, rocky headlands) can continue south on the beach, about 18 miles, to **Rialto Beach** near La Push (see the Forks and La Push chapter).

Important note: Cape Alava is accessible year-round, but overuse in the summer has led to permit restrictions. Between Memorial Day and Labor Day, all overnight campers must have a free backcountry permit; these are limited to 300 per day and should be reserved in advance. Call Olympic National Park's Wilderness Information Center, (360) 452-0300. The Cape Alava/Sand Point trailhead is well marked; follow signs from Ozette Ranger Station, near the north end of the lake.

Beaches

The trail to **Shi Shi Beach** (see Hiking/Backpacking, above) leads to this area's most spectacular shoreline—57 miles of it, to be exact. But you don't have to hoof it to the Pacific to spend a memorable day on the salt water here. Hwy 112 between Salt Creek Recreation Area (see the Port Angeles and Hurricane Ridge Chapter) and the town of Neah Bay is narrow, winding, and frustrating. But it offers plenty of opportunities for seaside leg-stretching and exploring on the Strait of Juan de Fuca. Here's a sampling:

The county park at **Pillar Point,** 37 miles west of Port Angeles on Hwy 112, is a fantastic beach access. Its launch ramp makes it a good place for kayakers and small-craft owners, although caution should always be exercised in the strait, where vicious winds can appear seemingly out of nowhere. Tides also are a concern here; they create substantial chop as well as a predominantly outgoing pull, sometimes as fast as 10 mph around rocky points.

Up the road a bit, the seaside village of Clallam Bay also offers up a public beach. At the waterfront **Clallam Bay Spit County Park,** you can walk 9,500 feet of shoreline, past the mouth of the Clallam River and out to intriguing tide pools near the Slip Point Lighthouse. Like the Sequim area just to the east, Clallam Bay has served up its share of natural history. A number of ancient marine fossils have been found at Department of Natural Resources' **Beach 426,** a stretch of tidelands beyond the lighthouse.

Just around the corner, downtown Sekiu has beach access too. The **"One Mile Beach" trail** begins at Olson's Resort and extends along a former railroad grade. It's mostly above the beach, but separate trails lead down to several very nice sandy spots on the water.

Between Sekiu and Neah Bay, stop at the beach pullouts for **Snow Creek Campground** (see Camping, below) and **DNR Beach 429,** a state access just east of Neah Bay. Both offer good beach access and views of sea stacks right offshore, and are noted for frequent seabird and marine mammal sightings (see Wildlife Watching, below).

In Neah Bay itself, the Makah Tribe's **Hobuck Beach** is open for picnics, horseback riding, surfing, and friendly arguments over tribal whaling.

Lake Pleasant Community Beach has swimming and a boat launch; on US 101 west of Sappho. **Lake Ozette** has small sections of pleasantly sandy beach near both campgrounds (see Camping, above).

Wildlife Watching

Neah Bay is a notable **seabird**-watching hot spot. More than 250 species are commonly seen at or near Cape Flattery, especially around Tatoosh Island. Mukkaw Bay, just over the Waatch River south of town, is another good birding area. A bird identification guide is available at the Makah Museum, or by contacting the Makah Planning Office; (360) 645-2201. Primary bird-watching season is the dead of winter. **Bald eagles** are most commonly seen in February and March, as they return north to British Columbia after wintering on Puget Sound rivers such as the Nooksack and the Skagit. Look for nesting **murres** on the cliffs of Tatoosh Island in the spring and summer.

Also from Cape Flattery, Shi Shi Beach, and the Cape Alava/Sand Point area, **gray whales** are often seen on their Pacific migration. They're going north in April and May, returning south in October and November. The best thing about seeing them here, as opposed to farther south on the coast, is that they tend to hug the shore off Cape Flattery. **Pilot and humpback whales** also are sometimes observed here, as are **Dall and harbor porpoises, white-sided dolphins,** and **Steller and California sea lions.** You'll only need a simple pair of binoculars to get that rare close-up view. The entire coastal area here is protected as Flattery Rocks National Wildlife Refuge, part of the 3,300-square-mile Olympic Coast National Marine Sanctuary offshore of the Olympic National Park coastal strip.

In the strait, watch for all of the above, plus **orca whales** and a growing population of **sea otters.** Large "rafts" of up to 100 or more male otters are often observed in the strait through the winter months. Females and pups are found primarily in the outer waters, between Cape Alava and Cape Flattery. Reliable wildlife-watching spots along the strait include the Clallam Bay Coast Guard Station, the Clallam River mouth at the county park in Clallam Bay (see Beaches, above), the mouth of the Sekiu River (west of the town of Sekiu), and Shipwreck Point.

If your heart is set on furrier mammals, the trail from Lake Ozette to Cape Alava is famous for its frequent **deer, black bear, raccoon,** and other wild animal sightings. On the lakeshore, especially near Ericsons Bay, marsh areas are habitat for wading birds such as **herons.**

For chartered marine wildlife-watching trips, scuba charters, and guided kayak expeditions in the region, contact Puffin Adventures, (888) 305-2437, www.olypen.com/puffinadventures/, located at Shipwreck RV Park, 8 miles west of Sekiu on Hwy 112.

Fishing

Salmon is king in Sekiu and Neah Bay. Or was. Washington's coastal and Strait of Juan de Fuca salmon-fishing seasons change substantially from year to year. In recent years, the summer salmon fishery here has been limited to "selective" fishing for **sockeye** or hatchery (marked) **coho,** with little or no fishing for chinook salmon, many of which are endangered stocks migrating to Puget Sound–area streams. Call the state Department of Fish and Wildlife, consult its web page, www.wa.gov/wdfw, or pick up a state game fish pamphlet at an outdoors store to get current season and bag limit information. Even when salmon fishing is curbed, the area remains a popular destination for **bottomfish** and winter **blackmouth** (immature chinook) salmon, when weather allows. Also, Neah Bay skippers go fishing for **halibut** in April and May. And keep in mind that salmon fishing sometimes is allowed from shore even when offshore waters are closed.

Once you decipher the fishing seasons, plenty of reputable charter skippers will be standing by, waiting. In Neah Bay, try Big Salmon Resort, (360) 645-2374. In Sekiu, contact Van Riper's Resort, (360) 963-2334, or Olson's Resort, (360) 963-2311. If salmon season is off, most charters will go in search of halibut, **cod, rockfish,** or other species. Ask the skippers.

Fishing is permitted without a license in Lake Ozette, which contains **trout, perch, kokanee,** and other species. Consult the ranger station for limits and restrictions. Boat ramps are found at Swan Bay and at the north end of the lake.

In the spring, Pillar Point Recreation Area (see Beaches, above) is a popular spot to dip **smelt** from the surf.

Camping

The primary public campground in the region is **Lake Ozette,** an Olympic National Park facility that's free but has only 14 sites (no hookups; RVs to 21 feet). The park is open all year. Sites cannot be reserved. *On the north end of Lake Ozette, 23 miles southwest of Sekiu via Hwy 112 and Hoko-Ozette Rd; (360) 452-0330.*

Also at Lake Ozette, **Ericsons Bay** is a small, primitive campground accessible by foot or boat only. The secluded refuge has 15 sites. It's a great overnight spot for canoeists exploring the lake—and the shallow shoreline here is a great swimming hole in summer, when the water warms nicely. A swampy trail leads about 2.2 miles west to the ocean just south of Sand Point. The campground is open all year. No fee; no reservations. *On the northwest shore of Lake Ozette; (360) 452-0330.*

A slew of **private campgrounds** also are available. Mostly gravel lots for anglers' RVs, they're not really suitable for tents, but RVers might favor amenities such as full hookups. Some have good views of the strait or the harbor at Neah Bay. The list includes Neah Bay's Tyee RV Park, (360) 645-2223; and Sekiu's spacious Van Riper's Resort, (360) 963-2334; Olson's Resort, (360) 963-2311; Surfside Resort, (360) 963-2723; and Coho Resort, (360) 963-2333.

Canoeing/Kayaking

The paddle from the north end of **Lake Ozette** to Ericsons Bay Campground on the lake's northwest shore (see Camping, above) is a delightful canoe trip, especially for beginners. The waters of Ozette often are dead calm in the summer, although paddlers should be prepared for a sudden blast of ferocious ocean weather. At the lake's southwest end at Allens Bay is another short trail to the ocean. The lake's many bays and the small Garden and Tivoli Islands make for lots of exploring. Lake Pleasant Community Beach has a **boat launch.**

On the strait, the relatively calm waters of **Clallam Bay** are a good bet for kayakers. The day-use park in downtown Clallam Bay is a good launch spot. For the extreme crowd only, **coastal beaches** south of Cape Flattery are considered prime territory for kayak surfing. Guided kayak tours in stable, ocean boats are offered by Puffin Adventures, (888) 305-2437, www.olypen.com/puffinadventures/; located at Shipwreck RV Park, 8 miles west of Sekiu on Hwy 112.

Scuba Diving

The reefs and kelp forests of the outer strait and Pacific Coast provide prime scuba habitat for experienced divers. The **"One Mile Beach" trail** in Sekiu (see Beaches, above) is a semipopular scuba-diving venue. For local advice, gear, and charter information, contact Curley's Resort and Dive Center, (800) 542-9680, or Puffin Adventures, (888) 305-2437.

Accessible Outdoors

Ozette Campground (see Camping, above) offers barrier-free camping and rest rooms.

More Information

Clallam Parks and Recreation: *(360) 417-2291.*

Clallam Transit System: *(800) 858-3747 or (360) 452-4511.*

Makah Tribal Council: *(360) 645-2201.*

North Olympic Peninsula Visitors and Convention Bureau:
(800) 942-4042; www.northolympic.com.

Olympic National Park Headquarters: *(360) 452-4501;*
www.nps.gov/olym.

Ozette Ranger Station (summer only): *(360) 963-2725.*

Road and Weather Updates: *(360) 452-0329.*

Visitors Center: *(360) 452-0330.*

Wilderness Information Center (summer only): *(360) 452-0300.*

U.S. Coast Guard, Neah Bay: *(360) 645-2311.*

Forks
and La Push

From the Olympic National Forest Information Center on US 101 south to the Bogachiel River, west to La Push, and east to Bogachiel Peak in Olympic National Park, including Rialto Beach, Mora Campground, Bogachiel State Park, and the lower Soleduck, Bogachiel, and Calawah Rivers.

Most of the sparkling rivers draining the mossy west slopes of the Olympics flow together near Forks. So, too, do the dueling passions that mark the past and probable future of the Olympic Peninsula.

The Olympics in general are a study in contrasts, with small oceans of clear-cut devastation yielding views of wilderness areas as pure as any on the planet. The dichotomy is particularly glaring in Forks, a longtime timber community now struggling to cash in on its unparalleled recreation venues—without denying a rich and deeply ingrained tradition of forestry. That's a tall order, and probably wouldn't be possible almost anywhere else in the state. Fortunately, the magnificent natural features surrounding Forks and La Push (a struggling native fishing village on the coast just to the west) have proven powerful enough to accommodate both uses for generations.

For the most part, people in Forks continue to look to the woods with an eye more toward cutting than camping. Likewise, the Quileutes in La Push hope for a renaissance in their own traditional craft, salmon fishing. But economic momentum is beginning to inch the other way. Logging and fishing have largely been halted on public lands by environmental restrictions—the result, it can be argued, of a century of sloppy, wanton overharvesting. And recreeation has—with only minimal urging from the local communities—begun to fill the void. That was inevitable, given the natural treasures that circle these two towns.

The string of ocean beaches to the north and south of La Push is the most pristine, fully accessible chunk of coastline in the Northwest, if not the nation. The surviving old-growth forests around Forks, most notably the upper Bogachiel River drainage, are priceless living memorials to the peninsula's wild past. And less than an hour away in either direction, the spectacular Hoh River Valley and Lake Crescent areas await with their own unique tourist-drawing power. Those are increasingly rare and—as the state's population continues to bulge—increasingly valuable commodities. More than any other towns on the coast, Forks and La Push are poised to take advantage of these assets. The free market of recreational opportunities might, by itself, lead both towns down a prosperous new path.

We wouldn't be surprised to drive through the old timber town of Forks in the year 2005 and see a brand-new placard popping up in local storefront windows: "This business supported by Gore-Tex dollars."

Getting There

Forks is located midway on the 175-mile, north-south Olympic Peninsula coastal stretch of US Highway 101. To reach it from the north, follow US 101 80 miles west and south of Port Angeles. From the south, Forks lies 95 miles north of Aberdeen. La Push, a small tribal fishing village at the mouth of the Quillayute River, is 14 miles southwest of Forks on Hwy 110, also known as La Push Road. Clallam Transit bus service is available from Port Angeles; (360) 452-4511 or (800) 858-3747.

inside out

Beaches

Wild ocean beaches are the primary drawing card for the Olympic Peninsula, and several of the finest are within walking distance of La Push. The center of attention is the Olympic National Park day-use area at **Rialto Beach,** just a stone's skip across the Quillayute River north of La Push, and a short walk or drive from Mora Campground (see Camping, below). Rialto has picnic facilities, a large parking lot, and other amenities. But the beach is the lure. It's a beauty—one of those very few picture-perfect Washington scenes you can drive right up to. A series of sea stacks lurk in the mist to the north, and the unusually steep-sloped beach makes for frothing, always picturesque surf. The beach is almost always windy, but great for strolling, with miles of unobstructed sand beckoning to the north. Rialto also is a major beach-hiking trailhead for coastal backpackers (see Hiking/Backpacking, below). Most single-day visitors walk 1.5 miles up the beach to **Hole in the Wall,** a nifty surf-carved tunnel beneath the jutting headlands. Note: Flooding occasionally plays havoc with some of Rialto's facilities. Check their status with Olympic National Park; (360) 452-0330.

Three other gorgeous ocean beaches are found just south of La Push, all reached from La Push Road/Hwy 110, which crosses the Quillayute River and continues to the ocean. About 3 miles from the river crossing, (12 miles west of US 101), look for the **Third Beach** trailhead on the south side of the road. The path leads 1.5 miles to the shore, where a nice waterfall plunges toward the beach's south end at Taylor Point, and tidal pools can be explored near Teahwhit Head, to the north. On the other side of that obstructing headland is **Second Beach,** reached via a three-quarter mile trail from La Push Road/Hwy 110 about a mile south of La Push. Third and Second Beaches are part of Olympic National Park. **First Beach,** on the Quileute Reservation and open to the public, is just south of La Push itself. All of these are great picnic/beachcombing spots, with big, awesome rock walls, kid-luring sea caves, and tons of unidentifiable sea gunk washing up on the beach.

Camping

The best campground in the region is **Mora,** an Olympic National Park site near Rialto Beach (see Beaches, above). Mora's 95 campsites (no hookups; RVs to 21 feet) are spread through several loops in a heavily wooded (dark, almost) flat not far from the Quillayute River. There's not much to see or do in the park itself, but the beach is a short walk away. A group camp for 15 to 40 campers is available and can be reserved on a first-come, first-served basis after March 1. Mora is open all year; sites ($10) cannot be reserved. *On Mora Rd (Hwy 110), 12 miles west of US 101—stay right at the Y where La Push Rd departs to the left; (360) 452-0330 or (360) 374-5460.*

Another good bet—especially for you multiple-days-without-showers US 101 vagabonds—is **Bogachiel State Park,** south of Forks on US 101. It's a simple place, with 40 sites (6 with hookups; RVs to 35 feet) a bit too close to the highway for our taste. But Bogachiel does have hot showers, the best investment of a quarter or two you'll make all summer. The park also has a picnic area and boat launch on the lovely Bogachiel River, a noted steelhead fishery (see Fishing, below). Bogachiel State Park is open all year. Sites cannot be reserved. *On US 101 6 miles south of Forks; (360)*

374-6356 or (800) 233-0321.

The final option is rustic **Klahanie,** a small (12 sites, no hookups), primitive Olympic National Forest site east of US 101. The campground, on the Calawah River, has no drinking water or facilities. It's open summers only. Sites (free) cannot be reserved. *On Forest Rd 29, 5.4 miles east of US 101; (360) 374-6522.*

Hiking/Backpacking

All the hikes below are in Olympic National Park, either its coastal strip or inland. Note that Wilderness Permits are required for all overnight stays in the Olympic National Park backcountry, and a per-hiker fee is charged. See the Olympic National Park: Overview chapter, or contact the park's Wilderness Information Center, (360) 452-0300, for current information.

Most of the prominent hikes in the area involve ocean beaches. The biggie is the **Rialto Beach to Sand Point** (moderate; 18.5 miles one way) trek north up the "Shipwreck Coast," where some scuttled seafaring remnants are still in evidence. It's a 2- to 3-day hike to the popular Lake Ozette area, with plenty of good streamside campsites along the way. (Note: Camping is not allowed on Rialto Beach south of Ellen Creek, about a half-hour's walk north of the Rialto parking lot). To the south of La Push, the **Third Beach trailhead** (see Beaches, above) is the departure point for a 17-mile, 3-day hike south to **Oil City,** near the mouth of the Hoh River. Long-distance beach hikers should be highly aware of tides, and be prepared to cross steep, rocky, often hazardous headlands on this stretch. Bring the rain gear, even if it is August.

If you're just out for the day, several good short beach hikes await. Campers at Mora often prefer to walk, roll, or run the 2-mile road from the campground to Rialto Beach, then walk north to **Hole in the Wall** (easy; about 3 miles round trip). On the south side of La Push, the hike to **Third Beach** (easy; 3 miles round trip) is a pleasant walk from La Push Road, as is the nearby **Second Beach** (easy; 1.5 miles round trip) trail.

Forest fans aren't completely shut out by clear-cuts around Forks. Just south of the town, a long finger of Olympic National Park follows the Bogachiel River toward the ocean, and the land on each side is protected. The **Bogachiel River Trail** (moderate; various lengths possible), which begins at the gated end of Undie Road, 5.5 miles east of Bogachiel State Park, is a fascinating but little-used trail up a lush old-growth valley. This is a wet and wild place. The trail has the look and feel of the famous Hoh River Trail, one valley to the south—but with a tiny fraction of the people. Great campsites are found all along the way, most overlooking the river, which will lull you to sleep at night. Strong trekkers can follow the Bogachiel Trail east all the way to High Divide, 31 miles (although we can't say we know anyone who's actually done this rather than take the shorter route up the Soleduck Valley). Weekend backpackers should consider a trek to the old Bogachiel Shelter site (moderate; about 6 miles one way) or Flapjack Camp (moderate; 8.25 miles one way). It's a very pleasant walk, mostly flat. But the trail can be a bear (a slug?) in the spring or during winter rainy periods, when gushing streams become difficult to ford. The Bogachiel gets hit by as much as 200 inches of rain every year. Watch for Roosevelt elk—and mondo banana slugs.

Fishing

Rivers draining the rain-soaked western Olympics around Forks are among the last best steelhead and salmon waters in the Northwest. The Soleduck, Bogachiel, and Calawah, all of which merge to become the Quillayute just west of Forks for a short, final run to the sea near La Push, are noted highways for winter and summer **steelhead** and numerous **salmon** species. Some form of game fish season is active most of the year, but these rivers' most famous—and productive—fisheries are for spring chinook and winter steelhead.

The Soleduck River's **spring chinook** fishery is legendary, with many salmon up to 50 pounds returning to the Sol Duc Hatchery north of Forks near Sappho. The chinook, because they're so fresh from the ocean, are uncommonly feisty and bright. Landing one from the beach or a drift boat is a thrill not soon forgotten. Because much of the Soleduck between its mouth and the hatchery runs through private property, bank fishing is difficult. Float trips from the **Sol Duc Fish Hatchery** downstream to a takeout off Salmon Road, just north of Forks, are popular. Guided trips are available in Forks. The spring chinook season typically runs April through May.

The **winter steelhead** fishery—which begins in December, peaks in January and February, and tails off by April—is more widespread, with good catch rates in all three local rivers. The trick here is timing. Because these rivers drain temperate rain forest, rain squalls can turn the waters from clear to chocolate-milk brown overnight. It's important to call for river conditions before you set out. And there's always the chance things will change by the time you drive all the way here from Seattle.

For guide referrals, tackle, licenses, season information, and river reports, see or phone Bob Gooding at Olympic Sporting Goods in downtown Forks; (360) 374-6330. For guided fishing trips, contact Three Rivers Resort; (360) 374-5300.

Kayaking/Surfing

First Beach in La Push has a surf often worthy of rides by surfers and/or aggressive sea kayakers. There's good parking and shore access, but you'll have to pack the gear down a substantial hill.

River runners will be challenged by the **lower Soleduck River,** which is rated intermediate (Class II to III) and is best run during the melt-off of spring and early summer. A popular route parallels a favorite fisherman's drift-boat course: from the Sol Duc Hatchery near Sappho downstream to a boat launch off Salmon Road, about 6 miles north of Forks. It's between 7 and 8 miles of river, and elk often are spotted along the banks. Note: Some major rocks lurk in this cold, fast river. Watch your bow.

The **Quillayute River,** the 6-mile stretch from the confluence of the Soleduck and Bogachiel Rivers to the coast near Rialto Beach, is another popular paddling destination. Most paddlers put in at Leyendecker Park near the confluence and take out in the salt water at Rialto. Upstream on the **Bogachiel,** the 15-mile stretch between Bogachiel State Park and Leyendecker County Park is a more challenging daylong trip for advanced paddlers.

Also in the area, Olympic Raft and Guide Service near Port Angeles (888) 452-1443 or online at www.northolympic.com/olympicraft, runs float trips on the Elwha, Hoh, and Queets Rivers.

Photography

Rialto Beach is a photographer's favorite. The hazy beach environment, marked by looming sea stacks and pounding surf, is a sure-fire target, especially at Hole in the Wall, to the north of Rialto Beach parking lot. Big-tree shooters should not overlook the **Bogachiel River Trail** (see Hiking/Backpacking, above). We've shot some grand, tiny-hiker-amid-gargantuan-trees portraits here. In fact, the world's largest silver fir stands proudly on the river's south banks. Look for it about a quarter mile beyond Flapjack Camp. It's that house-size thing with branches.

Wildlife Watching

Peaceful-but-skittish **Roosevelt elk,** high on our list of favorite creatures on the planet, are common in this area, particularly in lowlands near the lower Soleduck and upper Bogachiel Rivers. Bird lovers won't be disappointed by the region's beach sites. We haven't seen them, but rare **ospreys** are said to nest often in snags just north of Rialto Beach. And hundreds of other **shorebirds** are commonly seen from here, as well as at First, Second, and Third Beaches south of La Push. The La Push area is near the geographic center of the Quillayute Needles National Wildlife

Blacktail deer are constant companions to Olympic National Park visitors

Refuge and is part of the Olympic Coast National Marine Sanctuary, so all offshore rocks and islands are protected habitat. Also, we're told **gray whales** often pass very close to Hole in the Wall on their spring and fall migrations to and from Alaska. Finally, an acquaintance who knows one when she sees one reports seeing a **northern spotted owl,** of Northwest timber controversy fame, along the Bogachiel River, just up from Bogachiel State Park.

For chartered marine wildlife-watching trips, scuba charters, and guided kayak expeditions in the region, contact Puffin Adventures, (888) 305-2437, www.olypen.com/puffinadventures.

Accessible Outdoors

Sol Duc Hatchery north of Forks has barrier-free fish viewing. Just past milepost 204 on US 101, turn left on Mary Clark Road and immediately right on Pavel Road. The **Calawah River Public Fishing Access,** just north of Forks on the east side of US 101, has barrier-free rest rooms and river-viewing access. **Bogachiel State Park** (see Camping, above) offers barrier-free camping and rest rooms. **Mora Campground** (see Camping, above) has barrier-free campsites, rest rooms, and an amphitheater. Nearby **Rialto Beach** has a one-tenth-mile barrier-free trail with a Pacific Ocean view, as well as accessible rest rooms and picnic sites.

Restaurants

Si Señora ★ A family-style Mexican joint with more than the usual cheese-sauce-meat affairs. $; *90 Forks Ave, Forks; (360) 374-5414.*

Lodgings

Eagle Point Inn ★★ Cradled in a bend of the Sol Duc River, this lodge combines comfort and style. $$; *384 Stormin' Norman Rd, Forks; (360) 327-3236.*

Huckleberry Lodge The owners of Forks's most fun adventure lodge go the extra mile for guests. $$; *1171 Big Pine Wy, Forks; (360) 374-6008 or (888) 822-6008; www.huckleberrylodge.com.*

Shady Nook Cottage ★ English garden atmosphere at these two cottages just a few blocks from downtown. $$; *81 Ash Ave, Forks; (360) 374-5497; www.northolympic.com/shadynook.*

More Information

Forks Chamber of Commerce: *(800) 44-FORKS; www.forkswa.com.*
Olympic National Forest, Pacific Ranger District, Forks: *(360) 374-6522.*
Olympic National Park Headquarters: *(360) 452-4501; www.nps.gov/olym.*
Mora Ranger Station: *US 101; (360) 374-5460.*
Road and Weather Updates: *(360) 452-0329.*
Visitors Center: *(360) 452-0330.*
Wilderness Information Center (summer only): *(360) 452-0300.*
Olympic Sporting Goods: *(360) 374-6330.*

Central Coast: Hoh, Kalaloch, and Queets

From the Bogachiel River south to the Queets River, west to the Pacific, and east to Mount Olympus in Olympic National Park, including Ruby Beach, the Quillayute Needles National Wildlife Refuge, and Kalaloch and Hoh Rain Forest Campgrounds.

If they only let you out of town once a year to sample the Northwest's wilds, this is probably the place to cash in your pass. The Hoh River, which empties into the Pacific just north of Kalaloch, is the stuff of legend. At its headwaters, 7,965-foot Mount Olympus, the Olympic Peninsula's crown jewel, provides a constant glacial water source, which empties into the Hoh proper for a swift run downstream through one of the unique ecosystems of the world—the Hoh Rain Forest. This is a special, ethereal place, where average annual rainfalls approaching 140 inches fuel a vividly green environment.

The Hoh valley is almost surreal. It's filled with massive, moss-draped spruce, maple, and red cedar trees that are among the oldest living things on the planet. The quiet, misty river bottoms are home to thousands of plant species, as well as herds of Roosevelt elk, one of the state's most regal creatures. The 17-mile walk up the Hoh River to the shoulders—or even the top—of Olympus is one of the nation's classic outdoor treks.

But the charms of the upper Hoh are only half the attraction here. A dozen miles downstream, the river flows into the Pacific on a broad, pristine stretch of ocean beach that's still as wild as any coastline in the United States. Just to the south, Kalaloch (newcomers will quickly learn to say CLAY-lock), the only development on this central stretch of Washington's coastline, offers just enough amenities to make a pilgrimage to the ocean comfortable. Kalaloch's campground is unforgettable, with broad ocean views and a constant breeze to mix the sweet, salty aroma of the Pacific with campfire smoke and percolated coffee. And its comfortable lodge and cabins make for the definitive Pacific Northwest wet-weekend getaway.

Just to the south, the Queets River valley—thanks to a 1953 addition to Olympic National Park, the only rain-forest valley protected from mountains to sea—is an even wilder version of the Hoh, its cousin to the north. The Queets area, accessed by a rugged gravel road stretching 14 miles east of US 101, is a backpacker's heaven, with a lightly traveled trail beginning midway up the river and winding 14.5 miles toward the mighty river's headwaters. Compared to other peninsula river valleys, the Queets is seldom visited, with anglers making up the lion's share of humans most of the year. That's too bad, given the mighty river's status: it's the most powerful single stream on the peninsula, draining much of the park's southwestern interior.

Twin magnificent rain forests sandwiching a healthy serving of pristine ocean beach: no other single area in the Northwest is packed with as much beauty, intrigue, and splendor as this one. Washington, as a state and as a people, would be something much less without it.

Getting There

The Hoh River area, a 3- to 4-hour drive from Seattle via Port Angeles, is reached by traveling 13 miles south of Forks or 21 miles north of Kalaloch on US Highway 101, then following Hoh Rain Forest Road 18 miles east to the Hoh Ranger Station, campground, and day-use area. Kalaloch, an Olympic National Park campground, resort, and day-use area, is 34 miles south of Forks and 30 miles northwest of Lake Quinault on US 101. The Queets River basin is reached by turning east on Queets River Road, 13 miles south of Kalaloch and 20 miles north of Lake Quinault on US 101. The road is gravel, often heavily potholed, and not suited for RVs or very low-clearance vehicles.

inside out

Hiking/Backpacking

A pair of waterproof boots and a rain parka are your tickets to hiking nirvana here. Choose your pleasure: strike out either north or south of Kalaloch on a sprawling ocean beach with picturesque sea stacks and more seagulls than people. Or hoist your pack and walk in awe along two long, flat river valley trails through the planet's most fascinating rain forest, one leading onto the slopes of spectacular Mount Olympus. If there's a more fulfilling place to spend a summer week anywhere on Earth, we haven't found it. Note that Wilderness Permits are required for all overnight stays in the Olympic backcountry, and a per-hiker fee is charged. Contact the park's Wilderness Information Center, (360) 452-0300, for current information.

A series of wonderful rain forest walks begin at the Hoh Visitors Center. For kids and the aerobically challenged, the **Hall of Mosses Trail** (easy; three-quarter-mile loop), which begins and ends near the visitors center, is a good nature-trail primer. Nearby is the **Spruce Nature Trail** (easy; 1.25-mile loop) and a separate paved, quarter-mile **nature loop.**

But there's no reason just about anyone in love with the rain forest should fail to venture up the famous **Hoh River Trail** (easy; 2 to 35 miles round trip), which begins at the visitors center and runs all the way up the Hoh valley—17.5 miles—to Glacier Meadows backcountry camp on the flanks of Mount Olympus. The route is spectacular, winding through mile after mile of magnificent old-growth Sitka spruce, red cedar, bigleaf maple, and fir trees. Some of the trees in this valley are the largest of their kind in the world, and rank among the largest living things on Earth. That's reason enough to make the trek, but the trail provides another: The first 13 miles or so are totally flat, making this an easy walk for even inexperienced hikers. Grassy flats located along the trail make fine campsites, and established camps at **Happy Four Camp** (5.75 miles) and **Olympus Guard Station** (9 miles) are popular overnight spots (they're also good lunch-stop destinations for day hikers).

At 9.2 miles, some longer-distance trekkers turn north on the **Hoh Lake Trail,** which climbs sharply to the **High Divide** area. Many backpackers who have two cars or arrange for shuttle transportation use this trail to link the Soleduck and Hoh River valleys for weeklong backpack trips. Other long-distance hikers will want to follow the Hoh Trail for the full 17.5 miles (the last 4 being very steep) to **Glacier Meadows,** a stunning mountainside camp that serves as the base for Mount Olympus climbing expeditions. The Hoh's lower portions are hikable all year, the last 4 or 5 miles only from July to late October. Watch for stealthy herds of Roosevelt elk in the mossy forest. Also in the Hoh valley, the **South Fork Hoh Trail** (moderate; 7.5 miles round trip) is a more sparsely used trail that begins just beyond South Fork Hoh Campground (see Camping, below).

Beach hikes are plentiful, as well. From US 101 north and south of Kalaloch Campground, short paths lead steeply downhill to **Beaches 1, 2, 4, and 6** (we can't figure out what happened to Beaches 3 and 5, either).

Each runs one-quarter to one-half mile downhill to a beach with its own appealing character. **Beach 4,** marked by sheer walls, offshore rocks, and many explorable tidal pools, is a favorite. Kalaloch Campground itself is a good place to embark on a long beach hike. Many walkers enjoy heading north on the sand about 3 miles to **Beach 6,** one of the most scenic beach areas, then returning the same way. Long-distance beach backpackers often begin at **Oil City,** just north of the mouth of the Hoh River (from US 101, 17 miles south of Forks, take Oil City Rd west about 10 miles), for the rugged, spectacular 17-mile, 3-day walk **to Third Beach,** near La Push (see the Forks and La Push chapter).

A dozen miles to the south, the rain forest resumes. The **Queets River Trail** (moderate; various lengths), hidden up a rough, sparsely traveled road between Kalaloch and Lake Quinault, is a spectacular walk up an old-growth river valley, with a fraction of the foot traffic on the more popular Hoh River Trail one valley to the north. You guessed it: there's a small catch. Before the journey begins, hikers have to ford the Queets River.

Some people use rafts to make this crossing during heavy flow periods in early summer. But foot crossings are practical during low-flow periods, such as late summer and early fall, when the river can be safely waded. The river flow is more key than the season. Early spring crossings can be made during spells of dry weather, for example. But be aware that during spring storms, the river can rise several feet between the time you go in and the time you go out. Call the park for information and advice. (Tip: From the main trailhead at the end of Queets Valley Rd, it's usually easier to ford the Sams River, the smaller tributary flowing in from the south, and then cross the Queets farther upstream, where it's shallower.) Also be aware that two additional river fordings are required about 5 and 6 miles up the trail.

If and when you get across the river, this hike is a grand backpack trip. The trail runs 14.5 miles through lush old-growth to a dead-end at **Pelton Creek Camp,** with good campsites all along the route. Many backpackers opt to go in 5 miles to great campsites and fishing at Spruce Bottom. Day hikers can walk in 2.5 miles to find one of the largest Douglas firs in the world. Watch for Roosevelt elk here, particularly in the fall. The trailhead is about a mile beyond Queets Campground (see Camping, below).

Nearby, a 3-mile **loop trail** (easy) that begins and ends near the summer-only Queets Ranger Station makes a nice afternoon stroll through a rich, moss-draped rain forest. It's mostly flat, and elk sightings are possible.

Beaches

The beach right out in front of **Kalaloch Campground** is a state treasure. Incredibly broad, flat, and clean, it's often fog-shrouded and windswept. But that only seems to add to the allure. Barefoot beach-walking, kite flying, Frisbee games, and just plain gaping at the sea are the favorite activities here. Razor clam digging is allowed in season (see Fishing, below) From the campground, you can stroll for miles north or south, without ever running out of public beach—or enthusiasm. Even the least inspired walker can make it about a mile south to scenic **Kalaloch Rocks,** near the mouth of Kalaloch Creek just below Kalaloch Lodge. A couple miles farther south, you'll run into the mouth of the Queets River. It can be waded during certain tides, but use caution here.

The numbered beaches reached by short trails from US 101 (see Hiking/Backpacking, above) are great places to spend the day. **Beaches 4 and 6** are particularly scenic, with many sea stacks, offshore islands, and steep headlands separating them from the broader, sandy expanse to the south. Just to the north, **Ruby Beach,** a Northwest favorite, is reached via a short trail from a US 101 pullout, with good views of Destruction Island right offshore.

If Kalaloch is just a short stopover on the way to somewhere else, consider pulling into the **South Beach** overflow area (summer only), about 2 miles south of Kalaloch Lodge. It's essentially a flat parking lot used to accommodate extra campers. But the lot sits just yards above a delightful, driftwood-studded beach. South Beach is a drive-in mental-health break from US 101. Some Kalaloch campers actually prefer to camp here, as you're much closer to the surf line.

Camping

Kalaloch Campground, Olympic National Park's largest, is the star. Big surprise: the campground, one of the most wonderfully situated in the Northwest, can be difficult to get into during summer months. The campground's 175 sites (no hookups; RVs to 21 feet) fill up nearly every night, all summer long. It's still first-come, first-served here. And the park takes the rules seriously, requiring that you register for your site within an hour after arrival, and strictly discouraging saving sites for friends.

The best way to snag a site is to show up at midmorning, park in the day-use lot, and patrol the loops by foot or bicycle, swooping in vulture circles waiting for someone to leave. This Kalaloch Campground Cakewalk can be extremely frustrating. But it just makes it that much sweeter when you score that spot right on the bluff, overlooking the ocean. Some campers, particularly those with anxious, must-get-out-NOW children, adopt a longer-term strategy: they grab one of the less popular, dark sites that back onto US 101, then move up to a beachfront spot later in the week. Either way, it's worth the wait. Kalaloch is open all year. Sites ($10; 14-day maximum) cannot be reserved. *On US 101, 34 miles south of Forks and about 80 miles north of Hoquiam; (360) 452-0330 or (360) 962-2283.*

Just south of the campground is the **South Beach** overflow area, open summers only. This flat gravel lot began as a sloppy-seconds campground with no running water, tables, fire pits, or facilities of any kind. But now that a rest room has been built here, it's become the campground of choice for many, particularly RV owners who can set up just about anywhere. Reason: it's almost right on the beach, with only an 8-foot bank and a pile of driftwood separating the dinner table from the pounding Pacific surf. *On US 101, 3 miles south of Kalaloch; (360) 452-0330.*

Equally accommodating—and almost as popular—is **Hoh Rain Forest Campground,** a national park site near Hoh Visitors Center. The campground's 88 sites (no hookups; RVs to 21 feet) are spread through wooded loops near the river and famous rain-forest trails. Roosevelt elk are often seen in the area. One recent spring, in fact, the campground was shut down when a protective mother cow made a nursery of one of the camping loops. Hoh Rain Forest is another one of Olympic's favorite camps, and sites can be tough to land in summer months. It's open all year. Campsites ($10) cannot be reserved. *At the end of Hoh River Rd, 19 miles east of US 101 near milepost 176; (360) 452-0330.*

If Hoh Rain Forest and Kalaloch are full (or even if they aren't), don't overlook the string of very nice—and very free—state Department of Natural Resources campsites along the Hoh River. **Hoh Oxbow,** just south of the Hoh Rain Forest Road along US 101, has 7 sites for tents and small trailers, but no running water. A small boat launch makes it a favorite angler's hangout, especially during winter steelhead season. **Cottonwood,** just off Oil City Road (turn west off US 101 between mileposts 177 and 178, about 15 miles south of Forks) is similar, with 9 sites, primitive facilities, but no fee. On the Hoh Rain Forest Road itself are **Willoughby Creek** (3.5 miles east of US 101), which has 3 small campsites and limited facilities; and **Minnie Peterson** (4.5 miles east of US 101), which has 8 small riverside spots. Another primitive, but secluded, option is **South Fork Hoh,** reached by turning east on Hoh Mainline Road (about 15.5 miles south of Forks) and proceeding 14 miles east. South Fork Hoh, part of Bert Cole State Park, has 3 campsites and little else, except for those mind-blowing old-growth trees that clutter the place. The South Fork Hoh Trail (see Hiking/Backpacking, above) is just up the road from here. All five campgrounds are free and open all year. Sites cannot be reserved. *Contact the Washington DNR office in Forks; (360) 374-6131.*

A private campground in the vicinity is **Hoh River Resort,** near the river on US 101, which has 23 sites with hookups and other facilities. The park is open all year. Sites can be reserved by calling (360) 374-5566.

On the Queets River, **Queets Campground,** an Olympic National Park site, has 20 standard (moss on the picnic tables) tent sites near the river and the Queets River Ranger Station and trailhead. The campground and its access road aren't suitable for RVs or trailers. It's a nice spot, but primitive. No running water here. Queets is open all year. Campsites cannot be reserved. *On Queets River Rd 14 miles east of US 101; (360) 452-0330 or (360) 962-2283.*

Fishing

Spring and fall **razor clamming** seasons occasionally are available on the beach at Kalaloch, which gets crowded with hundreds of diggers seeking the succulent bivalves. Contact the state Department of Fish and Wildlife at Montesano, (360) 249-4628; www.wa.gov/wdfw, for seasons and restrictions.

Beaches around Kalaloch can be very productive for **surf perch** fishing. Beach 4, with a steeper, rockier surface than other local areas, is a prime producer. Some surf anglers also cast deep here for **Pacific skates,** a raylike bottom feeder whose meaty shoulders some fishermen consider a delicacy.

The Hoh and Queets Rivers are legendary game fish haunts. Both hold winter and summer **steelhead** and multiple **salmon** species. The Hoh gets hot for steelheading in December and continues to produce through April. Then it's salmon time, with a healthy hatchery **chinook** run available through the summer. The Queets also is a noted winter steelhead river. Most anglers head for the lower river, below the confluence of the Salmon River, where Quinault-tribe hatchery steelhead are placed. But the upper river is more scenic, and anglers searching for a big, wild steelhead can try here in March and April. Good bank access can be found all along Queets Rain Forest Road (see Camping, above). Some truly spectacular holes are found farther upstream, at Spruce Bottom on the Queets River Trail (see Hiking/Backpacking, above). For river conditions and seasons, call Olympic Sporting Goods in Forks; (360) 374-6330. For guided fishing trips, contact Three Rivers Resort in Forks; (360) 374-5300.

Photography

Sunset at **Kalaloch** can be fabulous for shutterbugs. Even on foggy days, the midday sun often bursts through the clouds at **Beach 4,** bathing the surf and rocks in an otherworldly light. By all means, photograph the famous **Hoh Rain Forest.** For similar pictures in an even more isolated

A rare view of the south face of Mount Olympus, from the Queets River

environment, venture up the **Queets valley,** where you can shoot magnificent moss-draped trees less than 30 feet from your car. The dark, cathedral-like canopy in both places makes for tricky light; use a tripod or bring fast film. Morning light usually is best, and bright, overcast days are better than sunny ones. A fast, 28-mm or shorter wide-angle lens is the tool of choice. And remember: The forest will be much more appreciated later if you include a human element for landscape perspective. People won't believe just how big these trees are without a known reference point.

Wildlife Watching

The entire coastline here is rich with wildlife; **seals, sea lions, seabirds,** and migrating **gray whales** are often spotted offshore. This is the southern end of Olympic National Park's 57-mile coastal strip. All rocks, islands, and other offshore formations north of Kalaloch are protected by the Quillayute Needles National Wildlife Refuge, and the entire Olympic coastal strip recently was protected from industrial exploitation when it received National Marine Sanctuary status. The US 101 pullout just north of Kalaloch, above Destruction Island, is a good, high post from which to watch, as is a similar, wheelchair-accessible overlook at the Beach 4 Trail parking lot.

The Hoh River is a famous wildlife habitat. It's a particularly good place to find yourself amid a herd of majestic **Roosevelt elk** in the winter months, when they migrate here from the highlands. The Hoh River Trail is your best bet. Elk also are seen along the Queets River Trail. Also keep your eyes peeled on all local trails for **cougars** and **black bears.**

Climbing

The route up the Blue Glacier to the summit of **Mount Olympus** is Olympic National Park's most popular climb. The route is fairly technical, but not impossible for inexperienced climbers—providing they have a guide who knows the mountain. From the base camp at Glacier Meadows, the summit can be bagged easily in one long day, conditions permitting. That's the catch. Weather is the biggest foe on Olympus. Because the mountain looms so high (7,965 feet) less than 40 miles from the Pacific, it's the first rain stop for approaching southwesterly storms. Major dumpage is always possible, and the route is very exposed.

Complicating matters is the relatively short climbing season. To be traversed safely, the Blue Glacier is best climbed in the spring (as early as April) or early summer. From July on, crevasses open quickly, and the route turns very hazardous. Consult with rangers at the Hoh Rain Forest Visitors Center well in advance of your climb. The Blue Glacier route is a solid day trip. It's 8 miles and about 3,500 feet from Glacier Meadows to the summit. But consider spending a solid week on the mountain, to accommodate bad weather. Most climbers take 2 days to make the 17.5-mile walk in and out the Hoh River Trail. Leaving 3 or 4 days to wait for clear skies at Glacier Meadows will dramatically increase your chance of success. Note: The last pitch to the summit is a rock scramble. Helmets are advisable. For guide service information, contact Olympic Mountaineering in Port Angeles; (360) 452-0240.

Rafting

Olympic Raft and Guide Service in Port Angeles, (888) 452-1443, www.northolympic.com/olympicraft; runs float trips on the Elwha, Hoh, and Queets Rivers. These are primarily placid, nonintimidating tours, with an emphasis on wildlife and natural history. It's well worth investing a day.

Accessible Outdoors

The **Spruce Nature Trail** and nature loop at the **Hoh Visitors Center** are wheelchair accessible, as are rest rooms, an amphitheater, and some campsites at nearby Hoh Campground (see Camping, above). **Kalaloch Campground** offers accessible camping, rest rooms, and picnic sites. The first

1,000 feet of the nearby Kalaloch Nature Trail are useable with assistance. **Beach Trail 4** near Kalaloch has a 200-foot, barrier-free trail to an ocean-viewing platform. **Ruby Beach** has an accessible viewpoint overlooking Ruby Beach and Cedar Creek, as well as barrier-free rest rooms.

Hoh Oxbow Campground (see Camping, above), offers barrier-free camping, rest rooms, and river viewing. **Minnie Peterson** (see Camping, above) also has wheelchair-accessible campsites and rest rooms, but no potable water.

More Information

Olympic National Forest, Pacific Ranger District, Forks: (360) 374-6522.

Olympic National Forest, Pacific Ranger District, Quinault: (360) 288-2525.

Olympic National Park Headquarters: *(360) 452-4501.*

    Hoh Rain Forest Visitors Center: *(360) 374-6925.*

    Kalaloch Information Station: *(360) 962-2283.*

    Road and Weather Updates: *(360) 452-0329.*

    Visitors Center: *(360) 452-0330; www.nps.gov/olym.*

    Wilderness Information Center (summer only): *(360) 452-0300.*

Lake Quinault
and the Quinault
River Valley

From the Queets River at US Highway 101 east to Anderson Pass in Olympic National Park, north to Low Divide, and south to Wynoochee Pass, including the Quinault River valley, the Colonel Bob Wilderness, the Enchanted Valley, and the Lake Quinault Lodge area.

For many Northwesterners, this rain-enriched valley is a touchstone. The Quinault—a name shared by an untamed river, a moss-draped valley, a glassy lake, and an indigenous people—is a survivor. The valley is in many ways an island of purity, an intact example of the startlingly beautiful rain-forest-to-glacier Olympic valleys first settled—but never tamed—by homesteaders in the late 19th century.

A sense of permanence pervades the place. Much of what was here before white settlers arrived remains. The valley's mighty rain forests, filled with Sitka spruce, western red cedar, and Douglas fir that sprouted from seeds 1,000 years ago, are still intact, at least above the lake. The glacier-carved lake, a quiet, fog-draped pool marking the halfway spot on the Quinault River's 60-mile march from Mount Anderson to the Pacific, is clean and largely undeveloped. Tying it all together is the river, an unruly force which, unlike most of its peninsula neighbors, has never been harnessed, even temporarily. The Quinault is one of the Olympic's largest and most vital arteries, draining more acreage than any single river in the range except the Queets to the north. Its east and north forks, which join just above Lake Quinault, drain the entire lower portion of the Olympics, from Low Divide south.

Many of the valley's early settlers stayed. Some of them helped build Lake Quinault Lodge, a cozy south-shore getaway that feels today much as it did when the doors opened in 1926. The lodge has become a symbol of a valley recognized as a treasure by three landlords: the Quinault Tribe, which owns the lake and all the land downstream to the north and west, and makes a living off reservation timber and fisheries; Olympic National Forest, which controls the rugged southern valley walls; and Olympic National Park, which manages the land from the river forks upstream, through the fabled Enchanted Valley and up to the Olympic Crest at Mount Anderson.

The Quinault would be beautiful in any setting, but it seems even more precious because of its immediate surroundings. Although the upstream lands survived wonderfully intact, public and private forest-lands both north and south of Lake Quinault—and tribal lands along the river to the west—were devastated by the harsh, clear-cut-and-run forestry of the first half of the century. Much of the land along US Highway 101 on either side of the Quinault looks like moonscape. But somehow, sitting beside Quinault Lodge's massive stone fireplace, walking through the old-growth forest, or straining to traverse an upper-valley trail, it's easy to forget—if not forgive—all that.

For outdoor lovers, the Quinault is a diversion powerful enough to make you forget a lot of things, not just clear-cuts. The basin represents both ends of the activity spectrum. Some of our most relaxing days have trickled by on the eerily quiet shores of Lake Quinault. And some of our most strenuous have zipped by in the mountain valleys above. The lake offers uncommonly good camping, fishing, canoeing, and kayaking. On both sides, lowland trails wind through magnificent old-growth rain forests. The mountains hold some of Washington's best alpine destinations: Enchanted Valley, Anderson, and O'Neil Passes, the Skyline Ridge, and a string of southern Olympic peaks in the Colonel Bob Wilderness.

The Quinault, unlike many other places in the Olympics, is a year-round destination. It goes without saying that the valley gets plenty of rain—170 inches in one recent year. But even during the wet season, when snows close the upper valley, the lake remains an enticement. Soggy walks along low-level rain-forest trails feel, frankly, natural in the rain. Roosevelt elk take up winter residence on the valley floor, delighting visitors—and annoying permanent residents. Lake Quinault Lodge reverts to the quiet, relaxing (no phones or TVs) retreat that first made it popular in the 1930s.

Which is probably why some of us keep coming back here, every winter, to check in on the way things were. And the way we'd like them always to be.

Getting There

Lake Quinault is 75 miles south of Forks and 38 miles north of Hoquiam on US Highway 101. It's a 3- to 4-hour drive from Seattle, either from the north via Port Angeles or from the south via Interstate 5 and US 101 (the southern route is probably faster for most Puget Sound residents). All Lake Quinault destinations are reached by a pair of narrow county/national park roads, North Shore Road and South Shore Road. The roads meet beyond the head of the lake, where a bridge crosses the Quinault. When both roads are open, they can be driven as a 25-mile, very scenic loop around the lake and along the upper Quinault River. The primary route is South Shore Road, which turns east from US 101 near the lake's southwest corner. The road passes Lake Quinault Lodge and continues 19 miles up the valley to Graves Creek (East Fork Quinault) campground and ranger station in Olympic National Park. North Shore Road provides access to Olympic's Quinault Ranger Station and continues east to the North Fork campground and trailhead. Be aware that the upper half of each road is gravel, and both can be quite rough. Washouts are common in winter. It's not at all unusual for one or both roads to be closed. Call before traveling.

inside out

Hiking/Backpacking

Whether you're in search of a short day-hike through old-growth trees or a two-week trek into some of the most spectacular alpine terrain in the Olympics, the Quinault valley is a good place to start. Several of the best short forest walks on the entire peninsula begin within walking distance of Lake Quinault Lodge. And two of Olympic National Park's classic trans-Olympic traverses start or end at trailheads only 30 minutes away. For trail conditions and updates, contact Olympic National Park or Olympic National Forest offices listed in More Information, below. Note that Wilderness Permits are required for all overnight stays in the Olympic National Park backcountry, and a per-hiker fee is charged. Quota systems are in place in some popular backcountry camps. Contact the park's Wilderness Information Center, (360) 452-0300, for current information. Also, a Northwest Forest Pass, $5 per day or $30 annually, is required to park in many Forest Service–administered trailheads in this area. They're available from ranger stations, from many private vendors, on-line at www.naturenw.org, or by calling (800) 270-7504. Here's a quick guide to the best of the region:

South Shore Lake Quinault

Short-term visitors, campers at Falls View or Willaby Campgrounds (see Camping, below), and guests of the Lake Quinault Lodge shouldn't miss the **Lake Quinault Loop** (easy; 3-mile loop), which circles along the quiet lakeshore and into a truly awesome grove of old-growth Douglas fir. This impeccably maintained trail is one of the best Forest Service paths in the state, and a great place to drain some vigor out of the kids. The setting is spectacular, particularly in Big Tree Grove, where there is a stand of 500-year-old fir trees. These are some of the best examples of what's left of Washington's original old-growth forests. It's pretty tough not to be awed. If the full loop is too far, park at the **Rain Forest Nature Trail** (easy; 1-mile loop) with a well-signed parking lot on South Shore Road, a half-mile west of the lodge, and walk that shorter loop through Big Tree Grove. An alternate hike, the **Willaby Creek Trail** (easy; 3.4 miles round trip), breaks off the Lake Quinault Loop trail about a mile from the Rain Forest parking lot. More big trees. *Really* big trees.

Farther up South Shore Road, near the Graves Creek Road's end, a series of popular hikes branch out from the Graves Creek Ranger Station and campground. Day hikers, especially those with children, will appreciate the **Graves Creek Trail** (easy; 1-mile loop), a nature walk that begins and ends near the ranger station. Note: When this book went to press, the Graves Creek Road was washed out 6 miles below the Graves Creek area. Call before you go.

A half mile up the road is the **East Fork Quinault Trail** (moderate; up to 26 miles round trip), which many backpackers say is as good as it gets in the Olympics, if not the country. The trail climbs gently through the river valley to a spectacular alpine basin with sheer rock walls, plunging waterfalls, and the picturesque **Enchanted Valley Chalet,** a 1930s hotel now used as a backcountry shelter for 30 or so hikers. It's often full, so bring a tent and camp in the beautiful surrounding meadows. This is one of the Olympic's most popular backcountry sites. It's usually snow-free by early summer and often remains so until late in the fall. Day hikers can go just 2.5 miles up the same trail to a truly excellent photo spot: **Pony Bridge,** which spans a deep canyon. Be warned, however, that the trail has been in disrepair in recent years. At publication time, the suspension bridge below Enchanted Valley was out; a river ford was necessary.

Backpackers should consider the worthwhile day trip from their Enchanted Valley campsite up to **Anderson Pass** (difficult; 10 miles round trip). Long-distance trekkers looking to put a full, 30-mile, one-way east-west Olympics crossing under their belts can exit down the east slope Olympics via the **West Fork Dosewallips River Trail.** Note that the High Dose Bridge, a vital link on the east half of this route, was washed out and impassable as of the summer of 2000. Call the park for updates. Another (longer) Olympic-crossing option is a steep climb from the Enchanted Valley area up to spectacular **O'Neil Pass** and an eastern exit via the **Duckabush River Trail.** (See the Olympic National Forest and the East Slope Olympics chapter for connections to east-slope trails.)

To get away from the crowds, consider alternate destinations that branch off the same trail system. (Some of these trails lead south into the 12,000-acre Colonel Bob Wilderness.) One mile up the East Fork Quinault Trail, the **Graves Creek Trail** breaks south, leading about 8 miles to nice high country at Wynoochee Pass, Sundown Lake, and Sundown Pass near Olympic National Park's southern boundary. (Ask rangers about the fording of Success Creek, about 4 miles up the trail.) From Sundown Pass, a high, rough trail leads 2 miles east to **Six Ridge Pass** (4,650 feet; excellent views), and another 8.5 miles east to a junction with the North Fork Skokomish River Trail. This is a rough alpine traverse. But more than likely, solitude will be easy to come by.

Gung-ho day hikers with more stamina than common sense might consider the **Colonel Bob Mountain Trail** (difficult; 14.6 miles round trip), which departs off South Shore Road, about 6 miles from US 101. It climbs quite steeply to an old shelter at 4 miles, then even more steeply to a true Kodak-moment mountaintop view. Good campsites are available along the route for backpackers, too.

North Shore Lake Quinault

For a quick, easy taste of the local rain-forest environment, the **Maple Glade Rain Forest Interpretive Trail** (easy, half-mile loop) is always a good bet. The trail, which begins 8.2 miles east of US 101 at Olympic National Park's Quinault Visitors Center, has a smooth, easy grade. Kids will like the big trees and beaver pond. Elk sometimes frequent these flat-lands.

Great backpack trips are launched from the trailhead near North Fork Quinault Ranger Station and Campground (see Camping, below.) The **North Fork Quinault Trail** (moderate; 31 miles round trip), the southern half of the popular Elwha-Quinault north-south Olympics crossing (see the Port Angeles and Hurricane Ridge chapter), follows the river 17 miles to Low Divide, 3,650 feet. Good campsites are found along the way. Many experienced backpackers use this route as one leg of the 44-mile **Skyline Loop,** completed by following the Skyline Ridge Trail west from Low Divide and back south on the Three Lakes Trail to the North Fork Quinault Trailhead area. The Skyline route, which winds through some of the most picturesque—and rough—high country in Olympic National Park, is passable only in late summer (mid-August to September). It's for veterans only.

Bunch Creek Falls is a year-round Lake Quinault–area favorite

The southern leg of that loop, the **Irely Lake and Three Lakes Trail** (moderate; 2.2 to 14 miles round trip) makes a good day hike or quick backpack trip for those walking it north from the North Fork Quinault area. The trail, just west of North Fork Campground, gradually climbs 1.1 miles to Irely Lake, a good bird-watching venue (osprey have been spotted here), passing through some magnificent old growth. About a mile east of

Three Lakes, you'll find the world's largest Alaska (yellow) cedar: a whopping 12 feet in diameter at the base. Have no shame: hug this baby. At 6.5 miles, the trail opens to some luscious, blueberry-filled meadows near three small lakes. Three Lakes Shelter, roughly marking the Queets-Quinault divide, is a half mile beyond. Note: This trail is very muddy in sections through midsummer.

Camping

In the south shore Quinault area, two fine Olympic National Forest sites are popular stopovers. The best one is **Willaby,** a well-kept Lake Quinault waterfront park with 24 sites (no hookups; RVs to 16 feet), a boat launch, and access to the Quinault Loop Trail. It's open from mid-April through mid-November. A half mile to the east, **Falls View** is another lakefront park, albeit with less privacy than Willaby, with 30 sites (no hookups; RVs to 16 feet) and a boat launch. Willaby and Falls View are open summer months only. Sites ($7.50 to $12) cannot be reserved. *Both are on South Shore Rd, between 1.5 and 2.5 miles east of US 101, near Lake Quinault Lodge and the Quinault Ranger Station; (360) 288-2525.*

Another nearby National Forest camp, **Gatton Creek,** functions primarily as an overflow to Willaby and Falls Creek. It has 5 tent sites and 8 (parking-lot-style) RV sites, and is open May through September. *3.5 miles east of US 101 on South Shore Rd; (360) 288-2525.*

Campers who continue east on South Shore Road to near the end of Graves Creek Road will encounter **Graves Creek,** an Olympic National Park campground near the trailhead for the East Fork Quinault and Graves Creek Trails. The campground has 30 sites (no hookups; RVs to 21 feet). They're free and open all year. *At the end of Graves Creek Rd/South Shore Rd, 15 miles east of US 101; (360) 452-0330.* Note: The road was washed out 6 miles below Graves Creek when this book went to press. Call before you go.

Just to the north is **North Fork,** a quiet but nondescript Olympic National Park campground with 7 tent sites set near the North Fork Quinault Trailhead. It's free but primitive (tents only), with no running water. North Fork is open all year. Sites cannot be reserved. *At the end of North Shore Rd; (360) 452-0330.*

Near midlake on the north shore of Lake Quinault is one of our favorites, **July Creek,** a walk-in Olympic National Park site with 29 tent spots. It's a great campground, with sites set in between some truly massive Douglas firs near the lake and creek mouth. It tends to be much quieter here than at campgrounds on the busier south side of the lake. July Creek is open all year. Sites ($10) cannot be reserved. Fees usually aren't collected in winter months, but the water is shut off: bring your own, or filter stream water. *On North Shore Rd 2 miles east of US 101; (360) 452-0330.*

An hour to the south, a more remote experience awaits at **Campbell Tree Grove,** an Olympic National Forest campground on the upper Humptulips River, near the southern border of the Colonel Bob Wilderness. It's a free campground with 8 tent sites and 3 small RV sites. Campbell Tree Grove is open from June through October. Sites cannot be reserved. *From US 101 north of Humptulips, follow Forest Rds 22 and 2204 about 23 miles northeast; (360) 288-2525.*

Canoeing/Kayaking/Boating

The clear, quiet waters of **Lake Quinault** are ideal for daylong paddle excursions. Both canoeing and kayaking are popular activities for campers at Willaby and Falls View Campgrounds on South Shore Road. Both sites have good launch areas and day-use parking. Canoes and rowboats can be rented during summer months from Lake Quinault Lodge; (800) 562-6672 from Washington only. Other rentals and **launch facilities** are available a mile up the road at Rain Forest Resort; (360) 288-2535.

Fishing

Lake Quinault offers good fishing for (occasionally quite large) **dolly varden,** as well as **kokanee** and **cutthroat trout.** The Quinault Tribe regulates the fishery. Licenses are $15. Ask at a ranger station or tribal office about restrictions, seasons, and limits.

The Quinault River has a strong winter **steelhead** run that produces some massive (25- to 30-pound) hatchery fish, as well as a respectable fall hatchery **coho salmon** run. Most fishable waters are below Lake Quinault, on the reservation. Anglers must be accompanied by a tribal guide to fish there. Call the Quinault Indian Nation, (360) 276-8211, for referrals. The season peaks in December and January, and anglers need a state license and steelhead punch card. Wild steelhead are harder to come by, but can be caught on the upper river (below the park boundary) in the spring. The upper-valley river inside the park can be very good trout-fishing water, no license required.

Wildlife Watching

Lake Quinault is a birder's bonanza. On recent visits we've seen dozens of aquatic birds (**mallards, loons,** and other waterfowl) along the shoreline portion of the Quinault Loop Trail near Lake Quinault Lodge. The broad floodplains along the river beyond the head of the lake are a primary winter habitat for one of Olympic's predominant **Roosevelt elk** herds. Watch for them in the bushes along North Shore Road, between the park's Quinault Ranger Station and the bridge connecting North and South Shore Roads. On the trails, be alert for **black bears.**

Accessible Outdoors

Falls Creek Campground offers barrier-free camping, rest rooms, picnic sites, and interpretive trails. **Gatton Creek Campground** offers barrier-free camping, picnicking, and rest rooms. **Campbell Tree Grove Campground** has barrier-free campsites and rest rooms. The **Humptulips Hatchery** offers barrier-free fish viewing and rest rooms; from Aberdeen, go north on US 101 for 22 miles, cross the Humptulips River Bridge, and turn left at the next road. Continue to the hatchery on the left.

outside in

Lodgings

Lake Quinault Lodge ★ A massive cedar-shingled structure, this grand old lodge was built in 1926. *$$–$$$; S Shore Rd, Quinault; (360) 288-2900 or (800) 562-6672 (WA and OR only); www.visitlakequinalt.com.* &

More Information

Olympic National Forest, Pacific Ranger District, Quinault: *(360) 288-2525.*
Olympic National Park Headquarters: *(360) 452-4501.*
Quinault Ranger Station (summer only): *(360) 288-2444.*
Road and Weather Update: *(360) 452-0329.*
Visitors Center: *(360) 452-0330; www.nps.gov/olym.*
Wilderness Information Center (summer only): *(360) 452-0300.*
Quinault Indian Nation: *(360) 276-8211.*

Grays Harbor: Westport and Ocean Shores

From Moclips south to Willapa Bay and east to Aberdeen, including Westport and Ocean Shores beaches, the Grays Harbor National Wildlife Refuge, and Twin Harbors, Grayland Beach, Westhaven, Westport Light, Pacific Beach, and Ocean City State Parks.

If geographic areas could seek therapy, Grays Harbor would be splayed out on the couch right now.

Washington's only coastal deepwater port grew up on the bounties that put the Olympic Peninsula on the map: timber and salmon. Timber built and nurtured the inner-bay towns of Hoquiam and Aberdeen, which gladly embraced—and just as gladly shipped off—entire forests of peninsula logs. More than 30 timber mills were humming along here in 1910. On the outer harbor, the pounding surf at Westport was muted by a seawall 50 years ago, and a thriving fishing village reached west for its own squirming handful of the coast's plentiful salmon runs. Across the bay, Ocean Shores sprang up 35 years ago as a resort community, feeding off the fishing-fueled tourist economy.

This worked out pretty well for Grays Harbor until the logs were gone and most of the salmon had died—two unexpected, but hardly unrelated, occurrences. Since then, the region has grappled with various new identities. Hoquiam and Aberdeen—strategically located, historically significant, and just Northwest-funky enough to attract the curious—are still seeking one. (Being known as the birthplace of rocker Kurt Cobain wasn't too popular when he was alive. It's not even discussed now that he's dead.) Westport and Ocean Shores, meanwhile, are farther along the road to where they're going. And it's increasingly obvious that outdoor recreation is going to help get them there.

Shortly after the Northwest's salmon stocks entered a death spiral a decade ago, Westport charter-boat operators scraped the fish scales off the seats, installed wave-proof latte holders, and discovered that many a Seattleite would pay to go out and chase migratory whales. Desperate motel owners, realizing that "it's the beach, stupid," started marketing rooms to beachcombers, bird-watchers, kite flyers, and other nature lovers who probably like Westport better without all the fishing commotion. Across the harbor, Ocean Shores, a prefab town launched with grand aspirations of megaconvention business in the 1960s, lowered its sights and realized that it, too, could make a pretty good living off little more than the sand upon which it sits.

In the 1980s and '90s, a new generation of outdoor lovers has been turned on to Grays Harbor, the closest and most accessible ocean beach area to Seattle. The former "Fishing Capital of the United States" still fishes—for fewer salmon and a lot more bottom fish—but its outdoorsy offerings have diversified. Westport has emerged as a Northwest surfing mecca, for instance. Ocean Shores and the North Beach area have become the Seattle area's backyard beachcombing getaway. On both sides of the harbor, tourists are increasingly drawn to ocean beaches for camping, kite flying, clam digging, and sand sculpting. Even the inner harbor is taking on a Gore-Tex feel: sea kayaking is gaining in popularity, and local rivers are becoming favored fishing destinations.

It took us more than 100 years to see through the industrial commotion, but the notion of Grays Harbor as a recreator's haven is catching on. Business leaders from Aberdeen to Ocean Shores should rise from the therapy couch and repeat their daily affirmations: "Grays Harbor is good. Our air is clean. We're folksy, friendly, and fun. We have a beach, it's only 2.5 hours from the Space Needle—and doggone it, people like us."

Getting There

The Grays Harbor area and its two popular oceanside destinations, Westport and Ocean Shores, are about 2.5 hours southwest of Seattle via Interstate 5 and US Highway 12. Drive I-5 south to Olympia, turning west on US 101. Six miles west of Olympia, the highway splits, with US 101 departing north to Shelton and the Hood Canal. Stay to the left, following Hwy 8 (which becomes US 12) 42 miles west to Aberdeen. There, follow signs 18 miles south via Hwy 105 to Westport and the South Beach area, or 16 miles north via Hwys 109 and 115 to Ocean Shores and the North Beach area. Watch your signs in Aberdeen, former home of some highly confused traffic engineers.

inside out

Beaches

Grays Harbor's productive tourist trade is tied to the beach. Make that *chained* to the beach. In fact, Ocean Shores wouldn't be worth supplying electricity to if it weren't for the beach. Luckily for them, some nice ones are in evidence here. One major caveat: The State of Washington, allegedly at the urging of local citizens, allows auto traffic—that's right, auto traffic—on most public beaches in this area for much of the year. (You know you're south of Olympic National Park when you have to stop, look, and listen before stepping into the surf.) Some beach strips are auto-bahns all year, others "only" from September to early April. This absurd anachronism turns some otherwise lovely, natural beaches into raceways for young 4X4 punks, who rarely heed the 25-mph speed limit. If you don't like car exhaust mixed with your sea smells, write a state legislator and complain. Or do what huge numbers of state residents have been doing for decades: vote with your feet, taking your tourist dollars with you north to Olympic National Park or south to the Oregon Coast, where beaches don't have passing lanes.

North Beach (Ocean Shores to Moclips)

Twenty-two miles of beach lie between Moclips and Ocean Shores, and most of it is publicly accessible (including automobiles). The strip, known only to state-government types as the **North Beach Seashore Conservation Area,** is open for exploration, but most beach uplands are private property. Access roads to this breezy, flat beach are numerous and well marked along Hwy 109, although few public facilities have been built here. The far northern stretch near Moclips is the most scenic in this region, making it the best local beachcombing area.

Exceptions are **Pacific Beach and Ocean City State Parks** (see Camping, below), both of which have good beach access, and **Griffiths-Priday State Park,** at the mouth of the Copalis River. The latter offers picnic facilities and rest rooms. From March to August, you won't be nesting in the uplands portions of the park, because the endangered snowy plover will. But the beach area is open all year. It's a fine spot for beachcombing, kite flying, surf fishing, and dumping sand on your sister's head. The river waters inside the spit are a good canoe/kayak spot, particularly for shorebird-watchers.

South Beach (Westport to Willapa Bay)

The 19-mile beach strip south of Westport comprises the **South Beach**

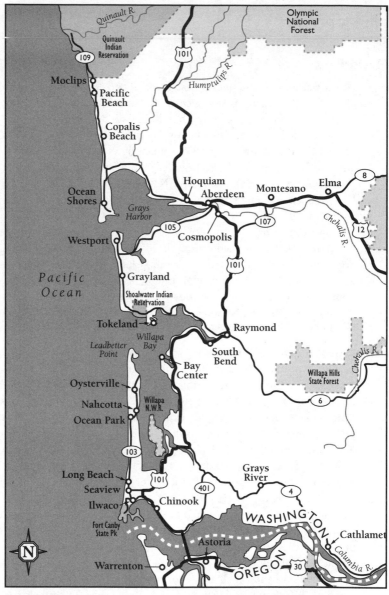

Pacific Coast

Seashore Conservation Area, which has good public access sites along Hwy 105. The most popular beach entrances are **Westhaven State Park** and **Grayland Beach** and **Twin Harbors State Parks** (see Camping, below).

Single-day visitors should make it a point to visit **Westhaven State Park,** just a short drive or bicycle ride from downtown Westport. The day-use park is in a spectacular setting—at the southern entrance to Grays Harbor, marked by an observation platform, a foghorn tower, and the wave-splashed South Jetty. Also strings of VW buses. High winds and waves bottled in by the jetty have made this a favorite hangout of Washington surfers (see Surfing, below). But Westhaven has been in a state of flux recently. Tidal action is literally carving much of the above-beach area away, wiping out a former parking lot and other day-use facilities. State parks planners are likely to wait and see if the whole place goes bye-bye before they pour much money into improvements. Still, this is by far the most convenient beach access in the Westport area, and the viewing platform is a great place to taste the wind, peer into the Pacific, and watch for whales, sailing ships, or a returning charter boat. On a clear day, look behind you and scan the horizon for the rising white hulk of Mount Olympus. Early explorer John Meares, who named the 7,965-foot mountain, probably had a similar view when he first admired the peak in 1788.

Camping

Two public campgrounds await on the north side of Grays Harbor; two more on the south. None of them are much to brag about, but their locations—all within a short walk of the ocean—keeps them in high demand throughout summer months. From north to south:

Pacific Beach State Park—a small (10-acre) in-town campground on Hwy 109—was renovated In 1995, with good results. The park now has fewer campsites (64; 31 with electrical hookups; RVs to 45 feet), but they're far better situated. They're still a bit too close together for most tenters' taste. But this campground is a hugely popular RV spot, particularly during razor-clam seasons (see Fishing, below). Get a reservation; this is one of the few Washington State Parks that accepts them year-round. Pacific Beach is open all year. Campsites can be reserved up to 11 months in advance through Reservations Northwest, (800) 452-5687. *On Hwy 109, 30 miles northwest of Hoquiam in the town of Pacific Beach; (360) 289-3553 or (800) 233-0321.*

Ocean City State Park, just north of Ocean Shores, is the main camper hangout near that town, with 181 sites (29 with full hookups; RVs to 55 feet) spread over 131 acres of pine trees and thick shrubbery. It gets windy here, but sites are very private. This is probably the best spot in the region for tenters. Unlike other parks in the area, Ocean City has more than just the ocean competing for attention. You'll find good picnic facilities here, as well as a group camp and a swampy area popular with bird-

Ready, set, dig: Pursuing razor clams on an Ocean Shores beach

watchers. And, of course, the Pacific is but a short walk away. This is a summer hot spot, but you can reserve sites during summer months. Ocean City is open all year. Sites can be reserved up to 11 months in advance by calling (800) 452-5687. *Just north of Ocean Shores 3 miles south of the Hwys 109/115 junction; (360) 289-3553 or (800) 233-0321.*

Twin Harbors State Park is a longtime favorite of beach fans. It's a big park, with 303 sites (49 with full hookups; RVs to 35 feet). The campground is split in two by Hwy 105, with half the sites on wooded lands east of the road, the other half on the windier, more exposed sand dunes on the west side. (The hookup sites, like many others installed for the benefit of visiting anglers, are crammed together, chockablock, on the east side.) The park has two trails to the ocean, as well as a nature trail that winds through the sand dune area between the campground and the beach. This is an older park, and many of its facilities are showing their age, but it's often booked during summer months. Reservations are a good idea. Twin Harbors campground is open from March to October; the day-use area is open all year. Sites can be reserved up to 11 months in advance by calling (800) 452-5687. *On Hwy 105, 3 miles south of Westport; (360) 268-9717 or (800) 233-0321.*

Of all the parks in this area, **Grayland Beach State Park** is probably in greatest demand. It's a newer state park, with nicer rest rooms and campsite facilities than nearby Twin Harbors. Its 63 sites (60 with full hookups; RVs to 40 feet) are well situated on loops through the shrubby tidal uplands, and the large number of hookup sites makes it a favorite destination for RV owners. Campsites here also are much quieter than at Twin Harbors, which is closer to the highway. Trails lead about a half mile through sand dunes to a very pleasant—and relatively lightly used—ocean beach. A separate trail leads about a mile to and around a small, marshy lake. Wildlife alert: Grayland Beach also is a popular camp spot for otters. We've seen them bouncing down a trail here, commuting between the lake and the ocean. Grayland Beach is open all year. Sites can be reserved up to 11 months in advance by calling (800) 452-5687. *Just south of Grayland on Hwy 105, 28 miles southwest of Aberdeen; (360) 268-9717 or (800) 233-0321.*

Fishing

Twenty years ago, fishing would have been the first Inside Out listing in this chapter. Not anymore. The gradual death spiral of Northwest wild coho and chinook stocks has reduced one of the nation's salmon capitals to a coastal community in the midst of an identity crisis. But charters still run from Westport during a sharply abbreviated summer season.

That season usually isn't set until mid-April, when coastal fisheries managers dole out meager shares of dwindling **salmon.** In recent years, Westport's summer season has been truncated, but gradually improving over the disaster scenario of the mid-1990s. Call for season openings.

But if you're not picky about your prey, a charter fishing trip from Westport is possible just about any time of the year. Many salmon-boat skippers have switched to bottom-fishing trips for **lingcod, perch, sea bass,** and other species from March to October. And several companies run **deep-sea tuna** fishing charters from Westport's harbor during summer months. Other skippers now spend most spring months conducting whale- and shorebird-watching trips (see Wildlife Watching, below).

Most **charter companies** and their rates are comparable. They include Cachalot, (800) 356-0323; Deep Sea, (360) 268-9300 or (800) 562-0151; Westport Charters, (360) 268-0900 or (800) 562-0157; Islander, (360) 268-9166 or (800) 322-1740; and Travis, (360) 268-9140. (Toll-free numbers often are in operation only during the season.) A tip: Managers at Westport Charters are particularly active in the regional fish-allotment process, and usually have first word on when fishing will begin and how long it will last.

Shore fishing also can be productive in this area. **Surf fishing** for perch and other species is possible virtually anywhere on the public beach. Use a long rod, a big spinning reel, flat surf-type sinkers, and hooks baited with natural bait, such as clam necks. No license is required. Bottom fish and even salmon are frequently caught on either side of the South Jetty, accessible through Westhaven State Park (see Beaches, above.) Similar fishing awaits at North Jetty, at Point Brown south of Ocean Shores.

An increasingly popular salmon-fishing option is a special fishery inside the Westport Boat Basin, where hatchery salmon can be caught from docks during September and October. A derby adds to the excitement. **Steelheaders** and those who prefer drift fishing for their salmon can make the short trip inland to the Humptulips River, a noted fall fishing venue for **chinook, coho,** and **chum.**

The shorelines on either side of Grays Harbor open periodically for **razor clams**—those sweet, meaty, highly sought coastal bivalves. State biologists usually open one or both beaches for several weeks of digging (usually on odd-numbered days only) twice a year. The fall season typically is in October; spring digging is in March, April, and/or May. Clammers need a state license ($7). Rental shovels and clam guns (plastic or metal suction tubes for digging) usually can be rented from local shops. Popular digging spots—when they're open—include Copalis, Moclips, Ocean City, downtown Ocean Shores, and Twin Harbors State Park.

Important note: Clam seasons are largely dictated by the presence of naturally occurring marine toxins that have killed razor clams or rendered them unsuitable for consumption in the past decade. At this writing, those toxin levels are in a period of decline, and clamming seasons are occurring more regularly. But seasons and limits change frequently. To learn where and when to dig, contact the state Fish and Wildlife office in Montesano; (360) 249-4628; www.wa.gov/wdfw.

Wildlife Watching

The Grays Harbor area is gaining increasing fame as a shorebird- and whale-watching destination, particularly during the spring whale-migrating season (March through May). Whale watching here was born largely of necessity. With dozens of fishing charter operators facing extinction because of shortened or canceled salmon seasons, whale-watching tours began sprouting like blackberry bushes around Westport. Thousands of **gray whales** migrate off Washington's coast each year, headed south to Baja in October and November, then north to the Bering Sea from March to May. Spring viewing is most productive, as whales seem to hug the coast more then, and ocean conditions are better for boat tours. Spring **whale-watching seminars** are conducted by experts on March and April weekends at the Westport Maritime Museum, 2201 Westhaven Drive; (360) 268-0078. Whales sometimes can be spotted from the harbor's North and South Jetties (use binoculars or a spotting scope, and look a mile or more offshore). But a whale-watching charter is your best bet.

They're offered by most charter companies. (See Fishing, above, or contact the Westport-Grayland Chamber of Commerce in More Information, below.)

The greater Grays Harbor area also is a bonanza to bird-watchers. The region has developed into a major destination for migratory birds in the Pacific Flyway. A half million Arctic-bound **shorebirds** migrate from as far south as Argentina and congregate on the beaches of the extensive North and South Beach Conservation Areas and the Grays Harbor National Wildlife Refuge at Bowerman Basin from mid-April through the first week of May. At high tide in Bowerman Basin, the birds rise in unison in thick flocks that shimmer through the air, twisting and turning, before settling back onto their feeding grounds. Trails lead through the marsh (located just beyond the Hoquiam airport). Be sure to wear boots. For more information and peak migratory days, call the Grays Harbor National Wildlife Refuge; (360) 753-9467.

Surfing

Huntington Beach this isn't, but the coastal surfing culture has woven itself into the fabric of Westport. Watching the neoprene-clad surfers bob around has become a leading spectator sport during Westport summers. (We knew it was serious when the town's second surf shop opened a few years ago.) Surfing grabbed its first toehold more than a decade ago at **Westhaven State Park,** where the South Jetty traps incoming southwesterly waves, creating a decent surf break. Tidal conditions have made that area less desirable in recent years, and many surfers have migrated to the **unnamed beach** just beyond the tall riprap jetty wall in downtown Westport.

Surfing is best on incoming tides. The break is tame in the summer, but can get pretty raucous during winter months. Whenever you go, wet suits are required equipment; the water never gets above 60°F here. For **rental gear,** advice, wax, and more, see California transplant Al Perlee at the Surf Shop in Westport; (360) 268-0992. Lessons are available if you call ahead.

Walking

Beach walking rules here, but at least one new path veers a ways off the sand. The **Westport Light Trail** (easy; 2.8 miles round trip) begins at Westhaven State Park and winds south to Ocean Avenue, near the historic Westport Lighthouse in Westport Light State Park. The concrete path runs atop the beach bluff. It's also open to wheelchairs, in-line skaters, and cyclists. A grand day hike can be made on the sandy beach and grassy uplands of **Damon Point State Park,** a day-use-only area near the Ocean

Shores Marina. Portions of the park are closed in the winter to protect snowy plover nests.

Cycling

Both the Westport and Ocean Shores areas are good road cycling venues, mainly because roads are flat, traffic is slow, and many miles of back roads wind through the sand dunes near the ocean. The paved 1.4-mile **Westport Light Trail** (see Walking, above), is open to cyclists. The Ocean Shores vicinity has become particularly good for cycling, with more than 100 miles of sparsely traveled roads, many optimistically constructed to accommodate tourism and convention business that still hasn't arrived here. Several good bike routes are marked, fanning out from **Duck Lake, Chinook Park,** or **North Bay Park.** The best are on the town's leeward side. All sorts of cycles—including four-wheel rigs big enough for the whole family—can be rented in downtown Ocean Shores. **Maps** and advice are available from Olympic Outdoors; (360) 289-3736.

Kayaking/Canoeing

Hot-dog whitewater kayakers often are found out among the surfers at **Westhaven State Park.** Quieter paddlers take to the more protected waters inside **Grays Harbor.** The harbor offers a full range of fascinating quiet-water destinations, most in wildlife-rich and historically significant waterways. Ocean Shores is ringed by a 23-mile **chain of canals and freshwater lakes** that are popular among canoeists. **Rental canoes** are available in town; call Resonance Canoe & Kayak; (360) 532.9176

Kite Flying

Go fly one. You won't be alone. Kite flying has emerged as a very popular coastal sport in the past decade, and Grays Harbor beach communities are natural magnets, thanks to persistent winds. **Ocean Shores,** in particular, is dotted with several well-stocked kite shops, and hosts a kite festival in early May.

Accessible Outdoors

Barrier-free campsites are found at **Pacific Beach** (31), **Ocean City** (29), **Twin Harbors** (3), and **Grayland Beach** (2) **State Parks** (see Camping, above); **Pacific Beach** has barrier-free rest rooms. The 1.4-mile **Westport Light Trail** between Westhaven State Park and Westport Light is paved and wheelchair-accessible (see Walking, above). In Ocean Shores, the **beach access** at Chance a la Mer has barrier-free rest rooms.

Restaurants

Alec's by the Sea ★   A good alternative to otherwise uninspiring dining options in Ocean Shores. $$; *131 E Chance a la Mer Blvd NE, Ocean Shores*; *(360) 289-4026.* ♿

Billy's Bar and Grill ★   At this historic pub, you can get a square-deal meal and an honest drink. $; *322 E Heron St, Aberdeen; (360) 533-7144.* ♿

Country Village Nutrition Shoppe and Café   A good place for a filling lunch before heading off to ocean beaches. $; *711 Vandercook Wy, Longview; (360) 425-8100.* ♿

Galway Bay Restaurant & Pub   Take off the chill in the best Irish fashion in this pub with a tasty menu. $$; *676 Ocean Shores Blvd NW, Ocean Shores; (360) 289-2300; www.galway-bay.com.* ♿

Parma ★★★   Adventurous, delicious Italian and French cuisine—who'd expect it in Aberdeen? $$; *116 W Heron St, Aberdeen; (360) 532-3166.* ♿

Lodgings

Best Western Lighthouse Suites Inn ★   Rooms are large and nicely decorated here, and each has an ocean view. $$$; *491 Damon Rd NW, Ocean Shores; (360) 289-2311 or (800) 757-SURF; www.bwlighthouse.com.* ♿

The Caroline Inn ★★   Four two-story suites await at this gleaming white Southern gothic mini-mansion. $$$; *1341 Ocean Shores Blvd SW, Ocean Shores; (360) 289-0450.*

Chateau Westport ★   Sixties-boxy on the outside, but pretty comfy and vaguely continental inside. $$; *710 W Hancock, Westport; (360) 268-9101 or (800) 255-9101.* ♿

Lytle House Bed & Breakfast ★   A B&B described as the county's finest example of pure Queen Anne architecture. $$; *509 Chenault, Hoquiam; (360) 533-2320 or (800) 677-2320; www.lytlehouse.com.*

Ocean Crest Resort ★   The tremendous view from this cliff-side resort perch is timeless. $$–$$$; *Hwy 109 N, Moclips; (360) 276-4465; oceanshores.com/lodging/oceancrest.*

Sandpiper ★★   The large, clean Sandpiper is a perfect place for a family reunion. $$–$$$; *4159 Hwy 109, Pacific Beach; (360) 276-4580; oceanshores.com/lodging/sandpiper.*

The Shilo Inn ★★   Something of a crown jewel in the nation's largest privately owned hotel chain. *$$$; 707 Ocean Shores Blvd NW, Ocean Shores; (360) 289-4600 or (800) 222-2244.*

More Information

Cranberry Coast Chamber of Commerce: *(800) 473-6018; www.cranberrycoastcoc.com.*

Grays Harbor Chamber of Commerce and Visitors Center: *(800) 321-1924.*

Ocean Shores–Grays Harbor County Visitor and Conventions Bureau: *(800) 76-BEACH or (360) 289-2451; www.oceanshores.org.*

Washington Coast Chamber of Commerce (Copalis area): *(360) 289-4552 or (800) 286-4552.*

Westport-Grayland Chamber of Commerce: *(360) 268-9422 or (800) 345-6223.*

Long Beach Peninsula and Willapa Bay

From North Cove south to Cape Disappointment and east to Chinook and Raymond; including Willapa National Wildlife Refuge and Fort Canby, Fort Columbia, Leadbetter Point, Loomis Lake, Pacific Pines, and Skating Lake State Parks.

We have to be careful here. A number of years ago, we got in big trouble by referring, in a newspaper article, to Long Beach as "the cheesy-souvenir capital of the Northwest." This was not at all popular with the locals, who called and wrote to extol the virtues of the Long Beach area's clean ocean beaches, friendly campgrounds, scenic lighthouses, kite-pleasing breezes, and other natural virtues. After long consideration and several more visits, we've come to a new conclusion: both reputations are correct.

Long Beach, which smells like taffy throughout, is the closest thing on Washington's coast to the well-developed, Super-8-and-GO-KART!-style summer havens on the Oregon Coast. It *is* the cheesy-souvenir capital of the Northwest. But it's also a quite delicious outdoor playground for those who venture off the beaten path—or boardwalk, as the case may be.

The Long Beach Peninsula, which begins at Leadbetter Point near the mouth of Willapa Bay and runs 27 straight, sandy miles south to the mouth of the Columbia River at Fort Canby, conceals a rich mix of outdoor wonders. On the inside of the long sand finger, portions of Willapa Bay are protected wildlife habitat, attracting thousands of migratory shorebirds in the spring and fall—and increasingly large hordes of chinook-salmon anglers in the summer. The inner bay's Willapa National Wildlife Refuge—particularly Long

Island, which is reached only by small watercraft—is a treasure.

On the outside of the peninsula is a wondrous stretch of flat, open beach—longer than any of its kind in the nation, according to the souvenir vendors. The beach leads south to one of Washington's truly memorable beach getaways, Fort Canby State Park, near the admirably untouristed town of Ilwaco. Lewis and Clark first set foot on the Pacific Coast here, and if you walk the beach today and squint just enough to block out the lighthouse on the bluff, you can drink in nearly the same view they had that day in 1805.

Such diversions—all within a short drive of the gift shops, tourist trappings, and uncommonly fine restaurants clustered around Long Beach—provide what for many Northwesterners is the perfect recreational mix: developed and undeveloped. Raw and (slightly over-) cooked. The Long Beach Peninsula has its share of cheese. But it can be served on the side, and the rest of the course is as satisfying as it is healthy.

Getting There

The Long Beach Peninsula and Willapa Bay are approximately 150 miles southwest of Seattle via Interstate 5, US Highway 12, and US Highway 101. Allow 3.5 hours to get there. On the peninsula itself, Hwy 103 (Pacific Highway) runs north between Seaview and Leadbetter Point, serving as the primary access road to most sites in this chapter. On the inner side of the peninsula, Sandridge Road, which runs roughly parallel to Pacific Highway, provides access to Oysterville and the west shores of Willapa Bay.

inside out

Camping

Nobody goes to **Fort Canby State Park** anymore; it's too crowded. Bad joke, especially if you're stuck without a campsite. This popular park, the only major public campground in the region, is frequently sold out during summer months. (Its popularity is further heightened during the increasingly brief ocean or "Buoy 10" salmon-fishing seasons, when anglers flock here to launch boats.) Fortunately—or unfortunately, if you're the spontaneous type—Fort Canby's campground now is on the Reservations Northwest system, meaning you can reserve sites by phone as much as 11 months in advance.

It's well worth the effort to get here. The park, sprawled out across 1,882 acres at the southwestern tip of the state, is marked on the north and south by twin-bookend **lighthouses**, North Head and Cape Disappointment. In between is a massive campground; a sprawling picnic area; a deliciously clean, flat ocean beach; miles of trails; and a rock jetty jutting into the roiling surf of the Columbia River bar. As at most coastal campgrounds, you can't see the beach from the campsites (it's a short walk away on many sandy trails). But the proud, beautiful North Head Light is always in view, even when the fog rolls in.

The scenery is only part of the allure here. This wind-blasted land has a rich history. Lewis and Clark ended their long journey here in 1805, plunking their sore feet into the icy Pacific. The place was an important transportation and trade center from that day forward. Its significance is best understood by visiting the park's **Lewis and Clark Interpretive Center,** which details the explorers' journey to the Pacific, as well as the history of the two local lighthouses. (When it first blinked on in 1856, the Cape Disappointment Lighthouse became the first in the state, and one of the first on the coast. North Head Lighthouse was added in 1898.) Fort Canby, as the name implies, has a long military history. The Army was in residence here for more than a century before surplusing the land to Washington State in the late 1950s. Fort Canby, the final incarnation of the military base, stuck as the park's name. But other evidence of Fort Canby's military past remains, most notably spooky abandoned gun bunkers at **McKenzie Head.**

Some of us who've been visiting Fort Canby since childhood continue to make new discoveries here. It's one of Washington's recreation treasures. For more details on park hiking, boating, fishing, picnicking, beaches, and other charms, consult individual sections below. Fort Canby State Park's campground has 254 sites (60 with hookups; RVs to 45 feet) that are spread in many small loops through the central part of the park, mostly between dunes. They rate only about a medium on the privacy and modernization scales, but you can't beat the setting. Trails lead to the beach, old gun bunkers, local lakes, and elsewhere. Kids love cycling on the miles of roadway. The park is also one of the only public camping areas in the state to offer a camping experience to folks without a tent: it contains three comfortable, wood-floored yurts in the main camping area, as well as three wooden cabins on **Lake O'Neill.** Reservations are strongly recommended. Fort Canby is open all year. Sites can be reserved up to 11 months in advance by calling (800) 452-5687. *From downtown Ilwaco on US 101, follow signs 3.5 miles south to the park, on Robert Gray Dr; (360) 642-3078 or (800) 233-0321.*

Long Island in the middle of Willapa Bay has several primitive campgrounds. Access is by small boat only. (See Canoeing/Kayaking, below.) **Private campgrounds** in this area are more numerous than anywhere else in the state. Contact the visitors centers listed in More Information, below, for referrals and information.

A lonely stretch of beach near Tokeland

Hiking/Walking

A slew of good opportunities await here, ranging from long strolls through wildlife-rich marshes to quick jaunts uphill to picturesque lighthouses. On the north end of the Long Beach Peninsula, **Leadbetter Point** (easy; various distances), part of the Willapa Bay National Wildlife Refuge and connected to an undeveloped state park, offers about 4 miles of beach-wandering on the sand spit, with the ocean on one side, Willapa Bay on the other. If you wander inland, beware the marshes! This is a prime bird-viewing venue, particularly when migratory species are landing here in the spring and fall. To get there, from Long Beach follow Hwy 103 north to the end of Stackpole Road.

The other, most popular, portion of the Wildlife Refuge, **Long Island** in the middle of Willapa Bay, also has a trail system. Access is by small boat only. (See Canoeing/Kayaking, below.) Long Island is unique. Scientists say the 5,000-acre refuge is the largest estuarine island on the Pacific Coast. Its most alluring attraction is an undisturbed, 274-acre grove of ancient cedars—believed to be the last surviving example of a coastal "terminal" forest. Because the trees have been isolated from fire damage and weren't reached by loggers who worked this island as late as the 1980s, the forest has remained much the same for thousands of years. The cedar grove is reached by a **2.5-mile trail** that runs northwest from the beach landing nearest the wildlife refuge parking area. The island is big enough for more lengthy explorations: more than **5 miles of trails** cut through the woods.

The central peninsula is known, of course, for its beach-strolling. **Long Beach** (easy; various distances) truly is just that: 28 miles of flat, hard, sand lie between Leadbetter Point and the mouth of the Columbia River. Long Beach is as good a place as any to start and finish, although more than a half-dozen good beach access points are marked along Hwy 103. For a short walk that won't put sand between your toes, try the city's nifty, half-mile **boardwalk.** Or for a longer stroll, head for the city's new **Dunes Trail,** which winds through the dune grass from 17th Street S to 16th Street NW, crossing beneath the boardwalk. It's open to cyclists, runners, and walkers.

To the south, **Fort Canby State Park** (easy/moderate; up to 5 miles) is a grand day-hiking destination. The prime draw here is the 43,000 feet of ocean beach. To walk the entire stretch, follow signs to the North Jetty parking area and hike the beach north about 2 miles to the rocky headland capped by the North Head Light. (Unmaintained way trails lead from the beach up to the lighthouse, but the light is more safely reached via one of two upland trails.) Other good day-hiking trails lead from the day-use area at **Waikiki Beach,** just inside the park entrance, up to the Cape Disappointment Lighthouse (difficult; 3.6 miles round trip) and the nearby Lewis and Clark Interpretive Center (see Camping, above).

On the far east side of the park, a pleasant nature loop, the **Coastal Forest Trail** (easy; 1.5 miles), begins and ends near the boat launch at Baker Bay, on the Columbia River. Closer to the camping area, a short trail climbs to an old gun bunker at **McKenzie Head.** Nearby, the **North Head Trail** (moderate; 3 miles one way) climbs through the east side of the park to the North Head Light. Note that both lighthouses can be reached more easily via short trails from Robert Gray Drive, the main access road to Fort Canby.

Fort Coumbia State Park, 1 mile east of Chinook on US 101, has about a mile of hiking trails through the historic, World War I–era former army base.

Picnics

The day-use area at **Waikiki Beach,** just inside Fort Canby State Park, is a great picnic site (see Camping, above). Tables are spread throughout the upper beach area, which is protected from the otherwise surly weather by the tall ocean headland topped by Cape Disappointment. The long public beach on either side of the town of Long Beach is accessible from many points along Hwy 103. Developed picnic sites can be found at **Pacific Pines** and **Loomis Lakes State Parks.**

Canoeing/Kayaking

The Willapa National Wildlife Refuge is a must-check-out scene for canoeists and kayakers. The broad tidal flat of the **Willapa Bay** is rich with bird and marine life, and paddling conditions are uncharacteristically calm for a coastal area. The one caveat is the tide: when it's low, many parts of the inner bay become chocolate pudding, without the taste appeal. The entire bay is accessible by small watercraft, but the most popular destination is **Long Island,** reached only by boat from a parking lot/launch area near the wildlife refuge headquarters along US 101, 10 miles north of Seaview. A short paddle to the landing, followed by a walk to the ancient cedar grove and back (see Hiking/Walking, above), makes a memorable day trip. Four of five primitive campgrounds found here are connected by 5 miles of trails. Most campgrounds, however, are more easily reached by boat. Deer, Roosevelt elk, and bear often are seen on the island. It makes a perfect base camp for waterborne exploration of Willapa Bay. Contact Refuge Headquarters, 8 miles northeast of Seaview on US 101; (360) 484-3482, for more information.

Kayak rentals are available from Willapa Bay Excursions, 270th and Sandridge Rd, Nahcotta; (360) 665-5557.

Photography

The **North Head Lighthouse,** above Fort Canby State Park, adorns the living room wall of many a Northwest amateur photographer. It's scenic whether shot from the beach in the state park below or from the hillside above it, reached by parking at the lighthouse trailhead off Robert Gray Drive (see Camping, above). **Sunsets** on partly cloudy days create nice lighting here.

Fishing

The town of Ilwaco was a major **salmon** charter center for decades before the bottom began to fall out of Northwest salmon runs in the 1980s. Charters still head to sea—and to nearby "Buoy 10," off the Columbia's mouth—when fishing is open during the summer. In recent years, that's only been for a few weeks in July and maybe August, depending on fish allotments. Spring **bottom-fishing** and summer **deep-sea tuna** trips have picked up some of the slack. Check with local charter operators for information on seasons and limits. Popular **charter operators** include Sea Breeze Charters, (360) 642-2300; Coho Charters, (360) 642-3333; and Pacific Salmon Charters, (360) 642-3466 or (800) 831-2695.

When the summer salmon season is on, the North Jetty at Fort Canby State Park becomes a popular place. Salmon often are hooked off the jetty in late summer by anglers fishing with herring or the occasional Buzz Bomb–style lure. If the salmon season is closed, remember that the jetty also is a good place to fish for surf **perch** and other bottom fish. Spring days seem most productive for perch fishing, and anglers favor incoming tides for all jetty fishing.

While the flow of anglers to Ilwaco's ocean fishery has dwindled, it has increased almost as rapidly just up the road at Willapa Bay. A thriving late-summer **chinook** season inside these sheltered waters has become known as one of the "last best" chances to catch a big king salmon in Washington waters. The fish, many upward of 40 pounds, are hatchery stock, returning to their birthplace on the Naselle River. The run usually shows up around mid-August, peaks around September 1, and tails off by month's end.

Loomis Lake State Park has a public fishing area north of Long Beach off Hwy 103. The public ocean beaches around Long Beach open sporadi-cally for **razor clam** digging in the spring and fall. Contact the state Fish and Wildlife office in Montesano, (360) 249-4628; www.wa.gov/wdfw, for seasons and limits.

Wildlife Watching

The 14,000-acre Willapa National Wildlife Refuge (see Canoeing/Kayak-ing, above) is rich with **shorebirds, migratory birds,** and other creatures. More than 250 bird species have been cataloged here. The best day-use area in the refuge, particularly for those on foot, is Leadbetter Point, on the northern tip of the peninsula. The Wildlife Refuge property here, which adjoins an undeveloped (except for trails) state park, is a stopover site for more than 100 species of migratory birds in the spring and fall. Follow signs to the parking lot at the end of Stackpole Road, 3 miles north of Oysterville. For information, stop at the refuge visitors center, 8 miles northeast of Seaview on US 101; (360) 484-3482. Also, Skating Lake State Park, north of Ocean Park at Surfside Golf Club, contains a marsh that often attracts trumpeter swans and other **waterfowl.**

Biking

The many miles of rural roads between the main drag (Hwy 103) and Willapa Bay are a favorite haunt of cyclists. Most of the roads are narrow, but traffic is light and plenty of turnouts are available. Several scenic cycling tours are marked and easy to follow. **Rentals** are available at Willapa Bay Excursions; (360) 484-3482. For a good half-day trip, park in Long Beach and cycle north up Sandridge Road (it runs parallel to Hwy 103, about a half mile east) all the way to Oysterville, then another 2 miles north to Stackpole Road and **Leadbetter Point State Park,** part of the Willapa National Wildlife Refuge. Follow one of the trails down to the beach for lunch, then ride back. It's a round trip of about 25 miles, taking you along some of the peninsula's most scenic, placid roadways near the shores of Willapa Bay.

Longer trips are possible on the east side of Willapa Bay. One highly popular route is the **Naselle-Seaview Loop,** a 42-mile circuit from Naselle on Hwy 104 and US 101 along Willapa Bay to Seaview and back the same way. For an even longer ride, continue south at Seaview, following US 101 up the Columbia to Chinook and Megler before turning north and returning to Naselle on Hwy 401.

A word to the wise for mountain bikers: enjoy your ride on the beach, because next time you come back to do it, your machine will be a pile of rust.

Horseback Riding

Clomp off (do they clomp on sand?) into the sunset on a **rental equine unit** from Back Country Wilderness Outfitters Inc., on 10th, west of Boulevard, (360) 642-7176; or Skipper's Equestrian Center Co., S 10th and Boulevard, (360) 642-3676—both in Long Beach. Those who bring their own can **board** them for a fee at the Peninsula Saddle Club's Rodeo Grounds in Long Beach, (360) 642-2576; or in Ilwaco at the Red Barn Arena, 6409 Sandridge Rd; (360) 642-2541.

Kite Flying

This is the tangled-string capital of the Northwest. Visit some of the many good **local shops** in Long Beach, such as Long Beach Kites, at the stoplight, (360) 642-2202; or Stormin' Norman's, one block south, (360) 642-3482 or (800) 4-STORMIN. Just looking? Kite lovers can visit the **Long Beach World Kite Museum and Hall of Fame,** Third and N Pacific Highway; (360) 642-4020; www.worldkitemuseum.com, or **buy their own** at August's International Kite Festival, which brings thousands of soaring creations to the skies. The entire peninsula swells with visitors for this event, so plan ahead; (360) 642-2400.

Accessible Outdoors

Leadbetter Point State Park (see Wildlife Watching, above) has barrier-free rest rooms and trail access. A barrier-free ocean **beach access** with rest rooms is found on Hwy 103 at Seaview. **Fort Canby State Park** near Ilwaco (see Camping, above) has extensive barrier-free facilities, including camping yurts, picnicking, and rest rooms. **Loomis Lake** (see Fishing, above) offers barrier-free rest rooms and fishing access. **Fort Columbia State Park** (see Hiking/Walking, above) has barrier-free rest rooms.

Restaurants

The Ark ★★   The Ark, run by owners who've authored several cookbooks, garners rave reviews. *$$$; 273rd and Sandridge Rd, Nahcotta; (360) 665-4133; www.arkrestaurant.com.*

The 42nd Street Cafe ★☆   Locals going out for a nice dinner head here; the menu is mostly Americana. *$$; 4201 Pacific Hwy, Seaview; (360) 642-2323.* &

The Heron and Beaver Pub ★   This tiny pub is a dining destination for lunch or a light dinner. *$$; 4415 Pacific Hwy, Seaview; (360) 642-4142; www.shoalwater.com/pub.html.* &

Las Maracas ★   The low-frills trappings of Las Maracas indicate how authentic the food is. *$; 601 S Pacific, Long Beach; (360) 642-8000.*

My Mom's Pie Kitchen and Chowder House   Pies here—from banana cream to chocolate-almond—always sell out fast. *$; 4316 S Pacific Hwy, Seaview; (360) 642-2342.*

The Shoalwater ★★☆   Native ingredients are employed in artful meals that fill a seafood-heavy menu. *$$$; 4415 Pacific Hwy, Seaview; (360) 642-4142; www.shoalwater.com.* &

Lodgings

Boreas Bed & Breakfast ★★   Each room at this romantic 1920s beach house has a private bath. *$$; 607 North Blvd, Long Beach; (360) 642-8069; www.boreasinn.com.*

Caswell's on the Bay Bed & Breakfast ★★★   This neo-Victorian B&B is possibly the peninsula's most romantic spot. *$$$; 25204 Sandridge Rd, Ocean Park; (360) 665-6535; www.caswellsinn.com.*

Inn at Ilwaco ★   Located on a quiet street overlooking town, this B&B is housed in an old church. *$$; 120 Williams St NE, Ilwaco; (360) 642-8686; www.longbeachlodging.com.*

Shakti Cove Cottages ★   Ten small cedar-shingled cabins are each funky-cozy, with their own kitchens. *$$; on 253rd Pl, Ocean Park; (360) 665-4000.*

The Shelburne Inn ★★★   Well worn and warm, the Shelburne is filled with antiques and friendly charm. *$$$; 4415 Pacific Hwy S, Seaview; (360) 642-2442; www.theshelburneinn.com.* &

More Information

Long Beach Peninsula Bed and Breakfast Association: (360) 642-8484.

Long Beach Peninsula Chamber of Commerce: (800) 642-2400.

Long Beach Peninsula Visitors Bureau: (800) 451-2542; www.funbeach.com.

Port of Ilwaco: (360) 642-3143.

South Bend Chamber of Commerce: (360) 875-5231.

Willapa National Wildlife Refuge: (360) 484-3482.

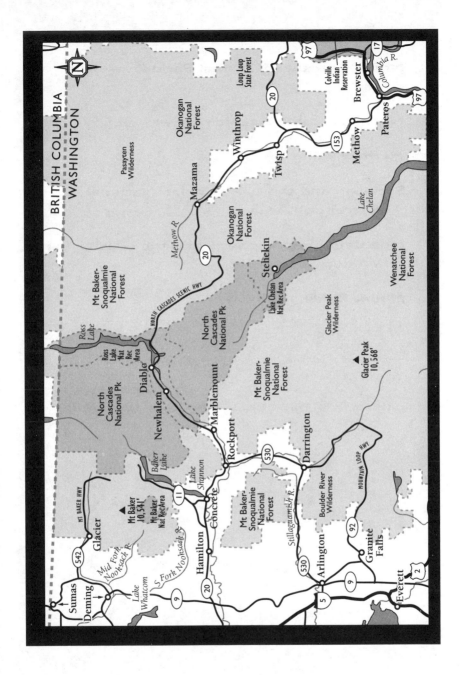

North
Cascades

North
Cascades

North Cascades National Park: Overview

From the Canadian border south to the Stehekin River, west to Mount Shuksan and east to Ross Lake, including nearly 700,000 acres of rugged, mostly unpopulated wilderness.

Follow the ice. That's a good general rule of thumb if you're looking for the wildest mountain lands in Washington. And it's particularly appropriate in the North Cascades National Park region, which contains the greatest collection of nature-cut crystal in the Lower 48 states. About 600 active glaciers are found in the United States outside Alaska, and more than half—318—are inside North Cascades National Park.

The park, which includes the adjoining Ross Lake and Lake Chelan National Recreation Areas, is 684,500 acres of the wildest, roughest, and most inspiring mountain valleys in the country. Like its wild-state cousin to the west, Olympic National Park, North Cascades was explored late in the local history of white settlers. The northern Cascade Range wasn't traversed by early trekkers until 1814, when an exploring party crossed Cascade Pass, following a route used for centuries by Native Americans. Development, such as it was, didn't hit the area until the late 19th century, when gold, lead, zinc, and other minerals drew miners high into the mountain valleys, where they left traces still evident today.

When the claims petered out, so did the human presence in the North Cascades—at least until the 1920s, when visionary City of Seattle engineer James Delmage Ross oversaw construction of the first of three Upper Skagit River dams, which continue to light the city today. The hydropower project—an engineering marvel then and now—put a permanent group of residents in the upper Skagit, and tourists followed.

The raw, craggy peaks, stunning alpine valleys, and sprawling glaciers in the area caught the eye of the 1920s and '30s adventuresome set, and much peak-bagging followed. In spite of frequent climbing treks, the North Cascades' interior peaks are so numerous and inaccessible that many were never scaled until 20 to 40 years later—an inordinate number of them by legendary Washington climber Fred Beckey, whose *Cascade Alpine Guide* series remains the region's climbing bible.

As is often the case in the mountains, where climbers led, hikers followed. Lots of them. Thanks in no small part to these backcountry pioneers, including prolific Washington guidebook author Harvey Manning, the North Cascades won national park status in 1968. Succeeding generations have trekked into the fantastic alpine terrain ever since, harvesting the fruit of these conservationists' indefatigable efforts.

Do the same yourself, and be prepared to be overwhelmed. The North Cascades are, with little argument, the wildest single place left in the Northwest, if not the United States. Ninety-two percent of the lands here are designated wilderness, meaning only feet and the occasional hoof ever mar the surface. Yet impressive as it is, the park is but a portion of the larger wilderness picture here. It is surrounded by other protected lands: the Mount Baker and Noisy-Diobsud Wilderness Areas to the west, the Glacier Peak Wilderness to the south, and the Pasayten and Lake Chelan–Sawtooth Wilderness Areas to the east. It's an impressive package, one that could consume a lifetime of exploration.

Around Puget Sound, many of us have pledged large amounts of our free time to that very pursuit. In the spring, we hike and camp in the Ross Lake valley, admiring the all-around mountain view and gulping down the clean air. In the summer, we lumber, curse, and grin our way high into the backcountry to stunning, wildflower-splashed vistas atop Desolation Peak, Cascade Pass, or Devil's Dome, rub our sore feet, and count our blessings. In the fall, we sneak out of the office at noon and drive the North Cascades Scenic Highway, past golden larches and blue skies, to a waiting bed or campsite in the Methow Valley. If we're feeling lucky, we call in well the following Monday, hop the boat up to Stehekin, walk into the backcountry, and take a world-class nap beneath the butterflies.

And all around, all year long, the glaciers are grinding away, beckoning, gleaming in some of the most memorable mountain vistas we've found, proving a universal mountain truth: for all its flaws and crevasses, ice is in good taste. A taste easily acquired.

Liberty Bell looms above a viewpoint along the North Cascades Highway

Getting There

Only three main access routes lead into the wild backcountry of North Cascades National Park. The most heavily used is Hwy 20, a wagon-path-turned-two-lane-highway that cuts through the mountains between Mount Vernon in the Skagit Valley and Winthrop in the Methow Valley. Primary national park hiking trails, campgrounds, and scenic vistas are reached via this highway, which closes between Ross Lake and Early Winters from November to April due to heavy snows. See the North Cascades Scenic Highway chapter for full details.

A popular alternate access is by tour boat or private boat to Stehekin, a mountain outpost at the north tip of Lake Chelan. Stehekin, reached by driving US Highway 2 and US 97 to Chelan, then catching a boat up the lake, isn't actually in North Cascades National Park. But the Stehekin Valley Road, which cuts west from Stehekin into the mountains, deposits hikers, cyclists, and campers at a string of remote trailheads and campgrounds inside the park's southern sector. See the Stehekin and the Lake Chelan National Recreation Area chapter for details.

The only other road into the park is the uneven, rocky Cascade River Road, which leaves Hwy 20 at Marblemount and penetrates 22 miles into the park's southern quadrant. From here, many hikers climb to Cascade Pass and drop down into the Stehekin Valley, linking with the Stehekin Valley Road, a park shuttle bus, and, ultimately, Stehekin Landing on Lake Chelan. The walk across Cascade Pass is about 9 miles.

Another foot route into the park, from the Hannegan/Ruth Creek area east of Mount Baker via Hwy 542, is the trail over Whatcom Pass through the high country west of Ross Lake.

inside out

Hiking/Backpacking

Without question, the best way to witness the wonders of North Cascades National Park is by hoofing it. The vast majority of rugged territory inside the park is reached only by trail, and some of it is reached only by scrambling off the trail for many miles. Park experts at the North Cascades Visitors Center in Sedro Woolley, (360) 856-5700, can advise you on suitable hikes. Two **trail guides** also will serve you well here. The definitive work is *100 Hikes in Washington's North Cascades National Park Region,* by Ira Spring and Harvey Manning (The Mountaineers Books). *Pacific Northwest Hiking,* by Ron C. Judd and Dan A. Nelson (Foghorn Press), also contains descriptions of most popular North Cascades hikes, as well as dozens more in the surrounding Glacier Peak and Pasayten Wilderness Areas. For a quick list of our favorite North Cascades hikes from Hwy 20 and the Stehekin area, consult the North Cascades Scenic Highway, and the Stehekin and the Lake Chelan National Recreation Area chapters in this section.

During many times of the year, your hiking choices will be dictated by **weather.** Although some lower-elevation trails (notably those in river valleys) are snow-free by June, many of this area's most popular hiking destinations are off-limits until July or later. The North Cascades receive unusually heavy amounts of snow, and Hwy 20 doesn't open until April or early May. Some alpine areas in the heart of the park don't melt out until late summer, if at all. North Cascades hikers should be prepared for bad weather at any time of the year. And backpackers bound for high-mountain passes above 6,500 feet should pack an ice ax and know how to use it for snowfield crossings, for most of the summer. If you're unsure whether your chosen trail will require **snow crossings,** consult a park official at one of the visitors centers listed in More Information, below. Never attempt to cross a steep snowfield without proper training and equipment. This mistake claims several lives in the Cascade high country every summer.

A word about rules. Like Olympic National Park, many trails in the North Cascades National Park area will pass through as many as three federal land-use jurisdictions: national park, wilderness area, and/or national recreation area. **Backcountry permits,** free and available at all park visitors centers and most trailheads, are required for all overnight stays inside the national park. Limited numbers are available for some of the more popular backcountry destinations, including the Pelton Basin and Sahale areas of Cascade Pass; Thornton and Monogram Lakes in Boston Basin; Copper Ridge; and the Sulphide Glacier climbing route on the south side of Mount Shuksan. Overnight permits are not required in the adjacent Glacier Peak and Pasayten Wilderness Areas, but group size and **stock-use limits** and other special restrictions apply there. Permits are not required for day-hiking in any portion of the national park, national recreation area, or wilderness areas.

Other considerations: **Group size** is limited to 12 living beings (people and stock) throughout much of the area; 6 beings in others. **Leashed dogs** are allowed only in campgrounds (note: on leashes here as well) and on trails in the Ross Lake and Lake Chelan National Recreation Areas. One exception is the Pacific Crest Trail, which cuts through the southern sector of the park. **Mountain bikes** are forbidden on all wilderness and national park trails, but allowed in the national recreation areas (but not on all trails). **Hunting** and **firearms** are forbidden in the park, but allowed according to state seasons in the national recreation areas. Confused? Employ the fail-safe method: ask someone in a position to have the answers.

Scenic Drives

Probably 90 percent of visitors to North Cascades National Park see it by car. Only one paved road ventures into the park, but it just happens to be one of the most magnificent in the state. The **North Cascades Scenic Highway,** Hwy 20, leaves Interstate 5 north of Mount Vernon and follows the Skagit River upstream through a steep, rocky gorge, culminating in the City of Seattle's extensive upper Skagit hydropower development. Guided tours of the area by railway and tour boat are conducted daily in summer by city crews. They're well worth the time, and a great introduction to the North Cascades ecosystem (see the North Cascades Scenic Highway chapter for details). From there, Hwy 20 climbs into the heart of the North Cascades, past 24-mile-long Ross Lake, the reservoir behind Ross Dam, and through mile after mile of inspiring mountain scenery. Notable pullouts are found at Rainy Pass and Washington Pass, where short trails lead to spectacular scenic vistas, with views you'd normally expect to see only at the end of a long, arduous hike. The highway then drops dramatically into the high, dry terrain of Mazama and the Methow River Valley at Winthrop.

That entire route can be driven easily in one day from Seattle, although doing so will leave little time to explore the high country on one or more of the many excellent day-hiking trails. Many Puget Sound area visitors make this a weekend trip, either camping in one of the park's campgrounds or picking from the many overnight spots in Winthrop. Hwy 20 is closed between Ross Lake and Early Winters (about 10 miles west of Mazama) from November to April or May. But in the summer, it makes a great northern leg on a 2- or 3-day **Cascade Loop.** To make the full circle, drive north on I-5 to Hwy 20, travel east through the Methow Valley to' its confluence with the Columbia at Pateros, then follow US 97 south to Wenatchee, and return west via either Hwy 2 (Stevens Pass) or US 97 (Swauk and Blewett Passes) and I-90. The loop is particularly popular in the fall, when slopes burst with colors both on Hwy 20 and, especially, US 2. For road conditions, consult the Department of Transportation pass report, (888) SNO-INFO; www.wsdot.wa.gov/sno-info.

Camping

The park has a number of good campsites along the Hwy 20 access route, and a wealth of nice, though primitive, walk- or shuttle-in back-country camps in the Stehekin area. See the North Cascades Scenic Highway, and Stehekin and the Lake Chelan National Recreation Area chapters for details.

Wildlife Watching

The North Cascades are a rich wildlife environment, and the full range of typical Cascades wild animals is found here: **black bears, coyote, cougars, bobcats, deer, elk, mountain goats,** and dozens of other, smaller species, most of which will crawl into your tent if you're not careful. The difference here is that they're more dispersed, and rarely visible from established viewing sites. Wildlife viewing up here is more by happenstance—usually on trails—than by careful planning.

The park's two most highly publicized creatures—**northern gray wolves** and the fabled **grizzly bear**—are rarely, if ever, seen. The U.S. Fish and Wildlife Service and the state Department of Fish and Wildlife have tracked one small family of wolves in the Hozomeen area, at the north end of Ross Lake near the Canadian border. Few wolf sightings have been reported by hikers in North Cascades backcountry. But biologists know wolves pass through the Cascades, whether or not they take up permanent residence there: reliable wolf sightings farther south in the Cascades have verified this. Park officials believe—and hope—that Canadian wolves will repopulate this former hunting territory. If you see one in the high country, give it a wide berth—and consider yourself very, very lucky.

Grizzly bears are yet more elusive. Even people charged with setting out for weeks at a time to find one have consistently come home empty-handed. Bear scat and fur found in some high, remote backcountry areas suggest the big carnivores do tour through the park—or at least have—

probably on their way to or from permanent homes in British Columbia. But no hiker has come back with a grizzly photograph, and no qualified observer has yet seen one in the North Cascades. That could change before the turn of the century. The U.S. Fish and Wildlife Service continues to mull plans to reintroduce the majestic beasts to the North Cascades, a former habitat. The plan has prompted a mixed reaction from backcountry users, but many North Cascades aficionados are excited at the prospect. They point out that grizzlies in the North Cascades would have much more isolated terrain in which to roam, play, and reproduce than do other Lower 48 populations in national parks such as Glacier in Montana. Stay tuned—and keep practicing good bear-country safety techniques, such as making plenty of noise out on the trail, cooking a considerable distance from your tent, and hanging all food and cooking supplies on a bear wire. Some North Cascades veterans would love to see a grizzly someday. But preferably not inside their tent vestibule.

A final wildlife note: Many people are surprised to learn that the park's critter list includes a squirmy one—the **rattlesnake.** They're not common, but rattlers are occasionally seen along trails and roads in the Stehekin Valley. Keep eyes and ears open.

Fishing

Trout fishing is a favorite summertime activity in many of the park's lakes, most notably Ross Lake, Diablo Lake, and Gorge Lake in the Ross Lake National Recreation Area. Good trout fishing also is found on the Stehekin River and at Domke Lake east of Lake Chelan. See the North Cascades Scenic Highway, and Stehekin and the Lake Chelan National Recreation Area chapters for details.

River Rafting

River rafting is a popular spring and summer activity on the **upper Skagit River,** below Newhalem. See the North Cascades Scenic Highway, and Stehekin and the Lake Chelan National Recreation Area chapters for details.

Mountain Biking

Mountain biking is a great way to see the **Stehekin River Valley,** thanks to the 22-mile Stehekin River Road. Mountain bikes are forbidden on nearly all trails in this area, however. See the North Cascades Scenic Highway, and Stehekin and the Lake Chelan National Recreation Area chapters for details.

More Information

North Cascades National Park: *www.nps.gov/noca.*
> **Glacier Public Service Center:** *(360) 599-2714.*
> **Golden West Visitors Center:** *Stehekin; (360) 856-5700, ext. 340, then ext. 14.*
> **Headquarters/Visitors Center:** *Sedro Woolley; (360) 856-5700.*
> **Newhalem Visitor Center:** *(206) 386-4495.*
> **Wilderness Information Center:** *Marblemount; (360) 873-4500, ext. 39.*

Park Service/Forest Service Joint Information Center: *Chelan; (509) 682-2549.*

Ross Lake National Recreation Area, Skagit District (Marblemount): *(360) 873-4500.*

Ross Lake Resort: *(206) 386-4437; www.rosslakeresort.com.*

Seattle City Light Diablo Tours: *(206) 684-3030; www.ci.seattle.wa.us/light/tours.*

North Cascades Scenic Highway

From Sedro Woolley east to Washington Pass, north to Hozomeen Campground at the Canadian border, and south to Cascade Pass in North Cascades National Park, including the upper Skagit River valley, Baker and Shannon Lakes, Diablo and Ross Lakes, Rasar and Rockport State Parks, Colonial Creek Campground, and Rainy Pass.

The howl of the wolf and the grunt of the grizzly don't sound at all out of place in Washington's North Cascades. Both creatures, previously believed to be extinct here, are now thought to be reinhabiting this raw wilderness, one of the wildest expanses of glaciated peaks in the Lower 48 states. Wolves have been seen and heard in the heart of this region, near Hozomeen Campground along the Canadian border. The griz have been more circumspect, leaving only small evidence of their incursions into Washington, probably on foraging commutes from the Cascades of British Columbia.

Seeing or hearing either one in the North Cascades would send a chill up your spine—either out of fear, respect, or both. But it could hardly be considered surprising. If there's one mountain region left in the United States that looks, smells, and feels like wild carnivore habitat, this is it. The North Cascades—divided into a national park, two national recreation areas, two Forest Service Districts, and a large, remote wilderness—are big, bad, beautiful—and mostly untouched.

Major exceptions come to mind, of course, such as the occasional abandoned mine shaft. And, most prominently, the City of Seattle's massive—almost mind-boggling—Skagit River hydropower project, which dammed the upper Skagit River, creating a valley-filling backwater, Ross Lake, that stretches north all the way into Canada. The most amazing thing about this man-made foothold in the North Cascades wilderness is not so much what it's done to the environment. It's how the environment's raw power accommodates it all with little more than a shrug. One of the most impressive construction projects in the history of the Northwest almost gets lost up here. That's how awesome the North Cascades appear, particularly to visitors who venture out into the backcountry.

Highway 20, the only major road in the area, provides a drive-through tour of all the best and worst of this majesty. From Mount Vernon, the highway leads up through the broad, fertile Skagit valley to a well-developed recreation area, Baker and Shannon Lakes (also the result of hydro handiwork, this time by Puget Sound Energy), then twists and turns along the upper Skagit's narrow gorge to Rockport, Marblemount, Newhalem, and Diablo, the latter two being rare examples of true "company towns" constructed for and by Seattle City Light crews building and maintaining Ross and Diablo Dams.

Viewing the massive hydro project from above brings mixed emotions. It's sad to see this river—one of the mightiest in the Northwest before its damming in the early 1920s—blocked by concrete. It's sad to see salmon stacked up below the Gorge Powerhouse in Newhalem, waiting in vain for the water to rise enough to allow their passage to the upper river. Old genes die long, slow, painful deaths. But it's also a thrill to realize even such a heavily altered area can remain so uniquely wild. The truth is that the power project here (aside from providing a century of cheap power, some of which produced this book and a billion other conveniences) opened an otherwise walled-off treasure trove to Washington recreators. If not for a handful of early City Light engineers with big plans, most of us likely would never witness the unforgettable view from the top of Desolation Peak, encounter a family of black bears beneath Devil's Dome, or watch in wonder as a glacier slowly carves away the face of Johannesburg Mountain. Those who take the time to study the area's early history will be impressed by the degree to which this area's sheer beauty turned its original human conquerors—the hydro crews—into its most ardent defenders, its most vigorous promoters.

Now as then, the North Cascades get under your skin. And there they stay. No area in the Northwest—and perhaps in the nation—is as wild as this. As Hwy 20 crosses the Cascade Crest and proceeds east, all other signs of human presence disappear. Animals outnumber drivers.

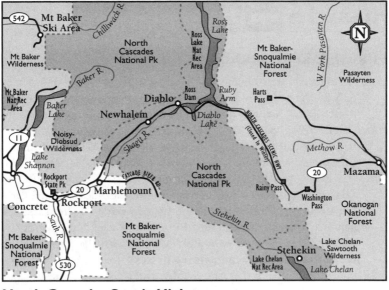

North Cascades Scenic Highway

The natural order here is as natural, and orderly, as it gets. Whether your visit is a short day trip to watch bald eagles feed on the Upper Skagit or a monthlong cross-country trek around, beside, and over countless 8,000-foot glaciated peaks, it likely will create a yearning for another.

The cure is simple: pick a trail, forge ahead, and keep your ears open. That grunt or howl you hear might be a wandering carnivore—or just another backcountry pilgrim with too big a load. Either way, it's a cry of freedom.

Getting There

The North Cascades Scenic Highway (Hwy 20) turns east from Interstate 5 at exit 230 near Mount Vernon, 63 miles north of Seattle. To reach the Baker Lake and Shannon Lake area, continue to Baker Lake Road (Forest Road 11), about 14 miles east of Sedro Woolley, which leads north to the lake. Other recreation sites in this chapter are farther east along Hwy 20, which continues over Rainy and Washington Passes to Mazama and ultimately to the Methow Valley. Note: The North Cascades Scenic Highway closes from mid-November through early April (depending on snow conditions) between Ross Dam, milepost 134, and milepost 170, about 10 miles west of Mazama. Consult the Department of Transportation pass report, (888) SNO-INFO; www.wsdot.wa.gov/sno-info.

inside out

Hiking/Backpacking

Hiking trails are so numerous—and so remarkable—in this area, we can only hit the highlights here. For full trail information, we strongly suggest a stop at the National Forest and National Park visitors center in Sedro Woolley, (360) 856-5700; the North Cascades National Park Visitors Center at Newhalem, (206) 386-4495; or the park's Wilderness Information Center at Marblemount, (360) 873-4500, ext. 39. All are along Hwy 20.

Remember that **overnight permits**, free and available at ranger stations and trailheads, are required for North Cascades National Park trails. Get them at the Marblemount information center, or from trailhead dispensers. In addition, beginning in the summer of 2000, North Cascades National Park formed an unholy alliance with the Forest Service and began requiring **trailhead parking passes** for some Forest Service–maintained trailheads in the park vicinity. The Northwest Forest Pass, $5 per day or $30 annually, is available at ranger stations, from many private vendors, on-line at www.naturenw.org, or by calling (800) 270-7504.

What follows is a list of perennial favorites, beginning in the Baker Lake and south slope Mount Baker area in the North Cascade foothills north of Concrete and heading east, concluding at trailheads at or near Washington Pass, at the Cascade Crest. This emphasis is on day hikes, although the most popular backpack routes are included.

Baker Lake and south slope Mount Baker

An easy hike along a chain of lakes in the shadow of the mountain culminates at **Elbow Lake** (easy; 7 miles round trip), where fishing can be good for trout. The trailhead for this trail system, which includes a dozen miles of other trails to lakes in the Middle Fork Nooksack drainage, can be reached from the north or south, via Hwy 542, Mosquito Lake Road, and Forest Road 38 or Forest Road 12.

High above in the same area, two trail systems climb to fantastic alpine territory on the south slopes of Baker. The **Park Butte Trail** (difficult; 7 miles round trip) is a walk into alpine heaven, climbing 2,250 feet through beautiful mountain parklands filled with wildflowers and backed by wonderful mountain views. The trail culminates at Park Butte Lookout, 5,450 feet. But surrounding areas, such as the adjacent Mazama Park and the nearby rugged Sulphur Moraine (accessible from a connecting path, the Scott Paul Trail), are worth a day's exploring on their own. Also from Park Butte Trail, a connecting path leads up the **"Railroad Grade"** (actually a glacial moraine) to the tip of the Easton Glacier, at about 7,000 feet. This is a primary Mount Baker summit route. Campsites in **Morovitz Meadows,** about midway up the trail, make a good base camp for mountainside exploration. The trailhead is on Forest Road 13, reached by turning north from Hwy 20 on Baker Lake Road, about 14 miles east of Sedro Woolley.

Just to the west, another spectacular alpine route is the **Cathedral Pass and Mazama Park Trail** (moderate/difficult; 10 miles round trip), which is an alternate route into the same high-country glacial meadow area reached via the Park Butte Trail. Good campsites are found in beautiful Mazama Park. Buggy in summer, this hike is at its best in early fall. The trailhead is on Forest Road 12, also reached from the Baker Lake Road.

A good route within a short drive of Baker Lake campgrounds, on the lake's west shore along Baker Lake Road, is the **Shadow of the Sentinels Nature Trail** (easy; half-mile round trip), a nice, family-friendly loop on a boardwalk through one of this heavily manhandled valley's last stands of old-growth Douglas fir. Another good day hike for Baker Lake campers is the **Baker River Trail** (easy; 6 miles round trip), which winds through a rain-forest environment along the river to Sulphide Camp in North Cascades National Park. Follow signs to Trail 606 from Forest Road 1168 at the north end of Baker Lake.

Near Baker Lake itself, try the newly expanded **East Bank Baker Lake Trail** (easy; up to 12 miles round trip), which runs along the shore of this scenic reservoir to Maple Grove Camp (see Camping, below), offering nice Mount Baker views. This is a decent cross-country ski route in the winter. The trailhead is near Upper Baker Dam, on Forest Road 1107. A good family hike within a short drive of Baker Lake campgrounds is the trail to **Watson Lakes** (easy; 5 miles round trip), a nice summer walk to a string of alpine lakes below Anderson Butte in the Noisy-Diobsud Wilderness. The trailhead is on Forest Road 1107-22, east of Baker Lake.

A good day hike from Rockport State Park is the **Sauk Mountain Trail** (moderate; 4.2 miles round trip), which climbs gradually to a 5,537-foot viewpoint (try it in late spring, when wildflowers are in bloom).

Marblemount area

Cascade Road, which leaves Hwy 20 at Marblemount and winds 22 rough (no RVs) miles into the southern district of North Cascades National Park, gets heavy traffic in the summer, and most people are headed for the same place. The **Cascade Pass Trail** (difficult; 7.4 miles round trip) is widely considered one of the top day hikes in the North Cascades. Hard to argue with that assessment. From the steep trail's 5,400-foot summit, you'll make eye contact with magnificent, 8,065-foot **Johannesburg Mountain,** whose front face contains a very active hanging glacier that often spits chunks into the valley below. The only drawback here is the crowds. How many other alpine day hikes end at a viewpoint with its own composting toilet? **Side trips** from the summit provide refuge for solitude seekers. They include the spectacular ridge walk up **Sahale Arm** to the **Sahale Glacier,** a trek to **Doubtful Lake,** the ridge walk south to **Mixup Peak,** and a trail northeast to lovely **Horseshoe Basin.** Through hikers can venture east 9 miles (from the Cascade Pass trailhead) down the upper Stehekin River valley to Cottonwood Campground, at the end of the road leading to **Stehekin** on Lake Chelan (see the Stehekin and the Lake Chelan National Recreation Area chapter). Note: No camping is allowed at Cascade Pass.

Newhalem area

Just west of Newhalem on rocky Thornton Creek Road is the **Thornton Lakes Trail** (moderate/difficult; 10.6 miles round trip), a popular walk to some nice alpine lakes (snowed-in until late summer). Closer to Newhalem itself, take the kids to the **Trail of the Cedars Interpretive Loop** (easy; one-third mile round trip) or the **Newhalem Campground Loop** (easy; half-mile round trip). Or better yet, stop on the edge of town at the Gorge Powerhouse, cross the footbridge, and embark on a fascinating historical/natural journey **to Ladder Creek Falls** (easy; half-mile round trip), an interesting rock garden built in the early 1920s by J. D. Ross, Seattle City Light's first superintendent. The falls themselves are a graceful showstopper.

Diablo area

Day trippers who arrive early for the Diablo ferry can stretch their legs on the **Stetattle Creek Trail** (easy; 7 miles round trip), a nice forest walk that begins near the Stetattle Creek bridge in Diablo. Near the tugboat pickup dock itself, the **Diablo Lake Trail** (easy; 7.6 miles round trip) climbs at a leisurely pace above the aqua-green lake and meanders east to Ross Dam. Consider making this a one-way trip by taking the tugboat up the lake, then walking back. For a climb that will test anyone's mettle, set out from "downtown" Diablo on the **Sourdough Mountain Trail** (difficult; 7 miles round trip), which climbs nearly 4,000 feet to the site of an antenna tower with sweeping views of the upper Skagit valley. The trailhead is behind the Diablo swimming pool. Note: The trail had some 40 trees across it in the summer of 2000.

Nearby, along Hwy 20 between Diablo and Colonial Creek Campground, look for the **Pyramid Lake** (difficult; 4.2 miles round trip) pullout parking area on the north side of the road, with the trail on the south side. The trail leads very steeply up to the picturesque lake, set below aptly named Pyramid Peak, 7,182 feet. No camping is allowed at the lake.

Watch for climbers on Pyramid Peak and nearby Colonial Peak. Up the road at Colonial Creek Campground, the **Thunder Creek Trail** (moderate; 12 miles round trip) is a main hiker's thoroughfare in this area, following the creek south all the way to the **Cascade River** drainage. This trail has been very brushy in recent summers, and bears have been active in the area. Day hikers and overnight backpackers use the lower portion only, cruising along Diablo Lake's Thunder Arm and passing through the cool, green forest to McAlester Camp, 6 miles in. Long-distance trekkers continue on to connecting trails to **Easy Pass,** spectacular (and highly popular) **Fourth of July Pass** (difficult; 10.5 miles round trip), or **Park Creek Pass** (difficult; 39 miles round trip), which serves as another trail entrance to the Stehekin area. Consult a trail map to consider the many loop-trip backpacking possibilities off this trail, which begins near the Colonial Creek Campground amphitheater.

Ross Lake

The giant reservoir cradled beneath stunning mountain peaks behind Ross Dam is one of Washington's most impressive wild areas. It's also one of the least accessible. To reach most of the wondrous lakeside campgrounds and trail systems on either side of this amazing Skagit River reservoir, you must take a boat—rentals and water-taxi drop-off are available through Ross Lake Resort, (206) 386-4437 (see Boating, below)—or do it the old-fashioned way: walk. The shortest route is the **Ross Dam Trail** (moderate; 5 miles round trip), which drops from a trailhead near milepost 134 to a small landing near Ross Dam. From here, you can cross the dam and continue 1.5 miles to Ross Lake Resort, where rental boats are available. Some hardy hikers carry kayaks in via this route, but heavy gear is best brought in by packing it onto the Diablo Lake tug, which stops at the foot of Ross Dam, then arranging for a truck pickup and portage (also contact Ross Lake Resort) from lower Ross Dam to the lake on the other side.

If you're boating up the lake, consider one of North Cascade National Park's classic backpack loops: the challenging, heavily forested **Big Beaver and Little Beaver Loop** (difficult; 28.2 miles round trip; allow 4 to 5 days). The best way to get here is to arrange a water-taxi drop-off at Little Beaver Camp trailhead, about 10 miles up the lake. You can also hike the Ross Dam Trail over the dam and about 6 miles up the lake's shore to Big Beaver trailhead and hike the loop in the other direction, arranging for a water-taxi pickup at Little Beaver. Either way, the route is challenging (trail maintenance is rare) but unforgettable, with awesome mountain views, 1,000-year-old western red cedars, and plentiful wildlife (black bears are common). You can also follow either the Big Beaver or Little Beaver Trail west to Whatcom Pass, for a one-way traverse with an exit near Mount Baker (see Whatcom/Hannegan Pass, in the Mount Baker Highway chapter under Hiking).

Some of the North Cascades' most memorable hiking awaits on the east shore of the lake. The **East Bank Ross Lake Trail** (moderate; 31 miles one way; allow 4 to 5 days) is a Northwest classic, winding along the reservoir through a series of beautiful lakefront camps. You can design a backpack trip of any length on this trail by arranging for a boat pickup at one of the campsites, most of which are equipped with docks. But to do it right, consider walking the entire length, hitting midway showstopper highlights such as **Desolation Peak** on your way to the destination, Hozomeen Campground, where you can arrange a boat pickup or a car pickup by a very, very nice friend who had to drive all the way through southern British Columbia just to get you. To reach the East Bank Trail, hike the Panther Creek Trail (the trailhead is near Panther Creek Bridge, near milepost 138 on Hwy 20) about 3 miles to its junction with the East Bank Trail. Consult a map and go wild with this one. (Warning: At some times of the year, the East Bank Trail is a walk along mudflats. See note on lake level fluctuations in Boating, below.)

If that sounds a bit too time consuming, you can sample the best of the region by hiking the **Desolation Peak Trail** (difficult; 9.4 miles round trip). It's possible to hike to the Desolation trailhead by walking 18 miles in from Hwy 20 via the Panther Creek and East Bank Ross Lake Trails. But most people make this a weekend trip by arranging a water-taxi ride to Desolation Landing or lakefront Lightning Creek Campground, then making the steep (4,400 vertical feet in less than 5 miles) hike to the top from a base camp at Lightning Creek or Desolation Camp (3.75 miles up the trail). Note that starting at Lightning Creek Campground adds about 4 miles to the round-trip hike, but provides a more convenient camping base for a weekend trip. Whichever route you choose, the summit is truly spectacular, with Ross Lake at your feet, wildflowers all around, and jagged Hozomeen Mountain (8,066 feet), Jack Mountain (9,066 feet), and its Nohokomeen Glacier in your face. At the meadow top is a fire lookout, occupied in 1956 by a then-unknown seasonal worker named Jack Kerouac. His stay here is described in his later beat-generation classic, *Desolation Angels*. (Note: Once the snow melts off, the only water source on the Desolation Trail is at about 3,200 feet, about halfway up. Be sure to stock up here, or be prepared for a dry night.)

Other classic North Cascades backpack loops lead from the Ross Lake area into the Pasayten Wilderness to the northeast. The **Devil's Dome Loop** (very difficult; 41 miles round trip; allow 8 days) is one of the most spectacular. This high-altitude route climbs to Crater Mountain and Devil's Park, turning west at Devil's Pass to Ross Lake, and returns via the

East Bank and Ruby Creek Trails. The trailhead is on the east shore at Devil's Junction Campground. Study your maps and eat your Wheaties for this one. For more Pasayten Wilderness backpack adventures, see the Methow Valley chapter.

Upper Highway 20 day hikes

On the south side of the highway in the eastern North Cascades high country is one of the more spectacular day hikes in the state. **Easy Pass** (difficult; 7.2 miles round trip) really isn't, whether you go in via the long route (20 miles from Colonial Creek Campground via the Thunder Creek Trail) or the short (3.6 miles from Hwy 20 on the east side). But it's worth it. If you have steely thighs, don't mind company, and want to do *the* North Cascades day hike, this is probably the one. Views at the 6,500-foot pass are stupendous, particularly in the fall, when larch trees paint the rocky slopes gold. Wildlife is plentiful (the last known resident grizzly bear in Washington State was shot not far from here in 1968), water is scarce. Be prepared for snow in the upper reaches well into summer. The trailhead is about 22 miles east of Colonial Creek.

A similarly popular hike with dual access is **Fourth of July Pass,** which can be reached via the Thunder Creek Trail (see above) or via the Panther Creek Trail, from a trailhead 8 miles east on Hwy 20 (near milepost 138). The latter route is longer (difficult; 11.5 miles round trip), but more direct. But many people do both by hiking the entire route as a 10.5-mile, one-way through hike.

Another good day hike, this one easier, is **Lake Ann** and **Maple Pass** (easy/moderate; 6.2 miles round trip), which gives you the choice of lounging at a pleasant lake (Lake Ann, stocked with cutthroat trout) or continuing 2 miles up the trail to superb views at Maple Pass, elevation 6,800 feet. The trailhead is in the Rainy Pass south parking lot. From the same spot, this highway's most heavily traveled path, the **Rainy Lake Nature Trail** (easy; 1.8 miles round trip) is a wheelchair-accessible path to a beautiful lakeside picnic spot, with views across the water of the Lyall Glacier and a nearby waterfall. Also from Rainy Pass, a popular day hike leads north on the Pacific Crest Trail to **Cutthroat Pass** (difficult; 11.5 miles round trip) with mind-blowing views at the pass, which PCT through-hikers say is one of the more spectacular spots on the entire route. The elevation gain is about 2,000 feet, and you can venture off on a side trip to Cutthroat Lake.

Blue Lake (moderate; 4.4 miles round trip) is a nice day hike to a very pretty lake just west of Washington Pass. Finally, another short-but-sweet walk is the **Washington Pass Overlook** (easy; half-mile round trip), a paved path offering a close-up look at Liberty Bell Peak, Silver Star Mountain, the Wine Spires, and Early Winters Spires. Perhaps nowhere else in the state is the dramatic difference between eastside and westside climates so evident from a single viewpoint. Watch for signs along Hwy 20. And be sure to check the parking area for the recently constructed Amazing Colossal Park Service Longhouse Outhouse. Your tax dollars at work!

Camping

In the Baker Lake area, any of the six National Forest campgrounds are worth visiting; call (360) 856-5700 for updates. Campsites can be reserved up to 240 days in advance by calling (877) 444-6777, or on-line at www.reserveusa.com.

Horseshoe Cove has 34 sites (no hookups; RVs to 35 feet). It's open from May through September, and has this area's best swimming beach. The campground also has a group site for 35 people, which must be reserved in advance. Many of the regular campsites can also be reserved in advance. *Hwy 20 to Baker Lake Rd near Birdsview, 15 miles north to Forest Rd 1118, 2 miles east to the campground.*

Boulder Creek, 1 mile west of the lake on Baker Lake Road, has 8 tent sites, 2 large group sites, and no drinking water. **Panorama Point** has 15 sites (no hookups; RVs to 21 feet). It's open from mid-May to mid-September. *Hwy 20 to Baker Lake Rd near Birdsview, then 18.5 miles north.*

Park Creek has 12 sites (no hookups; RVs to 22 feet). It's open from mid-May to mid-September. The campground has pit toilets and no piped water. *Hwy 20 to Birdsview, 19.5 miles north on Baker Lake Rd to Forest Rd 1144.*

Shannon Creek is a primitive site with 2 tent sites and 19 RV sites (no hookups). *At the far north end of the lake on Baker Lake Rd.*

Maple Grove is a paddle- or walk-in site on the east side of the lake, with 5 campsites along the East Bank Baker Lake Trail (see Hiking/Backpacking, above). It's free.

Two large **private campgrounds** in the Baker Lake area, Baker Lake Resort and Kulshan, both run by Puget Sound Energy, are good alternatives; (888) 711-3033.

Washington's newest state park, **Rasar,** awaits westside Hwy 20 campers with 52 campsites (22 with full hookups; RVs of any length) near the north bank of the Skagit River. Ten of the sites are cozy, walk-in tent sites, great for cyclists or car campers. Several nifty 4-person Adirondack shelters are located here. The park also has three designated hiker/biker (no vehicle) sites. The park is named after the family that donated most of this 168-acre former farm site to the state in 1986. Short trails lead to the banks of the Skagit. Watch for deer, elk, and bald eagles! The campground is open all year. Campsites cannot be reserved. *From Hwy 20 about 15 miles east of Sedro Woolley, turn right (south) on Lusk Rd, proceed three-fourths mile to Cape Horn Rd, turn left, and continue another mile to the park entrance; (360) 826-3942 or (800) 233-0321.*

Farther east along Hwy 20, **Rockport State Park** has 62 sites (50 with hookups; RVs to 45 feet) amid a stunning old-growth Douglas fir forest. It's amazing this campground was ever built here, amid these gentle giants. Enjoy it, and be nice to them. Good hiking is available on the premises, with a wheelchair-accessible Skagit River view trail and a great day-hiking trail at nearby Sauk Mountain (see Hiking/Backpacking, above). It's a short walk from here to the banks of the Skagit, where bald eagles can be viewed in winter months. With its equally nice picnic facilities and group campsite with four Adirondack shelters, this is one of the most pleasant campgrounds in the area, and one of the best state parks in the system. Hikers, take note: Showers! The park is open from April to late October. Campsites cannot be reserved. *North of Hwy 20 near Rockport, 7 miles east of Concrete, and a mile west of Rockport; (360) 853-8461 or (800) 233-0321.*

In Rockport proper, if there is such a thing, is **Howard Miller Steelhead Park,** a city campground with 59 sites (44 with hookups; RVs of any length). The park, near the confluence of the Skagit and Sauk Rivers, is open all year and popular with steelheaders and eagle-watchers from December through February. The campground is well equipped for winter or any season, with full RV hookups, flush toilets, showers, a playground, Adirondack shelters, and other niceties. Call well in advance for reservations. *From the Hwy 20/Hwy 530 junction at Rockport, turn south on Hwy 530 and proceed a short distance to the campground; (360) 853-8808.*

Continuing east on Hwy 20, Cascade Road leaves the highway at Marblemount and leads to three remote campgrounds. **Cascade Island,** a Department of Natural Resources camp, has 15 sites (no hookups) and no fees, and is open all year; (360) 902-1000. The next two campgrounds are National Forest camps. **Marble Creek** has 24 sites (no hookups; RVs to 31 feet), with no piped water and no fees. It's open from mid-May to mid-September; (360) 856-5700. **Mineral Park** has 5 primitive sites (no hookups; RVs to 15 feet), with no piped water, and it's open all year, weather permitting; (360) 856-5700. The latter is used mainly as a staging area for hikes into the Glacier Peak Wilderness.

Back on Hwy 20, the Newhalem area has two North Cascades National Park campgrounds. **Goodell Creek** has 20 campsites (no hookups; RVs to 22 feet). This Skagit-riverfront camp is a popular stopover for rafters. This park also offers a very rare road view of the North Cascades' jagged Picket Range, a string of 8,000-foot peaks south of

Whatcom Pass. The campground is open all year, with no services or fees in winter. Campsites cannot be reserved. The camp's group site can be reserved by calling (360) 873-4500, ext. 16. *Watch for signs along Hwy 20, near milepost 119 just west of Newhalem; (360) 856-5700.*

On the other side of Newhalem, **Newhalem Creek Campground** is a major summertime (mid-May to mid-October) stopover, with 107 standard sites (no hookups; RVs to 32 feet), a short nature trail, and nice forested environs. It's within walking distance of Newhalem, just across the suspension bridge. *Follow signs from Hwy 20; (360) 856-5700.*

Gorge Lake (6 tent sites), a tiny, peaceful riverfront campground on the river near the town of Diablo itself, is a good alternative to the larger campgrounds. Near Diablo Lake is the national park's most popular overnight spot, **Colonial Creek Campground,** right on the lake banks and just off Hwy 20. The park has 162 sites (no hookups; RVs to 32 feet). Many good hiking trails begin right in the campground (see Hiking/Backpacking, above), and the park offers great small-boat/canoe access to eerily turquoise Diablo Lake. You could swim here, too—for about 4 seconds, which is how long it will take you to feel frostbite take hold in this bracing, glacial water. Colonial Creek is open from mid-April to mid-October; campsites cannot be reserved. *At Hwy 20 milepost 130, 10 miles east of Newhalem and 4 miles east of the Diablo Lake turnoff; (360) 856-5700.*

Backcountry campers, kaykers, canoeists, and other human-powered travelers will find a string of 20 National Park campgrounds on Ross Lake, the behemoth body of water behind Ross Dam. They can be reached only by trail (primarily the East Bank Trail; see Hiking/Backpacking, above) or water, including **rental boats or water-taxi service** provided by Ross Lake Resort, (206) 386-4437. Contact any North Cascades visitors center for information.

Wildlife Watching

The lower Skagit River Valley is **bald eagle** central during winter months. Viewing the regal raptors has become such high sport for Puget Sound area residents, in fact, that the Forest Service recently adopted new restrictions to limit the number of bird-lovers' rafts on the river. Eagles arrive here in late November and peak in January, clearing out and heading for saltwater hunting grounds by early spring. (The Upper Skagit Bald Eagle Festival is in January; (360) 853-7009.) Roadside viewing can be good at times from Hwy 20 pullouts between Rockport and Marblemount. You'll need binoculars or a spotting scope; no wild eagle will let you get closer than about 50 yards without flying off. (Photographers, note: Unless you're very, very lucky, you'll need at least a 600-mm lens for good close-ups.) The designated pullouts are at Washington Eddy and a rest area a

A bald eagle makes a landing in a tree above the Skagit River

short distance to the east. A good place to watch the birds without standing along the road is the Skagit View Trail, a wheelchair-accessible loop
inside Rockport State Park (see Camping, above). The park is on the border of the Skagit Bald Eagle Sanctuary. Howard Miller Steelhead Park at
Rockport is another popular viewing site (see Camping, above).

For some reason, birds seem less wary of waterborne craft, which
means a raft seat is the best place from which to view the eagles. Many
outfitters book mellow, eagle-oriented raft trips on the river from November through January. For a full list of outfitters, or for information about
running the river yourself via raft, canoe, or kayak, contact the Forest Service's Mount Baker Ranger District in Sedro Woolley; (360) 856-5700. If
you've already been to the Skagit bald eagle view-a-thon, or the thought of
crowds makes you itch, consider driving one river drainage north to view
birds in the less-known, less-popular North Fork Nooksack drainage (see
the Mount Baker Highway chapter). Or take your binoculars north to
Lake Shannon near Concrete, home to one of the state's largest populations of resident **ospreys**.

While you're in the upper Skagit, don't overlook the very prey that bring
the eagles here. Spawning **chum salmon** can be viewed from several stops
along this route, including the Puget Power Visitors Center in Concrete,
where **sockeye salmon** are trapped for hauling around the two Baker River
dams to Baker Lake, where they used to wander on their own. Farther east,
the Marblemount Salmon Hatchery is open to the public all year. Stop here

in the fall to see spawning **coho.** Also check the waters at the Gorge Power-house in Newhalem for late-fall spawners, often schooled up here at the very end of the navigable Skagit, wondering why they can't go any farther.

For information on other North Cascades National Park wildlife, see the North Cascades Scenic Highway chapter.

Photography

For very scenic shots with minimal effort, hoof it down the short trails to **Rainy Lake** or the viewpoint at **Washington Pass** (see Hiking/Backpacking, above). Both are best photographed in early morning or evening light, as midday brightness washes out both scenes. Also, **Diablo and Ross Lakes** can be photographed from high above, from a series of pullouts along Hwy 20. Another photographer's favorite is **Easy Pass** (see Hiking/Backpacking, above), where golden larch trees in autumn make a spectacular complement to the awesome mountain scenery. The ultimate wide-angle perch in this region, however, is the meadow atop 6,000-foot **Desolation Peak,** where surrounding mountain views are simply stunning. Our favorite time to pack the tripod to this region is October, when larches are golden, other fall colors are present, and the first dusting of snow coats peaks higher than 7,500 feet.

Fishing

Fishing for **trout** and **kokanee** (landlocked salmon) is good in Baker and Shannon Lakes, each a reservoir behind a Puget Sound Energy dam on the Baker River. Note that the minimum-size limit for kokanee is 18 inches. Boat rentals are available from Baker Lake Resort; (360) 853-8325. Watch for submerged stumps. Ross and Diablo Lakes also hold trout, and rental boats are available at each lake. Diablo also has a popular boat launch inside Colonial Creek Campground. For best results at Ross Lake, rent a boat at Ross Lake Resort, (206) 386-4437, and troll a flatfish behind a flasher or pop gear. Note that Ross Lake is a "selective fishery" that's open only from July 1 through October 31, with a 13-inch minimum-size restriction and a three-fish daily limit. The lake has some huge **dolly varden,** but they must be released. Fishing is best around creek inlets, such as the deep, eerie Lightning Creek Gorge. Other good spots for **rainbow** and **cutthroat trout** are Gorge Lake, which is stocked with rainbows, and Watson Lakes, Thornton Lakes, Rainy Lake, Cutthroat Lake, and Lake Ann, all alpine lakes that can be reached by trail by late summer (see Hiking/Backpacking, above).

The upper Skagit holds a decent run of winter **steelhead,** with best results in January and February, and fewer numbers of summer-run steelhead. Fishing isn't as productive as lower-river sites below Concrete, however (see the Skagit Valley chapter). You'll find launch ramps in both Rockport and Marblemount.

Boating/Canoeing/Kayaking

The cold, clear reservoir waters of **Baker Lake, Shannon Lake, Ross Lake, Diablo Lake,** and **Gorge Lake** are all popular with canoeists and kayakers. The best access is at Baker and Shannon Lakes, both of which are ringed by campgrounds and launching points, and Diablo Lake, where a public boat launch is found at Colonial Creek Campground. See Hiking/Backpacking, above, and Lodgings, below, for information on paddle or boat trips on Ross Lake.

Waterborne adventures on Ross Lake deserve a special mention. Canoe or boat trips on the 24-mile waterway are a unique thrill. With careful planning, you can create a long backcountry itinerary combining paddling or boating with magnificent lakefront campsites (Ross Lake is ringed by an almost embarrassing assortment of campgrounds, all but one unreachable by road, therefore rarely crowded) and spectacular backcountry day hikes. A paddle up the narrow, winding **Lightning Creek Gorge** on the east side of the lake is fascinating—almost surreal. Keep in mind that Ross Lake is a reservoir, with large fluctuations in water level. Trips planned for spring, when the lake is drawn down and shores are expansive mudflats, are much less pleasant than in the late summer or fall, when the reservoir is full. And the water level commonly fluctuates as much as 5 feet in a single day. Call Ross Lake Resort, (206) 386-4437, or one of the information centers in More Information, below, for trip-planning guidance.

Kayakers often take to the waters of the **upper Skagit,** a Class II/Class III river most often floated downstream from Goodell Creek Campground (see Camping, above).

Rafting

The **upper Skagit River** contains Class II/Class III waters run by a number of professional river outfitters. Most trips begin near Goodell Creek Campground (see Camping, above) and continue 8 to 10 miles downstream. See Wildlife Watching, above, for information on eagle-viewing raft trips and outfitters.

Accessible Outdoors

On Hwy 20, **Rockport and Rasar State Parks** (see Camping, above) each offer quality, barrier-free trails with access to the Skagit River. They're popular with hikers, wheelchair users, and parents with strollers, particularly during the winter bald eagle–viewing season. Rockport also has barrier-free campsites and picnic sites. Rasar also has 2 barrier-free RV sites and 13 barrier-free standard campsites, as well as wheelchair-accessible rest rooms.

At Baker Lake, **Horseshoe Cove Campground** (see Camping, above) has barrier-free rest rooms and "usable" (wheelchair accessible with assistance) campsites. **Shannon Creek Campground** has barrier-free campsites, rest rooms, and lake access.

In **North Cascades National Park,** the long list of barrier-free facilities includes Park Headquarters in Sedro Woolley, the Shadow of the Sentinels Nature Trail, the park Wilderness Information Center, Goodell Creek Campground, the Goodell Picnic Shelter, Newhalem Creek Campground, the Newhalem Visitor Center, the Trail of the Cedars, Gorge Overlook Trail, Gorge Creek Falls, Ross Lake Resort, Seattle City Light Tours from Diablo, Ross Lake Overlook, the Rainy Lake Trail, and Washington Pass Overlook. See Hiking/Backpacking, and Camping, above, or call the park at (360) 856-5700 for more information.

outside in

Lodgings

A cab in the woods ★   These cozy cedar log cabins are one of the best values in the area. *$$; 9303 Dandy Pl, Rockport; (360) 873-4106; www.cabinwoods.com.*

More Information

North Cascades National Park Headquarters/Visitors Center:
   Sedro Woolley; (360) 856-5700.
North Cascades National Park Newhalem Visitor Center:
   (206) 386-4495.
North Cascades National Park Wilderness Information Center:
   Marblemount; (360) 873-4500, ext. 39; www.nps.gov/noca.
Ross Lake National Recreation Area, Skagit District (Marblemount):
   (360) 873-4500.
Ross Lake Resort: *(206) 386-4437; www.rosslakeresort.com.*
Seattle City Light Diablo Tours: *(206) 684-3030;*
   www.ci.seattle.wa.us/light/tours.

Methow Valley

From Washington Pass east to Loup Loup Ski Area, north to the Cana-dian border, and south to Pateros and the Lake Chelan–Sawtooth Wilderness boundary, including Winthrop, Mazama, the Methow Valley Community Trail System, Sun Mountain Lodge, the Pasayten Wilderness, Pearrygin Lake State Park, the Chewuch and Twisp River valleys, and portions of the Okanogan National Forest.

The Methow Valley fits like an old flannel shirt. Thousands of us revel in its familiar warmth every year. Whether we're pulling the valley's sleeves on for a day of blissfully lonesome fly-fishing, silent cross-country skiing, or high-altitude mountain bik-ing, the Methow always leaves us with a massage-like afterglow. The valley, which unofficially begins in Mazama and follows the liquid-crystal Methow River downstream to shake hands with the Columbia at Pateros, hasn't changed all that much in the past several decades.

Our appreciation for it certainly has. Once a mishmash of min-ing camps, trappers' cabins, hunting lodges, and apple orchards, the valley is fast becoming the favorite mountain getaway for wet-side cross-country skiers, mountain bikers, hikers, and yellow-leaf lovers. High, jagged North Cascades peaks loom over rocky river valleys filled with pine, aspen, and other dry-side flora, painting magnificent mountain canvases all year long: the valley explodes in greens in the spring, when melting snows turn the peaceful Methow River into an imposing force of nature, luring whitewater rafters and kayakers who ride it from top to bottom. In the summer, valley skies are dry and clear, and local mountains draw faithful legions of mountain bik-ers and hikers, who set out north into the Pasayten Wilderness,

The sign—and sore feet—say it all: Trail's End in Winthrop

one of the best places in Washington to enjoy an extended backpack trip.

The Methow is exceedingly beautiful—and pleasantly quiet—in the fall, when skies and apples turn crisp and the valley floor is colored a brilliant yellow and red. It is no less stunning in the winter, when the weather turns beastly cold but ample coats of fresh, dry snow coat a 175-kilometer Nordic ski trail system that ranks as one of the most magnificent in the country.

Local residents have made some smart decisions in the Methow, joining forces to create a recreation-based industry that draws a year-round stream of visitors to the valley's just-right number of inns and lodges. Collectively, the towns of Winthrop, Mazama, and Twisp have achieved a thriving ecology-based economy. Like other prospering mountain towns in the U.S. west, the Methow is taking full advantage of the nation's recreation-based vacation boom. Unlike most of them, it has managed to do so without the accompanying plague of overbuilt vacation homes, ugly commercial development, and corporate resort overkill.

Some residents say the latest abandonment of major resort plans for the valley will help keep things that way. The Arrowleaf development, the latest incarnation of what was, many years ago, to become Early Winters downhill ski resort, gave up in 2000. The developers, who had planned a large, "environmentally friendly" Mazama-area development with vacation homes and cabins, a golf course, and cross-country skiing/ mountain-bike trails, threw in the towel when they couldn't get necessary water permits. Some Methow types thought the resort, the lesser of all evils proposed for that property, would have fit nicely with the valley ecosystem. Others are glad it's dead.

Time will tell. Meanwhile, the development's initial toehold in the valley—Arrowleaf Resort—seems to fit in nicely with a recreation destination that feels more comfortable with itself with each passing year. Do yourself a favor and plan a cycling, hiking, fishing, or skiing trip to the Methow in the near future. Do the rest of us a favor and don't spread the word around too much: every time we get one of these flannel shirts nice and broken in, somebody else is constantly wearing it.

Getting There

The best access to the Methow Valley depends on the season. Between April and November, Hwy 20, the North Cascades Scenic Highway, is the preferred route, crossing Washington Pass and entering the upper Methow Valley at Mazama. Just east of Twisp, Hwy 153 travels south along the Methow Valley floor to a junction with US Highway 97 at the Columbia River at Pateros. In the winter, Hwy 20 is closed between Early Winters Campground (about 10 miles west of Mazama) and Ross Lake, and the best Methow Valley access route is east via US 2 (or Interstate 90/US 97) to US 97 at Wenatchee, then north to Pateros and Hwy 153. Allow 4 or 5 hours for the trip via either route. For highway updates, consult the Department of Transportation pass report, (888) SNO-INFO; www.wsdot.wa.gov/sno-info. In the valley itself, should you poop out on your mountain bike or skis, you can get from one place to another year round on the Methow Mountain Transporter; (509) 996-8294.

inside out

Cross-Country Skiing/Snowshoeing

Anyone who says Washington has no truly world-class skiing has never been to the Methow Valley in the dead of winter. The valley, tucked into the dry side of the North Cascades, garners little attention on the national ski scene because it has no high-profile alpine ski resort (although more than one developer has tried, and failed, to produce one at Early Winters). But the valley's cross-country skiing terrain and facilities just might be the best Nordic skiing combination in the country.

The winter's cold skies and abundant dry snow create perfect cross-country touring conditions, while the **Methow Valley Sport Trails Association,** a conglomeration of skiers and local businesses, maintains a 175-kilometer trail system that literally winds through the entire valley, offering ski terrain ranging from easy loops near cozy Sun Mountain

Lodge to experts-only mountain ascents and deep-powder telemark plunges in the Rendezvous region. The trail system largely falls into three separate, groomed chunks: **Sun Mountain's trail network** on the slopes of Gobbler's Knob, just west of Winthrop; the **Mazama system** near Mazama, between the Methow River and Early Winters Creek; and the challenging **Rendezvous Trail System** in the highlands between Rendezvous and Grizzly Mountains, northwest of Winthrop. In between, the 30K **Methow Community Trail** runs the length of the Methow River from Mazama to a trailhead near Winthrop.

Just how you go about choosing your starting point depends largely on your choice of accommodations. Most visitors to Sun Mountain Lodge can work full time for several days and never ski the same trail twice on the 50 miles of Sun Mountain loops. Likewise for those staying around Mazama/Early Winters, where major trailheads are found at Mazama Country Inn and near the (closed in winter) Early Winters Ranger Station. Trust us: wherever you choose to roost in the Methow Valley during winter, a great cross-country ski trail is nearby, with your name on it.

In one part of the valley, lodging is even more closely tied to the ski trail. In fact, it sits on it. **Hut-to-hut skiing** is a favorite activity on the Rendezvous Trail System. Rendezvous Outfitters, 800-257-2452, or Methow Central Reservations, (800) 422-3048, can make the arrangements to ski between three spartan huts, each of which bunks up to 8 people and comes equipped with wood stove and propane cookstove.

Use of the valleywide trail system requires a **ski pass,** widely available at sport shops, visitors centers, and lodgings, for $14 a day on weekends, as of this writing. Valley skiing usually begins in December and lasts into March. Keep in mind that the Sun Mountain trail system, most of which is about 1,000 feet higher than the Methow Valley floor, usually opens first. A variety of ski-related festivals and races take place throughout the winter, including biathlons, a ski rodeo, and numerous distance races. **Ski rentals** are widely available, but Winthrop Mountain Sports, 257 Riverside Avenue, Winthrop; (509) 996-2886 or (800) 719-3826, rates as one of the finer full-service Nordic shops in the state. It's open every day except Thanksgiving, when employees stay home to wax the bases and file the edges of their turkeys. **Lessons** also are widely available, but the Sun Mountain Lodge Ski School, (800) 572-0493, and Methow Valley Ski School, (509) 996-2451, are local favorites.

For ski conditions, check with the Methow Valley Sport Trails Association, (800) 682-5787; www.mvsta.com. Central reservations for the entire valley can be made at (800) 422-3048. Sun Mountain Lodge ski packages are available by calling (800) 572-0493 (see Lodgings, below).

Two large cross-country trail systems are found at **Loup Loup Ski**

Bowl between Twisp and Okanogan on Hwy 20. Loup Loup Sno-Park, on the north side of Hwy 20, has 21 kilometers of mostly easy-to-intermediate trails. Trail fees are charged only when the ski area is running on Wednesdays, Sundays, and holidays. South Summit Sno-Park, across Hwy 20, has 30 kilometers of trails for all abilities. State **Sno-Park parking permits,** available at outdoor retailers and ranger stations, are required. But plenty of other, lesser-visited Sno Park opportunities await skiers—and, especially, snowshoers seeking some solitude—in this area. The list: **Black Canyon,** 5 miles south of the town of Methow; **Goat Creek,** 2 miles east of Mazama; **South Summit,** 12 miles east of Twisp on Hwy 20; **South Fork Gold Creek,** 6 miles south of Carlton; **North Summit,** 13 miles east of Twisp; **Eight Mile,** 8 miles north of Winthrop; **Boulder Creek,** 7 miles north of Winthrop; **South Twisp River,** 11 miles west of Twisp; **Yellow Jacket,** 5 miles northwest of Mazama; and **Kerr,** 4 miles northwest of Conconully.

Downhill Skiing

Alpine skiing in the Methow is mostly limited to **backcountry telemark** trips—unless you're willing to fly to the powder. North Cascades Heli-Skiing is your express ride to vast powder fields rarely touched by skis. **Heliskiing** is pricey, but owner Randy Sackett's rates are actually quite reasonable compared to similar services to the north in British Columbia's Bugaboos, Selkirks, and Monashees. Mazama-area lodging packages are available. Call (800) 494-HELI for reservations and information.

An intriguing ski operation also offers downhill not far from the Methow Valley proper. **Loup Loup Ski Bowl,** between Twisp and Okanogan on Hwy 20, hit the big time in 1999, going straight from surface lifts to a fixed-quad chair. The area now has one hurkin' chair, two poma lifts, and a rope tow to service about 1,200 feet of vertical over 550 acres, as well as 30 kilometers of groomed cross-country trails (and many more at the nearby Sno-Park, see above). The lifts run on Wednesdays, Sundays, and holidays; (509) 826-2720 or (509) 826-0945.

Mountain Biking

The very same community trail system that thrills cross-country skiers in the winter turns into a mountain-biking fast track once the snow clears. The Methow is increasingly becoming a favorite mountain-bike destination, offering rides for literally all abilities. The hilly, challenging, single-track terrain in the **Rendezvous Trail System** draws many expert riders, while novices and intermediates love the long, relatively flat course of the **Methow Valley Community Trail** between Mazama and Winthrop. Riders who begin at Mazama can ride the entire 17-mile course to Winthrop, following the river on its downhill journey through the scenic valley. Guests at **Sun Mountain Lodge** have their own 30-mile trail system that serves all skill levels.

Infinite loop possibilities present themselves. Consult **Methow Valley Sport Trails Association,** (800) 682-5787, for trail conditions and suggestions. There's plenty of riding outside the trail system, too. **Pipestone Canyon** southeast of Winthrop is a popular backcountry road-riding destination, with a wide variety of terrain in the state-managed Methow Wildlife Area. From Winthrop follow Center Street and Park Avenue south to Bear Creek Road. Turn left and proceed to the end of the pavement, about 2 miles beyond the golf course. The variable-distance **Buck Lake/Buck Mountain Loop** is another old-time favorite. From US 20 at Winthrop, take the W Chewuch River Road about 10 miles to a parking area at the junction with Eightmile Creek Road. Ride north on Eightmile Creek Road to Road 100, where signs indicate Buck Lake. The route is fairly steep, but the lake and a nearby campground are a nice reward. Riders can turn around at the lake for a 6-mile round trip or continue on Road 100 for another 6 miles, connecting once again with Eightmile Creek Road for an easy, paved voyage back to the car. The latter loop is about 16 miles. Another popular road ride is the 12-mile round trip from **Winthrop to Pearrygin Lake State Park** (see Camping, below). A fair number of trails in the surrounding Okanogan National Forest also are open to mountain bikes. Call the Methow Valley Visitors Center, (509) 996-4000, for a list of open trails. **Rentals** are available at Winthrop Mountain Sports, 257 Riverside; (800) 719-3826.

Prime time for mountain biking in the valley is the first weekend in October, when valley businesses host the annual **Methow Valley Mountain Bike Festival.** A full range of rides—both for fun and for hot competition—introduce riders to the valley trail system, and a series of competitive races take place on Sun Mountain Trails. Call the Methow Valley Sport Trails Association, (509) 996-3287, for details.

Hiking/Backpacking

The dry alpine country on the east slopes of the North Cascades is a favorite of many Washington hikers, particularly backpackers making extended journeys to the headwaters of the Methow, Pasayten, and Chewuch Rivers in the half-million-acre Pasayten Wilderness, one of Washington's loneliest wildlands. More than 400 miles of trails wind through this sprawling, meadow-dominated highland area. Note that a **Northwest Forest Pass,** $5 per day or $30 annually, is required to park in many Forest Service–administered trailheads in this area. They're available from ranger stations, from many private vendors, on-line at www.naturenw.org, or by calling (800) 270-7504.

Two favorite backpack routes on the west side of this massive wilderness are the **West Fork Pasayten** (moderate; 31 miles round trip) and **Robinson Pass** (difficult; 55 miles round trip), both of which begin near Harts Pass (see Camping, below) and wind into the heart of the wilderness, which is particularly beautiful in the fall. Another pair of trails provide quick access to the wilderness from Forest Road 51/Chewuch Road north of Winthrop. **Andrews Creek** (difficult; 31 miles round trip) and **Peepsight** (moderate; 28 miles round trip) are both outstanding backpack routes that follow pretty streams to scenic alpine meadows loaded with wildflowers, wildlife, and good campsites.

But you don't have to devote a week's worth of walking to see the mountain splendor in the upper Methow drainage. The east side of US 20 west of Mazama offers great day hikes. An easy walk and free of barriers, **Lone Fir Trail** (easy; 2 miles round trip) begins in Lone Fir Campground 11 miles west of Mazama (see Camping, below) and winds along—and over, via four very stylish wood bridges—Early Winters Creek. It's a great family walk. Another local hike is the **Monument Creek Trail** (moderate/difficult; up to 51 miles round trip), a good backpack trip that begins at Lost River trailhead off Harts Pass Road (see Camping, below, for directions to Harts Pass Road) and climbs up the Monument Creek drainage to a ridgetop with sublime views. Day hikers will find even the lowest several miles an enchanting walk, and stronger hikers can get to great views and back in a single day. Around Winthrop itself, the **Methow Valley Community Trail,** even though it's often dominated by the sounds of whirring spokes and schussing skis (see the Mountain Biking, and Cross-Country Skiing/Snowshoeing sections), makes for great summer day hiking between Mazama and Winthrop. Pick up a map at Methow Mountain Sports or any inn or lodge in the valley.

A number of good day and overnight hikes are also found west of Twisp in the Twisp River drainage, which provides the primary access to the east side of the Lake Chelan–Sawtooth Wilderness. Popular day hikes in the area include the **Eagle Creek Trail** (moderate; 14.5 miles round trip), which follows a placid, quiet creek valley to good views at Eagle Pass; and **War Creek South** (moderate; 12 miles round trip), which follows the stream through a forest to an alpine area rich with mule deer and other wildlife. Both trailheads are on Twisp River Road near War Creek Campground (see Camping, below). Contact the Methow Valley Ranger District at Twisp, (509) 997-2131, for more guidance on hikes in this remote, wild area.

Camping

For information on all but the state park, call the Methow Valley Visitors Center; (509) 996-4000.

Winthrop area

Pearrygin Lake State Park is the premier campground in the region. The 580-acre lakefront park has 83 campsites (30 full hookups, 27 water hookups; RVs to 60 feet), a 48-person group camp, good picnic sites, a swimming beach and bathhouse, and a boat launch. It's very popular with anglers and boaters, and usually remains full through the summer. Pearrygin is open from April through October. Campsites can be reserved up to 11 months in advance by calling Reservations Northwest; (800) 452-5687. *From Winthrop, follow Bluff St (it becomes E Chewuch Rd) about 2 miles north to County Rd 1631. Turn right (east) and proceed less than 2 miles to the park entrance, on the right (follow signs); (509) 996-2370 or (800) 233-0321.*

North of town in the Chewuch River valley is a string of Forest Service campgrounds. They're open summers only and offer limited facilities, but most are very scenic sites along streams or lakes with decent trout fishing. In the Eightmile Creek drainage, **Buck Lake,** 12 miles north of Winthrop on Road 100, has 9 sites (no hookups; RVs to 16 feet). **Flat,** 11 miles north of Winthrop on Road 5130, has 12 sites (no hookups; RVs to 18 feet). **Nice,** 13 miles northwest of Winthrop on Road 5130, has 3 tent sites, as does **Ruffed Grouse,** 4 miles farther up the same road. Nearby **Honeymoon** has 6 tent sites. In the Chewuch River drainage along Forest Road 51 are **Falls Creek** (7 sites and a short hiking trail to Chewuch Falls), **Chewuch** (4 tent sites), and **Camp 4** (5 tent sites). *The campgrounds are reached by following Forest Rds 51, 5130, or 5130-100 north of Winthrop.*

Mazama/Early Winters area

Three Forest Service campgrounds offer good camping just off US 20 in this area. **Lone Fir,** near milepost 168 (27 miles northwest of Winthrop) has 27 sites (no hookups; RVs to 20 feet). **Klipchuck,** near milepost 175 (19 miles northwest of Winthrop), has 46 sites (no hookups; RVs to 34 feet). **Early Winters,** near milepost 177, has 13 sites (no hookups; RVs to 24 feet).

The Lost River/Harts Pass area in the Upper Methow Valley offers more scenic, remote campgrounds. **Ballard** (6 sites; no hookups; RVs to 20 feet) has no piped water, but it's near Robinson Creek trailhead, a major horsepacking departure point (see Hiking/Backpacking, above). *From Hwy 20 about 15 miles west of Winthrop, follow Harts Pass/Lost Creek Rd northwest for about 7 miles until the pavement ends and the road becomes Forest Rd 5400. Continue about 2 miles to the campground.*

River Bend (5 sites; no hookups; RVs to 16 feet) is similarly primitive, and is used most often by horse packers and hikers bound for destinations such as the West Fork Methow Trail (an angler's favorite). *From Ballard Campground, continue about 2.5 miles on Harts Pass Rd to Forest Rd 54-060. Turn west and proceed less than half mile to the campground. (Note: Road is rough and usually not suitable for RVs or trailers past Ballard Campground.)*

Farther up the road, **Harts Pass** (5 walk-in sites) is a true thin-air special. It's only about 300 feet below the Slate Peak overlook, which at 7,200 feet is the highest place you can drive to in Washington. Harts Pass Campground is about 10.5 miles beyond River Bend Campground. The last in this string, **Meadows,** with 14 tent sites, is more like a backcountry camp than a car campground. But you can't beat the scenery. *On Forest Rd 5400-500, 1 mile south of Harts Pass.*

Twisp area

Similar Okanogan National Forest campsites are found to the south, in the Twisp River drainage. They're popular with anglers, hikers, horsepackers, and backpackers headed up and over Sawtooth Ridge, through the Sawtooth Wilderness, to the Stehekin area of Lake Chelan in North Cascades National Park. These camps are open all year—or at least as long as they're accessible via County Road 9114 and Forest Road 44. From east to west, they are: **War Creek** (11 sites), **Mystery** (4 sites), **Poplar Flat** (16 sites), **South Creek** (4 sites), and **Road's End** (4 sites). Other remote Twisp-area campgrounds are **Black Pine Lake** (23 sites), via Poorman Creek Road/Forest Road 300; and **Foggy Dew** (13 sites), via Gold Creek Road/Forest Road 4340. East of Twisp, just off Hwy 20, are **Loup Loup** (25 sites) and **JR** (6 sites). Call the Methow Valley Visitor Center; (509) 996-4000.

Rafting/Kayaking

The **Methow River** has a split personality. The upper stretch, from Carlton to just north of Methow, is fast in the spring, but fairly tame. The lower section downstream from Methow to the Columbia River is fast and raucous, earning an honest Class IV rating for many rapids in **Black Canyon.** Call the Methow Valley Visitors Center, (509) 996-4000, for a list of qualified **river outfitters.**

Fishing

The Methow drainage is prime-time fly-flipping territory, with many clear, cold streams and lakes cranking out good numbers of **rainbow** and **cutthroat trout,** plus a few steelhead. Favorite local spots are Buck Lake (north of Winthrop), and Twin, Patterson, and Pearrygin Lakes, all close to Winthrop; the Twisp River; and the Chewuch River, a selective fishery (artificial flies and lures/single barbless hooks only) stream accessible from many campgrounds north of Winthrop (see Camping, above). Pearrygin Lake is the most popular, both because of the state park on its banks and the extra-plump trout it seems to produce every year.

In the lower part of the valley, the Methow River itself is a noted **steelhead** stream, with a decent run of summer steelies that somehow manage the incredibly long journey through the Columbia River's hydropower gauntlet, out to sea and all the way back again. Methow River fish usually show up in September and October, but luring a Methow steelhead is no easy task. The water here is often so low and clear that the fish can see you coming a mile away. Very light leaders and a dose of good luck are required. Camouflage is optional. Many anglers fare better by fishing with bobbers and jigs on the lower river at its confluence with the Columbia near Pateros. Remember: All wild steelhead (if there are any left) must be released, and selective fishery regulations are in effect along most of the Methow. The Methow Valley Visitor Center, (509) 996-4000, has more information.

Horseback Riding

The upper Methow River drainage and Pasayten Wilderness look like they're right out of some old Western movie. You can put yourself in one by signing up for a **guided jaunt** with Early Winters Outfitting, (509) 996-2659 or (800) 737-8750, which arranges trips ranging from 1-hour rides to weeklong pack trips into the heart of the Pasayten Wilderness.

Other Activities

Tired of skiing, biking, and hiking? Take a **dog-sled ride** (winters only, of course) with Malamute Express Dog Sledding in Twisp; (509) 997-6402. In the summer, consider getting up close and personal with a llama on a frontcountry jaunt or backcountry trek. Contact Poorman Creek Llamas, (509) 997-LLMA, or Pasayten Llama Packing, (509) 996-2326, two of the more notable **llama ranches** in the greater Twisp metropolitan area.

Accessible Outdoors

Lone Fir Campground has a wheelchair-accessible, 1-mile interpretive trail, barrier-free rest rooms, and "usable" (wheelchair accessible with assistance) campsites. **Pearrygin Lake State Park** has barrier-free campsites and rest rooms.

outside in

Restaurants

Duck Brand Restaurant and Hotel ★   This funky, eclectic restaurant is a popular gathering spot. *$$; 246 Riverside Ave, Winthrop; (509) 996-2192; www.methownet.com/duck.*

Freestone Inn ★★★   A candlelit restaurant for dinners featuring Northwest specialties. *$$$; 17798 Hwy 20, Mazama; (509) 996-3906 or (800) 639-3809; www.freestoneinn.com.*

Sun Mountain Lodge ★★   This restaurant has long been regarded as one of the region's finest. *$$$; Patterson Lake Rd, Winthrop; (509) 996-2211 or (800) 572-0493; www.sunmountainlodge.com.* &

Lodgings

Freestone Inn and Early Winters Cabins ★★★   This inn sets an elegant, rustic tone for the 1,200-acre Wilson Ranch. *$$$; 17798 Hwy 20, Mazama; (509) 996-3906 or (800) 639-3809.*

Mazama Country Inn ★★   This spacious lodge makes a splendid year-round destination. *$$; 42 Lost River Rd, Mazama; (509) 996-2681 or (800) 843-7951 (in WA); www.mazamainn.com.*

Mazama Ranch House ★   The rural ranch atmosphere here is the real deal: bring your horse. *$$; 42 Lost River Rd, Mazama; (509) 996-2040.* &

Sun Mountain Lodge ★★★   Guest rooms at this hilltop lodge offer casual ranch-style comfort. *$$$–$$$$; Patterson Lake Rd, Winthrop; (509) 996-2211 or (800) 572-0493; www.sunmountainlodge.com.* &

Wolfridge Resort ★★   This lodge has an impressive 60-acre riverside setting. *$$–$$$; 412-B Wolf Creek Rd, Winthrop; (509) 996-2828 or (800) 237-2388.*

More Information

Department of Transportation pass report: *(888) SNO-INFO; www.wsdot.wa.gov/sno-info.*
Methow Central Reservations: *(800) 422-3048; www.mvcentralres.com.*
Methow Valley Home Pages: *www.methownet.com and www.methow.com.*
Methow Valley Ranger District: *Twisp; (509) 997-2131.*
Methow Valley Sport Trails Association: *(509) 996-3287 or (800) 682-5787; www.mvsta.com.*

Methow Valley Visitors Center: *Winthrop; (509) 997-4000.*
North Cascades Heli-Skiing: *(509) 996-3272 or (800) 494-HELI.*
Okanogan National Forest Headquarters: *1240 S Second Avenue, Okanogan, WA 98840-9723; (509) 826-3275; www.fs.fed.us/r6/oka.*
Sun Mountain Lodge: *(800) 572-0493; www.sumountainlodge.com.*
Tonasket Ranger District: *Tonasket; (509) 486-2186.*
Winthrop Chamber of Commerce: *(800) 4METHOW; www.winthrop.com.*
Winthrop Mountain Sports: *(800) 719-3826.*

Stehekin
and the Lake Chelan National Recreation Area

From Stehekin west to the Pacific Crest Trail, east to the Lake Chelan–Sawtooth Wilderness boundary with Okanogan National Forest, and north to Washington Pass, including upper Lake Chelan and portions of North Cascades National Park and the Glacier Peak Wilderness.

Stehekin is the only place in this guide—and one of the few in this outdoor-blessed state—that you can't get your car anywhere close to. Enough said.

Well, almost enough. Stehekin, year-round population 70, is a special place in an unforgettable setting. Accessible only by foot, passenger ferry up Lake Chelan, or floatplane, the sprawling backcountry in the Stehekin River valley east of town is virtually unchanged from the time of the first white settlement (if you can call miners "settlers") here in the 1850s.

The Stehekin valley, filled with fresh, cold streams, peaceful meadows, awesome gorges, and rocky peaks so high your neck will be hurting, has changed little, in fact, since long before that. The valley has provided a convenient access route from the east Cascades to the west for millennia. When early peoples moved from one climate to the other to hunt, trade, or perhaps just vacation, they came through here, using the same general route—Stehekin River to Cascade Pass, then down the west side to the Skagit drainage and Puget Sound—as many backpackers do today.

Backpacking trails in the upper valley mostly lie in the Lake Chelan National Recreation Area (NRA), with many reaching into

Tailor-made for boaters: Lake Chelan State Park

North Cascades National Park and Glacier Peak Wilderness. Some legendary routes are found here, many crossing fantastic alpine passes to Highway 20, though the average Stehekin admirer never dons anything heavier than a fanny pack. The town itself is a great retreat, a charming mountain village that would be spectacular anyplace. But its physical dislocation from the rest of the world enhances its adventure/intrigue factor at least tenfold. Setting out from Stehekin with your weekend gear, you get the feeling you're really out there.

Once in your life, before you die or have both knees 'scoped, you owe it to yourself to pack a duffel with a firm set of boots, a stout book, a sleeping bag, a pack of moleskin, some beef jerky, and your favorite doo-rag and set out for a week in the wilds around Stehekin. Compared to most other alpine destinations, this area is tricky to get to, requires some advance planning, and therefore is easy to bypass. That's the whole idea. So make a commitment, make a reservation, make a memory. For at least 150 years, Stehekin has specialized in those.

Getting There

Access to the village at the head of Lake Chelan and the foot of the North Cascades is by boat, floatplane, or foot only. By boat is the preferred route. From the town of Chelan on US Highway 97, you can take the old-fashioned tour boat, The Lady of the Lake II *(4 hours one way), the zippier* Lady Express

(2 hours and 15 minutes one way), or a new high-speed catamaran, the Lady Cat (1 hour and 15 minutes one way), which makes two round trips daily in the summer. Round-trip fares range from $23 to $89, based on (you guessed it) the season and the speed of your chosen mode of transport. Reservations are a good idea, particularly in the summer. Some factors to mull: The Lady II stops at Lucerne (about three-quarters of the way up the lake)—and at any of the Forest Service campgrounds/trailheads on the lake—by request in summer. During summer months, when all three boats run full schedules, it's possible to take them in various combinations to get into and out of Stehekin just about any time you need to. Lake Chelan Boat Company, (509) 682-4584; www.ladyofthelake.com.

If time is short, you can fly up to Stehekin by floatplane, tour the valley, and be back the same day via Chelan Airways, (509) 682-5555. Rates at this writing were less than you might expect: $80 per person one way, $120 round trip.For those on foot, several routes lead south from Hwy 20 into the Stehekin River valley—and to the Stehekin Valley Road, where you can hijack the bus back to the lake. But the shortest route is the one people have used for thousands of years: Cascade Pass, east of Marblemount (see the North Cascades Scenic Highway chapter). It's a 9-mile crossing—and a stunning one at that—from Cottonwood Campground at the end of Stehekin Road to the Cascade Pass trailhead, 22 miles east of Newhalem.

Once you're in Stehekin, the only way around is by shuttle bus. The National Park Service runs a 14-seat van twice a day from Stehekin Landing. How far it takes you depends on how late in the year you visit. In a typical year, the bus goes as far as High Bridge Campground from May to mid-June; to Bridge Creek Campground until early July; and all the way to Cottonwood from July through September. In recent years, however, flood damage has prevented the shuttle from running beyond Glory Mountain, about 20 miles west of Stehekin Landing. A trail has been established around the large washout to get people, horses, and bikes up to or down from Cottownood, which is 2.7 miles beyond. Shuttle reservations are required, and can be made up to 2 days in advance at visitors centers, or farther in advance by calling the Golden West Visitors Center; (360) 856-5703, ext. 340, then ext. 14. You'll need to reconfirm the reservations 2 to 4 days before you leave, or they'll be canceled.

In addition, a private contractor, Stehekin Adventures, runs a 36-seat bus four times a day in the lower valley (from Stehekin Landing to High Bridge) from June to mid-September. Seats are $4; reservations are not needed; bikes and packs are accommodated. Ask about the special doughnut run—it costs only a buck to get you as far as Stehekin Pastry Company.

Seasonal note: Prime time in Stehekin generally is late June through September. To miss the crowds, consider a visit in late May/early June or—better yet—September, just before the shuttles shut down.

inside out

Hiking/Backpacking

Most people come here to hike. And most people who don't come here to hike wind up hiking, in spite of themselves. That's how alluring the sunny, wildflower-painted high country around Stehekin is. Listed below are some of the Stehekin valley's most popular hikes. For full trail information, particularly for longer backpack routes, contact the North Cascades Visitors Center in Sedro Woolley, (360) 856-5700 (all year), or stop at the national park's Golden West Visitors Center at Stehekin Landing (summers only). Free **overnight permits** are required for trips inside North Cascades National Park, northwest of Stehekin. They're available at the Golden West Visitors Center. No permits are required for hikes within the Lake Chelan National Recreation Area, unless the trailhead uses a Forest Service lot requiring a **Northwest Forest Pass.**

Right at Stehekin Landing, find the **Chelan Lakeshore Trail** (moderate; up to 18 miles), a pretty shoreside walk with a split personality. You can make it a brief, 4-mile (one way) walk to a nice campsite, or tighten down your pack and walk the whole thing, 18 miles to Prince Creek Campground, where you can hitch a ride home on *The Lady of the Lake* (make prior arrangements). Or arrange a drop-off at Prince Creek and hike it north to Stehekin. Either way, a fine walk, hilly in a sore-knee (but not cartilage-shredding) kind of way. Good campsites are found all along the way. Backpackers should note, however, that this trail in the Lake Chelan–Sawtooth Wilderness on the lake's north shore can be extremely hot and dusty in midsummer.

If you have an hour to kill, walk, ride, or shuttle up the valley road to the Rainbow Creek Bridge and find the trailhead to **Buckner Orchard** (easy; 1 mile), one of the older (1889) valley homesteads, complete with a still-producing apple orchard. Nearby is a short walk to **Rainbow Falls,** which leaps a remarkable 312 feet into the Stehekin River. The popular **Rainbow Loop** (moderate; 6.5 miles) begins (or ends) at an upper trailhead a half mile beyond Harlequin Bridge and ends (or begins) at a lower trailhead about 3 miles up the road from Stehekin Landing. Good views and wildflower meadows are found only a short distance up this trail. About 2.5 miles from the upper trailhead is a junction with the **Rainbow Lake Trail,** which leads to High Camp and McAlester Pass (8 miles) and connects to the Pacific Crest Trail. You can use this trail to make a one-way through hike from Stehekin to Rainy Pass on Hwy 20. If you have time, wander up this trail just a half mile beyond its junction with the Rainbow Loop to a scenic overlook; views are well worth the walk.

For serious oat burners who brag about vertical gain, the **Goode Ridge Lookout** hike (painfully difficult; 10 miles round trip) just might be the ticket—to fame or breakdown, depending on your pain threshold. The path gains a rather remarkable 5,000 vertical feet in just under 5 miles, and much of it comes in the final 2 miles. It ends at a 6,600-foot lookout site. We've heard the views are grand. The trailhead is near the Bridge Creek Bridge, 16 miles west of Stehekin. Another brutal, but extremely rewarding, high-altitude haul is **McGregor Mountain** (difficult; 14.2 miles round trip). From the trailhead near High Bridge Ranger Station, it zigs, zags, zigs, zags—144 times (really) and 6,400 vertical feet (ditto) straight up to Heaton Camp, 6.6 miles, where you can set up the tent and perhaps recover enough to make the final mile-long scramble (for experienced hikers only, even then only late summer) to the summit, an 8,000-foot former lookout site that will blow what's left of your oxygen-deprived mind. On a lighter scale, walk the trail from High Bridge Campground to **Agnes Gorge** (easy; 5 miles). The trail follows the west bank of Agnes Creek, with great views into the steep creek gorge and of 8,115-foot Agnes Mountain. A good picnic spot waits at the end.

Backpackers should consider several marvelous loop trips in this area. The **Rainbow Lake Trail** (moderate; 20 miles round trip), makes a fine weekend backpack trip to McAlester Pass. The **Park Creek Pass Trail** (moderate; 16 miles round trip) is an occasionally steep (the trail gains 3,900 feet), but spectacular, route through a valley surrounded by 9,000-foot peaks, including 9,160-foot Goode Mountain, one of the highest peaks in the Cascades. Good campsites are found at Five Mile Camp, and from Park Creek Pass you can continue west 19.4 miles to Colonial Creek Campground on Hwy 20 (see the North Cascades Scenic Highway chapter).

Other favorites for backpackers are the **Company/Devore Creek Loop** (difficult; 28 miles round trip), a long, delightfully lonesome backcountry walk that's best in fall; **North Fork Bridge Creek** (moderate; 19 miles round trip), a very scenic backpack getaway to a fantastic glacial cirque—suitable for the more aerobically challenged, with good views throughout and great early-season access; and the **Chelan Summit Loops** (difficult; 19 to 48 miles), a design-it-yourself trip up Chelan Summit Trail and down any number of creek drainages to a water pickup (or walk out via the Lakeshore Trail) on Lake Chelan (see the Chelan and the Middle Columbia chapter for details on the Chelan Summit Trail).

Camping

A string of 10 fine (primitive, but anything else would seem out of character here) North Cascades National Park campsites await all along the Stehekin Valley Road and the northern lakeshore. You'll need to stop at the Golden West Visitors Center in Stehekin and pick up a free **permit** on your way there. Choose from **Purple Point** (7 sites), a short walk from the landing; **Harlequin** (7 sites), near the airstrip; **Rainbow Bridge** (2 sites), **High Bridge** (2 sites), **Tumwater** (2 sites), **Dolly Varden** (2 sites), **Shady** (1 site), and **Bridge Creek** (6 sites), all along the Pacific Crest Trail between Agnes and Bridge Creeks; **Flat Creek** (4 sites); and **Cottonwood** (4 sites), at the end of the road, or a half dozen other walk-in sites. Consult a ranger, and try to get a campsite nearest any hikes or sites you're most interested in. Remember that upper-valley campsites don't melt out until early July. Campers seeking RV shelter before taking the boat ride to Stehekin should consider **Lakeshore Park,** (509) 682-8024, in Chelan (reservations suggested); or **Lake Chelan State Park** on S Lakeshore Road. Sites can be reserved by calling (800) 452-5687. In addition, a series of remote campgrounds northwest of Stehekin on Stehekin Valley Road are accessible only by the shuttle bus from Stehekin. Call for details. For other Chelan-area camps, see the Chelan and the Middle Columbia chapter.

Lake Chelan's shorelines also offer some of Washington's better walk-in or boat-in (or some creative combination thereof) camping experiences. Primitive U.S. Forest Service camps, all with floating docks or fixed moorage piers, ring the upper lake. A $5 per night fee is charged at most boat-in sites. **Moore Point** (4 sites, 3 boats) is on the north shore 5.5 miles south of Stehekin on Chelan Lakeshore Trail; **Flick Creek** is farther up on the north shore; **Manley Wham** is on the south shore near Bridal Veil Falls; and **Weaver Point** (22 sites) is near the mouth of the Stehekin River.

Speaking of water pickups, good hiking trails also emanate from Lucerne, farther south on the Lake, and Holden Village, 11 miles up a gravel road. Near Lucerne, pack the fly rod and follow the Railroad Creek Road a short distance to the **Domke Lake Trail.** It leads an easy 1.5 miles to Domke Lake—which has a private fishing resort—then continues another three miles—gaining 3,000 feet—up tp good views on Domke Mountain. For a pleasant overnighter, follow signs from the Domke Lake Trail to the **Emerald Park Trail** (moderate; 16 miles round trip). This is a beautiful valley walk into the eastern Glacier Peak Wilderness, with lighter crowds than Stehekin-area trails. You can make it a one-way trip to a car pickup in the Entiat River drainage.

From Holden, the **Railroad Creek Trail,** a major eastern access to the

Glacier Peak Wilderness, climbs to spectacluar **Lyman Lakes** (moderate; 19.4 miles round trip), at the foot of the Lyman Glacier. From there, very experienced hikers can climb along the glacier and pass through 7,100-foot Spider Gap, then drop to Spider meadows and an eventual exit on US 2. Bunk-style lodging can be arranged at Holden Village, operated as a Lutheran Conference Center, (509) 687-3644.

Mountain Biking

Stehekin Valley Road is the one, the only, route to ride here. But you could do a lot worse. Mountain bikes actually are the preferred mode of transportation up here, unless you ride the shuttle bus. Many people find a pedal up the valley road from Stehekin Landing a perfect way to sample Stehekin's beautiful valley floor without gearing up for a full backpack adventure. You can bring your own bike on the tour boat from Chelan, but it'll cost you $13 round trip. It's easier to **rent** at Stehekin; both Stehekin Lodge and Discovery Bicycles have ample supplies of mountain bikes and helmets right near Stehekin Landing. For a fun day trip, consider Stehekin Day Tours' **cycle trip;** (509) 682-3014. For a modest fee, they'll haul you and your (provided) bike up the road to Harlequin Campground, and leave you to ride back down. They also offer a locally famous "Ranch Breakfast Ride," with breakfast at Stehekin Valley Ranch followed by a ride down the valley.

Fishing

Pack the fly gear. The Stehekin River and its many feeder streams are a decent **cutthroat** and **rainbow trout** fishery, with some absolutely gorgeous waters. It's catch-and-release from March through June, but you can catch and keep from July through October (minimum size is 15 inches). The Stehekin is closed to fishing above Agnes Creek; most anglers take the bus there and work their way down. The river also has a **chinook salmon** run in late August and September. For **gear, licenses, advice,** and the occasional lie, call North Cascades Stehekin Lodge, (509) 682-4494, www.stehekin.com; or inquire at McGregor Mountain Outdoor Supply at Stehekin Landing. Fair trout fishing for rainbows and cutthroat also can be found at Domke Lake (see Chelan and the Middle Columbia chapter).

Cross-Country Skiing/Snowshoeing

Stehekin is a lonely place in the winter, but you can stay at North Cascades Stehekin Lodge and explore some remarkable snowshoeing or cross-country touring terrain, even if you never venture from the snowed-over **Stehekin Valley Road.** The peak season is December through May.

Dress warmly, and bring your own food and supplies: the rest of the town is mostly gone till summer. **Snowshoe and ski rentals** are available at the lodge, and sometimes are included in winter lodging packages.

Horseback Riding

Trail-riding trips for cowpokes of all abilities are offered in the valley by the Courtney family, which runs Cascade Corral and Stehekin Valley Ranch; Cragg and Roberta Courtney, Box 67, Stehekin, WA 98852; (509) 682-7742; www.courtneycountry.com.

outside in

Lodgings

Silver Bay Inn ★★   The inn offers a gracious, memorable retreat on 700 feet of waterfront. *$$–$$$; 10 Silver Bay Rd, Stehekin; (509) 682-2212 or (800) 555-7781 (WA and OR only); www.silverbayinn.com.*

More Information

Chelan Chamber of Commerce: *(800) 4CHELAN; www.lakechelan.com.*
Lake Chelan Boat Company: *(509) 682-4584; www.ladyofthelake.com.*
North Cascades National Park: *www.nps.gov/noca.*
  Glacier Public Service Center: *(360) 599-2714.*
  Golden West Visitors Center: *Stehekin; (360) 856-5700 ext. 340, then ext. 14.*
  Headquarters/Visitors Center: *Sedro Woolley; (360) 856-5700.*
  Newhalem Visitor Center: *(206) 386-4495.*
  Wilderness Information Center: *Marblemount; (360) 873-4500, ext. 39.*
North Cascades Stehekin Lodge: *(509) 682-4494; www.stehekin.com.*
Park Service/Forest Service Joint Information Center: *Chelan; (509) 682-2549.*

Mountain Loop Highway
and the Glacier Peak Wilderness

Highways 92 and 530, from Granite Falls north to Arlington, and east to the Pacific Crest Trail, including the Boulder River, Glacier Peak, and Henry M. Jackson Wildernesses and Mount Pilchuck State Park.

The Mountain Loop Highway is our recreational backyard. The fact that the Loop, on the east edge of Snohomish County, is not exactly the kind of place for croquet and pink flamingos says a lot about where we live—on the edge of true wilderness.

The Mountain Loop, actually more of a square, is a grand collection of tall mountains; magnificently clear, strapping rivers; and patches of wondrous old-growth forest on the western foothills of the Cascades. It is an area defined by—and indeed still shaped by—wild rivers flowing out of the high, wet Glacier Peak Wilderness just to the east.

The bold, bubbling Stillaguamish reigns supreme here. The Mountain Loop Highway's north edge is defined by its North Fork, which cuts a broad, fertile valley from the foothills town of Darrington to the lowland town of Arlington along Interstate 5. The Loop's south edge is marked by the South Fork Stilly, a swift, clear, boulder-strewn stream that always seems to be flowing straight off one nature calendar and onto another. In between is the raucous Sauk, blasting its way north as if perpetually late for a downstream meeting with the Skagit.

Entire generations of Washingtonians have spent lifetimes exploring what lies in between these flowing crystals. The Mountain

Loop is one of the greater Seattle area's favorite hiking getaways, for obvious reasons. More than three dozen quality, old-growth-to-alpine hikes are found along its borders—most within an hour's drive of the major Puget Sound population areas. Longer trails provide the quickest access to the lands around 10,568-foot Glacier Peak—one of the most pristine alpine areas in the Cascades. Hiker pressure along the Mountain Loop is very heavy in the summertime. Often disconcertingly so.

As the population continues to mushroom, particularly in Snohomish County suburban areas, the pressure on Mountain Loop trails will continue. Not good news for anyone who's hiked the Mount Pilchuck Lookout Trail on a recent summer weekend. Mount Pilchuck, in that sense, illustrates one constant about human interaction with the Mountain Loop area: it's where suburbia meets the wilderness, literally and figuratively. This is where civilized Washington, whether it plans to or not, goes to learn about life in the woods. All too often, the lesson comes the hard way. Every year, it seems, half a dozen people get lost on Mount Pilchuck, which to a veteran hiker seems a simple ascent on a well-marked trail. Not so if it's your first or second time in the high country, fog sets in, and panic follows. Year after year, decade after decade, people head to the fabulous backyard playground of the Mountain Loop. Year after year, goof after gaffe, some don't come back.

It's a point worth bearing in mind. The mountains inside the Mountain Loop are mountains, no more or no less beautiful—or fearsome—than their cousins 50 miles from the nearest road. Approach them with respect, and they'll provide a lifetime of memories. Approach them with disregard, and you'll be film at 11.

End of sermon. For most of us—the practical, the cautious, the fun-loving, and, especially, the overworked—the Mountain Loop is a godsend, a quick escape from reality. Or to it, depending on one's degree of mountain Zen. Hiking, rafting, kayaking, fishing, and camping here are surprisingly fine, especially for a place within short reach of Seattle. Just driving the loop on a sunny summer day makes you feel like you've done something wholesome.

Go forth and recreate. It's too close at hand to ignore. Even if time is short, take a half day, drive the loop, get out of the car, and do what we do. Walk to the water and launch into a good riverbank daydream, letting the effervescent bubbles at the tail of a whitewater washboard scrub, boil, and wash away the knots in your nerves.

Remember, it's your backyard. And yardwork is good for the soul.

Getting There

The Mountain Loop Highway is actually more of a square, consisting of Interstate-5 (or the parallel Hwy 9) on the west, Hwy 530 on the north, Forest

Road 20 (narrow, unpaved; summer only) on the east, and Hwy 92 on the south. Hwy 530 continues north of Darrington, ultimately connecting with Hwy 20 at Rockport; about halfway along, the Suiattle River Road heads east into the heart of the Glacier Peak Wilderness. Recreation sites are centered on the upper portion of Hwy 530 north of Darrington; along Forest Road 20, which follows the Sauk River; and along all of Hwy 92 from its east end at Barlow Pass west to Verlot.

Most Puget Sound area visitors arrive from the south, taking I-5 north to exit 194 in Everett and following US 2 and Hwy 9 north to Granite Falls, where the "loop" begins by following the South Fork Stillaguamish upstream on Hwy 92 east. To approach from the north, drive north on I-5 to Arlington, follow Hwy 530 east to Darrington, and turn south on Forest Road 20. Remember: The loop is closed between Darrington and Barlow Pass (or lower) in the winter.

inside out

Hiking/Backpacking

The Mountain Loop slices through some of the best close-in Cascades day hiking in the Puget Sound region. Expect crowds in the summer, and remember to go prepared. Just because these trailheads are less than an hour from home doesn't mean you can't get lost—or worse—if you're ill prepared. Listed below is a sampling of the more popular hikes here. Dozens more trails are maintained in this mountainous region, which includes the Darrington Ranger District of Mount Baker–Snoqualmie National Forest, the Boulder River and Henry M. Jackson Wilderness Areas, and western portions of the Glacier Peak Wilderness. For full trail information, contact the Verlot Public Service Center, 33515 Mountain Loop Hwy, (360) 691-7791 (summer only); or the Darrington Ranger District, 1405 Emmons Street, Darrington; (206) 436-1155. Note that a **Northwest Forest Pass,** $5 per day or $30 annually, is required to park in many Forest Service–administered trailheads in this area. They're available from ranger stations, from many private vendors, on-line at www.naturenw.org, or by calling (800) 270-7504.

Mountain Loop Highway

Near the start of the Mountain Loop's southern leg, Hwy 92, are three of its most popular day hikes. **Mount Pilchuck Lookout** (moderate/difficult; 6 miles round trip) offers a great mountaintop view of the entire Puget Sound area from the 5,300-foot lookout site. This trail is one of the most underestimated in the state. Things have improved somewhat since portions of the trail were rebuilt in the late 1990s, but still, every summer brings a report of lost hikers on Mount Pilchuck. Usually, they're people who've strayed off the trail on one of many "shortcuts" and lost their way in bad weather or fog. Go prepared. The trailhead is on Mount Pilchuck Road, which turns south about a mile beyond the Verlot Public Service Center. Also on Mount Pilchuck Road is the trail to **Heather Lake** (moderate; 3.8 miles round trip), a very pretty alpine lake set in old-growth forest below Mount Pilchuck. This heavily used trail usually is accessible all year. Just to the east, **Lake Twenty-two** (moderate; 4 miles round trip) is an equally popular family hike, this one climbing through more old-growth trees and a half-dozen waterfalls on the way to a sterling lake on Pilchuck's northeast ridge. The trailhead is well marked on the Mountain Loop Highway, about 1.5 miles east of Verlot Public Service Center.

Farther up the road, the trail to **Big Four Ice Caves** (easy; 2 miles round trip) is another year-round draw. These actually aren't ice caves at all, but wind- and stream-melted tunnels beneath a remnant snowfield on the north face of 6,153-foot Big Four Mountain. Access to their tempting, ice blue arches is probably too easy. Many people ignore warning signs and logic, and venture into the caves. Bad idea. They can, and do, collapse suddenly. The short trail to the ice caves is a popular cross-country ski and snowshoe route in the winter, and hikers often trudge over the snow to get here in the spring. But visitors should never venture out of the forest and into the slide plain around the ice caves while snow is present on Big Four. Avalanches off the mountain are very frequent, and very deadly.

On the north side of Hwy 92, two arduous, but rewarding, day hikes head north from the Mountain Loop Highway. **Mount Forgotten Trail** (moderate; 7.8 miles round trip) passes pleasant waterfalls (Perry Creek Falls, 2 miles in, is a good short-trip turnaround spot) before opening to vast meadows—and a steeper grade—below 6,005-foot Mount Forgotten. Experienced scramblers can swallow hard, climb all the way to the summit, and take a memorable mental picture of the great view. **Mount Dickerman** (strenuous; 8.6 miles round trip) is a good overnight trip to open meadows and a grand, 5,723-foot summit with views of Del Campo, Glacier, Sloan, and Monte Cristo Peaks. This is a favorite hike in the fall, when the meadows are filled with ripe huckleberries and crimson berry bushes. Bring the Backpacker Oven and a boxed crust, and you're in business.

South of the highway at the end of Forest Road 4065 (Sunrise Mine Road) is the **Sunrise Mine Trail** (difficult; 5.2 miles round trip), which climbs to 4,700-foot Headlee Pass, among the triple spires of Del Campo, Morning Star, and Vesper Peaks. Not for the faint of heart or those untrained in the art of snowfield crossing.

At Barlow Pass, the pavement ends and the fun begins for many hik-

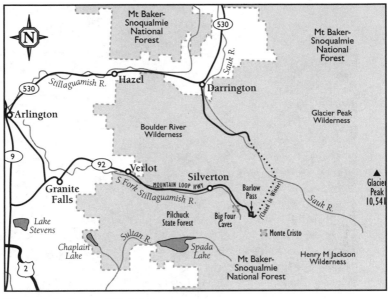

Mountain Loop Highway

ers and mountain bikers. The **Monte Cristo Road** (easy; 8.6 miles round trip), now closed to traffic, is an easy walk into Monte Cristo, the mostly ghost-town remnants of an early-century bustling mining village. A walk-in campground is open near the townsite (see Camping, below), and a slew of great Cascade backcountry hikes depart from the same area. Among them: Gothic Basin via the **Weden Creek Trail** (difficult; 10 miles round trip from Barlow Pass), Poodle Dog Pass **to Twin Lakes** (difficult; 16.8 miles round trip from Barlow Pass), and **Glacier Basin** (difficult; 12.2 miles round trip from Barlow Pass). All three are tough climbs up rocky trails, but serve up stunning alpine views as a reward. Consider camping around Monte Cristo and hiking them as day hikes.

Popular hikes on the northern (unpaved) leg (Forest Road 20) of the Mountain Loop Highway include **Mount Pugh and Stujack Pass** (difficult; 7 miles round trip), a late-summer scramble that begins 1 mile up Mount Pugh Road, 15 miles south of Darrington; **Old Sauk River** (easy; 6 miles round trip), a nice river walk near the Clear Creek Campground; and **Squire Creek Pass** (moderate; 7.4 miles round trip) at the end of Squire Creek Road, south of Darrington.

Glacier Peak Wilderness

Northeast of Darrington, the wild Suiattle River drainage contains several great day hikes and longer backpack routes providing westside access to

Peering into an ice tunnel at Big Four Ice Caves

Glacier Peak. The **Huckleberry Mountain Trail** (difficult; 14 miles round trip) is a tough climb through old-growth forest to a 5,900-foot lookout site. Warning: The views don't begin until right near the top. Most people make this an overnighter. The trailhead is near Buck Creek Campground (see Camping, below). Nearby **Green Mountain** (moderate; 8 miles round trip) is an area favorite, thanks to its extensive wildflower meadows and lakeside campsites in the valley below the summit. At the 6,200-foot top is a still-functioning lookout site with the best mountain views in this area. A winner.

Farther east on Suiattle River Road, a backpacker's favorite is the **Downey Creek and Bachelor Meadows Trail** (moderate; 13.2 miles round trip). This trail has it all: old-growth forest on the Suiattle, and a stunning alpine meadow below 8,264-foot Spire Peak in the Glacier Peak Wilderness. The trailhead is near Downey Creek Campground. Another popular day hike in the same area climbs up **Sulphur Creek** (moderate; 3.6 miles round trip) to a hot springs, of sorts (too small and too cool to soak in, but fun to look at). At the end of Suiattle River Road, the **Suiattle River Trail** (moderate; various lengths possible) leads up the river and onto the northwestern flanks of Glacier Peak itself. Some of the most popular destinations in the Glacier Peak Wilderness—Image Lake, Suiattle Pass, and a very scenic stretch of the Pacific Crest Trail—are reached via this trail system. Ambitious backpackers can cross through the entire wilderness north of Glacier Peak, east to Holden Village, and ultimately to Lake Chelan (see Stehekin and the Lake Chelan National Recreation Area chapter).

One drainage to the south (reached from the Mountain Loop Highway on Forest Road 23), backpackers flock to the **White Chuck River Trail** (moderate/difficult; various lengths possible), which leads to the popular (and scummy, by our taste) Kennedy Hot Springs and beyond to the Pacific Crest Trail on Kennedy Ridge of Glacier Peak. Alpine campsites, explorable moraines of the Kennedy and Scimitar Glaciers, and up-close views of 10,541-foot Glacier Peak are simply stupendous. A very memorable, 18-to-20 mile round trip, if the weather cooperates. A very horrible one if it doesn't.

Camping

A dozen—count 'em, 12—Forest Service campgrounds are offered for your tent-pitching pleasure (this isn't really good RV territory, although those little Barbie Toyota Campers will fit into some of these). In addition, the Darrington Ranger District handles eight small, reservation-only campsites along the Mountain Loop Highway. Call (360) 436-1155 for information on all the campgrounds listed here.

Turlo has 19 sites (no hookups; RVs to 31 feet) near the South Fork Stillaguamish. Campsites can be reserved up to 240 days in advance; (877) 444-6777; www.reserveusa.com. Turlo is open mid-May to late September. *On Mountain Loop Hwy near Verlot Public Service Center, 10.8 miles east of Granite Falls.*

Nearby **Verlot** has 25 sites (no hookups; RVs to 31 feet), some with river views. The Lake Twenty-two and Mount Pilchuck Trails are nearby (see Hiking/Backpacking, above). Verlot is open from mid-May to late September. Campsites can be reserved up to 240 days in advance; (877) 444-6777; www.reserveusa.com. *On Mountain Loop Hwy near Verlot Public Service Center, 11 miles east of Granite Falls.*

The largest and most popular campground in the area, **Gold Basin,** is several miles east. The campground has 92 sites (no hookups; RVs to 31 feet) and a 25-person group camp along the South Fork Stillaguamish. It's open from mid-May to late September. Campsites can be reserved up to 240 days in advance; (877) 444-6777; www.reserveusa.com. *On Mountain Loop Hwy, 13.5 miles east of Granite Falls.*

Boardman Creek has 8 large sites (no hookups; RVs to 31 feet) and access to the popular Boardman Lake Trail. It's open mid-May to early September. Campsites cannot be reserved. *On Mountain Loop Hwy, 16.6 miles east of Granite Falls.*

Red Bridge, a very pretty but primitive South Fork Stillaguamish site, has 16 campsites (no hookups; RVs to 31 feet). Hiking trails are nearby. No piped water. The park is open late May to early September. Campsites cannot be reserved. *On Mountain Loop Hwy, 18 miles east of Granite Falls.*

The hike- or bike-in campground at **Monte Cristo** has 8 free sites, with pit toilets and piped water. It's open summers only. See Hiking, above, for access.

On the north-south (unpaved) highway portion (Forest Road 20) is **Bedal,** which has 18 sites (no hookups; RVs to 21 feet) near the confluence of the north and south forks of the scenic Sauk River. The campground has no piped water, and is open from June to early September. North Fork Sauk Falls, a true gusher, is only a mile away, and worth a visit. Campsites cannot be reserved. The Forest Service began collecting fees here in 1998. *On the Mountain Loop Hwy about 6.5 miles north of Barlow Pass (southeast of Darrington 20 miles).*

Closer to Darrington, **Clear Creek** (13 sites), 2.5 miles south of Darrington on the Mountain Loop Hwy, is a small seasonal campground with no piped water. The Forest Service recently began collecting fees at this once-free campground. Sites cannot be reserved.

On the Suiattle River Road (Forest Road 26) northeast of Darrington off Hwy 530, choose from **Buck Creek** (26 sites; no hookups; RVs to 30 feet) or **Sulphur Creek** (20 sites), seasonal (June through October) campgrounds with no piped water, but with good river and hiking access—the Huckleberry Mountain Trail (see Hiking/Backpacking, above) is near Buck Creek Campground. Buck Creek's sites are spaced through a small patch of lush, lovely old-growth forest, and the campground has a nifty Adirondack (three-sided) shelter under which you can flee in bad weather. Campsites cannot be reserved.

Some other options: three Forest Service group camps are nicely located near the South Fork Stillaguamish River, along the Mountain Loop Highway: **Esswine** (facilities for 25 campers, 16 miles east of Granite Falls), **Tulalip Millsite** (facilities for 60 campers, 18.5 miles east of Granite Falls), and **Coal Creek Bar** (facilities for 25 campers near the South Fork Stillaguamish, 23 miles east of Granite Falls). Additional group-camp sites are located at **Marten Creek** and **Wiley Creek.** All of these campgrounds can be reserved in advance; all have pit toilets and no piped water or showers. For reservation and fee information, contact the Mount Baker–Snoqualmie National Forest's Darrington Ranger District, (360) 436-1155.

The Department of Natural Resources oversees five small, free, primitive campgrounds in the Mountain Loop corridor. Four are hike-in sites from the Ashland Lake trailhead, reached via Forest Roads 4020 and 4021: they are **Beaver Plant Lake** (5 sites, 2.1 miles from the trailhead), **Lower**

Ashland Lake (6 sites, 2.5 miles), Upper Ashland Lake (6 sites, 3 miles), and Twin Falls Lake (5 sites, 4.5 miles). All are primitive, free sites with no piped water. Another remote DNR site, William C. Dearinger (12 sites, no piped water), is located on the south bank of the Suiattle River, northeast of Darrington on SW-D-5400 Road. Contact the DNR's Sedro Woolley office, (360) 856-3500.

Fishing

The rivers defining the Mountain Loop itself—the North and South Fork Stillaguamish, Sauk, and Suiattle—are wild, unspoiled waterways, with plenty of good rod-bending opportunities. The Stillaguamish—or "Stilly," as it's locally known—is a famous **steelhead** waterway. The North Fork is a particularly notable fly-fishery, for both summer and winter fish. The river also holds **cutthroat trout.** The Sauk also is a locally famous steelhead stream, known for its occasional large fish. Catch rates aren't what they used to be, though. The Suiattle produces a fair number of steelhead itself. Be sure to check steelhead regulations before you fish. Sections of all these rivers now are closed during part of the year and open only to catch-and-release fishing during other periods.

The Mountain Loop offers a wealth of alpine lake fishing for **rainbow and brook trout.** Easy-to-reach lakes such as Lake Twenty-two and Heather Lake offer decent fishing amid fantastic alpine scenery. Other good bets are Boardman Lake, Island Lake, and Lake Evan (all nearby); Goat Lake, via Forest Road 4080; the many small lakes accessible by short trails off the Suiattle River Road (Forest Road 26); and the string of lakes in the upper Suiattle and White Chuck River drainages inside the Glacier Peak Wilderness. More than two dozen are there for the choosing, and many are periodically stocked with packed-in fingerlings. See Hiking/Backpacking, above, for access ideas.

Rafting/Kayaking

The **Sauk** and **Suiattle Rivers** are two of the favorite whitewater haunts of Seattle-area rafting companies. Both receive heavy spring use. The Suiattle is a better choice for novices, although the mostly Class II/Class III stream shouldn't be considered tame, by any means. The Sauk is the wild child in this area, with a score of Class III/Class IV rapids from Bedal to White Chuck, and a serious set of Class IV/Class V rapids between White Chuck and Clear Creek Campground, a popular get-out-and-check-for-missing-body-parts spot. Many kayakers will be found racing the rafts through these chutes. This is not for beginners, however. Rookies should stick to the rafts. A large number of good **commercial rafting**

companies run these rivers. For references, contact the Darrington Ranger District, (360) 436-1155. Generally, it gets tamer the farther north you go. The lower Sauk River along Hwy 530 between Darrington and Rockport is a scenic, semi-advanced paddle route, with good takeout access. Most kayakers and canoeists in search of calmer waters float the **North Fork and South Fork Stillaguamish Rivers** downstream from Granite Falls and Darrington, respectively, to Arlington.

Mountain Biking

The **Monte Cristo Road** at Barlow Pass (see Hiking/Backpacking, above) is one of the best family-friendly mountain-bike routes in the near Cascades. It receives heavy use in the summer; consider a weekday. Mountain bikes are forbidden from most trails in this area, but a wealth of Forest Service roads await the more serious biker looking for a healthy dose of vertical. Check with the Darrington Ranger District, (206) 436-1155, for road conditions, including washouts and logging truck traffic.

Cross-country Skiing/Snowshoeing

Snow levels can be iffy along the Mountain Loop. But when the freezing level drops, some good cross-country ski/snowshoe trails stand out in the white. For beginners, the **Big Four Ice Caves Trail** (see Hiking/Backpacking, above) makes for a pleasant day outing. It's reached by driving to the winter-closure end of the Mountain Loop, about 12 miles east of Verlot, and hiking about 2 miles up the snow-covered road to the Big Four Trail, then another mile to the ice caves viewpoint. It's an easy, family-friendly route, but be aware that snowmobiles also frequent the area. Remember: In the winter it's never safe to ski or snowshoe into the open area near the Big Four Ice Caves. It's an avalanche zone. More advanced skiers and snowshoers often make their way up a wide range of other trails in this region (see Hiking/Backpacking, above, for most of these), including **Kennedy Hot Springs, Rat Trap Pass** (via Forest Roads 25 and 27), **Mount Pilchuck, Heather Lake, Lake Twenty-two, Boardman Lake, Marten Creek** (off Hwy 92 east of Red Bridge Campground), and **Coal Creek** farther east. Call the Darrington Ranger District, (360) 436-1155, for snow and trail conditions.

Horseback Riding

Horse Country, 8507 Hwy 92, Granite Falls; (360) 691-7509, offers lessons, horse leasing, picnics, and day camps, and features **guided rides** up into the Cascades and then down to the Pilchuck River. Kids age 5 and up are welcome, riders over 200 pounds are not.

Accessible Outdoors

For a rough-and-tumble area, the Mountain Loop corridor provides a surprising number of barrier-free outdoor venues. From west to east on the Mountain Loop: **Turlo Campground** offers barrier-free rest rooms and drinking water. **Verlot Campground** has barrier-free river views and drinking water, and campsites and picnic sites rated "usable" (wheelchair accessible with assistance). **Verlot Public Service Center** provides barrier-free interpretive displays (also in Braille), rest rooms, and an interpretive trail, as well as "usable" picnic sites. **Hemple Creek Picnic Area,** about 13 miles east of Granite Falls, has barrier-free picnic sites and rest rooms, and is known as a good bird-watching area.

Gold Basin Campground (see Camping, above) offers barrier-free rest rooms, campsites, and drinking water. The nearby **Gold Basin Millpond Interpretive Trail** offers barrier-free access to a floating wildlife-viewing dock. **Red Bridge Campground** (see Camping, above) has barrier-free campsites and rest rooms. The nearby **Youth on Age Interpretive Trail,** which winds through a deep forest, is a wheelchair-accessible path that's also popular with families. Pick up an interpretive brochure at the Verlot Public Service Center.

The **Big Four Ice Caves** parking area (see Hiking, above) includes barrier-free rest rooms, picnic sites, and some trails, although the entire path to the Ice Caves themselves is not wheelchair accessible. **Bedal Campground** has "usable" campsites and barrier-free rest rooms and river access. A popular accessible wildife-viewing site is **the White Chuck Overlook.** To get there, follow the Mountain Loop Highway about 12 miles southeast of Darrington (near the Sauk River/White Chuck River confluence) and turn east on Forest Road 23. Continue about 3 miles to the overlook, where you'll find barrier-free rest rooms and picnic sites, as well as grand views of White Chuck Mountain, where mountain goats often are spotted in late summer and early fall. **Clear Creek Campground** has "usable" sites and barrier-free rest rooms.

More Information

Darrington Ranger District, Darrington: *(360) 436-1155.*
Mount Baker–Snoqualmie National Forest Headquarters:
 (425) 775-9702 or (800) 627-0062; www.fs.fed.us/r6/mbs.
Verlot Public Service Center (summer only): *(360) 691-7791.*

Mount Baker Highway

From north Bellingham east to Artist Point near Mount Shuksan and south to Mount Baker summit, including Glacier, Mount Baker Ski Area, Heather Meadows, Glacier Ranger District of the Mount Baker–Snoqualmie National Forest, and western portions of North Cascades National Park.

This is the back-door entry to Washington's alps. Arguably the most rugged, untamed mountain slopes in the Northwest, if not the country, the North Cascades are the truest test of many a recreator's mettle. Everything about them is raw, from their awesome, jagged peaks to their massive glaciers, charging rivers, and inhospitable access routes.

Lucky for us, the Mount Baker Highway is a fairly civilized crack in the North Cascades' stony armor. From the outskirts of Bellingham, the wandering two-lane road does its best imitation of the Nooksack River it follows into the craggy mountains—winding, curving, climbing, and falling through a beautiful river valley surrounded by snowy peaks. All along its route are places to pull off the road and into Washington's wild natural past.

No matter what time of the year you drive it, the Mount Baker Highway locks onto your alpine guidance system and begins priming your adrenaline pump, ultimately dragging you to a spectacular destination—the alpine ridgeline between 10,778-foot Mount Baker and 8,268-foot Mount Shuksan, two of the state's most magnificent alpine peaks. In the summer and fall, hiking, camping, and climbing from this area are outstanding. Backcountry areas are rich with hundreds of acres of wildflowers, chill-raising alpine views, and secluded backcountry campsites. This is rugged, wild country—the kind you normally have to hike for days to reach. The summer season is short but sweet. Most of Mount Baker's alpine area doesn't melt out until August.

In the winter, access gets tough, but the tough keep going—directly to Mount Baker Ski Area, which has a well-earned national reputation for steep slopes and deep snow. The mountain's average annual snowfall— more than 700 inches, or 60 feet—is tops among North American ski resorts. That gives Mount Baker the longest ski season in the state. And one of the best. At Baker, however, the very term "ski season" is a misnomer. This is one place where the number of snowboarders typically equals—if not surpasses—skiers. In the past 15 years, Baker's wild, rugged terrain has made it an international snowboarding mecca, turning the tiny valley town of Glacier into a snow-rider's enclave. Craig Kelly, snowboarding's first international superstar, is a local here.

Nowhere else in the state is a large recreation area so vividly and accurately personified by a single user group: in this case, Baker's clan of highly skilled, mildly motivated (at least in traditional senses) snowboard hounds, many of whom forsake all else to get their regular mountain fix. Watching a world-class snowboard rider float in graceful, sweeping arcs down Shuksan Arm is a unique thrill, even for nonriders. Without so much as a sound, their descents say all there is to be said about the special place Mount Baker holds in the hearts of Washington recreators: poetic grace in the midst of natural chaos.

On Mount Baker, whether you're on a snowboard or skis, Vibram soles or a river raft, a boat or a rope, the game can be risky, but the payoff is always rich. Baker is often moody, occasionally ugly, and always challenging. It is alternately relentless and magnificent. But in the end, it usually is simply inspired. It's easy to see why we feel its pull: that's the way a lot of us like to think of ourselves.

Getting There

The Mount Baker Highway (Hwy 542) is 100 miles north of Seattle on Interstate 5. From I-5 north of Bellingham, take exit 255 (Hwy 542) and drive east. Another option is to take I-5 exit 230 at Burlington, travel Hwy 20 east to Sedro Woolley, and follow Hwy 9 north to its junction with Hwy 542 near Deming. All activities in this chapter are reached via Hwy 542, which ends at Artist Point, a scenic vista 58 miles east of Bellingham. Note: In the winter, Hwy 542 ends at Mount Baker Ski Area, just below Austin Pass. In an average year, the final 2 miles of road to Artist Point don't melt out until late July or August.

inside out

Hiking/Backpacking

The Mount Baker and Mount Shuksan area at the end of Highway 542 is one of the most awe-inspiring hiking areas in the state. From this region's high, rugged ridges, you'll find mile-long blankets of wildflowers, goose-bump-popping views of glacier-shrouded alpine peaks, and heavenly backcountry campsites. The only catch: none of these come easy. The very topography that makes the heart soar will make the thighs scream. Most long hikes in this area are steep day hikes, some of them being old miners' trails. (Which, incidentally, is the correct answer to the Jeopardy question: "Why are there no old miners anymore?") In that sense, many of the Baker area's woods-to-views climbs are classic Northwest ascents. Even a day hike here can send you home feeling like you've conquered something. The burn in the legs is a good one.

But you don't have to kill yourself to sample the North Cascades alpine country. The Mount Baker Highway ends at a parking lot/viewpoint between Mounts Baker and Shuksan that ranks right up there on our list of Most Amazing Places You Can Drive to in the State. The Heather Meadows, Austin Pass, and Artist Point area is true high-alpine country, interlaced with short day-hiking trails that loop to and from the parking lot. If you're not into sweating, this is your spot. Two important visitors' tips: On the average, this area of the North Cascades receives as much snowfall as any auto-accessible (or even chairlift-accessible; see Skiing/Snowboarding, below) site in the United States. The Artist Point parking lot doesn't melt out until early August. Call the Glacier Public Service Center (see More Information, below) to check road conditions. Also, once the snow melts, the bugs proliferate. Mid-August in the Baker high country can be a miserable experience in years when black flies are particularly bad. They bite. They're fast. They're relentless. You've been warned. The swarms die down in early autumn—a prime time to visit and stroll through alpine fields of ripe wild blueberries. Also note that a **Northwest Forest Pass**, $5 per day or $30 annually, is required to park in many Forest Service–administered trailheads in this area, including Artist Point and all parking areas in the Heather Meadows recreation area. They're available from ranger stations, from many private vendors, on-line at www.naturenw.org, or by calling (800) 270-7504. A list of our favorite Baker-area hikes follows. For more information on these and others, call the Glacier Public Service Center; (360) 599-2714.

Starting at the top, several good day hikes emanate from the parking

Resting hikers take in the grandeur of Mount Baker from Skyline Divide Trail

lot at Artist Point. At the south end of the parking lot, the **Chain Lakes Loop** trail (moderate; 6.5 miles round trip) makes a circle around Table Mountain, with starting points either at Artist Point or the Heather Meadows parking lot, just south of Mount Baker Ski Area. You'll pass by a string of sparkling alpine lakes—Mazama, Iceberg, Hayes, and Arbuthnot, then climb steeply over Herman Saddle before dropping to another lake and an exit through beautiful Heather Meadows. For a full loop, walk back up the road about 2 miles to Artist Point. Even the road is a pleasant walk, with stunning views. Allow about 4 hours to take it all in. And do not forget your camera.

Also from the Artist Point lot, the **Table Mountain Trail** (difficult; 3.5 miles round trip) will take you to the top of its namesake peak, where some truly memorable views of Mount Shuksan await. This is a steep one. You'll zigzag up what seem like several hundred switchbacks, most of them chipped into rugged volcanic rock. And no matter when you go, there's likely to be snow at the top. (Chances are you'll find snowboarders up here, riding down the far side of the mountain.) If you're up for the climb, this one is well worth it.

Nearby, the route up **Ptarmigan Ridge** (difficult; 9 miles round trip) doesn't really follow a trail at all. This is a ridge walk, up the north flanks of Mount Baker. The lower portion is snow-covered for much of the year, and its upper reaches are under snow all year long. That makes it a favorite path of summertime backcountry skiers or snowboarders, or climbers looking for snowfields on which to practice self-arrests. But for experienced hikers who know how to use an ice ax, this is a beautiful late-summer snow walk: follow the cairns or trail markers. The route leads to Camp Kiser, a bivouac camp for climbers taking this secondary route to the summit of Mount Baker. Mountain goats are often seen in the area.

On the highway just below Artist Point but above Heather Meadows, a wide spot in the road marks the parking area for the trail to **Lake Ann** (moderate; 8 miles round trip). The trail drops down for 2 miles to Swift Creek, then climbs up a boulder-strewn (and marmot-inhabited) meadow before dropping into a basin holding jewel-like Lake Ann. Behind the lake, the view is drop-dead amazing. You're looking right at the Lower Curtis Glacier and the full glory of 8,268-foot Mount Shuksan. Campsites are found around the lake. A well-used climbers trail continues on, up the south flank of Shuksan. It's a great day trip; the trail takes you right above Curtis Glacier.

A wealth of long day hikes or weekend backpack routes can be found lower on the Mount Baker Highway, in the upper Nooksack drainage. Two favorites are **Skyline Divide** (moderate/difficult; 6 miles round trip), which is an express route to a lovely ridgeline painted with purple lupine; and **Heliotrope Ridge** (difficult; 6.5 miles round trip), the main climbing route on the mountain, but a good day hike for strong hikers who want a close look at the Coleman Glacier. The trailheads are on Forest Roads 37 and 39, respectively—both just east of Glacier.

Other great view hikes in this region are **Church Mountain** (difficult; 8.4 miles round trip), off Forest Road 3040 2.5 miles north of the highway at Nooksack Campground; **Welcome Pass** (difficult; 3.6 miles round trip), a 2,200-vertical-foot climb to a great mountain viewpoint above Forest Road 3060, which turns north from the highway 12.3 miles east of

Glacier Public Service Center; **Excelsior Pass** (difficult; 6 miles round trip), an alpine lookout site off Forest Road 31, which turns north from the highway 1.8 miles east of Glacier Public Service Center; **Yellow Aster Butte** (difficult; 6 miles round trip), **Winchester Mountain** (easy; 4 miles round trip), and **Tomyhoi Lake** (difficult; 10 miles round trip), all off Forest Road 3065, near Silver Fir Campground on the highway; and **Goat Mountain** (moderate; 6 miles round trip), a hike with stunning views, and **Whatcom/Hannegan Pass** (easy/moderate; 10 miles round trip), a popular backpackers' entry into Ross Lake and the remote backcountry of North Cascades National Park—both off Forest Road 32, which also leaves the highway near Silver Fir Campground. For the latter hike, overnighters will need a **backcountry permit.** They're available at the Glacier Public Service Center.

Camping

Three small-but-pleasant Mount Baker–Snoqualmie National Forest campgrounds are found along Hwy 542. **Douglas Fir** has 15 tent and 15 RV sites (no hookups; RVs to 31 feet) in a wooded loop near the North Fork Nooksack River. The park is open from May to October. Campsites can be reserved up to 240 days in advance; (877) 444-6777; www.reserveusa.com. *2 miles east of Glacier; (360) 599-2714.* Farther east on Hwy 542, **Silver Fir**'s 20 sites (no hookups; RVs to 31 feet) also are on the North Fork Nooksack. The campground is open from May to October. This is a nice camp; sites along the river are particularly private. And campsites can be reserved up to 240 days in advance; (877) 444-6777; www.reserveusa.com. *On Hwy 542, 14 miles east of Glacier; (360) 599-2714.* **Excelsior Group Camp** has 2 group sites for 25 campers each, and must be reserved through the Forest Service. *On Hwy 542 6.5 miles east of Glacier; (360) 599-2714.*

One of the nicest camping (and lodging—see Lodgings, below) venues in the area is **Silver Lake Park,** a Whatcom County facility on a quiet mountain lake with acres of green space. The park has 80 sites (53 with water/electrical hookups; RVs of any length). Fishing and canoeing in the calm lake are family favorites. Rental craft are available. Silver Lake Park also is home to a small museum, rental cabins, a 28-site horse camp, a large kitchen shelter, and a day-use lodge with a dining room, which can be rented for meetings or retreats. Kids will love the swimming beach. Note: The campground has piped water, flush toilets, and showers. Campsites can be reserved by Whatcom County residents only; (360) 599-2776. *On Silver Lake Rd, 3.5 miles northwest of Maple Falls, which is on Hwy 542 about 5 miles west of Glacier; (360) 599-2776.*

Picnics

Heather Meadows, the general name for the gardenlike alpine area encompassing Austin Pass and Artist Point, has been a favorite Washington lunch spot for decades. Austin Pass, in fact, was the site of a grand lodge in the 1920s, but it burnt and never was replaced. In the winter, this is the end of the road for Mount Baker Highway, and only cross-country skiers and snowshoers make tracks here. But in the late summer and fall, the road continues to Artist Point. Picnickers, however, often gather in the newly revamped Heather Meadows or **Austin Pass** parking areas for lunches. Lower on the mountain, the **Shuksan Picnic Area** at the beginning of Forest Road 32 is an enjoyable spot.

Snowboarding/Skiing

Mount Baker taught the Northwest—and by extension, a lot of the world—how to ride a snowboard. Its unusually steep slopes, deep snow, and laid-back air have made **Mount Baker Ski Area** (actually on the foothills of Mount Shuksan) a cult favorite among deep-powder skiers for decades. But in the early 1980s, a new breed of snow play was born here, mostly at the inquisitive whim of young Bellingham-area adventurers and college students seeking to mix their skateboard and surfing affinity with the mountain's deep, steep powder snowfields. Most people in the snow business will swear snowboarding as we know it today was invented by Jake Burton Carpenter at Stratton Mountain, Vermont. The truth is that snowboarding was bursting out at Stratton and Mount Baker simultaneously. But it blossomed most quickly at Baker, which was the first established ski area in the country to embrace the sport.

The snowboard relationship has only flourished over the past decade. Most of the first professional and world champion–caliber snowboarders (including Amy Howat, daughter of ski-area manager Duncan Howat) sprang from the deep-powder pockets of Mount Baker in the mid-'80s, and it continues to be a globally recognized snowboard mecca. Craig Kelly, widely regarded as the sport's first superstar, is a longtime Glacier resident. Dozens of these top riders and snowboard pros gather at the mountain every year to compete in the Legendary Baker Banked Slalom, a rather amazing slalom-gate race down a steep, high-walled creek bed. (It's on Super Bowl Sunday, and the Slalom makes for a great spectator event for skiers who line the course.)

None of which means Baker is any less of a draw to legions of faithful ski fans. Recent additions at the mountain, such as the fixed-grip quad chairlift to the shoulder of Shuksan Arm, have increased its draw among Seattle-area skiers. Baker is not the most rookie-friendly area (the chair system remains tricky to negotiate, at least until you learn its intricacies). But intermediate-to-advanced skiers love the mountain's ungroomed glades and deep-powder chutes. And beginner terrain has improved in the past several years. So have the mountain's creature comforts. The White Salmon Day Lodge—a winner of architectural awards for its Cascade styling that incorporates local timber, stone, and other trappings—is destined to become a Northwest classic. Its front-window view of Mount Shuksan will thrill even the nonskiers among us.

Baker's main lure, however, remains the same: snow. Lots of it. The mountain's average annual snowfall—between 650 and 750 inches—is the highest average of any ski area in the United States. By far. Just how far was demonstrated during the winter of 1998–99, when it started snowing at Baker in October—and hardly ever stopped. By the next spring, Baker had shattered the all-time record for seasonal snowfall anywhere on Earth: 1,140 inches—or 95 feet—fell on Mount Baker Ski Area between July 1, 1998, and June 30, 1999. That eclipsed the old mark of 1,122 inches set in the winter of 1971–72 at Paradise on Mount Rainier. The mondo dumpage gives Baker the state's longest ski season: it usually opens by Thanksgiving and runs strong until early May (although the schedule shifts to weekends-only late in the year).

The ski area's biggest drawbacks: access and lack of slopeside lodging. Most of the winter, the drive to Baker is a long haul (3 to 4 hours, depending on weather) from Seattle. And the nearest lodging is down the mountain in Glacier. But the pros outweigh the cons here. The skiing is fantastic, and the setting might be unequaled in the country. Anyone who's stood atop Shuksan Arm on one of those clear, crisp, 20-degree January mornings will be a changed person.

Mountain stats: Elevation: 3,550 feet to 5,050 feet. Lifts: 8 (2 fixed quads, 6 double chairs, 2 ropetows). Skiable acres: 1,000. Season: Late October through May. Lift tickets: $33, weekend adults, midweek discounts, (2000–2001 season). Full ski and snowboard rentals, sales, repairs, and lessons are available on the mountain. Mount Baker also offers day care, and has a small maintained cross-country ski area (see below). *Mount Baker Ski Area is at the end of Mount Baker Highway/Hwy 542, 56 miles east of Bellingham; mountain info (360) 734-6771, snow phone, (360) 671-0211; www.mtbakerskiarea.com.*

Snowshoeing/Cross-Country Skiing

Many snowed-in trails and Forest Service roads in the North Fork Nooksack drainage make sublime snowshoe/skinny ski getaways, although visitors must be prepared for cold, wet weather in the lower drainage. For a full winter trail report, call the Mount Baker Ranger District in Sedro Woolley, (360) 856-5700. Some local favorites: The trail to **Coat Pass** (moderate; 10 miles round trip) begins at the winter end of Road 39, Glacier Creek Road, about a mile east of the Glacier Public Service Center. The route climbs a road through Glacier Creek valley to a scenic, 4,700-foot pass on Lookout Mountain. Watch for snowmobiles! From the same trailhead, you can access a trail to Mount Baker's **Coleman Glacier** area (difficult; 14 miles round trip)—a classic backcountry snowshoe trek that climbs Heliotrope Ridge (see Hiking/Backpacking, above) and offers grand views of Mount Baker. A great family outing in the area is **White Salmon Creek** (easy; various distances), where 'shoers can follow snow-covered Road 3070 along the North Fork Nooksack River. The route begins in the Salmon Ridge Sno Park, about 12.5 miles east of Glacier near the North Fork Nooksack River bridge.

Climbing

Both **Mount Baker** and **Mount Shuksan** are popular spring and summertime alpine climbs. Both are semitechnical ascents but negotiable by most climbers with basic glacier-climbing experience, and both are used extensively as training routes by climbing schools preparing alpinists for larger peaks. Baker, in particular, is a popular climb, drawing 100 to 200 climbers a day on spring weekends. Two primary routes are used: the **Coleman Glacier,** on the mountain's northwest slopes, and the **Easton Glacier,** on the south side. For details on **permits,** logistics, and conditions, contact the Glacier Public Service Center, (360) 599-2714, or Base Camp Inc., 901 W Holly in Bellingham; (360) 733-5461. And if you're looking for **instruction,** this is a good place to find it. The American Alpine Institute, 1513 12th St, Bellingham; (360) 671-1505, is one of the best climbing schools in the country, offering novice-to-expert instruction, as well as **guided climbs** on Baker and Shuksan.

Mountain Biking

Road riding is not impossible on Mount Baker Highway, but it is not advisable. The highway, particularly the upper stretches, is narrow and winding, and shoulder space is nil. Lower portions of the highway, between Bellingham and Glacier (31 miles), are more manageable, but less than optimal. Mountain bikers, however, have a choice of **a few backcountry trails** and many, many miles of **Forest Service roads.** Call the Glacier Public Service Center, (360) 599-2714, to find out which roads are open, either by regulation or by snowmelt.

Wildlife Watching

For a river basin less than 30 miles from a fairly large population center, the North Fork Nooksack is surprisingly wild. The best evidence is found on its banks in the winter months, when hundreds of **bald eagles** arrive to feed on spawning **chum salmon.** The North Fork is often overlooked by Puget Sound–area eagle watchers, who flock instead to the Skagit River, one drainage basin to the south. But the Nooksack, thanks to its lighter crowds, actually may be a better place to view eagles in their habitat. The big birds begin to arrive here in November and stay through January, feasting on hatchery runs of winter chum salmon. Public access to the riverbanks is far from ideal. But good viewing points are found at the Nooksack Salmon Hatchery (a mile south of Kendall along Hwy 542) and at the Welcome Bridge on Mosquito Lake Road (turn east from Hwy 542 about 2.5 miles east of the Hwy 9 junction). Recent winter counts on the river have shown as many as 500 eagles on the 4 miles of river between the hatchery and the bridge. For more information, call the state Department of Fish and Wildlife; (206) 775-1311.

In past years, wintering **elk** often were seen in valley fields along the North Fork Nooksack. This herd has been badly depleted by overhunting in recent years, however, so sightings have become more rare.

Fishing

Trout fishing is usually excellent in Silver Lake, which has ample dock and shore access from Silver Lake Park (see Camping, above). The lake gets a hefty spring plant, and less fishing pressure than many other westside ponds. Silver Lake also is said to hold some **cutthroat trout.** The season opens the last Saturday in April, and it's best early on. Other potential trout haunts are the region's alpine lakes, including Tomyhoi and the Galena Lakes chain (see Hiking/Backpacking, above).

Most of the Nooksack River is also a fair trout fishery. Check the state regulations pamphlet for seasons and special restrictions. If they're feeling lucky, steelheaders can give the Nooksack system a try. The river's north and middle forks are accessible from Hwy 542, and hold some winter-run fish. Catch numbers in recent years have been very low, however, particularly on this upper-river portion. Most of the Nooksack's **steelhead** now come out of the lower river, near Lynden and Everson. The river also can be a fair **chinook, coho,** and **chum salmon** fishery.

Photography

One of the most often-snapped photos in the state is the view of **Mount Shuksan** from a small reflecting pond just below Mount Baker Ski Area.

It's a winner—even if you can shoot it from the front seat of your car. Walk a ways, and the views get even better. Morning shots of Mount Shuksan from the **Lake Ann** area, and afternoon wildflower meadows at **Skyline Divide, Chain Lakes,** and other local day-hiking trails offer fabulous shutterbug possibilities (see Hiking/Backpacking, above). This is a particularly beautiful area in the fall, when alpine berry bushes turn brilliant crimson.

Rafting

All that melted snow charging down the **North Fork Nooksack** makes for hot whitewater-rafting action in the summer. The most commonly floated stretch on this mostly Class II river is between Douglas Fir Campground and Maple Falls. For a list of **rafting vendors,** contact the Mount Baker–Snoqualmie National Forest's Mount Baker Ranger District; (360) 856-5700.

Accessible Outdoors

The **Glacier Public Service Center** (summers only) has wheelchair-accessible picnicking and interpretive displays, as does **Shuksan Picnic Area,** 40 miles east of Bellingham on Road 32, just off Hwy 542. But the real star in accessibility in this area is the Heather Meadows area at the end of the highway. From the **Heather Meadows Visitor Center,** just beyond Mount Baker Ski Area, three short, barrier-free trails traverse the splendid North Cascades alpine terrain, offering grand views of Mount Shuksan and other local peaks. In the fall, the area is lush with ripe blueberries and huckleberries. This is one of the best wheelchair-accessible alpine areas in the Northwest. For information, call the Glacier Public Service Center, (360) 599-2714.

outside in

Restaurants

Deming Steakhouse ★ One of the few real steak houses in the region. $$; 5016 Deming Rd, Deming; (360) 592-5282. &

Lodgings

Diamond Ridge ★★ A luxurious, log-style B&B overlooking the Nooksack River. $$$; 9216 Mt Baker Hwy, Deming; (360) 599-3297 or (800) 424-1966; www.diamondridgebb.com.

The Logs at Canyon Creek ★ Five log cabins nestled among dense stands of alder and fir. $$; *9002 Mt Baker Hwy, Deming; (360) 599-2711; www.telcom plus.net/thelogs.*

More Information

Base Camp Inc. (mountaineering/outdoor gear, supplies, rentals): *Bellingham; (360) 733-5461.*

Carter's Carving Edge (snowboard rentals and repairs): *3206 Orleans Street, Bellingham; (360) 671-9738.*

Department of Transportation pass report: *(888) SNO-INFO; www.wsdot.wa.gov/sno-info.*

Fairhaven Bike & Mountain Sports: *1103 11th Street, Bellingham; (360) 733-4433.*

Glacier Public Service Center: *(360) 599-2714.*

Mount Baker Ranger District, Sedro Woolley: *(360) 856-5700.*

Mount Baker Ski Report: *(360) 671-0211; www.mtbakerskiarea.com.*

Mount Baker–Snoqualmie National Forest Headquarters: *(425) 775-9702 or (800) 627-0062; www.fs.fed.us/r6/mbs.*

Mt. Baker Snowboard Shop (rentals, repairs, gear, and mountain information): *Glacier; (360) 599-2008.*

Northwest Avalanche Hotline: *(206) 526-6677.*

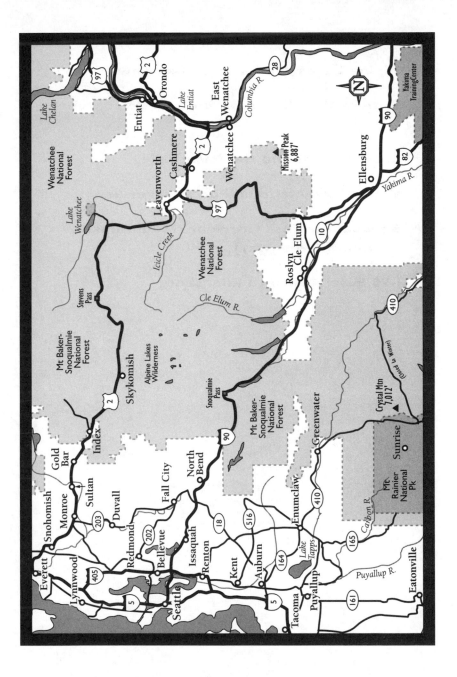

Central
Cascades

Central
Cascades

Alpine Lakes Wilderness: Overview

A 393,000-acre, mostly alpine wilderness backcountry area in the Central Cascades sandwiched between Snoqualmie and Stevens Passes.

It's the ultimate Washington paradox: the kind of mountain solitude you hope to find in the Alpine Lakes Wilderness is the very reason many nature lovers move to Washington, but on some sunny summer afternoons, you might think every last one of them is up here. Occupying most of the high Central Cascades between Interstate 90 and US Highway 2, Alpine Lakes Wilderness contains some of the most splendid alpine territory in the Lower 48. It's also the most heavily trod wilderness in the country, thanks—or no thanks—to its proximity to more than four million (and counting) Puget Sound residents, most of them card-carrying REI members.

Veterans of this beautiful alpine territory know its popularity has been more curse than blessing. Alpine Lakes, which received federal wilderness designation in 1976, includes 393,000 acres, more than 600 lakes, 615 miles of trails, and countless rugged alpine peaks, many of them glaciated. Yet dozens of its most popular hike-in destinations are overused to the point of serious permanent damage. The sheer weight of hundreds of thousands of hikers and their accompanying gear, tents, candle lanterns, and the like has pounded fragile lakeshores into permanent mud fields. Human waste has fouled once-pristine waterways. Trail maintenance can't keep pace with trail use. As a result, the Forest Service in the 1990s announced new backcountry permit regulations, stock and pet restrictions, and other safeguards for more fragile areas (see Alpine Lakes Wilderness Rules and Regulations, below, for details). This, coupled with the 1997 addition of trailhead fees (latest incarnation: the "Northwest Forest Pass") makes exploring the Alpine Lakes a lot less carefree than it was in the days when Harvey Manning was but a young tyke.

The surprising thing is that supervisors of the Mount Baker–Snoqualmie and Wenatchee National Forests, which jointly manage this enterprise, haven't gotten even tougher on access: a series of strict overnight-use quotas, and perhaps even day-hiking quotas, were mulled during the late 1990s, and wilderness fans braced themselves for their implementation. But most of them still await, gathering dust on shelves in proposed policy manuals, while the Forest Service dawdles and decides how far to go, and when. But it still seems only a matter of time before these Alpine Lakes areas join the Enchantments near Leavenworth in strict crowd-control measures.

Tougher access rules probably won't reverse damage already done, but they should limit future degradation, saving this awesome wilderness for those lucky enough to gain access to it in succeeding generations. Let's be honest: the notion of phoning a vendor (heaven forbid, TicketMaster!) in advance for permits, entering your name in a lottery, or paying a trail-use fee for a weekend hike sounds frightfully alien to many backcountry fans. But take a trip into the Alpine Lakes interior, and it's easy to see why so many endure so much bureaucracy to get here. The glacier-carved terrain—an endless chain of clear lakes surrounded by bursting meadows framed by magnificent granite peaks—truly is spectacular. Some of Washington's most precious natural features are found here—the Enchantment Basin, considered one of the nation's most beautiful backcountry destinations; the Necklace Valley; Chain Lakes; Tuck and Robin Lakes—the list goes on and on. Cascade peaks here are the stuff of Washington mountaineering legend: the Tooth, Chair Peak, Summit Chief, Mount Snoqualmie, Kendall Peak, Mount Alta, Three Queens, Chikamin Peak, Big Snow Mountain, Bears Breast, Cathedral Rock, and the most impressive granite structures of all—Mount Stuart, the Stuart Range, and the Enchantment Crags.

Topography in the wilderness ranges from lush, green rain forest on the west slopes to dry, ponderosa-pine-and-big-skies country on the east. Most Alpine Lakes territory is snowbound for all but a brief, August-to-October recreational window (porthole might be more appropriate). That means that seeing the best of this region requires careful planning, not only to avoid foul weather and deep snowfields, but to time your visit between road washouts and permit hangups.

Somehow, that makes spending time here all the more special, that much more desirable. In future years, we hope, some of the hiker pressure

Hyas Lake, part of the Alpine Lakes Wilderness

will be taken off the wilderness area by developing more trails on all sides of it. The Mountains-to-Sound Greenway effort—which seeks to develop much of the Interstate-90 corridor (and the Middle Fork Snoqualmie Valley) for hiking, camping, and mountain biking—is the best hope toward that end.

In the meantime, exercise special caution on the trails, around the lakes, and on the mountaintops of the Alpine Lakes Wilderness. Consider visiting your favorite area as a day trip, not a backpack venture. Tread even more lightly than normal. The Alpine Lakes Wilderness is worth every ounce of extra effort.

Getting There

> Most of the interior Alpine Lakes Wilderness is reached by a combination of
> Forest Service logging roads and hiking paths, most originating on US High-
> way 2 on the north side of the wilderness, Interstate 90 on the south side, or
> US 97, Blewett Pass Highway, on the east side. From the south, the most
> widely used access roads from I-90 are Middle Fork Snoqualmie Road, Taylor
> River Road, Forest Road 9030, Kachess Lake Road, and Salmon La Sac Road;
> and from US 97, North Fork Teanaway Road and Ingalls Creek Road. From
> the north, the primary access points along US 2 are Miller River Road, Foss
> River Road, and Icicle Road near Leavenworth.

inside out

Alpine Lakes Wilderness Rules and Regulations

In 1994, after many years of study, the Mount Baker–Snoqualmie and
Wenatchee National Forests, which co-manage the Alpine Lakes Wilderness, published a list of new user rules for overused areas in the wilderness. However, it turned out that the Forest Service couldn't afford to
enforce its own rules. Forest officials in 1997 said the new rules will be
phased in "as budgets allow." In spite of recent law changes that allow the
Forest Service to collect user fees from recreators every time they turn
around, forest managers were saying essentially the same thing in 2000. In
spite of all that, there are some things we do know about life in the Alpine
Lakes Wilderness in the near future. It's critical to check with a local
ranger district about permit **requirements and use restrictions** for any
Alpine Lakes venture, even if it's a simple day hike. A phone call could
save you a major headache—not to mention a wasted trip if your destination turns out to have been booked up a year in advance by other hikers
who were savvy to the rules. See More Information, below, for a list of
phone numbers, and note the following:

A **Northwest Forest Pass,** $5 per day or $30 annually, now is
required to park in most Forest Service–administered trailheads in the
Alpine Lakes Wilderness. They're available from ranger stations, from
many private vendors, on-line at www.naturenw.org, or by calling (800)
270-7504. Day hikers also must fill out **wilderness trail permits,** which
at least for now are free, unlimited, and available at all trailheads and
ranger stations. The permits are required between May 1 and October 31.
Backpackers also must have a **backcountry permit** between May 1 and
October 31. At this writing, these permits are free and available at trail-

heads for most Alpine Lakes trails. Some major exceptions:

Limited numbers of overnight permits are issued for the popular Enchantments Basin southwest of Leavenworth. In the summer of 1996, the traditional Enchantments Permit Area nearly doubled in size, and **overnight quotas** now extend to Snow Lakes, Eightmile and Caroline Lakes, the Upper Ingalls drainage, and the Stuart Lake/Mount Stuart area. Permits are required for any travel in these areas between June 15 and October 15, and you'll probably need to get a reservation to land one during midsummer. An experiment with phone reservations for Enchantments permits was deemed a failure; you now once again must apply in writing or in person at the Leavenworth Ranger District, 600 Sherbourne Street, Leavenworth, WA 98826; (509) 548-6977; www.fs.fed.us/r6/wenatchee.

Other overused areas in the Wilderness are likely to see similar overnight limits in the future. Candidates include the West Fork Foss River drainage in the Skykomish Ranger District and a large area north of Snoqualmie Pass including Snow Lake and Rampart Ridge. The latter permit area is the largest and will be by far the most significant because it's less than 1 hour from Seattle and its trails are the most heavily used in the wilderness area. At this writing, however, it remains unclear when or how these long-rumored quotas will descend on these popular areas. Call the Leavenworth, Snoqualmie (formerly North Bend), or Skykomish Ranger Districts at the numbers listed under More Information, below, for current permit information.

Mountain bikes, or any other "mechanized" mode of transport, aren't allowed (and likely never will be) in the Alpine Lakes, or any other federal wilderness area. **Other no-nos** that apply to all wilderness areas: cutting switchbacks; caching food or equipment; cutting any trees or portions thereof; washing dishes or bodies in streams and lakes; dumping litter in backcountry toilets; or burying human waste less than 200 feet from a water source.

The **maximum number** of living souls allowed in one party (human or stock) is 12. In the Enchantments Permit Area, it's 8 humans (stock is not allowed). You can't lead a horse to water unless you make him drink: pack and saddle animals are not allowed within 200 feet of lakes, except to get a drink. Go figure. Bring your own horse feed, and make sure it's seed-free (we don't want to know how the rangers check this after the fact). Consult ranger districts for other **stock restrictions.**

Dogs are allowed in the wilderness, but must be leashed on all trails off I-90 and US 2 west of Stevens Pass. No dogs are allowed in the Enchantments Permit Area.

Camping is allowed only in designated areas at most backcountry sites. Check with your local ranger district for a list of affected areas.

Whenever possible, camp on snow, rock, or bare ground. Camping is not allowed within 200 feet of Cradle Lake, Lake Edna, Cup Lake, Larch Lake, or Escondido Tarns. **Campfires** are prohibited above 4,000 feet west of the Cascade Crest and above 5,000 feet east of the Crest. (If you can't locate the Crest, you shouldn't be operating a fire anyway.) Campfires are prohibited at most lakes and popular backcountry camps. Also, consider that just because you are allowed to have a fire in some areas doesn't mean you should. Stoves are recommended throughout the wilderness.

Hiking/Backpacking

This is the big-ticket item. Some of Washington's most spectacular high-country destinations lie within the Alpine Lakes Wilderness. You can hike all the way across the wilderness on any of several routes, one of which is the 69-mile north-south stretch of the Pacific Crest Trail between Snoqualmie Pass and Stevens Pass. But even a short enumeration of the best hikes in the region is too long to list here. (For a healthy start, consult the Snoqualmie Pass Corridor, I-90 East: Roslyn to Ellensburg, Stevens Pass Corridor and Lake Wenatchee, and Leavenworth and the Icicle Valley chapters.)

Camping

No organized campgrounds lie within the Alpine Lakes Wilderness. Back-country campsites are sublime, but most are subject to "low-impact" restrictions (see Alpine Lakes Wilderness Rules and Regulations, above). A large number of excellent Forest Service campgrounds ring the wilderness border, however. (See the Camping sections of the Snoqualmie Pass Corridor (Mountains-to-Sound Greenway), I-90 East: Roslyn to Ellensburg, Stevens Pass Corridor and Lake Wenatchee, and Leavenworth and the Icicle Valley chapters for details.)

Fishing

The Alpine Lakes are a high-lake angler's paradise. Many of this region's 700 lakes and tarns contain **rainbow** or **brook trout,** most of them brought here in water tanks packed in on the backs of volunteers. Keep in mind, however, that most high lakes don't fully melt out until July or later, and even then fishing can be slow until waters warm in the very late summer. Anglers 15 and older need a Washington fishing license to fish all Alpine Lakes Wilderness rivers, lakes, and streams. (See the Camping sections of the Snoqualmie Pass Corridor, I-90 East: Roslyn to Ellensburg, Stevens Pass Corridor and Lake Wenatchee, and Leavenworth and the Icicle Valley chapters for more information, or call a local ranger district.)

Climbing

Many of Washington's best-known climbing routes and pitches lie on granite peaks within the Alpine Lakes Wilderness. (Consult the Snoqualmie Pass Corridor, I-90 East: Roslyn to Ellensburg, and Leavenworth and the Icicle Valley chapters for details.)

Wildlife Watching

You won't find designated animal-watching sites in the Alpine Lakes Wilderness. You won't need them. The wilderness itself is a wildlife refuge in its own right, containing healthy populations of **black-tailed deer, black bears, cougars, mountain goats, raccoons,** and even the occasional migratory **northern gray wolf.** Some people will swear **grizzlies** dip this far south from their journeys though the North Cascades. Doubtful. And if so, extremely rare. We'll believe it when we see one. In general, the biggest predators in the Alpine Lakes Wilderness are black bears and cougars, and troublesome human encounters with either species are exceedingly rare. Still, it's a good idea to exercise good backcountry food-storage and -preparation techniques, such as hanging all food and cook gear from a bear wire, and refraining from sleeping with slabs of fresh bacon.

Horseback Riding

Much of the Alpine Lakes Wilderness is open to stock use. **Guided tours** are available in some portions. (Consult the I-90 East: Roslyn to Ellensburg chapter for trip information.)

More Information

Cle Elum Ranger District: *(509) 674-4411.*
Lake Wenatchee Ranger District: *(509) 763-3103.*
Leavenworth Ranger District: *(509) 782-1413.*
Mount Baker–Snoqualmie National Forest Headquarters:
21905 64th Avenue SW, Mountlake Terrace, WA 98043;
(425) 775-9702 or (800) 627-0062; www.fs.fed.us/r6/mbs.
Skykomish Ranger District: *(360) 677-2414.*
Snoqualmie Pass Visitors Center: *(425) 434-6111.*
Snoqualmie Ranger District, North Bend office: *(425) 888-1421.*
Wenatchee National Forest Headquarters: *215 Melody Lane,*
Wenatchee, WA 98801; (509) 662-4335; www.fs.fed.us/r6/wenatchee.

Stevens Pass Corridor and Lake Wenatchee

From Gold Bar east to Highway 207 near Lake Wenatchee, north to Dishpan Gap on the Pacific Crest Trail, and south to the Necklace Valley in the Alpine Lakes Wilderness, including Stevens Pass Ski Area, the Skykomish River, Wallace Falls and Lake Wenatchee State Parks, and parts of the Henry M. Jackson and Glacier Peaks Wildernesses

They don't call it a National Scenic Byway for nothing. Perhaps no other Northwest highway is as deserving of that moniker as Stevens Pass Highway (US Highway 2), a road that mimics the rivers it follows from the Puget Sound lowlands to headwaters high in the Central Cascades. Like the nearby lumbering Snoqualmie River, US Highway 2 begins as a boring four-laner through cow country in the lower Snoqualmie Valley, gets narrower and more interesting between Monroe and Sultan, then downright skinny and squirrelly between Gold Bar and Skykomish.

The roadside views as you enter this upper Skykomish River gorge say more about this region than any words ever mustered. Coming around a bend on an autumn day, motorists are blindsided by the sudden presence of 5,990-foot Mount Index, the most impressively jagged slab of rock in the Cascades. Snow clings to a handful of narrow ledges on this near-vertical beast, one of many similar behemoths forming the walls of the upper Skykomish drainage.

In a mountain setting like this, the beauty and mystique of every inch of land is magnified. The Skykomish is a federally designated Wild and Scenic River, and rightly so. Hiking trails leading north into the Henry M. Jackson and Glacier Peaks Wildernesses and south into the Alpine Lakes Wilderness are packed with mountain lakes and alpine meadows as majestic as any in North America. Skiers harden thigh muscles—and strain smile muscles—on trails and ski lifts near the Stevens Pass summit. Anglers wade into the Skykomish and Wenatchee River systems, which drain the west and east slopes of this region, respectively, and come home with sizable fish and unwieldy tales.

The Stevens Pass Corridor is wild by accident. Unlike some other state mountain areas set aside early for conservation regions, this one is so rugged that it largely preserved itself. Miners, railroads, developers, and contractors have given their all on both sides of this corridor, but here the rivers and mountains continue to reign supreme. Mine shafts have crumbled. Roads routinely wash out. More than one railroad has picked up its ties and gone home.

A single thin ribbon of concrete—the Stevens Pass Highway—is the lone enduring human presence in this geographic center of the Central Cascades. For recreationalists, that's the ideal compromise. Thanks to the highway, reaching the heart of the mountains is easy. Thanks to the mountains, a lot of us still have trouble getting back out.

Getting There

All destinations in the Stevens Pass Corridor are reached via US Highway 2, Stevens Pass Highway, which runs east from Interstate 5 at Everett to Wenatchee on the central Columbia River. Stevens Pass summit is some 80 miles northeast of Seattle; allow about 2 hours. Lake Wenatchee is an additional 20 miles to the east. Snow often socks in Stevens Pass near the summit, where one 10-mile stretch can be particularly hazardous for drivers. The pass rarely is closed by snow, but chains sometimes are required. Consult the Department of Transportation pass report, (888) SNO-INFO; www.wsdot.wa.gov/sno-info.

inside out

Hiking/Backpacking

Trails in this region run the gamut, from close-in, overcrowded day hikes (Wallace Falls) to lonely treks through some of the more remote wilderness areas in the state. From US 2, hikers can head north into the Glacier Peak or Henry M. Jackson Wilderness Areas, or south into the heavily traveled but still spectacular Alpine Lakes Wilderness. Note that a **Northwest Forest Pass,** $5 per day or $30 annually, is required to park in many Forest Service–administered trailheads in this area. They're available from ranger stations, from many private vendors, on-line at www.naturenw.org, or by calling (800) 270-7504. For full trail information, including ever-evolving **permit requirements** and reports on high-mountain roads (which often wash out in this area), contact the Skykomish Ranger District for westside trails, (360) 677-2414, or Lake Wenatchee Ranger District for eastside trails, (509) 763-3103. But just to get your mind drooling, here's a short list of popular hikes on both sides of US 2, arranged generally west to east.

US 2 from Gold Bar to Scenic

Everyone should haul themselves up to **Wallace Falls** (moderately difficult; 7 miles round trip) at least once. Visible from US 2 in the winter, the falls have been luring Stevens Pass travelers for decades. From a trailhead in Wallace Falls State Park just north of Gold Bar (see Camping, below), the path climbs fairly steeply, coming to a fork. The left route follows an old railroad grade to the top. It's a mile longer, but a bit easier on the lungs. The right fork is the direct route, direct meaning painful if you're not in shape. The paths meet at a bridge over the North Fork Wallace, then take you another mile or so to a lower-falls viewpoint. Stop here, or continue another 1.5 miles to an upper-falls viewpoint. Either way, the payoff is rich. Wallace Falls, a 250-foot drop on the South Fork Wallace, is arguably the most magnificent in the Cascades. The mist is a great elixir.

Mount Index area

The recently rebuilt (1998) trail to **Lake Serene** (moderate; 7 miles round trip) now is more than worth your day-hiking time. Get there by turning right (south) on Mount Index Road, just past milepost 35, then turning right at the first junction, (about a quarter mile). The trail follows an old road for about 1.5 miles, then splits. The right fork goes less than a half mile to a grand viewpoint of Bridal Veil Falls; the left goes another 2 miles up, up, up to Lake Serene, tucked into the armpit of magnificent Mount Index. No camping is allowed at the lake. Total elevation gain to the lake: about 2,000 feet.

North Fork Skykomish River/Henry M. Jackson Wilderness

Follow Road 63, the North Fork Skykomish River Road, northeast from Index for access to the Henry M. Jackson Wilderness:

A pleasant backpack route is the **West Cady Ridge Trail** (moderate; various loop distances possible) in the North Fork Skykomish drainage. From a trailhead about 20 miles up Road 63 (stay left at the fork at about 15 miles), the path climbs through thick forest before breaking out on a scenic, 5-mile-long stretch of ridge-top meadows. Highlights include Benchmark Mountain and access to a spectacular stretch of the Pacific Crest Trail that passes Skykomish Peak and skirts Lake Sally Anne on the

Deception Falls is a short walk from US 2, west of Stevens Pass

way to Dishpan Gap in the Henry M. Jackson Wilderness. Pick up a copy of Green Trails' Monte Cristo and Benchmark Mountain maps (numbers 143 and 144) and plan your own route. Don't tell anyone, but you can find summer solitude here.

For a more direct, river-valley access to the same area, the **Dishpan Gap Trail** (moderate; 14.6 miles round trip) begins at the end of Road 63 and follows the North Fork Skykomish directly to Dishpan Gap. A trying day hike in the same area is the **Blanca Lake Trail** (difficult; 7 miles round trip), which climbs from Road 63 about 2,700 feet in the first 3 miles before dropping to the lake, which offers beautiful views of Columbia, Monte Cristo, and Reyes Peaks in the Henry M. Jackson Wilderness.

Miller River drainage (south side US 2)

Follow the Old Cascade Hwy south from US 2 near Money Creek 1 mile to Miller River Road; proceed about 9 miles south:

The trail to **Lake Dorothy** (easy; 3 miles round trip) is a big hit, thanks to the fact that you can practically drive to it on logging roads. This trail is almost too easy, drawing large crowds to the alpine lake. Keep going for a good example of how logging roads very nearly cut the Alpine Lakes Wilderness in two. Those who continue around the east side of Lake Dorothy can proceed another 6.5 miles up the trail, passing **Bear** and **Deer Lakes** on the way to **Snoqualmie Lake,** in the Taylor River drainage. If you were so inclined, you could walk another couple of miles west down the Taylor River and—voilà!—be back on road, the abandoned Road 5630, which ultimately leads to Forest Road 56. Before you know it, you're all the way down the Middle Fork Snoqualmie and into North Bend for a hot-fudge sundae.

Beckler River drainage (north side US 2)

Take Beckler River Road 65 about 7 miles north from Skykomish, then Rapid River Road 6530 about 4 miles east:

Fortune Ponds (moderate; 13 miles round trip) is a very popular back-country destination—a string of lakes in the heart of the Henry M. Jackson Wilderness. This access, one of several, puts you on the **Meadow Creek Trail,** which climbs gently from the Rapid River along Meadow Creek, through a 1960s burn, to the ponds, a series of lakes in the shadow of Fortune Mountain. You'll find lots of good—and overused—campsites. You can make a long shuttle hike out of this one by joining the **Pacific Crest Trail** near the ponds and hiking south about 12 miles to Road 6700, which exits on US 2 east of Stevens Pass Ski Area. Or continue south on the PCT via **Lake Valhalla** and **Stevens Creek** for a total of about 20 miles, exiting directly at Stevens Pass.

West Fork Foss River drainage (south side US 2)

Follow Foss River Road 68 south from US 2, about 1.75 miles east of the Skykomish Ranger Station:

Tonga Ridge (easy; 9.2 miles round trip) is a great way to sample the Alpine Lakes high country, because it starts out high. The first mile or so is in second-growth forest, then the trail breaks out into meadows. You'll find good campsites at Sawyer Pass (3.5 miles), amid one of the largest blueberry patches you'll ever find (a major early autumn bonus). A side trail leads to pretty Fisher Lake. To reach the trailhead, follow Road 68, continue right on Road 68 at the first fork (1.25 miles) and proceed 3.5 miles to Tonga Ridge Road 6830. Turn left and proceed 7 miles to Spur Road 310. Turn right and find the trailhead in about 1.5 miles.

Higher in the same drainage, the **West Fork Foss Lakes** (moderate; 13.5 miles round trip) are one of the most popular destinations in all the Alpine Lakes Wilderness. (For more on Alpine Lakes permits, see the Alpine Lakes Wilderness: Overview chapter.) It's easy to see what draws the crowds. This chain of beautiful alpine lakes, surrounded by stunning peaks and fed by waterfalls, begins with Trout Lake at 1.5 miles and ends more or less at Delta Lake, 7.5 miles in. Day hikers will find that crowds thin measurably after Trout Lake. The trailhead is on Road 6835, which turns left from Road 68 about 4.5 miles south of US 2.

Road 68 about 4.5 miles south of US 2

The string of jewel-like lakes in the nearby **Necklace Valley** (moderate/difficult; 15 miles round trip) is another loved-nearly-to-death destination. From a trailhead 4.1 miles south on Foss River Road/Road 68 from US 2, the **East Fork Foss River Trail** climbs to Jade, Locket, Jewel, Emerald, Opal, and a half dozen other too-small-to-name lakes, nearly all set in dramatic alpine cirques in the very heart of the Alpine Lakes Wilderness. The walk is easy for the first 5 miles, following an old miners railroad grade up the East Fork Foss River. Then the path crosses the river and zooms (okay, plods, if you're an average hiker laden with backpack) straight up, gaining about 2,500 feet in just over 2 miles to the first of the lakes. This area, too, is likely to see limits on permits in coming years. Ask at the Skykomish Ranger Station, where you should also be sure to ask about road conditions.

Deception Falls area

Deception Falls is a lovely Cascade gusher you can see right from US 2. But it's worth getting out here (about 8 miles east of Skykomish) and walking the lovely **nature trail** (easy, about 1.5-mile loop), which drops down into the forest, loops along the creek, and returns to a spectacular footbridge just below the falls, on the north side of the highway. **Deception Creek Trail** (moderate; various lengths possible) is a great midsummer, hot-day hike, mainly because it'll keep you out of the sun. To reach the trailhead, turn right on Road 6088, about a quarter mile beyond the Deception Falls parking area. The trail, following Deception Creek south through deep forest, makes for a steady-but-moderate pace. You can hike it a mile to break in the new boots—or new kid—or keep going about 3 miles to some nice campsites. Shuttle-hiking backpackers (assuming it's late July or beyond, and the snow is melted) can continue south all the way through the Alpine Lakes Wilderness to **Deception Lakes, the Pacific Crest Trail, Deception Pass** (10.5 miles), and, ultimately, an exit in the upper Cle Elum River drainage above Salmon La Sac (see the I-90 East: Roslyn to Ellensburg chapter). It makes for a one-way north-south Alpine Lakes Wilderness crossing of about 17 miles. (Note: The upper portions of Deception Creek must be crossed several times on foot logs, which may or may not have survived the winter storms and spring floods before you visit. Check with a ranger.)

Surprise Creek Trail (moderate; 8 miles round trip to Surprise Lake), which begins near Scenic, about 10 miles east of Skykomish (turn right just before the bridge over the railway, just before milepost 59), is another grand hot-day excursion. This very pretty creekside trail climbs about 2,300 vertical feet through cool, waterfall-lined forest to the lake. Call it a day there, or continue south to the **Pacific Crest Trail**, 6,000-foot **Pieper Pass**, and **Deception Lakes** (about 10 miles).

Stevens Pass vicinity

The **Iron Goat Trail** (easy; 8 miles round trip), a newly reclaimed Great Northern Railroad right-of-way, is a great family hike, or a good leg-stretcher for Stevens Pass travelers. From US 2, 6 miles east of Skykomish, take the Old Cascade Highway (Forest Road 67) 2.3 miles north to Road 6710, turn left, and find the trailhead at road's end, 1.4 miles farther on. Awaiting your strolling pleasure are about 8 miles of reclaimed railroad trail, complete with interpretive signs to link the present ruins (collapsed snowsheds and long-abandoned tunnels) with the railroad past. This particular stretch was abandoned by the Great Northern in 1929, when the second Cascade Tunnel, a 7.8-mile passage beneath Stevens Pass, rendered it obsolete. Today, it's a fascinating walk, and one of the best places in this area to enjoy blooming wildflowers in the spring and early summer. Much credit goes to Volunteers for Outdoor Washington and other trail groups, who have built this trail system almost exclusively with volunteer labor. Because of this constant work, the trail is in a state of flux, with new trailheads and trail grades being added regularly. Call the Skykomish Ranger District (see More Information, below) for current information.

Chain Lakes (difficult; 24 miles round trip), reached by hiking the **Pacific Crest Trail** south from Stevens Pass Summit (park near the ski area), are among the more dramatic backpacking destinations in this area. The trail, occasionally very steep and always snowbound until late summer, climbs to Josephine Lake, where the **Chain Lakes trail** heads south then east to Chain and Doelle Lakes, which lie in a cirque below 6,807-foot Bulls Tooth peak. This area also can be reached by hiking the **Icicle Creek Trail** west from Icicle Road, crossing Frosty Pass. Through hikers can do a one-way Stevens-Pass-to-Icicle trip of about 31 miles. It's a beauty.

Lake Wenatchee area

About 9 miles east of Stevens Pass on US 2, watch for the **Rock Mountain Trail** (painfully difficult; 10 miles round trip) near milepost 73. This is the direct—very direct—route to the top of Nason Ridge, which runs from Stevens Pass east to Lake Wenatchee. It climbs 3,500 feet in the first 4 miles, black flies are deadly, and there's little water. Still game? The ridge-top view (from 6,200 feet) is grand, and you can drop several hundred feet and about a mile down to Rock Lake. Conscience forces us to advise you that there's an easier way to get here. The **Snowy Creek Trail**, reached via Smith Brook Road 6700 (it turns off US 2 about 4.5 miles east of Stevens Pass), is a much gentler, 4.5-mile route. But you wouldn't have nearly the same blisters to show for it. **Merritt Lake** (moderate; 6 miles round trip), on the other hand, is a rather pleasant day trip for Lake Wenatchee visitors. The trailhead is on Spur Road 657, marked "Merritt Lake," just off

US 2 about 12 miles east of Stevens Pass. You'll gain about 1,700 feet in the first 2 miles, climbing to a junction with the Nason Ridge Trail. Stay right and climb another 500 feet or so over the final mile to Merritt Lake, which holds some trout.

Closer to Lake Wenatchee itself, the **Dirty Face Trail** (difficult; 9 miles round trip), which departs near the Lake Wenatchee Ranger Station on Hwy 207, is a fine place to work off all those s'mores from last night. This is another major gasser, gaining 4,000 feet on its 7.6 billion-switch-backs route to a 6,000-foot summit lookout. Carry lots of water on this one; little is available. More sensible day hikers will enjoy the **South Shore Trail** (easy, 2.4 miles round trip) and the short walk to **Hidden Lake** (easy; 1 mile round trip), both of which begin near Glacier View Campground (see Camping, below). Campers or day visitors to Lake Wenatchee State Park will find a pair of short, easy hiking trails up both banks of the **Wenatchee River** as it flows from the lake.

Wenatchee River drainage

Follow Road 6500 west from the Lake Wenatchee area to reach Little Wenatchee Ford, the staging area for a number of excellent Glacier Peak Wilderness hikes. One of the more popular is the **Cady Creek/Little Wenatchee Loop** (difficult; 18.8 miles round trip). Take the Cady Creek Trail west to Cady Pass, turn north for a 5.7-mile walk along the Pacific Crest Trail to Dishpan Gap, proceed 1 mile to Meander Meadow, then turn south and return on the 7-mile Little Wenatchee Trail. It's a spectacular loop, through the heart of a rather amazing alpine wilderness. Also from the Little Wenatchee Ford area, the **Poe Mountain Trail** (excruciatingly difficult; 5 miles round trip) climbs 3,000 feet in 2.5 miles to a 6,015-foot viewpoint. Eat your Wheaties—twice.

White River drainage

Anybody who survived the hike up Poe Mountain—and enjoyed it—shouldn't miss the trail up an even higher peak four mountains to the east, **Mount David** (difficult; 14 miles round trip). From the Indian Creek trailhead at the end of Road 6400 northwest of the Lake Wenatchee area, hike the Indian Creek Trail a short distance to the Panther Creek Trail to the Mount David Trail—and muster up some courage. The trail gains more than 5,000 feet on its way to what's left of an old lookout tower (basically, an outhouse with a billion-dollar, 7,400-foot view). This is a tough climb in places, with the trail sometimes lost in scree or snow. Don't go before late summer, and don't ever go unprepared. Also from this trail-head, the **White River** and **Indian Creek Trails** depart west and north into the heart of the Glacier Peak Wilderness.

Camping

Lake Wenatchee State Park is the camp-o-rama in this region. One of the few state parks in a truly alpine-lake setting, it's a perennial favorite of hikers, boaters, anglers, and regular old chaise-lounge power snoozers. Spread across both sides of the Wenatchee River's outlet from the lake, this park is big and diverse, with 197 standard campsites (no hookups; RVs to 60 feet), an 80-camper group camp, extensive picnic facilities, a boat launch and moorage, swimming area, and horse stables. Good hiking, mountain biking, cross-country skiing, kayaking, and fishing await nearby (see appropriate sections in this chapter). Lake Wenatchee is open all year. Camping loops are closed November 1 through mid-April, but camping is allowed in the day-use area for those with Sno-Park winter ski permits. Sites can be reserved up to 11 months in advance by calling (800) 452-5687. *From Coles Corner on US 2 (about 20 miles east of Stevens Pass or 11 miles northwest of Leavenworth), turn east on Hwy 207 and follow signs 3.8 miles to the campground entrance; (509) 763-3101 or (800) 233-0321.*

On the west side of US 2, **Wallace Falls State Park,** 2 miles north-weast of Gold Bar (follow signs from US 2), offers 6 tent sites, with piped water and flush toilets—a rarity at tents-only campgrounds. It's open all year; (800) 233-0321 or (360) 793-0420.

Elsewhere in the Stevens Pass Corridor, **public camping** facilities are primarily Forest Service campgrounds, with varying levels of service.

Skykomish Ranger District; (360) 677-2414

Money Creek has 12 tent and 12 tent/RV sites (no hookups). It's in a pretty setting beside the Skykomish River. The campground is open Memorial Day through Labor Day. Campsites can be reserved up to 240 days in advance; (877) 444-6777; www.reserveusa.com. *West of Skykomish on US 2.*

Beckler River, just north of US 2, has 7 tent sites and 20 tent/RV sites (no hookups; RVs to 21 feet) scattered along the tantalizing—and often unruly—Beckler River. The campground is open Memorial Day through Labor Day. Some campsites can be reserved up to 240 days in advance; (877) 444-6777; www.reserveusa.com. *On Forest Rd 65, 1.5 miles north of US 2 just east of Skykomish.*

Two more remote campgrounds in the North Fork Skykomish area are reached via Forest Road 65 from the south or the Index-Galena Road from the west. **Troublesome Creek** has 24 sites (no hookups; RVs to 21 feet). Campsites can be reserved up to 240 days in advance; (877) 444-6777; www.reserveusa.com. **San Juan,** which has no piped water, has 8 sites (no hookups; RVs to 21 feet). Both are open Memorial Day through Labor Day only. *On Index-Galena Rd (summer only) 12 and 14 miles, respectively, east of Index.*

Lake Wenatchee Ranger District; (509) 763-3103

Two Forest Service camps in the Lake Wenatchee area stand as alternatives to Lake Wenatchee State Park:

Nason Creek, on the Wenatchee River just south of the lake, has 73 sites (no hookups; RVs to 31 feet). Most people go right by it on their way to the state park. This one is almost as close to the lake, and serves as a good alternative if the other campground is full. But don't bet on finding open spaces here in the dead of summer, either. The campground is extremely popular with boaters, anglers, and other Lake Wenatchee vacationers. The campground is open May through October. Campsites cannot be reserved. *From Coles Corner on US 2, turn north on Hwy 207 and proceed 3.5 miles to Cedar Brae Rd. Turn left and proceed a short distance to the campground entrance.*

Glacier View, on the lake's southwest shore (elevation 1,900 feet), has 23 tent sites, 16 of which are walk-in sites near the lake, making this a popular boater/angler camp. The campground also has a boat launch and piped water. It's open May through September, and campsites cannot be reserved. *From Coles Corner on US 2, turn north on Hwy 207 and proceed 3.5 miles to Cedar Brae Rd. Turn left and drive about 5.5 miles to the campground.*

Lake Wenatchee–area campers seeking a more remote experience in the upper Wenatchee River drainage (northwest of Lake Wenatchee) can seek out three small, primitive Forest Service camps in the shadow of Glacier Peak, on the Little Wenatchee River. **Soda Springs** (5 tent sites); **Lake Creek** (8 tent sites), and **Little Wenatchee Ford** (3 tent sites). The latter is the staging area for many Glacier Peak Wilderness expeditions, such as the popular Cady Creek/Little Wenatchee backpacking loop (see Hiking/Backpacking, above). All three campgrounds are open summers only and are free but primitive, with pit toilets and no piped water or other services. *All are on Forest Rd 6500, off Lake Wenatchee's N Shore Dr.*

One river valley to the north of the Little Wenatchee lies the White River, another major Glacier Peak drainage. It's the site of three more small, primitive Forest Service campgrounds. The first, **Napeequa Crossing** (5 sites), serves as a popular staging area for expeditions into the Glacier Peak Wilderness (the popular Twin Lakes trailhead is nearby). The second, **Grasshopper Meadow** (5 sites), is only about a mile from the third, **White River Falls** (5 sites), which is set near the impressive falls of the same name. All three camps are primitive, free, and open summers only, with pit toilets but no piped water or other services. *On Forest Rd 6400 (White River Rd).*

A similar string of campgrounds is found northwest of Lake Wenatchee, along the eastern border of the spectacular Alpine Lakes Wilderness. From lower Chiwawa River to upper, they are: **Alder Creek**

Horse Camp (24-horse capacity; dispersed camping); **Goose Creek** (29 sites), with lotsa dirt bikes and ATVs; **Grouse Creek Group Camp; Finner Creek** (3 sites); **Riverbend** (6 sites); **Rock Creek** (4 sites); **Chiwawa Horse Camp** (21 sites); **Schaefer Creek** (10 sites); **Atkinson Flats** (7 sites); **19 Mile** (4 sites); **Alpine Meadows** (4 sites); and **Phelps Creek** (7 sites), near Trinity. All are primitive, with pit toilets and no piped water. Some of these campgrounds are free, but require a Northwest Forest Pass (see Hiking/Backpacking, above) for parking. *On the remote Chiwawa River Rd (Forest Rd 6200), which turns northeast from Hwy 207 near Lake Wenatchee State Park.*

Four other small, free, primitive Forest Service camps in the upper Wenatchee drainage are: **Theseus Creek** (3 sites), *on Rd 6701 (take Forest Rd 6500 to Little Wenatchee Falls and turn left);* **Meadow Creek** (4 sites), *on Rd 6300 from N Shore Dr;* **Deep Creek** (3 sites), *on Rd 6100 off Chiwawa River Rd;* and **Deer Camp** (3 sites), *on Rd 6101 off Rd 6100.* For information on all, contact Wenatchee National Forest, Lake Wenatchee Ranger District, (509) 763-3103.

Downhill Skiing

Stevens Pass Ski Area, a longtime favorite of Seattle-area day-skiing commuters, is the main attraction here, offering some of Washington's best all-around skiing when snow conditions cooperate. Stevens, with 1,800 of vertical spread broadly across 1,125 acres on both sides of the Stevens Pass Summit, has a great mix of alpine terrain. That, coupled with an improving chairlift system and quite consistent snowfall, makes the mountain a must-visit for the serious Puget Sound–area skier.

Stevens, owned by the same Harbor Properties group that now owns Mission Ridge and Schweitzer, in Idaho, offers something for every skier. Options on the front side range from broad, smooth beginner and intermediate runs to a set of downright nasty bump runs under the lifts and, for the experts, the knee-shaking steeps of Seventh Heaven. The back side, a portion of Mill Creek Valley, was opened in 1987 with the addition of two fixed quad chairs—and many acres of groomed and ungroomed fun. The back side, which expanded Stevens' acreage by 40 percent, is medium-steep, a touch wild, and usually not as heavily skied as the front, making it the location of choice for fans of unbroken snow. When it's open (often not until a month's worth of skiing on the front side has passed), the back side is the place to be.

Stevens took another step toward regional ski-resort respectability in 1996 with the installation of its first high-speed detachable quad lift, the Skyline Express, which replaced the popular front-side Barrier chair. It proved to be a boon both to intermediate skiers, who love Barrier's long, flowing runout, and experts, who now can zip to the base of the Seventh Heaven chair without the use of an annoying midmountain rope tow. That lift was followed in 1998 by the Hogsback Express, which provides quad-chair access to lovers of the mountain's middle, intermediate slopes.

The base area at Stevens got its own full-blown, $5 million face-lift for the winter of 1999–2000, with a large, new, quite stylish day lodge, Granite Peaks. The base village offers full services, including a quality ski school, a **rental** and gear shop, several restaurants, a nice brown-bag lunch area, and an efficient ski-check (use it; stolen skis are as much a problem here as anywhere else). Skiing typically begins here around Thanksgiving (in recent years, the mountain has given perennial early opener Mount Baker a run for its money, although veterans know the skiing usually doesn't get really good until January) and lasts through the first week of April. The base area is just under 4,000 feet, not exactly high as ski resorts go, but a full 800 feet higher than competing Snoqualmie Pass areas. Stevens tops out at 5,845 feet.

Snowboarders are warmly welcomed at Stevens, and have proliferated on the slopes. They like the same things about the mountain as skiers: lots of mixed terrain, reliable snow, room to spread out. Until recently, you could add reasonable lift rates to that list. Stevens' midweek rates as recently as the later 1990s were a great deal midweek, when tickets cost $13 to $15. Not anymore. All those capital improvements have displaced bargain days at Stevens, which at this writing charged $41 for an all-day lift ticket, 7 days a week. It was the first ski area in the state to break the $40 lift ticket barrier.

The biggest drawback to skiing Stevens is getting there. For much of the winter, it's an easy 90-minute to 2-hour commute from the Seattle area, 78 miles away. But when the weather turns sour, US 2 can be a hellish drive, particularly for the 10 miles or so on either side of the summit. Carry chains, or you'll regret it. The closest lodging is in Skykomish on the west side, and at Lake Wenatchee and Leavenworth on the east.

Stevens stats: Elevation: 3,850 to 5,845 feet. Lifts: 10. Skiable acreage: 1,125. Season: Late November to mid-April, snow permitting. Hours: 9am to 10pm daily. Lift rates: $41 adults, daily. *On US 2 at Stevens Pass Summit; mountain info (206) 812-4510, snow phone (206) 634-1645; www.stevenspass.com.*

Cross-Country Skiing

Nordic skiers have several options in the Stevens Pass area. The first is the increasingly popular **Stevens Pass Nordic Center,** 5 miles east of the main ski area along US 2. The Nordic Center has 25 kilometers of groomed trails running up Mill Creek Valley. It's a nice trail system, the primary drawback being the high-tension power lines that run through the valley, making you wonder what all that snap, crackle, and pop is doing to your brains as you slide underneath. Even so, this is an enjoyable day outing. Some longtime Stevens Pass Nordic fans lament the construction of this facility in the early '90s (the Mill Creek Valley formerly was an unpatrolled backcountry ski area, with parking access provided by a state Sno-Park). But the new facilities make for a fair trade-off, considering how much trail grooming is done here now. The Nordic Center is open Fridays through Sundays, plus holidays, from 9am to 4pm; (206) 634-1645.

Another option is the extensive trail system at **Lake Wenatchee State Park,** where a Sno-Park provides trail access all winter long for skiers whose autos have a Sno-Park parking sticker ($20 annually). This is one of the better Sno-Park areas in the state, with 35 kilometers of trails spread out across lands owned by Washington State Parks, the Forest Service, and a couple of private timber companies. The tracks lead to six main loops, ranging from 1 to 4 kilometers in length. The most scenic is the easy 1K lake loop, which skirts the shore of (frozen) Lake Wenatchee. This isn't the quietest Sno-Park, however. It's a huge staging area for snowmobilers bound for backcountry trips on local logging roads. But there's something here for everybody in the Nordic-skiing family. Call the Lake Wenatchee Ranger District, (509) 763-3103, for snow conditions and information. Other Sno-Park turnouts are found along Chiwawa Road north of the lake. They include **Chiwawa Road** (1.2 miles east of the Hwy 207/County Road 22 junction) and **Kahler Glen** (from Hwy 207 near Lake Wenatchee, left on Cedar Brae Road and left on Kahler Drive), both of which have groomed trails.

Another great backcountry ski option is truly in the backcountry. Privately operated **Scottish Lakes High Camp,** reached only by skiing or by riding a sno-cat 8 miles north of US 2, offers a unique ski experience. Skiers are shuttled into a cluster of seven rustic cabins and a newly expanded day-use building in the heart of the high, dry forest. A very extensive (24 kilometers, total) and well-maintained trail system awaits for skiers of all abilities. Backcountry telemarkers also find a nice range of fresh powder in the local mountains. Rates at this writing were $40 per person per night (adults), with an additional fee for sno-cat transportation. It's a reservation-only affair, so call early. High Country Adventures, PO Box 2023, Snohomish, WA 98291-2023; (888) 9HICAMP or (425) 844-2000 office, (509) 763-3044 base camp; or www.scottishlakes.com.

Snowshoeing

Many of the popular trailheads listed under Hiking/Backpacking, above, double as snowshoe jump-off points in the winter. Popular backcountry snowshoe treks along US 2 include the **East Fork Foss River** (difficult; 14 miles round trip), at the winter end of Forest Road 68; **Tonga Ridge** (easy; 7 miles round trip); **Skyline Lake** (difficult; 3 miles round trip), on the north side of Stevens Pass parking lot; **Surprise Lake** (difficult; 8 miles round trip; see Hiking, above for trailhead information); and **Lanham Lake** (moderate; 3.5 miles round trip), accessed from the Mill Creek/Nordic Center parking area 5 miles east of Stevens Pass. In the **Lake Wenatchee** area, try local ski trails around the lake, originating in the state Sno-Park (see Cross-country Skiing, above), or, for more backcountry adventure, make your way to the **Wenatchee Ridge Trail** (moderate; 10 miles round trip) or **Chiwaukum Creek** (difficult; 10.4 miles round trip) trails or **Little Wenatchee River Road** (moderate; 16 miles round trip). Snowshoes also are **rented,** and trails are available, at the Stevens Pass Nordic Center (see Cross-country Skiing, above).

Fishing

The middle flanks of the rushing Skykomish River settle into a string of deep pools just east of Gold Bar, forming the fabled Reiter Ponds, one of the state's most active **steelhead**-fishing venues. The Sky's winter run is one of the largest in the state. It usually peaks in December and January, but can remain productive until early March, when fishing switches to catch-and-release through April. The Sky also has a very productive summer-run fishery. Reiter Ponds can—and often does—get ridiculously crowded. But there are many other good shore-fishing spots on the river from Sultan downstream to the Hwy 203 bridge at Monroe. This river also has a healthy autumn return of **coho, chum,** and (during odd-numbered years) **pink salmon.** Check the state's fishing regulations pamphlet for information on seasons, limits, and conservation closures. If you're a newcomer who's really serious about learning the Sky, consider one of the **guided float trips** run by most Puget Sound–area river guides. Inquire at any local tackle shop.

The east side of the Stevens Pass Corridor offers an interesting mix of **kokanee, trout,** and occasionally **sockeye salmon** fishing. In a good year, Lake Wenatchee holds all three. The sockeye run is a spotty one—no surprise, considering the obstacles these fish must endure to return here (see notes on migratory salmon and steelhead in Leavenworth and the Icicle Valley chapter). When it's open, most anglers employ the same method used successfully for salmon in Lake Chelan and Lake Washington—a bare hook trolled behind a flasher or spinner. The lake's kokanee population is quite healthy, a fact reflected by large bag limits in recent years. Best success comes in a boat, trolling with pop gear or active, flashy spinners.

Both the Little Wenatchee and White Rivers, the lake's two tributaries, offer decent trout fishing. The White, true to its name, often carries glacial silt from the Glacier Peak Wilderness downstream, so fishing can be tough. No bait is allowed above the Napeequa River confluence. The Little Wenatchee, conversely, can make trout fishing seem like child's play—particularly if you arrive just after the state plants catchable **rainbows** here. The river opens in late June, and can be productive all summer. (See Camping/Parks, above, for a list of good access points to the upper river.)

Trout fishing also can be very good on nearby Fish Lake, which holds rainbows and some big **brown trout,** as well as **perch** and **bass.** Decent bank access for fly anglers can be found at various points around the lake, and boats can be rented at a lakeside resort. If the crowds at these spots are a turnoff, consider that most of the high-country lakes in the Alpine Lakes Wilderness offer some semblance of a sport fishery. Check with the Lake Wenatchee or Skykomish Ranger District offices for information on which lakes are open, accessible—and thawed. State licenses are required for all freshwater fishing in this region. See More Information, below.

Mountain Biking

In the Skykomish drainage, hundreds of miles of abandoned or nearly abandoned logging roads provide good fodder for fat-tire fans. A popular ride just off US 2 is **Money Creek Road 6420,** reached by turning south at Money Creek Campground (10 miles east of Index; see Camping, above) and following the Old Cascade Highway and Miller Creek Road a short distance to the road start at a gate (open in summer if the road isn't washed out). You can climb about 12 miles on this road, with grand views along the route, all the way **to Lake Elizabeth.**

Other good day or multi-day trips can be made on the **Beckler River Road,** which, combined with the **North Fork Skykomish Road** heading north from Index, creates a loop of about 30 miles off US 2. Riders can make it a multi-day trip by camping at Beckler River, Troublesome Creek or San Juan Campgrounds (see Camping/Parks, above). In the summer, the **Mill Creek Valley,** winter site of Stevens Pass Nordic Center (see Cross-Country Skiing, above), is a worthy mountain-biking destination, with more than 15 miles of roads and trails.

Other good mountain-bike routes can be found all around Lake

Wenatchee, where winter ski and snowmobile trails become summer bike and off-road-vehicle routes. If you don't mind some gas-powered company, abandoned and rarely used logging roads on **Nason Ridge, Pole Ridge, Minnow Ridge** (north of Chiwawa River), and up **Chikamin Creek** (north of Minnow Ridge) all are easily accessible from the Lake Wenatchee area. Get a recent Forest Service map and consult the rangers at the Lake Wenatchee Ranger District (see More Information, below) for road information.

Rafting/Kayaking/Canoeing

The **Skykomish River** between Gold Bar and Skykomish is one of the state's more notable and frequently ridden whitewater stretches, with many Class III rapids and one particularly hairy obstacle—Boulder Drop, a notorious Class IV-to-V rapid. Whitewater kayakers and rafters run it regularly, but it's no place for wannabes. The river is numbingly cold all year long, and its treacherous waters seem to claim a handful of ill-advised amateur river-runners every year. Helmets and life jackets are required by law. Also rated expert is the **North Fork Skykomish,** often run by experienced whitewater paddlers between Galena on the North Fork Skykomish Road and the river confluence just below Skykomish. If running any portion of the Sky is on your to-do list, go with a pro. Consult the Skykomish Ranger District (see More Information, below) for a list of qualified **guides and outfitters.**

On the east side, even more disconcerting are the frothing whitewater drops in Tumwater Canyon, where the **Wenatchee River** plunges from Lake Wenatchee to Leavenworth. Look, admire—and stay out. Rapids in this stretch are Class IV to VI—and there are a lot of them. Relatively placid float trips can be taken on the lower Wenatchee, below Leavenworth. (See the Leavenworth and the Icicle Valley chapter.)

Canoeists will find **Lake Wenatchee** to their liking, although excessive motorboat traffic can be a hassle. Glacier View Campground (see Camping, above) near the head of the lake is a great canoe camp. The walk-in sites allow easy access to the lakeshore for launching.

Accessible Outdoors

Bechler River Campground has barrier-free rest rooms and river access that provides excellent fall-color viewing. The campground also has "usable" (accessible to wheelchairs with assistance) camping and picnicking sites. **Deception Falls Picnic Area** has excellent barrier-free facilities, including picnicking, rest rooms, and a lovely interpretive trail along Deception Creek, with a viewing area of Deception Falls. **Troublesome**

Creek Campground has barrier-free camping and picnic sites, as well as "usable" rest rooms and drinking water. The **Bygone Byways Interpretive Trail,** 28 miles west of Lake Wenatchee on US 2, is a barrier-free inter-peretive trail that extends for about three-quarters of a mile. **Nason Creek Campground** offers campsites rated "usable" for wheelchairs (accessible with assistance), and wheelchair-accessible rest rooms and water. **Chi-wawa Horse Camp** also has "usable" campsites and barrier-free rest-room facilities.

More Information

Department of Transportation pass report: *(888) SNO-INFO;* *www.wsdot.wa.gov/sno-info.*
Lake Wenatchee Ranger District: *(509) 763-3103.*
Mount Baker–Snoqualmie National Forest Headquarters: *(425) 775-9702 or (800) 627-0062; www.fs.fed.us/r6/mbs.*
Northwest Avalanche Hotline: *(206) 526-6677.*
Skykomish Ranger District: *(360) 677-2414.*
Stevens Pass Ski Area: *(206) 812-4510 snow report, (206) 634-1645; www.stevenspass.com.*
Wenatchee National Forest Headquarters: *215 Melody Lane, Wenatchee, WA 98801; (509) 662-4335; www.fs.fed.us/r6/wenatchee.*

Leavenworth and the Icicle Valley

From Tumwater Campground on US 2 south to Mount Stuart, north through the Chiwaukum Creek drainage, west to the Chelan–King County border near the Pacific Crest Trail, and east to Cashmere, including the Cashmere Crags, Enchantment Lakes Basin, Tumwater Canyon, and Peshastin Pinnacles State Park.

Everyone together now: Do the polar-fleece polka! If there were such a jig, it would feature lots of wheezing accordions played by hefty, pasty-faced mountain boys swilling dark German beer after a long day's free-climb up a rock called "Cruel Thumb." Which means it could be written, produced, and performed only in Leavenworth, the tiny Bavarian (hunch your lips up horse-style and say "Bah-VAHR-ian") village clinging to the edge of one of the Northwest's grander wilderness areas.

Indeed, hang around Leavenworth long enough, and that cornball license-plate-frame slogan "Washington, America's Alps" might begin to seem downright appropriate. If the Bavarian-kitsch town doesn't have you reaching for the lederhosen, the local hiking trails probably will. As with a real Bavarian village, the beauty of Leavenworth is mostly outside it.

Generally, it's in the Icicle Valley, stretching south, then west from town. Specifically, it's in Icicle Creek Canyon, which reaches into the eastern heart of the Alpine Lakes Wilderness. Bordered on the north by Icicle Ridge and on the south by the Stuart Range, the Icicle drains a truly Alps-like highland heaven. The south side is dominated by 9,415-foot Mount Stuart, a freak of nature whose angry face is marked by 2,000-vertical-foot granite scowls.

But the lands around the fantastic peak are more famous than the old mountain itself. Lying in a basin below Enchantment Peak, one mountain east of Stuart, is fabled Enchantments Basin, a string of high-country lakes surrounded by soaring, knife-edged granite spires. This is one of the most awe-inspiring backpack destinations in the country. The Enchantments' soaring popularity, in fact, made it the first alpine area in Washington with enforced limits on overnight visitors. The area has created many a lifetime memory, both among backpackers weary from the long, steep haul in to the 7,000-foot basin, and rock climbers who challenge the basin's magnificent granite spires, collectively known as the Cashmere Crags.

In a state filled with many valuable outdoor jewels, this is one of the true irreplaceable treasures. In the summertime, few backcountry areas in the country rival the sheer beauty of the Icicle Canyon and its guardian Stuart Range. In the winter, most of that backcountry is locked away, but Leavenworth and its surroundings take on what in many ways is an even greater charm. For Puget Sound residents, Leavenworth's always-frosty winter face is a welcome one—a chance to escape the wet, windy winter warmth for a brief taste of good old-fashioned, dry-air mountain shivers; a place to go ski hard all day beneath the silent pines, then build a fire in the woodstove and curl up with a good book (or even this one) at night. Thanks to its relative wealth of lodging options, Leavenworth is perhaps the best place to do just that within 2 hours of Seattle.

This mondo-lodging scenario is crucial for us outdoors enthusiasts. If it wasn't for the Bavarian Blitz, your mothers, fathers, aunts, and uncles would never bother to come to Leavenworth, and many of the hotels, B&Bs, and eateries that make the town such an easy-to-book weekend adventureland would dry up and blow to Peshastin.

Not long ago, nature very nearly accomplished that on its own. In the summer of 1994, many of the local wildlands around Leavenworth were charred by the Rat Creek and Hatchery Creek wildfires, which burned nearly all summer, destroying thousands of acres of timber and blackening earth right to the gates of Little Bavaria. But a rebirth has swiftly taken place in the valley, with acres of wildflowers and young trees sprouting forth and prancing in spring breezes created by helicopters hauling out the last of downed "salvage" timber. Nature, in other words, continues to do its thing here.

And the Leavenworth Bavarian Chamber of Commerce continues to do its thing too. For lovers of the pure and natural, the high and quiet, these accordion-huffing lowlands can be a shock to the system. Like unnaturally dark beer, Leavenworth prompts an initial shudder. But after a while . . . well, it sort of grows on you. Which is not to suggest that the polar-fleecers and the polka dancers are, or ever will be, in perfect step

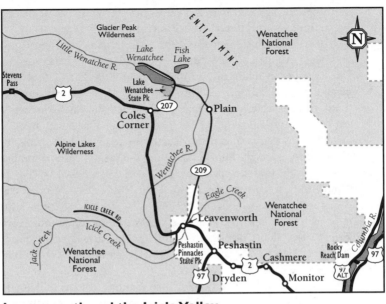

Leavenworth and the Icicle Valley

with each other. But they have made something of an art of avoiding one another's toes.

Getting There

Leavenworth is about 100 miles east of Everett on US Highway 2 and north of Cle Elum/Interstate 90 via US 97. Recreation sites in Icicle Canyon are reached via Icicle Road (Forest Road 7600), which turns south from US 2 on the west side of Leavenworth.

inside out

Hiking/Backpacking

As mentioned above, Leavenworth has become the launching point for some of the Northwest's most memorable backcountry jaunts. Thankfully, they don't all require the extensive advance preparation—or thigh muscles—needed for long trips into the Enchantments. Some of them, in fact, start right next to your favorite downtown doodad shop. A new Leavenworth city-center trail system, used as a cross-country skiing byway in the winter, leads along the Wenatchee River and over wheelchair-accessible ramps to Blackbird Island. Connecting paths lead up into the Icicle drainage and the Leavenworth Golf Course. A good starting point for the **Waterfront Interpretive Trail** is Front Street Park.

Just about every other trail outside town—the good ones, anyway—requires an **Alpine Lakes Wilderness permit,** either the day-use kind (free and unlimited at trailheads) or the overnight kind (call ahead and pray). Beginning in the summer of 1996, additional Alpine Lakes Wilderness destinations accessible from Leavenworth joined the Enchantments on the advance-reservations-required list. These included the Stuart and Colchuck Lakes area, as well as an expanded zone around the Enchantments. If you're planning an overnight hike anywhere in the region, check permit requirements with the Leavenworth Ranger District; (509) 548-6977. (For more on Alpine Lakes permits, see the Alpine Lakes Wilderness: Overview chapter.)

Also note that whether you're going day hiking or backpacking, most popular trailheads in this region now require the ubiquitous **Northwest Forest Pass,** $5 per day or $30 annually. The parking pass is available at ranger stations, from many private vendors, on-line at www.naturenw.org, or by calling (800) 270-7504.

Once you're thoroughly permitted, all that remains to trip you up is nature, and this area has seen more than its fair share of natural temper tantrums in the 1990s. Nearly all the trails in the Icicle drainage—everything from flat, easy creekside paths to trying alpine routes over mountain passes—were, for better or worse, altered by the awesome Rat Creek and Hatchery Creek wildfires in the summer of 1994. Much of the Icicle Canyon burned in those fires, taking thousands of acres of forests with it, and most Icicle Canyon trails have reopened, with new looks. The fire had its upside, too. Spring visitors to the Icicle will encounter proliferations of wildflowers and wildlife perhaps never before seen here.

For full details on the range of hikes available around Leavenworth, call or stop by the Leavenworth Ranger District. For further pondering, trail guides worthy of consultation are *Pacific Northwest Hiking,* by this author and Dan A. Nelson (Foghorn Press), and The Mountaineers' *100 Hikes in Washington's Alpine Lakes Wilderness.* Two excellent topographic maps of the region are Green Trails Nos. 177 and 178, Chiwaukum Mountains and Leavenworth.

Here's a list of some favorite hikes.

North side Icicle Road

A longtime favorite of early-summer wildflower fiends, the **Icicle Ridge Trail** (moderate/difficult; 26 miles one way) is a Leavenworth-area classic that ties all other north-side trails together. From a trailhead about 1.5 miles down Icicle Road, this trail gets serious fast, zipping and zagging to the ridge top, which it follows northwest nearly all the way to Stevens

Pass. Views from along the route are grand, and backpack loops of various distances through the Chiwaukum Mountains can be made by combining the Icicle Ridge Trail with northern connecting trails such as **Hatchery Creek** (moderate; 13 miles round trip from Tumwater Canyon), **Chiwaukum Creek** (moderate/difficult; 24 miles round trip from Tumwater Canyon to Ladies Pass), or **Frosty Creek** (moderate; various distances), which connects in the north valley at Frosty Pass.

Day hikers also might find themselves at high viewpoints on the Icicle Ridge Trail by climbing the **Chatter Creek/Lake Edna Trail** (moderate; 10 miles round trip) or **Fourth of July Creek Trail** (difficult; 10.6 miles round trip), both of which begin on the north side of Icicle Road. For much of its length, the ridge trail is a great place to survey the path of the Hatchery Creek fire, which burned on both sides of the ridge, nearly all the way to Lake Augusta.

South side Icicle Road

The **Snow Lake Trail** (moderate; 13 miles round trip) is best known as the primary access to the Enchantment Lakes Basin. But it's a superb overnight backpacking or long day-hike destination in its own right, often serving as a second option when Enchantment permits are all booked up. The trailhead is about 4 miles down Icicle Road, on the left. Strong hikers won't be disappointed by an in-and-out trip to the two Snow Lakes, which are much like the Enchantments higher up. The **Enchantment Lakes Trail** (difficult; 29 miles round trip) actually begins as the Snow Lake Trail, switching names—and degree of difficulty—after upper Snow Lake. The difference between backpackers and day hikers on this trail is that backpackers die more quickly and get it over with. Switchbacks climb up, up, up through the trees into the Enchantments, which will be beautiful if you can stay awake long enough to see them. Remember: This is a limited overnight permit area. Call well in advance of your trip (six months is minimum) to find out about permits. No fires, no dogs, no trombones.

Heads or tails, you win: that choice awaits visitors to the **Stuart/Colchuck Lakes** area (difficult; 8 to 9 miles round trip). The trail—which begins at the end of Forest Road 7601 (an Icicle Road offshoot)—climbs steeply up Mountaineer Creek, coming to a fork at about 2.5 miles. Stuart Lake, with awesome views of the north face of Mount Stuart, is 2 miles to the right; Colchuck is 1.6 miles to the left. From Colchuck, a way trail skirts the lake and climbs nearly 4 miles along a high-ridge route over **Aasgard Pass,** then down into Isolation Lake, easternmost of the Enchantments. This back-door access to the Enchantments can be a stunning trip, but the pass is snowbound much of the year and shouldn't be crossed by neophytes. Note that Stuart and Colchuck

Lakes, like the Enchantments, are limited-permit backcountry areas. Call well in advance for permits. No fires, no dogs, etc.

A trailhead slightly lower down Road 7601 is the start of a popular valley day hike to **Eightmile Lakes** (moderate; 6.6 miles round trip). The short round-trip distance is the key, and the destination, Little Eightmile and Eightmile Lakes, is well worth the walk. But keep in mind that only the last portion of the trail is inside the Wilderness. Much of the lower portion has been logged and, more recently, burned. A very pretty, and easily accessible valley hike is **Icicle Gorge Trail** (easy; 3 miles round trip), which makes a loop through lovely old-growth forest along Icicle Creek. From a trailhead near the Chatter Creek Guard Station, the trail follows the river to Rock Island Campground, then returns on the other side.

Backpackers, meanwhile, cluster along three upper-valley trails. The **Trout Creek Trail** (difficult; 12.6 miles one way) allows a unique, one-way shuttle hike through the area. The path runs south 3 miles, then turns back east and climbs to amazing views at 7,200-foot Windy Pass before dropping to Eightmile Lakes (see above) and a shuttle-hike exit on Road 7601. The nearby **Jack Creek Trail** (moderate; 24 miles round trip) is a beautiful walk south to a meeting with the mountain gods at Stuart Pass, where you can continue on into the Ingalls Creek drainage (see the I-90 East: Roslyn to Ellensburg chapter) in the US 97 corridor near Blewett Pass. Hikers up for a long, luscious valley walk can do the entire 27-mile route and walk nearly all the way around—but never into—the Stuart Range. The trail is a relaxing, moderately paced, valley-bottom walk, with good campsites all along the route. Short-trip backpackers will be more than happy with overnight jaunts on its lower portions.

A similar valley-bottom hike is the **French Creek Trail** (moderate; 22.8 miles round trip), which follows a peaceful creek drainage south to Paddy Go Easy Pass, a 3-mile downhill walk away from the headwaters of the Cle Elum River in the Salmon La Sac area (see the I-90 East: Roslyn to Ellensburg chapter). French Creek's lower portions are commonly employed as one leg on an upper Icicle drainage loop trip when combined with the **French Ridge Trail** to the north, or the **Snowall Creek or Meadow Creek Trails** to the south. The trailhead is 1.5 miles up the Icicle Creek Trail, which begins near Blackpine Horse Camp (see Camping, below) at the upper end of Icicle Road.

Camping

The Forest Service will leave the light on for ya. Well, maybe a citronella candle or something. There are eight Forest Service camps in this area. All have piped water and vault toilets, all charge a fee, all are open summers

An early morning scene along the Icicle River

only, and campsites cannot be reserved at any of them. For information, call (509) 548-6977.

Tumwater is an expansive Forest Service campground on the main route into Leavenworth. Tumwater has 84 tent/RV sites (no hookups; RVs to 22 feet). The camp also has a group site with a kitchen shelter. This is an almost-always shady, peaceful site along the Wenatchee River in Tumwater Canyon, with nearby access to the Hatchery Creek and Chiwaukum Creek trailheads (see Hiking/Backpacking, above). *On US 2, 10 miles northwest of Leavenworth.*

A string of seven campgrounds is located along Icicle Rd (mileages are given from Leavenworth); from east to west, they are: **Eightmile**—oddly enough, just about 8 miles down Icicle Road—offers 45 sites (no hookups; RVs to 21 feet) and a group site. It's a nice little campground, not far from the trailheads to Stuart/Colchuck and Eightmile Lakes. **Bridge Creek** (9 miles), just over a mile farther, is tiny, with 6 tent sites (no RVs) and 1 group site (must be reserved). **Johnny Creek** (12.5 miles), split into upper and lower loops, has a total of 8 walk-in tent sites and 65 tent/trailer sites (no hookups; RVs to 21 feet); great river access. **Ida Creek** (14 miles) has 5 tent spots and another 5 tent/trailer sites (no hookups; RVs to 21 feet). **Chatter Creek** (16 miles) is as centrally located as any campground in this area. It has 12 sites (no hookups; RVs to 21 feet) and 1 reservation-only group site. The Chatter Creek, Icicle Gorge, Jack Creek, and Trout Creek trailheads all are nearby, making this a favorite bivouac spot for backpackers.

Rock Island (17 miles), in the upper Icicle Canyon, offers 12 tent sites and 10 tent/RV spots (no hookups; RVs to 21 feet). At the head of the valley (and the end of the road) is **Blackpine Horse Camp** (18 miles), which has 10 pull-through sites (no hookups; RVs to 21 feet). The camp, located at 3,000 feet next to a major trailhead for excursions into the heart of the Alpine Lakes Wilderness, is horse-packer central. It's the valley's only campground with horse facilities. Non-horse people: your mission, should you choose to accept it, is to put your ground cloth down between those road apples without getting any on you.

Cross-Country Skiing

A wealth of overnight lodgings and quick access from Seattle make the Leavenworth area one of the leading winter weekend getaways for fans of the quiet sport of Nordic skiing. The big catch is snow. Leavenworth gets plenty of it, but ice, a four-letter word to the skinny-ski set, can be a problem here. And the season is rather unpredictable. It generally gets under way by Christmas and extends into March. But in some years, the season might be over by January. Call to check snow conditions before you make the drive.

That said, the abundance of good, impeccably maintained trails makes Leavenworth and the Icicle Canyon a great ski getaway, particularly for families and groups. Facilities are scattered around town, which is good, because so is lodging. If you're staying in Leavenworth in the winter, chances are some nice groomed tracks are not far away. All the ski trails are well maintained by the Leavenworth Winter Sports Club, which grooms 23 kilometers of trails and sells **trail passes** (at this writing, $8 per day, with children 12 and under free) from 8am to 4pm daily at each venue. For snow conditions, general information, and placing orders for homemade peanut brittle by ticket-booth personnel, call the **Leavenworth Winter Sports Club;** (509) 548-5115. Ski passes are sold at the following ski venues:

The **Icicle River Trail,** south of town, has 7.5 kilometers of groomed tracks and skating lanes in two loops at the mouth of Icicle Canyon. This is a family favorite. It's beautiful, especially on a crisp, sunny day, and the terrain is gentle. The 4K Meadow Loop is lovely and a good place to spot winter wildlife (true beginners, beware Dune Hill—take the bypass!). Take Icicle Road south from US 2 and watch for the thicket of Range Rovers and Explorers.

The **golf course** has Leavenworth's most extensive trail system, with 10 kilometers of trail in three chunks. Choose from the 3K, aptly named Lazy River Loop; the 5K Tumwater Loop (a bit more curvy and challenging); and the 2K Waterfront Park Trail, the winter version of the Waterfront Interpretive Trail (see Hiking/Backpacking, above). The latter crosses a bridge to Blackbird Island and connects to downtown at the end of Ninth Street. The golf course is located a short distance down Icicle Road; you can also ski here from downtown on the Waterfront Trail. Breakfast, lunch, and snacks are available in the **clubhouse** Thursdays through Saturdays from 9am to 3pm; Sunday brunch is served from 10am to 2pm.

Aggressive intermediates, free-wheeling free-heelers, and suicidal beginners congregate up the road at **Leavenworth Ski Hill,** which has 5 kilometers of trail split into a 2K and a 3K loop. Both are challenging, hilly, and—if you know what you're doing—lots of fun. A bonus when the weather cooperates is an oh-gosh view of icy-topped Mount Stuart. Ski Hill's 3K loop is lighted for skiing until midnight—or beyond, if diehards are present. Ski Hill is 1.5 miles north of downtown Leavenworth on Ski Hill Road.

For a more natural ski setting, hop in the rig and head out of town to one of several local **Sno-Park areas.** (You'll need a Sno-Park pass, available at ranger stations and ski shops.) Popular areas are Swauk Pass, 25 miles south of Leavenworth on US 97—watch for snowmobiles (see the I-90 East Roslyn to Ellensburg chapter), Lake Wenatchee State Park, which has 35 kilometers of groomed tracks in two very extensive cross-country ski-trail complexes, and other turnouts along Chiwawa Road north of the lake (see Stevens Pass Corridor and Lake Wenatchee chapter). **Shuttle buses** run from downtown Leavenworth to Lake Wenatchee State Park. Call the Leavenworth Ranger District, (509) 548-6977, for Sno-Park ski conditions. Some Leavenworth overnighters drive back west to the Stevens Pass Nordic Center to do their skiing (see the Stevens Pass Corridor and Lake Wenatchee chapter).

Ski **rentals** are available at several Leavenworth shops.

Snowshoeing

Popular snowshoe day-hiking areas include **Icicle Road** (easy; 5 miles round trip) at the winter-closure end; **Hatchery Creek Road** (moderate; 5 miles round trip), northwest of Leavenworth on US 2; **Chiwaukum Creek Trail** (difficult; 10.4 miles round trip), on Chiwaukum Creek Road, 12 miles northwest of Leavenworth on US 2; and **Wenatchee River Road** (easy; 4 miles round trip), east of of US 2 near Tumwater Campground. Another good 'shoe course can be found in the **Eagle Creek area** (easy; 4 miles round trip). Take US 2 to Chumstick Road/Hwy 209, and follow signs north toward Plain; at 2.1 miles, turn right on Eagle Creek Road and drive 5 miles to the end of the road, just past Eagle Creek Ranch. For details and snow conditions, call the Leavenworth Ranger District, (509) 548-6977.

Climbing

Mount Stuart, a 9,415-foot wall of solid granite, is climbed via more than 10 separate ice-and-rock summit routes. Some of them go straight up the mountain's 2,000-foot vertical faces, which rank right up there with the Northwest's most challenging alpine routes. The peak and its stony companions—**Sherpa Peak** (8,605 feet), **Argonaut Peak** (8,453 feet), and **Ingalls Peak** (7,662 feet)—shouldn't even be considered by less-than-experienced climbers.

Smaller granite spires in the Enchantments and elsewhere in the Icicle drainage are famous among rock aficionados. The legendary **Cashmere Crags** in Enchantment Valley are among the most challenging pitches in the country, drawing ratings from 5.0 to a couple of off-the-scale 5.11 routes (such as one **Dragontail Peak** route). Many climbers come here for a lifetime and never summit all of these routes, whose names are enough to scare most people away. Notable rocks in this forest of granite spires include **Prusik Peak, Razorback Spire, Cruel Thumb, Crocodile Fang,** and **Bloody Tower.**

Other popular local rock-climbing venues are **Icicle Buttress, Memorial Buttress, Eightmile Buttress, Egg Rock, Trick or Treat, Rat Creek Boulder, Condor Buttress, The Sword, Bridge Creek** and **Little Bridge Creek Walls,** and the **Fourth of July Group.** If you're even thinking about setting out on Icicle Canyon rock, consult the bible—Fred Beckey's *Cascade Alpine Guide* series (The Mountaineers Books). And you'll need a permit, available at the Leavenworth Ranger District; (509) 548-6977.

About 8 miles east on US 2, rock climbers increasingly gather at **Peshastin Pinnacles State Park,** the only Washington State Park designed specifically for that activity. Actually, the climbers were here long ago, when these were just big rocks sticking up in the middle of orchard territory. Frustrated farmers sold the property to the state in 1991, and the state had the good sense to leave the area basically au naturel, adding only a few signs, outhouses, and parking areas. A dozen or so climbing routes make this a favorite practice site for climbers of all abilities (the highest-rated pitch here is about 5.8), especially in the off-season when other rocks are under snow. Note, however, that Peshastin Pinnacles is closed in December and January. No camping. Follow signs from US 2, 8 miles east of Leavenworth. Beginners seeking a list of qualified **guides** should contact Leavenworth Ranger District; (509) 548-6977.

Mountain Biking

Most local trails are closed to fat tires, but a good selection of Forest Service roads is available. For more information, inquire at the Leavenworth

Ranger District; (509) 548-6977. Cycle **rentals** are available at several outdoor stores (see More Information, below). For bicycle **pickup and drop-off service,** contact Leavenworth Outfitters, (509) 763-3733 or 800-347-7934. A few time-honored favorite roads:

Wenatchee River Road (Forest Road 7903), which begins on US 2 just west of Tumwater Campground (see Snowshoeing, above), is a pretty ride, with several good river-access points. You can only go about 5 miles before the road turns private, but it makes for an enjoyable round trip of just under 10 miles. Other popular road rides around Leavenworth include **Mountain Home Road** and **Icicle Road** (see Hiking/Backpacking, above). **Freund Canyon Road,** just north of town via Chumstick Road/Hwy 209, is a popular singletrack trail, about 8 miles round trip.

A series of Forest Service roads in **Derby Canyon** near Peshastin (just east of Leavenworth off US 2) have become popular fat-tire hangouts. Loops of various lengths are possible on these rolling, dry public roads. In addition, most of the side roads beginning on US 97 near Swauk Pass are prime mountain-bike territory, as long as you don't mind sharing the road with motorcyclists. And many more good routes run through the Lake Wenatchee area (see the Stevens Pass Corridor and Lake Wenatchee chapter). Finally, right in Leavenworth, a couple of decent riding loops can be found at **Leavenworth Ski Hill** (see Cross-Country Skiing, above).

Rafting/Canoeing/Kayaking

The frothing whitewater drops in **Tumwater Canyon,** where the Wenatchee River plunges from Lake Wenatchee to Leavenworth, are disconcerting. Look, admire—and stay out. Rapids in this stretch are Class IV to VI—and there are a lot of them. Tamer float trips can be taken on the lower Wenatchee where the big melt-off makes for lots of whoops and cheers each spring, however. March through April, a number of commercial rafters take thrill-seekers down the lower Wenatchee, which is wide, fast, and exciting. Float trips continue through the summer. For a list of **outfitters,** contact the Leavenworth Ranger District; (509) 548-6977. The lower river (downstream from Leavenworth) is a popular canoe and kayak route during summer months. For raft **pickup and drop-off service,** contact Leavenworth Outfitters, (509) 763-3733 or (800) 347-7934.

Wildlife Watching

For those middle-of-the-week, resting-your-bones days, ride or bike down to the fish hatchery on Icicle Creek, 12790 Fish Hatchery Road, off Icicle Road; (509) 548-7641, to watch the **chinook salmon** run (June and July) and spawn (August and September). The spawning season prompts (what else?) another Leavenworth festival, the Wenatchee River Salmon Festival in late September. Icicle Canyon itself—one of the deepest in Washington, with more than 8,000 feet separating the floor from the highest peak—is a wildlife treasure trove. It's a state-designated wildlife area, with common sightings of **mule deer, golden eagles, harlequin ducks, ospreys,** and **great blue herons.** A 2-mile interpretive trail near the fish hatchery is a good starting point. But any of the many trails listed (see Hiking/Backpacking, above) will get you into the animals' home turf.

Fishing

Without question, the most highly sought scaly creatures in this region swim in the Icicle. They're spring **chinook salmon**—hatchery fish that return each year at the end of a flat-out astonishing journey from the Pacific way up the Columbia, up the Wenatchee, then 2 miles up the Icicle from its mouth to the hatchery. Spring chinook are the cream of the salmon crop, and some of these fish are the crème de la crème. Some big ones (25 pounds or more) make it up the Icicle, but the run usually is so brief (a few weeks in May) that proper amounts of luck and skill must meet before you take one home. When the Icicle kings are running, lay those egg clusters out there and hang on tight. The Icicle also produces a handful of **steelhead** every year—not many, considering the number of smolts sent downstream, probably to meet their maker in a hydroelectric turbine.

Steelhead and **sockeye salmon** in the Wenatchee River seem to suffer the same fate, but a few summer runs return every year to swim up Tumwater Canyon. The upper river (above the Icicle) is a selective fishery, with barbless hooks and artificial flies or lures required. Wild steelhead must be released. This stretch is popular with fly fishers, but steelheaders who are looking for something to keep generally fish the lower river, downstream from Leavenworth. A short section of the Wenatchee near Leavenworth (downstream from the Icicle) also is open for spring chinook fishing most years.

Mountain-stream **trout** fishing can be decent around Leavenworth. Most streams are overfished, but the quality of the experience makes up for results that at best are spotty. The upper Wenatchee River (above Lake Wenatchee) is a fair bet, and Chumstick Creek and Eagle Creek, both crisp streams that flow into the Wenatchee near Leavenworth, produce a few fish in the summer.

Horseback Riding

Hourly, daily, and multi-day **horse-riding** adventures can be arranged with Eagle Creek Ranch, (509) 548-7798, or Icicle Outfitters, (800) 497-3912.

Hay rides and **sleigh rides** are offered all year-round at Mountain Springs Lodge, (509) 763-2713; or Red Tail Canyon Farm, (800) 678-4512.

Accessible Outdoors

Some campsites in the Leavenworth Ranger District are rated "usable" for wheelchairs. Call (509) 548-6977.

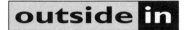

Restaurants

Lorraine's Edel House Inn ★★   A pleasant restaurant with an international menu. $$; *320 9th St, Leavenworth; (509) 548-4412.* &

Restaurant Osterreich ★★★   One of Leavenworth's finest Austrian restaurants. Come hungry. $$; *633 Front St, Leavenworth; (509) 548-1031; www.leavenworthdining.com.* &

Lodgings

Abendblume Pension ★★★   This is one of the most elegant, sophisticated inns in town. $$$; *12570 Ranger Rd, Leavenworth; (509) 548-4059 or (800) 669-7634; www.abendblume.com.*

All Seasons River Inn ★★   A modern two-story cedar house with a relaxing riverside location. $$; *8751 Icicle Rd, Leavenworth; (509) 548-1425; www.allseasonriverinn.com.*

Bosch Garten A stylish, newly built two-story home at the outskirts of town. $$; *9846 Dye Rd, Leavenworth; (509) 548-6900 or (800) 535-0069; www.boschgarten.com.*

Haus Lorelei Inn ★★   Here's a rarity: a bed-and-breakfast that welcomes kids. $$; *347 Division St, Leavenworth; (509) 548-5726 or (800) 514-8868; www.hauslorelei.com.*

Mountain Home Lodge ★★★☆   This lodge is a mile above Leavenworth in a breathtaking mountaintop setting. $$$; *8201 Mountain Home Rd, Leavenworth; (509) 548-7077 or (800) 414-2378; www.mthome.com.*

Mountain Springs Lodge ★★   This big, sunny mountain retreat is best when you've got a group. $$$; *19115 Chiwawa Loop Rd, Plain; (509) 763-2713 or (800) 858-2276; www.mtsprings.com.*

Natapoc Lodging ★★★   Each log house claims 1 to 5 piney acres and 200 feet of riverfront. $$$; *12338 Bretz Rd, Leavenworth; (509) 763-3313 or (888) NATAPOC; www.natapoc.com.*

Run of the River ★★★★   An elegant log inn on the bank of the Icicle River. *$$; 9308 E Leavenworth Rd, Leavenworth; (509) 548-7171 or (800) 288-6491; www.runoftheriver.com.*

Sleeping Lady Retreat and Conference Center ★★★   A quintessential Northwest retreat with an acute awareness of the environment. *$$; 7375 Icicle Rd, Leavenworth; (509) 548-6344 or (800) 574-2123; www. sleepinglady.com.* &

More Information

Department of Transportation pass report: *(888) SNO-INFO; www.wsdot.wa.gov/sno-info.*
Der Sportsmann (gear and rentals): *837 Front Street; (509) 548-5623.*
Lake Wenatchee Ranger District: *(509) 763-3103.*
Leavenworth Chamber of Commerce: *(509) 548-5807; www.leavenworth.org.*
Leavenworth Mountain Sports: *940 US 2; (509) 548-7864 or (800) 344-8884.*
Leavenworth Outfitters Outdoor Center (gear and rentals): *(800) 347-7934.*
Leavenworth Ranger District: *(509) 548-6977.*
Leavenworth Ski and Sports Center (gear and rentals): *US 2 and Icicle Road; (509) 548-7864.*
Leavenworth Winter Sports Club: *(509) 548-5115; www.ncw.net/lwsc.*
Wenatchee National Forest Headquarters: *215 Melody Lane, Wenatchee, WA 98801; (509) 662-4335; www.fs.fed.us/r6/wenatchee.*

Wenatchee National Forest: Overview

From Lake Chelan south to the Yakama Indian Reservation; west to Glacier Peak, Alpine Lakes, Norse Peak, William O. Douglas, and Goat Rocks Wildernesses; and east to US Highway 97 and the upper Naches and Tieton Rivers, including more than two million acres of eastern Cascade lands from the North Cascades to the Goat Rocks Wilderness.

Here's a national forest with big potential. Make that huge. As in, 2.2 million acres worth of high, mostly dry, east-slope Cascades alpine territory that ranks right up there on the outdoor-inspiration scale. Wenatchee National Forest, Washington's largest single forest jurisdiction, controls (or has a hand in managing) almost half of the state's prime forestlands.

Sadly, much of Wenatchee's potential is unrealized. Although some wilderness areas under its full or partial care—such as the Alpine Lakes, Glacier Peak, and Lake Chelan–Sawtooth Wildernesses—draw large numbers of visitors, Wenatchee's nonwilderness lands are foreign territory to many Western Washington campers, hikers, and backpackers. Why? Dirt bikes and other off-road vehicles, for starters. This national forest has 2,500 miles of trails, but all too many of them have been turned into high-speed raceways for smoke-belchers. These trails—which dominate most of the forest's prime Central Cascades hiking territory—are euphemistically called "dual-use" paths by the Forest Service. But no hikers in their right minds want to risk their bones amid the madness of dirt bikery.

The result: in spite of the fact that Washington hikers outnumber off-road violators exponentially, hundreds of thousands of acres of national forest lands have essentially been reserved for the few. This made no sense during the 1960s, when Wenatchee's forest brain trust was converting many forest trails to "dual use." It makes even less sense now that the state's hiking population has mushroomed in the past two decades. Write your representatives. Write your ranger (for an address, see More Information, below). Write your mother. Write someone—and hope for change.

None of which is meant to suggest that the entire Wenatchee National Forest is unworthy of your recreation time. Hardly. Not even the U.S. Forest Service could fully screw up an area this large and unpatrollable.

Many of the forest's hiking trails are closed to motorized vehicles. And a slew of other mountain-high recreation gems can be found throughout the forest, particularly in its isolated, often-primitive, but frequently beautiful campgrounds. More than 150 of them dot the pine-treed landscape of this national forest, which fans out north, south, and west from its headquarters in Wenatchee.

The most popular, not surprisingly, are in the forest's Central Cascades heartland. An example is the Cle Elum Ranger District, the closest jurisdiction to Seattle. The Cle Elum and Teanaway River valleys, in particular, are premium getaways, with many gorgeous campgrounds near hiking trails climbing into the southeastern Alpine Lakes Wilderness. Both areas are an easy, 2-hour drive from Seattle on Interstate 90. Consult the Snoqualmie Pass Corridor (Mountains-to-Sound Greenway), I-90 East: Roslyn to Ellensburg, Alpine Lakes Wilderness: Overview, and Leavenworth and the Icicle Valley chapters for recreation details.

Equally popular are the lush alpine lands overseen by the Leavenworth and Lake Wenatchee Ranger Districts, which administer eastside Stevens Pass areas such as Lake Wenatchee, the Wenatchee River, and Icicle Creek drainages, and northeastern fringes of the Alpine Lakes Wilderness. Campgrounds and trails in this region are among the most heavily used in the state—for good reason. It's beautiful here, and overuse is the primary concern of forest rangers. Primary access is via Stevens Pass Highway (US Highway 2) and Blewett Pass Highway (US Highway 97). (Consult the Leavenworth and the Icicle Valley, and Stevens Pass Corridor and Lake Wenatchee chapters for full details.)

To the south, under the watch of the Naches Ranger District, are similarly lush, popular campgrounds and trails around Bumping and Rimrock Lakes, and on the east side of the Norse Peak, William O. Douglas, and Goat Rocks Wilderness Areas. Access, at least in summertime, is easy via Chinook Pass (Highway 410) and White Pass (US Highway 12). (Consult the White Pass Corridor and Mount Rainier National Park chapters for recreation details.)

To the north, the Entiat and Chelan Ranger Districts manage the dry Cascade valleys between Leavenworth and Lake Chelan, as well as eastern approaches (by trail) to the Glacier Peak Wilderness. These rugged lands are primarily the home of small-stream anglers, mountain campers, long-distance backpackers, off-road vehicle enthusiasts, and, in the fall, hunters. Major access is via US Highway 97A and the Entiat River Road, Highways 207 and 209 and the Chiwawa River Road north from Plain, and via the Lake Chelan water-taxi service. (For details, consult the Chelan and the Middle Columbia, and Stehekin and the Lake Chelan National Recreation Area chapters.) The Chelan Ranger District also administers the wildlands of the Lake Chelan–Sawtooth Wilderness north of Lake Chelan. Access is via the Lake Chelan water taxi or Twisp River Road. (Consult the Methow Valley, and Stehekin and the Lake Chelan National Recreation Area chapters for details.)

Also, don't overlook the forestlands around Wenatchee itself, home to some fine camping, hiking, and skiing. (See the Wenatchee and Mission Ridge chapter for details.)

Getting There

The only major roadway that samples this vast area is US 97, which roughly parallels the forest's eastern border from Yakima to Chelan. As mentioned above, interior portions of the forest are reached via the White Pass, Chinook Pass, Snoqualmie Pass, and Stevens Pass Highways, as well as Entiat Valley Road, Twisp River Road, and the water-taxi service on Lake Chelan.

inside out

Activities

The Wenatchee National Forest is home to many of Washington's most remote, wild recreation lands, which are particularly popular with fans of high, pine-dominated mountain slopes and small, rocky, sparkling creek valleys. **Camping** (151 campgrounds), **fishing** (1,800 miles of streams and rivers), **hiking** (2,500 miles of trails), **skiing** (seven ski areas), **whitewater rafting** (primarily on the Wenatchee River), **climbing** (on Alpine Lakes Wilderness peaks), **canoeing** (nearly 250 lakes and reservoirs), **kayaking** (nine rivers under Wild and Scenic River review), **mountain biking,** and other outdoor activities too numerous to count all are popular in Wenatchee National Forest. For full details on all those and more, consult these chapters: Methow Valley; Stevens Pass Corridor and Lake Wenatchee; Leavenworth and the Icicle Valley; Wenatchee and Mission

Ridge; Snoqualmie Pass Corridor (Mountains-to-Sound Greenway); I-90
East: Roslyn to Ellensburg; and White Pass Corridor.

Wenatchee National Forest Rules and Regulations

Forest users should note that parking in most popular Wenatchee
National Forest trailhead parking areas now requires a **Northwest Forest
Pass.** The permits are $5 per day or $30 annually, and are available from
ranger stations, from many private vendors, on-line at www.naturenw.org,
or by calling (800) 270-7504.

More Information

Chelan Ranger District: *(509) 682-2576.*
Cle Elum Ranger District: *(509) 674-4411.*
Entiat Ranger District: *(509) 784-1511.*
Lake Wenatchee Ranger District: *(509) 763-3103.*
Leavenworth Ranger District: *(509) 548-6977.*
Wenatchee National Forest Headquarters: *215 Melody Lane,*
   Wenatchee, WA 98801; (509) 662-4335; www.fs.fed.us/r6/wenatchee.

Snoqualmie Pass Corridor (Mountains-to-Sound Greenway)

From Issaquah east to Lake Easton along Interstate 90, including the Issaquah Alps, Snoqualmie Summit ski areas, southern portions of the Alpine Lakes Wilderness, and Olallie, Iron Horse, and Lake Easton State Parks.

This is wilderness made easy. Too easy, actually. And hence, not so wild anymore. Detect a pattern?

For as long as Seattleites have called themselves Seattleites, the upper Snoqualmie River drainage—a convenient crack in the otherwise impenetrable wall of the Central Cascades—has been a backyard playground. Early exploring clubs such as the Mountaineers cut their climbing teeth and hiking boots along an eastbound roadway that, over time, evolved from the "Yellowstone Highway" to the "Sunset Highway" to Interstate 90. Today, the corridor's rich collection of trails, creeks, waterfalls, and forests allow Seattleites to be out away from it all in less than 30 minutes—a temptation many have found impossible to resist. As the city and highway have grown, so have crowds of hikers, skiers, horseback riders, and other "solitude" lovers seeking escape. Few metropolitan areas in the United States have a wild, wooded land so close to their back door, and few have taken advantage of it to the extent that Seattle-area residents have.

The lure of these woods has been so great, in fact, that not even the systematic clear-cutting of the upper Snoqualmie River's once-grand forest system was enough to dissuade us. By the late

Mountain bikers getting up the nerve to enter the Snoqualmie Tunnel

1980s, the Snoqualmie Pass corridor had become an unlikely combination of ugly, vegetation-mined slopes and a nonstop stream of hikers, who figured a clear-cut trail close to home beat an old-growth hike 4 hours away. Worse yet, the clear-cutting acted as a springboard to send hordes of hikers farther east, into the pristine but fragile lands of the Alpine Lakes

Wilderness, which have been badly trampled in some places.

In this case, however, two bad things have combined to create what ultimately could be a greater good. In 1991, a group of business and community leaders—headed by attorney Jim Ellis, the father of the Metro plan that cleaned up Lake Washington in the 1950s—formed the Mountains-to-Sound Greenway Trust, whose purpose was to create, or perhaps re-create, a broad swath of green on both sides of I-90 from Seattle to Cle Elum. From the beginning, the group's approach has been subtle. They persuade rather than coerce. They shape development rather than oppose it. And people have listened. Greenway's vision has evolved into a plan, and the plan is getting results.

Land swaps have been made with timber companies, trading small amounts of visible forest for larger plots hidden from sight. Key historical and natural sights have been preserved. The Greenway, as the Snoqualmie Pass corridor increasingly is known, is slowly taking shape. How it will end up is anyone's guess. For the time being, though, the group has succeeded in at least maintaining status quo in the battle to preserve recreation lands in Seattle's forested backyard. Eventually, they hope to develop newly protected lands for recreation use, easing the substantial burden on existing forestlands and reestablishing what's lacking here: a wilderness ethic—a caring connection between people and land.

Today, as you drive east from Seattle, you can squint a little and actually sort of see it: green lands on both sides of the highway, beginning with the Issaquah Alps and continuing to North Bend, the front door to the upper Snoqualmie. From there, devastated forestlands are slowly coming back to life, painting the corridor a bit greener every year. Tiny steps in trail construction could lead to giant leaps in future years, when the state's Iron Horse Trail State Park will link the entire Greenway in one long, skinny string. The corridor already is, thanks to decades of exploration and exploitation, a highly developed outdoor getaway. The Greenway plan promises to make it better. But only time will tell if improvement can outpace growth, and whether the Greenway, which is being closely watched by other national groups, will be remembered as a brilliant success or just a nice try.

Unfortunately, no one with the Greenway group or outside it has answered the Big Question posed by the use/abuse pattern: Can freeways and greenways coexist? Doesn't attracting more people to a natural area—no matter how thinly they're dispersed and how well they behave—ultimately lead to its degradation?

History says yes. Greenway optimists say no. The reality will probably be somewhere in the middle. And when the middle is as scenic, resilient, and fun to explore as Snoqualmie Pass, there are worse places to be.

Getting There

The Mountains-to-Sound Greenway's easy access from Seattle is its biggest draw. From anywhere in the Seattle area, hop on Interstate-90 and drive east. Hundreds of recreation chances await between Issaquah (10 miles east of Seattle) and Easton (70 miles east). Seasonal note: Snoqualmie Pass is frequently snowed upon during the winter, but chains rarely are required and road closures are unusual. (Even so, it's a good idea to carry chains between October and May.) Typically, drivers won't encounter snowy roads until about 4 miles west of the summit, where the highway begins a 1,000-foot climb to Snoqualmie Summit, elevation 3,022. For road conditions, call (888) SNO-INFO or tune car radios to 530 AM at Eastgate or 1610 AM at North Bend.

inside out

Hiking

The Snoqualmie corridor's proximity to greater Seattle makes it a natural first choice when sunny Saturday morning skies crash through the blinds and implant the word "hike" on the brain. That is both this area's greatest blessing and its greatest curse. In the early part of the century, trails leading up peaks along the corridor were familiar only to hardy, wool-covered explorers from get-out-and-get-wet adventure groups such as the Mountaineers. (Mountaineers' hiking parties, in fact, carved out many of the best trails still in use here today.) But these days, the Mountaineers' old haunts are familiar to everybody, from young rock climbers and mountain bikers to your weak-kneed Aunt Ethel. You're liable to run into both age groups—and about 400 others—on many I-90 corridor trails on a given weekend.

Without question, **overcrowding** is a problem in these parts. It's not unusual to see 400 cars in the Mount Si parking lot on a sunny Sunday, an equal number at Snow Lake, and perhaps even more at the High Point trailhead for Tiger Mountain, near Issaquah. The amazing—and for many local hikers, frustrating—thing is that more obscure trails in between also will be packed from end to end with hikers. There is, it seems, no way to escape the crush of humanity along I-90 in the summer. Take that as a given. For most people, particularly those who manage to sneak off during midweek, the short drive makes up for crowded conditions. And it is still possible to find little-used trails in this area. Besides, there's one major upside to the intense trail use here: intense pressure to keep the trails up to snuff and build new ones in the future. Many I-90 trails have been "adopted" by Seattle-area corporations, whose workers, coordinated by

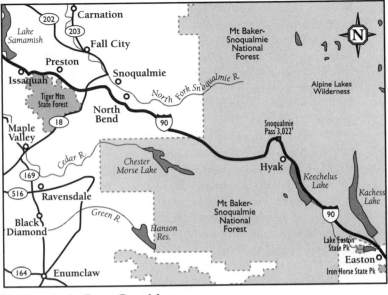

Snoqualmie Pass Corridor

groups such as Washington Trails Association, devote weekends to fixing bridges, cutting brush, hauling gravel, and shoring up switchbacks. Consider joining one. Good for the soul, if not the back.

A word about **permits:** some trails on the north side of I-90 enter the Alpine Lakes Wilderness. Permits are required, for both day hikes and overnighters. Permits are free, unlimited (so far), and available at trailheads. No sweat, but fill them out. In the near future, limits on overnight campers are expected in some highly popular areas, such as Snow Lake north of Alpental. Check with a local ranger district office about these and other restrictions (see More Information, below). For more on permits, see the Alpine Lakes Wilderness: Overview chapter. Permits are not required for nonwilderness trails in this area, most of which are governed by the Mount Baker–Snoqualmie National Forest. But since the summer of 1997, hikers have been required to purchase a parking pass for most popular trailheads. The current incarnation is the **Northwest Forest Pass,** $5 per day or $30 annually. They're available from ranger stations, from many private vendors, on-line at www.naturenw.org, or by calling (800) 270-7504.

Dogs are allowed on most trails, but be courteous and keep the beast on a leash. Remember, not everyone is a dog lover, and prudent doggie-watching helps quiet the voices crying out for more extensive dog bans.

Finally, a word about **seasons:** Declaring when a trail will be snow-free and walkable is a risky business. Snow levels vary enough from year to year to make those dates shift by a month or more. But some things you can (pretty much) count on when it comes to seasonal snow levels. Valley trails that begin below 1,000 feet in elevation—such as Tiger Mountain near Issaquah, and Little Si, Twin Falls, and Rattlesnake Ledge near North Bend—are snow-free virtually all year. Each makes a nice, if sloppy, winter walk. Lower sections of the Iron Horse Trail also usually are free of snow all year.

Midlevel trails beginning between 1,000 and 2,000 feet usually open by May. Note that trails with southern exposure melt off much more quickly than those along north-facing slopes. Higher-elevation trails, such as those beginning at between 2,000 and 3,000 feet in the Snoqualmie Pass area, often don't melt out until July. The only way to know for sure is to ask at the appropriate ranger district (see More Information, below).

So you're ready to walk. Where? Good question. Choices are rich here, and we won't attempt to list them all. For a full inventory, we recommend *Hiking the Mountains-to-Sound Greenway,* by Harvey Manning (The Mountaineers Books). The book, chock-full of color and local history, has full details on hikes from Snoqualmie Summit west. Or consult *Pacific Northwest Hiking* (Foghorn Press), by this author and Dan A. Nelson, which contains a long list of hikes in the Greenway area. But here's a healthy sampling of the best.

Issaquah to North Bend

In the world of hiking, closest is busiest. That's certainly the case at **Tiger Mountain State Forest** (easy/moderate; various distances), where green slopes are laced by the most heavily trod trail system in the region. From the main trailhead at **High Point** (I-90 exit 20, 2 miles east of Issaquah), trails fan out in many directions, making loops of 1 to 12 miles through mostly deciduous forest, with occasional grand views of the Snoqualmie valley, Lake Washington, and, from the 3,000-foot top, Mount Rainier. You'll find more than 60 miles of trails here, all best discovered through the art of trial and error. A popular introductory route is the **Tradition Lake Loop,** a 2.5-mile walk from the High Point trailhead. Additional Tiger Mountain trailheads are located near Issaquah High School and along Hwy 18. (From the High Point trailhead, you can cross under the freeway and catch the old rail-trail to Preston and beyond to Snoqualmie Falls and North Bend.) For maps and details, call the Department of Natural Resources, (360) 825-1631.

Up the road a piece, actually 15 miles of pieces, is North Bend, home of the **Mount Si Trail** (difficult; 8 miles round trip). Everyone, it seems, at one time or another puts foot to trail on Mount Si, the single most overused trail in the state, with as many as 50,000 people a year huffing and puffing their way to the top. On sunny summer days, the Mount Si trailhead looks like the parking lot at Larry's Market: overcrowded with misbehaving yuppies. The trail up Mount Si, named for local settler Josiah "Uncle Si" Merritt, is nothing to write home about. It's almost entirely in dark second-growth forest until the summit. But it does go up 3,200 feet in 4 miles—a good workout pace for training hikers, climbers, and backpackers. That, coupled with its easy access and grand summit view, makes it irresistible to most of us. To give in to your own urge, take the main drag out of North Bend and turn north on Mount Si Road. Look for the Amazing Colossal Trailhead Parking Lot on the left in about 2.5 miles.

One easier, though nearly as crowded, alternative is **Little Si** (moderate; 5 miles round trip), the 1,500-foot thumb of a peak sticking up on Mount Si's southwest shoulder. Park in the signed lot just across the Middle Fork Snoqualmie on Mount Si Road and walk a short distance down the residential street (you guessed it, residents aren't thrilled with all you hikers) to the signed trailhead. The path climbs steeply for the first half mile, then winds through the cool, dark, glacier-carved valley between Si and Little Si before climbing steeply again for the final half mile. Nice views of the upper valley from the top. Little Si's inside walls also are a longtime practice hotbed for rock climbers. You'll see them—or at least hear them—directly overhead.

On the opposite side of the valley, a trail system is ever expanding on **Rattlesnake Mountain,** that long hulk of green south of North Bend that looks like it lost a knife fight with logging companies. (It did.) Houses are creeping up into the clear-cuts these days, but the mountain's top ridgeline, thankfully, was recently purchased and reserved for public use. A good way to see its tremendous potential is by walking (climbing, actually) the **Rattlesnake Ledge Trail** (difficult; 2.6 miles round trip). From a trailhead near Rattlesnake Lake (take exit 32, then drive 3 miles south), this recently improved route climbs steeply through mostly second-growth trees to an exposed rocky knob with awesome views of the upper valley, and into the marvelously protected forests of the City of Seattle's Cedar River Watershed. Careful around the top. It's a loooong (400 to 500 feet) way down. Not a good place for kids or dogs. But a very good workout for the rest of you. Below and a short distance east is a newly developed parking area and trailhead, the westernmost access to the **John Wayne Pioneer Trail,** aka Iron Horse State Park (see Mountain Biking, below).

North Bend to Snoqualmie Summit, north side I-90

A string of good valley-to-peak hikes is lined up along the north shoulders of I-90. In order: **Bandera Mountain** (moderate; 7 miles round trip) begins at the end of Forest Road 9031 (take exit 45) and climbs 2,800 feet to nice views of Rainier from the fire-scarred, 5,200-foot summit. This trail melts out sooner than many of similar height in the area. Also from exit 45, you can follow Forest Road 9030 to its end to find the trailhead for one of the Greenway's more popular destinations, **Talapus** and **Olallie Lakes** (easy; 4 miles round trip). Lots of campsites here. Lots of overused, always full campsites.

Two miles east, take exit 47 (Denny Creek/Asahel Curtis), cross the freeway to the north, and turn left to the signed **Pratt Lake Trail** parking lot. This is a dual-purpose trailhead, with access to **Pratt Lake** (moderate; 11 miles round trip) to the west and **Granite Mountain** (difficult; 8.6 miles round trip) above and to the east. Pratt Lake, also reachable via the Talapus and Olallie Lakes Trail, is a very nice walk along this route, climbing about 1,600 feet to the lake, whose many campsites are shockingly trampled. Make this a day hike. Granite Mountain is a bear of a climb, a leading source of chronic Thighus Fryus. You'll huff, puff, and claw 3,800 feet in 4.3 miles to an old fire lookout at the 5,600-foot summit. The upper slopes often are snowbound (and very prone to avalanche) until midsummer. Is the view worth it? Absolutely.

Also from exit 47, take a right at the T on the north side of the freeway and drive beyond Denny Creek Campground, past some private cabins, a total of about 3 miles, to the road's-end trailhead for **Denny Creek Trail** (moderate; 9 miles round trip to Melakwa Lake). This is one of the more pleasant walks in the region, offering a choice of a short stroll along Denny Creek to lovely **Keekwulee** (1.5 miles) or **Snowshoe** (2 miles) **Falls,** a longer day hike to **Hemlock Pass** (4,800 feet), or another half mile down to **Melakwa Lake.** The trail continues 3 miles west around Tuscohatchie Lakes and connects to the Pratt Lake Trail (see above). Another wildly popular local hike, particularly for parents with youngsters, is the short (half-mile) walk to spectacular 75-foot **Franklin Falls,** on Road 58 off Denny Creek Road. Note: Heavy flood damage is common in the Denny Creek drainage. Check road and trail conditions with the North Bend Ranger District before setting out.

At Snoqualmie Pass proper, take exit 52 (West Summit), turn north under the freeway and follow the Alpental Road 2 miles to its end at Alpental Resort parking lot, aka the summertime (July onward) trailhead for **Snow Lake** (moderate; 7 miles round trip). A grand alpine walk, this. And absolutely mobbed on your average weekend. On the relatively gentle (1,300-vertical-foot-gain) ascent, you'll find great views of craggy Cascade peaks such as Chair Peak and the Tooth, then wonderful shoreline lounging along the mile-long lake. The lake is inside the Alpine Lakes Wilderness, so special camping restrictions (follow signs and use established sites only) are in effect. Limited overnight permits are on their way to this overused spot. But there's no getting away from the fact that it's a great day hike.

Also from exit 52, follow signs a short distance on the north side of I-90 to the **Pacific Crest Trail** parking lot, where several hiking options await. Of course, you're welcome to hitch up your shorts and walk north to Canada or south to Mexico. But most of us prefer shorter day jaunts, such as the popular hikes to lovely **Commonwealth Basin** (moderate; 5.5 miles round trip), view-rich **Red Pass** (moderate; 10 miles round trip), or the cliff-clinging **Kendall Katwalk** (difficult; 10.5 miles round trip). The "Katwalk" section of the latter hike is a narrow ledge blasted from solid rock, with stone walls above and lots of open air below. Definitely not for the faint of heart or people with really wide packs. The trail is dangerous until all snow is gone, usually by July.

North Bend to Snoqualmie Summit, south side I-90

Parents and baby-sitters of visiting Nebraskans, pay attention. If the recalcitrant interlopers of whom you're in charge want a dose of Northwest-style fresh air (possibly including eye-to-radula encounters with banana slugs as long as your hand), you needn't venture all the way to, say, Stehekin to do it. The long, skinny public place known as **Twin Falls/Olallie State Park** just east of North Bend should do the trick. From the park's western entrance (take exit 34, Edgewick Road, turn right, and follow signs), the **Twin Falls Trail** (easy/moderate; 2.6 miles round trip) is a nice, family-friendly walk. You'll pass through an actual moss-draped rain forest (90 inches of rain a year) along the South Fork Snoqualmie River, pass some rare old-growth trees, then climb moderately (about 500 feet) up the river gorge to an overlook of the lower of two (actually, there are three) Twin Falls. The waterfall, once known as Upper Snoqualmie Falls, isn't as grand as it used to be. A small power plant now robs much of its thunder, diverting water underground through an invisible turbine. But it's still a splendid sight. Continuing, you'll reach an impressive bridge spanning the 125-foot gorge just above the lower falls. Look pretty pricey for a State Parks trail? It was. The power company undoubtedly paid to helicopter this baby in as part of its public-impact funding in exchange for a hydro permit. Proceed beyond the bridge, up one more switchback, for a view of the upper falls. Most people turn around here, but you can go on to connect to the Iron Horse Trail, which leads east to Olallie State Park.

Olallie State Park, the upper portion of the South Fork Snoqualmie gorge public/hydropower area, offers several hiking options. To get there, take exit 38, turn right, and follow the old highway three-quarters of a mile to a road veering left, near a brown house. A parking lot here provides access to the river on the short, flat, very peaceful **Olallie Nature Trail** (easy; 1 mile round trip). It's a nice walk for kids, or for adults who want to escape the big-city noise for an hour or so. At trail's end is another parking lot, this one near the Olallie hydro project. Just beyond, **Weeks Falls,** another formerly awesome cascade, can be viewed in its now muted state. A sign on the turbine house says the project, which siphons a goodly portion of the South Fork Snoqualmie underground, provides enough power to light about 800 homes. You decide if it was worth it.

Olallie State Park also offers a secondary west-end access to Iron Horse Trail State Park, the old Milwaukee Road right-of-way now being converted to a cross-state walking, cycling, and equestrian path. The trail actually begins near Rattlesnake Lake near Tiger Mountain (see Issaquah to North Bend, above), where a new trailhead recently was developed. But many hikers and bikers have been trained to use this access, because it's closer to other popular trails, and because for years it was the most direct route to the cross-state **Iron Horse Trail.** A major washed-out trestle here (at Hall Creek) used to necessitate separate routes for eastbound and westbound Iron Horse travelers. Eastbounders would climb up the steep slopes to the east end of the chasm, westbounders would take a right at the bottom of the exit 38 off-ramp, then another hard right up the hill to a trailhead parking lot.

Thankfully, the split is no longer necessary. Everyone can use the more easily accessible former westbound trailhead, because the trestle gap was rebridged in the winter of 1999 by Washington State Parks. It's worth walking out to the trestle to take a look below; it's more than 150 feet down to Hall Creek. It's also worth surveying exactly what caused the trestle, which bore the weight of freight trains for more than 75 years, to wash out. The middle third of the bridge's superstructure was blasted away by dead logs, the result of a blatant timber strip-mining of this drainage (the land is denuded as far as the eye can see up and around the small valley). It's a grand example of the cut-first, worry-later thinking that's in evidence all the way over Snoqualmie Pass. From this amazing spectacle, it's about 1.5 miles west (or 1 mile from the trailhead) to a dramatic trestle over a waterfall on Washington Creek. Pleasant spot. But greater riches await to the east, and now that the bridge is decked you can get to them all from here, traveling east to the McClellan Butte and Annette Lake trailheads (see below), crossing beneath Snoqualmie Pass in the Snoqualmie Tunnel, and continuing all the way to Easton and beyond.

Back on I-90, the next stop east is exit 42 (West Tinkham Road), where a right turn off the exit takes you past a Transportation Department office and to the **McClellan Butte** (difficult; 9 miles round trip) trailhead. This one can suck the life out of you. It starts steep and stays steep, gaining 3,700 feet on the way to the spectacular 5,100-foot summit perch.

North-facing slopes make the upper portions dangerous well into summer. Don't try it before July, and say no thanks to the final couple hundred feet unless you're adept at rock scrambling. That said, the view from the ridge top just below the summit is stupendous in both directions: north all the way up the Cascade Range; south into the lovely green carpet of the Cedar River Watershed and into the glaring north face of Rainier.

Five miles east, take exit 47 (Denny Creek/Asahel Curtis), turn right to a T intersection, then go left about a half mile to the trailhead for highly popular **Annette Lake** (moderate; 7 miles round trip). The trail climbs about three-quarters of a mile beneath a thick canopy (a "recovering" clear-cut) to a junction with the Iron Horse Trail, then switchbacks steadily upward through older forest to a pretty alpine lake. Some nice (overused) campsites are found on the north shore, probably occupied by Boy or Girl Scouts wearing Glad Trash Bags in a feeble attempt to keep dry. This trail receives heavy use. (Note: The lower portion is a good I-90 exit route for one-way hikers from the Snoqualmie Tunnel. See below.)

People can argue until their Scarpa boots rot off about the Evergreen State's best hiking trails. But there's little quarrel over its most unusual. The **Snoqualmie Tunnel** (easy but creepy; 5.6 miles round trip from Keechelus trailhead) is proudly billed by its overseers, Washington State Parks, as "the longest hiking tunnel in the United States." Well, okay. That's either saying a whole lot or very little, considering how much underground hiking takes place in the United States. But this historical oddity, in its time an engineering marvel, has attracted thousands of Puget Sound-area walkers since 1994, when its heavy wooden doors swung open for the first time in decades. The tunnel is 2.3 miles long, and cuts a straight path from Hyak, beneath millions of tons of rock (and the Snoqualmie Pass ski areas), to a western portal hidden in the trees just south of I-90, where the highway curves and begins to climb steeply to Snoqualmie Summit. The tunnel was built in 1912—blasted and chipped by crews cutting through the mountain from both ends. Legend has it they met in the middle only several feet apart. The walls are lined with concrete, and trail crews have replaced the old flooded floor with smooth gravel.

Walking the tunnel is a unique experience, to say the least. It's chilly inside, the temperature hovering in the 50s even on 90° days. And a constant wind funnels from west to east. It's also nearly pitch dark. There are no lights in the tunnel, only a small pinpoint of daylight visible at the far end. A strong flashlight, extra batteries, and warm clothes are required, no matter when you visit. Those easily inclined to cases of the willies should consider taking a friend. The tunnel is spooky, perhaps because of the lingering ghosts of railroad workers past. Or perhaps because the tunnel itself looks, smells, and feels alive. The wind blasting from its eastern portal makes a constant roar. When it reaches the warm eastside air, it billows out as steam, like the breath of a snoozing mountain dragon. This giant west-to-east suckage has been a problem in the tunnel since its early days. The wooden doors were kept closed between trains in the wintertime to block the wind, which, combined with seepage from the roof, created 8-foot icicles. The doors are still kept closed in the winter by State Parks, which shuts the tunnel from November to May.

The best tunnel access is from the newly developed (1999) **Keechelus Lake/Iron Horse** trailhead near Summit East ski area (formerly Hyak). Take exit 54 and follow signs. From the parking lot, walk a half mile west to the tunnel entrance, hidden in the weeds just below the parking lot for Hyak Ski Area. You can walk the 2.3-mile tunnel down and back in about 90 minutes. But for a fun day trip with more mileage, bring two cars. Leave one at the trailhead for Annette Lake (see above), and take the other to the Keechelus trailhead. It creates a one-way, moderately downhill walk (or mountain-bike ride) of just over 5 miles from car to car.

Downhill Skiing

Snoqualmie Pass taught the Northwest to ski. And it continues to do so. Skiing at the summit began in the 1930s, when a weekly ski train from Seattle brought hordes of weekend warriors to the snowy slopes to make big, heavy turns on even bigger, heavier wooden skis. These days, the equipment has improved (a lot) and the lifts are better, but the setting—and the attraction—is the same: reliable skiing, only 45 interstate minutes east of Seattle. The four summit ski areas—previously known as Alpental, Snoqualmie Summit, Ski Acres, and Hyak, and now known as Alpental, Summit West, Summit Central, and Summit East—form one of the largest ski operations this close to a major metropolis in the country. Little surprise that perhaps more youngsters learn to ski and snowboard here than at any other single place in America.

The place got a major boost in 1997, when the Moffett family sold the entire operation to George Gillett Jr., the high-rolling ski-resort developer who was the original force behind Vail, Colorado. Gillett, who also owns a chain of other resorts, including Grand Targhee, Wyoming, promised a $30 million makeover, with not only new lifts and facilities, but also a completely relocated main base area at Summit Central, moved downhill nearer to the freeway, thus increasing the area's vertical drop by several hundred feet. Small portions of those promises have been kept. The resorts, particularly Summit Central and Summit West, got new quad lifts and a general spiffing up. A new chair also has been installed at Alpental, which, thankfully, has kept its rather quaint demeanor. But there's much work to be done here to bring **The Summit at Snoqualmie,** as the four areas now are known, up to eye level with the best ski facilities elsewhere in the area, including Crystal Mountain to the south, Stevens Pass to the north, and, regionally, Mount Hood Meadows and Mount Bachelor, Oregon, and Whister, British Columbia.

When it comes to snow, the Pass, only about a racing ski higher than 3,000 feet, is no Alta, Utah. It's no Mount Baker, for that matter. The borderline altitude makes snow conditions iffy; in the peak season, rain is just as likely as (generations of soggy ski-school students will say more likely than) snow. But the base is reliable, usually providing a Thanksgiving-to-spring-break ski season. That's good enough for **ski schools,** dozens of which operate at the four areas (mainly Summit West and Summit Central).

Snoqualmie's other big draw? **Night skiing.** All things being equal, skiing at night is pretty much the same wherever you do it: cold, dark, icy. Squint a bit on a run at Summit Central, and you could very well be in Aspen—so, many skiers who spit in the general direction of Snoqualmie Pass in the daylight lower their standards and head up I-90 at night. Prices are good, access unbeatable: barring major I-90 traffic problems, Seattle workers can go from the 76th floor of Columbia Seafirst Center to a summit chairlift in 1 hour. Try doing that in New York, Chicago, Los Angeles, or even Denver. The snow usually is wet, the vertical drop (1,100 feet at Central) puny by Western U.S. standards. But as much as Seattle skiers talk trash about the Summit, we'll probably continue to sneak up there, because, well, we love to ski, and it's too close to resist.

The Summit is a full-service operation, with ample ski schools, **rentals,** cafeterias, and the like. The day lodge at Summit Central is recently renovated. More lodging has been promised by Gillett's people. In the meantime, slopeside lodging is limited to the Snoqualmie Summit Inn; (425) 434-6300. A single lift ticket ($35 on weekends and holidays, less for kids and on weekdays) gets you access to lifts at all four areas. **Summits West, Central,** and **East** are connected by ski trails, and can be viewed as one large area. Terrain at all three is similarly nondescript: wide-open, untreed, and not very steep. The longest—and arguably best—runs are those on the upper portion of Summit Central.

Not so at **Alpental.** This small, tucked-away area, a 2-mile shuttle-bus ride away on the north side of I-90, is the demon seed of this ski family. Alpental strains thigh muscles throughout its respectable 2,200 feet of vertical. Its slopes, particularly upper knee-knockers such as Internationale, are as steep as any in the Northwest. For experts, Alpental's unpatrolled backcountry areas can provide incredible, Rocky Mountain–quality experiences when snow conditions are good. Really.

The Summit stats: Skiable acreage: 2,000. Elevation: 3,200 feet to

5,400 feet. Lifts: 22 (4 recently installed quads, the rest triples, doubles, or surface lifts). Hours: Generally 9am to 10pm daily; no night-skiing on Sundays. Season: Mid-November to mid-April, conditions permitting. Lift rates: $35 for weekends and holidays at this writing. *On I-90 at Snoqualmie Pass; mountain information (425) 434-7669, snow phone (206) 236-1600; www.summit-at-snoqualmie.com.*

Cross-Country Skiing

Cross-country skiing in the I-90 corridor comes in two flavors: commercial and public. The commercial offering is **The Summit at Snoqualmie Nordic Center,** located at Summit East ski area (see above), one of the best full-service Nordic skiing operations in the Northwest. Choose from 55 kilometers of nicely groomed trails, some in the lower areas across the street from Summit Central, but most on the plateau atop Snoqualmie Summit's three downhill ski areas. The upper areas, reached by riding the Silver Fir chair near Summit Central, are a joy to intermediate and advanced skiers. On a sunny day, the **Mount Catherine Loop** is a grand cross-country tour, with stunning views. The Nordic Center also serves as a summertime base for the Summit's mountain-bike operation (see below). Summit Central offers another rare cross-country bonus: night skiing. The lower track area is lighted on Wednesday nights and weekends. Call (425) 434-7669, ext. 4531 for details.

Public opportunities, found at a string of Washington State Parks–maintained Sno-Parks, are rich all along the I-90 corridor. Sno-Parks (roadside pullouts or trailheads kept plowed for winter parking) are a great recreational bargain for Washington skiers. An annual **Sno-Park pass** ($20 at this writing, with an additional $20 fee for annual access to regularly groomed trails in the I-90 corridor) grants seasonal access to more than 50 of them in the state, as well as dozens more in Oregon. Buy the sticker at any ski shop and stick it on your windshield. Then pick a Sno-Park and kick-glide away. The permit fees pay for parking-area plowing, plus machine grooming on many of the tracks. For more information on Sno-Parks and permits, contact Washington State Parks, (800) 233-0321; www.parks.wa.gov, "winter recreation" link.

Popular Sno-Parks include **Cabin Creek North** (easy/difficult; 10K) and **Cabin Creek South** (easy; 2K), both off exit 63; **Lake Keechelus** (easy; 11.2K on the west shore of Lake Keechelus) off exit 54; **Gold Creek** (moderate; various lengths) off exit 54; **Crystal Springs** (easy; 11.2K connecting to the Lake Keechelus Sno-Park); and **Lake Easton** (easy; 5K) off exit 70. The grooming crew, (509) 656-2230, for these trails operates out of Lake Easton State Park.

Snowshoeing

Snowshoers generally make their own trails from one of the Sno-Park areas listed above. And major trailheads listed under Hiking, above, are starting points for backcountry treks for more experienced snowshoers along the I-90 corridor. Popular routes include **Talapus Lake** (difficult; about 10 miles round trip); **Source Lake** (moderate/difficult; 10 miles round trip), on the summertime Snow Lakes route; **Commonwealth Basin** (difficult; up to 10 miles round trip); **Kendall Peak Lakes** (difficult; about 9 miles round trip from Gold Creek Sno-Park); the **Gold Creek valley** (easy/moderate; variable distances); and **Mount Margaret** (easy/moderate; about 9 miles round trip from Gold Creek Sno-Park). Avalanche danger can be severe in the area; call the Northwest Avalanche Center Hotline, (206) 526-6677, before you set out. A good, detailed guide for day trips on snowshoes in this area is *Snowshoe Routes Washington* by Dan A. Nelson (The Mountaineers Books).

Snowshoe **rentals** are available at the Nordic Center at Summit East (see Cross-country Skiing, above). Rangers with the Mount Baker–Snoqualmie National Forest often offer **guided snowshoe treks** from the Snoqualmie Pass area from January through April; they're free (a donation is suggested) and open to novices. For scheduling and reservations, call the Snoqualmie Pass Visitor Center, (425) 434-6111 (it's open Friday to Sunday).

Snow Play

Snow-tubers bound for Snoqualmie Pass are in luck. Old-fashioned, pull-off-the-road-and-slide opportunities are few, and usually dangerous. But Summit Central's **Mount Tubemore** area is a tuber's delight. Rope tows. Rental tubes. Hot chocolate. Heaters! The discarded innards of truck tires don't get much more fun than that. Mount Tubemore, located just east of the main Summit Central parking area, generally operates weekends and holidays during ski season. A new day lodge, (425) 434-7669, recently opened there.

Mountain Biking

Most I-90 corridor hiking trails are off-limits to mountain bikes, but Forest Service and fire **roads** emanating from I-90 offer a wealth of gravel mountain-bike opportunities. Ask about open roads at the Snoqualmie Ranger District's North Bend office, (425) 888-1421, or the Snoqualmie Pass Visitors Center, (425) 434-6111.

Two other grand mountain-bike opportunities are available. The **John Wayne Pioneer Trail** in Iron Horse State Park is an ideal beginner's path, with a broad, smooth surface that never gets steep. A good starting point is the Lake Keechelus trailhead (see Hiking, above). From here, the trail can be ridden east all the way to Easton, or west through the Snoqualmie Tunnel to a pickup car at one of several trailheads: Lake Annette (5.5 miles), McClellan Butte (16 miles), or Olallie State Park (about 20 miles). Westbound riders can continue another 5 miles to Rattlesnake Lake, just south of North Bend off exit 32 near Tiger Mountain.

A second option is the summer mountain-bike operation at **Summit Central,** which opens its upper-mountain cross-country ski trails (see Skiing and Snow Play, above) to cyclists during summer months. A chairlift ride up the hill puts you into an intermediate mountain biker's heaven. Call (206) 236-1600 for details.

Camping

Choices are limited here. On the west side of the pass, two small Forest Service campgrounds are the only options. Campsites at both can be reserved up to 240 days in advance; (877) 444-6777; www.reserveusa.com. For more information, contact the Snoqualmie Ranger District's North Bend office, (425) 888-1421.

Denny Creek (33 sites; RVs to 35 feet) is the most popular, often crowded because of the flood of I-90 traffic. The campground also has a group site for 35 people. Denny Creek is open summers only, generally late May to mid-October. Note: Flood damage to the Denny Creek access road is common; call before you head this way in the spring. *Off I-90 exit 47, take a right at the T on the north side of the freeway, then a left onto Denny Creek Rd.*

Tinkham (48 sites, no hookups; RVs to 21 feet) isn't exactly beautiful, with most sites set in shady, second-growth trees not far from the roar of I-90. But it'll do for an overnighter. This campground also has been closed periodically because of flood damage. *Follow signs off I-90 exit 42.*

Things get a bit better on the east side. **Crystal Springs** has 25 sites (no hookups; RVs to 21 feet) near Lake Keechelus. The campground is open summers only. Campsites cannot be reserved. *Take I-90 exit 62, 10 miles east of Snoqualmie Summit; (509) 674-4411.* **Kachess,** on a large reservoir northeast of Easton, is the largest local campground, with 182 sites (no hookups; RVs to 32 feet). This Wenatchee National Forest camp has a summer store, a boat launch, and boat rentals. It's a good base camp for exploring many Alpine Lakes Wilderness trails. Kachess is open late May to mid-September. Campsites can be reserved up to 240 days in advance; (877) 444-6777; www.reserveusa.com. *From I-90 eastbound, take exit 62 (Crystal Springs), cross over the freeway, and follow signs; (509) 674-4411.*

The lone local state park, **Lake Easton,** is a very nice one, with 137 sites (45 with hookups; RVs to 60 feet). And it's located just off I-90 (convenient, but noisy). Spaces are spread through wooded loops on bluffs above Lake Easton, a reservoir on the upper Yakima River. The park has a boat launch, and Lake Easton is a decent late-summer trout fishery. The park is open all year, but camping loops are open mid-April to mid-October only. Campsites can be reserved up to 11 months in advance by calling Reservations Northwest; (800) 452-5687. *From I-90 eastbound, take exit 70 and follow signs a short distance to the park, about a mile west of Easton;* (800) 233-0321 or (509) 656-2230.

A **private campground,** the Snoqualmie River Campground, on the banks of the river at Fall City, has 50 tent sites and 30 RV sites (hookups; RVs to 60 feet); (425) 222-5545.

Wildlife Watching

No established wildlife-viewing areas grace the Mountains-to-Sound Greenway, but it's a rich wildlife zone. Hikers and backcountry trekkers (lucky ones) might encounter one of the dozen or so **mountain goats** happily at home on the north side of Mount Si. **Black bears** are sporadically seen on local trails, as are **deer** and, increasingly, **cougars.** It's common to see **coyotes** in the upper Snoqualmie Valley, and people who know what they're seeing have spotted **wolves** even this far south in the Cascades. Many of these local critters are spillover from the Cedar River Watershed, a vast protected area hidden one ridge to the south. The watershed's **Rocky Mountain elk** herd is particularly infamous, both among hunters, who drool over the 600-animal herd's massive bulls (hunting is forbidden inside the watershed), and among upper Snoqualmie Valley residents, who frequently chase the nosy beasts out of their carrots and peas. Seeing a local elk is a hit-and-miss proposition. But hang out in the area between Rattlesnake Lake and Mount Washington in the winter long enough, and the odds get pretty good.

Picnics/Swimming

First, the essentials: stop at George's Bakery (main street, North Bend) and stock up on fresh bread and buttermilk crullers. Properly equipped, proceed up I-90 to one of several good picnickeries.

The grassy shores of **Rattlesnake Lake,** just south of North Bend (see Hiking, above), are a pleasant place to partake of sandwiches, frosty beverages, and giant monkey-shaped clouds floating overhead—especially since the City of Seattle, the local landlord, spiffed up the place recently. This is a very pleasant, peaceful spot. Good picnic spots are found near the main parking area—watch for goose leavings—and around the corner to the right, where there's a shaded area. (For cheap entertainment on windy summer nights, those of us who live close to Rattlesnake Lake will drive down to watch the evening breeze kick up and push all those float-tubers, like overgrown rubber duckies, all the way to the far end of the lake, where they have to get out and walk back.) Take I-90 exit 32, continue 4 miles south on SE Cedar Falls Road.

At Rattlesnake Lake, where you sit depends on when you get here. The lake is fickle, filling itself right to the roadway in the winter and early spring, then shrinking away in the summer until it's just a big puddle by autumn. You have only yourselves to blame—at least if you live in Seattle. Rattlesnake Lake was an unexpected by-product of the Seattle watershed operation on the nearby Cedar River. The city's Masonry Reservoir, a holding pond for Seattle drinking water, sits 1.3 miles to the south and—more importantly—about 600 feet above Rattlesnake Lake. When the reservoir is full, so is the lake, which is connected by glacial gravel. Result: spring and early summer visits are best, when the lake is full-up.

Up the road a piece is **Olallie State Park** (see Hiking, above), where nice, grassy picnic spots are found near the old house along the South Fork Snoqualmie River. Take I-90 exit 38, turn right, and watch for the access road in about three-quarters of a mile on the left. The **Denny Creek Campground** (see Camping, above) is a good picnic spot. And near the Snoqualmie Pass summit, a peaceful but seldom used rest area on **Gold Creek Pond** is a fine summertime picnic spot. Take exit 54, follow the frontage road north under the freeway, then east to signs for Gold Creek Rest Area. To the east, **Lake Easton State Park** (see Camping, above) has a delightful waterfront picnic area, complete with a children's play area and rest rooms with running water.

Asahel Curtis picnic area has a split personality: the picnic area is to the east of I-90, but a path goes under the freeway to connect with a nature trail on the west side of I-90. Take I-90 exit 47 for the picnic area or exit 50 for the nature trail. The **Gold Creek Pond Picnic Area,** off I-90 exit 51, has an interpretive trail and picnic sites in a converted gravel quarry.

Canoeing/Kayaking

Whitewater kayakers and canoeists are a common sight on both the **South Fork** and **Middle Fork Snoqualmie.** The activity is heavily dependent on water levels, which vary rapidly and generally are too low during summer and fall months. Both streams provide multiple access points. Most kayakers hit the Middle Fork by following Middle Fork

Road to one of a half dozen decent put-in spots (take exit 34, turn north, and follow signs). The South Fork, when it's high enough, can easily be run between Twin Falls State Park (see Hiking, above) and downtown North Bend. Another put-in can be found about midway on this route—just off 432nd Avenue, reached by turning south from exit 32. This one requires a tricky portage down from a bridge over the river, however. Canoeists and beginning kayakers will love the placid waters of **Rattlesnake Lake,** which are almost always smooth. A Seattle Water Department park around two sides of the lake allows excellent flat-bank access. **Lakes Keechelus, Kachess,** and **Easton** also are popular canoe destinations, especially for campers.

Fishing

The Snoqualmie River is a major destination for Seattle-area steelheaders. Its lower portions that is. Nearly all the fishable waters below Snoqualmie Falls are mined regularly in winter months by **steelhead** enthusiasts. Two spots draw the biggest crowds—and, not surprisingly, the highest catch totals. One is the confluence of the Snoqualmie and Tokul Creek, where a strong run of winter steelhead returns each year to the Tokul Creek Hatchery. This is a productive fishery, but way down there on the aesthetics scale. Most of the fish hooked here are caught within yards of the inlet stream to the hatchery, and the banks of Tokul Creek below the hatchery come as close as anyplace in the state to approximating shoulder-to-shoulder Alaskan "combat fishing" conditions. But if you want your steelhead badly enough, you'll probably find yourself here at least once. The run typically peaks in late December or early January. Tokul Creek has one other major advantage over other local streams—it's relatively flood-proof. Even when the mainstem Snoqualmie and other local rivers are blown out by winter flooding, the shallow waters of Tokul Creek are usually fishable. Take Hwy 202 east from Fall City or west from Snoqualmie to Fish Hatchery Road, near the Tokul Creek Fish Hatchery.

Another productive and popular Snoqualmie River fishery—probably more because of its easy access than any other single factor—is the area on either side of the Fall City bridge. You'll find good bank access here, and anglers properly equipped (with hip waders) will usually find good drifts just below the confluence with the Raging River. Skunkees should proceed directly up the street to the Short Fries drive-in for a pleasing infusion of hot grease.

Trout anglers can fish the Snoqualmie after it opens in June (check the state regulations pamphlet for special restrictions and limits in some areas). Most of the river above the falls, including most of the fishable

South Fork and Middle Fork, is a selective fishery, with single, barbless hooks only, and no bait is allowed.

Those same restrictions apply at Rattlesnake Lake (see Picnics/Swimming, above), a very popular fly-fishing venue. Fly tiers, particularly those who like to fish from float tubes, love Rattlesnake for its ample parking, unparalleled bank access, and convenient, lightly sloping shores. Fishing can be pretty good. The lake gets a plant of 12,000 pan-size **rainbows** every spring. And unlike many Puget Sound–area lakes, this one usually isn't fished out on Opening Day in late April. The bite tends to pick up later in the summer when waters warm. Remember: No bait or gas motors.

At higher elevations, the Keechelus and Kachess Lakes hold some **kokanee, rainbows,** and even **burbot,** although fishing in both is generally slow because of their massive acreage and slow-warming waters. Keechelus has the added challenge of being nearly impossible to launch a boat into in late summer, when the water level drops far below the lone boat launch near Summit Central at Snoqualmie summit. Lake Easton is another fair-to-good summer bet for state-planted rainbow trout. Bank access here isn't great—a small boat makes fishing easier.

Horseback Riding

Tiger Mountain Outfitters, 24508 SE 133rd Street, Issaquah; (425) 392-5090, specializes in 3-hour **rides** to a lookout on Tiger Mountain, often on horse celebrities. (No kidding—nobody from *Mr. Ed* here, but many were used on *Northern Exposure* and other TV shows.) Most of the 10-mile round trip is along logging roads, and the rest is in dense forest. No tykes under 10.

Accessible Outdoors

The **High Point trailhead** for hiking trails on Tiger Mountain has barrier-free rest rooms, picnicking, and access to an interpretive trail, as does the Mount Si trailhead. **Tinkham** and **Denny Creek Campgrounds** offer barrier-free camping and rest rooms. **Asahel Curtis picnic area** offers barrier-free picnicking, rest rooms, and access to a path in old-growth forest off I-90 exit 50. The **Gold Creek Pond Picnic Area,** off I-90 exit 51, has barrier-free rest rooms and wheelchair access to an interpretive path. **Kachess Campground** has barrier-free rest rooms and campsites rated "usable" (usually with assistance) for wheelchairs. **Lake Easton State Park** has barrier-free campsites.

outside in

Lodgings

The Salish Lodge & Spa ★★★☆   The falls may be the initial draw, but the rooms are just as nice. *$$$; 6501 Railroad Ave SE, Snoqualmie; (425) 888-2556; www.salishlodge.com.* &

More Information

Cle Elum Ranger District: *(509) 674-4411.*

Department of Transportation pass report: *(888) SNO-INFO;*
   www.wsdot.wa.gov/sno-info.

Mount Baker–Snoqualmie National Forest Headquarters:
   (425) 775-9702 or (800) 627-0062; www.fs.fed.us/r6/mbs.

Mountains-to-Sound Greenway Trust: *(206) 382-5565.*

Northwest Avalanche Hotline: *(206) 526-6677.*

Snoqualmie Pass Visitors Center: *(425) 677-2414.*

Snoqualmie Ranger District, North Bend office: *(425) 888-1421.*

Summit at Snoqualmie: *Snow phone (206) 236-1600; www.summit-at-snoqualmie.com.*

Wenatchee National Forest Headquarters: *(509) 662-4335;*
   www.fs.fed.us/r6/wenatchee.

I-90 East:
Roslyn
to **Ellensburg**

From Lake Easton east to the Kittitas Valley, north to the Stuart Range, and south to the Yakima River Canyon, including Swauk and Blewett Passes and portions of Alpine Lakes Wilderness.

If you listen hard, you can almost hear the thud. Right here smack-dab in the center of the state, the wet, cold Cascades collide headlong with the dry, crisp plateau country, sending magnificence flying every which way. Giant pieces of that splendor remain lodged in the high, spectacular mountain-meets-plateau lands between Roslyn and Ellensburg.

This is ponderosa country, both in the tree sense (pine) and in the squishy old TV series sense (we keep expecting Hoss and Little Joe to ride out of the woods somewhere in the Teanaway River valley). This land also happens to offer perhaps the most user-friendly backcountry interface to the Alpine Lakes Wilderness, which otherwise is forever locked away from the longing gaze of the nonbackpacking public.

Here at what was ground zero in the state's early-century mining explosion, you can drive right to the edge of that vaunted wilderness—even inject yourself through its skin by hiking one of many fairly easy trails. And once you're in, you're in for good. The sprawling, splendid lands north of Interstate 90 between Easton and Ellensburg are some of the "last best places" in Washington. And we steal that phrase from writer William Kittredge on purpose: this land comes as close as any we've found in the Evergreen

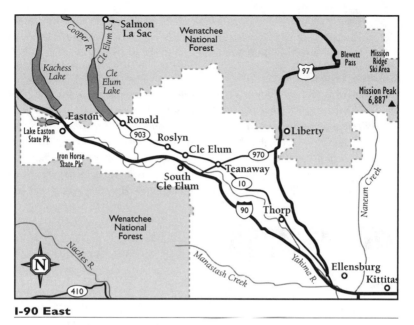

I-90 East

State to duplicating Northwest Montana. It's Big Sky without big (Hollywood) stars. And whether you're a hiker, fly caster, camper, or just an unrepentant cloud-gazer, that's a good thing.

These lands boast some of the highest critter-per-capita ratios of any in the Northwest. The steep, narrow valley of the upper Cle Elum and the broad, peaceful plains of the Teanaway drainage are teeming with deer, elk, cougar, bear, raccoon, beaver, and other mammals too numerous to count. The area has far more year-round hooved residents than shoed ones. So many, in fact, that extra caution should be taken driving here. Deer and elk are the main roadside attraction. Trust us: if you ran one over, both you and it would feel very, very badly.

This is a brittle, desolate land in the wintertime, when everything and everyone freezes solid and most mountain roads close to all but snowmobiles, four-legged creatures, and a few Jim Bridger throwbacks. (You know you're really in the mountains when roadside speed limits are posted for cars and snowmobiles.) But this land is vigor personified in the spring and early summer, when the snow melt-off creates a high-mountain waterfall crescendo that echoes all the way down to overflowing lower-valley lakes and reservoirs.

Our favorite time to visit, though, is fall, when the bugs are dead, and the "tourons" from Ohio and the kids from everywhere are back where they belong: at work and at school, respectively. Fall colors are beautiful in these mountains. Fall skies are crisp. Fall travel is slow but unencumbered. Falling in love with this place is easy. For the nature lover, it's too close to home to ignore and too close to the heart to forget.

Getting There

Roslyn is an easy 80-mile drive east of Seattle on Interstate-90. Cle Elum and Ellensburg are farther out on the same route, 85 and 110 miles, respectively. Recreation sites in the Cle Elum River drainage are reached on the Salmon La Sac Road/Forest Road 4330, an extension of Hwy 903 through Roslyn around the east shore of Cle Elum Lake. Recreation sites in in the Teanaway River drainage are reached on the North Fork Teanaway River Road, which becomes Forest Road 9737 at 29 Pines Campground; take Hwy 970 east from Cle Elum.

inside out

Hiking/Backpacking

The I-90 corridor of Snoqualmie Pass will transport you into some of the most glorious hiking terrain in the Central Cascades. The mountainous land north of Roslyn is drained by the Cle Elum and South Fork Teanaway Rivers, both favorites among fans of this region's pine-dominated forest valleys. And the Middle and North Fork Teanaway River valleys stretching north from Cle Elum provide backdoor access to the spectacular Stuart Range in the Alpine Lakes Wilderness. Hundreds of trails fan out to explore this area. For full details on area trails and roads, as well as **permit requirements** for trails in the Alpine Lakes Wilderness, contact the Cle Elum Ranger District (see More Information, below; for more on permits, see the Alpine Lakes Wilderness: Overview chapter). Note that a **Northwest Forest Pass,** $5 per day or $30 annually, is required to park in many Forest Service–administered trailheads in this area. They're available from ranger stations, from many private vendors, on-line at www.naturenw.org, or by calling (800) 270-7504. Below is a sampling of some of the area's best hikes.

Cle Elum River drainage

The Cle Elum Lake/Salmon La Sac area north of Roslyn is a hiking/camping paradise. One popular overnight route is the **Deception Pass Loop** (difficult; 15 miles round trip), at the end of Forest Road 4330 in the upper Cle Elum River valley, 28 miles north of Roslyn. The alpine scenery is stunning. Hiked clockwise, the loop follows Cathedral Rock Trail to Cathedral Pass (5,600 feet), turns north on the Pacific Crest Trail to

Deception Pass, then exits south on the Deception Pass Trail, past Lakes Hyas and Little Hyas, back to the Cle Elum River valley. A side trip on the way out is the short, trampled path to **Tuck and Robin Lakes,** below Granite Mountain. Strong day hikers can do an in-and-out trip on this trail to Cathedral Rock, but it's 18 miles round trip, with a lot of vertical (about 2,200 feet one way) to complete in a single day. More sensible day hikers might consider walking the latter portion of the Deception Pass Loop in the reverse direction for a family-friendly, beautiful excursion into the Alpine Lakes Wilderness. From the trailhead at the end of Road 4330, it's an almost level walk to **Hyas Lake** (easy; 4 miles round trip), which has some nice lakeshore campsites, and a pleasant (though crowded) hike on the same trail to **Deception Pass** (moderate; 10 miles round trip). This route usually is snow-free by July, and campsites at Hyas Lake make a good first backpacking trip for the kids. Ask at the Cle Elum Ranger District about permits.

For another taste of the same alpine splendor, try the popular day hike to **Paddy Go Easy Pass** (difficult; 6 miles round trip), which begins on Road 4330 2 miles north of Scatter Creek Campground. It's a gasser: the trail gains 2,700 feet in 3 miles. But the view from the top is stupendous. This trail is the entry route for a long cross-Cascades trek to the Icicle Creek drainage via the French Creek and Meadow Creek Trails (see the Leavenworth and the Icicle Valley chapter).

Campers at Salmon La Sac Campground (see Camping, below) can (and should) take advantage of the beautiful long day-hike or pleasant overnight trip into **Waptus Lake** (moderate; 16 miles round trip). The trail follows the Waptus River to the lake, one of the grandest in the wilderness. A trail junction there provides access to greater glories on the Pacific Crest Trail, Waptus Pass, and Dutch Miller Gap. From lakeside campsites, views of local peaks such as Summit Chief will melt your synthetic Thor-Lo socks. The truly adventurous can make a side trip from Waptus Lake's north shore up a steep, nasty path to **Spade Lake** (difficult; 3.5 miles one way), a usually frozen tarn below Mount Daniel. Remember, you'll need an overnight permit to camp in this area.

Owners of monster thighs, however, should settle for nothing less than the trail to **Jolly Mountain** (difficult; 12.5 miles round trip), which begins from the Salmon La Sac Road/Forest Road 4330 area near Cayuse Horse Camp and goes straight up, up, up to a grand viewpoint. The trail gains more than 4,000 feet in its 6-mile climb, and hikers should pick up a good trail map (Green Trails' Kachess Lake and Snoqualmie Pass maps are a good choice) to avoid getting lost on the confusing, interlaced trail system. As an added challenge, you'll need to cross Salmon La Sac Creek, which can be an unruly gush monster during the spring melt-off. Those who keep their heads above water, their eyes on the path, and their lunches in their stomachs will be rewarded with a postcard view of the Stuart Range to the north, and just about every other peak within gazing distance of this high perch. Plant the flag and scarf a PowerBar. You will have earned it.

Also, from the north end of Salmon La Sac Campground, a nice day trip is the trail to **Cooper Lake** (easy; 5 miles one way), where you'll find a pleasant walk-in campground (Owhi; see Camping, below) and another major trailhead for hikers bound for **Pete Lake** (moderate; 15 miles round trip).

Teanaway River drainage

Day hikers seeking a quick fix of some of the most scrumptious scenery the Alpine Lakes Wilderness has to offer should proceed immediately to the **Ingalls Lake/Esmerelda Basin/Longs Pass** (easy/moderate; 4 to 8 miles round trip) trailhead high in the Teanaway Valley at the end of Forest Road 9737 (North Fork Teanaway River Road). This single trailhead is the front door to a trio of great alpine destinations. From the parking lot, what begins as an old mining road turns into a pleasant trail. Less than a mile in, a side trail climbs to the Esmerelda Basin/Fortune Creek Pass area, home of a spectacular summer wildflower display. The main trail continues 2 miles to a second fork, where one trail leads 1.5 miles up and over Ingalls Pass to Ingalls Lake, where views of ruggedly handsome Mount Stuart are sublime. The other path leads a half mile to the right to Longs Pass, elevation 6,250 feet, with its own seemingly stone's-throw views of Stuart. Each is a winner in its own right. And all are used rather heavily most of the summer.

The **Beverly-Turnpike Trail** (difficult; 13 miles round trip) is probably more heavily used by Mount Stuart climbers than by hikers. But it makes for a great long day trip in the upper Teanaway drainage, passing through many spectacular wildflower meadows. This path also is the primary western access route to the Ingalls Creek Trail (see below), which leads to Stuart Pass. Backpackers making shuttle hikes from the Blewett Pass area to the North Fork Teanaway often take advantage of this route. To reach the trailhead from Hwy 970 east of Cle Elum, drive north on Teanaway River Road, which becomes Road 9737 at 29 Pines Camp. Proceed about 16 miles from 29 Pines Camp to Spur 112 and turn right.

Longer-distance backpackers should strongly consider the **Ingalls Creek-to-Stuart Pass Traverse** (moderate; 29 miles round trip), one of the longest valley hikes in the Alpine Lakes Wilderness. From a trailhead on Ingalls Creek Road (west off US 97 12.5 miles north of Blewett Pass), this trail follows an easy grade west through a long, luscious alpine valley, all within the shadow of the mighty Stuart Range looming to the north.

Pursuing trout in Cooper Lake, near Owhi Campground

Good first-night campsites are found at **Falls Creek** (6 miles; good turn-around for day hikers). The trail continues through gorgeous meadows (most with good campsites) in the Falls, Cascade, Hardscrabble, Fourth, and Turnpike Creek drainages, each of which is flanked by its own steep side trail south. The main route continues west, skirting the foot of 9,415-foot Mount Stuart and climbing steeply to **Stuart Pass**, 6,400 feet. This is a good turnaround point for a 4- to 5-day backpacking trip, but experienced hikers can find an off-trail route down to the Lake Ingalls area for a shuttle-hike exit in the North Fork Teanaway drainage via the Esmerelda Basin Trail (see above). This is a limited-permit wilderness area; consult the Cle Elum Ranger District.

Camping

The primary campsites in the area are small, limited-facility (but quite beautiful) campgrounds maintained by Wenatchee National Forest; call the Cle Elum Ranger District, (509) 674-4411, for information on most of them.

Cle Elum River drainage

A half dozen campgrounds are strung along Hwy 903 (Salmon La Sac Road) along the Cle Elum River north of Roslyn—mileages from Roslyn are given below. Also, wide areas along the north shoulder of that road often turn into unofficial campgrounds during the busy summer months, when hundreds of visitors rough it in riverside pullouts between Salmon La Sac and Scatter Creek Campgrounds.

The first campground, **Wish-Poosh,** has 17 tent sites and 22 RV sites (no hookups; RVs to 21 feet). This attractive campground is on Cle Elum Lake, a reservoir, which is often full right up to the campground in the early summer. The north side of Wish-Poosh has the busiest boat launch on Cle Elum Lake. An added treat in the camping loop: 4 double-wide spots, able to accommodate two RVs. Perfect for families camping out together. Wish-Poosh is open summers only. Campsites cannot be reserved. *6.5 miles north of Roslyn.*

Next in the valley is **Cle Elum River,** which has 2 tent sites and 33 RV sites (no hookups; RVs to 21 feet). The campground is at the head of Cle Elum Lake and is open summers only. Campsites cannot be reserved. *12 miles north of Roslyn.*

About a mile upstream is **Red Mountain,** which offers 9 sites (no hookups; no piped water) and some small group sites. It's primitive, but free. Red Mountain is open summers only. Campsites cannot be reserved. *13 miles north of Roslyn.*

One of the most popular is **Salmon La Sac,** a pretty spot on the west bank of the Cle Elum River. The campground has 127 sites (no hookups; RVs to 21 feet). The camp is wheelchair accessible, and has a horse camp and a group camp (but no horse group camp). It's a prime location for hikers (see Hiking/Backpacking, above) and anglers (see Fishing, below). Salmon La Sac is open late May through late September. Twenty-six campsites can be reserved up to 240 days in advance; (877) 444-6777; www.reserveusa.com. *15.5 miles north of Roslyn.*

Beyond Salmon La Sac, the road turns to (steep, rough) gravel, and the campsites become more, well, rustic. Two established campsites are found here, **Scatter Creek,** at the south end of Tucquala Lake, and **Fish Lake,** at the north end of the marshy valley. Both are more open, grassy areas than actual campgrounds, and tenters seem to fan out just about everywhere. Scatter Creek is particularly heavily used. In the early summer, a stream running over the road just beyond the Scatter Creek camp prevents most campers from venturing farther north. For more solitude, cross the stream (the crossing has a paved bottom, and usually can be driven by cars and trucks with moderate to high clearance—but be conservative in your guessing!) and camp in an area farther up the valley, near Fish

Lake. Camping in this area is free, but facilities are few (no tables, very few outhouses, water from the river only). The access road can be treacherous; trailers and RVs are not recommended. The area is open summers only. Campsites cannot be reserved. *Near the end of Salmon La Sac Rd (Forest Rd 9330), 29 miles north of Roslyn.*

Equally far afield is **Owhi,** a 23-site walk-in campground on the Cooper River. This is a beautiful spot, primitive but free. It's a short walk from the parking lot to the campsites, scattered in the woods above lovely Cooper Lake. The backdrop, the snow-clad Three Queens peak, is magnificent. Cooper Lake also is home to a popular trailhead for backpackers bound for Pete or Spectacle Lakes (see Hiking/Backpacking, above). Open mid-June to October. Owhi campsites cannot be reserved. *21 miles northwest of Roslyn via Salmon La Sac Rd and Forest Rd 46.*

Teanaway River drainage and US 97

To the east, **Beverly,** in the North Fork Teanaway River valley, has 13 tent sites and 3 RV spots (no hookups; RVs to 16 feet), and has no potable water. Decent stream fishing can be found nearby, and this is a prime launching spot for Alpine Lakes hikers. Beverly is open summers only. Sites cannot be reserved. *On Forest Rd 9737 (North Fork Teanaway Rd), 25 miles north of Cle Elum.*

A remote, free Department of Natural Resources campground in the area, popular with horse packers, is **Indian Camp** (9 tent sites). *19 miles northeast of Cle Elum on Middle Fork Teanaway Rd; (509) 925-8510.*

Ken Wilcox Campground at Haney Meadows (19 sites), a remote campground/horse camp at 5,500 feet, is primitive, with pit toilets, but no piped water or other services. *8 miles west of US 97 on Liberty Rd/Forest Rd 9712.*

Mineral Springs, at 2,700 feet along US 97, has 5 tent sites and 7 RV spots (no hookups; RVs to 21 feet). The campground, which has running water, is at the confluence of Medicine and Swauk Creeks. It's a popular winter-sports stopover. A group camp also is located here. Mineral Springs is open summers only. Campsites cannot be reserved. *On US 97, 21 miles northeast of Cle Elum.*

Nearby small but very scenic **Red Top,** at 5,500 feet, is a primitive spot with 3 campsites. Red Top is a notable wildlife-watching area (see Wildlife Watching, below). *West off US 97 near Mineral Springs on Forest Rds 9738 and 9702, at the end of the road near Red Top Lookout, 28 miles northeast of Cle Elum.*

Swauk, the major campground along US 97, offers 23 sites for tents or RVs (no hookups). At 3,200 feet, it's close to many popular hiking trails. The old Blewett Pass Highway intersects with US 97 about 1.5 miles south of the campground, which is open summers only. Campsites cannot be reserved. *On US 97, 27 miles northeast of Cle Elum.*

North and east of Ellensburg

And for the truly out-there crowd: A handful of remote campgrounds operated by the Cle Elum Ranger District, 674-4411, offer alternatives to the more popular campsites listed above. All are primitive, with pit toilets, but no piped water or other services. Some of these campgrounds are free. They are: **Buck Meadows** (5 sites), on South Fork Manastash Creek, 24 miles west of Ellensburg on Manastash Road/Forest Road 31; **Quartz Mountain** (3 sites), beyond Buck Meadows, 33 miles west of Ellensburg on Road 3100; **Tamarack Spring** (3 sites), 18 miles south of Cle Elum on Taneum Road/Forest Road 33; **Taneum** (13 walk-in sites), 18 miles south of Cle Elum on Taneum Road/Forest Road 33; **Icewater Creek** (17 sites), 20 miles south of Cle Elum on Taneum Road/Forest Road 33; **Taneum Junction** (group site for 75 people), 20 miles south of Cle Elum on Taneum Road/Forest Road 33; and **Lion Rock Spring** (3 sites), 23 miles north of Ellensburg on Reecer Creek Road/Forest Road 35.

Finally if you're stuck in windy Ellensburg visiting the kid in college, your best bet is a **private campground,** the Ellensburg KOA; (509) 925-9319.

Fishing

The Yakima River, which flows through the heart of this region, is one of the state's best **trout**-fishing streams, drawing increasing numbers of fly casters each year. The Yakima may be as close as Washington State can come to a classic dry-country, high-mountain, Montana-style trout stream. Fishing for wild **rainbows** is good, the setting sublime. The catch: you can't keep a trout caught between Easton and Roza Dams—it's catch-and-release only. This is a selective fishery, with bait forbidden and single barbless hooks (either on flies or small spinners or spoons) the only acceptable hardware. Access is good from I-90 downstream from Easton. For information on the Yakima River Canyon south of Ellensburg, see the Yakima Valley chapter.

The waters of the upper Cle Elum River along Salmon La Sac Road look like they should be a fly-caster's heaven, but fishing, by most accounts, is fairly slow. The river and its large valley reservoir, Cle Elum Lake, do yield some rainbows, however. Cooper Lake, which has a boat launch (no gas motors) at Owhi Campground (see Camping, above), is usually a fair summer bet for **brook** and rainbow trout and a few **kokanee.** Several backcountry Alpine Lakes Wilderness lakes, such as Hyas, Waptus, and Spectacle, also can provide fair trout fishing.

Cycling

Road cyclists should strongly consider a **Cle Elum-to-Salmon La Sac** tour, which makes a great day trip. Park at the Cle Elum Ranger Station (or nearby Safeway) on the west side of town, and follow Hwy 903 several miles northwest through Roslyn, then on up the Cle Elum River valley. Numerous rest/lunch stops are found all along the route, notably at Wish-Poosh and Cle Elum River Campgrounds (see Camping, above). The scenery is gorgeous, and Salmon La Sac Campground, at about 15 miles, is a great turn-around spot. Shoulders are narrow on this highway, but sight lines are very good, and traffic generally not too frantic (the speed limit is 35 mph for long stretches and never higher than 50). This trip should become more interesting in a few years. Cle Elum, Roslyn, and Kittitas County, with help from the Mountains-to-Sound Greenway Trust, have purchased the old Burlington Northern Railroad right-of-way between Cle Elum and Ronald, just east of Roslyn. The plan is to convert it to a multiple-use trail.

Mountain Biking

Salmon La Sac campers have a grand mountain-bike option: **Road 9330** turns to gravel at the campground, climbing sharply to the **upper Cle Elum River valley.** The first steep stretch is the worst—it's mostly rolling hills after that. Traffic is light (and dust-raising), and the mountain and river-gorge views are fantastic. This is a great mountain-bike ride in the late season, such as in September and October, when few cars are encountered and the air is cool enough to prevent cranial overheating. There are lots of great rest stops along this 18-mile (one way) route, and other Forest Service roads will take you even higher into the valley's eastside mountains.

Mountain bikers can ride long, uninterrupted stretches of the **John Wayne Trail** in Iron Horse State Park in either direction from a major trailhead at Easton. See the Snoqualmie Pass Corridor (Mountains-to-Sound Greenway) chapter.

In addition, most of the side roads beginning on US 97 near **Swauk Pass** are prime mountain-bike territory, as long as you don't mind sharing the road with motorcyclists.

Canoeing/Kayaking

Camping canoeists would be hard-pressed to find a better getaway than Owhi Campground at **Cooper Lake** (see Camping, above). The portage distance from campsite to lake is very short, and paddlers with heavy boats can drop them right at the lakeshore using the campground's boat launch. From the lake center, views of the Three Queens and other Alpine Lakes Wilderness peaks are splendid. The shallow, quiet waters of

Tucquala Lake near the headwaters of the Cle Elum River also are good, though fairly confined, canoeing waters. In the early summer melt season, waterfalls roar right overhead down the sheer westside walls of the Cle Elum River valley. Views of Cathedral Rock and other peaks are magnificent; lake waters are shallow and clear.

Wildlife Watching

Savvy **hawk** fans already know about the spot, and casual bird lovers should discover it: Red Top Mountain on Teanaway Ridge (west of US 97) is one of the state's top hawk-watching posts. Also seen in this locale are **ospreys, eagles, turkey vultures, Rocky Mountain elk,** and **mule deer.** The experts suggest visiting in September and October for birds, and right after the spring melt if you're after mammals. A small campground is found near the Red Top Lookout (see Camping, above). From US 97 south of Blewett Pass, follow Forest Roads 9738 and 9702; (509) 674-4411. In the winter, the state Department of Fish and Wildlife feeds a large elk herd in Joe Watt Canyon, near Thorp. Feeding is at 8am daily. Take the Thorp exit from I-90 and follow Old Thorp Cemetery Road to Joe Watt Canyon Road.

Horseback Riding

This is some of the most spectacular country in the Northwest for extended mountain horse-packing trips. Two **outfitters,** 3 Queens Outfitter/Guide Service, (509) 674-5647; and High Country Outfitters of Issaquah, (425) 392-0111, www.highcountry-outfitters.com; run day or multiple-day trips into the high country above Roslyn and Cle Elum. High Country Outfitters operates a summer alpine base camp in the North Fork Teanaway drainage, while 3 Queens specializes in the upper Cle Elum/Salmon La Sac area. High Country also operates a children's horse/outdoors camp (Camp Wahoo!), annual "Women in the Wilderness" Workshops, and horse and cattle drives. Also, Hidden Valley Guest Ranch, (509) 857-2344 or (800) 526-9269, offers **guided rides** on its 780-acre ranch. Horse owners seeking backcountry experiences on their own should consult the Camping section, above, which contains a number of Forest Service horse camps.

Rafting

The **Yakima River** between Cle Elum and the large diversion dam near Thorp is a popular, not-too-wild float of about 14 miles. Contact the Cle Elum Ranger District, (509) 674-4411, for **guide referrals.**

Photography

The **upper Cle Elum** and **Teanaway River valleys** are shutterbugs' paradises. Since both valleys are sheer-walled, the best summertime light is early morning when sunlight from the east lights western peaks. The Teanaway River valley, in particular, puts on a spectacular autumn color display.

Cross-Country Skiing/Snowshoeing

For skiers who don't mind commingling with snowmobilers, the Swauk/Blewett Pass area (US 97) offers good winter opportunities. The main attraction, **Swauk Creek Sno-Park,** is a large trailhead to dozens of miles of backcountry ski, snowshoe, and snowmobile roads for all ability levels. Some of these trails are machine-groomed when equipment and staff are available. The Sno-Park is 25 miles east of Cle Elum on US 97. Skiers need a state Sno-Park vehicle pass, available at ranger stations and outdoor stores. A number of other, smaller parking areas along US 97 also offer ski opportunities. Check with the Cle Elum Ranger District, (509) 674-4411, to see which have been plowed out and are accessible.

A good long-day or overnight ski tour can be made by following Forest Road 46 from the Salmon La Sac Road 6 miles into Owhi Campground at **Cooper Lake** (see Camping, above). Strong skiers can continue another 5 miles from Cooper Lake to **Pete Lake.** Avalanche danger exists along this route. Call the Northwest Avalanche Hotline, (206) 526-6677, before setting out.

Climbing

The Alpine Lakes Wilderness in the northern part of this region is home to several noteworthy alpine ascents, including the **Three Queens** (6,678 feet), **Chikamin Peak** (7,000 feet), and **Lemah Mountain** (7,840 feet) in the Cooper River drainage. In the upper Cle Elum drainage, experienced climbers get all the mountain they can handle from **Bears Breast Mountain** (7,197 feet), **Mount Daniel** (7,899 feet), **Mount Hinman** (7,500 feet), and **Cathedral Rock** (6,725 feet). Most ascent routes on these peaks are rated between 3.0 and 5.7. For a list of qualified **guides,** contact the Cle Elum Ranger District; (509) 674-4411.

Accessible Outdoors

Salmon La Sac Campground has barrier-free rest rooms and campsites. **Taneum, Beverly,** and **Haney Meadows Horse Camp** have barrier-free rest rooms and campsites rated "usable" for wheelchair users. The **Fiorito Ponds,** just off I-90 near Ellensburg, offer bank trout-fishing access for wheelchair users.

outside in

Restaurants

Austin's Roadside Deli ★★   Organic ingredients flavor items such as seasonal soups and deli dishes. *$; 311 N Main St, Ellensburg; (509) 925-3012.*

Roslyn Cafe   This formerly funky eatery is now a family stop with homestyle cooking. *$; 201 W Pennsylvania Ave, Roslyn; (509) 649-2763.*

The Valley Cafe ★★★   Who would expect to find this gourmet gem in the cowboy town of Ellensburg? *$$; 105 3rd, Ellensburg; (509) 925-3050.*

Lodgings

Hidden Valley Guest Ranch ★★   The state's oldest dude ranch, on 700 private and beautiful acres. *$$; 3942 Hidden Valley Rd, Cle Elum; (509) 857-2322 or (800) 5-COWBOY; www.ranchweb.com/hiddenvalley.*

The Inn at Goose Creek   Theme rooms allow you to pick your mood, from romantic to year-round Christmas. *$$; 1720 Canyon Rd, Ellensburg; (800) 533-0822.* &

Iron Horse Inn B&B ★   This 1909 bunkhouse is pleasantly furnished with reproduction antiques. *$$; 526 Marie St, Cle Elum; (509) 674-5939 or (800) 2-2-TWAIN; ironhorseinn.uswestdex.com.*

More Information

Wenatchee National Forest Headquarters: *(509) 662-4335; www.fs.fed.us/r6/wenatchee.*
Cle Elum Ranger District: *(509) 674-4411.*
Cle Elum/Roslyn Chamber of Commerce: *(509) 674-5958.*
Department of Transportation pass report: *(888) SNO-INFO; www.wsdot.wa.gov/sno-info.*
Ellensburg Chamber of Commerce: *(509) 925-3137 or (888) 925-2204; www.ellensburg-chamber.com.*

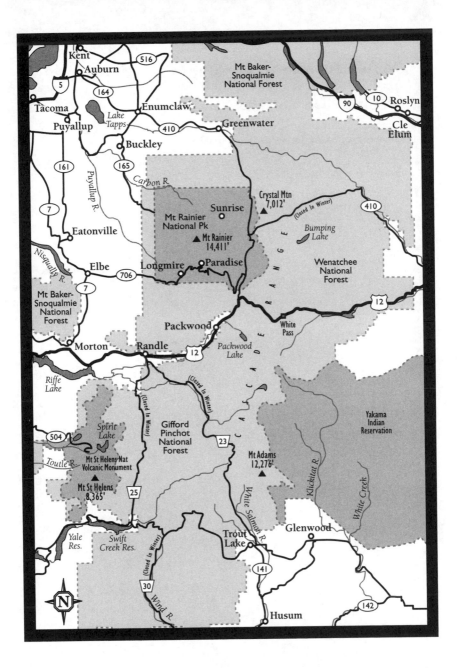

South Cascades

South
Cascades

Mount
Rainier
National Park

From Elbe west to Cayuse Pass, north to the Carbon River valley, east to Crystal Mountain Resort, and south to the US Highway 12–Highway 123 junction.

Those magical Tahoma moments strike swiftly and, it seems, always at the least opportune time. In heavy freeway traffic, for example. Anyone who's lived here very long has been there: driving down Interstate 5, focused on the bumper ahead, trapped in the permafunk gloom of a Washington winter. Suddenly, storm clouds part to the south, a shaft of light slices through, and—whoa—there she is. Mount Rainier, the Northwest's most powerful, enduring landmark, thrusts its head through the clouds and reminds us all why we live here. It's enough to make you cry, and some of us occasionally do. For those of us whose homes lie scattered helter-skelter below its heavily glaciated slopes, the mountain is a source of inspiration, fear, and respect. This personal, often emotional connection to a hulking, 14,411-foot rock defies explanation. But it is undeniable. Just look at the thing, and you'll know. This is a mountain that truly moves people.

Rainier—or Tahoma, as it is known to Native Americans—is all things to most people. Some of us are dabblers, visiting only on sunny summer days and fighting the crowds in visitors-center parking lots to give the Pennsylvania relatives a quick glimpse of Sunrise or a taste of Paradise. Some of us are fair-weather regulars, meeting with Rainier each year to sample its crystal streams, camp beneath its old-growth hemlocks and firs, hike its 300 miles of trails, and sleep in its endless meadows. Some of us, preferring to face the mountain one-on-one, avoid the summer crush altogether and visit only in winter, when the peak's full face stays hidden and only one road goes in and out of the park. Some of us have become downright hard-core, swinging through the national park's developed facilities just long enough to park the car, and heading by foot, ski, or snowshoe into the true heart of the mountain's wilderness. And for some of us, none of that is enough: we can no longer bear the sight of the mountain from afar without knowing we've set foot on top of it.

Rainier clearly is one of the most diverse outdoor haunts in the United States. The mountain's high-altitude visitors centers at Paradise and Sunrise are spectacular enough, but the backcountry can be mind-numbingly beautiful when weather cooperates. It also can be deadly when the weather does not. Mount Rainier, it is often (correctly) said, creates its own weather, and in doing so, rarely seems to take our vacation plans into account. People die from exposure every year—occasionally in August—in Rainier's deceptively beautiful alpine country. And not all of them are climbers. Backpackers and backcountry skiers, in particular, should heed the advice of Rainier veterans and never—at any time of the year—venture far into the wilds without overnight gear and the good sense to use it.

That said, something about days spent outside on the slopes of Mount Rainier sets the park apart from all other sections of the state. The hills seem steeper here, the ice a bit slicker, the sun a lot brighter, and the air thinner. Lifetimes have been spent exploring this magnificent rock, extremely rich lifetimes. It's our firm belief, based on years of trying, that no day spent poking around Rainier is a wasted one. Whether you're a climber or a loafer, more often than not you will go home with a self-satisfied glow.

Entire books have been written about Rainier's many special fresh-air nooks and deep-snow crannies. We offer instead a mere outline—a road map to get you rolling. Trust yourself, respect the mountain, and, for heaven's sake, carry extra long johns. Which brings to mind a rule about the rarity of those "Tahoma moments," and about enjoying Rainier's hard and soft sides—a rule that might well fit the Washington outdoor experience as a whole: The only thing worse than underestimating Mount Rainier is taking it for granted.

Getting There

In the summer, Mount Rainier is approached by two main access routes: Highways 7 and 706 from the Puyallup/South Tacoma area (to the Nisqually entrance, Longmire, and Paradise); and Hwy 410 from Enumclaw (take Hwys 18 and 169 to Enumclaw from Interstate 5) to Crystal Mountain Resort, the White River entrance, and Sunrise. Allow 2 to 3 hours from the Seattle area

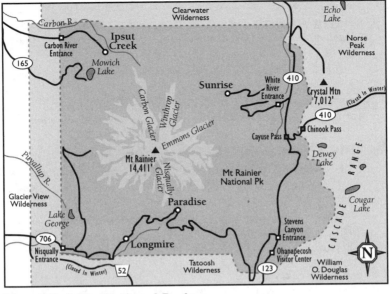

Mount Rainier National Park

via either route when snow isn't a concern. In the winter, Hwy 410 (Chinook Pass Highway) closes near the National Park border, at the Crystal Mountain Boulevard turnoff. That leaves Hwy 706 as the only winter park entrance— the Park Service keeps Hwy 706 open to Longmire all winter. The road beyond, to Paradise, is open daily as soon as plows have cleared it—usually by 10am, but sometimes as late as noon. The road is closed during periods of particularly heavy snow or avalanche danger. Always carry chains when entering the park in the winter. Cheating not only is ill-advised, it's basically impossible: park rangers check for chains or four-wheel drive. If you don't have either, you're going back home.

The park has three other entrances. The Stevens Canyon entrance is on Hwy 123 (Cayuse Pass Highway) on the southeast side of the park. This entrance can be reached via US Highway 12 from the south or Hwys 410 and 123 from the east, via Enumclaw or Yakima. Hwys 410 and 123 are closed in the winter. On the northwest side of the park, both Mowich Lake Road and Carbon River Road are unpaved entrances to the scenic (and less heavily vis-ited) north side. Both are accessed via Hwy 165, which runs south into the park from Buckley just south of Enumclaw. These roads are open summer only, and often are in rough condition. For updates on road conditions, call (360) 569-2211, the park's recorded information line.

Daily-use fees (presently $10 per carload) are collected at the Nisqually, Stevens Canyon, White River, and Carbon River entrances—unless you arrive *very early or late, in which case you can sneak by without paying. Frequent park visitors usually fork over $20 for an annual pass or $50 for a pass granting admission to all U.S. national parks for one year. Gray Line Tours of Seattle, (800) 426-7532, runs summer tours of the park.*

inside out

Scenic Drives/Visitors Centers

The vast majority of Mount Rainier's 2.2 million annual visitors pack a lunch, grab a map, and make a day trip to the mountain. And most of them wind up at one of two places: Paradise or Sunrise. Summer ranger stations are located at Sunrise, Ohanapecosh, White River, Carbon River, Nisqually, and Longmire. All dispense park information, hiking permits, and other information. See More Information, below, for phone numbers.

Longmire/Paradise

Hwy 706, the road to Paradise on the southwest side of Rainier, passes through the Nisqually entrance and climbs gradually to Longmire, a small village where you'll find the National Park Inn, (360) 569-2275; a small wildlife museum with plant and animal displays; several day-hiking trails (see Hiking/Backpacking, below) and a hiking information center; there's also a rental outlet for cross-country skiing. It has the only place that sells gas in the park. The restaurant at the National Park Inn is very familiar to backcountry skiers and snowshoers, who often bide their time here waiting for snowplows to finish their work on the Paradise Highway.

From Longmire, the road climbs steeply, crosses the massive rubble path of the Nisqually Glacier and river drainage, then climbs to Paradise, elevation 5,400 feet. (Notable spots to pull off the road on the way up are beautiful **Narada Falls**—a good picnic spot—and the **Canyon Rim Viewpoint,** which overlooks the upper Nisqually River.) You'll know you've arrived at Paradise when you happen upon the other 217,000 cars parked in the massive lot. Okay, maybe not that many, but on summer weekends, Paradise is so heavily visited that you'll likely have to patrol, shopping-mall-the-week-before-Christmas style, for a parking spot.

The attractions here are obvious: an up-close view of the mountain (too close, really, for photographers, because you're standing *on* the mountain rather than looking *at* it), many hiking trails through beautiful alpine meadows (see Hiking/Backpacking, below), picnic sites with killer views, and the **Henry M. Jackson Visitors Center,** housed in a saucer-shaped building that looks as if it just arrived from the planet Zendar. The

Snowshoers tromp up the Reflection Lakes Trail in Mount Rainier National Park

Jackson Visitors Center exhibits are interesting, but most people never see them, so impressed are they by the view of the mountain. Nearby, the folksy Paradise Inn offers accommodations from May to October; call Rainier Guest Services, (360) 569-2275, for reservations.

Paradise is a treat for many southern-clime visitors, because snow is present nearly year-round. The site for many years held a world record for the largest single-season snowfall in history; 1,122 inches, or 93 feet was recorded here in the winter of 1971–72. The mark finally fell in the winter of 1998–99, when Rainier had another near-record year, but was bested by the phenomenal 1,140 inches—or 95 feet—that fell on Mount Baker Ski Area between July 1, 1998, and June 30, 1999.

Paradise averages more than 700 inches a year, so it's not unusual to find accumulated snow on the ground from October through April; 20 feet of snow on the ground by midwinter is not unusual. Only in late summer and early autumn do the slopes above Paradise completely clear of snow, and even then permanent snowfields and glaciers remain to entice visitors. Generally, hiking trails around Paradise are free of snow by early July, but this varies widely with weather conditions.

Paradise is also the departure point for most climbing expeditions headed up the mountain (see Climbing, below), creating a fascinating parking-lot mishmash of hardened mountaineers and tourists in RVs with Nebraska plates. People-watching here is almost as good as mountain-viewing. In the winter, the Paradise parking lot takes on an entirely different, and by this we mean nasty, character. Weather can turn brutal in an instant, with winds gusting routinely to 30 mph, and snowstorms a constant threat. Woe is the winter Paradise visitor who ventures more than 100 feet from the car without a pack full of basic survival gear. Still, Paradise is surprisingly busy in the winter, when cross-country and telemark skiers flock here for some of the best backcountry skiing in the Northwest. Inner-tubers and snowboarders also flock to Paradise in the winter (see Skiing and Snow Play sections, below).

Sunrise

The park's second most-frequented—and arguably its most beautiful—auto-accessible spot is the Sunrise area at 6,400 feet on the northeast side of the mountain. Sunrise, which opens only after snow melts off the access road (usually by the Fourth of July), has a historic day lodge/visitors center, a ranger station, and a substantial picnic area. But most visitors come for the stunning views of the mountain—the best from any vista in the park. A multitude of both short and long hiking trails fan out from the parking lot (see Hiking, below), most winding through alpine meadows. Naturalists lead guided walks daily; stop by Sunrise Ranger Station for a schedule, or set out on your own. If you venture more than a couple of miles from the car, there's a better than even chance that you'll encounter deer, mountain goats, Rocky Mountain elk, or marmots.

Remember to bring your binoculars or spotting scope. From the parking lot, you can see the entire Emmons Glacier climbing route, where ant-size climbers inch their way up and down steps kicked into the snow. If you can't spot the route yourself, stop by Sunrise Ranger Station, which monitors climbing expeditions with a spotting scope. The station can turn into a beehive of activity if a mountain rescue operation is under way.

Hiking/Backpacking

The slopes around Mount Rainier, though heavily visited, contain some of the most splendid hiking terrain in the Northwest, if not the country. More so than other parks that share its stature, Rainier is best experienced on foot, either on one of its many short, paved interpretive trails, or on its magnificent 94-mile Wonderland Trail (see below), which circles the entire mountain. All hikers should note, however, that weather on Rainier is even more unpredictable than in most other Cascade hiking destinations. It can snow on the mountain any time—and we do mean any time. Hikers should never set out on a Rainier trail of any significant length without carrying extra clothing and the other "10 essentials" of backcountry travel (see the Washington Outdoors Primer, page vii). Many trails in the park are at high altitudes, where skin can sunburn quickly and dehydration and minor altitude sickness are significant concerns. Route-finding can become difficult when snow and fog set in. If that's not enough, flash floods are not uncommon in the park's heavily glaciated valleys. You've been warned.

Also, heed the rules, which are consistent with those in most other fragile wilderness areas: **no dogs, no bikes, no fires.** Groups are limited to 12 people. Day-hiking permits aren't required, but you must have a free **backcountry permit** to stay overnight, and they're limited for some popular backpacking areas. Campsite reservations at popular backcountry camps during the May-to-September peak season aren't required, but they're a good idea if you're headed into the backcountry during peak summer times, particularly on weekends. For a fee of $20, you can reserve a site up to two months in advance through the Longmire Wilderness Information Center; (360) 569-HIKE; fax (360) 569-3131. About 60 percent of the backcountry sites in the park are reservable in this fashion. Permits for the remaining sites are available first-come, first-served at Hiker Information Centers, found at Longmire, White River, and Carbon River. Overnight permits also are required for winter snow camping, which is allowed in virtually all of the park (at least as much of it as you can get to). Permits are available at all ranger stations, but your best bet is to shoot for one of the park's Hiker Info Centers.

All that said, enjoy yourself. We've rarely completed a hike on Rainier that wasn't memorable in some way—good or bad. This is raw, unfiltered Washington at its alpine best. Entire books have been written about Mount Rainier hiking and climbing trails, so we won't attempt to list the entire 300 miles here. That's what your spare time and hiking boots are for. Below are some favorites to get you started, grouped into the most popular park destination areas.

Longmire area

One of the most popular day hikes in the park is the **Comet Falls/Van Trump Park Trail** (moderate; 5.5 miles round trip), which begins at a trailhead on the Paradise Highway about 4 miles beyond Longmire, just before the Christine Falls Bridge. The trail, which doesn't melt out until midsummer, climbs steeply about 1.5 miles to great views of the 320-foot falls. The path continues up to Van Trump Park, a lovely alpine meadowland. Watch for mountain goats. Lower on the road, about 3 miles inside the park, is the **Kautz Creek Trail** (moderate/difficult; 11.4 miles round trip), which showcases the magnificent devastation wrought by a 1947 flood from a burst ice dam at the foot of the Kautz Glacier. The trail climbs steadily to Indian Henry's Hunting Grounds, one of Rainier's most beautiful alpine parklands, and a great place to see wildflowers in the summer.

From Longmire itself, options include the moderately scenic **Rampart Ridge Loop** (easy/moderate; 4.5 miles round trip), with connections to the Wonderland, Van Trump Park, and Comet Falls Trails (see above); and the kid-friendly **Trail of the Shadows Nature Trail** (easy; three-quarter mile round trip), an interesting walk to the former site of the Longmire Springs Hotel, as well as the ruins of an 1888 homestead cabin once occupied by the Longmire family. The trailhead is across the highway from the National Park Inn. Also near Longmire, a trail on the far side of the suspension bridge over the Nisqually River leads to **Eagle Peak** (difficult; 7.2 miles round trip), where views of Rainier and the Nisqually drainage are sublime. It's a steep hike, though, gaining some 3,000 feet in the 3.6 miles to the 5,700-foot saddle just below the summit. North of Longmire near Cougar Rock Campground is the **Carter Falls Trail** (easy; 2 miles round trip), which leads along the Paradise River to the remains of an old hydropower plant, then through a nice forest to Carter Falls.

West Side Road

Great hiking terrain in the Puyallup River drainage on the west side of Rainier is a bit lonelier than most other mountain locales, largely because the West Side Road, which turns north from Hwy 706 (Paradise Highway) about a mile beyond the Nisqually entrance, is washed out and permanently closed at Fish Creek, about 3.5 miles. The closure adds as much as 8 miles of road walking (one way) to the most popular trails in this area, turning short day hikes into long ones, or even overnighters. Some hikers ride mountain bikes up West Side Road beyond the washout to the trailhead of their choice.

A good destination here is **Klapatche Park** (difficult; 21 miles round trip), a spectacular backpacking route. Campsites on this route at Aurora Lake, Saint Andrews Lake, and Saint Andrews Park are so great they're overused, even with the washout's addition of 16 miles of road walking. A long but spectacular day hike in the same area is **Emerald Ridge Trail** (difficult; 16 miles round trip), which begins 4.5 miles up from the washout and climbs steeply to a connection with the Wonderland Trail.

Go left to Saint Andrews Park or right to the Tahoma Glacier and Glacier Island. Both are magnificent. A bit shorter, but only slightly less scenic, is the **Gobblers Knob/Lake George Trail** (moderate; 12 miles round trip), which begins 3 miles up from the washout and follows a very easy path to Lake George, a pleasant lunch spot. Fully fortified, you can proceed another mile up the hill to a fire lookout site atop Gobblers Knob, where the view of the Tahoma Glacier on the western face of Rainier is likely the best in the park.

Paradise

A number of short-but-memorable nature trails begin at the Paradise visitors center. All pass through alpine meadows and offer great views of Rainier and other Cascade peaks. They include the **Alta Vista Trail** loop (easy; 1.5 miles round trip), which climbs through some nice meadows to a viewpoint; and nearby **Nisqually Vista Trail** (easy; 1.2 miles round trip), a similar walk. Both can be hiked in about an hour. For a slightly longer walk, take the **Deadhorse Creek** and **Moraine Trails** about 1.25 miles to a great viewpoint high above the Nisqually Glacier. To get more altitude and better views, hop on the **Skyline Trail** and climb about 600 vertical feet in a mile to the **Glacier Vista Loop.**

For a more serious day hike, **Skyline Trail** loop (moderate/difficult; 5.8 miles round trip) is a great option. The trail climbs north beyond the Alta Vista Trail and short Glacier Vista Loop before coming to a fork at about 2 miles. The lower route leads across a permanent snowfield—if it's early in the day or cold, making the snow hard and slippery, take the upper route, which climbs around the snow and adds about three quarters of a mile to the trip. The steep climb to Camp Muir (see below) begins nearby. The trail tops out at about 7,000 feet, granting superb views at **Panorama Point** before connecting with the **Golden Gate Trail** (the quickest way back) or the **Mazama Ridge Trail,** which can be followed to the **Lakes Trail,** then back to the parking lot. The latter option adds about 2.5 miles to the loop distance. Note: Weather can turn nasty at 7,000 feet on Mount Rainier any day of the year. Bring proper gear.

Another great day hike is the **Mazama Ridge/Lakes Loop** (moderately difficult; 5 miles round trip), which begins above Paradise and follows the Mazama Ridge to the Reflection Lakes area, then climbs back to the Paradise parking lot. This is a busy, beautiful trail, offering the best mix of terrain and views in the Paradise area. Another popular day trip, particularly among backcountry skiers who flock here in spring and early summer, is **Paradise Glacier** (moderately difficult; 6 miles round trip), which begins on the Skyline Trail before branching off up Mazama Ridge and climbing to the toe of the Paradise Glacier, 6,400 feet. The path continues up the glacial moraine, which can be difficult to negotiate. Venturing out on the glacier—where the Paradise Ice Caves remain buried—is very hazardous, particularly in the late summer when hidden crevasses might lie just below the surface. The view is awesome, however, making this a great place to pack in a lunch and escape some of the Paradise-area masses.

The ultimate Paradise day hike, of course, is the straight-up climb to **Camp Muir** (difficult; 9 miles round trip), the 10,000-foot base camp for summit expeditions. The route begins on the Skyline Trail, then turns straight north up the mountain from either Pebble Creek or Panorama Point. From there on, it's a snow slog most of the year. This isn't for the meek. The route gains 4,600 feet—much of it in snow—from the Paradise parking lot. Don't do it if you're not properly trained and equipped for snow travel.

Two great day hikes begin just below Paradise, in the Reflection Lakes parking area on Stevens Canyon Road. The trail to **Bench** and **Snow Lakes** (easy; 2.6 miles round trip) is extremely crowded, largely because it's immensely beautiful and very accessible. The lakes, jewel-like ponds below Tatoosh Ridge, about 700 feet below Paradise, don't thaw out until late July, and the trail stays quite muddy most of the summer. Wildflowers are beautiful here through August. Some campsites are found here, but the trails are too busy to allow any semblance of an enjoyable overnight stay. Pick another trail for that. If all the people here drive you nuts, mark your calendar to come back in the winter, on snowshoes (see Skiing/Snowshoeing, below).

To escape some of the crowds, you can get up on Tatoosh Ridge by following the **Pinnacle Peak Trail** (moderate; 2.6 miles round trip) from the same parking area. The trail climbs steadily to 6,000-foot Pinnacle Saddle, between Pinnacle Peak (6,562 feet) and Plummer Peak (6,370 feet). Because it's detached a bit from the peak, this might be the best place in the Paradise area to photograph Mount Rainier.

Many hikers also choose the Paradise area as their departure point for hikes on the **Wonderland Trail** (very difficult; 94 miles round trip), the spectacular route that skirts the entire mountain. This is one of the nation's most magnificent backpacking adventures, requiring significant planning (food caches and campsites must be arranged with rangers before departure) and substantial stamina. The route passes through every conceivable Cascade Mountain landscape on its long journey, from placid meadows to deep forest to open snow and ice to frustrating, rocky moraines, and harrowing stream fords. In many respects, circumnavigating Rainier on the Wonderland Trail is more difficult than climbing the mountain: the trail gains and loses about 20,000 feet of elevation on the loop, and gains and losses of 4,000 feet in a day's hike are not uncommon.

Contact park rangers for information about cache points and designated campsites. And carry plenty of moleskin.

Sunrise

Many short, easy trails lead from the Sunrise parking lot to Emmons Glacier views. They include the half-mile **Emmons Vista Trail** and the placid **Sunrise Rim Trail,** which makes a nice, 1.5-mile (one way) stroll into the walk-in campground near Shadow Lake. Wildflowers, deer, and elk are thick here in the summer. The most popular day hike from Sunrise very likely is the **Fremont Lookout Trail** (moderate; 5.6 miles round trip), which leads to great views of the entire central Cascade Range. Mountain goats often are seen in this area. By branching in different directions from the same trail, you can pack your lunch to **Grand Park** and **Berkeley Park** (moderate; 13 miles round trip), or up the steep, occasionally dangerous route to **Burroughs Mountain** (difficult; 7 miles round trip), where views are magnificent (but don't try to cross the permanent snowfield without an ice ax).

Lower on the mountain, near the White River entrance station, are two memorable mountain routes. Both are great overnight backpacking routes—which naturally makes them among the most crowded trails in the park. The **Glacier Basin Trail** (moderate; 7 miles round trip) begins at White River Campground, following the White River past some old mining-operation remnants to a side path that leads to the foot of the massive Emmons Glacier, the largest ice sheet by surface area in the Lower 48. The trail ends at Glacier Basin Camp, a staging area for summit climbs via the Emmons/Winthrop Glacier route. From From the White River Road at a small parking lot near the Fryingpan Creek Bridge is the **Summerland/Panhandle Gap Trail** (moderate; 8.6 miles round trip), which climbs 4 miles through the Fryingpan Creek drainage before breaking into open slopes and, ultimately, the alpine wonderland of Summerland, rich with wildflowers and jaw-dropping views of Rainier, Little Tahoma, Goat Island Mountain, and the Fryingpan Glacier. Watch for mountain goats. If you've strategically placed another car or consider yourself an ace hitchhiker, you can make a longer trip by proceeding from Summerland to the Wonderland Trail and heading south to **Indian Bar** and an exit on the Stevens Canyon Road at Box Canyon. It's a one-way hike of about 16 miles, and a great way to get away from the crowds. (Another good option is to hike it with another party starting from the opposite end and swap car keys in the middle.)

Carbon Glacier

The northern slopes of Rainier are extremely rugged and extremely beautiful. They're also extremely popular, although the steep, rocky nature of many trails here tends to weed out all but the most determined backcountry travelers. (Note: The Carbon River Road has suffered from frequent washouts in recent years, particularly at one point 5 miles below Ipsut Creek Campground. Call for road information before you go.) An uncharacteristically easy, and lovely, day hike is the **Green Lake Trail** (easy; 3.6 miles round trip), which begins at Ranger Creek, 3 miles beyond the Carbon River entrance station. This is a grand family hike, passing through a wonderful old-growth forest, and beyond gushing Ranger Creek Falls to placid Green Lake, where (thankfully) no overnight camping is allowed.

From the main trailhead near Ipsut Creek Campground, hikers can venture up one leg of the Wonderland Trail to the impressive **Carbon Glacier** and beyond to magnificent alpine backcountry. Options include **Windy Gap** (difficult; 13 miles round trip), a strenuous but beautiful backpack trip; and the **Carbon Glacier/Mystic Lake Trail** (moderate/difficult; up to 15.2 miles round trip). The latter can be either a moderately easy (except for the rickety suspension bridge) 7-miles-round-trip hike to the toe of the lowest-elevation glacier in the Lower 48, or a curse-inducing haul to Mystic Lake, where you can stare directly into Rainier's magnificently sheer north face, the Willis Wall. You can also follow the Wonderland Trail south from Carbon Glacier to the meadowlands of **Seattle Park** and **Spray Park.**

Mowich Lake

Rough, gravelly Mowich Lake Road ends at a walk-in camping area that also serves as trailhead for the **Spray Park Trail** (moderate/difficult; 6 miles round trip). This extremely popular day-hiking trail drops slightly to the Wonderland Trail, then climbs steeply through the forest to Spray Falls before opening to the wildflower meadows and parklands of Spray Park. It's beautiful in midsummer, providing easy off-trail access to snow-play and skiing areas on the remnant Flett Glacier. Backpackers can continue north on the Wonderland Trail to Seattle Park and Ipsut Campground, then take the connecting Ipsut Creek Trail back to Mowich Lake, for a loop of 15.5 miles. Another popular day hike from Mowich Lake leads to **Tolmie Peak Lookout** (moderate; 6.4 miles round trip), which offers great views of the northwest side of Rainier. Many hikers walk only as far as **Eunice Lake,** a pretty spot about 3 miles up the trail. The short access trail to the lookout is very steep. No camping is allowed at the lake, although a few permits are issued for designated sites nearby.

Stevens Canyon/Ohanapecosh

Day-hiking trails in the southeast corner of the park don't offer views of the mountain, but they're scenic, nonetheless. The **Grove of the Patri-**

archs (easy; 1.3-mile loop) is a resilient stand of ancient Douglas fir, hemlock, and western red cedar trees that have been nursing on the rich, clean waters of the Ohanapecosh River for centuries. The trail crosses the river on a steel suspension bridge and loops through trees as big as 35 feet in circumference. Some are believed to be 1,000 years old. The trailhead is on Stevens Canyon Road, just north of Ohanapecosh Campground and Visitors Center (just beyond the Stevens Canyon entrance station/fee collection booth). This is a popular cross-country skiing destination in the winter (see Cross-Country Skiing, below).

For a longer taste of the same, get on the nearby **Eastside Trail** (moderate; 9 miles one way), which follows the river between Ohanapecosh Campground and a second trailhead about 6 miles north on Cayuse Pass Highway. Another easy, primo day hike, the **Silver Falls Loop** (easy; 3 miles round trip), begins near the Ohanapecosh Visitors Center and leads to a former hot springs resort site and 75-foot Silver Falls, where the Ohanapecosh River powers through a stunning gorge crossed by a log bridge. The trail also is accessible from Loop B of the Ohanapecosh Campground and the Laughingwater Creek Trail off Hwy 123. For a nice day hike, start at Ohanapecosh Campground, hike the Silver Falls trail north, cross the highway and walk the Grove of the Patriarchs Loop, then return the way you came. It's one of the most scenic forest walks in the entire park.

Climbing

We look up there every day (well, at least in the summer) and see The Mountain. And some of us just can't resist climbing it. Mount Rainier is attempted by thousands of climbers every year, with skill levels ranging from world-class alpinist to first-time weekend warrior. Many people make it, many don't. Nearly all who do make it come home at least partially whipped, saying the summit trek was the most difficult physical thing they've ever done—and ever plan to do. While the primary climbing route on the south face of Rainier isn't technically difficult, the elevation, 14,411 feet, is enough to make a summit climb very challenging. Altitude affects many climbers, and fickle weather can very quickly turn a sunny snow slog into a wintry hell. Generally, the summer climbing season is relatively safe. Good-weather days can see dozens of climbers reach the summit. But would-be summiteers should not underestimate the mountain's considerable peril. Many climbers—including many experienced alpinists—have died on Rainier. And many, many more have turned back, exhausted.

Thanks largely to the considerable expertise of Rainier Mountaineering, Inc., one of the nation's top **climbing-guide services** (it's co-owned by Lou Whittaker, twin brother of Jim, first American climber atop Everest), you don't need climbing experience to get up Rainier. You do need to be in good shape and to have the good sense to follow the directions of a veteran guide. The typical guided climb on Rainier includes a partial day of training, followed by a long trek from Paradise to Camp Muir, at 10,000 feet. Climbers rise early and head for the summit via Disappointment Cleaver and the Ingraham Glacier. For guide information, call RMI at Paradise, (360) 569-2227, in the summer, or Tacoma, (206) 627-6242, in the winter. You can also climb the mountain without a guide, although anyone who does so without considerable experience is a fool. A $15 climbing fee is charged. Call the park; (360) 569-2211. Rainier can be, and is, climbed all year-round, but peak climbing season is from May to July.

Camping

Campers are limited to 14 days at all Mount Rainier campgrounds. And after the trouble you go through to score a space, you'll want to stay the full two weeks. Nabbing one of Rainier's 600 campsites in midsummer can be a lot like winning the lottery. Everybody's looking for one, and only a fraction wind up happy when the sun goes down. Rainier's campgrounds are generally open June through mid-October, except for Sunshine Point, which is open all year. They provide water and flush toilets, but no showers or RV hookups. Sites, at this writing $6 to $14, are first-come, first-served, with notable exceptions: Reservations at the park's two most popular campgrounds, Ohanapecosh and Cougar Rock, are *required* from late June through the end of Labor Day weekend; 800-365-CAMP; www.reservations.nps.gov.

Paradise-area visitors can choose from **Sunshine Point** (18 sites along the Nisqually River; open all year) or **Cougar Rock** (200 sites and 5 group sites, about 2.5 miles beyond Longmire). Sunrise visitors head for **White River,** which has 112 sites near the White River entrance. Note that White River, at 4,400 feet, opens later than other campgrounds, usually in late June. If you're entering at Stevens Canyon, **Ohanapecosh** is the best bet, with 205 sites along this pretty river. It's open from late May to mid-October. (An alternative is **La Wis Wis,** a Forest Service campground near Packwood; see the White Pass Corridor chapter.)

On the north side of the park, **Ipsut Creek** offers 28 campsites, plus a group camp. The campground, which has no piped water, is at 2,800 feet, and is open when snow conditions allow. A large walk-in campground with 30 sites is found at **Mowich Lake,** 4,950 feet. The campground, at the end of often rough, unpaved Mowich Lake Road, is generally open from July to mid-October. Campers need backcountry permits, available on-site on weekends or from the Carbon River Ranger Station other times. Mowich Lake has no piped water.

Downhill Skiing

Widely regarded as the state's premier alpine ski resort, **Crystal Mountain** is not inside the national park—but you can see Rainier from its summit. Crystal, on Hwy 410 on the mountain's northeast side, has the state's biggest vertical drop, most lifts, and by far the most diverse terrain. This is a big ski area, offering an in-bounds terrain with enough variety to keep any skier happy and an unpatrolled backcountry area that ranks with the best in the West.

The resort also offers a small number of condominium-style slopeside lodgings—a rarity for Washington skiers (see www.skicrystal.com for rates and information). That's a particular blessing, given how difficult Crystal can be to drive to. Thousands of people make it on winter weekends, but the commute to Crystal can be trying. Most of the drive is two-lane road, the upper portions of which get nasty when the snow is dumping.

The mountain got a major boost in 1998, when the longstanding local ownership group sold its entire holdings to Boyne USA, owners of Big Sky in Montana, and Brighton, in Utah, and a number of other notable destination winter resorts. The new owners sank more than $10 million into mountain improvements, expanding and updating the day lodge and rental facilities and adding two new "six-pack" detachable chairs to combat Crystal's chronic lift-line problems. Another long-awaited improvement was scheduled for the winter of 2000–2001: a high-speed, detachable quad chair to replace the old double chair in Green Valley, a choice area at the resort. Long-range plans call for expanded lifts into the area's fabled North and South Backcountry areas, as well as a 100-passenger tram, which would shuttle passengers to a ridgetop restaurant/day lodge all year around. In all, Boyne plans to spend about $40 million at Crystal over the next decade. Possible plans include a new hotel and conference center.

Skiers give mixed grades to the new management (chief complaint: higher midweek prices) but generally agree things are on the upswing at Crystal. All of them agree that Crystal, on a good snow day, is tough to beat. The ridgetop view of Mount Rainier from the top of the Rainier Express lift is truly spectacular, and the mountain's open bowls provide a great mix of fast, steep ski terrain. Experts usually ride the Rainier Express and turn right, headed for areas such as Green Valley or the North or South Backcountry.

Most of that, however, depends on good snow, which can be wildly inconsistent here. A bare base area has been a consistent problem at Crystal, although upper-mountain lifts typically have a very reliable base from early December through mid-April. It can dump hard and fast here. A major storm in the winter of 1994 dumped 65 inches of snow on the resort in a single 24-hour period. Astonishing, but unfortunately fairly rare. Crystal's most consistently heavy snowfall comes late in the winter, during February and March. That makes it a great spring skiing area. In recent years, such as the record Cascade snowfall winter of 1998–99, the mountain actually reopened for skiing in Green Valley for a couple weekends during the early summer. The resort also has a small summer operation, ferrying hikers, mountain bikers, and Summit House diners to the top of the Rainier Express lift for a fee.

Crystal stats: Elevation: 4,400 to 7,012 feet. Lifts: 10; two high-speed detachable six-passenger lifts, one express quad, two triples, four doubles, one surface lift. Skiable acreage: 2,300, including 1,000 acres of backcountry terrain. Prices: Adult tickets are $39 daily at this writing. Hours: 9am to 4pm Monday through Friday, 8:30am to 4pm Saturdays, Sundays, and holidays; night skiing 4pm to 8pm Friday, Saturday, and Sunday. Season: Mid-November through mid-April; weekends through May, snow permitting. *On Hwy 410 39 miles southeast of Enumclaw; mountain information (630) 663-2265, snow line (888) SKI-6199; www.skicrystal.com.*

Cross-Country Skiing

Mount Rainier is the backcountry skiing capital of the Northwest. For cross-country skiers and snowshoers, an abundance of great terrain is found both inside and outside the park. Paradise usually has skiable snow by late October, and almost always by Thanksgiving. Whenever you go, make sure you're equipped with tire chains. The road to Paradise is plowed and kept open all winter, but it can be treacherous above Longmire, and rangers will turn you away if you attempt it without four-wheel drive or chains (see Getting There, above).

Inside the park, **Paradise**—the only National Park area open all winter—is the skiing focus. Many good cross-country and telemark routes begin here. Beginners will enjoy the flat, easy pace of the **Stevens Canyon Road,** which is closed to auto traffic (and buried in about 30 feet of snow) at the Paradise parking lot. The road drops about 500 feet in a 3-mile descent through Paradise Valley to Reflection Lakes. There's no grooming here, but it's usually easy to follow the tracks made by previous skiers. Stronger skiers can continue on a trail to **Narada Falls** parking lot, where a cozy, heated changing room is open all winter. If you have friends nice enough to come pick you up, you can thaw out and ignore the steep ski back up the hill. Also good for beginners is the 1.2-mile **Nisqually Vista Loop** from Jackson Visitors Center.

When there's enough snow down low, ski-touring trails also can be found at **Longmire,** 2,700 feet lower on the mountain. Another popular ski route is the east end of the Stevens Canyon Road, which can be skied from the Stevens Canyon entrance to the **Grove of the Patriarchs Trail** (see Hiking/Backpacking, above). Similarly, many of the Longmire- and Paradise-area trails listed under Hiking/Backpacking, above, can also be skied in the winter. Check with rangers about avalanche danger. Ski **rentals** are available at Longmire Ski Touring Center; (360) 569-2411.

More advanced cross-country and telemark skiers go straight up the mountain from Paradise to any of a number of wide-open winter snowfields. Popular intermediate routes include the 1-mile **Alta Vista Trail,** the 2.5-mile **Panorama Point Loop**, and the 3-mile **Mazama Ridge Route,** which leads to the Paradise Glacier year-round snowfield. Get a good topographic map and know where you're headed. Make no mistake: Backcountry skiing is an inherently risky activity made even more dangerous by the weather at Paradise. Avalanche danger is considerable, and winter storms often are so strong that skiers are completely blinded very quickly. It's easy to get lost, even if you think you know where you're going. Don't ski alone. Newcomers should hook up with at least one other skier who's expert at route-finding. Always carry a pack with survival gear sufficient to wait out a long storm. Many telemarkers in this area carry avalanche transceivers.

West of the park, the **Mount Tahoma Scenic Trails Association** maintains an extensive 145-kilometer (103-mile) **trail network,** mostly on logging roads and trails on both sides of Hwy 706, below Rainier's south slopes. The trails are free, and reservations are available for overnight stays in the association's yurts and backcountry cabins. About 32 kilometers of trails are groomed. Skiers parking in trail lots must have state Sno-Park stickers, available at outdoor retailers, ranger stations, and ski shops. Stop by the MTSTA office in Ashford, or call (360) 569-2451, for a trail map and information.

Snow Play

Paradise isn't just a snooty skinny-ski heaven. Kids love it, too, particularly those of the inner-tube persuasion. The park makes a fuss every year about kids scalping off trees and colliding with themselves and other objects as they hurtle down the lower slopes at Paradise. But they ultimately wind up establishing an organized, groomed inner-tube area every winter, with separate chutes for little kids and big kids. Before you go, call the park to make sure the tubes are flying. **Tubing** often doesn't get good at Paradise until mid- to late December, when the snow gets deep enough to cover the small trees and fragile alpine plants above Paradise.

Snowshoeing

Paradise is a snowshoer's dream, with walkable snow available at least nine months out of the year. Newcomers to the sport are welcome here. Park rangers lead **guided snowshoe walks** from Paradise on weekends and during holiday seasons. The walks are free, with the park usually requesting a small donation to cover snowshoe rentals. No experience is necessary. It's a lot of fun. Call the park information line, (360) 569-2211, for details.

If you want to go it on your own, two particularly good novice snowshoe routes can be found in the Paradise area. From the **Narada Falls** parking lot on the road between Longmire and Paradise, follow the orange-wand-marked trail up through the trees (to your left, as you pass the rest room/warming hut) to the snow-covered Stevens Canyon Road, which can be followed just over a mostly flat mile to **Reflection Lakes,** which offers a grand view of Rainier's south face. The area around the lake, frozen in winter, is a good lunch/overnight camp spot. The round trip is about 3 miles. More advanced 'shoers can continue from here on a trail up **Pinnacle Peak** in the Tatoosh Range.

From the Paradise parking lot itself, most of the ski trails described in Cross-country Skiing, above, make good snowshoe routes. A popular novice route begins at the far end of the parking lot, where you can climb over the snowbank and follow the **Stevens Canyon Road** about 2 miles downhill through Paradise Valley to the Reflection Lakes area (see Cross-country skiing, above). **Rental** snowshoes are available at Longmire Ski Touring Center; (360) 569-2411.

Bicycling

Rainier's highways are open to cyclists, and some park roads—notably the **Stevens Canyon Road** between Paradise and Ohanapecosh—make beautiful summertime rides. But none of Rainier's 300 miles of trails are available to the fat-tire fans—largely because virtually all of the park is designated wilderness. The only place mountain bikes are commonly seen in Rainier is **West Side Road** above the washout 3.5 miles up from the Paradise Highway. There, hikers often bring bikes to reduce their time walking up the abandoned roadway to several popular trailheads in the Puyallup River drainage (see Hiking/Backpacking, above).

Fishing

An angler's paradise Rainier is not. Some **trout** are caught in Green Lake in the Carbon River drainage, and in nearby Mowich Lake (see Hiking/Backpacking, above). But like all other lakes in the park, these don't receive planted fish. Dewey Lake—a popular backpacking destination just outside the park's boundaries south of Chinook Pass, along the Pacific Crest Trail—holds some **brook trout.**

Wildlife Watching

Mount Rainier National Park is one of the richest wildlife areas in the state. **Mountain goats** are frequent visitors to alpine campsites along the park's 300 miles of trails. The easiest to negotiate probably is the Mount Fremont Lookout Trail from Sunrise Visitors Center. Backpacking destinations such as Summerland/Panhandle Gap and Van Trump Park also are consistently reliable goat haunts. See Hiking/Backpacking, above, for details. The Sunrise area in general is rife with wildlife. We almost always see friendly **black-tailed deer** here, and very often encounter **Rocky Mountain elk.** Spring and fall are the best times to spot elk.

Photography

Any fool with a camera should come home with at least one great photograph from a summertime visit to Mount Rainier. Pick a direction, pick a time of day, pick an exposure. Everywhere you look, Rainier is photogenic. Some nature photographers we know have spent the better part of their lifetimes exploring the nooks and crannies of Rainier. They keep coming back for more, swearing the mountain is one of the most diverse nature-shooting havens on the planet.

Generally, it's a given that the very best pictures produced at Mount Rainier have two characteristics. They're usually taken some distance off the road, often on one of the park's 300 miles of trails. And they're usually not pictures of the mountain, which is too close to be squeezed into a fitting landscape from most areas of the park. What to shoot, then? Wildlife. Wildflowers. Ice formations. Waterfalls. Clouds. Marmots. Rivers. Big trees. Ferns. Park rangers' Smokey Bear hats or mint green patrol cruisers. You name it. Rainier is a Kodachrome gold mine.

If you insist on shooting the mountain—and who among us has ever been able to resist?—don't go to Paradise to do it. The **Sunrise Visitors Center** on the northeast side of the mountain provides far better vistas. Or try the **Pinnacle Peak Trail** (see Hiking/Backpacking, above). As usual, very early or very late light is best. **Rainier** sometimes lights up in brilliant crimson alpenglow just after sunset. Choose your spot and bring a tripod.

Accessible Outdoors

Wheelchair-accessible dining facilities are found at the **Paradise Inn** (summer only), the **Jackson Visitors Center** at Paradise (via steep paved ramps), and the **Sunrise Lodge** snack bar. Barrier-free campsites are found at **Sunshine Point** (sites 1 and 3), **Cougar Rock** (5 of the sites), and **Ohanapecosh** (3 sites in Loop D). Those campgrounds also offer barrier-free rest rooms. Facilities with wheelchair access include the **Longmire Museum,** the Jackson Visitors Center at Paradise (wheelchairs also may be borrowed here; inquire at the front desk), the **Ohanapecosh Visitors Center,** and the **Sunrise Visitors Center.**

Accessible rest rooms are found at Sunshine Point Campground, **Kautz Creek picnic area,** Longmire, Cougar Rock Campground, the Paradise Plaza near the Paradise Inn, the Jackson Visitors Center, Ohanapecosh Campground and **White River Campground.** Accessible picnic tables are located at Kautz Creek and Cougar Rock picnic areas.

Several barrier-free interpretive trails also make pleasant journeys for wheelchair users or parents with strollers. These include the **Kautz Creek Trail;** the 0.7-mile **Trail of the Shadows** at Longmire, across from the National Park Inn; the **Nisqually Vista Trail,** just south of the visitors center at Paradise (difficult for wheelchairs, accessible to strollers); the first mile of the **Grove of the Patriarchs Trail** near the Ohanapecosh River, near the Stevens Canyon entrance (difficult for wheelchairs, often used by strollers); and the **Ohanapecosh Hot Springs Trail** in the Ohanapecosh Campground (also difficult for wheelchairs, often used by strollers.) At Sunrise, the **Sourdough Ridge Trail** makes a 1-mile loop through mountain meadows. It's not technically accessible to wheelchairs, but often is used by families with strollers. For questions or other special access needs, call (360) 569-2211, ext. 3314, to speak to a ranger. The park's TDD line is (360) 569-2177.

outside in

Restaurants

Naches Tavern ★   Now this is the way to do a country tavern. $; 58411 Hwy 410E, Greenwater; (360) 663-2267. ♿

Lodgings

Mountain Meadows Inn and B&B ★★   This inn is privately situated on 11 landscaped acres. $$; 28912 Hwy 706E, Ashford; (360) 569-2788; www.mt-rainier.net.

Nisqually Lodge ★   Just a few miles west of the Nisqually entrance to Mount Rainier National Park. *$$; 31609 Hwy 706, Ashford; (360) 569-8804; www.mtrainier-mt.com.*

Silver Skis Chalet ★★   These condos are your best bet if you want to stay right on the mountain. *$$; Crystal Mountain Blvd, Crystal Mountain; (360) 663-2558 or (888) 668-4368; www.crystalmtlodging-wa.com.* &

Wellspring ★★   Two spas nestled in a sylvan glade surrounded by evergreens. *$$; 54922 Kernahan Rd, Ashford; (360) 569-2514; www.info atmtrainier.com.*

More Information

Crystal Mountain snow phone: *(888) SKI-6199.*

Department of Transportation pass report: *(888) SNO-INFO; www.wsdot.wa.gov/sno-info.*

Mount Rainier National Park Headquarters: *Tahoma Woods, Star Rte, Ashford, WA 98304; (360) 569-2211; www.nps.gov/mora.*

> **Backcountry reservations:** *(360) 569-HIKE.*
> **Camping reservations:** *(800) 365-2267.*
> **Jackson Visitor Center:** *(360) 569-2211, ext. 2328.*
> **Longmire Ranger Station:** *(360) 569-2211, ext. 3314.*
> **Mount Rainier Guest Services** (park lodging): *(360) 569-2275.*
> **Nisqually Ranger Station:** *(360) 569-2211, ext. 2390.*
> **Ohanapecosh Ranger Station:** *(360) 569-2211, ext. 2352.*
> **Paradise Ranger Station:** *(360) 569-221,1 ext. 2314.*
> **Sunrise Ranger Station:** *(360) 569-2211, ext. 2357.*
> **White River Ranger Station:** *(360) 569-2211, ext. 2356.*
> **Wilkeson Ranger Station:** *(360) 829-5127.*

White Pass Corridor

From Packwood east to Naches, north through the William O. Douglas Wilderness, and south through the Goat Rocks Wilderness to the Yakama Indian Reservation, including Rimrock Lake, the Tieton River, White Pass Ski Area, and Tatoosh Wilderness.

The place rocks. And the rocks of the place are some of the grandest anywhere. White Pass visitors who aren't geology buffs when they leave Packwood likely will be before they arrive in Naches. The White Pass corridor provides a cutaway glimpse into the violent volcanic past of the South Cascades. Evidence is everywhere you look, from fascinating layers of volcanic rock in highway road cuts to 6,000-foot cinder cones that look like they might have erupted only recently—and could once again at any time.

Most who explore the White Pass area on foot, however, are struck less by the area's volcanism than by the stunningly beautiful alpine terrain it has left in its wake. White Pass is the drive-through window for Washington wilderness. As you travel east between Packwood and White Pass summit, you're literally surrounded by it. To the north is Mount Rainier National Park and the 167,000-acre William O. Douglas Wilderness, named for the late Supreme Court justice who hiked extensively here, chronicling his journeys in *Of Men and Mountains*. The volcano-pocked wilderness is dotted with small lakes, sprawling meadows, and fantastic alpine ridges. To the south is the spectacular 105,000-acre Goat Rocks Wilderness, whose centerpiece, the Goat Rocks, is a series of impressive 8,000-foot crags that mark the site of an ancient extinct volcano.

Both wilderness areas are reached by hiking a short distance north or south of US Highway 12. This rugged country lures hikers

Hikers skirt a large lava flow in the Gifford Pinchot National Forest

up steep mountain paths to stunning vistas and down cool, quiet paths along the Clear Fork Cowlitz and Tieton Rivers. But you don't have to invest a lot of sweat to be awed by the sights of White Pass. US Highway 12 through White Pass is one of the more beautiful mountain highways in the state, particularly in the autumn, when aspens, alders, and larches on the east side of the pass burst into a brilliant yellow. It is perhaps even more fantastic in the winter, when deep snows lure skiers to one of the state's most scenic alpine ski areas.

White Pass is open all year, except for occasional snow closures near the 4,500-foot summit. A central stretch of about 20 miles often is coated with packed snow and ice. Carrying chains is a must in the winter. No matter when you visit, the roadside views are grand. A short distance from the highway are vistas of the Goat Rocks and the massive Rimrock Lake, a prominent wildlife-viewing area, and a string of serene campsites along the liquid-crystal Tieton, a favorite of anglers and whitewater rafters.

The total package is impressive enough for the mixed-in volcanic remnants to be a bit troubling. Normally we take it for granted that the wonders left in the wake of volcanoes are potentially temporary (see Mount St. Helens for proof). But we'd sure hate to see White Pass, in its present state, go before we do.

Getting There

*The White Pass Highway (US 12) turns east from Interstate 5 south of
Chehalis, then continues about 85 miles to White Pass and another 35 miles to
Naches, east of Yakima. Allow 3 hours' travel time from Seattle to White Pass
summit. US 12 at Morton is connected north to Elbe/Hwy 706 (the Longmire
Road into Mount Rainier National Park) via Hwy 7. On US 12 between Packwood and the summit, Hwy 123 goes north into Mount Rainier National Park
to Ohanapecosh and Hwy 410, which loops down to meet US 12 again just
west of Naches.*

inside out

Hiking/Backpacking

The White Pass Highway is the primary access route to dozens of good
short day hikes and extended backpack trips into the William O. Douglas
Wilderness to the north and the spectacular Goat Rocks Wilderness to the
south. For a full trail inventory, maps, and current permit information,
contact the Packwood Information Center, (360) 494-0600, or Naches
Ranger District, (509) 653-2205. Note that a **Northwest Forest Pass,** $5
per day or $30 annually, is required to park in many Forest
Service–administered trailheads in this area. They're available from ranger
stations, from many private vendors, on-line at www.naturenw.org, or by
calling (800) 270-7504. Following is a list of favorites, arranged from west
to east beginning at Packwood.

Just north of Packwood is **Tatoosh Ridge** (difficult; 9 miles round
trip), a prominent high point popular for its awesome views of Mount
Rainier. The trail begins on Forest Road 5272 (reached from US 12 near
Packwood via Forest Roads 52 and 5270) and climbs steeply to a spectacular view at the old Tatoosh Lookout. Hikers with two cars can walk the
entire ridge as a through hike, exiting at a southern trailhead along Road
5292. There are more good day hikes a short distance to the north, near
the Stevens Canyon entrance to Mount Rainier National Park.

For a sampling of the greater wonders that await south of the high-
way, drive about 4.5 miles east of Packwood, turn south on Roads 4610
and 4612, and try the **Bluff Lake Trail** (difficult; 13.2 miles round trip).
The going is very steep at first, but relents somewhat after the first couple
of miles. Your reward is a beautiful lake and beautiful views of the Goat
Rocks Range from the ridgeline of Coal Creek Mountain. Nearby, the
Three Peaks Trail (moderate; 10.8 miles round trip), which begins on
Road 1266 (turn south 2 miles east of Packwood), is a fairly uneventful

trail, but views of the area are good from the top of a ridge above Packwood Lake, on the west border of the Goat Rocks Wilderness.

Moving east, two delightful day-hiking trails weave through the cool forests of the upper Cowlitz River drainage. The first, **Clear Fork** (easy; up to 19.2 miles round trip), begins on Forest Road 46, about 5 miles east of Packwood, and follows the Clear Fork Cowlitz River on a very flat trail (it gains only about 1,200 feet in 8 miles). It's an easy walk, suitable for children most of the year. Trout fishing is fair in the river, and small Lily Lake is a nice bonus attraction. The **Clear Lost Trail** (moderate; up to 13.2 miles round trip), on US 12 about 17 miles east of Packwood, drops steeply for about 2 miles to the Clear Fork. Here, it ends—unless you're willing to get wet. Hikers who ford the river can proceed up the other side of the valley to fine views from Coyote Ridge.

White Pass is a crossing for the **Pacific Crest Trail,** which can be hiked south from here through the entire Goat Rocks Wilderness—a stretch that many through-hikers say is among the most spectacular sections of the 2,600-mile Mexico-to-Canada trail. If you're heading south, you'll climb up through the forest to the top of Hogback Ridge and find great campsites at **Shoe Lake** (about 6.5 miles). The route continues south past Lutz Lake and Elk Pass, and ultimately to Cispus Pass in the Mount Adams Wilderness (about 13 miles in). Northbound hikers head into the heart of the William O. Douglas Wilderness on a grade that's uncharacteristically flat for the PCT. Many good campsites are found on this 29-mile stretch between White Pass and Chinook Pass. Highlights include **Deer Lake, Sand Lake, Cowlitz Pass, Snow Lake,** and **Dewey Lakes,** which is a popular backpack destination for Mount Rainier National Park visitors. Backpackers usually can hike the stretch from one pass to the other in about 3 days. Note: If you're headed this way in late summer, the mosquitoes can be maddening.

Just east of White Pass summmit, on US 12 near Leech Lake, is the trailhead for the **Dumbbell Lakes Loop** (moderate; 15.7 miles round trip), a popular overnight trip that starts on a leg of the PCT, then heads north between Cramer Mountain and Spiral Butte to a plethora of lakes in this volcanic area, returning south back to US 12 via the Cramer Lake and Dark Meadows Trails. The best campsites are at Buesch Lake (3.8 miles) and Dumbbell Lake (4.3 miles). It's a beautiful area, but mosquitoes are intolerable here in midsummer. Try it in the fall, after the first freeze. Five miles farther east, also on the north side of the highway, is **Spiral Butte** (difficult; 12 miles round trip), a steep climb to the top of an interesting old cinder cone. The 5,900-foot summit offers grand views of the Goat Rocks Range and beyond. Just east of Rimrock Lake, between Hause Creek and Riverbend Campgrounds (see Camping, below), Forest Road

1500 heads north to Road 199, where you'll find the Cash Prairie trailhead and the **Ironstone Mountain Trail** (moderately difficult; up to 13 miles one way). This is a very quiet, scenic trail that stays high on an east-west ridgeline, with a multitude of possibilities. Day hikers can proceed just a couple of miles to great William O. Douglas Wilderness vistas; backpackers can drop north into the Rattlesnake Creek drainage or find great views and camping meadows on the flanks of Burnt Mountain (6,536 feet) and Shellrock Peak (6,835 feet). A highlight, and the best camping destination, is Fox Meadow below Ironstone Mountain, at about 6.5 miles. You can return the way you came or continue north to an exit in the Bumping Lake area, for a one-way trip of about 10.5 miles.

Some of the most beautiful hikes in the White Pass Corridor lie farther south, in the upper Tieton River drainage of the Goat Rocks Wilderness. A joint trailhead for three of them is reached by driving 29 miles east of Packwood to Forest Road 12 near Clear Lake, turning south, and proceeding to Road 1207. From the end of this road, the **Tieton Meadows Trail** (moderate; 9.4 miles round trip) is a great midsummer hike for wildflower fans, with meadows full of blossoms a short distance down the trail. Then it gets serious, climbing sharply up 7,000-foot Pinegrass Ridge, which offers great views, but no water or campsites. From the same trailhead, the **North Fork Tieton Trail** (moderate; 9.8 miles round trip) winds through a nice forest for a couple of miles before breaking into open, boulder-strewn meadows, where the grade gets steep but the wide-open alpine scenery is spectacular. The trail climbs all the way to Tieton Pass, where it joins the Pacific Crest Trail. A third enticing option here is **Hidden Springs Trail** (moderate; 7 miles round trip), which branches off the North Fork Tieton Trail at about 1.5 miles and climbs steeply to beautiful alpine campsites in a meadow around a cold-water spring. Great side trips are available on the nearby PCT.

From the nearby Conrad Meadows trailhead (at the end of Road 100, reached via Tieton River Road, which leaves US 12 near Rimrock Lake), hikers can take **Bear Creek** (moderate; 15 miles round trip) and **South Fork Tieton** (moderate; 9 miles round trip) **Trails.** The first climbs to breathtaking views at a former lookout site atop 7,336-foot Bear Creek Mountain; the second is a top-notch backpacking route through some beautiful (and relatively flat) meadows, then moderately uphill to lovely **Surprise Lake.**

The other highly popular Goat Rocks Wilderness area is reached by driving south from US 12, 2 miles west of Packwood on Forest Roads 21 and 2150 to Chambers Lake. Here, a connecting path leads about 5 miles to **Snowgrass Flat** and a nearby junction with the Pacific Crest Trail on its most spectacular local stretch, past the Goat Rocks themselves and a beautiful alpine vista at Cispus Pass. You can combine the trail with the PCT and the **Goat Ridge Trail** for a memorable backpacking loop trip. Mountain goats, oddly enough, are frequently seen in the Goat Rocks.

Camping

West-side White Pass (Gifford Pinchot National Forest)

Packwood Information Center; (360) 494-0600:

The largest campground in the region, **La Wis Wis,** is on the Ohanapecosh River, just north of US 12 about 7 miles east of Packwood. This Forest Service camp, which sits at 1,400 feet, has 90 sites (no hookups; RVs to 24 feet), as well as picnic grounds and a scenic river overlook. It gets a lot of overflow traffic from Mount Rainier National Park (only about 7 miles away), where reservations are required from July 1 through Labor Day. La Wis Wis is open from late May through September. Campsites can be reserved up to 240 days in advance; (877) 444-6777; www.reserveusa.com. *From US 12 just west of the junction with Hwy 123, turn north on Forest Rd 1272 and proceed a half mile to the campground.*

Two smaller Forest Service camps about 20 minutes east of Packwood, **Summit Creek** (6 sites) and **Soda Springs** (8 sites), are free campgrounds (although all vehicles must have a **Northwest Forest Pass,** available at ranger stations and retail outlets) along Summit Creek, open summers only, with no piped water. *On US 12 about a mile east of the Hwy 123 junction, turn left onto very bumpy Forest Rds 45 and 4510.*

Another option is the **private** Packwood RV Park, with showers, hookups, and full services. *On US 12 at Packwood; (360) 494-5145.*

White Pass's cross-country ski venue (see Skiing, below) turns into a campground in the summer, when it's the site of **White Pass Lake Campground.** The primitive (no piped water) camp has 16 sites (no hookups; RVs to 20 feet) on the east side of pretty Leech Lake. It's open from June to November. Note that the elevation is 4,500 feet, so dress accordingly. The Pacific Crest Trail (see Hiking/Backpacking, above) is a short walk away, as is a boat launch. An adjacent horse camp has 6 campsites, hitching rails, and other equestrian facilities. *On US 12 at the summit.*

East-side White Pass (Wenatchee National Forest)

Naches Ranger District; (509) 653-2205:

Reservations note: Several of the campgrounds in the Naches Ranger District formerly accepted reservations through the Forest Service's contractor, the National Recreation Reservation System. As of 2000, none of them do. Too many problems, rangers say.

On the north side of the highway just east of White Pass is **Dog Lake,** another small (11 sites) free campground with no piped water. Farther east on the south side of the highway is **Clear Lake,** which has 65 sites spread throughout two separate campgrounds (north and south) on Clear Lake, part of the Rimrock Lake reservoir. Fishing and wildlife viewing are the primary activities here (see appropriate sections in this chapter, below). The campgrounds are open summers only.

Three other Forest Service campgrounds encircle scenic Rimrock Lake reservoir. **Indian Creek** (39 sites; RVs to 32 feet), **Peninsula** (dispersed camping), and **South Fork/South Fork Bay** (15 sites) all are on or near Rimrock Lake, which is massive when it's full in the early summer, but becomes a large mudflat by late fall. All these campgrounds are open summers only. Only Indian Creek has piped water. Peninsula and South Fork are both about 4 miles south of US 12 via County Road 1000.

Farther down the Tieton drainage are two more small campgrounds: **Hause Creek** (42 sites; RVs to 30 feet) and **Willows** (16 sites; RVs to 20 feet). These are wild, fairly primitive campgrounds, but exceptionally beautiful in the fall, when aspen, alder, and larch trees burst into brilliant gold. They're popular with anglers and, in the fall, river rafters (see Rafting, below). Both campgrounds provide drinking water and are open from April or May through November. Note: Two former small campgrounds in this area, Wild Rose and River Bend, reverted to day-use only in summer 2000. Farther east is **Windy Point** (15 sites; RVs to 22 feet), the campground closest to Naches and the Oak Creek Wildlife Area (see Wildlife Watching, below). The campground is open from April to late November.

Downhill Skiing

Long one of Washington's better-kept skiing secrets, **White Pass Ski Area** is best known for producing Phil and Steve Mahre, regarded by many as the greatest U.S. alpine racers ever to strap on boards. The quasi-retired Mahres still ski here, but they've been joined by plenty of skiing-purist compadres in recent years, now that White Pass has added a high-speed, detachable quad lift to the top of the mountain.

Nestled along the northern boundary of the Goat Rocks Wilderness, White Pass is treated to healthy doses of snow that's typically drier than the normal Northwest fare. Even on weekends, the mountain's slightly remote location leaves it far less crowded than nearby areas such as Crystal Mountain. Show up here on a crisp, clear, winter midweek day, and you'll feel like you have the place all to yourself.

The terrain is mostly intermediate, making this a great destination for families, beginners, and cruisers who love smooth, uncrowded runs. But it's far from boring. While no super-steeps exist to prime the adrenaline pumps of experts, they'll find plenty of short, steep, powder-filled chutes to keep them entertained.

The ski area's primary disadvantage—an extra hour of driving time from Seattle, compared to Crystal Mountain—is largely overcome by slopeside lodging, a rare feature for a Washington resort. The 55 Village Inn condos ($80 to $172 a night) right across US 12 from the base area are privately owned, but many are available nightly through the mountain's rental office; (509) 672-3131. If you're not up for longish commutes for day skiing, this is a good way to go. White Pass is a great, very quiet weekend getaway. But be warned: Weekends book up fast. There are alternate lodgings in Packwood (see Lodgings, below) and Yakima, 51 miles east.

White Pass gets solid amounts of snow from early December through early April. An annual highlight is the White Pass Winter Carnival the first weekend in March, which includes a Children's Hospital charity event during which you can actually race Phil Mahre. Hey, you never know: he might fall.

White Pass stats: Elevation: 4,500 to 6,000 feet. Lifts: 5; one high-speed quad, "Great White." Lift tickets: $33 adult daily on weekends at this writing; substantially lower midweek. Hours: Daily 8:30am to 4pm; night skiing until 10pm. Day care is available daily. *On US 12 at the summit; mountain info (509) 672-3101, snow phone (509) 672-3100; www.ski-whitepass.com.*

Cross-country Skiing/Snowshoeing

The most convenient cross-country skiing in the corridor is also at **White Pass Ski Area,** which maintains 18 kilometers of mostly intermediate groomed trails, open Thursdays through Sundays from 8:45am to sunset, and daily during the Christmas holiday season. **Rentals,** lessons, and other services are available.

For more remote skiing and snowshoeing, two state Sno-Parks are found on the east side of White Pass Highway. They are **Goose Egg,** 22 miles west of Naches on Road 1201; and **North Fork Tieton,** 32 miles northwest of Naches on Road 1207 (see the Tieton Meadows Trail in Hiking/Backpacking, above). A string of similar Sno-Parks is found on Hwy 410 east of Naches. Another popular option is the ski up Stevens Canyon Road from the Stevens Canyon entrance to Mount Rainier National Park, north of Packwood.

Wildlife Watching

The 42,000-acre Oak Creek Wildlife Area, just east of Naches on US 12 (about 20 miles west of Yakima, only a 30-minute drive), is one of the state's most popular wildlife-viewing areas. For more than 50 years, this has been the annual winter feeding site for the state's biggest single herd of **Rocky Mountain elk,** the thriving descendants of a couple dozen elk released here decades ago to start a population for hunting. The elk— which have few natural predators in this area—prospered, and many began moving down the valley in search of feeding grounds just as homes and orchards were creeping up it. The Oak Creek feeding program, coupled with hundreds of miles of 12-foot elk fences, solved that problem. Without the hay-feeding program—largely financed by sportsmen's groups—most of these elk would normally congregate in the winter in valley lowlands where they'd feed on grass—and crops. The elk now venture only as far down the valley as the feeding station, where they're fed every morning through the winter by sportsmen's club volunteers. It's an impressive sight, to say the least.

The feeding station is definitely worth a trip in the winter. It's as close to wild elk as you're likely to get, and kids absolutely love it. Several hundred elk typically line up for their hay here every day, and visitors can stand as little as 20 or 30 yards away behind a wood fence. It's a great place to photograph or just watch elk, and plenty of people take advantage: The visitors center logs around 100,000 onlookers a year. Feeding typically begins as soon as snows creep down to 3,000 feet, and lasts through the winter. The feeding area is just beyond the Hwy 410/US 12 junction east of Naches; follow Old Naches Road from the US 12/Hwy 410 junction.

A separate feeding area for **California bighorn sheep,** which are fewer in number but still often seen, is just off US 12 on Old Clemens Road, at the base of Clemens Mountain near the US 12/Hwy 410 junction. The herd was reintroduced here in 1967, using bighorn sheep stock captured in British Columbia. For feeding times and other information, contact the Washington Department of Fish and Wildlife office in Yakima, (509) 575-2740; www.wa.gov/wdfw, or the Oak Creek refuge, (509) 653-2390.

Farther west, **mountain goats** often are spotted from the old lookout site atop Timberwolf Mountain, reached by driving Road 1500 north from US 12 near Hause Creek Campground to Forest Road 190. **Mule deer** and elk also are commonly seen at the mountain and along the road on the way up. Rimrock and Clear Lakes also are rich wildlife areas. Watch for nesting **bald eagles** and **osprey** around Peninsula Campground. Clear Lake Campground (see Camping, above) is usually a good place to spot wildlife. An interpretive trail along the lake has wildlife-viewing information, and the North Fork Tieton, which flows into the lake, is a great place to watch spawning **kokanee** (land-locked sockeye salmon; they'll be bright red).

Rafting

The scenic **Tieton River** becomes a raging gusher alive with whoops and screams of river rafters every September, when irrigation water released from Rimrock Lake creates a wild ride down the canyon toward Naches. About two dozen Seattle-area outfitters run trips down the Tieton in September, when it's really the only game in town for Washington whitewater fans. Contact the Naches Ranger District, (509) 653-2205, for a list of qualified **guides.**

Fishing

The Tieton River receives annual state plants of **rainbow trout,** and bank access is excellent from the Forest Service campgrounds along US 12 (see Camping, above). The lower river also has a productive winter **whitefish** season. Nearby Oak Creek (also on Hwy 12), a clear, swift tributary of the Tieton, produces some trout. It also receives annual rainbow plants from the state Department of Fish and Wildlife. Farther up the pass, Rimrock Lake Reservoir has a very beautiful **kokanee** (landlocked sockeye) fishery. The limit is 16, and many people get there during the hot fishing season in midsummer. The lake becomes unfishable late in the summer, when irrigation water is released from Tieton Dam and the reservoir shrinks to a puddle. Just upstream, Clear Lake also is planted with **rainbow trout.**

Near White Pass summit, Dog Lake and Leech Lake (see Camping, above) are decent trout lakes (once the ice melts). Note that Leech is fly-fishing only. Backpackers with portable rods will find plenty of good fishing in the William O. Douglas Wilderness north of White Pass. The Pacific Crest Trail north from White Pass, or the Dumbbell Lake Loop (see Hiking/Backpacking, above) are good routes for backpacking anglers.

Accessible Outdoors

Clear Lake day-use area in the Naches Ranger District offers barrier-free picnicking, rest rooms, and a half-mile interpretive path over the lake. From Naches, drive west on US 12 for 38 miles to the Clear Lake turnoff. Turn left and continue to the site on the north side of the lake. **Oak Creek Wildlife Area** offers barrier-free rest rooms and wildlife viewing. Campsites, picnic facilities, and rest rooms at **La Wis Wis Campground** are rated "usable" (with assistance) for wheelchairs. In the Naches Ranger District east of White Pass, **Hause Creek Campground** has one barrier-free site and barrier-free rest rooms; **Clear Lake North** has barrier-free vault toilets.

outside in

Lodgings

Hotel Packwood ★　This spartan lodge (open since 1912) remains a favorite. $; 104 Main St, Packwood; (360) 494-5431.

More Information:

Cowlitz Valley Ranger District, Randle: (360) 497-1100.

Department of Transportation pass report: (888) SNO-INFO; www.wsdot.wa.gov/sno-info.

Gifford Pinchot National Forest Headquarters: (360) 891-5000; www.fs.fed.us/gpnf.

Gifford Pinchot National Forest, Packwood Information Center: (360) 494-0600.

Naches Ranger District: (509) 653-2205.

Wenatchee National Forest Headquarters: (509) 662-4335; www.fs.fed.us/r6/wenatchee.

White Pass Ski Area: (509) 453-8731; www.skiwhitepass.com.

Mount
St. Helens

From Randle on US Highway 12 south to Swift Reservoir along Forest Road 25 and west to Silver Lake, including the national volcanic monument and the Cowlitz and Toutle Rivers.

Words cannot do it justice. Nor can photos, slide shows, fancy interpretive exhibits, or even a big-screen IMAX movie. The colossal volcanic explosion of Mount St. Helens on May 18, 1980, was one of the most cataclysmic natural events in recorded history, and succeeding years have done little to minimize the awe visitors feel upon exploring the Mount St. Helens National Volcanic Monument.

The only way to begin to imagine the spectacular force of the eruption is to poke through the rubble of what's left. And in that sense, Washington nature lovers are fortunate. Rather than lock the curious public out of this remarkable, blasted-apart mountain, managing federal agencies have, in effect, invited all of us to act as our own scientists. The Mount St. Helens National Volcanic Monument—a specialized federal designation that includes elements of both natural parks and federal research sites—is with few exceptions wide open for public use.

Nearly two decades after the eruption, St. Helens has gone relatively dormant, and the volcano—one of the youngest and still most active in the country—calls out for exploration. Just about the only place you can't go on foot around Mount St. Helens is a restricted zone inside the crater itself. And nobody in their right mind would want to go there, anyway. The volcano may be dormant, but the ominous black lava dome inside its mouth still looks like a living, breathing creature—one prone to violent tantrums with little or no warning.

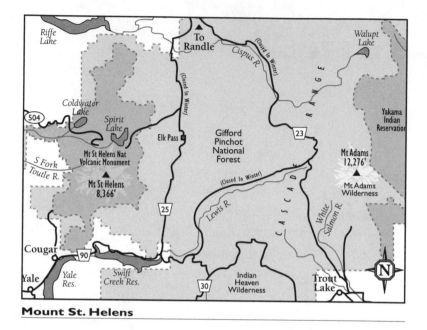

Mount St. Helens

In a way, that's a large part of the allure of hiking, biking, or fishing around the volcano, or just warily watching it. It's a little like the scary—but oddly welcome—feeling you get when hiking in grizzly country: there's a constant element of danger here, a unique sense that the world through which you walk is one over which you have absolutely no control. For many recreationists, that's the very definition of a "wild" encounter. At Mount St. Helens, where the evidence of nature's power is present everywhere you look for 50 miles around, the feeling is impossible to ignore.

It lives in the eyes of hikers standing on the shores of Spirit Lake, amid an otherworldly landscape—a city-size circle of land that was rearranged from top to bottom in one volcanic blink of an eye. It lives in the minds of visitors who walk into one of the monument's interpretive centers and attempt to assimilate the numbers: 6.6 billion tons of mud, ice, and rock moving at 150 mph and settling 650 feet deep; 500°F winds blasting at 650 mph; ash and rock bursting 12 miles into the sky before circling the Earth; 230 square miles laid waste. It lives in the souls of those of us who remember the mountain as it once was—a pristine, symmetrical cone standing as a shrine in one of the most beautiful, forested recreation playgrounds of the Pacific Northwest. Then Mount St. Helens was a thing of beauty, a place to escape to and relax. Now it is the ultimate monument to humility, a place to stand in awe and reflect.

There will be no attempt here to describe the event, the result, or the rebirth now taking place in its wake. The only way to know is to go. The St. Helens National Volcanic Monument does an excellent job—especially considering the unprecedented logistical obstacles—of providing human access to an incredible natural work-in-progress. It's a pilgrimage everyone who loves and reveres the natural world ought to make.

Getting There

The primary access to Mount St. Helens National Volcanic Monument is from the northwest, via Highway 504, the Spirit Lake Memorial Highway, which turns east from Interstate 5 at Castle Rock (exit 49) and travels 53 miles into the heart of the volcanic blast zone. Hwy 504 is the only paved route into the blast area; allow at least 3 hours from Seattle. The northeast side of the mountain, including popular hiking trails and viewpoints near Norway Pass and Windy Ridge, is reached by following Forest Roads 25 and 99 about 45 miles south from Randle on US Highway 12. Allow about 4 hours from Seattle, and note that winter flood damage to roads is common in this area. The south side of the mountain is reached via Hwy 503 from I-5 at Woodland, then Forest Road 90 (which connects with Forest Road 25 on the east).

inside out

Scenic Drives/Visitors Centers

The vast majority of those visiting Mount St. Helens do so in a daylong auto tour from the Seattle or Portland area. The most popular route is Hwy 504, which leads east into St. Helens National Volcanic Monument from Castle Rock. Hwy 504, the only paved highway into the monument, connects with four interesting visitors centers. The other popular access route, Forest Road 99, reached by driving 45 miles on forest roads from Randle, is more difficult, but leads to Windy Point, which has the best drive-to views of the volcano.

Beginning in 1997, the Forest Service, which manages the Volcanic Monument, began charging what many users considered outrageous **access fees**—$8 per person for a 3-day pass to all monument visitors centers. Beginning in the summer of 2000, that fee structure changed, but still causes significant confusion and consternation. The new system, in fact, changes so often, and at this at this writing is so Byzantine, convoluted, and indecipherable, we won't kill the thousands of trees it would take to describe it here. Suffice to say you must pay a per-person access fee for any (or, for a higher price, all) monument visitors centers, *and/or* you must have a **Northwest Forest Pass** (see Hiking, below) to park at most popular trailheads and viewpoints. (Monument staff, in a news release, explain the addition of the Northwest Forest Pass as an effort to "provide a simple, convenient, and affordable pass program for Monument visitors." And they're apparently serious.) Contact the monument visitors center at the numbers below for their fee-system du jour.

Once you're properly permitted, a good first stop is the **Mount St. Helens Visitors Center,** (360) 274-2100, 5 miles east of Castle Rock on Hwy 504 (follow signs from I-5, exit 49). The center, open daily, has impressive interpretive displays, maps, literature, and—most important— rangers and specialists who can help you get the most out of your visit. On very clear (rare) days, the volcano itself can be seen in the distance from an area behind the center.

Highway 504 is an impressive piece of construction. As you wind your way high above the Toutle River valley, several pull-off **viewpoints** offer impressive overlooks of the massive mudflow that scoured the valley, which now is being revegetated in a forest of green shrubs and trees. Bring binoculars: you might spot some members of St. Helens' burgeoning elk herd below.

The first views of the volcano are at **Hoffstadt Bluffs Visitors Center,** near milepost 27, which has a memorial to mountain characters such as Harry Truman, the stubborn Spirit Lake man who refused to leave before the eruption that took his life. Also at the center is a gift shop filled with cheesy volcano memorabilia, a snack/espresso bar (naturally), and a large restaurant—the only sit-down dining in the monument. A bit farther up the road, the **Forest Learning Center** is another worthwhile stop, with plenty of hands-on exhibits particularly popular with children.

The **Coldwater Ridge Visitors Center,** 43 miles east of Castle Rock; (360) 274-2131, offers the first good naked-eye views of St. Helens, as well as Coldwater Lake, a large, eruption-formed lake directly below. Inside, the interpretive displays feature a lot of whiz-bang gadgetry (including a theater with an eruption film you shouldn't miss) that's highly informative, and impressive on its face. Ultimately, however, all the glass, steel, and electronics (not to mention the obligatory gift shop) seem wildly out of character with the stark, moonscapelike terrain that surrounds the modern building. A series of trails begins here—most of them dropping steeply into the blast zone (see Hiking/Backpacking, below). Coldwater Ridge is open daily, although snows can close Hwy 504 in winter. Note: Bring your jacket. Coldwater Ridge is 5,000 feet above sea level—higher than just about any of Washington's major mountain passes.

The newest section of Hwy 504 proceeds beyond Coldwater Ridge and drops to **Coldwater Lake** (where there's a small boat launch and

Day hikers approach the summit of Mount St. Helens

interpretive trail; see Fishing and Hiking/Backpacking, below). The road then climbs through the blast zone to the new **Johnston Ridge Observatory,** 52 miles east of Castle Rock, (360) 274-2140, which provides the closest views into the volcano crater. The center, open 10am to 6pm daily,

May 1 to September 30, provides interpretive exhibits, a wide-screen theater presentation on the eruption, interpretive walks, and other volcano facts and figures. The nearby, half-mile **Eruption Trail** is an easy interpretive path through the heart of the blast zone.

From the north, Forest Roads 25 and 99 lead 45 miles south from US 12 at Randle to the aptly named **Windy Ridge Viewpoint,** which looks directly into the crater from the south shore of volcano-revamped Spirit Lake. This also serves as one of the monument's major trailheads (see also Hiking/Backpacking, below). Note: The road to Windy Ridge is prone to winter washouts. Call monument headquarters in Amboy, (360) 247-3900 or (360) 247-3903 (recorded information), before you go. On your way, stop by the **Woods Creek Information Center** on Road 25 south of Randle.

Visitors entering the monument from the south, via Hwy 503, can get visitors information at the summers-only **Pine Creek Information Center,** near Swift Creek Reservoir at the junction of Forest Roads 90 and 25 (about 45 miles east of Woodland).

Hiking/Backpacking

Setting off on foot in the St. Helens blast zone is an unforgettable experience. The sheer magnitude of destruction in evidence all around (including in your hair and under your fingernails, if you're hiking when winds stir the volcanic ash) is overwhelming, the rebirth of plant and animal populations inspiring. It's an experience you won't find anywhere else on the continent, and in few places on the planet.

A hike around the **volcano** can be particularly unforgettable if you don't go prepared. This is still very much an active volcano. While geologists say large-scale eruptions aren't likely to happen without seismographic warnings, smaller steam and ash eruptions are not uncommon. It's vital to carry **survival gear,** which should consist minimally of "10 essentials" supplies (see the Washington Outdoors Primer). Footing is shaky, at best, on some trails. Use your head. Also keep in mind that the gritty ash can destroy your camera, clog your water filter, and perhaps render your cookstove inoperable. Carry **repair kits** for the filter and stove. Backup iodine tablets for treating water are a good idea.

Hiking trails inside the volcanic monument are in a constant state of flux, due to the instability of both the area itself and of the federal budget. **Trail maintenance** is a problem here, because of a lack of funding and an abundance of open slopes and unstable soils highly prone to erosion. The same is true of roads, particularly the Forest Service access roads in the north monument area, south of Randle. **Flood damage** closed many of them in 1996. Call monument headquarters in Amboy, (360) 247-3900, before you set out. Generally, however, more and more trails are being added, and Northwest hikers only recently have begun to catch on to the thrill of climbing near, on, or all the way around an active volcano. As of this writing, more than 200 miles of trails are open inside the Volcanic Monument.

Some rules: **Dogs** are prohibited on many trails, and must be leashed on all others. **Mountain bikes** are allowed on some trails. Keep in mind that the restricted area is a living laboratory. Pack out everything you pack in, and practice very **low-impact travel techniques.** Backcountry camping is allowed, but with restrictions (consult monument headquarters). **Fires** are prohibited. **Group size** is limited to 12.

Permits aren't required unless you're bound for blast-zone areas above 4,800 feet (see Climbing, below), although free backcountry **camping permits** now are required for all campsites in the Mount Margaret Backcountry north of the volcano. Permits are available by mail or fax from Monument Headquarters and the Coldwater Ridge Visitors Center (see More Information, below) beginning May 1 each year. They're free, but must be accompanied by a valid **Northwest Forest Pass.** This parking pass, $5 per day or $30 annually, also is required to park in many Forest Service–administered trailheads in this area. They're available from ranger stations, from many private vendors, on-line at www.naturenw.org, or by calling (800) 270-7504. For maps, trail reports, and a full list of routes, contact monument headquarters or stop at any of the visitors centers described above. Following are some popular routes, divided by area.

Coldwater Ridge

The volcano's most heavily visited area is the launching point for three short, worthwhile interpretive trails and a longer hike through the blast zone. The **Winds of Change Trail** (easy; quarter-mile loop) begins just outside the visitors center and loops along the ridgeline, with interpretive signs describing landscape changes under way here. A short distance down the road is the **Birth of a Lake Trail** (easy; 0.6-mile loop) another short, easy path on a boardwalk above Coldwater Lake, which was formed by a massive mud slide that dammed the creek drainage. Both trails are barrier-free. A short distance farther down the road, the **Hummocks Loop Trail** (easy; 2.3-mile loop) begins just beyond the Coldwater Lake pullout. The trail winds through the hummocks—hilly remnants of the massive landslide that swept this area the day of the eruption. An overlook of the area is found a short distance down the trail. Keep your eyes peeled for elk. An easy, half-mile interpretive trail in the blast zone begins at the Johnston Ridge Observatory (see Scenic Drives, above).

Back on the ridge near the visitors center, the **Coldwater** aka **Lakes**

Trail (moderate; 12 miles round trip) drops steeply via a connecting path, the **Elk Bench Trail,** to Coldwater Lake, then follows its north shore. The first portion of the trail is an access route used by trout anglers (see Fishing, below). It's an interesting walk through what once was a pretty, forested valley and now looks like a massive, bare crater with a water-filled bottom. The trail travels 5.2 miles around the lake, then connects with Coldwater Trail 230, and ultimately the Truman Trail (see below).

Norway Pass area

Access south from Randle on Forest Roads 25, 99, and 26:

The **Goat Mountain Trail** (moderate; up to 12 miles round trip) begins on Forest Road 2612 near Ryan Lake and climbs steeply to a ridge with excellent views into the volcano crater. It's a good place to compare what's left of St. Helens with the dormant (for the time being), snow-covered dome of Rainier, visible to the north. The first views of the crater are less than a mile up the trail, but you can continue along the ridge top, weaving into and out of the blast zone, to Deadman's Lake and ultimately Vanson Peak. A short, easy hike in the same area is the **Ryan Lake Interpretive Loop** (easy; 0.6 mile round trip).

The **West Boundary Trail** (moderate; up to 10 miles round trip) is the remnant western portion of the Boundary Trail that bisected the Gifford Pinchot National Forest before the volcano wiped out much of the western end. This section draws less attention from backpackers than the longer eastern route. From Road 26 near Norway Pass, the trail climbs to Bear Pass and 5,858-foot Mount Margaret, where views into the volcano are unforgettable. The counterpart **East Boundary Trail** (difficult; 30 miles one way) begins at the same place, but heads east along the ridge tops all the way to Council Lake Campground near the Mount Adams Wilderness. It's a popular one-way backpack route, with several good campsites along the way. Volcano views are good, but not as easily accessible as on the West Boundary Trail. A great primer on the survival and recovery of life in the blast zone is the **Meta Lake Trail** (easy; half-mile round trip), where much of the plant and animal life was spared from the May 1980 eruption by a 10-foot blanket of snow.

Windy Ridge area

Access through Randle on Forest Roads 25 and 99:

If you're looking for good crater and Spirit Lake views without investing many hours and gallons of sweat, the **Independence Pass Trail** (moderate; up to 7 miles round trip) is a good option. From its Road 99 trailhead, the path climbs a short distance to a fine viewpoint, then proceeds to a junction with the Boundary Trail. For a close look at the volcano-remodeled Spirit Lake, proceed about a mile up Road 99 to the

Harmony Trail (moderate; 2 miles round trip), which drops about 600 feet through blast-devastated forest to the lakeshore. This currently is the only way to hike all the way to Spirit Lake, and it's a stunning experience, particularly for those who remember Spirit Lake in its former pristine state. The eruption raised the lake level 200 feet, creating a giant wave of water that destroyed everything standing on the far shore. Harmony Falls, a once-magnificent cascade, is now half its former height, thanks to the millions of cubic yards of earth, logs, and muck that reshaped the lake.

At the end of the road near Windy Ridge, the **Truman Trail** (moderate; up to 13 miles round trip), named for the Spirit Lake Lodge owner who died in the eruption, drops through the blast zone on the south shore of Spirit Lake, then climbs to a junction with the Boundary Trail above the west side of the lake. It's also a common entry point to the Loowit Trail (see below), which connects several miles down the path via the Windy Trail. The Truman Trail is one of the best, most direct footpaths into the very heart of the blast zone. Be aware that there's no shade or water, making this a very hot, dry walk in midsummer. It's a particularly fine autumn hike, however.

A similar experience can be had on the nearby **Plains of Abraham Trail** (moderate; up to 8 miles round trip), which turns south into the blast zone from the Truman Trail just before that path turns north, up to Spirit Lake. The Abraham Trail continues south to a junction with Loowit Trail. A 9-mile loop can be made by combining the upper Truman, Loowit, and Windy Trails (if you haven't already done so, consult a map!).

Many hikers also favor the Windy Ridge Viewpoint as a drop-off/starting point for their journey all the way around St. Helens on the **Loowit Trail** (very difficult; 27 miles round trip), which roughly circles the volcano. Loowit, the native name for this volcano, is the granddaddy of all St. Helens backpack routes, exposing hikers to a bewildering array of environments, old and new. We advise starting at Windy Ridge and traveling clockwise, although other popular starting points are reached via the Ptarmigan Trail near the Climber's Bivouac on the south slope (see Climbing, below) and the June Lake Trail, off Forest Road 83. This is a rough, often treacherous route. Middle sections through the blast zone are marked only by cairns. Don't attempt the hike unless you're well equipped and proficient at route-finding. If you are, by all means do it. This is one of the most fascinating backpack routes on the planet today. Give yourself a week, though.

South side
Access from Cougar via Forest Roads 83, 8303, 81, and 8122:

This lesser-ravaged side of the volcano is still interesting, as evidenced by the awesome **Lava Canyon Interpretive Trail** (easy; half-mile round trip), which leads you on a tour of the Muddy River Canyon, an ancient lava flow remodeled by floodwaters from the 1980 eruption. The trailhead is on Road 83, north of Cougar, and guided interpretive hikes sometimes are offered in the summer. The trail continues down this steep gorge in spectacular fashion, ending at a second trailhead on Road 8322 below. The 3-mile walk between them is very difficult and very spectacular, clinging to steep canyon walls and at one point crossing the chasm on a wobbly suspension bridge.

For a look at a St. Helens forest spared from the blast, try the **Jackpine Shelter Interpretive Trail** (easy, 0.8 mile round trip), which winds through a lovely stand of old-growth firs. The trail begins on Road 83 and includes some views of the volcano and its eruption floodpath in the Pine Creek drainage. A nice day hike nearby is the **June Lake Trail** (moderate; 3 miles round trip), which climbs moderately (about 500 feet) from Road 83 to a small, picturesque lake, also connecting to the Loowit Trail. Another interesting interpretive trail, the **Trail of Two Forests Loop** (easy; one-third mile round trip), begins on Road 8303, a half mile from the Road 83 junction.

A half mile farther up Road 8303 is one of the most popular trails in the monument, if not in all southwest Washington: **Ape Cave** (moderate; 1 mile one way). You can take two routes into the cave, the longest intact lava tube (12,800 feet) in the continental United States. Explorers can walk through a lower (three-quarter-mile) or upper (1.25-mile) section of the caves, then return on a mile-long trail. The lower section is by far the easiest (best for kids), with a relatively smooth floor surface. The upper cave requires scrambling over large rocks and one particularly steep rock face. Oh, yes: don't expect any apes. The cave is named after an outdoor club, the Mount St. Helens Apes, who first explored it in the 1950s. Kids love the cave, but beware the uneven cave-floor surface and the temperature: it's quite cold (about 42°F, year-round) inside. Strong flashlights and good hiking shoes are a must. Lantern rentals and **guided walks** are available daily at the parking area in the summer.

A very nice southside weekend backpacking destination is **Butte Camp** (moderate; up to 6.8 miles round trip). The trail, which begins on Road 81 at Red Rock Pass, crosses an ancient lava flow and mudflows from the recent eruption before climbing through an old-growth forest to Butte Camp, a pretty backcountry site that serves as a climber's bivouac for an alternate route to the summit. The campsite is a good launching point for a 1.25-mile side trip through scenic alpine meadows to a junction with the Loowit Trail, which offers views of the jagged southside crater rim. For more easily attainable views in this area, the **Sheep Canyon Trail** (easy; up to 4 miles round trip) has a fine viewpoint of the upper Toutle Valley about a quarter mile from the trailhead on Road 8123. The trail, which passes through a nice noble fir forest and offers views of a 75-foot waterfall, connects with the Loowit Trail at 2.2 miles, 4,600 feet. (For a scenic loop of about 5 miles, follow Loowit Trail north to the Toutle Trail, which can be followed south back to Sheep Canyon Trail.)

Climbing

If you think St. Helens is impressive from 5 miles away, try looking straight down into its throat. About 15,000 climbers get that opportunity every year by following the **Monitor Ridge route** up the southwest side of St. Helens. The climb to the top isn't technical at all in the summer, when it's mostly free of snow. It's a mildly technical snow-trudge in the winter and spring, accessible to anyone with an ice ax and basic snow-travel skills. The most popular climbing time—by far—is spring, when stable snowfields cover the upper portion of the route. Why? Footing. Ironically, for even moderately experienced trekkers, footing is better—certainly easier—on the snow than on the aggravating, loose pumice that dominates the upper route in summer. Climbing in the pumice is like hiking up a sand dune—or doing your federal tax forms: You feel like you're sliding 2 feet back with every one step up.

The vast majority of climbers follow the established route from Climber's Bivouac, reached by following Forest Roads 8100 and 8100-830 a total of 14 miles northeast from Cougar. It's common practice to drive to Cougar one day, snare a climbing permit (see below), and set up camp at the Bivouac (bring your own water!), elevation 3,765 feet, then set out for the summit early the next morning.

The route—just over 2 miles up **Ptarmigan Trail** and about 3 miles on open slopes—isn't technically challenging. But it is relentless, gaining about 4,500 feet in 5 miles to the crater rim. There, peering over the rocky lip, you literally are gazing into the depths of the Earth. The crater's steaming lava dome looks very much alive, and large rockslides and steam eruptions are common. It's awesome to consider that, from the point where you're standing, the former Mount St. Helens rose an additional 1,300 feet before the blast. Be very careful near the 8,350-foot rim, where rock and snow often are unstable. It's 2,000 feet straight down off the other side, and no one—we do mean no one—will be coming to pick up your remains. Most climbers take 7 to 12 hours to make the ascent.

In the spring or early summer, climbers trained with an ice ax and comfortable with self-arrest skills will find the return trip an absolute hoot. It's basically a 3-mile, uninterrupted glissade, one of the longest and best in the Northwest. This is a serious way to get hurt if you don't know what you're doing, however. Bringing along slick plastic or some other sliding device to facilitate your speed, as some foolhardy guidebooks suggest, is only for those with a death wish.

Permit roulette: You must have a **climbing permit** to be above 4,800 feet on St. Helens. Permits are required all year, but during the peak climbing season, April 1 to October 31, they're limited to 100 a day, and a $15 **climbing fee** is charged. To request a reserved permit, call the monument's climbing hotline, (360) 247-3961, for instructions. From November 1 to March 31, permits are free and available at Jack's Restaurant and Store, 23 miles east of Woodland on Hwy 503. If you reserved your permit in advance, you can pick it up and pay for it at Jack's, (360) 231-4276. To get one of the remaining 40 spots, show up at Jack's the day before you intend to climb and sign the list for a daily 6pm drawing. You must be present to claim your prize. A single lottery permit covers up to 4 climbers; if you have a party of 12, 3 reasonably warm bodies must play the odds at Jack's. Permits are good for 24 hours. All parties must sign in at Jack's before climbing and sign out on the way home. Otherwise the search-and-rescue army will come looking for you—and they won't be too happy if they find you back home in Bothell.

Cross-Country Skiing

Many of the backcountry trails described in Hiking/Backpacking, above, are gaining favor with backcountry skiers. Call monument headquarters for ski-trail information, which changes significantly with snow levels throughout the winter. The most commonly skied cross-country areas are on the south side of the mountain, north of Cougar. The focal point is the **Cougar Sno-Park,** 8 miles east of Cougar on Forest Road 83. The lot has spaces for 30 cars; state Sno-Park passes are required. Trails here are not groomed, but good skiing can be found on snowed-under Forest Service roads. Several other unofficial backcountry skiing pullouts are found farther up Road 83, including the **Lahar Viewpoint trailhead** in Ape Canyon. Rental skis are available at Jack's Restaurant and Store on Hwy 503 west of Cougar; (360) 231-4276.

Fishing

Some of us used to kid the fish biologist in Mount St. Helens National Monument about having the easiest job in the world: watching over fish in a blast zone where everything within 10 miles is dead? The joke was on us. The fact is that many fish species survived the 1980 blast because they were protected beneath alpine lakes still covered with spring ice. Not only that, but the volcano—by completely wiping clean the local landscape and starting over—gave biologists a unique opportunity to study marine-life development in waterways relatively uninfluenced by other living organisms.

A good example is 700-acre Coldwater Lake, which formed in Coldwater Creek valley after the volcano mudflow built a natural dam at its mouth. State Fish and Wildlife biologists planted **rainbow trout** here in 1989, and the population has flourished, with many now measuring 24 inches or more. Fishing is allowed all year in the lake, but selective fishery regulations are in effect (single, barbless hooks; no bait; one-fish limit; minimum size 16 inches). The lake can be fished in a couple of places from the west shore along the Coldwater Lake Trail (see Hiking/Backpacking, above), but most anglers launch float tubes or small boats at a parking area at the south end of the lake on Hwy 504. Amazingly, Coldwater also contains **cutthroat** that just might be the hardiest creatures in the state. Scientists believe they rode out the blast in one of several local lakes protected by ice, later migrating through blast-zone streams into Coldwater Lake. You can fish here for cutthroat, too—but after all that, how could you possibly kill one?

Another popular monument fishing spot, this one much tougher to reach, is Castle Lake, which holds a healthy stock of rainbows. It's also under selective-fishery rules. Call monument headquarters for details on access to this lake, which is reached by driving a string of old Weyerhaeuser logging roads off Hwy 504. The other notable trout fishery here is in the upper Green River lakes, which lie north of the volcano in the upper Green River drainage. **Brook trout** and some big rainbows are caught in this string of five small lakes, which also are reached by navigating a string of Weyerhaeuser roads.

Steelhead action can be found here, too. A decent summer hatchery steelhead run is beginning to reestablish itself in the South Fork Toutle River, which can be reached from Weyerhaeuser Road 4100. Wild fish (those with intact adipose fins) must be released. (The North Fork, more heavily scoured by volcanic mudflows, also holds some steelhead, but usually is too cloudy to fish easily.) A Toutle tributary on the north side of the mountain, the Green River, also has a small summer steelhead run.

Silver Lake, a shallow, broad wetland near Castle Rock, is open all year for **largemouth bass** fishing, and some hefty ones are landed here. The lake also holds **crappie, perch,** and a few rainbow trout. Bank access is fairly good at any of several resorts here, or at the state boat launch.

Photography

It goes without saying that St. Helens is on the must-do list for every Washington shutterbug—novice, pro, or in-between. For a big mountain with a gaping crater, St. Helens can be surprisingly difficult to photograph well. Good panoramic vistas are available at the **Coldwater Ridge, Johnston Ridge,** and **Windy Ridge viewpoints.** But some of the best scenic shots of the blast zone actually are taken from a bit farther back, on high ridge-top trails north of the volcano (see Hiking/Backpacking, above). The advantage is height and perspective: photos from here can show not only the volcano, but the broad blast zone in relation to the forest that survived on the edges. As with most scenic shots, very early or late light will bring best results here. The volcano crater is almost always photographed looking south, so midday light is troublesome.

If you're serious about capturing the entire volcano experience on film, take a walk on one of several trails that lead into the **blast zone.** In some areas, felled trees laid out like matchsticks and the nearly black-and-white moonscape environments create fascinating landscape scenes. Increasingly, though, local photographers have turned their attention to the rebirth of life here. The blast zone gets a little greener every year. Forest Road 99, which ends at the Windy Ridge overlook, is a good place to photograph **Spirit Lake,** now packed with dead trees.

Important note: The fine, gritty **volcanic ash** in the blast zone can wreak absolute havoc with camera gear, particularly zoom lenses with moving parts. Keep your camera and all lenses sealed away tight—not only inside a camera bag, but sealed in zipper pouches—anytime you're near the ash. And try to minimize the number of times you open your camera to change film or lenses.

Camping/Parks

Options are limited here. The best destination by far for campers is **Seaquest State Park** on Hwy 504, near the National Volcanic Monument Visitors Center. The park, which includes a nice grove of old-growth trees, has 96 campsites (16 with hookups) and a large day-use area with picnic grounds and playfields. Silver Lake, one of the state's better bass fisheries, is across Hwy 504. That, coupled with the convenient location for volcano visitors, makes this a very busy park. Seaquest is open all year. If you're counting on a campsite here in the summer, reserve up to 11 months in advance by calling Reservations Northwest; (800) 452-5687. *On Hwy 504 (follow signs from I-5 exit 49) 6.5 miles east of Castle Rock; (360) 274-8633 or (800) 233-0321.*

On the north side of the Monument is **Iron Creek,** a Forest Service campground with 98 campsites (no hookups; RVs to 42 feet) and piped water. It's not fancy, but the location is good for north-side volcano hikers. It's open summers only. Campsites can be reserved up to 240 days in advance; (877) 444-6777; www.reserveusa.com. *10 miles south of Randle via Forest Rds 23 and 25; (360) 497-1100.*

The other camping options around the mountain are on the far south side—out of easy reach if you're visiting the volcano via Hwy 504. Several campgrounds are available in the Gifford Pinchot National Forest north of Carson. A handful of others are operated by Portland's Pacificorp—**Swift** (93 sites), **Cougar** (60 sites), **Beaver Bay** (78 sites), and **Cresap Bay** (73 sites). *Near the Swift Creek and Yale Reservoirs along Hwy 503; (503) 813-6666.*

Wildlife Watching

Many mammals began moving back into the St. Helens blast zone almost as soon as the ash cooled. But none took advantage of the outdoor remodeling job to the extent of the Toutle River **Rocky Mountain elk** herd. Mudflows scoured out the entire floor of this broad river valley in 1980, but thousands of acres of grass and shrubs—primo grazing fodder—sprouted the following spring. Elk, needless to say, were ecstatic, and the herd now is proliferating on the valley floor. Bring your binoculars, and you might see them from any of a number of pullouts along Hwy 504. Elk also often are seen on the bare (of trees, anyway) slopes around Coldwater Lake.

Mountain Biking

Frankly, the ubiquitous ash and stark terrain don't appeal to many mountain bikers. But some surprisingly good riding can be found on monument trails (not all are open to bikes; check at headquarters first) and local logging roads. Some bikers' favorites are the **Plains of Abraham Trail** from Windy Ridge Viewpoint, and the **Ape Canyon Trail** on the southeast side of the mountain off Forest Road 83 (see Hiking/Backpacking, above). Another very popular route south of the volcano is the **Upper Lewis River Trail,** a 14-mile singletrack ride up or down the river through a beautiful old-growth coniferous forest. Access is off Forest Road 90. Also, several private outfitters have been running **guided tours** on Weyerhaeuser roads north of the volcano, above Coldwater Ridge, in recent years. Contact monument headquarters, (360) 247-5473, for referrals.

Kayaking/Canoeing

Silver Lake, near Seaquest State Park (see Camping, above), is an interesting place for paddlers, with lots of old snags, and fields of grass and pond lilies. It's a big lake, but it's less than 10 feet deep almost all the way across. Small boats and canoes also can be launched in **Coldwater Lake** (see Fishing, above). Be advised that it's often windy here. If your craft is blown down the lake, there's no convenient way for you to get out and walk back.

Accessible Outdoors

Many **volcanic monument trails** are barrier-free interpretive paths. These include the Birth of a Lake Loop, Eruption, Silver Lake Wetlands, Winds of Change, Iron Creek Old Growth, Meta Lake, Woods Creek Watchable Wildlife, Lava Canyon, and Trail of Two Forest Trails. **Iron Creek Campground** has barrier-free rest rooms and picnicking. **Seaquest State Park** has barrier-free campsites, rest rooms, and picnic sites. All of the National Volcanic Monument **visitors centers** are barrier free.

outside in

Lodgings

Blue Heron Inn ★   A great base for exploring Mount St. Helens, and for being pampered. *$$$$; 2846 Spirit Lake Hwy, Castle Rock; (360) 274-9595; www.blue heroninn.com.* &

More Information

Coldwater Ridge Visitors Center: *3029 Spirit Lake Highway, Castle Rock, WA 98611: (360) 274-2131, fax (360) 274-2129.*
Cowlitz Valley Ranger District, Randle: *(360) 497-1100.*
Johnston Ridge Observatory: *(360) 274-2140.*
Mount St. Helens Climber's Hotline: *(360) 247-3961.*
Mount St. Helens National Volcanic Monument Headquarters: *4218 NE Yale Bridge Road, Amboy, WA 98601; (360) 247-3900, fax (360) 247-3901, recording (360) 247-3903; www.fs.fed.us/gpnf/mshnvm.*
Mount St. Helens Visitors Center, Silver Lake: *(360) 274-2100.*
Wind River Information Station, Carson: *(509) 427-3200.*

Mount Adams

From Trout Lake north through the Mount Adams Wilderness, west to Takhlakh Lake, and east to the Yakama Indian Reservation, including Walupt Lake and Mount Adams and Indian Heaven Wildernesses.

They should issue head nets at this wilderness boundary. The rough, volcano-forged lands around Mount Adams lead the state in mosquitoes-per-capita. The whiny little critters (and by that we mean bugs, not forest rangers) buzz incessantly in the early summer, forming in clouds at the door to your Explorer before you even slow to a stop. It's enough to make you scream, pull a U-turn, and drive back to the Vancouver Holiday Inn. Assuming you found your way here, that is. Mount Adams is as hard to get to as it is bug-ridden. No matter which way you drive here, it's a long trip, requiring the better part of a day.

Discouraged yet? Well, we tried.

Those factors do discourage a good number of would-be Mount Adams explorers. But they don't even faze hard-core wilderness fans. And that, more than anything, shapes the confused degree of activity at Mount Adams, in many respects the most alluring of the state's string of Cascade volcanoes. Generally, the mountain's reputation for being the loneliest, wildest, and least-seen of the bunch is true: it's visited by far fewer tourists, largely because it's difficult to get to. On the other hand, it's a misnomer to think of Adams as a remote, lonely wilderness. Some areas of the mountain, such as the popular Around the Mountain Trail and South Spur summit climbing route, have become so crowded that limited-use permits are being mulled by Forest Service managers.

All things considered, though, the Mount Adams area offers a much more remote experience than its neighboring peaks. Rainier, St. Helens, and Hood, which form a volcanic triangle around Adams, are all overrun by tourists and hikers in the summer. Adams is Mayberry RFD by comparison. Hikers, campers, climbers, and skiers who do happen upon the peak tend to get hooked. The bait is appealing. At 12,276 feet, Adams is the second-highest peak in the state. But it wins the sheer bulk award hands down. This is a huge mountain, with shoulders broad enough to wear some of the Northwest's most magnificent hanging glaciers.

The peak and much of the surrounding volcanic plain is protected territory. The Mount Adams Wilderness, nearly 43,000 acres, surrounds the mountain to the north, west, and south. The Yakama Indian Nation controls all access to the east, where some truly wild lands still exist.

The natural beauty that brought wilderness protection in 1964 had been attracting nature lovers for nearly 100 years. Mount Adams was first scaled in 1854, and quickly became a destination for weekend mountaineers drawn to one of several early-century outpost hotels. The word got out—the big, beautiful peak just up the road from the Columbia Gorge had an easy summit route. Adams has drawn large numbers of mountaineers ever since.

More than two dozen ascent routes have been climbed and reclimbed. They range from the extremely difficult to the fairly easy snow trudge up the south side. Climbing, however, no longer is the sole focus of activity here. The mountain's north, west, and south slopes make magnificent backpacking territory for strong hikers. Much of the terrain here is even more spectacular than mountainside routes on Mount Rainier. Word of the wonders of Adams is spreading fast, and backcountry use has increased rapidly in the past decade.

In the western shadows of the mountain lies one of the state's most fascinating geologic areas. The South Cascades are a volcanic wonderland, with broad lava plains, extinct craters, collapsed mountain peaks, and long lava tubes dotting the landscape. This is among the most rugged, least-visited land west of the Cascade Crest. Intrepid visitors willing to put in their time on winding Forest Service roads will happen upon some true gems: forest lookouts with stunning mountain views, little-used trails, and lakefront campgrounds with nature-calendar views out the tent flap.

The *zipped* tent flap, that is. Like a lot of other Adams fans, we might have been trying to scare you away to save the place for ourselves. But we weren't kidding about the bloodsuckers. If you're visiting in early to mid-summer, pack an extra plasma unit in your fanny pack. You're going to need it.

Getting There

No matter how you hold the map, there's no really easy way to drive to Mount Adams. Primary access ("primary" meaning most pavement) is from the south. Take Hwy 14 east from Vancouver to White Salmon, then travel north on Highway 141 to Trout Lake. From there, Forest Road 23 leads to the west side of the mountain, while Forest Roads 80 and 82 lead north to most southside Mount Adams trailheads. The Yakama Indian Nation's Bird Creek area (Tract D, open July 1 to September 30 only) on the mountain's southeast side is reached from the east through Glenwood or from the south via Roads 82 and 8290. A fee is charged to enter Tract D. Finally, you can get here from the north by driving Forest Road 23 south from Randle on US Highway 12. It's the shortest route, in terms of mileage, and the best way to reach campgrounds in the Takhlakh Lake area. But if your destination is Trout Lake, Road 23 is a long, slow haul. Note that many Forest roads in this area are closed in winter and often washed out by spring. Call the Mount Adams Ranger District at Trout Lake, (509) 395-3400, for road conditions before setting out.

inside out

Hiking/Backpacking

The north, west, and south slopes of Mount Adams have a lot of what we all sweat to get to: fantastic hanging glaciers, sprawling alpine meadows, and broad views of the rest of the Cascade Range. Mount Adams Wilderness hiking trails in many ways have the feel of alpine routes on Mount Baker—except you'll generally find fewer people down here in the oft-overlooked South Cascades. Dozens of quality hiking trails skirt the lower and middle slopes of Adams, particularly on the south and west sides. They range from short climbs to great mountain viewpoints to long, spectacular backpack routes above 7,000 feet. (Some, such as the Around the Mountain Trail, are so popular that limited-use permits are being contemplated by rangers.) Don't forget the bug dope. This land, heavily scarred by both volcanic and glacial forces, is pitted with little lakes and swamps, which become full-fledged mosquito factories in the summer. For a full trail roster, trail reports, and road information, contact the Mount Adams Ranger District at Trout Lake; (509) 395-3400. Note that a **Northwest Forest Pass,** $5 per day or $30 annually, is required to park in many Forest Service–administered trailheads in this area. They're available from ranger stations, from many private vendors, on-line at www.naturenw.org, or by calling (800) 270-7504.

The star of the Adams trail system is its most popular backpack route—the somewhat misnamed **Round the Mountain Trail/Trail 9** (difficult; 16.6 miles round trip). The trail doesn't go around the mountain at all (although you can go halfway around by combining this trail with the Pacific Crest Trail, which runs up the west side), but it does skirt a large portion of Adams's south slopes. And a spectacular portion, at that. This is an excellent 2- to 3-day backpack route. From a trailhead on Forest Road 8810, the route follows the Pacific Crest Trail 5 miles, then climbs steadily to good campsites at Horseshoe Meadows, 8 miles. It then continues east around the mountain, passing through some beautiful alpine meadows, with grand views all along the route. As you travel east, the trail passes junctions with trails connecting to Morrison Creek and Cold Springs Campgrounds—allowing one-way through hikes if you've arranged to leave a car. The trail ends at the Yakama Indian Reservation Tract D border—the turnaround point unless you've obtained tribal permission and paid an access fee to hike on and exit in the beautiful Bird Creek Meadows on the southeast side of the mountain. The Bird Creek trailhead is reached via Forest Road 8290-285. Note: The Round the Mountain route also offers views of a massive debris avalanche that occurred in 1997, beginning in the Avalanche Glacier cirque, at 12,000 feet elevation on the southwestern flank of Mount Adams.

A similarly beautiful—and challenging—route on the north side of the mountain is the **Highline Trail** (moderate/difficult; 16 miles round trip), which begins on the Killen Creek Trail along Forest Road 2329 near Takhlakh Lake and climbs very steeply along a route that follows a portion of the Pacific Crest Trail. This is a tough trail, looping up and down steeply across rocky moraines and ravines and climbing as high as 7,800 feet. But the terrain is spectacular, as are the views of the Lyman and Lava Glaciers, the Goat Rocks and Mount Rainier from this glacier-carved mountainside. Note that the path crosses streams that form the two branches of the Muddy Fork. Creeks can be high and difficult to cross on warm afternoons.

Day hikers also will find plenty to keep them busy on the northwest side of the mountain. **Divide Camp** (moderate; 5.6 miles round trip), on Forest Road 2329 southeast of Takhlakh Lake, is a surprisingly easy hike (the elevation gain to the end point on the PCT is about 1,300 feet), considering the payoff: lovely meadows along Adams Creek and up-close views of the Adams Glacier, at about 6,000 feet. Campers at Takhlakh Lake itself don't have to walk very far for their own great views of the mountain. **Takhlakh Loop Trail** (easy; 1.1 miles round trip) begins in Takhlakh Lake Campground (see Camping, below) and skirts the lakeshore. For a similarly good view of Adams from just outside the wilderness area, try the **Steamboat Viewpoint Trail** (moderate; 1.4 miles round trip), northwest of Trout Lake on Forest Road 8854-021, which

Takhlakh Lake reflects Mount Adams on a quiet August morning

climbs to a former lookout site on Steamboat Mountain. Goats are often spotted in the area.

If you're looking for day hikes on the mountain's south side, **Stagman Ridge** (moderate; 8.2 miles round trip), on Forest Road 8031-120, is a moderate climb to a nice lunch/view spot at a junction with the Pacific Crest Trail, elevation 5,800 feet. (If you can ignore the big clearcut on the trail's lower stretches, it's almost a real wilderness experience, with great views of the Avalanche and White Salmon Glaciers.) This is another good place to view the amazing debris avalanche that occurred in the Avalanche Glacier cirque in August 1997. The elevation gain is about 1,600 feet.

The **Shorthorn Trail** (easy/moderate; 5.6 miles round trip), which begins in Morrison Creek Campground (see Camping, below), is a not-too-tough walk to a 6,200-foot view of Mount Adams's south face. If you don't like it, blame its original developers: sheep herders, following old Native American paths. The elevation gain is 1,400 feet. The **Snipes Mountain Trail** (moderate; 11.4 miles round trip) on Forest Road 8225-150 climbs along the 4-mile-long Aiken Lava Bed, formed by an eruption 2,000 to 4,000 years ago. It offers good views of the mountain, but water is sparse in midsummer. The trail, named for Ben Snipes, a local cattleman involved in "range wars" with sheepherders, has an elevation gain of about 2,500 feet.

Many more trails are within a moderate driving distance in the buggy-but-beautiful Indian Heaven Wilderness west of Trout Lake on Forest Road 24.

Climbing

The very best high-altitude hike in this region actually qualifies as a climb. It's the **Mount Adams summit route.** The climb up 12,276-foot Adams, the second-highest point in Washington (and arguably its loveliest peak, now that St. Helens has taken itself out of the running), requires plenty of stamina, but only basic alpine-climbing skills. It's one of the most climber-friendly summits we've found in the Northwest—basically a long, steep snow trudge, much like the route to the summit of the South Sister in Central Oregon. That doesn't mean it's easy, or—when the weather turns nasty—even safe. The easy routes on Adams are south-face climbs such as the **South Spur** from Cold Creek Campground. Even this one is 5.7 miles and 6,700 vertical feet one way. Most people take 6 to 8 hours to reach the summit. Crampons and ice axes are recommended all year. The route is well marked. Some climbers choose to spend the night at the "Lunch Counter," a flat area above the Crescent Glacier, at about 9,000 feet and then head for the summit the next morning. Other popular routes include the **North Glacier** and **Adams Glacier** climbs.

No matter which way you go, you're exposing yourself to about 6,500 vertical feet of above-tree-line steep snow climbing. Don't attempt it unless you know what you're doing. For experienced climbers—or rookies climbing with veterans—the south slopes of Adams often turn into an early-season training ground. Adams is famous for its early-summer climb-up, ski-down trips.

Overnight **wilderness permits,** free and available at trailheads, are required for all trips in the Mount Adams Wilderness. And since the fateful summer of '00, you'll need an additional **climbing permit** to go above 7,000 feet on Adams anytime between April 1 and October 31. The new "Cascades Volcano Pass" is $15 per person for climbs involving any weekend days—Friday through Sunday, $10 per person for trips on Mondays through Thursdays, or $30 per year. It's also good for Mount St. Helens, and the parking permit that comes with it replaces the **Northwest Forest Pass** you'd otherwise need to park at trailheads leading to summit routes. Passes are available from the Cowlitz Valley Ranger District at Randle, and from self-issuing machines at the Mount Adams Ranger District at Trout Lake, or Killen Creek trailhead parking area (see Hiking, above.) For more information, call the Mount Adams Ranger District, (509) 395-3400. Order forms can be printed from the Gifford Pinchot web site (see More information, below) and mailed in. For climbing-route updates, call the Adams climbing hot line, (360) 891-5015.

Camping

Some very pleasant, relatively untrampled backcountry campgrounds are found in this area—uncrowded largely because they're not easy to drive to from any major highway. All these campgrounds are open summers only, charge a fee, and offer no utility hookups or campsite reservations.

Mount Adams northwest side

Cowlitz Valley Ranger District; (360) 497-1100):

The nicest spot in the area is **Takhlakh Lake Campground,** where 62 campsites ring a lovely lake, with good fishing (see below) and drop-dead gorgeous views of Mount Adams. It's open from mid-June to late September. Campsites can be reserved up to 240 days in advance; (877) 444-6777; www.reserveusa.com. *34 miles southeast of Randle via Forest Rds 23 and 2329.*

Nearby **Olallie Lake Campground** is similar but much smaller, with only 5 sites. *On Rd 5601.* Another option in the same area is **Chain of Lakes Campground,** a walk-in camp area with 3 established sites. It's pretty dusty, however, and a popular dirt-bike trail runs nearby. Camp here as a last resort. *Off Rd 2329.*

Farther north, in the Killen and Spring Creek drainages, are **Horse-shoe Lake** (10 sites; RVs to 16 feet), **Keene's Horse Camp** (12 sites and hitching facilities), and **Killen Creek** (8 sites; RVs to 22 feet, essentially a wilderness trailhead). *All are reached via Rds 23 and 2329 south from Randle.*

Mount Adams south side

Mount Adams Ranger District; (509) 395-3400:

Cold Springs is a high (4,200 feet) site with 9 primitive campsites and not much else, unless you count lots of huckleberry bushes and good access to south-side hiking trails and climbing routes (see the Hiking and Climbing sections, above). *Follow Rds 80 and 8040 north from Rd 23.*

Nearby is **Morrison Creek Campground,** a very small (12 tent sites) campground/horse camp at 4,600 feet.

The Yakama Indian Nation also operates three small campgrounds in the Bird Creek drainage on the south side of the mountain: **Bird Lake** (20 sites), **Mirror Lake** (12 sites), and **Bench Lake** (44 sites) are east of Trout Lake *via Rds 82 and 8290.* Call the Yakama Nation's Forestry Development Program, (509) 865-5121, ext. 657, for information.

Mount Adams east side

The Department of Natural Resources operates **Island Camp** (6 sites) and **Bird Creek** (8 sites), both priitive campgrounds with access through the

Goldendale area. Call the DNR's Southeast Region in Ellensburg, (509) 925-8510.

Indian Heaven Wilderness

Remote Forest Service campgrounds surrounding this fascinating geologic area include **Cultus Creek** (51 sites; no hookups; RVs to 32 feet), reached from Hwy 14 west of White Salmon by following Hwy 141 25.5 miles north to Forest Road 24 and proceeding 15 miles northwest; **Goose Lake** (37 sites; no hookups; RVs to 18 feet), on Forest Road 60, also reached from Hwy 14 west of White Salmon by following Hwy 141 and Forest Road 24; **Tillicum** (32 sites; no hookups; RVs to 18 feet), 4 miles beyond Cultus Creek on Road 24; **Little Goose** (28 sites, used primarily during fall berry season, also on Road 24); **Saddle** (12 tent sites), a poor campground with bad road access near Tillicum (above); and **Atkisson Group Camp** (space for 50 campers, reservations only, on Hwy 141). Call the Mount Adams Ranger District, (509) 395-3400.

Berry Picking

The alpine meadows on and around Mount Adams are Washington's most prolific **huckleberry** producers. The sweet, juicy berries thrive on the region's marshy, volcano-pocked landscape—the same factors that combine to create bumper crops of mosquitoes. Peak picking time is mid-August to mid-September, although this varies from year to year depending on the weather. Your best bet is to call the Mount Adams Ranger District at Trout Lake, (509) 395-3400, to find out what's ripe, when, and where. (You'll need to get a free **picking permit** there, anyway). Prizes go to anyone who can pick enough berries for an 8-inch pie—then successfully bake it on a Whisperlite camp stove. Also please note: Black bears like huckleberries, too, and they were here first!

Fishing

Takhlakh, Council, Horseshoe, and Olallie Lakes, all easily accessible from Forest Service campgrounds in the Randle Ranger District (see Camping, above), offer decent spring and summer trout fishing. Stocked with **cutthroat, brown,** and **brook trout,** they're fun to fish from canoes or other small craft launched from the campgrounds. If you don't catch anything, you won't care, so spectacular is the view of Mount Adams on a clear day.

Cross-Country Skiing/Snowshoeing

Two maintained Sno-Parks are northeast of Trout Lake on Forest Road 82. **Smith Butte** is a small (10-car) parking area providing access to a number of ungroomed backcountry trails. **Pineside** is more developed, with intermediate 8K and 2.2K loops on either side of Road 82. For the deluxe treatment, however, the place to go is Flying L Ranch near Glenwood. The ranch maintains about 3 kilometers of **private** groomed trails, but a much more extensive **trail network** (about 14K) is on nearby state Department of Natural Resources land. (See Lodgings, below.)

Accessible Outdoors

Takhlakh Lake Campground offers barrier-free rest rooms, campsites, and an interpretive trail ringing the lake.

Lodgings

Flying L Ranch ★   If you never went to camp as a kid, the Flying L Ranch gives you the chance. *$$; 25 Flying L Ln, Glenwood; (509) 364-3488 or (888) MT-ADAMS; www.mt-adams.com.*

Serenity's Village ★   These cabins set among firs are a good base for exploring the Trout Lake Valley. *$$; Mile 23, Hwy 141, Trout Lake; (509) 395-2500 or (800) 276-7993; www.gorge.net/serenitys.* &

More Information

Cowlitz Valley Ranger District, Randle: *(360) 497-1100.*
Gifford Pinchot National Forest Headquarters, Vancouver:
   (360) 891-5000; www.fs.fed.us/gpnf.
Mount Adams Climber's Hotline: *(360) 891-5015.*
Mount Adams Ranger District, Trout Lake: *(509) 395-3400.*
Yakama Indian Nation, Forestry Development Program:
   (509) 865-5121, ext. 657.

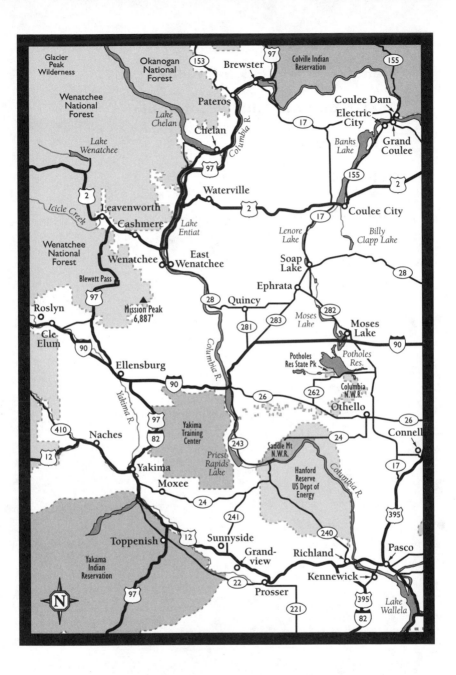

Central Washington

Central Washington

Wenatchee
and Mission Ridge

From Cashmere east to the Columbia River, west to US Highway 97, and south to Mission Ridge Ski Area, including Wenatchee Confluence and Squilchuck State Parks.

Make no mistake: for a city that lies at the junction of the spectacular Wenatchee and the mighty Columbia Rivers, the greater Wenatchee area isn't great at all. It's miles of strip malls, truck stops, apple warehouses, and a maddeningly slow, one-way thoroughfare through downtown. Wenatchee's cluttered sprawl (a unique land-use achievement!) can make you downright loopy, particularly if you're fresh off one of the many 70-mph highways leading into town.

Yet we're forced to admit that some local amenities—one old, a couple new—are making the Apple Capital a tasty year-round destination, particularly for cyclists, campers, and skiers. The key to Wenatchee's new recreation luster is its smartly designed Apple Capital Loop trail, which winds 11 miles along and over the Columbia River. The trail has encouraged both heavier use and sprucing up of existing Columbia River waterfront parks in the north section of Wenatchee. Spend a day on the path, and Wenatchee's ugly side fades from view, literally and figuratively.

Depending on your taste in skiing, Wenatchee also can be a worthy winter destination. When the deep, dry stuff collects on Mission Ridge (which is not nearly as often as anyone would like), the local ski mountain turns into a high, dry, downhill racecourse guaranteed to test your base wax.

Granted, getting there means doing the downtown Wenatchee crawl, which is only slightly more pleasant than driving through

A cyclist crosses the Columbia River on the Apple Capital Loop

Lynnwood at rush hour. But if you squint really hard, it looks like paradise . . . or you just rear-ended a big ol' pickup truck. In Wenatchee, save yourself some time and look north and south of town.

Getting There

Wenatchee is 138 miles (about 2.5 hours) east of Seattle via US 2, the Stevens Pass Highway. It can also be approached via Interstate 90 east and then north on US 97 over Blewett Pass. Recreation sites in the Mission Ridge area are 13 miles above and south of town. Take Mission Street south from downtown Wenatchee and follow signs.

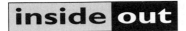

Camping/Parks

Campers in the Wenatchee area have their choice of . . . well, basically one site, but it's a particularly good one. (At this writing, a longtime alternative, Wenatchee River County Park near Monitor, was closed, its fate uncertain.) **Wenatchee Confluence State Park,** just north of town on US 97A, is a modern (established 1990) park that sits at the confluence of the Wenatchee and Columbia Rivers. This sunny, flat space, surrounded on two sides by cool waters, is a superb spot for family campers, particularly those with kids on bikes. The Apple Capital Loop trail (see Cycling, below) runs right through the campground, providing year-round riding fun, not to mention easy pedal or foot access to downtown Wenatchee. The park's 59 campsites (51 with full hookups; RVs to 65 feet) are spread throughout a nicely manicured, grassy field (exposed to sun until the planted shade trees gain a few stories in height) that's a delight for tent campers. Also on site are a volleyball court and play area, basketball courts, a boat launch on the Columbia River, swimming area, 300-person group camp, and more than 100 picnic sites, most of them along or near the Columbia River. Wenatchee Confluence is open all year. Campsites can be reserved up to 11 months in advance by calling Reservations Northwest; (800) 452-5687. *Immediately north of the US 2/US 97A junction near Wenatchee, follow signs north on US 97A; (509) 663-6373 or (800) 233-0321.*

Another nearby campground, **Squilchuck State Park,** near Mission Ridge Ski Area, is a reservation-only group camp for up to 168 people. It reverts to a ski hill operated by Wenatchee Valley College on winter weekends (see Skiing, below). *Follow Mission St south from Wenatchee, then follow signs along Squilchuck Rd; (800) 233-0321.*

Cycling

At first blush, Wenatchee seems an unlikely destination for two-wheelers. Its topography—rolling hills and hot, sunny summertime skies—is fairly pedestrian (sorry), and most streets in the area are either busy interstates or dusty back roads. The **Apple Capital Loop,** however, turns that image on its head. The loop, which runs through Wenatchee Confluence State Park (the best parking area and starting point; see Camping, above), crosses the Wenatchee River on a newly constructed bridge and rolls through some lovely green city and utility-company waterfront parks near Wenatchee before crossing the Columbia on a railroad-bridge-turned-footbridge. On the east side, it follows the Columbia's shoreline north for 4 or 5 miles, then recrosses the river on a concrete highway bridge and returns to Wenatchee Confluence State Park. The total loop of about 11 miles makes a great day trip for campers at Wenatchee Confluence, or for any travelers who find themselves in Wenatchee for a day. It's all asphalt, with smooth riding, few hills, and plenty of walkers and in-line skaters for company. Even on hot days, a cooling breeze off the river makes this path a treat. The west side of the trail is lighted until midnight. Plans call for a northern extension of the trail to Rocky Reach Dam.

Hiking/Walking

For downtown Wenatchee visitors, the **Apple Capital Loop** (see Cycling, above) offers a pleasant walk along the Columbia and Wenatchee Rivers. From downtown, a walk north on the trail, through the city's waterfront parks and over the Wenatchee River footbridge to Wenatchee Confluence State Park, makes a perfect half-day round trip of about 7 miles.

Outside town, many unmarked fire trails lead into the dry forest area around **Squilchuck State Park** (see Camping, above), and fire roads and hiking trails also emanate from **Mission Ridge Ski Area** (see Skiing, below), some connecting with trails and roads in the Swauk Pass area to the west, along US 97.

Rafting/Kayaking/Canoeing

The **lower Wenatchee River** is perhaps Washington's whitewater favorite. It's easy to see why. From Leavenworth downstream through Cashmere to—ultimately—the Columbia River confluence, the Wenatchee is a broad, rushing stream throughout the spring and early summer, when it carries millions of gallons of Central Cascades snowmelt from Tumwater Canyon and Icicle Gorge. Peak months are April through June, and most commercial rafters focus on the 18 miles of rapids between Leavenworth and Monitor. The river's appeal: big, fast water, lots of speed; pleasant, sunny surroundings (high bluffs topped by apple orchards); and good put-in and take-out spots below Leavenworth and at Cashmere. A large number of commercial **rafting companies** run trips on the lower Wenatchee. Contact the Leavenworth Ranger District, (509) 548-6977, for references. Kayakers and experienced whitewater canoeists are drawn to the same waterway for the same reasons. Good put-ins are found just east of Leavenworth, at Peshastin, in downtown Cashmere, and at the Monitor Wildlife Area. You'll see plenty of kayakers in the area throughout the summer. Even after water levels drop too low to make large rafts practical, this remains runnable water for kayak paddlers. Note: There's a **nec-**

essary portage over an irrigation dam at Dryden, just below Peshastin Creek, and several Class III to IV rapids to negotiate.

Downhill Skiing

Mission Ridge Ski Area, 13 miles southwest of Wenatchee, is a favorite of many Washington dry-snow skiers. The mountain indeed gets dusted with a much drier-than-usual base, and a small-but-efficient resort creates a nice, homey feel here. Mission, since 1998 under the stewardship of Harbor Mountain Company, a subsidiary of the same Harbor Resorts that owns Stevens Pass Ski Area and Schweitzer Mountain Resort at Sandpoint, Idaho, has taken some major customer-service strides, following through with previous owners' plans to regrade and widen ski trails and upgrade facilities. The resort's goal: convince all those Seattle-area skiers that Mission is worth driving another 90 minutes beyond Stevens Pass, a longtime state favorite.

To that end, they've organized some very economical weekend packages with Wenatchee-area motels. Hit Wenatchee on that one midwinter weekend when the sky is blue and powder is deep, and you'll have a true Rocky Mountain–style ski getaway—at a fraction of the price. Chronically light snowfall continues to plague Mission Ridge, however.

Physically, Mission is somewhat unique among Washington ski resorts. The upper mountain is distinguished by a panel of steep canyon walls—the Bomber Cliffs—sometimes jumped from by hard-core ski vaulters (not recommended). Upper-mountain chutes and glades collect deep snow, and make excellent expert skiing after snow dumps. Below, most runs are long, fairly narrow trails through mixed forest. Most of this mountain is a treat for intermediate cruisers and lovers of light, groomed surfaces. Favorite fast cruiser run: Bomber Bowl. Favorite white-knuckle, jump-turn run: Wa Wa or Ka Wham Chutes.

Mission has no slopeside lodging, but plenty is available in Wenatchee, which runs a shuttle bus to the mountain. For package-deal information, call the ski area or the Wenatchee Visitors Bureau (see More Information, below), or consult the ski area's web site (see below).

Mission Ridge stats: Elevation: 4,600 to 6,740 feet. Skiable acreage: 2,080. Lifts: six (two rope tows, four double chairs). Hours: Daily, 9am to 4pm. *Mission Ridge is 13 miles southwest of Wenatchee on Squilchuck Rd— follow Mission St south from downtown and watch for signs; mountain information (509) 663-6543, snow phone (800) 374-1693; www.missionridge.com.*

Just down the road a few big GS turns is **Squilchuck Ski Bowl,** a small (one rope tow) operation run by Wenatchee Valley College. It's a fun beginner slope, and a grand place to rent out for the weekend (the 200-person ski lodge can be reserved by calling Reservations Northwest; (800) 452-5687.

Cross-country Skiing

A series of unimproved cross-country trails also begins at **Squilchuck**. Fire trails and snowed-in Forest Service roads in the **hills above Mission Ridge** Ski Area are favorites of backcountry telemarkers. A favorite winter activity is the **Hog Loppet**, a 21-mile cross-country ski traverse from the top of Mission Ridge to Blewett Pass; *(800) 572-7753*.

Wildlife Watching

The South Confluence area, a marshy natural set-aside at the Wenatchee-Columbia confluence, is a productive creature-spotting venue. Park at Wenatchee Confluence State Park, follow the trail south over the Wenatchee River Footbridge, and turn left on the waterfront interpretive trail. Watch for **blue herons, pheasants, hawks, eagles, ducks**, and small mammals such as **beavers** and **raccoons**. This 100-acre, wildlife-rich spot has an equally rich history: it's an ancient campsite of Columbia River tribes, who were here more than 10,000 years ago. The first white settlers in the Wenatchee area also took up residence here.

Accessible Outdoors

Wenatchee Confluence State Park offers barrier-free camping (51 sites), picnicking (5 sites), rest rooms, water, and access to the wheelchair-accessible **Apple Capital Loop trail.**

outside in

Restaurants

Garlini's Ristorante Italiano ★   Dim lighting, dark wood, and festive music bring Italy to the senses. $; *810 Valley Mall Pkwy, East Wenatchee; (509) 884-1707.*

John Horan's Steak & Seafood House ★★   The chef at this 1899 Victorian farmhouse makes his mark with seasonally fresh seafood, but you'll be equally impressed with the sirloin. $$$; *2 Horan Rd, Wenatchee; (509) 663-0018; www.johnhoranhouse.com.* ♿

The Windmill ★★   Meals at this offbeat-looking place are western American classics. $$; *1501 N Wenatchee Ave, Wenatchee; (509) 665-9529.*

Lodgings

The Warm Springs Inn ★   The pillared entrance lends majesty to this five-room B&B. $$; *1611 Love Ln, Wenatchee; (509) 662-8365 or (800) 543-3645; www.warmspringsinn.com.*

West Coast Wenatchee Center Hotel ★   This is the nicest hotel on the strip (a very plain strip, mind you). $$; *201 N Wenatchee Ave, Wenatchee; (509) 662-1234 or (800) 426-0670; www.westcoasthotels.com.* &

More Information

Arlberg Sports (outdoor gear; in-line skate rentals): *(509) 663-7401.*
Asplund's Sports (outdoor gear; rentals; info): *(800) 922-2038; www.asplundsports.com.*
Mission Ridge Ski Area: *(509) 663-7631; www.missionridge.com.*
Ski Link Bus (Mission Ridge shuttles): *(509) 662-1155.*
Wenatchee Chamber of Commerce: *(800) 57-APPLE; www.wenatchee.org.*
Wenatchee Visitors and Convention Bureau: *(800) 572-7753; www.wenatcheevalley.org.*

Chelan
and the Middle Columbia

From Rocky Reach Dam north to Pateros, west to the Glacier Peak Wilderness, and east to US Highway 97 and the Columbia River, including lower Lake Chelan, the Entiat River Valley, and Alta Lake, Twenty-five Mile Creek, and Lake Chelan, Daroga, and Lincoln Rock State Parks.

By all rights, this area should be one mondo mudhole. Consider the ingredients: thousands of square miles of empty, dry land. Billions of gallons of clear, standing water. Nowhere else in the Northwest will you find so much wet surrounded by so much dry. Get the two together, and you should have a first-class slophole on your hands. But wet and dry stay nicely separated, thank you, in the middle Columbia area, which is distinguished mainly—okay, only—by two of the more impressive waterways in the state.

One is the middle Columbia River itself, a once-magnificent stream now relegated to lake status by an endless series of hydropower dams. Even in its dammed state, the Columbia, once the greatest free-flowing Western river, is an impressive waterway. Surrounded by massive, crumbling-basalt cliffs, its water irrigates millions of Central Washington apple trees, making this once-barren stretch of drylands an agricultural gold mine.

An equally impressive waterway, Lake Chelan, creates gold of its own—recreation dollars—thanks to the natural handiwork of ancient Central Washington glaciers, which carved a lake trough that ranks among the deepest in North America. Lake Chelan, 55 miles long and never more than 2 miles wide, redefines "deep and clear." The lake bottom is 1,500 feet down in places, a mark that's surpassed in the United States only by Lake Tahoe and Crater Lake.

That in itself doesn't make Lake Chelan a great outdoor getaway. But its location does. The heavenly waterway just happens to be surrounded on three sides by celestial mountain peaks. To the southwest rise the magnificent, glacier-draped mountains of the Glacier Peak Wilderness. To the northwest are the rugged peaks of North Cascades National Park. And due north is the impressive Sawtooth Range and other peaks in the Lake Chelan–Sawtooth Wilderness.

All these mountains are visible on a leisurely trip up the lake, either on the popular *Lady of the Lake* or *Lady Express* tour boats or by private watercraft. The setting is so spectacular, in fact, that many Lake Chelan visitors never leave the lake at all, choosing to while away the days on a houseboat or at a lakeside campsite. Lake Chelan is a watersport wonderland that draws thousands of boaters, sailors, windsurfers, water-skiers, Jet-ski riders, big-fish anglers, and swimmers. The surrounding delights— hiking or backpacking from Stehekin or the mountain village of Holden; cycling down impressive canyons and coulees; riding never-ending thermals on a hang glider from tall, open buttes; cross-country skiing on unobstructed, sunny slopes—make the Chelan area one of the state's most richly stocked recreation treasure chests.

And there's no need to rough it in order to drink this all in. The Chelan area's wealth of sunshine and just plain wealth (imported by retirees and vacation-home builders) have sparked an amenities boomlet here, with condos, hotels, B&Bs, and resorts sprouting in Chelan and Manson. At first glance, in fact, Lake Chelan's southern shores look more like a condo-infested Malibu than a Cascades mountain getaway. Don't be fooled. Lake Chelan is a massive, cold-water dogleg, and only its southernmost little pinkie is touched by development. Get on the boat to Stehekin, and you leave time—and time-shares—far behind.

Together, the middle Columbia and Lake Chelan represent the best and worst of the Washington experience: an unstoppable river stopped by dams. A prehistoric lake skimmed by Jet-skis. Condos with views of actual wilderness areas. Summertime-dream-worthy campsites—booked up before Valentine's Day. It's Washington in a bottle. Somebody please put the cork in—and by all means, refrain from shaking.

Getting There

The middle Columbia area is reached by driving US Highway 2 or Interstate 90 east from the Puget Sound area and following US 97 (on the east bank of the Columbia) or US 97A (on the west bank) north to Pateros. The two highways are linked by bridges only at Wenatchee and Chelan, US 97A's northern terminus. Allow 3 to 4 hours for the 170-mile drive from Seattle. In the summer, an alternate route is driving Hwy 20, the North Cascades Highway, through Winthrop and Twisp, then Hwy 153 south down the Methow Valley to US 97 at Pateros. Access to the shores of lower Lake Chelan is provided by Hwy 150 on the north shore and S Lakeshore Road; Entiat River Road provides access to the Wenatchee National Forest south of the lake.

inside out

Camping

Columbia River

A string of modern campgrounds is found on the shores of the Columbia between Wenatchee and Pateros. The many riverside campgrounds in this region feature sprawling grassy playfields, boat launches, a swimming area, and flat, open trailer and tent sites separated by young shade trees. All of these parks are popular with boaters, who flock here in summer months to water-ski and soak up the sun.

On the east bank is **Lincoln Rock State Park,** within sight of Rocky Reach Dam. The park has its own unique physical oddity: a rock face across the Columbia that, if you squint pretty hard, looks a lot like a profile of Abraham Lincoln. (We must confess it really does look like Lincoln. On the other hand, the fact that someone actually took the time to discover this is more than a little disconcerting.) Lincoln Rock has 94 campsites (32 full hookups, 35 water/electrical hookups; RVs to 65 feet), extensive playgrounds and ballfields, two boat launches and moorage floats, tennis and volleyball courts, horseshoe pits, and large, well-developed picnic facilities. Just across the river (actually, they call the impoundment behind Rocky Reach "Entiat Lake") is the Rocky Reach Dam visitors center, which you can only get to by driving back south to Wenatchee, crossing the river and driving up US 97A. Lincoln Rock State Park is open from mid-March to late October. Campsites can be reserved up to 11 months in advance by calling Reservations Northwest; (800) 452-5687. *On US 97, 7 miles north of East Wenatchee; (509) 884-8702 or (800) 233-0321.*

Farther north on US 97, **Daroga State Park** is another welcome oasis in this dry, brown canyon. This relatively new state park is one of the best in the region, with an interesting layout, particularly for tent campers. It's actually two campgrounds in one: Daroga, a former ranch site, has a lagoon separated from the main Columbia by a narrow earthen bar, which has been equipped with 17 walk-in campsites (the park provides wheelbarrow-type devices to help you move your gear.) These are very nice spots, well worth the effort to get here. The park, which has nearly a mile and a half of

A camper soaks up the silence at Alta Lake State Park

riverfront, also has a nice waterfront group campsite on the south border and a neatly kept trailer loop in an upland area at the far north end. (Note that the entrance for the walk-in sites is a short distance south of the main park entrance on US 97.) In all, Daroga offers 17 walk-in campsites, 25 RV sites with water/electric hookups, two 100-person group camps (booked by reservation only), and extensive picnic facilities on the shores of the Columbia. Also on the premises are a swimming area and bathhouse, boat launch and moorage, short cycle paths, and a playground. When the weather cooperates, winds that kick up here are sufficient for windsurfing. Since you asked about the name: former property owner Grady Auvil developed a new strain of peach, which was named "Daroga" by local nurseryman Pete Van Well Sr. The name contains the letters of the names of three Auvil brothers, Dave, Robert and Grady, who began working the ranch in 1928. Daroga is open mid-March through mid-October. Campsites cannot be reserved. *On US 97, 18 miles north of East Wenatchee, 15 miles south of Beebe Bridge; (509) 664-6380 or (800) 233-0321.*

Entiat City Park, a 50-acre muncipal campground, offers 81 sites (31 water/electrical hookups; RVs of any length), a nearby boat launch, picnic facilities, showers, a swimming beach, and other amenities. It's open April through September. It's a popular RV stopover, so reservations are recommended. *On US 97A 16 miles north of Wenatchee, at Entiat; (800) 736-8428 or (509) 784-1500.*

Entiat River Valley

Lovers of dry Central Washington plateau country are drawn to the long, narrow Entiat Valley, which connects the Columbia River Valley to the alluring alpine country in the Glacier Peak Wilderness. A string of picturesque Forest Service campgrounds await, between 1,600 and 3,100 feet in elevation, in the upper Entiat Valley. They're primitive, but strategically located. The remote campgrounds are filled in summer months with small-stream anglers, horse or dirt-bike riders, or hikers and backpackers headed into the wilderness; in the fall they're filled with hunters. Note that much of this valley was devastated by the massive Tyee Creek wildfire of 1994, one of the worst in modern history. The fire burned uncontrolled from midsummer to the first snows of October, stretching north nearly all the way to Lake Chelan. But vegetation and wildlife have been quick to spring back.

All these campgrounds are open mid-May through October, all have pit toilets, and all except Pine Flat have piped water. Most are suitable for tents and small RVs. Fees range from $3 to $10 per vehicle per night. Campsites cannot be reserved. Call or visit the Wenatchee National Forest's Entiat Ranger District, 2108 Entiat Wy, (509) 784-1511.

The campgrounds, all on Entiat River Road unless noted otherwise (mileages are from the town of Entiat), are: **Pine Flat** (7 sites and a 30- to 50-person group camp), *10 miles up Entiat River Rd and then left onto Mad River Rd*; **Fox Creek** (16 sites), *27 miles*; **Lake Creek** (18 sites), *28 miles*; **Silver Falls** (31 sites and a 30- to 50-person group camp), *32 miles*; **North Fork** (9 sites), *33 miles*; **Spruce Grove** (2 tent-only sites), *35 miles*; **Three Creek** (3 tent-only sites), *36 miles*; and **Cottonwood** (25 sites), *38 miles*.

For an even more rustic setting, dozens of unofficial campsites are found along the river on Entiat River Road, which climbs high into the river's headlands between the Entiat and Chelan Mountains. Many classic Glacier Peak Wilderness backpacking trips begin from this area. (See Hiking/Backpacking, below.)

Lake Chelan and environs

Two well-developed state parks on this massive lake's south shores are camper and boater favorites, while a string of walk-in or boat-in campgrounds farther up the lake are popular with people who don't mind packing in their gear.

Lake Chelan State Park is a boater's heaven. This beautiful campground on the shores of the deep, crystal-clear lake was built with boating in mind, and rates as one of the most popular waterfront campsites in the state. The park has 144 sites (17 with water/electric hookups; RVs to 30 feet). The hookup spots are clustered side by side in a grassy upland area of the park. Far nicer are the spectacular walk-in sites along an access road in the park's southern section. Each has a flat tent pad, a table, and a fireplace, all within a lazy rock's-throw of the lakeshore, which is well equipped with modern boat-moorage floats. Absolutely killer views, right from your vestibule. Also on site are a swimming area, playfields, picnic shelters, a bathhouse, and boat launch. In the winter, the park is a popular snow-play area, with local cross-country skiers using it as a warming base for ski trips on the area's roads and trails. Lake Chelan State Park is open all year, but weekends only from late October to late March. You're not likely to get in during the summer without a reservation. Campsites can be reserved up to 11 months in advance by calling Reservations Northwest; (800) 452-5687. *From US 97A about 8 miles north of Entiat, turn north on Hwy 971 (Navarre Coulee Rd) and proceed about 9.5 miles to the park, on S Lakeshore Rd; (509) 687-3710 or (800) 233-0321.*

Just up the road is **Twenty-five Mile Creek State Park,** an interesting old resort site that became a state park in 1975. Boating also dominates the scene here; the park has a boat launch, ample moorage, a fuel dock, and other amenities. The campground offers 86 campsites (23 with hookups) and an 88-person group camp, all in wooded sites near the lake and along Twenty-five Mile Creek. Kids can test their fishing gear on a fishing pier or in the stream, which holds rainbow trout. Twenty-five Mile Creek is open from April through September. Campsites can be reserved up to 11 months in advance by calling Reservations Northwest; (800) 452-5687. *On S Lakeshore Rd, about 10 miles north of Lake Chelan State Park; (509) 687-3710 or (800) 233-0321.*

For campers who think the "it" in "getting away from it all" means automobiles, **Lake Chelan's shorelines** also offer some of Washington's better walk-in or boat-in (or some creative combination thereof) camping experiences. A string of primitive U.S. Forest Service camps, all with floating docks or fixed moorage piers, rings the lake. A $5 per night fee is charged at most boat-in sites. From Chelan on the lower lake up to Lucerne on the south shore, they are: **Big Creek** (4 campsites, 4-boat moorage capacity), **Corral Creek** (2 sites, 6 boats); **Graham Harbor** (5 sites, 10 boats); **Graham Harbor Creek** (4 sites, 6 boats); **Domke Falls** (3 sites, 6 boats); **Refrigerator Harbor** (4 sites, 4 boats); and **Lucerne** (2 sites; 11 boats). From Chelan on the lower lake up to Prince Creek on the north shore, they are: **Mitchell Creek** (6 sites, 17 boats); **Antilon** (dispersed sites), north of the lake near Mitchell Creek; **Deer Point** (4 sites, 8 boats); **Moore Point** (4 sites, 3 boats); **Safety Harbor** (2 sites, 6 boats); and **Prince Creek** (6 sites, 3 boats), 18 miles south of Stehekin on Chelan Lakeshore Trail.

South Navarre (4 tent sites at 6,475 feet) is a primitive, tents-only

U.S. Forest Service campground 40 miles northwest of Chelan near Chelan Summit and South Navarre Peak. *On Forest Rd 3001, reached from Hwy 150 on the north shore.*

The Forest Service also maintains a half dozen primitive walk-in sites along the Chelan Lakeshore and Prince Creek Trails (see Hiking, below). All of these hike-in campsItes are free. They are: **Cub Lake** (3 sites), *6.5 miles from Lake Chelan on Prince Creek Trail;* **Boiling Lake** (3 sites), *10 miles from Lake Chelan on Prince Creek Trail;* **Surprise Lake** (3 sites), *6 miles from Lake Chelan on Trail 1246 (north of Prince Creek);* and **Domke Lake** (8 sites), *2 miles from Lucerne via Trails 1230 and 1280.*

Another possible remote destination is **Holden Ballpark** (2 sites), near the Lutheran Camp/mining burg of Holden Village, reached by boating to Lucerne and riding the shuttle bus. Call Wenatchee National Forest's Lake Chelan Ranger District, (509) 682-2576, for more information.

Finally, a handful of primitive, tents-only, U.S. Forest Service campgrounds are scattered in the rugged hills above Lake Chelan's southern shore. All are on or near Forest Road 5900 (Shady Pass Road), reached by continuing a short distance beyond Twenty-Five Mile Creek State Park on S Lakeshore Road. These campgrounds, most of which have pit toilets but no piped water or other services, are, in order: **Snowberry Bowl** (3 sites), *3.7 miles southwest of the lake;* **Ramona Park** (8 sites), closed in 2000 due to flood danger—call first; **Windy Camp** (2 sites), *15 miles southwest of Ramona Park on Rd 8410;* **Grouse Mountain** (4 sites), *8 miles west of the lake;* **Junior Point** (5 sites), *14 miles west of the lake;* and **Handy Springs** (1 site), *15 miles west of the lake.*

All the lakeshore campsites can be reached either by private watercraft or **floatplane;** call Chelan Airways, (509) 682-5555. Or arrangements can be made for drop-offs by *Lady of the Lake* passenger boats ferrying visitors from Chelan to Stehekin in North Cascades National Park; (509) 682-4584; www.ladyofthelake.com. The most popular dropoff camps are **Prince Creek,** where Chelan Lakeshore Trail walkers depart for an 18-mile walk north to Stehekin, and **Lucerne,** the drop point for hikers bound for Holden Village along Railroad Creek in the Glacier Peak Wilderness. See the Stehekin and the Lake Chelan National Recreation Area chapter for more details.

Pateros area

A little-known but very nice campground, **Alta Lake State Park,** is tucked away in the foothills of the lower Methow River Valley. The 180-acre park is nestled into a dry pine forest between impressive rock cliffs and peaceful Alta Lake, a popular trout fishing, swimming, and picnicking site. The campground's four loops offer a choice of 180 sites (32 with electrical hookups; RVs to 45 feet) nicely scattered through the thin pine forest. Also available is an 88-person group camp. The lakeside picnic area is a great stopover spot for tired travelers, and a short, steep hiking trail leads from the park to a viewpoint of the middle Columbia valley (watch for snakes!) Alta Lake State Park is open from April through October. Campsites cannot be reserved. *From US 97 just south of Pateros, follow Hwy 153 north about 2 miles, turn left on Alta Lake Rd and proceed about 2.5 miles to the campground at the end of the road; (509) 923-2473 or (800) 233-0321.*

A **private resort** with a store and boat rentals is nearby.

Boating

Whether the activity of choice is water-skiing, boat camping, hiking, fishing, or just waterborne lollygagging, **Lake Chelan** clearly is one of the state's premier recreational boat getaways. The deep, long lake offers exceptionally clear water and almost always sunny skies. Boater/camper families often queue up for sites at Lake Chelan or Twenty-five Mile Creek State Parks, both of which offer camping spots with nearby boat moorage. For more solitude, head for one of the many boat-in campgrounds along Lake Chelan, most of which have boat docks (see Camping, above).

There are **public boat launches** at Lake Chelan State Park, at Twenty-five Mile Creek State Park, at Riverwalk Park and Chelan City Park in Chelan, and at Old Mill and Manson Bay Parks near Manson on the north shore. Launches also are available at **Wapato Lake** and **Roses Lake,** just northwest of Chelan. **Boat fuel** is available at Chelan City Marina, Lake Chelan Marina, Kelly's Resort, Twenty-five Mile Creek State Park, and Stehekin Landing. **Boat dump stations** are found at Chelan City Marina and Old Mill Park, east of Manson. Boats, Jet-skis, and water-skiing gear can be **rented** at Chelan Boat Rentals, (509) 682-4444, and at Ship 'n' Shore Boat Rental, (509) 682-5419.

Hiking/Backpacking

The middle Columbia area doesn't have many interesting hikes inside its borders, but it's the gateway to some of the most spectacular hiking destinations in Washington. A **Northwest Forest Pass,** $5 per day or $30 annually, is required to park in many Forest Service–administered trailheads in this area. They're available from ranger stations, from many private vendors, on-line at www.naturenw.org, or by calling (800) 270-7504. Free **overnight permits** (unlimited, at this point) are required for hikes in the Lake Chelan–Sawtooth and Glacier Peak Wildernesses. They're available at the Entiat and Lake Chelan Ranger Districts (see More Information, below). Most of these trails are in three primary areas:

Entiat River drainage

Many mixed-use trails (mixed meaning hikers, horses, mountain bikes, and dirt bikes) emanate from Entiat River Road. But a couple of trails stand out as spectacular.

The **Ice Lakes/Entiat Meadows Trail** (moderate/difficult; 29.5 miles round trip) leads into a fantastic alpine area in the heart of the Glacier Peak Wilderness. From a trailhead near Cottonwood Campground (as far as you can drive up the Entiat), this popular trail follows the river 4.3 miles northwest to the wilderness boundary (bye-bye, mountain and dirt bikes), passing junctions with the Larch Lakes and Snowbrushy Creek Trails, then joins the Ice Creek Trail about 8 miles in. Options: Turn left and hike just under 4 miles to spectacular **Ice Lakes,** which lie in a cirque below 9,100-foot Mount Maude. Or continue straight on the Entiat River Trail another 5 miles, into the alpine wonderland of **Entiat Meadows.** Views of Mount Maude, 9,077-foot Seven Fingered Jack, 9,249-foot Mount Fernow, and the Entiat Glacier are unforgettable. Our advice: Plan enough time to visit both areas. That adds about 8 miles to the round-trip total, which is measured to the end of the Entiat River Trail. Note: Long-distance shuttle hikers can do a truly fantastic through trip by taking the Entiat River Trail to the Snow-brushy Creek Trail, which can be followed over Milham Pass east through Emerald Park (see below) to Domke Lake and a Lake Chelan water-taxi pickup at Lucerne. It's a grand 20-mile (one way) traverse.

Also high in this valley, at the end of Forest Road 113 (from Entiat River Road near Lake Creek Campground, following Forest Road 5900 to Forest Road 113), is the **Pyramid Mountain Trail** (difficult; 18.5 miles round trip), a rugged climb with a magnificent payoff: an airplane-seat view of Lake Chelan from an 8,245-foot fire lookout site. This trail is open to mountain bikes and horses, but closed to dirt bikes. Be warned that the road to the trailhead is rough, and the trail itself isn't for slouches. Due to the long climb and big-time vertical, most mortals make this an overnighter, camping on the summit.

Note also that this entire valley continues a slow recovery from the massive Tyee Creek wildfire of 1994. Check trail and road conditions with the Entiat Ranger District, (509) 784-1511, before departing.

East side Glacier Peak Wilderness (Lucerne/Holden Village area)

Good hiking trails emanate from Lucerne, on the lake's south shore, and Holden Village, 12 miles up a gravel road west from Lucerne. *Lady of the Lake* drop-off passengers can combine a stay in the Lucerne or Holden Village area with a trek into the backcountry for a truly unique wilderness weekend.

From Lucerne, pack the fly rod and walk a quarter mile up Railroad Creek Road, where a trail leads east to **Domke Lake** (easy; 3 miles round trip). You'll find a private resort here, with decent fishing at Domke Lake. Another trail continues about 3,000 vertical feet to the top of **Domke Mountain** (difficult; 6 miles round trip from Domke Lake), which has grand Lake Chelan views. Domke Lake also is a good launching point for backpackers seeking high-altitude solitude at **Emerald Park** (moderate; 16 miles round trip from Domke Lake). This valley walk into the eastern Glacier Peak Wilderness is part of the Entiat-to-Lake Chelan traverse described above under Ice Lakes/Entiat Meadows; it's an excellent overnight getaway to some beautiful alpine meadows.

For more Glacier Peaks splendor, take the shuttle bus from Lucerne 12 miles up Railroad Creek Road to the old mining village of Holden, now a Lutheran conference center. For a remote backpack getaway, it's tough to beat the **Lyman Lakes** (moderate; 19.4 miles round trip), reached from Holden by hiking the Railroad Creek Trail, a major eastern access to the Galcier Peaks Wilderness. The route is spectacular, passing Crown Point Falls on the way to Lower Lyman Lake, about 7 miles. A side trail leads through beautiful meadows to the upper lakes, near the toe of the Lyman Glacier below Chiwawa Mountain. Many skilled hikers climb a way trail up the glacier to Spider Gap, 7,100 feet, then drop down the Spider Glacier to Phelps Creek Pass and an exit route in the Chiwawa River drainage north of Leavenworth (see Hiking/Backpacking in the Stevens Pass Corridor and Lake Wenatchee chapter). If you know your way around a glacier and can save yourself and/or a friend with an ice ax, it's a rewarding cross-country jaunt. Few hikers, however, are disappointed with a backpack trip into Lyman Lakes and back. Remember that this is an exceptionally fragile, heavily used area. It's important to practice low-impact camping techniques. (To break up a long trip, consider booking lodging at a bunkhouse in Holden Village; (509) 687-3644.

Lake Chelan–Sawtooth Wilderness

The **Chelan Lakeshore Trail** (easy; 18 miles one way) can be walked campground to campground (see Camping, above) for a fantastic, low-difficulty backpack trip all year long except for the deep winter months. Consider a water-taxi drop-off at Prince Creek on the north shore, then an 18-mile walk north on the trail to Stehekin, where the boat can be reboarded for a return trip to Chelan. Two major caveats: The trail is very, very hot and dry during summer months, with little shade and little running water. And rattlesnakes are common hazards along the route.

Vertical-gain fans have a wealth of other options. Using the Chelan Lakeshore Trail as a shoreline leg, hikers can create a number of challenging loops by climbing any of numerous creek-drainage paths up, up, up to the **Chelan Summit Trail** in the Chelan–Sawtooth Wilderness. The Summit Trail follows a ridgeline above the lake on its north side, never dropping below 5,500 feet on its 28-mile journey from South Navarre Campground (see Camping, above) high above the lake (also reached by a maze of roads from Manson) to War Creek Pass, a 6,800-foot lookout above Stehekin. By combining the Summit and Chelan Lakeshore Trails with routes up and down drainages such as Fish and Prince Creeks, hikers can make loops ranging from 19 to 48 miles.

Cycling

A hilly but picturesque scenic loop of about 30 miles starts right in Chelan, providing a full sampler of the area's rocky buttes, steep coulees, and magnificent lakeshores. Follow **S Lakeshore Road** about 9 miles west of town to Lake Chelan State Park. Rest up for the coming onslaught: **Navarre Coulee Road** climbs steeply from the park, eventually dropping into the very scenic coulee and continuing about 8.5 miles south to US 97A. From there, it's up again for about 2 miles on **US 97A,** then down steeply back into Chelan, about 11.5 miles from the Navarre Coulee Junction. For a more relaxing tour from Chelan, consider the 8.5-mile (one way) ride north to **Manson.** Follow Columbia Street to Hwy 150. Manson Bay Park is a nice midpoint lunch stop.

Mountain Biking

An unusually high percentage of trails in the high, pine-forested area of the Entiat Ranger District are open to mountain-bike use. The 10.6-mile **Lake Creek Trail** is a favorite; the trailhead is on Road 5900, 28 miles up Entiat River Road. In the Chelan Ranger District, popular mountain-bike trails are the **Domke Lake Trail** (see Domke Lake in Hiking/Backpacking, above) and paths in the **Echo Ridge ski area** (see Skiing/Snowshoeing, below).

Fishing

Washington's deepest lake holds some of its most highly sought fish. Present and quite often accounted for in Lake Chelan are **rainbow** and **lake trout** ("Mackinaw," sometimes weighing in at 20-plus pounds), **kokanee** and **chinook salmon, freshwater lingcod (burbot),** and a number of other species. All these are worthy of pursuit, but the chinook fishery is a truly unique one. Chinook have been stocked in the deep, cold lake since 1974, and now provide a popular all-year fishery. The average size is 4 to 6 pounds, but bring a rod with some backbone: the lake-record chinook is 29 pounds! Successful anglers troll herring, often very deep, making downriggers an almost necessary tool. Rick Graybill of Graybill's Guide Service, (509) 682-4294, www.rgraybill.com, is the leading **local**

guide and Lake Chelan fishing expert.

Just up the road in Manson, Wapato Lake is a noted trout pond, with a decent reputation among fly fishers. It also holds some **largemouth bass.** Nearby Roses Lake also is a good trout fishery, but it's open winters only. Bring the **ice-fishing** gear. To the north, up Grade Creek Road, Antilon Lake and Long Jim Reservoir are popular mixed-species fisheries, and Dry Lake is a productive bass-fishing lake.

Trout anglers shouldn't overlook the many clear, high-mountain streams in the Entiat River Valley and on Wenatchee National Forest land west of Lake Chelan. For details, inquire at the Entiat Ranger Station (see More Information, below). Wherever you fish in this region, watch where you step. Local anglers say rattlesnakes are commonly encountered in brushy and rocky lakeshores and creek banks.

Picnics

Nearly all of the campgrounds listed above have good picnic facilities, many with reservable group shelters. In the town of Chelan, **Lakeshore City Park** is a nice waterfront picnic venue, as is **Manson Bay Park**. For weary US 97A travelers, **Rocky Reach Dam** has nice picnic grounds as do Lincoln Rock and Daroga State Parks, across the Columbia River.

Cross-Country Skiing/Snowshoeing

The Lake Chelan area is a notable cross-country ski/snowshoe destination, provided snow levels drop enough to blanket local hillsides' elevations. Examples of good Nordic tours include the roads and trails around **Twenty-five Mile Creek State Park. Rentals** are available at Lake Chelan Sports, 132 E Woodin Avenue in Chelan; (509) 682-2629. The premier cross-country venue in the area, though, is **Bear Mountain Ranch,** which has more than 55 kilometers of trails on hillsides above the lake. Rentals are available on-site. The ranch is on Country Club Road, about 6 miles west of downtown Chelan. Call for schedules; the area generally is open only late in the week and weekends; (509) 682-5444. The **Lake Chelan Golf Course** also maintains a small cross-country ski operation; (509) 682-8026 or (800) 246-5361. **Echo Ridge,** operated, like Echo Valley (see below), by the Lake Chelan Ski Club, has 35 kilometers of groomed cross-country trails, but also plenty of snowmobilers in the vicinity.

Downhill Skiing

Echo Valley, northwest of the town of Chelan on Hwy 150, offers three rope tows and a poma lift on gentle slopes. It's open Christmas through February; (509) 682-4002 or (509) 682-3167.

Photography

It's tough to go wrong with a camera in the Lake Chelan area, particularly if you have boat access to **the lake.** Its aqua blue waters spread out before a magnificent alpine backdrop of peaks in the Lake Chelan–Sawtooth and Glacier Peak Wildernesses. At 3,800 feet, **Chelan Butte Lookout,** 9 miles south of town, provides an almost aerial view of the lake, the Columbia River, and the orchard-blanketed countryside. You're also likely to see hang gliders here, launching off the bluff for extended glides over the lake. Follow Chelan Butte Road south from West Chelan.

Wildlife Watching

The Swakane Canyon, reached by turning west on Swakane Canyon Road just north of Rocky Reach Dam on US 97A, is a major habitat for **mule deer** and **bighorn sheep.** This is one of the most reliable sites for viewing them in the winter. From December to March, both species are fed at stations in the canyon, reached by snowshoes or cross-country skis. For feeding and access information, contact the Entiat Ranger District; (509) 784-1511. The canyon also is home to **golden eagles** and other raptors, as well as many smaller birds. Entiat River Canyon is another area rich in wildlife. Lake Chelan also attracts wildlife. On your boat journey up or down the lake, watch for mule deer, **mountain goats, ospreys, eagles,** and beautiful **harlequin ducks.**

Accessible Outdoors

Lincoln Rock and **Daroga State Parks** offer barrier-free picknicking, camping, trails, and shoreline access. Daroga has wheelchair-accessible rest rooms. In the Entiat Ranger District, **Fox Creek, Lake Creek,** and **Silver Falls Campgrounds** have some "usable" (not barrier-free, but open to wheelchair use with assistance) campsites, picnic sites, and rest rooms. **Lake Chelan** and **Twenty-five Mile Creek State Parks** offer barrier-free shoreline access and picnic facilities. Twenty-five Mile Creek has wheelchair-accessible rest rooms. **Alta Lake State Park** offers barrier-free camping.

outside in

Restaurants

Campbell House Cafe ☆☆   This is where you'll find Chelan's freshest seafood. *$$$; 104 W Woodin Ave, Chelan; (509) 682-4250; www.campbells resort.com.* &

Deepwater Brewing & Public House ☆ This brewpub features tasty pub food to match a gregarious mood. *$$; 225 Hwy 150, Chelan; (509) 682-2720; www.deepwaterbrewing.com.* &

Lodgings

Amy's Manor Inn ☆☆ This enchanting manor is your best bet for miles. *$$; 435 Hwy 153, Pateros; (509) 923-2334.*

Best Western Lakeside Lodge ☆ Nice extras include spacious rooms and an indoor pool. *$$$; 2312 W Woodin Ave, Chelan; (509) 682-4396 or (800) 468-2781.* &

Campbell's Resort on Lake Chelan ☆☆ The draw here is prime lakeside property and a sandy 1,200-foot beach. *$$$; 104 W Woodin Ave, Chelan; (509) 682-2561 or (800) 553-8225; www.campbellsresort.com.*

Kelly's Resort ☆☆ This getaway is like summer camp for families who return year after year. *$$–$$$; 12801 S Lakeshore Rd, Chelan; (509) 687-3220 or (800) 561-8978.*

More Information

Chelan County Tourism: *www.chelan.org.*
Chelan Ranger District: *(509) 682-2576.*
Entiat Ranger District: *(509) 784-1511.*
Lake Chelan Chamber of Commerce: *(800) 4CHELAN;*
    www.lakechelan.com.
North Cascades National Park, Stehekin District/Lake Chelan
    National Recreation Area: *(509) 682-2549.*
Wenatchee National Forest Headquarters: *(509) 662-4335;*
    www.fs.fed.us/r6/wenatchee.

Grand Coulee:
Coulee Dam
to Soap Lake

From the town of Coulee Dam south to Soap Lake, west to Bridgeport, and east to Fort Spokane at the Spokane/Columbia Rivers confluence, including Grand Coulee Dam, the Lake Roosevelt National Recreation Area, Lake Roosevelt, Banks Lake, Dry Falls, the Channeled Scablands, and the Sun Lakes, Steamboat Rock, and Bridgeport State Parks.

The Columbia River is on vivid display here. All incarnations of it.

The Old, Old Columbia once washed through here in a gush unequalled in the prehistoric history of the West. The Big Flow came between 10,000 and 15,000 years ago, when glacial dams holding back a lake that covered much of what is now Montana abruptly gave way, and the lake swept Eastern Washington with a wall of water. Geologists believe this process repeated itself hundreds of times as glaciers advanced and retreated, washing a series of deep coulees—ancient flood scars—into the landscape. These coulees survive today, and the Grand Coulee, true to its name, is the largest. The head of this massive canyon is near present-day Coulee Dam, its foot far to the south, near Soap Lake.

Along the way, the floodwaters wreaked havoc almost beyond imagination, restructuring the landscape and forming a colossal waterfall now known as Dry Falls. At their peak flow, the falls—more than 3 miles wide and 400 feet high—likely created the largest waterfall on the planet. Even without water, the dry face remains impressive today. A series of lakes at its base, collectively known as Sun Lakes, remains as a lingering scar of the ever-moving falls' splash pools.

The Old Columbia—the river of our era, before it was dammed—took a different path, turning west toward Chelan and leaving the Grand Coulee dry. It stayed that way until 1941, when completion of 550-foot-high Grand Coulee Dam across the head of the coulee created Franklin D. Roosevelt Lake, the 150-mile flooded basin that stretches northeast all the way to Kettle Falls. Water from Roosevelt Lake was (and still is) pumped into the coulee, now sealed off at each end by the North and Dry Falls Dams. The result is a 30-mile-long reservoir—Banks Lake—that serves as a holding pond for irrigation water bound for the Columbia Basin Reclamation Project.

Thus, the New Columbia is a tamed beast, at least for the time being. The damming of the great river and reflooding of the Grand Coulee have helped create an agricultural empire in Eastern Washington. And the soothing waters have proved equally beneficial to outdoor recreators. Today, Roosevelt Lake provides year-round thrills for tens of thousands of boaters, swimmers, sailors, anglers, and houseboat devotees. Banks Lake is a noted wildlife refuge, boater's paradise, and fishing venue. Steamboat Rock—another Old, Old Columbia River creation—looms like an island in the center, with one of Washington's most popular state parks at its base.

Today, this is a place to soak under the big, open sky, drink up the sunlight, and imagine these surroundings before humans set foot here. If not for the behemoth dam, the old land scars would look much the same as they must have 10,000 years ago.

Getting There

For the most direct route (about 200 miles) from Seattle, take Interstate 90 over Snoqualmie Pass and east to George, then follow Hwy 283 northeast to Ephrata and Hwy 28 north to Soap Lake. Allow about 3.5 hours. For an alternate route from North Puget Sound, follow US Highway 2 east over Stevens Pass to Wenatchee, US 2/US 97 north to Orondo, then US 2 east again over the Waterville Plateau and through the Moses Coulee to Dry Falls. It's slower but more scenic. The length of the Grand Coulee can be navigated by driving Hwy 17 north from Soap Lake to Dry Falls/US 2, and Hwy 155 (east of Banks Lake) north from Coulee City to Coulee Dam.

inside out

Camping/Swimming/Picnics

The Grand Coulee is one of those rare Evergreen State regions where "the thing to do" is obvious: get on (or in) the water, stupid. Outdoor activities here begin, continue, and end on Roosevelt Lake, Banks Lake, or the chain of lakes south of Dry Falls. Following is a rundown of the Grand Coulee's many lakefront parks, all of which offer a combination of camping, fishing, boating, and sunbathing.

Lake Roosevelt

Small campgrounds, managed either by the National Park Service (because they lie within the Lake Roosevelt National Recreation Area) or the Colville or Spokane tribes, literally ring Roosevelt Lake, the massive, 150-mile long reservoir behind Grand Coulee Dam. Stop by the Lake Roosevelt NRA office in the town of Coulee Dam, (509) 633-9441, or visit the NRA web site (see More Information, below) for a full list. All these campgrounds provide water access, most are open all year, and some have boat launches. Rangers say only about half of the NRA's 1.4 million annual visitors list "camping" as their reason for coming, but that still makes for a lot of folks behind the wheel of RVs, particularly in early summer. It's a good idea to have a contingency plan if you're headed to popular campgrounds such as Fort Spokane or Porcupine Bay. Some of the 28 campgrounds (18 accessible by land, 10 by boat only) are so far up the lake that they land in a separate chapter of this guide (see the Kettle Falls, Colville, and the Pend Oreille chapter). But a few of the most popular are within a short drive of the Coulee Dam visitors center. As of 2000, NRA campgrounds charge $10 per night per from May 1 to September 30, $5 per night from October 1 to April 30. A $6 fee is charged to use most campground boat launches.

Spring Canyon, just east of Coulee Dam on Hwy 174, is the leading campsite for all those dam visitors. It's a nice one, overlooking the lake just behind the massive dam. The federally managed campground has 87 campsites (no hookups; RVs to 26 feet) spread throughout a series of loops in this dry, sagebrush and light-air country. The park also has a boat launch, making it a favorite home base for anglers and water-skiers. It also has a very popular swimming area, with a lifeguard on duty from July through Labor Day weekend. The campground is open all year, weather permitting, with limited winter facilities. Campsites cannot be reserved. *On Hwy 174 about 3 miles east of Coulee Dam; (509) 633-9441.*

Keller Ferry, at the south side of the Roosevelt Lake ferry crossing on Hwy 21, is off the beaten path unless you're taking the ferry. It has 50 sites (no hookups; RVs to 16 feet). The Colville Confederated Tribes' boat ramp and moorage facility is nearby, and there's a playground for kids. A lifeguard is on duty at the swimming area from July through Labor Day weekend. Keller Ferry is open all-year, weather permitting, with limited winter facilities. Campsites cannot be reserved. *On Hwy 21, 14 miles north of Wilbur; (509) 633-9441.*

Farther upstream are **Hawk Creek,** which offers 21 newly renovated standard sites in a quieter setting, and **Fort Spokane,** which has 67 sites (no hookups; RVs to 25 feet) and interesting historical exhibits describing the late-19th-century Indian wars. Fort Spokane has a noted swimming area (lifeguard included during summer months), a boat launch, and other goodies. Both parks are open from mid-April to mid-October, and campsites cannot be reserved. *from US 2 at Davenport, follow Hwy 25 north 23 miles to the Spokane/Columbia River confluence, then turn south on Miles-Creston Rd (Fort Spokane) and continue south 10 miles (Hawk Creek); (509) 633-9441.*

Note: These two campgrounds are often full during summer months. As alternatives, rangers suggest **private campgrounds:** Two Rivers Marina and R.V. Park (100 sites with full hookups), (509) 722-4029 or (800) 722-4031); or the Colville Tribe's Seven Bays RV Park (35 RV sites, most with full hookups, and some tent sites), (509) 725-1676; www.colville-tribal.com/RRE. Both accept reservations.

Banks Lake

And you thought irrigation was only good for growing asparagus. Banks Lake, nature's own holding tank (with a little help from those big pumps at Grand Coulee), offers a whole lot more to recreators—particularly the lie-in-the-sun-till-you-bake type. Banks also is a first-class fishing lake, and most of its shorelines are managed as state wildlife habitat (see Fishing and Wildlife Watching, below).

Most of the focus here is on **Steamboat Rock State Park,** one of Washington's premier sunny-side vacation getaways. It's a mondo park—3,500 acres—with a very well-groomed, very well-attended campground. Steamboat was one of the first parks in the state to leap onto reservation status, and if you're seeking a campsite between Memorial Day and Labor Day, it's a good idea to get one. The park has 126 campsites (100 with full hookups; RVs to 60 feet) and a dozen or more isolated, boat-in campsites. Most are on flat, grassy land that's well suited for tents (be warned, however, about nasty winds and predatory late-night sprinklers). Steamboat Rock is a water-sports recreation hub, with boat launches and moorage, a sandy-bottom swimming area, a water-ski float, bathhouses, and extensive waterfront picnic facilities. For water-skiers, the 27-mile-long, 4-mile-wide lake is paradise. If the weather's not baking hot, you can take to the park's trail system (see Hiking and Wildlife Watching, below). In the winter, the park keeps hopping, with ice fishing and cross-country skiing drawing small but happy crowds. Steamboat Rock is open all year. Campsites can be reserved up to 11 months in advance by calling Reservations Northwest; (800) 452-5687. *On Hwy 155, 9.5 miles south of Electric City,*

26.5 miles north of Coulee City; (509) 633-1304 or (800) 233-0321.

Boaters will find two other **public boat launches** on the northeast side of Banks Lake, just off Hwy 155. One is at Osborne Bay, the other at the mouth of Northrup Creek, both with picnicking and primitive camping facilities nearby. The two sites are jointly managed by State Parks and the Department of Fish and Wildlife. Several other **primitive boat-in sites** can be found elsewhere on the lake.

Park Lake, Blue Lake, and Sun Lakes

Sun Lakes State Park, another extremely popular summertime getaway, is an odd mix of private amenities and public facilities amid a gaggle of small lakes at the south end of the Grand Coulee. If you don't mind camping next to a Palm Springs–style golf course, rental cabins, and other businesses, you might enjoy all the commotion. If you do mind, go elsewhere. The main development is on the south boundary at Park Lake, where you'll find a private resort complex (see below) as well as a state park picnic area, camping area, and large group camp. To the north, trails lead to a half dozen other small lakes, all believed to be former splash pools from the awesome Dry Falls just to the north. In all, the state park offers 192 campsites (18 with full hookups; RVs to 50 feet), a large group camp, and day-use picnic facilities, a boat launch, and more than 16 miles of hiking trails (watch for snakes). Most of the campsites are in a partially shaded, dirt-floored area near the lake, with little privacy between sites and little grass or ground vegetation to speak of. Not our favorite tent area, to say the least. Good fishing is found throughout this multi-lake park (see Fishing, below). And don't miss the Dry Falls Interpretive Center just up the road, or the Lenore Caves (see Hiking, below) just up the trail. Sun Lakes is open all year. State park campsites can be reserved up to 11 months in advance by calling Reservations Northwest; (800) 452-5687. *On Hwy 17, 6 miles south of Coulee City, 17 miles north of Soap Lake; (509) 632-5291.*

Sun Lakes Resort Lodge, next door to the state park, adds cabins, a golf course, boat ramps and rentals, a store, laundromat, and other amenities, plus 110 RV sites and a stable for horseback trips to the surrounding lakes. The concession-operated resort is open summers only. The **resort** campsites can be reserved by calling (509) 632-5291.

Another pleasant oasis in this dry area is **Summer Falls State Park** on Billy Clapp Lake, which has a small picnic area near an impressive waterfall. *Follow signs from US 2 in Coulee City.*

Boating/Houseboat Rentals

Roosevelt Lake and its neighbor, **Banks Lake,** are among the most popular boating destinations in the state. (See Camping/Swimming/Picnics,

Imagine it with water: Peering into Dry Falls in the Grand Coulee

above, for a list of launch facilities.) Boaters bound for Roosevelt Lake should note that most of its 16 public boat launches are unusable in the spring, when the lake is drawn down to accommodate the spring melt-off. The waters reach a stable level by early July. A hot-line number, (800) 824-4916, gives updated lake levels. Until recently, this big reservoir was untapped by the RV-on-pontoons fleet. Now more than 40 houseboats are available to explore the 150-mile-long lake, and most book up early for the summer.

The **houseboat rental** service is managed by the Colville Confederated Tribes. The sun's almost guaranteed, and all you need to bring is food, bed linens, towels, fishing gear, and your bathing suit. Operators promise: no TV, no phones, no cell-phone reception. Boats are moored at Kelly Ferry Marina, 14 miles north of Wilbur. Rates vary widely depending on season and boat type, from around $650 for a 46-foot boat over a winter weekend to more than $3,500 for a luxury 54-footer for a week in the dead of summer. Most of the boats will sleep a dozen or more guests; (800) 648-LAKE; www.colville-tribal.com/RRE. Houseboat rentals also are available at the north end of the lake at Kettle Falls Marina through Lake Roosevelt Houseboat Vacations, (509) 738-6121 or (800) 635-7585; www.lakeroosevelt.com.

Fishing

The dry shores and deep, clear reservoirs and lakes in the ancient Grand Coulee contain more than a few monstrous, waterborne links with the past. Big fish await anglers in these waters, which hold some of the most prized lunkers in Washington. Lower Roosevelt Lake is known for its productive **walleye, rainbow trout, largemouth** and **smallmouth bass, kokanee, whitefish,** and **perch** fisheries. This is a huge, diverse lake, where a variety of methods will yield different species. The big fish—rainbows, kokanee, and walleye all grow to impressive sizes here—are usually caught trolling spoons or spinners. The state record for kokanee is broken almost annually here. It currently stands at about 5.5 pounds. Get after it. Roosevelt also contains some truly massive **white sturgeon,** which grow to 20 feet in the deep, cold waters. Most fishing action centers around stream inlets or rocky shorelines providing underwater structure. Hot temperatures send many fish scurrying for the lake's depths in midsummer. Best fishing usually is early and late in the summer season. That's particularly true for bank anglers, who can be successful here, but usually find fishing much more hit-and-miss than do boaters. Keller Ferry Marina, (509) 647-5755, is a good source of **supplies** and advice.

Banks Lake is another monstrous waterway with a mess of marine life lurking below. Walleye also are the prominent species here, but largemouth and smallmouth bass, **crappies,** rainbow trout, and whitefish also are solid. Steamboat Rock State Park (see Camping, above) is a great base camp for Banks Lake anglers.

To the west, Jameson Lake is a longtime favorite **trout**-fishing spot, particularly when it first opens in the spring. Then, anybody—and we do mean anybody—should be able to hook into a chunky rainbow or two with a bit of effort, even by bank casting. Flip your glob of Power Bait out there among all the hand-tied flies and hang on tight. (Just don't get your glob hooked up to our glob; this is a favorite guidebook-author fishing spot.) Check the state regulations pamphlet for seasons on Jameson, which closes during midsummer and reopens in the fall. Jameson Lake Resort, (509) 683-1141, dispenses **supplies** and advice.

Most of the many lakes below Dry Falls in Sun Lakes State Park are open from late April through September, and they offer uncommonly good fishing early in the season. The largest, Park Lake, is another can't-miss rainbow trout fishery on or around Opening Day. Healthy catches are made here every spring, with most bank and boat anglers limiting on some of Washington's healthiest trout. When the bite is on, just about anything works. Access is good through the state park and along Hwy 17. **Rental boats** are available at Sun Lakes Resort Lodge; (509) 632-5291. Expect unbelievably huge crowds during the first two weeks of fishing.

Conditions at Blue Lake, outside the Sun Lakes Park just to the south, are nearly identical, with excellent bank access, excellent catch rates early in the year, and very large crowds. If the mob scene makes you nuts, try this lake (or any in this area) later in the summer. Crowds thin out—and fishing usually is still productive—before the lakes close in September.

You'll have to work a bit harder in the Sun Lakes cluster's smaller, less accessible lakes, all reached by walking or driving several miles on very rough roads from the state park. But that seems to make the experience more rewarding. Deep Lake, at the south end of the Sun Lakes complex, holds planted rainbows, which are fairly bite-happy on Opening Day in late April every year. To the north, Dry Falls Lake is a selective fishery. Bait and barbed hooks are prohibited, but the lake has become a favorite of fly casters, who report fair-to-good trout catches. Perch Lake, in the center of the Sun Lakes group, also is a hot Opening Day lake, as is nearby Rainbow Lake. Both reportedly get fished out pretty early in the season.

To the south, below Blue Lake, is Alkali Lake, a warmwater lake that's being groomed as a walleye fishery. Immediately to its south is Lake Lenore, home of a fascinating—and amazingly successful—stocking program. **Lahontan cutthroat trout** planted here have grown huge—some up to 6 pounds or more—and strict selective fishery regulations are in place to prevent overfishing. The lake is fast becoming legendary among fly casters, who flock here in March for the start of a three-month catch-and-release-only fishery. A one-fish bag limit goes into effect for the rest of the summer, but many of Lenore's fly casters have taken to releasing fish all season—a very healthy trend.

Another alternative in this region are three Colville Tribe-controlled lakes north of Grand Coulee Dam: McGinnis, Buffalo, and Rebecca. **Tribal fishing permits** are required, but fishing can be quite good in all three, without the big crowds of lakes in the lower Coulee.

Hiking

The impressive Steamboat Rock State Park in the midst of Banks Lake (see Camping/Swimming/Picnics, above) has an interesting 25-mile trail system, including one short, steep jaunt (800-foot elevation gain) up a crack in **Steamboat Rock** (difficult; 3 miles round trip) to the broad, flat, 700-foot summit. Nice view! Bring lots of water, however. It's dry, hot, and miserable in the dead of summer. Be sure to stay back from crumbly basalt cliffs. And do watch for rattlesnakes along the way. As a local tourist brochure advises, "rattlesnakes are generally not lethal, but they should be avoided."

To the south, Sun Lakes State Park has more than 15 miles of trail, although some of it is shared by horses and four-wheel-drive rigs. Roads or paths link all of the half-dozen largest lakes in the Sun Lakes cluster. The region is geologically fascinating. But it can be very exposed and dry in summer months. Protect yourself from the sun, and watch for snakes. For the most interesting route (moderate; 3 miles one way), follow the path from the end of the campground loop around the east side of **Rainbow Lake,** past **Perch Lake,** and on to the shore of **Dry Falls Lake,** where the massive Dry Falls cliff band is an awesome sight from ground level.

On the east shores of Lake Lenore—just off Hwy 17 about 10 miles south of Dry Falls—a short trail leads to a cliff band concealing **Lenore Caves** (moderate; half-mile round trip), a series of rock caverns carved by the ancient river. Some of these caves have produced significant archaeological finds, believed left by passing bands of ancient hunters. Pictographs are visible on the rock walls. These caves are worthy of exploration, but be careful.

Wildlife Watching

The entire, 44,000-acre reservoir at Banks Lake is a state wildlife area, a significant stopover point for migratory birds, with access at several primitive camping/boat-launch sites on the east shore (see Camping/Swimming/Picnics, above). The lake attracts a fair number of **waterfowl,** and hunting is allowed here in season. In the winter, keep your eyes peeled for **bald eagles,** which winter here in fairly large numbers. A more obscure attraction near here is across the highway from Steamboat Rock State Park's northern rest area/boat launch (about 3.5 miles north of the main entrance): Northrup Canyon, the only natural forest in Grant County (if not farther). The 3,120-acre area is filled with forested ravines between coulee walls, where bald eagles and other **raptors** sometimes are spotted. Lake Roosevelt also has become a popular spot to scan for wintering bald eagles.

The Channeled Scablands, a bizarre mix of gullies, rocks, caves, and cliffs on the high, dry east side of the Columbia Basin, were formed by the same series of prehistoric floods that carved out the Grand Coulee and created Dry Falls. They're now home to various waterfowl; hundreds of **desert songbird** species; range birds such as **partridge** and **quail;** and large numbers of raptors, including **great horned owls, golden eagles, falcons,** and numerous **hawks.** This area—roughly bordered by Wilbur, Davenport, Odessa, and Ritzville—is best experienced by following a 150-mile **wildlife-viewing loop** from Ritzville. A visitors guide to the loop, which takes about 5 hours and includes six major stops on a mix of public and private property, is available from the Odessa Economic Development Committee, (509) 982-2232.

For single-stop viewing of the same type of shrub-steppe environment, visit Wilson Creek Canyon, south of US 2 off Govan Road (just west of Wilbur). A short trail leads to an overlook where various **hawks, owls, eagles,** and **falcons** are often seen, as well as waterfowl such as the beautiful **redhead duck** and the **cinnamon teal.**

Cycling

A good day trip suitable for the whole family is the **Down River Trail,** which follows the Columbia downstream from the city park in the town of Coulee Dam. It's about 6.5 miles one way.

Accessible Outdoors

The **Sun Lakes State Park** complex has barrier-free rest rooms and interpretive exhibits. **Steamboat Rock State Park** offers barrier-free camping, water, and rest rooms. **Jameson Lake** fishing access has barrier-free rest rooms and primitive campsites. Excellent barrier-free viewing of Lahontan cutthroat trout can be found at the **Lake Lenore Fish Trap.** From Soap Lake, drive north on Hwy 17 for 9 miles and turn left at the public-fishing sign. The nearby **Lenore Boat Launch** has barrier-free rest rooms.

Restaurants

La Presa ★   The decor is velvet paintings and wool blankets; the food is authentic Mexican. *$; 515 E Grand Coulee Ave, Grand Coulee; (509) 633-3173.* &

Lodgings

Notaras Lodge   The log cabin style lodges are lakeside and the decor reflects western history. *$$; 236 E Main St, Soap Lake; (509) 246-0462; www.notaraslodge.com.* &

Victoria's Cottage ★★   Staying here is like having your own wing in an impressive Coulee Dam home. *$$; 209 Columbia Ave, Coulee Dam; (509) 633-2908; www.reitpro.com/victoriascottage.*

More Information

Colville National Forest, Kettle Falls Ranger Station: *(509) 738-7700.*
Dry Falls Interpretive Center: *(509) 632-5214.*
Grand Coulee Visitors Center: *Hwy 155, near Coulee Dam; (509) 633-9265.*
Lake Roosevelt National Recreation Area: *(509) 633-9441; www.nps.gov/laro.*
Lake Roosevelt water-level hot line: *(800) 824-4916.*
Soap Lake Visitors Information Center: *300 Beach Street; (509) 246-1821; www.soaplakecoc.org.*

Columbia Basin

From Ephrata south to Othello, west to Vantage, and east to Ritzville, including Moses Lake Columbia National Wildlife Refuge, Wanapum Recreation Area, and Gingko Petrified Forest, Moses Lake, and Potholes State Parks.

So what if Dave Matthews lured you over here? The white pelicans might bring you back. That could well be the fate of music fans who've flocked in recent years to the Columbia River Amphitheater near George, which has emerged as one of the state's leading concert venues. All those people heading to Moses Lake and George have had to scratch and sniff for campsites, and their search has put them on a collision path with a little-known fact about the Columbia Basin: a lot of wildlife passes through this endless flatland. And by that we do not mean Beck.

The Columbia Basin, Washington's largest stretch of desert before the Columbia Basin Reclamation Project turned it into a fertile agricultural center, doesn't attract many full-time residents. But its singular asset—water—draws plenty of part-timers. The list includes white pelicans and countless other bird species, which flock to the Potholes and the Columbia National Wildlife Refuge every year as they migrate along the Pacific Flyway. That's long been known to the state's avid birders. But the bird species dropping in on the basin are attracting new bird lovers by sheer force of numbers. They're giving the region what it really has long lacked: a long-term tourism draw.

Of course, it doesn't take birds—no matter how many or how fancy—to draw another segment of the outdoors community that's been trekking to the Columbia Basin for years: anglers. The basin's broad waterways and relatively clean environs have combined to create one of the most productive freshwater fisheries in the state.

Most of the water here is seepage from the grandiose Reclamation Project, which pumps millions of gallons of water from Banks Lake onto surrounding fields. When earthen O'Sullivan Dam was completed in 1949, the water backed up and filled a series of low-lying glacial depressions: the Potholes. At about 29,000 acres when full in the spring, Potholes Reservoir is by far the largest body of water here. But literally hundreds of other small ponds and water canals are linked to it by the artificially high water table, creating a navigable paradise for anglers and paddlers. Like the Potholes to the south, the waters of Moses Lake also were augmented by the irrigation project. The diverted Columbia River water expanded the lake to a skinny, 17-mile-long waterway that keeps Moses Lake bearable during the blazing summers.

That's about all there is to offer the outdoor lover in the Columbia Basin. But it's enough for the people of Moses Lake, George, and Ephrata. Bring your tackle box. Bring your spotting glasses. Fish and fowl are taking center stage.

Getting There

Moses Lake, the heart of the Columbia Basin (and arguably the only civilized spot therein), is 176 miles east of Seattle on Interstate 90. It's about a 3-hour drive. Highway 283 from George and Hwy 17 from Moses Lake head north to Ephrata; from Moses Lake, Hwy 17 heads south to Othello. At Vantage, Hwy 26 heads east to Othello, continuing beyond to US Highway 395, which heads northeast to connect with I-90 at Ritzville.

inside out

Camping/Swimming/Picnics

The best thing to do in Moses Lake in the summer is wish it were winter. Well, that's not entirely true, considering that winters are as ferociously cold as summers are hot—and besides, lots of people flock to the Columbia Basin during the hot season specifically for its arid, Palm Springs–like climate. But even sun worshippers need a place to cool off once in a while. In the Columbia Basin, a series of waterfront parks are the cool places to be.

Potholes State Park is the hub of waterborne activity in the Columbia Basin. To be totally honest, the 640-acre splash of green amid the rather harsh surrounding desert won't be everyone's idea of a grand vacation getaway. But if fishing or canoeing are even medium-high on your list, the

Roadside highlights are few and far between in the Columbia Basin

place deserves at least one visit. The water, naturally, is the star here. The park, which sits on the southwest shore of the reservoir, offers 126 campsites (60 with full hookups; RVs to 50 feet), a mondo boat launch and day-use parking area, picnic facilities, and a playground. The campground is a mix of pleasant-enough RV pads and rougher-cut tent sites (they're set in sand and sagebrush, exposed to the wind). This is a very popular springtime destination for Washington anglers and, increasingly, bird-watchers. Hundreds of species of birds migrating on the Pacific Flyway make stops here and at nearby Columbia Wildlife Refuge. Potholes State Park is open all year. Campsites can be reserved up to 11 months in advance by calling Reservations Northwest; (800) 452-5687. *From I-90 west of Moses Lake, take exit 164 to Dodson Rd and follow signs about 10 miles south and west to the park, on Frenchman Hills Rd; (509) 765-7271 or (800) 233-0321.*

Nearby, a notable private development on the Potholes, **Mar Don Resort,** offers 300 sites (full hookups; RVs of any size), a store, motel, and extensive boating and fishing services (see Fishing, below). The resort is open all year. Campsites can be reserved. *On O'Sullivan Dam Rd (Hwy 262) at the west end of O'Sullivan Dam; (800) 416-2736 or (509) 346-2651; www.mardonresort.com.*

Moses Lake State Park, a day-use area just off I-90 in Moses Lake, is a welcome oasis of rolling green lawns, covered picnic shelters, playgrounds, and other summer fun equipment. The 80-acre park is on the lakeshore, with good access for swimmers, paddlers, and bank anglers. The bathhouse and swimming area (lifeguard on duty during the summer) is one of the best in the region. The park also has a boat ramp and mooring dock. Easy freeway access to this park makes it a popular lunch stopover for road-weary I-90 travelers. In the winter, bring your skates: ice skating on a portion of the frozen lake near the park is a popular activity. Moses Lake State Park is open all year. *Follow signs from I-90 exit 175 in Moses Lake; (800) 233-0321.*

Other pleasant Moses Lake waterfront picnic spots include **Cascade Park** (which also has limited camping facilities) on Valley Road, **Montlake Park** on Beaumont Road, and **McCosh Park,** at Dogwood and Fourth, which has a popular water slide and outdoor pool complex. RV-equipped Gorge Ampitheater concertgoers should note that other Moses Lake **private RV campgrounds** are Big Sun Resort (60 sites, 50 with hookups), (509) 765-8294; and Willows Trailer Village (85 sites, 65 with hookups), (509) 765-7531.

To the north, in the thriving hub of Ephrata, a **private campground** is a good possible stopover spot for travelers bound to or from Grand Coulee. Oasis RV Park Resort on Hwy 28 is a quiet spot, complete with shaded picnic facilities, a swimming area, fishing ponds, and 105 campsites, some with utilities. The park is open all year. Campsites can be reserved. *On Hwy 28 in Ephrata; (877) 754-5102 or (509) 754-5102.*

In the Vantage area, two options await I-90 travelers or Gorge concertgoers. At **Wanapum Recreation Area** (part of Ginkgo-Wanapum State Park), a riverfront site on the west side of the Vantage bridge over the Columbia, you'll find a slew of individual picnic sites, a swimming area and bathhouse, a boat launch, and 50 partially shaded campsites (all with full hookups; RVs to 60 feet). They'd work for a tent in a pinch, but are geared for RV use. The park, the only one in this area along I-90, is crowded during the summer. Ginkgo Petrified Forest is nearby. Wanapum Recreation Area is open all year. Campsites cannot be reserved. *Follow signs from the Vantage exit on I-90; (509) 856-2700 or (800) 233-0321.*

Tent campers likely will be happier scooting over to the nearby Vantage Riverstone Resort (formerly KOA Vantage), which offers 125 campsites (100 with hookups) and the usual private-resort amenities. The campground is open all year. Campsites can be reserved. *North of Vantage off I-90 exit 136; (509) 856-2230.* Gorge Amphitheater visitors also might consider another **private campground,** Shady Tree RV Park in George, which offers 74 campsites (44 with hookups). George and Martha Lakes are nearby. The park is open all year. Campsites can be reserved. *At the Hwy 281/283 junction just north of George; take I-90 exit 151; (509) 785-2851.*

Fishing

No other region of the Evergreen State provides the wealth of angling opportunity found in the Columbia Basin. The literal flood of fresh water provided by the Columbia Basin Reclamation Project combines with warm weather and a wealth of species for some of the hottest fishing action in the Northwest. The list of lakes, canals, and reservoirs with good fishing in this region would be monstrous. We've grouped them into over-all areas, and urge you to spend some time at each, discovering your own tucked-away fishing water. Take a good map and a state regulations pamphlet. Like the fishing venues themselves, seasons, catch limits, and special restrictions are all over the map here. Anglers who get an itchy casting finger early in the year should note that many Columbia Basin fishing waters are either open all year or have March 1 opening dates, and some of the hottest fishing here is in early spring, before it even gets under way in much of Western Washington.

If you can't catch your favorite fish at Potholes Reservoir, you're just plain unlucky. Chances are, the one you want is down there. The Potholes are famous for their production of **largemouth** and **smallmouth bass, walleye, trout, kokanee, crappie, perch,** and other species. Finding your way around this massive jigsaw waterway is the tricky part. It comes with experience (either your own or hired, through one of the **local guide services**). The south end of the Potholes near the dam is the most easily negotiated by boat, and also offers plenty of good bank access. Fishing for bass and walleye can be very good from the bank here. The north end is a maze of small waterways, making it easy to get lost if you're not careful. Still, fishing for warm-water species is excellent in these shallower waterways, which are guaranteed to provide a memorable day on the water, at the very least.

Trout anglers take some hefty ones home from the Potholes, either by trolling deep in the south end, or by fishing from the bank at deep-water drop-offs or the fishing pier at Mar Don Resort. Boat-launch facilities are found at Potholes State Park and Mar Don (see Camping/Swimming/Picnics, above), which offers guide services and serves as the best **information and gear** source for Potholes fishing; (509) 346-2651.

An equally impressive—and equally bewildering—array of "seep lakes" and waterways is found to the south in Columbia National Wildlife Refuge (see Wildlife Watching, below). Many of these lakes and ponds are very productive fisheries for trout, **whitefish,** perch, bass and other species. The largest, Warden, opens March 1 for an extremely popular fishery of planted **rainbow trout.** Many smaller lakes are stocked with rainbow trout. You can find good fishing just about any time of the year here. Many of the lakes are open all year, including Upper and Lower Goose, which are among the most popular for warm-water species. Call Columbia National Wildlife Refuge, (509) 488-2668, for access information.

Lenice, Merry, and Nunnally, three tiny lakes southeast of Vantage on Hwy 243 near Beverly, have a reputation beyond their size among fly casters, who flock to the selective-fishery (single barbless hooks, no bait) lakes for monster-size rainbow and **brown trout.** The lakes are open April through October, but veterans say the best fishing almost always is early in the season. Also on the western side of the basin near George, George and Martha Lakes provide decent fishing for planted rainbows. Like many lakes in this region, they open March 1.

Wildlife Watching

Pelicans like the taste of Columbia River irrigation water every bit as much as potatoes do. The Columbia Basin's vast array of open waterways is visible from miles up in space, so it's no surprise that migratory birds on the Pacific Flyway include the region on their annual travel itinerary. So do most Washington birders. Springtime visits to the Potholes, Columbia National Wildlife Refuge, and the Channeled Scablands are rites of the season for bird lovers. These rich bird refuges, in fact, have converted many otherwise disinterested visitors into bird lovers, simply on the strength of overwhelming numbers of species. Birds and other wildlife are commonly seen in fields and on waterways throughout the basin, but viewing is best in these areas:

Potholes Reservoir may well be the single richest bird-viewing area in the state. The sprawling waterway is home to large numbers of migratory Canada **geese, mallards,** and other waterfowl in the fall and winter. Also watch for **cormorants, herons, egrets,** a variety of **songbirds,** and some **white pelicans. Avocets** are commonly seen on the Winchester Wasteway (northwest of Potholes Reservoir off Dodson Road) during the spring. A trail along the Frenchman Hills Wasteway near the southwest corner of the reservoir (south on Dodson Road) is another popular bird-viewing spot, although serious birders will enjoy the best success by launching a canoe or other quiet craft from Potholes State Park (see Camping/Swimming/Picnics, above.) Spring is the peak viewing time in the Potholes.

To the south, Columbia National Wildlife Refuge is a sprawling, 23,000-acre refuge comprising hundreds of small lakes and waterways with adjacent nesting fields. This is migratory waterfowl central, with hundreds of thousands of geese and ducks stopping over in the fall migration. Wading birds such as avocets and **curlews** also are commonly seen, and **sandhill cranes** are often spotted in March and April. An overlook site is maintained at Royal Lake, in the south end of the refuge north of Hwy 26, and trailheads are found along Morgan Lake Road. A more remote, but no less fascinating, site is Crab Creek Coulee, which contains the famed Lenice, Merry, and Nunnally fishing lakes (see Fishing, above). The coulee is home to large numbers of raptors, waterfowl, and **range birds,** as well as **coyotes** and **badgers.** Because the refuge is large and access roads often confusing, it's best to stop first at refuge headquarters, 44 S Eighth Street in Othello, for maps and information. The Moses Lake Area Chamber of Commerce (see More Information, below) dispenses copies of an Audubon Society brochure and map detailing bird-viewing in the area.

Canoeing/Kayaking

Both **Moses Lake** and **Potholes Reservoir** are popular with canoeists and kayakers, particularly those interested in viewing wildlife. (See Wildlife Watching and Camping/Swimming/Picnics, above, for major access points.)

Hiking

Hiking "trails" per se are a rarity out here. Why build a trail through a wide-open, flat space? But plenty of hiking can be done by the enterprising walker, particularly one with a set of field glasses and a bird guide. **Potholes Reservoir** (see Camping/Swimming/Picnics, above) is a good place to set out for a stroll, as is the **Columbia National Wildlife Refuge,** where several short trails lead to bird-viewing blinds. **Ginkgo Petrified Forest State Park** has a mile-long interpretive trail and a 2.5-mile loop trail through brushy desert that is home to more rattlers and lizards than people. (It's said to be nice in the spring, when some wildflowers are in bloom. But we suspect "nice" is a relative term here.)

Accessible Outdoors

Potholes State Park offers barrier-free picnicking (2 sites), camping (2 sites), trails, water, rest rooms, and boat launching. A large number of state Fish and Wildlife water accesses in this area also have barrier-free facilities: **Canal Lake** and **Windmill Lake** in the state Department of Fish and Wildlife's Seep Lakes fishing access provide barrier-free fishing and rest rooms. From Moses Lake, travel south on Hwy 17 for about 5 miles, turn right at County Road M SE. Travel 6.5 miles and turn left at O'Sullivan Dam Road. At the half mile, turn right at the public fishing sign. Proceed 3.75 miles and turn left at the Canal Lake sign. Continue about a mile to the parking area. Wheelchair-accessible rest rooms are found at **Long Lake, Corral Lake, Lind-Coulee Island, Warden Lake, Potholes Blythe Access** (all located along or near O'Sullivan Dam Road), and **Moses Lake North** and **South Outlet fishing accesses.** Moses Lake

North also offers year-round, barrier-free fishing access. From Moses Lake, drive west on I-90 for about 1 mile to the Mae Valley exit. Turn left and cross the freeway. Turn left at the T and proceed about a half mile. Turn right at the public fishing sign and continue 1.5 miles to the parking area. The **Columbia Basin Hatchery** has a barrier-free trail leading to four accessible hunting/fishing platforms along Hatchery Creek, which is stocked with rainbow and brown trout. From Moses Lake, drive east on Broadway Extension for a half mile, then turn north on Road K NE and proceed 2.5 miles to the hatchery, on the right. The **Rocky Creek Overlook** southeast of Ephrata off Hwy 17 has a wheelchair-accessible, reservable duck blind; (509) 754-4624. The **Stan Coffin** and **Burke Lake East accesses** in the Quincy Seep Lakes Hunting and Fishing area (west of Hwy 281) have barrier-free rest rooms.

outside in

Restaurants

Michael's on the Lake   Diners get a view of the lake and fairly standard entrees. $$; 910 W Broadway Ave, Moses Lake; (509) 765-1611.

More Information

Grant County Tourism: (509) 754-2011, ext. 331;
   www.tourgrantcounty.com.
Moses Lake Area Chamber of Commerce: 324 S Pioneer Wy;
   (509) 765-7888 or (800) 992-6234; www.moseslakechamber.org.
Moses Lake Area Tourism: www.moses-lake.com.

Yakima
Valley

From Ellensburg south through Yakima Canyon, west to Naches, and southeast to Prosser, including Toppenish, Sunnyside, the Yakima Wine Country and Yakima Sportsman and Fort Simcoe State Parks.

Here's the best place, bar none, to live and play in Washington. Assuming you're asparagus.

The Yakima Valley, which for our purposes begins in the Yakima River Canyon south of Ellensburg and stretches southeast to Prosser, truly is Washington's fertile crescent. Some of the most productive soils in the state make the valley a national leader in cranking out apples, cherries, asparagus, corn, grapes, and other crops. All of this is made possible, of course, only by the cooperation of the Yakima River, which bubbles to life high on Snoqualmie Pass and leaves a swath of green in its wake as it flows southeast to the Columbia. The river, or at least that portion of it not siphoned off for irrigation, also serves as the recreation lifeblood of the Yakima Valley.

The Yakima provides a world-class trout fishery—and regionally significant wildlife habitat—in the Yakima River Canyon. It's also the star attraction along the Yakima River Greenway, this valley's leading recreation venue, as well as in most valley campgrounds.

It's hard to imagine life here without it. Any life. The Yakima Valley sans river would be a dust bowl. It rains less than 10 inches a year here (less than you might get in three days during the occasional Western Washington winter storm). Vegetation is sparse and—unless you get really excited about sagebrush and tumbleweeds—nondescript. Take away the Yakima River, and all that's left is a long downtown strip of motels, ringed by more bowling alleys than you'll find anywhere this side of Omaha, Nebraska.

Lucky for you the river is here to stay, at least in some form. And the recreation venues it creates are surprisingly interesting, some even unique. The key to visiting this area—even more so than in most other places—is timing. The valley has become one of our favorite weekend getaways during the spring or late autumn, when local temperatures have cooled and conditions elsewhere (on the coast or in the mountains) are inhospitable. The Yakima River Canyon, in particular, is stunningly beautiful in both of these "shoulder seasons," decked out in bright fall leaves or brilliant spring wildflowers. Trout fishing in the river may be as pure an angling thrill as you can get in Washington, with catch-and-release restrictions designed to keep it that way. Hikers, particularly those who enjoy sweating a bit to share space with wild birds and mammals, can find refreshingly under-visited wildlife habitat in and around the valley, and a world of mountain exploration awaits a short distance to the east, in the Tieton River drainage.

The Yakima Valley, like the asparagus that sprouts from its floor, is a great natural product hampered by bad packaging. It might look funky and unappealing, but get it while it's fresh, and the flavor is hard to beat.

Getting There

Yakima is 142 miles east of Seattle via Interstate 90 and I-82/US Highway 97—an easy, all-freeway drive of about 2.5 hours. If there's time to spare, don't hesitate to drive Hwy 821, the Yakima Canyon Road, between Ellensburg and Selah, rather than take I-82 over Manastash and Umtanum Ridges. It's one of the state's more visually lovely drives, and adds only about 30 minutes to the trip. In the summer, highly scenic routes to Yakima skirt Mount Rainier, via either Cayuse or Chinook Pass or US 12 (White Pass). Note: White Pass is the only Rainier-area mountain pass open all winter. US 97 and I-82 continue south of Yakima on either side of the river. At Toppenish, US 97 heads south for the Columbia Gorge; I-82 continues southeast along the river to Prosser and the Tri-Cities.

inside out

Fishing

It might be dry. It might be dusty. It might be hot and windy. But there's fishin' to be done here. The Yakima River north of Roza Dam (about 5 miles north of Selah) is an intergalactically famous trout stream. The river's gentle pace, brushy bank cover, ample highway access, and Montana-like terrain make it an absolute favorite of fly casters. The Yakima is home to a healthy population of plump **wild rainbow trout,** which you must catch and release. This is a selective fishery, meaning only single, barbless hooks can be used, and no bait is allowed. A wide variety of flies are effective, but you can also fish with light spinning lures, provided they're equipped with single barbless hooks. The Yakima will test your casting mettle: most of the river's feisty trout hide from the sun under brushy bankside cover, which provides constant target practice. The river is open all year, and access is quite good from all along the Yakima Canyon Road. The Umtanum Creek parking area (about 12 miles south of Ellensburg/I-90) is popular because a suspension bridge allows foot access to the west side of the river. Watch for snakes!

Not far from the canyon's south outlet at Selah is Wenas Lake (take Wenas Road west some 15 miles), an irrigation reservoir that holds some lunker-size **brown trout,** plus a mess of nice rainbows. It's open all year, and boat trollers have the best success.

West of Yakima in the Tieton River alley, both the Tieton River and one clear, swift tributary, Oak Creek, offer decent rainbow trout fishing. Both receive annual rainbow plants from the state Department of Fish and Wildlife. Follow Hwy 12 west from Yakima.

Cowiche Creek, northeast of town (see Hiking and Wildlife Watching, below), is a very scenic stream with good trail access and a healthy number of smaller rainbows. Outstanding bank access can be found at all seven of the Freeway Ponds, just west of I-82 between Union Gap and Zillah. This chain of small lakelets offers productive fishing for nearly every species imaginable. Warm-water fish—**bass, walleye, perch,** and the like—are very active here, but you can also find brown and rainbow trout.

A unique kids-only fishery is found at Yakima Sportsman State Park east of town (see Camping, below), where ponds stocked with rainbows are open to anglers 15 and younger. Follow signs from I-82 exit 34. Gary's Fly Shoppe/Yakima River Outfitters, 1210 W Lincoln; (509) 457-3474, is your best **local-expert** contact.

Camping/Picnics

Yakima Sportsman State Park is the leading campground in the Yakima Valley, where campsites are sparse, to say the least. The park has 67 sites (37 with full hookups; spaces are pull-throughs!), a playground, kids' fishing ponds, and extensive (shady) picnic facilities. The park provides good access to the Yakima River and the Yakima River Greenway Trail (see Hiking, below). Historical trivia: The park owes its existence to members of the Yakima Sportsman's Association, who, noting the lack of public parks in Yakima, purchased the land and began development here in the 1940s.

The park was later turned over to Yakima County and, subsequently, Washington State Parks in 1949. Yakima Sportsman is open all year. Campsites can be reserved up to 11 months in advance by calling Reservations Northwest; (800) 452-5687. *From I-82 east of Yakima, take exit 34 and follow signs about 2 miles east to the park; (509) 575-2774 or (800) 233-0321.*

The other major (private) campground in the area, **Yakima KOA,** has 50 tent sites and 90 RV sites with full hookups and the usual KOA amenities. The riverside campground is open all year, and campsites can be reserved. *On Keyes Rd in Yakima—take I-82 exit 34; (800) 562-5773 or (509) 248-5882; www.koa.com.* West of the city, in the Ahtanum Creek drainage, the state Department of Natural Resources maintains four small, free campgrounds. Unless you're riding a dirt bike or really enjoy the exhaust from other people's, don't bother.

Fort Simcoe State Park, 27 miles (it'll feel like 57) west of Toppenish via Hwy 220, offers 52 picnic sites and an interpretive center describing local Indian wars of the 1850s.

Hiking

The dry, dusty lands around the Yakima Valley don't seem like hiker heaven, but some choice slices of it can be found by the industrious lugged-soler. The **Yakima Greenway National Recreation Trail** (easy; 7 miles one way) is a pleasant, mostly paved walkway along the Yakima River's west bank between Selah Gap and Nob Hill Boulevard. The trail also is an excellent bikeway and wildlife-spotting venue. Major access points are at the Resthaven Road exit off I-82, Harlan Landing in Selah Gap, and Sarge Hubbard and Sherman Parks in Yakima. The Yakima Greenway folks—who developed and maintain this trail through a nonprofit agency—have done a great service to the valley. Pick up trash, follow the posted rules, and keep it pleasant.

A very interesting diversion, **Cowiche Canyon Conservancy Trail** (easy; 3 miles round trip), follows an abandoned railroad right-of-way along (and over, 11 times) Cowiche Creek, which cuts through basalt and andesite cliffs. This is another prime wildlife-watching area, with more than 50 bird species spotted in the canyon (also some rattlesnakes). At last check, the trail ended where a bridge is out, just over 1.5 miles from the start. But it should extend along the full 3 miles of right-of-way in years to come, and plans call for a connecting link to the Yakima Greenway Trail. It's a very nice walk, particularly in morning or evening, out of the harsh sunlight. The trailhead is off Weikel Road, 3 miles northwest of the city limits (take Summitview Avenue west, then northwest).

In the Yakima River Canyon, a number of trails skirt the high cliffs of

The Yakima River Gorge on a crisp autumn morning

Umtanum Ridge, with views of the river. A good day hike is the short, steep climb up the old road from the Umtanum Creek Recreation Area parking lot, about 12 miles south of Ellensburg (cross the river on the suspension bridge). The trail leads about 1.5 miles to the ridge top, which offers sweeping views of the canyon. On the same (west) side of the river, the **Yakima Rim Skyline Trail** (moderate; 15 miles one way) stretches along the ridge top. The best of several tough-to-find accesses to this high, dry (no water) trail is the northern trailhead, found on the old Jacob Durr Wagon Road (from Selah, take N Wenas Avenue and Wenas Creek Road, turn right on Sheep Company Road, and proceed to Durr Road). This mostly flat ridge-top hike with sweet mountain and canyon views is very popular in the spring, when wildflowers are aburst along the path, and other Cascade trails remain snowed in. The surrounding lands are part of the L. T. Murray Wildlife Area.

A wide range of scenic hikes in the Tieton River Valley is found off of Hwy 12, about 1 hour east of Yakima. (See the White Pass Corridor chapter.)

Cycling

The most popular cycling out here involves following the grape: riders can enjoy **loop tours** of the Yakima Valley by visiting its wineries. Contact the Yakima Valley Wine Growers Association for maps and information; PO Box 39, Grandview, WA 98930; (800) 221-0751.

Wildlife Watching

The Yakima Valley is a standout on the Washington Watchable Wildlife tour. Two popular trails, the Greenway Trail and the Cowiche Canyon Trail (see Hiking, above), are great places to see a wide range of birds and small mammals. The Greenway Trail, which runs along the west bank of the Yakima, is an increasingly popular **bald eagle** hangout. Many of the regal birds are attracted here to feed on fish. The Yakima Arboretum, near the south end of the 3,600-acre Greenway, is another rich bird-watching spot. Take I-82 exit 34. Yakima Sportsman State Park's ponds and Yakima River banks also are prime bird-watching territory. (See Camping, above.)

The entire length of the Yakima River Canyon, reached by driving Hwy 821 between Ellensburg and Yakima, is rich with wildlife. Broad expanses of canyon uplands west of the river are managed as wildlife habitat in the L. T. Murray Wildlife Area. It's mostly designed as a reserve for **mule deer, elk,** and **California bighorn sheep,** but the high cliffs and valley shrub-steppe also draw large numbers of raptors. Twenty-one raptor species have been observed here, and 10 are known to nest in the valley. As you drive the canyon, use roadside pullouts as a chance to get out of the car and watch for bald eagles, any of 11 **hawk** or **falcon** species, 5 **owl** species, and other rare birds, such as **American kestrels** and **ospreys.** If you want to get out on foot, consider the Umtanum Canyon Trail (see Hiking, above), which begins across the suspension bridge from the Umtanum Recreation Area parking lot. (Watch for snakes.) For an excellent booklet detailing the bird species of the canyon—and better yet, when they're likely to appear—write the Bureau of Land Management's Wenatchee Resource Area, 915 Walla Walla Avenue, Wenatchee, WA 98801. The free booklet and a pair of binoculars can make for a very inexpensive, but quite memorable, daylong outing.

Birders also will enjoy the Boise Cascade Park and Bird Sanctuary, 5 miles west of Selah on Wenas Road. It's a 40-acre preserve where more than 100 bird species have been spotted.

Finally, one of Washington's most popular wildlife-watching venues, the Oak Creek Wildlife Area just east of Naches, is only a 30-minute drive from downtown Yakima. It's the annual winter home to the state's biggest single herd of **Rocky Mountain elk.** (See the White Pass Corridor chapter for details.)

Rafting

Very scenic, not-too-raucous float trips can be made down the **Yakima River Canyon** between Ellensburg and the Roza Dam. Good public access is along Hwy 821. Call River Raft Rentals in Ellensburg, (509) 964-2145, for **rentals.** These are relaxing, beautiful trips, with a good chance of spotting deer, elk, bighorn sheep, and other wildlife.

See the White Pass Corridor chapter for details on rafting the **Tieton River** near Naches, to the west.

Skiing

Terrific downhill and cross-country ski facilities are less than 1 hour's drive west of Yakima at **White Pass** on US 12. (See the White Pass Corridor chapter for details.)

Accessible Outdoors

Yakima Sportsman State Park has barrier-free camping (37 sites), rest rooms, and water. **Buena Lake** (Pond No. 6) off I-82 southeast of Yakima provides barrier-free fishing access for stocked rainbow trout. Take exit 50, turn left toward Buena and proceed a half mile. Turn left onto Buena Loop Road and proceed about a half mile to the access on the left. The state Fish and Wildlife **Sunnyside Wildlife Area** has a reservable duck blind at **Griffin Lake.** From I-82, take exit 67 and go south on Midvale Road to Green Valley Road. Turn west and proceed 1 mile, then turn left (south) onto Snipes Pump Road; (509) 837-7644.

outside in

Restaurants

Birchfield Manor ★★ Birchfield offers French-country dining and a good list of Washington wines. $$$; *2018 Birchfield Rd, Yakima; (509) 452-1960.* &

Deli De Pasta ★ This intimate Italian-influenced cafe is in the historical district. $; *7 N Front St, Yakima; (509) 453-0571.*

Dykstra House Restaurant Entrees are seasonally good, but the stars are the homemade desserts. $$; *114 Birch Ave, Grandview; (509) 882-2082.*

El Pastor ★★ Flavorful, reasonably priced Mexican fare includes enchiladas and fajitas. $; *315 W Walnut St, Yakima; (509) 453-5159.*

El Ranchito ★★ El Ranchito is the perfect midday stop for authentic tortillas. $; *1319 E 1st Ave, Zillah; (509) 829-5880.*

Gasperetti's Restaurant ★★ The two dining rooms here are the place to be seen in Yakima. $$; *1013 N First St, Yakima; (509) 248-0628.* &

Grant's Brewery Pub ★ This brewpub—the first in the U.S.—has beer that runs the gamut of styles. $; *32 N Front St, Yakima; (509) 575-2922.*

Santiago's Gourmet Mexican Cooking ★   Santiago's continues to serve popular gourmet chalupas, tostadas, and tacos. $; *111 E Yakima Ave, Yakima; (509) 453-1644.*

Snipes Mountain Microbrewery & Restaurant ★   Tasty beer brewed on the premises complements good-quality steak-house fare. $; *905 Yakima Valley Hwy, Sunnyside; (509) 837-2739.* ♿

Taqueria la Fogata   The small, simple Mexican taqueria reflects local tastes, including posole. $; *1204 Yakima Valley Hwy, Sunnyside; (509) 839-9019.*

Lodgings

Cozy Rose Inn ★   The Cozy Rose offers four rooms, each with a private entrance and fireplace. $$–$$$; *1220 Forsell Rd, Grandview; (800) 575-8381.*

Oxford Inn ★   Each of the 96 basic rooms has a small balcony overlooking the Yakima River. $; *1603 Terrace Heights Dr, Yakima; (800) 521-3050.* ♿

Sunnyside Inn Bed & Breakfast ★   This B&B's 13 rooms occupy two houses, one built in 1919, the other in 1925. $$; *804 E Edison Ave, Sunnyside; (800) 221-4195.*

A Touch of Europe B&B ★★   This Queen Anne Victorian house, built in 1889, wins rave reviews. $$; *220 N 16th Ave, Yakima; (888) 438-7073.*

Whistlin' Jack Lodge ★★   This 1957 mountain hideaway is ideal for hiking, skiing, or just escaping. $$; *20800 Hwy 410, Naches; (800) 827-2299.*

More Information

Greater Yakima Chamber of Commerce: *(509) 248-2021;*
   www.yakima.org.
Naches Ranger District: *(509) 653-2205.*
Wenatchee National Forest Headquarters: *(509) 662-4335;*
   www.fs.fed.us/r6/wenatchee.
Yakima Valley Visitors and Convention Bureau: *(800) 221-0751;*
   www.visityakima.com.

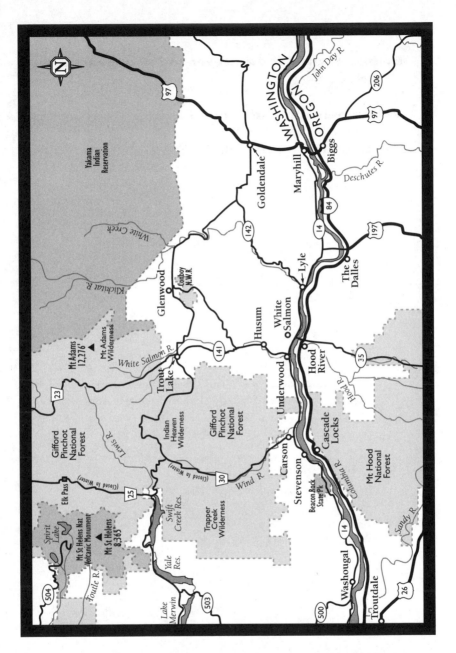

Columbia River Gorge

Bridge of the Gods: Stevenson and Beacon Rock

From Woodland east to Carson and Dog Mountain and north through the Wind River Gorge, including North Bonneville, Stevenson, Home Valley, the Skamania Lodge area, Trapper Creek Wilderness, and Beacon Rock State Park.

Trust us on this one: Lewis and Clark never skimmed across the surface of the Columbia River—or any other body of water—at 40 mph. At least not on purpose. And never in a wet suit.

Gale-force winds that would've beached the Lewis and Clark boys in 1805 simply mean surf's up these days in the Columbia River Gorge, where thousands of windsurfers launch from the beaches on both the Washington and Oregon sides to chase after the hottest board-sailing action in the country, if not the world. The Gorge, particularly this stretch of it, is board-sailing central, U.S.A. The sport has turned the little town of Hood River, just across the Columbia, into a thriving sports hub with year-round action, and much of that activity spills across Columbia River bridges to the Washington side. Windsurfing is the hottest participatory and spectator sport in this region, but it's far from the only one. The terrain here is unique on the planet, and in most ways as alluring today as when Lewis and Clark passed by on their way to a date with salt water. And in any direction you look, recreation fiends are taking full advantage.

To the north, a rich, volcano-forged mountain wonderland in the Gifford Pinchot National Forest provides top-rate camping and hiking action, in the Wind River drainage south of Mount St. Helens. It's a particularly grand place to get lost in during the spring, when some of Washington's most spectacular wildflower fields burst into bloom, and in the fall, when wild huckleberries and blueberries turn ripe on Cascade slopes. Throughout the summer, you can negotiate the back roads and drive practically right to St. Helens itself.

But plenty of wonder is found right outside the motel room (or tent) door. The Columbia Gorge is one of the most awesome physical wonders in North America, and this stretch is the most scenic on the Washington side. The Gorge, a river-carved swath through the Cascades so deep and wide that it literally creates its own weather, is a showcase for the awesome natural features of the Northwest. Its walls, sliced cleanly by the most powerful river in the country, are visible cross-sections of the Cascades, revealing volcanic features such as massive Beacon Rock and graced by countless plunging waterfalls and stunning vistas.

A sight even more fantastic exists, however, in the imagination of visitors to the Stevenson area. The small bridge crossing the Columbia today to Cascades Locks, Oregon, is a "Bridge of the Gods" in name only. The real bridge, according to Native American legend, was a natural one: a massive stone arch that bridged the river after a landslide clogged the waterway, forcing the river to tunnel beneath it. The bridge, as the legend goes, eventually gave way, forming the raucous Cascades of the Columbia rapids that Lewis and Clark encountered on their way west (since flooded by Bonneville Dam). Geologists believe the tale has merit, noting that eruptions of Mount Hood and Mount Adams, which loom close by to the south and north, could have caused such massive land shifts. (See the interpretive display in a roadside pullout, just east of the Bridge of the Gods.)

From the top of Beacon Rock, elevation 1,048 feet, it doesn't take much imagination to look east up the Gorge and imagine the natural bridge. The rock, an old volcano core, is one of the most striking features in the Gorge. That somehow seems comforting. All those hydro plants down below will, like the legendary Bridge of the Gods, give way to Mother Nature one day—offering as little resistance as the windsurfers flitting about between them.

Getting There

From Vancouver at Interstate 5/I-205, Stevenson is 40 miles east on Highway 14, which follows the Washington side of the Columbia River Gorge. Allow about 3 hours from the Seattle area. From Hwy 14 near Washougal, Hwys 500 and 503 go north to Mount St. Helens; from Hwy 14 at Carson, the Wind River Road goes north as well.

inside out

Hiking

Along Hwy 14 itself, several options await weary drivers itching for some quick vertical followed by great scenery. Beacon Rock State Park has its own 14-mile trail system. The highlight is the **Beacon Rock Trail** (moderate/difficult; 2 miles round trip), which follows a meticulously carved path (most of which clings to the south rock face, and thankfully is guarded by handrails) up 53 switchbacks to the summit of the ancient, 850-foot volcanic plug. (Keep a tight rein on the kids here; the handrails make the steep trail fairly safe, but short people can slide underneath.) A major-league view awaits at the top of this rock, which is considered the largest monolith in North America, second on the planet only to Gibraltar. One suggestion: don't take people up here who get nervous about heights. Although it's proven perfectly safe, the trail can be unnerving to ardent adherents of terra firma.

On the north side of Hwy 14, Beacon Rock State Park proper offers a dozen miles of other pleasant trails. The most popular one begins in the main day-use area and climbs about a mile up Hardy Creek to beautiful **Rodney** and **Hardy Falls** (easy; about 2 miles round trip) and ultimately the top of **Hamilton Mountain** (difficult; about 4 miles round trip). These paths, which can be combined with a string of fire roads (see Mountain Biking, below) for daylong loop hikes, make Beacon Rock a great place to spend a day, whether you're camping here, passing through, or staying at Skamania Lodge. Note: The park's campground closes from late October to late March, so you might find the main gate closed, but cyclists can park below and still access the trail system.

Just to the east on Hwy 14, a little-known interpretive trail that overlooks the Bonneville Dam makes a good leg-stretcher. The **Fort Cascades Trail** (easy; 1.5 miles round trip) loops along the river bluff through the site of the former fort and town of Cascades. The turnoff is near the North Bonneville Powerhouse, just past milepost 38.

Farther east on Hwy 14, near milepost 53, about 9 miles east of Carson, is the **Dog Mountain Trail** (difficult; 6.5 miles round trip), which climbs swiftly from the Gorge floor to a trail fork (one part of this trail is a former route of the Pacific Crest Trail) about a half mile up. Take either path, but the left one is a steeper, more direct route to the summit, where the view of the Gorge and Mount Hood from a former lookout site (dismantled in 1967) is absolutely splendid. This heavily trod trail makes for a beautiful hike in the spring, when wildflowers, especially balsam root, are blooming on the upper reaches. But bring plenty of water, and watch out: poison oak and rattlesnakes present dual hazards on this trail. Total elevation gain is about 2,800 feet. Also note that the Canada-to-Mexico **Pacific Crest Trail** crosses the Columbia at Bridge of the Gods, then heads northwest through the Gifford Pinchot National Forest. The section of the trail within short day-hiking distance of the Gorge isn't very scenic or interesting, but you can park at the trailhead near the bridge and follow the trail north for several hours or several weeks: it's only about 500 miles to the Canadian border.

Some very scenic hiking awaits in the volcano-shaped lands of the southern Gifford Pinchot National Forest, north of Carson in the Wind River drainage. For a full list, as well as for local road and trail conditions, contact the Wind River Information Center in Carson; (509) 427-3200. Note that a **Northwest Forest Pass**, $5 a day or $30 annually, available at ranger stations and from private vendors, is required for most Gifford Pinchot hikes. Following are a few favorites.

In the upper valley, the **Lava Butte Trail** (easy; 1.2 miles round trip) begins across from site 30-D at Paradise Creek Campground on Wind River Road and climbs to a clear-cut butte with a good regional view of the surrounding volcanic landscape. It's far from spectacular, but makes a nice day hike for campers in the area. The elevation gain is about 900 feet. Warning: You'll need to cross the river to access the trail. Just off Forest Road 64, which turns west of the Wind River Road about 16 miles north of Carson, the **Paradise Trail** (moderate; 5 miles round trip) climbs to the top of Paradise Ridge, then follows it north to a second trailhead. Good views all along. One of the most popular hikes in this area is **Upper Falls Creek** (moderate; 8 miles round trip), which climbs about 3 miles to a 100-foot waterfall plunging from a magical deep, clear pool. It's a grand picnic spot. The trail continues on to a dead end at Forest Road 6053. The trailhead is at the end of Forest Road 3062, which turns east off Wind River Road about 15 miles north of Carson. An easy hike that's palatable and engaging enough for children is the **Lower Falls Creek Trail** (easy; 3.4 miles round trip), which climbs gently through a cool, mossy forest to a bridge vista of a 100-foot waterfall. Follow Wind River Road north to Road 3062, turn east for 1.5 miles, then turn right on Road 57.

On the west side of the Wind River drainage are a handful of other worthwhile Gifford Pinchot National Forest hikes. The **Observation Trail** (moderate; 16.5 miles round trip) climbs through forest before breaking out to grand views on the slopes of Observation Peak and Sisters Rocks. The view from the top of Observation Peak (reached by a short way trail, about 6 miles from the trailhead) is stupendous, with Rainier, St. Helens, and Hood all on display. Decent campsites are found along the route,

Walk a crooked mile—or two—on the unique Beacon Rock trail

although the climb to Observation and back (about 11.5 miles) can be made in a day by strong hikers. The heavily used trailhead is on Forest Road 5401, reached by following Wind River Road 8 miles north to Mineral Springs Road and following it west. Nearby, off Forest Road 34, the **West Crater Trail** (easy/moderate; 1.5 miles round trip) climbs along the rim of an ancient volcano crater, a fascinating spot. Follow Wind River and

Hemlock Roads to Forest Road 54, then turn left on Road 34. Slightly to the south is **Zig Zag Loop** (moderate/difficult; 1 mile round trip), a short but steep trail through a nice forest to an alpine lake that contains Eastern brook trout. The trailhead is on Forest Road 42 off Wind River Road.

Fans of big, wide-open views won't be disappointed by the **Bunker Hill Trail** (moderate; 3 miles round trip), which follows the Pacific Crest Trail for about a mile before climbing steeply (about 1,300 feet) to this former fire lookout site, elevation 2,383 feet, where fantastic views await in all directions. Follow Wind River Road to Hemlock Road, turn west for just over a mile to Road 43, then turn right and drive a half-mile to Road 43-417. Watch for Pacific Crest Trail markers to the trailhead.

Camping

Beacon Rock State Park is the primary campground in this region, with two separate camping areas and a 200-person group camp. In all, the park offers 33 campsites (no hookups; RVs to 50 feet). The best ones are in the main, upland camping area, but a handful of more primitive (also more scenic, and more windy) sites are found across the narrow Hwy 14 bridge in the park's marine area, where a boat launch is located. (Note: The marine area suffered flood damage in the spring of 1996. Call the park for updates.) Beacon Rock is open from late March to late October. Campsites cannot be reserved. *35 miles east of Vancouver on Hwy 14; (509) 427-8265 or (800) 233-0321.*

A handful of slightly more removed, but still quite pleasant Gifford Pinchot National Forest campgrounds are found in the Wind River drainage, reached by following Wind River Road north from Carson. Panther Creek and Beaver, both near the Wind River Ranger Station, are the closest. **Panther Creek** (33 sites, 26 reservable; RVs to 25 feet), a lightly used streamside camp in a forested area off Forest Road 65, is at 1,000 feet. **Beaver** (24 sites, 15 reservable; RVs to 25 feet), located off Road 30, on the Wind River, is shady with paved sites (good RV parking) and a large, grassy day-use area. The elevation is 1,100 feet. Farther north, near the south border of Indian Heaven Wilderness on Forest Road 30, is **Paradise Creek** (42 sites, 31 reservable; RVs to 25 feet). The road is paved all the way to this lightly used campground at 1,500 feet. All three are open summers only and have piped water and other standard Forest Service amenities, but no RV hookups. Campsites may be reserved in advance; 877-444-6777; reserveusa.com. A more rustic option is the **Falls Creek Horse Camp** (6 sites), adjacent to Forest Road 65. It's used mostly as a staging area for horse treks to the Pacific Crest Trail and other areas. Not recommended for RVs. Check campground and road status with the Wind

River Information Center, (509) 427-3200; www.fs.fed.us/gpnf. Winter washouts are common in this area.

Windsurfing

The Washington side of the Gorge isn't as widely known for windsurfing as the Oregon side. But savvy riders know several beaches that are as good as the Gorge gets when winds cooperate. Here's a list of Washington windsurfing beaches and vista points for those seeking to get wet or just to watch.

Rock Creek Pond in Stevenson is on a shallow, protected inland lake better suited to beginners than most Gorge locations. It's on Rock Creek Drive between Stevenson and Skamania Lodge. Another local hot spot, **Bob's Beach** at Stevenson Landing, draws large crowds of intermediate-to-expert surfers, who are advised to watch out for the big paddlewheeler that docks here. Farther east, **Home Valley Park** is a favorite beginner-to-intermediate spot, and **Drano Lake** is a noted area for beginners. Follow signs to the Drano Lake boat launch from Hwy 14. In this area, expert sailors usually are found farther east at Swell City (see the White Salmon and Bingen chapter).

To discover the world's foremost collection of windsurfing gear, supplies, lessons, and lore cross the Columbia at Bridge of the Gods or White Salmon and trek to Hood River, home to a dozen **sailing shops.** Beginners, you'll be wasting valuable time if you don't take a **lesson.** They're available from a dozen board shops in Hood River and usually cost about $125 for full gear and 2 days of instructions. Traveling tourists who just want to know where to go to watch should tune radios to 104.5 FM, a Hood River station that offers wind updates and "noteworthy boardhead news" all day long. For planning a Gorge board-sailing vacation, pick up a copy of *The Gorge Guide,* available at most Seattle-area outdoor stores or by phoning (800) 98-GORGE; or contact the Columbia Gorge Windsurfing Association; (541) 386-9225. For real-time, online wind reports, visit www.iwindsurf.com.

Canoeing/Kayaking

Paddlers, particularly sea kayakers, are drawn to the rocky shores, towering cliffs, and interesting inlets of the **Columbia River.** Frequent high winds, coupled with heavy boat and barge traffic and dangers from dams and river locks, make the Columbia itself an experts-only area. Good **launch points** include Beacon Rock State Park, Skamania Landing, North Bonneville boat launch, Rock Creek Park, Stevenson Landing, Stevenson boat launch, and Home Valley Park. The one good beginner area here is **Drano Lake,** also an interesting canoe venue, where waters are calm most of the time. Follow signs to the boat launch from Hwy 14. The **upper Wind River** is a noted whitewater kayak stretch.

Fishing

The lower Columbia River below Bonneville Dam is a world-famous fishery, noted both for its once abundant **salmon** (now troubled; seasons are truncated) and its healthy **steelhead** populations. Fishing for steelhead still can be productive here, both from boats and banks. Keep in mind that all wild steelhead must be released.

If you're after the big one—the really, really big one—consider a guided lower-river **sturgeon** trip. These babies are literally monsters, with some growing to 20 feet. They're uglier than sin, with giant sucker mouths and long, reptilian bodies. You can only keep sturgeon between 42 and 66 inches, but, for the catch-and-release experience of a lifetime, many Columbia guides steer clients to fish that are longer than the boat. The peak season is June and July. Experienced anglers hook a good number of sturgeon from the shore, fishing a shad or smelt bait off the bottom.

An increasingly popular Columbia fishery is the robust lower-river **shad** run, which peaks in June. The hot spot is the water below Bonneville Dam. Bank casters on both sides of the river do well with just about any kind of cast-and-retrieve tackle. Shad, basically overgrown herring, aren't much for eating. But they're fun to catch, and as of this writing, there's no limit on them.

For years, the **Wind River** was known for a productive chinook salmon run. But as with other Columbia chinook runs, hydropower, overfishing, and a half dozen other factors have combined to snuff most of it. The river does still have a semiproductive, hatchery-produced summer steelhead run, with the best fishing in July and August. All wild steelhead must be released here. Reliable river reports sometimes can be had by inquiring at Carson Hot Springs, (509) 427-8292.

Wildlife Watching

For fish fans and kids young and old, the **Bonneville Dam Fishway** and Visitors Center is a must-stop, particularly if you're in the area during a summer salmon migration. Fish runs in the mighty Columbia are mere fractions of their former numbers, but because all steelhead and salmon stocks returning to dozens of rivers in eastern Washington, Oregon, and southern Idaho must pass through this hydropower funnel, the fish windows at Bonneville usually are alive with movement. Spring chinook pass through in April and May, but other **chinook, coho, sockeye,** and **steelhead** pass through the ladder for most of the summer. The center is open daily until 5pm, 8pm during summer months. Follow signs from Hwy 14 near milepost 40, between Beacon Rock and Stevenson; (509) 427-4281. Another fish-viewing area is the Carson National Fish Hatchery near the Wind River Ranger Station on Wind River Road north of Carson. The hatchery, which raises salmon and **trout** smolts, welcomes visitors.

If you're looking for a more natural setting, look no further than Pierce Island, a Nature Conservancy preserve, a former salmon-harvesting site left to revert to its natural, willow-and-ash-covered state. The 85-acre island is one of the last surviving "natural" islands in the Gorge, and in the early '80s narrowly avoided becoming a dumping ground for river dredge spoils. Acquisition by the Nature Conservancy in 1984 protected habitat for **great blue heron, osprey,** and **beaver,** as well as a population of a rare plant species, persistent sepal yellowcress (a mustard plant), which grows on the gravel shoreline. It's found in only a dozen places in North America, and is protected only here. Pierce Island is due east of the boat launch at Beacon Rock State Park (see Camping, above). It's accessible only by boat.

Mountain Biking

The hilly, forested Wind River drainage north of Carson is home to some excellent fat-tire terrain—mostly on paths that double as winter ski trails in the Oldman Pass area. From the upper Wind River Winter Sports Area parking lots (see Cross Country Skiing/Snowshoeing, below), riders will find well-marked trails, most suitable for beginning trail riders. Look for **Trails 150, 151, 154, 157,** and **159.** Most of the paths are 50-foot-wide ski and snowmobile trails through short vegetation, making for easier, non-threatening riding. Six loops beginning at the Sno-Park range from 1 to 13 miles. Get a trail map at the Wind River Information Center. Down lower, in the Gorge, options are somewhat limited. But fat-tire hounds can work up a good sweat on the 13 miles of fire roads in the upland area of **Beacon Rock State Park** (see the Camping and Hiking sections, above). From the main park entrance, follow signs to the group camp area and watch for the gated road on the right. The road leads about 5 miles north, and a 10-mile loop **around Hamilton Mountain** is possible.

Climbing

The front face of 848-foot **Beacon Rock** is a major rock-climbing destination, attracting experts who take on some 60 routes, many among the most technically challenging in the Northwest, with ratings up to 5.10. Climbing was halted recently because of concerns about nesting peregrine falcons on the rock, but it has since resumed. An access trail leads down from the parking area on the south side of Hwy 14.

Cross-Country Skiing/Snowshoeing

The Wind River Winter Sports Area, at and around **Oldman Pass**, about 25 miles north of Carson on Wind River Road, is a launching pad to 22.5 kilometers of cross-country trails, which are groomed from December 15 to April 1. The Sno-Park—actually four separate winter parking areas spread along the highway, at about 3,000 feet in elevation—is a great place for beginner and intermediate skiers; all of the trails are rated easy. Grooming usually is repeated on Thursdays or Fridays. The more adventurous skier can head off on an additional 25 kilometers of marked but unmaintained ski trails on local Forest Service roads. Some trails in this area, so-called **"Snofoot Trails,"** are for skiers and snowshoers only. Others are shared with snowmobiles. All cars must have a state **Sno-Park permit,** available at ski and outdoor stores and Ranger District offices. For snow updates, call the Wind River Information Center at Carson, (509) 427-3200, or visit the Gifford Pinchot National Forest web site (see More Information, below).

Accessible Outdoors

The **Hemlock Lake Recreation Area** north of Carson near the Wind River Information Center has a handicapped-accessible fishing pier and quarter-mile interpretive trail; (509) 427-3200. **Beaver Campground** (see Camping, above) has barrier-free sites.

outside in

Lodgings

Skamania Lodge ★★ Just like a national park lodge, but with a golf course, saunas, and spa. $$$; 1131 Skamania Lodge Wy, Stevenson; (509) 427-7700 or (800) 221-7117; www.dolce.com/properties/skamania.

More Information

Columbia River Gorge National Scenic Area: (509) 493-3323.
Columbia Gorge Windsurfing Association: (541) 386-9225.
Gifford Pinchot National Forest Headquarters: 360-891-5000; www.fs.fed.us/gpnf/.
Skamania County Chamber of Commerce: (800) 989-9178; www.skamania.org.
Wind River Information Center: (509) 427-3200.

White Salmon
and Bingen

From Drano Lake north to Trout Lake and east to Lyle, including the lower White Salmon and Little White Salmon River valleys and Doug's Beach State Park.

White Salmon itself isn't an outdoor lover's paradise, but you can certainly see one from here. Any direction you look, as a matter of fact. Located as it is near the geographic center of the Northwest, White Salmon has a South Cascades wonderland (the Mount Adams Wilderness) to the northwest, Hood River and Mount Hood across the Columbia River to the south, and the Columbia Gorge extending east and west from either end of town.

That makes the outdoor lineup predictable but rich. In the summertime, White Salmon is a good launching point for Gorge windsurfing or fishing expeditions; hiking on Mount Adams Wilderness trails to the north, near Trout Lake; and rafting or just general cavorting on the scenic White Salmon River. In the winter, roads to the north are closed, and White Salmon becomes a quiet, peaceful getaway, with rich wildlife-viewing opportunities in the Gorge and at its many fish hatcheries. All things considered, White Salmon is a good, central location for many days worth of Gorge exploration.

Getting There

White Salmon is 65 miles east of Vancouver on Highway 14. For travelers driving the Oregon side of the Columbia River Gorge, White Salmon is directly across the Columbia River bridge from Hood River, Oregon. Hwy 141 goes north from White Salmon to Trout Lake; Hwy 142 goes northeast from Lyle to eventually connect with Goldendale and US Highway 97.

inside out

Windsurfing

The White Salmon area is home to some of the best windsurfing on either side of the entire Columbia River Gorge. When the wind is strong, the bulk of the area's board-sailing faithful might start the day in Hood River, Oregon, but many board sailors quickly become part of the northbound traffic on the Hood River–White Salmon bridge.

One of Washington's board-sailing hot spots, **Swell City,** is found close by, near Hwy 14 milepost 61, 4 miles west of the Hood River Bridge. The spot seems made for windsurfing: a small, protected bay gets you on your feet, and several yards farther south, the big winds turn on the gas. The river here is known for its consistently ripping west gales, making Swell City a top spot for advanced Gorge sailors. Parking is limited and is maxed out quickly on good wind days.

A half mile east is another area mostly for experts, **Spring Creek Hatchery.** Access to the river through the fish hatchery isn't great, and parking is very limited. Launching also can be tricky on the riprap bank. Winds are slightly tamer, amenities certainly more comforting, at the **Klickitat Point** windsurfing beach near Bingen Marina. The parking area is spacious, and the site offers plenty of rigging room. Veterans advise: watch out for deadheads (logs that float just beneath the surface)!

Farther east, 2.5 miles beyond Lyle, is another longtime access point, **Doug's Beach State Park,** named after Doug Campbell of Hood River Windsurfing. Parking is along the south shoulder of Hwy 14, where you'll need to cross the busy Burlington Northern tracks. A small, sandy beach makes a good launching point, and big waves and big winds (30-mph gales aren't unusual) make this an experts-only beach. Beware of barge traffic close to the shore.

For more information on windsurfing **lessons and supplies** and on Hood River, Oregon, see the Bridge of the Gods chapter.

Hiking

Hiking terrain is scarce on the floor of the steep-sided Gorge, but many quality hikes are found in the Mount Adams and Indian Heaven Wilderness areas around Trout Lake (see the Mount Adams chapter for hikes north of Trout Lake). And two Gifford Pinchot trails in the region are a short distance north of White Salmon off Hwy 141.

A fairly easy trail that climbs to nice views at a former lookout site is the **Monte Cristo Trail** (easy; 8 miles round trip), which begins south of

Views are plentiful in the central Columbia River Gorge

Trout Lake and climbs very gradually to the twin summits of Monte Cristo and Monte Carlo. To reach the trailhead from Hwy 141, turn south on Road 80 3 miles west of Trout Lake, then turn west on Road 86-080.

A more difficult hike, the **Little Huckleberry Trail** (moderate/difficult; 5 miles round trip) climbs steeply to a summit with a grand view of the Big Lava Bed and Goose Lake. The trailhead is about 2 miles west of Little Goose Horse Camp on Hwy 141, which becomes Forest Road 24 at the National Forest boundary.

Fishing

Much of the sport-fishing action here centers on Drano Lake, at the mouth of the Little White Salmon River east of Cook. Seasonal highlights are the spring (April/May) **chinook** fishery, and the fall (August/September) chinook and **steelhead** seasons. The spring season has been iffy in recent years because of troubled chinook stocks in the Columbia system, so call the Mount Adams Ranger District, (509) 395-3400, before you go. A boat launch is located on the north side of the lake.

Conditions are similar on the White Salmon River to the west, where strong numbers of steelhead and salmon catches are made around the river's mouth in the spring and fall. Upriver several miles on Hwy 141, decent **trout** fishing breaks out every spring in Northwestern Lake, a reservoir on the White Salmon. Trout also are stocked in Rowland Lake, a

Columbia River pond bisected by Hwy 14 east of Bingen.

The pooled-up Columbia River in this region also is a productive fishery. See the Fishing/Boating section of the Goldendale and Maryhill chapter for details.

Camping

Options are somewhat limited here, unless you want to drive an hour north up Hwy 141 to one of the two dozen small-but-scenic Forest Service campgrounds in the Trout Lake area of the White Salmon River drainage. See the Mount Adams chapter for details. Closer to the Gorge are two other Forest Service camps, **Moss Creek** with 17 sites (no hookups; RVs to 32 feet) and **Oklahoma** with 23 sites (no hookups; RVs to 22 feet), which are 8 and 14 miles north of Cook, respectively (drive north on County Road 1800). Both are open May to September. Campsites can be reserved; (877) 444-6777; www.reserveusa.com. Contact Mount Adams Ranger District in Trout Lake; (509) 395-3400.

Wildlife Watching

A good Gorge fish-watching station, the Little White Salmon National Fish Hatchery, is at the mouth of the Little White Salmon River between Home Valley and White Salmon. The hatchery, about 12 miles east of Stevenson, produces 3.7 million upriver bright fall **chinook**, 1.35 million spring chinook, and 2.5 million **coho salmon** every year. Chinook and coho spawn in the lower river, attracting flocks of **ospreys** and **bald eagles,** which feed on the spent carcasses. Eagles are commonly seen here throughout the winter, and salmon are visible in the hatchery ponds. Best viewing times are during the spring chinook run in June and July and the fall chinook run in September and October. The hatchery is managed by the U.S. Fish and Wildlife Service; (509) 538-2755.

Farther north, toward Mount Adams, is Conboy Lake National Wildlife Refuge, home to large populations of migratory **geese, ducks,** and **swans** every spring. This refuge also is the only known state nesting spot for **sandhill cranes,** and **elk** often are spotted in the fall. An interpretive loop trail begins near the headquarters for the 5,600-acre refuge, located 6 miles southwest of Glenwood on the Glenwood-Trout Lake Road off Hwy 141 at BZ Corner; (509) 364-3410.

Rafting/Kayaking

A popular summertime rafting venue, with some Class III and Class IV rapids, the **White Salmon River** also is a good ride for whitewater kayakers. The upper portion (downstream from Glenwood Road, a couple miles south of Trout Lake) is extremely hazardous, with many Class V obstacles. Several falls are impassable, and other stretches are navigable only during heavier flows. The middle portion (between BZ Corner and Husum) is an intermediate stretch, with mostly Class III obstacles. The lower portion from Husum to Northwestern Lake is gentler, with a couple Class II rapids. For detailed river information and **guide referrals,** contact the Mount Adams Ranger District in Trout Lake; (509) 395-3400.

outside in

Restaurants

Fidel's   Lively Mexican music accompanies carne asada, chile verde, and chile colorado. $; *120 E Stuben St, Bingen; (509) 493-1017.*

Lodgings

Inn of the White Salmon ★★   This 1937-vintage jewel offers the privacy of a hotel with the comfort of a B&B. $$; *172 W Jewett, White Salmon; (509) 493-2335 or (800) 972-5226; www.gorge.net/lodging/iws.*

More Information

Columbia Gorge Windsurfing Association: *(541) 386-9225.*
Columbia River Gorge National Scenic Area: *(509) 493-3323.*
Mount Adams Ranger District: *(509) 395-3400.*
Skamania County Chamber of Commerce: *(800) 989-9178;*
   www.skamania.org.

Goldendale
and Maryhill

From Lyle northeast to Satus Pass and southeast to John Day Dam, including the Klickitat River Gorge and Horsethief Lake, Maryhill, Goldendale Observatory, and Brooks Memorial State Parks.

We hate to say a place has a little of everything, but Goldendale really does. No matter which way you look at it, the little town perched high on a bluff above the Columbia River Gorge is a transition zone. This is where wet turns to dry, flat turns to mountainous, Oregon turns to Washington. The result, for outdoor lovers, is a nice mix of all the activities and ecosystems found up and down the Gorge.

South of Goldendale is the Columbia, where Maryhill and Horsethief Lake State Parks lure campers, anglers, and windsurfers all year round. To the north are the beautiful rocky outcrops and dry pine forests of the Satus Pass area—a past and present home to the Yakama Indian Nation. And the giant, hulking form of Mount Adams, a constant backdrop, is a reminder that only a short distance to the west the serious mountains begin. The Goldendale area is a prominent gateway to the Mount Adams Wilderness, most frequently explored on its south slopes.

And there's a bonus. If the weather goes haywire on you (not an unusual occurrence in the Gorge), the Goldendale area offers plenty of tourist curiosities to distract your attention. The intriguing Maryhill Museum, Stonehenge Monument, and other legacies of the late Sam Hill, a quirky industrialist who shaped this area, all are worth a stop, as is the Goldendale Observatory—a bit of everything, and a big telescope to boot.

Getting There

The Goldendale/Maryhill area is a long haul from Seattle, with a choice of two scenic routes. Take Interstate 90 east to I-82, and continue southeast to Toppenish. Turn south on US Highway 97 and proceed 50 miles, crossing Satus Pass, to Goldendale. Or, from I-5 at Vancouver, follow Hwy 14 about 100 miles east to US 97 at the Sam Hill Bridge over the Columbia; Goldendale is a dozen miles north. Allow about 4 hours either way.

inside out

Camping

Maryhill State Park is one of the best-developed and nicest campgrounds in the Columbia River Gorge. Located on a long stretch of riverfront with ample green lawns and mature shade trees, Maryhill is a favorite of road-weary Gorge travelers as well as boaters and windsurfers. Maryhill has a boat ramp, large group picnic facilities, a swimming beach, fishing pier, broad playfields, and 70 campsites (50 hookups; RVs to 50 feet). The Maryhill Museum and Stonehenge Memorial are nearby. Maryhill is open all year. Campsites can be reserved up to 11 months in advance by calling Reservations Northwest; (800) 452-5687. *Immediately east of the Sam Hill (US 97) Bridge; (509) 773-5007 or (800) 233-0321.*

To the west, near The Dalles Dam is **Horsethief Lake State Park,** a smaller, less-developed riverfront site than Maryhill. The park has 14 campsites (no hookups; RVs to 30 feet) near the Columbia and Horsethief Lake, standing water created by the backup from The Dalles Dam. It's an interesting historical area: Lewis and Clark reported a permanent Indian camp here, and discernible petroglyphs can be seen at the end of a short trail from the park. Another hiking trail leads up Horsethief Butte (see Hiking/Climbing, below). Horsethief Lake itself is a popular spot for windsurfing and fishing (see sections for both, below). The campground is open from April to November. Campsites cannot be reserved. *On Hwy 14 1.5 miles east of The Dalles (US 197) Bridge, 28 miles west of Goldendale; (509) 767-1159 or (800) 233-0321.*

To the north, **Brooks Memorial State Park** straddles US 97 just south of 3,100-foot Satus Pass. With its group camp, large picnic shelters, and educational facilities, the park is most heavily used by groups. But it has a pleasant area for individual campers in the portion of the park on the west side of the highway. Here, 45 campsites (23 full hookups; RVs to 50 feet) are scattered through two pine-forested loops. The park's high elevation makes it a popular cross-country skiing/snowmobiling base camp in the winter. Brooks Memorial is open all year. Campsites cannot be reserved. *On US 97 15 miles north of Goldendale; (509) 773-5382 or (800) 233-0321.*

Another camping option—a long drive east on Hwy 14—is **Crow Butte State Park.** See the Tri-Cities chapter for details.

Somewhat primitive, but also usually quite private, camping can be found in the **Klickitat Wildlife Area,** a state Department of Fish and Wildlife preserve west of Goldendale. (See Wildlife Watching, below.)

Windsurfing

A nice mix of beginner and expert waters can be found along the **Columbia** below Goldendale. From west to east:

A good beginner area is **Horsethief Lake State Park,** which has the advantage of a sheltered **inland lake** large enough for neophyte sailors to roam. From the same location, experts can launch into the Columbia proper. The dual action makes this a good spot for windsurfing families or for campouts for groups whose members are far apart on the skills list. The lake is safe for beginners because there's no boat or barge traffic. But beware of winds that seem perpetually to blow rookie sailors to the far side—with no easy way to return on foot. And be particularly cautious about walking along the very actively used railroad tracks. The park is about 1.5 miles east of The Dalles Bridge.

Avery Park, 6 miles east of The Dalles Bridge, is a primitive Corps of Engineers parking lot/river access. It's an intermediate-skills area with strong west winds and big waves. Steer clear of fishing boats launching here, and of the Indian fishing platform at one end of the park. Also note that most barge traffic is funneled to this side of the river, between the bank and Brown's Island.

Maryhill State Park, immediately east of the Sam Hill Bridge, is a favorite expert's hangout, with plenty of room for rigging, a nice launching beach, and rest rooms. The river here can be a challenge even for the expert windsurfer, with smoking west winds coupled with very strong currents, particularly in the spring.

Two other frequently surfed experts-only areas, **Peach Beach** and **The Wall,** are found between Maryhill and the John Day Dam, but access is difficult and launch areas hazardous. For information on windsurfing lessons, vendors, and wind conditions, see the Bridge of the Gods and the White Salmon and Bingen chapters.

Kayaking/Rafting

Experienced paddlers can launch at any of the beaches identified in Windsurfing, above, for raucous, whitewater-style action in the big winds and

Windsurfers in the central Columbia River Gorge

waves of the **Columbia.** The scenic **Klickitat River Gorge,** home to a
wealth of Class IV rapids, is frequently run by experienced paddlers.
Many commercial rafting companies lead **guided expeditions** down the
Klickitat. Contact the Mount Adams Ranger District at Trout Lake, (509)
395-3400, for references.

Fishing/Boating

The Klickitat River, accessible along Hwy 142 between Lyle and Goldendale, consistently ranks as one of the state's favorite summer **steelhead**
streams. Fishing is best early in the season (late June/early July) and late
(September). Even when the fishing slows, the setting—in the spectacular
Klickitat Gorge—is unbeatable. Note that all wild steelhead must be
released. Fishing for fall **chinook** also can be productive. Most successful
steelhead and salmon anglers float the upper part of the river in drift boats.

The broad, deep waters of the Columbia River in this Gorge midsec-
tion used to be famous for spring and fall chinook salmon fishing. Both
have been curtailed dramatically in recent years because of concerns over
struggling wild salmon stocks. Check the state regulations pamphlet for
information about river openers. There's plenty of other fishing to be done
here, however. A fair number of **sturgeon** are horsed ashore at the Mary-

hill State Park boat launch in the early summer, before catch-and-release rules take effect in July. This section of the river also holds **walleye, shad, largemouth** and **smallmouth bass,** and steelhead.

Public boat launches are found at Lyle, Horsethief Lake State Park, Avery, and Maryhill. Horsethief Lake is stocked with **rainbow trout** (best in the spring) and offers a decent bass fishery. Bank access is decent for both.

Hiking/Climbing

Several short but interesting trails fan out through Horsethief Lake State Park. One climbs a short distance from the day-use area to some interesting **ancient petroglyphs** on the hillside. Another climbs from Hwy 14 about a mile east of the park entrance to the top of 500-foot **Horsethief Butte,** which looms east of the lake. It's a 2-mile round trip from the (limited) parking area on the north side of Hwy 14, or a 4-mile round trip walk from the campground. The last part is a rock scramble. Watch for snakes, and please refrain from digging for arrowheads. Most of the good mountain hiking trails in this region are on the southern slopes of Mount Adams, in the Mount Adams Wilderness around Trout Lake. See the Mount Adams chapter for details. The **short pitches** on the north side of Horsethief Butte are popular beginner rock-climbing areas.

Wildlife Watching

Black-tailed deer are thick in winter months throughout the Klickitat Wildlife Area, a very scenic mix of grasslands, mountain ridges, and forests of oak and ponderosa pine; (509) 773-4459. The area's Soda Springs Unit, a 13,000-acre site west of Goldendale bisected by the Klickitat River (see Fishing/Boating, above) is home to a variety of game birds (including **wild turkeys**) and raptors. The headquarters is 16 miles northwest of Goldendale on the Glenwood Highway, which heads north from Hwy 142. In the winter, chances of spotting deer on south-facing slopes along this road are excellent. Other wildlife common in the area are **Rocky Mountain elk, ruffed** and **blue grouse, Merriam's turkey,** and **California quail.** Note that hunting seasons for deer and game birds take place every fall. Two smaller areas, the Mineral Springs and Dillacort Canyon units, are downstream in the Klickitat River Canyon. The Goldendale Trout Hatchery, about 4 miles west of town, also is part of this collection of properties managed by Washington Department of Fish and Wildlife.

Photography

Just about anywhere you go in the Gorge area is rich with photo opportunities, but this particular section shines even brighter. The lower **Klickitat**

River Gorge, accessible along Hwy 142, is gorgeous, with plenty of white-water and canyon scenic spots. For an overall Columbia Gorge view looking west from the dry side of the state to the wet, the **Stonehenge memorial** offers a grand vista, with the Sam Hill Bridge providing a humbling degree of scale in the foreground.

Accessible Outdoors

Maryhill State Park has handicapped-accessible campsites, Columbia River access, and rest rooms.

outside in

Lodgings

Timberframe Country Inn B&B   The Timberframe, surrounded by ponderosa pines, has two private-entrance suites. *$$; 223 Golden Pine, Goldendale; (800) 861-8408.*

More Information

Columbia Gorge Windsurfing Association: *(541) 386-9225.*
Columbia River Gorge National Scenic Area: *(509) 493-3323.*
Gifford Pinchot National Forest Headquarters: *360-891-5000;*
   www.fs.fed.us/gpnf/.
Goldendale Chamber of Commerce: *(509) 773-3400.*
Klickitat County Travel Information Center: *(509) 773-4395;*
   www.klickitatc ounty.org/Tourism.
Mount Adams Ranger District, Trout Lake: *(509) 395-3400.*

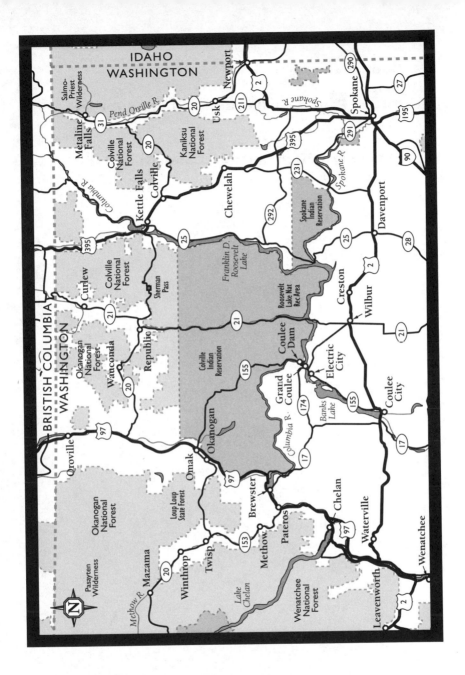

Northeast Washington

Northeast Washington

Spokane

From downtown Spokane north to Mount Spokane, south to Sprague, east to the Idaho border, and west to Long Lake Reservoir, including the Spokane and Little Spokane Rivers, the Centennial Trail, Riverfront Park, the Turnbull National Wildlife Refuge, and Riverside and Mount Spokane State Parks.

Locals call it "the Capital of the Inland Empire." They point out that it was the site of the first white settlement in the Northwest. They insist it's the biggest city between Seattle and Minneapolis. Big deal. For many of us, the important thing about Spokane is something a lot more practical: it has the only REI between Redmond and Boise.

Before you summarily dismiss that little fact, consider the implications. They only locate REI (Recreational Equipment Inc.) stores in urban centers containing plenty of (a) cash and (b) outdoor-recreation enthusiasm. Spokane, it could be argued, from time to time is short on the former. But it certainly suffers no lack of the latter. Long the center of commerce, education, medicine, manufacturing, transportation, and religion for a broad Northwest inland area comprising Eastern Washington, Idaho, Western Montana, Northeastern Oregon, and southern British Columbia and Alberta, Spokane also holds the regional focus for outdoor enthusiasts. Many of the Spokane area's 375,000 residents are newbies, and a high percentage of those were attracted by the regional lifestyle. It includes plenty of clean air, medium-size mountains, clear-running rivers, and hospitable pine forests. Not to mention actual seasons. Unlike the state's other major population centers, Spokane has real weather: blazing hot summers, stormy autumns, frequently brutal winters, and magical springs.

Spokane Falls is a highlight of Spokane's fine municipal park system

Even more so than most other parts of the state, Spokane is a city shaped by its environment. From the time of explorer David Thompson's initial white settlement here in 1810, through the growth boom of Western railroad expansion, the harsh era of the Great Depression, and a current rebirth related to high-tech industry and light manufacturing, the people of Spokane always have been dragged down—and lifted up—by the landscape. It's not a gentle place to live.

That perhaps explains why Spokane residents—and many of their frequent visitors—deal with the natural elements the only way they know how: head on, face first. Whether they're whitewater kayaking on the Spokane River, running till they drop in the Bloomsday Race, backcountry telemark skiing on Mount Spokane, or hauling a state-record cutthroat out of a local lake, Spokane outdoor enthusiasts are serious about their craft. When your environment is constantly in your face, freezing your radiator, challenging your mind, serious is the only way to be.

Not that a visit to the Spokane Valley necessarily requires wearing your best outdoors game face. Spokane can provide a wonderful, relaxing experience for the visiting recreator. Local fishing, kayaking, recreational running, cross-country skiing, and just plain walking all rate as excellent. The city is rightfully proud of its fine 37-mile Centennial Trail, which plays a role in each of those activities. It's equally fond of its lakes (76 within a 50-mile radius), streams, wildlife reserves, campgrounds, hiking trails (1,635 miles worth in the region), and even a ski mountain. If all that's a little too raucous for you, break out the clubs: the Spokane area is home to two dozen golf courses, many very highly rated.

Make a visit to this little big city, and you'll see why the city fathers all have moleskin on their heels. Ultimately, you're likely to find yourself in the aisles of REI, rubbing elbows with the locals. You'll be buying maps and lattes, and they'll be buying moleskin and duct tape. Never mind that. Once you step outside, into the river or onto the trail, you're all playing the same game. For once, being the visiting player holds a distinct advantage: when the going gets tough, you can fold up the board and go home.

Getting There

Spokane is 280 miles east of Seattle on Interstate 90. Allow 5.5 to 6 hours— less if you're under the influence of caffeine and/or radar-detection devices. US Highway 2 also goes through Spokane, where it turns north through Newport to Idaho. Other highways running north from Spokane are Hwy 291 (to Long Lake), US 395 (to Chewelah), and Hwy 206 (to Mount Spokane). US 195 heads south from Spokane to the Palouse.

Many major airlines, including Horizon, Northwest, Alaska, and South-west, offer daily flights from Sea-Tac to Spokane International Airport. Other transportation options are Greyhound, (800) 231-2222, and Amtrak's Empire Builder; (800) 872-7245.

inside out

Parks

Spokane has a very nicely maintained city park system, with some of the more pleasant urban parks in the Northwest. **Riverfront Park** is the green heart of the old city. Developed from old railroad yards by Expo '74, the

100-acre park is now an airy place full of meandering paved paths (see Cycling, below) and mesmerizing whitewater rapids, with entertainments ranging from ice-skating to an IMAX theater. Just strolling the grounds and pausing over one of the multiple bridges over Spokane Falls is a favorite activity any time of the year. Head west from any of the main downtown exits off Interstate 90, and you'll eventually run into it. **Manito Park,** at Grand Boulevard and 18th on the South Hill, has theme gardens and a duck pond you can splash in. **Finch Arboretum** (a couple of miles west of downtown Spokane along the interstate), a pleasant picnic site, holds a modest but attractive collection of trees and shrubs among ravines and a stream. For a panoramic vista of Spokane, visit **Cliff Park** at 13th and Grove.

Cycling

By all means, bring the bikes. Perhaps the best urban-to-rural walking-and-cycling path in the state, the 39-mile **Centennial Trail** from Riverside State Park to Coeur d'Alene, Idaho, is the recreational focus of the Spokane area. The trail follows the Spokane River, and its entire length is open to strolling and cycling (in some sections, wheeled and nonwheeled users are channeled onto separate paths), with some portions open to horseback riding. The primary access point is Riverfront Park in downtown Spokane (see Parks, above.) The trail passes by Gonzaga University, Mission Park, the Walk in the Wild Zoo, and other local attractions. If hills are your worst enemy, start downtown and ride east; the only substantially hilly portions are to the west, in Riverside State Park (see Hiking, below). Note: Most of the trail east of Spokane is open territory. Bring sunscreen. For details, maps, and trail events, contact Friends of the Centennial Trail; (509) 624-7188; www.spokanecentennialtrail.org. If you couldn't squeeze the bikes into the van, **rentals** are available at Riverside State Park and from Serendipity Cycles in Riverfront Park; (509) 455-9167. Plenty of good road trips await outside the city. Locals cite the lonely roads in the **Turnbull National Wildlife Refuge** (see Wildlife Watching, below), **Hangman Valley** to the south, and the **Indian Prairie** and **Four Mound Prairie** areas to the west.

Mountain Biking

Mountain bikers find plenty of singletrack and fire-road riding in **Mount Spokane State Park** (see Camping, below).

Hiking

The **Centennial Trail** (see Cycling, above) is a grand place for a short walk or a very long trek along the Spokane River. The 37-mile trail begins at Nine Mile Falls in Riverside State Park northwest of Spokane and runs east to Idaho. By Washington standards, the trail isn't wildly scenic. But it's a walk with plenty of historical flavor. Indian petroglyphs are visible from the trail near Long Lake, and the trail itself follows a route pounded out over the centuries by Native peoples—and after that, white fur traders. For lovers of wilder territory, the western trail portions inside Riverside State Park are the most alluring. The path in this section passes through the scenic Bowl and Pitcher picnic area and campground. This is also the only trail portion where you're likely to find significant hills. **Riverside** also contains an intricate network of its own hiking trails, with some 36 miles of combined hiking, equestrian, and ORV paths.

A bit more on the wild side is another family-friendly trail, this one a stroll through the **Little Spokane Natural Area** north of Spokane, adjacent to Riverside State Park (see Wildlife Watching, below). About 6 miles of mostly flat trails lead through this preserve, where deer, beavers, coyotes, blue herons, and other bird species are commonly seen. (No mountain bikes allowed.) The **Turnbull National Wildlife Refuge** and **Dishman Hills Natural Area** also have some hiking trails (see Wildlife Watching, below for more information and directions). The latter features a 4-mile hiking trail in an area home to 400 plant species, 100 bird species, and 50 types of butterflies.

A number of good day hikes are found at **Mount Spokane State Park,** leading from the camping area to the Mount Spokane Vista House, Mount Kit Carson, Smith Gap, and other areas. The trails here are usually snow-free from June through October (the hight point is just over 5,200 feet.) This is another favorite horseback-riding area. See Camping, below, for directions and other information.

Wildlife Watching

Two areas just a couple of miles outside Spokane's city limits are excellent places to hike and to see birds and wildlife: the Little Spokane Natural Area (watch for **songbirds, herons, osprey, waterfowl, deer, coyotes, beavers,** and **porcupines**), accessed from the Indian Rock Paintings parking lot on Rutter Parkway, (509) 456-3964, and the Spokane Fish Hatchery, 2927 W Waikiki Road; (509) 625-5169. The Dishman Hills Natural Area, (509) 456-4730, a 460-acre preserve in the Spokane Valley east of downtown, has a network of trails with mixed wildlife habitats. Take I-90 east to the Sprague Avenue exit, go east 1.5 miles to Sargent Road; turn right a half mile to the parking area. Just 25 miles south of Spokane south of Cheney, you'll find the 17,000-acre Turnbull National Wildlife Refuge, especially interesting during fall and spring **waterfowl** migration. Watch for **Canada geese, ducks,** and **teal,** as well as **badgers, coyotes and Rocky Mountain elk.** A 6-mile, self-guided auto tour leads through the refuge, which—unlike most others in the state—never allows hunting. Take I-90 west, exit at Cheney, go south through the town, and turn left on Smith Road; (509) 235-4723; www.r1.fws.gov/turnbull/turnbull.html.

Liberty Lake County Park has a marsh at the lake's south end, where a trail winds up Liberty Creek. Watch for herons, osprey, mule deer, and **marmots;** (509) 456-4732 (from I-90 exit 295, follow Liberty Lake Rd south).

Camping

Riverside State Park is scattered in separate parcels along 9 miles of the Spokane River. The camping area is in a broad meander curve, in a park section known as the Bowl and Pitcher area, named for unique rock formations along the river. With 101 campsites (no hookups; RVs to 45 feet), it's the largest public campground in the area and a popular spot, although it rarely fills up. The campground, however, is only one of a dozen good reasons to venture to Riverside. Inside the park's 7,600 acres are 36 miles of hiking, mountain-bike, and equestrian trails; a large group camp; multiple picnic areas; fascinating rock formations; Indian petroglyphs; whitewater rapids on the Spokane and Little Spokane Rivers; an off-road vehicle park; a scenic river gorge; and Spokane House Interpretive Center. The latter, which has been open sporadically of late because of budget problems, is on the site of Spokane House, explorer David Thompson's 1810 Hudson's Bay fur-trading outpost. Riverside State Park is open all year. Campsites cannot be reserved. *From Division St/US 395/US 2 in downtown Spokane, take Francis Ave west to Hwy 291, and follow signs northwest to the park's multiple entrances—the main park offices and camping area are in the Bowl and Pitcher section; (509) 456-3964 or (800) 233-0321; www.riversidestatepark.org.*

It's known mostly as a day-use area, but **Mount Spokane State Park** has a small campground with 12 sites (no hookups; RVs to 30 feet). The park also has an extensive trail system, and is open in winter for crosscountry and downhill skiing. The view from Vista House atop the 5,800-foot mountain is outstanding. Mount Spokane is open June through September, weather permitting. Campsites cannot be reserved. *30 miles northwest of Spokane via Division St/US 395/US 2, US 2, and Hwy 206; (509) 456-4169 or (800) 233-0321.*

Long Lake Campground, a DNR facility on the Spokane River northwest of Spokane, offers camping and picnic sites (12 sites for tents or small trailers; no hookups). The campground is open April through September and does not accept reservations. Drive US 2 west to Reardan, drive north on Hwy 231 for 14.2 miles, turn right on Hwy 291 (Long Lake Dam Rd), and proceed 4.7 miles to the campground on the right; (509) 684-7474.

Another DNR campground, **Dragoon Creek** (22 sites; no hookups), is a primitive campground near the Little Spokane River. It's free, open April through September, and does not accept reservations. Drive 10 miles north of Spokane on Hwy 395, turn left on Dragoon Creek Road, and proceed a half mile; (509) 684-7474.

A number of **private resorts** are located west of town on the shores of Medical Lake, including West Medical Lake Resort, (509) 299-3921; Mallard Bay Resort, (509) 299-3830; and Rainbow Cove Campground, (509) 299-3717. Several large **private campgrounds,** including summer-only KOA Spokane, (800) 562-3309; www.koa.com, 13 miles east of town, have reserved sites and other amenities. Many of the lakes around Spokane (see Fishing, below) also have private campgrounds. Call the Spokane Visitors Center, (800) 248-3230, for a full list.

Downhill Skiing

Only one downhill area, **Mount Spokane Ski and Snowboard Park,** in the foothills of the Selkirks, is within a short drive of Spokane. This state-owned day-use area is recovering from a recent shutdown and reopening under new management. It's also recovering from a major access road closure in the winter of 1999–2000; check by phone before making the drive. The mountain has no slopeside lodging. The day-use area has five lifts and a respectable 2,065 feet of vertical and 1,500 skiable acres. Weekend lift tickets are $21, and midweek passes are an even better bargain. *30 miles north on Hwy 206; (509) 238-2220, snow reports (509) 443-1397; www.mtspokane.com.*

A wealth of even better skiing is found within about 2 hours of town. The list includes **49 Degrees North,** (509) 935-6649, 58 miles north of Spokane near Chewelah (see the Kettle Falls, Colville, and the Pend Oreille chapter); **Schweitzer Mountain Resort** in Sandpoint, Idaho, (800) 831-8810; www.schweitzer.com, with excellent facilities for family skiing; and the region's newest destination ski resort, **Silver Mountain** at Kellogg, Idaho, (208) 783-1111; www.silvermt.com. Any one of these areas can provide a good day's skiing for reasonable prices, but if you have time to sample only one, Schweitzer is the star in this cluster.

Cross-country Skiing

For cross-country skiers, **Mount Spokane Sno-Park** is a longtime favorite. A large (180-car) state Sno-Park at the mountain offers 25 kilometers of groomed ski trails for all skill levels, plus two warming huts. A

Sno-Park pass, available at local outdoor retailers and ranger stations, is required. Closer in, two short ski trails are found at the **Indian Canyon Golf Course** just west of town, which operates as a state Sno-Park in the winter. Easy 0.3K and 4.5K loops begin near the main parking area at Assembly Street and West Drive. Another good beginner area is the **Downriver Golf Course Sno-Park,** which offers two loops totaling 5 kilometers; 3225 N Columbia Circle. The 6-mile **Little Spokane Natural Area trail** (see Wildlife Watching, above) is another popular beginner-to-intermediate area northwest of the city.

Fishing

Plenty of good trout fishing is available in the greater Spokane area. Noted spring and summer **rainbow** and **brown trout** producers are Medical and West Medical Lakes, Silver Lake, and Clear Lake, all in a cluster southwest of the city. West Medical Lake Resort, (509) 299-3921, is a good contact. Fishtrap Lake near Sprague is a noted early-season hot spot, and nearby Sprague Lake is a good mixed-species fishery. Other good trout lakes are Fish Lake near Cheney; Newman Lake to the east, via Hwy 290; and Long Lake, a Spokane River reservoir west of the city. The Spokane River itself, much of which is under selective fishery regulations, is a fair fly-fishing stream.

Kayaking/Canoeing/Rafting

Kayakers run the **Spokane River** primarily in two sections—an intermediate (Class II) 6-mile stretch below Harvard Park off I-90 east of the city, and an advanced (Class III) stretch on the lower river between Downriver Drive and Riverside State Park. Highlights on the lower stretch are the Class III rapids at Bowl and Pitcher and Devil's Toenail, both viewed from Riverside State Park (see Camping, above). The Spokane is best run in May and June. It's a big, fast river—not for novices. For **raft trips** on the Spokane River, contact Wiley E Waters in Liberty Lake; 888-502-1900. Reasonably experienced canoeists will enjoy the float along the **Little Spokane River,** in the Little Spokane Natural Area (see Wildlife Watching, above). A good put-in is near the Spokane Trout Hatchery on Waikiki Road. Note that inner-tubing and swimming are prohibited in this area.

Horseback Riding

You can bring your own horse or rent a steed for a **guided ride** at **Riverside State Park** (see Camping above), where Trailtown Riding Stables, (509) 456-3964, offers rides at a rate of $12 per hour.

Accessible Outdoors

West Medical Lake Public Fishing Area has an accessible dock access for rainbow trout fishing. From Spokane, go west on I-90 to Four Lakes exit; drive northwest to Medical Lake, then south 1 mile to the public fishing sign. **Riverside State Park** offers accessible camping and picnic sites. **Liberty Lake Public Fishing Area** has an accessible dock for fishing for warm-water species. From Spokane, drive 5 miles east on I-90 to the Liberty Lake exit, turn south, and follow signs. **Long Lake Campground** offers barrier-free shore access, camping, and picnic sites.

outside in

Restaurants

Café 5-Ten ★★   The short menu at this intimate spot focuses on inventive pasta dishes. *$$$; 2727 S Mount Vernon St, Spokane; (509) 533-0064.* &

Chicken-n-More ★   Spokane's sole soul-food joint, specializing in slow-cooked brisket and ribs. *$; 502 W Sprague Ave, Spokane; (509) 838-5071.*

Cannon Street Grill ★   This cozy little spot is a cut above the average breakfast place. *$; 144 S Cannon St, Spokane; (509) 456-8660.* &

The Elk Public House ★   A lively neighborhood watering hole with an ever-changing choice of microbrews. *$; 1931 W Pacific Ave, Spokane; (509) 363-1973.* &

Hill's Someplace Else ★★   You'll get topnotch food in this dark, smoky spot that feels a lot like a bar. *$$; 518 W Sprague Ave, Spokane; (509) 747-3946.* &

The Italian Kitchen ★   This stylish trattoria turns out the most authentic Italian fare in Spokane. *$$; 113 N Bernard St, Spokane; (509) 363-1210.* &

Luna ★★★   This classy neighborhood spot will remind you of sun-drenched California dining. *$$$; 5620 S Perry St, Spokane; (509) 448-2383.* &

Mizuna ★★   Spokane's only upscale vegetarian restaurant, known for its seasonal offerings. *$$$; 214 N Howard St, Spokane; (509) 747-2004.* &

Moxie ★★   Step inside this unlikely gem and find some of the prettiest plates around. *$$$; 1332 N Liberty Lake Rd, Spokane; (509) 892-5901.* &

Niko's II Greek and Middle East Restaurant ★★   A popular downtown eatery with a lively vibe and a cozy wine bar. $$; *725 W Riverside Ave, Spokane; (509) 624-7444.* &

Paprika ★★★   This intimate little dining room has the most imaginative food in town. $$$; *1228 S Grand Blvd, Spokane; (509) 455-7545.* &

Lodgings

Angelica's Bed & Breakfast   This 1907 Arts and Crafts mansion was designed with a European sensibility. $; *1321 W 9th Ave, Spokane; (509) 624-5598 or (800) 987-0053; www.angelicasbb.com.*

Cavanaugh's Inn at the Park ★   A fine base for exploring downtown Spokane and Riverfront Park on foot. $$; *303 W North River Dr, Spokane; (509) 326-8000 or (800) 843-4667.*

Fotheringham House ★★   Pampering of guests is a hallmark of this restored Queen Anne-style mansion. $$; *2128 W 2nd, Spokane; (509) 838-1891; www.fotheringham.net.*

The Kempis Hotel Suites ★★★   A vintage Rolls Royce delivers guests to the door of this boutique hotel. $$$; *326 W 6th Ave, Spokane; (509) 747-4321 or (888) 236-4321; www.thekempis.com.*

Marianna Stoltz House ★   This 1908 foursquare home is on a tree-lined street near Gonzaga University. $$; *427 E Indiana Ave, Spokane; (509) 483-4316 or (800) 978-6587; www.mariannastoltzhouse.com.*

Waverly Place Bed & Breakfast ★★   This pretty 1902 Victorian has four rooms; the grandest is the two-story suite. $$; *709 W Waverly Pl, Spokane; (509) 328-1856; www.waverlyplace.com.*

More Information

General outdoors information: *www.inlandadventure.com or www.spokaneoutdoors.com.*

Northwest Map and Travel Book Center: *525 W Sprague; (509) 455-6981.*

REI (outdoor equipment sales and rentals): *1125 N Monroe; (509) 328-9900;*

Spokane area Convention and Visitors Bureau: *801 W Riverside, Ste 301; (888) 776-5263 or (509) 747-3230; www.visitspokane.com.*

Kettle Falls, Colville, and the Pend Oreille

From Kettle Falls north to British Columbia, east to Idaho, and south to Newport, including 49 Degrees North ski area, the Salmo-Priest Wilderness, Sullivan Lake, portions of the Colville and Idaho Panhandle National Forests, and Crystal Falls and Crawford State Parks.

Go where the moose go. Anywhere you go in the West, that's a fairly reliable rule for finding the wildest, least-spoiled mountain areas. It certainly works in Washington, where the moose population mostly limits its range to the still-wild hillsides of the Pend Oreille valley in extreme northeast Washington.

The moose are not alone in choosing this out-there, away-from-it-all region. The state's most constant population of grizzly bears is believed to roam the rocky peaks of the Selkirk Range. Bighorn sheep are a common sight, and the Lower 48's last herd of woodland caribou live—and struggle to survive—in patches of preserved land such as the Salmo-Priest Wilderness.

This is a last refuge, of sorts. That's true of the wildlife population and of the human one. No other place in the state is less geared for tourists than this one. That's not the result of hostility toward encroachers. It's just that the northeast corner of the state isn't on the way to anything. (If you enter the region via the U.S. border crossing north of Metaline Falls, you pull your car up over a gas-station-type rubber hose that rings a bill and wakes the border agent from a nap inside a small cottage.)

Whether you're measuring distance in miles of asphalt or state of mind, this place is a long way from your local Larry's Market. Which probably explains why many native Evergreen State out door lovers (all seven of them) at some point in their lives make a Pend Oreille pilgrimage. They come to see the animals, taste the luscious alpine meadows of the Shedroof Divide Trail in the Selkirks, fish for trout on lonely mountain streams. They come to breathe the same air their great-great-grandparents might have breathed. Stop looking for the last and only uncivilized part of Washington. This is it: Section 119—the very last page in the Washington Atlas & Gazetteer. It's been pushed right up against the back corner, and the SUV caravan is visible on the horizon.

Getting There

The Kettle Falls/Colville area can be reached by driving US Highway 2 east to US 97, then north to Hwy 20, the Sherman Pass Scenic Byway, east from Tonasket. The area can also be reached from US 2 farther east, via Hwy 25 north from Davenport or Hwy 231 north from Reardan. Or take Interstate-90 east to US 395 north in Spokane. No matter how you get there, it's a full day's journey from the Seattle area. From Kettle Falls, US 395 and Hwy 25 continue north to Canada; Hwy 20 continues east to the Pend Oreille River and south to Newport. From Hwy 20 at the Pend Oreille, Hwy 31 runs north through Metaline to Canada.

inside out

Camping

Most public campgrounds in the area are Colville National Forest sites. Among the more popular in the Sullivan Ranger District (Metaline Falls area) are Sullivan Lake and Noisy Creek, both on Sullivan Lake northeast of Metaline Falls. **Sullivan Lake** has 44 sites divided between two campgrounds separated by a grass landing strip. East Sullivan has 38 sites, West Sullivan 6 (no hookups; RVs to 50 feet) on the lake's north shore, near the south boundary of the Salmo-Priest Wilderness. East Sullivan has a pleasant, lakefront day-use area and a fine swimming beach. The landing strip often is the sight of fly-in campouts in the summer, when dozens of small planes will light here, their pilots pitching small tents under their wings. **Noisy Creek** has 19 sites (no hookups; RVs to 35 feet) on the lake's southeast shore. A bighorn sheep feeding station, which operates in the winter only, is nearby, as are several great hiking trails (see Wildlife Watching and Hiking/Backpacking, below). These two campgrounds are popular with anglers, water-skiers, boaters, and canoeists. Both are open late May through September, and campsites can be reserved in advance; (877) 444-6777; www.reserveusa.com. *On Sullivan Lake Rd (County Rd 9345), 6.5 and*

Boundary Dam: A lonely spot north of Metaline Falls

10 miles, respectively, northeast of Metaline Falls; (509) 446-7500.

Note: An alternate campground, **Millpond** (10 sites), is the first campground encountered by motorists driving east on Sullivan Lake Road. East and West Sullivan and Noisy Creek, both beyond, are more pleasant campgrounds, but keep this one in mind as a backup. The popular Red Bluff Trail (see Hiking/Backpacking, below) starts nearby; (509) 446-7500.

An alternative site not far away to the south on the Pend Oreille River is **Edgewater,** which has 23 campsites (no hookups; RVs to 20 feet) and limited picnic facilities. It's open May through September, and campsites cannot be reserved. *On County Rd 3669, 2 miles northeast of Ione; (509) 446-7500.*

Farther south along Hwy 20 are **Panhandle** (11 sites)—cross the river at Ione and take LeClerc Road south; **South Skookum Lake** (25 sites) and **Brown's Lake** (18 sites)—from Hwy 20 at Usk, cross the Pend Oreille River on Kings Lake Road and proceed about 6 and 9 miles, respectively, north on Forest Road 5030; and **Pioneer Park** (14 sites)—from Newport drive northeast on US 2, cross the Pend Oreille River, and turn northwest on LeClerc County Road 9305 for 2 miles. All the campgrounds charge a fee, and all are open between Memorial Day and Labor Day. Call the Newport Ranger District; (509) 447-7300.

In the Colville Ranger District, in the area northeast of Colville off Hwy 20, are five campgrounds, all open summers only and all fairly remote (listed here east to west). For directions and information about

Big Meadow Lake (16 campsites), **Lake Leo** (8 campsites), **Lake Thomas** (15 tent sites), **Lake Gillette/East Gillette** (44 campsites), or **Little Twin Lakes** (20 campsites; quite pleasant, but no piped water), contact the Colville Ranger District; (509) 684-7010. Big Meadow Lake has a wildlife-viewing platform (see Wildlife Watching, below).

In the Kettle Falls Ranger District between Kettle Falls and the Canadian border is another free, remote campground, **Pierre Lake,** which has 15 sites and good fishing access to the lake. *Northeast of Orient off US 395; (509) 738-7700.*

Several state Department of Natural Resources campgrounds offer more options. Most of these campgrounds are open all year, and all are free and offer limited services. For details, call the DNR's Northeast Region office in Colville; (509) 684-7474. Listed here roughly north to south: **Sheep Creek**—on Sheep Creek Road, just off Hwy 25 near the Canadian border—has 11 small campsites along the scenic creek. **Upper Sheep Creek,** just up the road, has 2 primitive sites. Sheep Creek Falls is nearby. **Williams Lake,** on Williams Lake Road north of Kettle Falls, has 8 sites. **Douglas Falls Grange Park,** on Douglas Falls Road north of Colville, has 8 sites. **Flodelle Creek,** just south of Hwy 20 about 20 miles east of Colville, has 8 sites—and lots of dirt bikes using the nearby ORV area. Avoid it. **Starvation Lake,** about 8 miles east of Colville just south of Hwy 20, has 8 small sites and canoe/fishing access on a shallow, weed-choked lake. The Little Pend Oreille National Wildlife Refuge Headquarters (see Wildlife Watching, below) is nearby, south on Narcisse Road. **Rocky Lake,** off Hwy 395 south of Colville, has 7 unimpressive sites, but it's also near the Little Pend Oreille National Wildlife Area. **Skookum Creek,** on the Pend Oreille River near Usk off Hwy 20, has 10 sites and access to an Indian painting interpretive site.

In addition, several Lake Roosevelt National Recreation Area campgrounds on upper Lake Franklin D. Roosevelt are nice facilities with good lake access for boaters, water-skiers, and swimmers. They're scattered along either the Kettle River Arm of the backed-up Columbia near Kettle Falls, or on the east shore of the Columbia itself (actually the northern extremes of Franklin D. Roosevelt Lake). From north to south: **North Gorge** (12 sites), **Evans** (43 sites), and **Marcus Island** (27 sites) are on Hwy 25 on the east shore; **Kettle River** (13 sites) **and Kamloops** (14 sites) are on the Kettle River Arm off US 395; and **Kettle Falls** (76 sites), by far the most heavily used, is just south of the junction of Hwy 20 and US 395 on the east shore. These camps are open from mid-April to mid-October, and do not accept reservations. For information, contact the Lake Roosevelt National Recreation Area office in Kettle Falls; (509) 738-6266; www.nps.gov/laro.

Hiking/Backpacking

The Pend Oreille region offers some of Eastern Washington's finest high-forest day-hiking and backpacking, especially in motorcycle-free areas such as the Salmo-Priest Wilderness. A healthy menu of day-hiking trails also is available for campers at any of the dozen state or federal campsites listed in Camping, above. For road and trail reports and full trail information, contact the Sullivan Lake Ranger District; (509) 446-7500. Note that a **Northwest Forest Pass**, $5 per day or $30 annually, is required to park in many Forest Service–administered trailheads in this area. They're available from ranger stations, from many private vendors, on-line at www.naturenw.org, or by calling (800) 270-7504. Following is a list of area favorites.

Sullivan Lake/Metaline Falls area

Campers at any of the Sullivan Lake campgrounds will find pleasant walking on the **Sullivan Lakeshore Trail** (easy; 4 miles one way), which extends along the lake to Noisy Creek Campground. Noisy Creek campers are within a short distance of the **Noisy Creek Trail** (moderate; 10.6 miles round trip), which begins at the campground and climbs fairly steeply up the creek drainage to several good viewpoints and ultimately a junction with the Hall Mountain Trail. If you're here in midsummer, try the **Hall Mountain Trail** (moderate/difficult; 5 miles round trip), which climbs steadily to the summit of the big rock butte, and is one of the most reliable places in the state to view bighorn sheep. Sheep are visible here all year, but the access road (Road 500, off Sullivan Creek Road) is closed from August 15 to June 30 every year to provide solitude for the sheep during fall mating and spring birthing seasons.

Northwest of Metaline Falls, several good vista hikes are found in the Abercrombie-Hooknose Roadless Area. One of the most popular is **Abercrombie Mountain Trail** (difficult; 8 miles round trip), which climbs about 2,000 vertical feet to the 7,300-foot summit of Abercrombie, the tallest Selkirk peak. Views of the entire region are outstanding. To reach the trailhead from Metaline Falls on Hwy 31, take Boundary Road north to near Flume Creek, and turn west on Forest Road 350.

Salmo-Priest Wilderness

The Sullivan Lake/Metaline Falls area also is a good staging ground for treks into the beautiful Salmo-Priest Wilderness, a 40,000-acre wild area that contains some of Eastern Washington's largest remaining old-growth forests. Viewed on a map, the protected area is shaped like a horseshoe, with 6,828-foot Salmo Mountain located at the head. The westernmost prong extends south almost to Sullivan Lake, and the easternmost traces the Idaho border on a route defined by a string of 6,500-foot-plus mountains: Shedroof, Thunder, Helmer, Mankato, and Round Top. The western summit line is defined by Crowell Ridge and Gypsy Ridge, the eastern by Shedroof Divide.

Not surprisingly, trails follow both ridgelines, with a series of short connectors climbing from the heavily clear-cut slopes outside the wilderness boundary into the unspoiled highlands. Popular hikes on the north (Hwy 31) side of the wilderness include **Halliday** (moderate; 15.6 miles round trip), a popular wilderness connector trail that climbs from the junction of Hwy 31 and Road 180 (about 4 miles north of Pend Oreille Village) to the Halliday Fens, a string of beaver bogs that attracts deer and moose; **Slate Creek** (moderate; 8.4 miles round trip), which begins on Slate Creek Road (just to the north of Road 180 off Hwy 31) and goes up, down, up, down, and up a series of ridges that also draw large numbers of wildlife (and autumn hunters); **North Fork Sullivan Creek** (difficult; 19.2 miles round trip), a rugged backpackers' route that begins near Lime Lake (north off Sullivan Lake Road just east of Hwy 31) and climbs steadily up the drainage to the top of Crowell Ridge, where mountain goats sometimes are spotted; and **Red Bluff Trail** (difficult; 10.5 miles round trip), a lowland route that begins near Mill Pond Campground (see Camping, above).

The **Crowell Ridge Trail** (moderate/difficult; 15.6 miles round trip)—a high route that connects with the North Fork Sullivan Trail and other access paths—is a regional highlight. If you start at the upper trailhead just below the summit of Sullivan Mountain off Forest Road 245 (reached from Sullivan Creek Road via Road 242), this becomes one of those rare backpack routes that starts very high (6,200 feet) and stays there, offering grand views of BC's Kokanees and the Pend Oreille valley. Lovely meadows surround you all along the route, and good campsites are abundant. Note: Unless you visit very early in the summer, you'll need to carry all your own water. Little is found along the ridgetop, although strong hikers can drop to one of several lakes below the ridge to replenish supplies.

In the more remote, northern portion of the wilderness, **Salmo Loop** (difficult; 18 miles round trip) is a popular 2- to 3-day backpack route through the South Salmo River valley to Shedroof Divide Trail, following the divide past Shedroof Mountain and Snowy Top, then down a long ridgeline back to the trailhead at the end of Forest Road 2220 (Sullivan Creek Road). Good day hikes in the same area, off Road 2220, include **Thunder Creek** (moderate; 5.8 miles round trip), which follows the creek through a cool old-growth forest, and **Shedroof Cutoff** (moderate; 3.4 miles round trip), a steep shortcut to the Shedroof Divide Trail.

In the eastern wilderness, the shining star is the **Shedroof Divide Trail** proper (moderate; 31.4 miles round trip). Like its westside counterpart, Crowell Ridge, the Shedroof trail begins high and follows the ridgeline, this time to a turnaround point near Idaho. Allow 4 days for a long,

memorable walk through this inspiring alpine area. The Shedroof Divide
Trail is accessible via the Thunder Creek, Salmo Loop, and Shedroof Cutoff Trails, but the main trailhead is near Pass Creek Pass, on Forest Road
22 (south of Sullivan Creek Road). Side trips allow short-but-difficult
hikes to the summits of Round Top, Helmer, Thunder, Shedroof, and
Snowy Top Mountains (try to find the old lookout access trails, and be
careful). A long day hike from the Shedroof Divide trailhead is the **Pass
Creek/Grassy Top Trail** (moderate; 15.5 miles round trip), which is a
wonderful summer wildflower hike.

Pend Oreille River valley

Near the southern Colville National Forest boundary on Hwy 20 a few miles
west of the river are three notable trails, each easy and interesting enough for
the whole family: the **Tiger** and **Coyote Rock Loops** (easy; 5-mile round trip
each), which begin near Frater Lake on Hwy 20 (a popular winter cross-
country skiing/snowshoe area); **Sherry Loop** (easy; 3.8-mile loop), a very
pretty riverside walk near Sherry Lake that's popular with summer anglers
and winter cross-country skiers; and **Springboard Interpretive Loop** (easy;
2.4 miles round trip), which begins in East Gillette Campground (see Camping, above) and winds through an interesting old homestead site.

To the southeast, campers at Skookum Lake Campground shouldn't
miss the **South Skookum Loop** (easy; 1.3 miles round trip), which meanders along the lake through a truly beautiful forest and affords the chance
to see the occasional wandering moose. At Pioneer Park Campground, try
walking the **Pioneer Park Interpretive Trail** (easy; half-mile round trip),
site of a Kalispell tribe camas-root harvesting area. To get to these, see
Camping, above.

Kettle River area

In the northwest corner of this area, north of Lake Roosevelt, another
campground-centered walk, the **Pierre Lake Trail** (easy; 1.6 miles round
trip), leads through a nice forested area on the shore of the lake. The trail
begins in the campground (see Camping, above) and follows the west
shore. It's a good family walk.

Wildlife Watching

This is where the really wild things are. Some of Washington's—and,
indeed, America's—rarest creatures roam the woods of extreme northeastern Washington. A herd of 30 to 50 **woodland caribou,** an endangered
species, divide their time between Washington, British Columbia, and
Idaho in the rocky Selkirk Range. Rarely seen, they're struggling to hang
on. This is the very last herd of the animals in the Lower 48 states. State

Fish and Wildlife biologists have been supplementing the herd with animals from British Columbia, and most of the caribou are tracked and loosely monitored by radio collars. The most recent group of caribou was released in the winter of 1995–1996 at Gypsy Meadows, near the border of the Salmo-Priest Wilderness.

Two other endangered species, the **grizzly bear** and the **northern gray wolf,** also are believed to dip into the area from BC habitats. They're even more scarce, and hikers who encounter either one not only would be extremely fortunate, but important eyewitnesses. Fish and Wildlife managers need all the help they can get to monitor both species. Report any sightings to a ranger district office (see More Information, below).

Though not endangered, **moose** are rare in the Lower 48, and the northeast corner of the state is home to as many as 200. Keep your eyes peeled around lakes and boggy areas in this region. Moose sightings aren't common, but they're by no means unusual. If you are fortunate enough to encounter a moose, keep in mind these massive beasts aren't always as genteel as their smaller deer-family cousins. Bull moose and protective cows have been known to charge people, cars, outhouses, radio towers, and anything else they suddenly find offensive. Keep your distance.

Two high-cliff dwellers, **mountain goats** and **Rocky Mountain bighorn sheep,** are found in the northeast corner of the Colville National Forest, in and around the Salmo-Priest Wilderness. An excellent place to view mountain goats, moose, and deer is the Flume Creek Mountain Goat Viewing Area, on Boundary Road (County Road 2975) just north of Metaline Falls. Bighorns are commonly seen in the Hall Mountain area east of Sullivan Lake (see Hiking/Backpacking, above). State wildlife managers have relocated many of these majestic beasts from Rocky Mountain states to this area, and sometimes place salt licks at the summit peak to supplement the sheeps' diets. The animals are even easier to find in the winter, when many of them feed at Noisy Creek Sheep Feeding Station near Noisy Creek Campground on Sullivan Lake (see Camping, above).

A popular wildlife-viewing area is Big Meadow Lake (see Camping, above), where deer, moose, **beaver,** and **osprey** often are seen from an observation tower over the wetlands. Another popular wildlife viewing area is the Little Pend Oreille Wildlife Area north of Chewelah, where deer, bear, and various **waterfowl** species often are seen. From Hwy 20 about 8 miles east of Colville, turn south on Narcisse Creek Road to reach the refuge headquarters.

Wherever you go in this region, chances are good you'll eventually encounter **mule** and **white-tailed deer.** This corner of the state is home to the bulk of the state's whitetail population, making this a wildly popular hunting area in the fall.

Fishing

Good trout-fishing waters dot the region. Deep Lake, between Metaline Falls and Northport on Deep Lake Boundary Road; Sullivan Lake east of Metaline Falls; and Pierre Lake northeast of Orient (see Camping for these last two) all are productive **trout** waters. A string of lakes on either side of Hwy 20 east of Colville—Rocky, Hatch, Starvation (all to the south), Little Twin, and Black Lakes (these last to the north)—also offers good **rainbow** and **cutthroat** trout fishing (for most of these, see Camping, above). In the Little Pend Oreille Wildlife Area south of Starvation Lake, McDowell Lake and Bayley Lake are fly-fishing–only waters popular with trout anglers. Another popular fly-only venue is Browns Lake, north of the Skookum Lakes (also good trout fishing) near Usk (see Camping, above).

The Kettle River above the confluence with the Columbia at Kettle Falls has good spring trout fishing (check special regulations and seasons here). The upper portions of the lake are open all year and are particularly known for **walleye** fishing. For Franklin D. Roosevelt Lake fishing information, see the Grand Coulee chapter.

Downhill Skiing

Downhill skiers are in for a treat at **49 Degrees North,** a small but often outstanding day-use ski area on 5,775-foot Mount Chewelah. The area is small, with 1,851 feet of vertical on 16 runs accessed by four double chairlifts and one surface lift. But the snow typically is light, cold, and dry—often as close as snow in Washington State comes to a true "powder" rating. Mountain managers close off some of the best of the ski area for weekend skiing. 49 Degrees North normally operates Friday through Tuesday, except during holidays, when they're open 7 days a week. All-day weekend adult lift tickets are $30; the closest lodging is in Chewelah. *From US 395 in Chewelah, go 11 miles east on Flowery Trail Rd; snow phone (509) 880-9208, mountain information (509) 935-6649; www.ski49n.com.*

Cross-Country Skiing

About 9 miles of cross-country ski trails are found **near 49 Degrees North** (see above). Two groomed cross-country-skiing areas lure skinny-ski riders near Newport, one long schuss from the Idaho border. **Geophysical Nordic Ski Trails Sno-Park,** on Indian Creek Road east of Newport, has 10 kilometers of groomed trails that wind through a cold, very scenic pine forest. The **Upper Wolf Nordic Trail** system—the winter incarnation of the Wolf Donation Trail north of Newport—offers 4 kilometers of short, often steep, groomed trails. State **Sno-Park passes,** available at local ranger stations and ski shops, are required. For directions and snow reports, call the Newport Ranger District; (509) 447-7300. The **Sherry Lake area** along Hwy 20 east of Colville also is a popular, nongroomed cross-country area, as are the **Tiger** and **Coyote Rock Loops** at Frater Lake farther east, in the Little Pend Oreille Lakes area on Hwy 20 (see Hiking/Backpacking, above). Frater Lake offers ample parking, a warming hut, pit toilets, and other facilities provided by local Nordic ski clubs.

Boating/Canoeing/Kayaking

Upper Franklin D. Roosevelt Lake, the flooded backwater from Grand Coulee Dam, is a boater's and water-skier's dream. See Camping, above, and the Grand Coulee chapter for launch and campground information. **Sullivan Lake** is a clear, beautiful waterway, but Jet-skiers and fast motorboats can ruin the experience for canoeists. Better bets for quiet paddlers are **McDowell Lake** and **Bayley Lake** in the Little Pend Oreille Wildlife Area (see Fishing, above). The fast waters of the **Kettle River** below Orient Bridge are popular kayak/rafting/inner-tubing rapids when water conditions allow; call the Kettle Falls Ranger District, (509) 738-7700, for details.

Picnics

A nice roadside stop, **Crystal Falls State Park** offers views of the cascades on the Little Pend Oreille River; 14 miles east of Colville on Hwy 20. **Frater Lake,** in the Little Pend Oreille Lakes area on Hwy 20 a few miles east of the Pend Oreille River (see Hiking/Backpacking and Cross-Country Skiing, above), is a great roadside picnic spot in the summer. Break out the bug dope!

Horseback Riding

Overnight **trail rides, cattle drives,** short rides, and lessons all are offered at Bull Hill Ranch and Resort, a family-owned, 50,000-acre spread northeast of Kettle Falls on Bull Hill Road, off Northport Road on the north side of Lake Roosevelt; (509) 732-4355.

Accessible Outdoors

In the Sullivan Lake area, the **Noisy Creek Trailhead** and **Campground** offers shore access and accessible rest rooms. The **Mill Pond Historic Site** (see Camping, above) has a 0.6-mile interpretive trail leading to a fascinating wood flume, as well as barrier-free picnic sites. **East** and **West Sullivan Campgrounds** offer accessible picnic sites, wildlife viewing, and bank fishing.

In the Newport area, **Pioneer Park Campground** offers a moderately challenging, quarter-mile interpretive trail with possible viewing of ospreys and eagles. To the north, **Brown's Lake Campground** has a barrier-free interpretive trail with a viewing platform over a beaver pond; spawning cutthroat are visible in the stream in the spring.

In the Colville area, **Big Meadow Lake** (see Camping, above) has a half-mile, barrier-free trail through wetlands and a wildlife viewing area where moose are frequently seen. **Starvation Lake** (see Camping, above) has a barrier-free fishing pier, and moose are frequently seen here. **Pierre Lake Campground** also has barrier-free fishing.

outside in

Restaurants

Cafe Italiano   This inviting cafe reveals its Greek heritage, but the fare is mostly Italian. $$; 153 W 2nd, Colville; (509) 684-5957.

Katie's Oven ★   Indulge in a gooey-good bun at this bakery in the historic Washington Hotel. $; 225 E 5th, Metaline Falls; (509) 446-4806.

The Loose Blue Moose ★   Every Friday is "Fondue Night" at this funky, slightly out-of-place coffeehouse. $; 1015 S Clark, Republic; (509) 775-0441; loosebluemoose@hotmail.com.

Lodgings

My Parent's Estate ★   This 43-acre historic spot has a religious past (mission then convent, now B&B). $$; Hwy 395, Colville; (509) 738-6220.

More Information

Colville National Forest Supervisor's Office: (509) 684-7000.
Colville Ranger District: (509) 684-7010.
Department of Natural Resources, Colville: (509) 684-7474.
Kettle Falls Chamber of Commerce: (509) 738-2130.
Kettle Falls Ranger District: (509) 738-7700.
Mill Creek Outfitters, Colville: (509) 684-9782.
Newport Ranger District: (509) 447-7300.
Sullivan Lake Ranger District: (509) 446-7500.

Okanogan Highlands and Sherman Pass

From Omak west to Loup Loup Summit, north to Lake Osoyoos, east to US Highway 395, and south to the Colville Indian Reservation, including Republic, Wauconda Summit, portions of the Okanogan and Colville National Forests, the Sherman Pass National Scenic Byway, and Conconully, Osoyoos Lake, and Curlew Lake State Parks.

Anyone who grew up in high country marked by tall, straight ponderosa pines, crisp air, and autumn's yellow larch-tree fireworks would call the Okanogan Highlands "God's country." Those of us who grew up anywhere else would be hard-pressed to disagree.

The Highlands are rolling ranges of quiet, clean, unpeopled mountains just south of the Canadian border between the Okanogan and Columbia River drainages. This is wide-open country, a place where backpackers can still set out for two weeks—even in midsummer—and meet more bears and deer than people. Spacious, virtually unpopulated (save for a handful of interesting outpost communities), and largely left alone by Washington's recreating masses, this is prime discovery territory for anyone feeling the pinch of population in the "wilderness" closer to home.

You can choose your level of lonely here. The Okanogan valley clings to the fringe of civilization, drawing occasional campers, anglers, hikers, and skiers from the wildly popular Methow Valley, one river drainage west. It's wild enough to be refreshing, close enough to semi-equipped towns such as Omak and Okanogan to offer comfort. Venture farther north and hang a hard right on Highway 20, however, and it's easy to throw your mind back to the early 19th century, when the first hardy white explorers began following fur-trapping lines—and insatiable curiosity—down the Pend Oreille, Okanogan, and Columbia Rivers, in search of adventure and a water route to the Pacific.

For them, this was the last great frontier land in what would become the northwestern United States. For many of us, it still is. Today it's easy to get swept up in the same awe of discovery by parking the car at Sherman Pass and heading off on a trail into some of the least-traveled wildlands in the state. Hiking and backpacking are a treat in this region, but (and perhaps because) they're not the main focus. Fair numbers of Northwest hikers discovered the wonders of this section of the Okanogan National Forest some time ago. But it still never attracts the uncomfortable summer hordes often encountered in the North or South Cascades or the Alpine Lakes or Glacier Peak Wilderness.

Most who visit the Okanogan Highlands do so just to drive through and look, following Highway 20, a National Scenic Byway, to Sherman Pass, at 5,575 feet the highest in the state. Those who stay on for a while usually do so to fish. Trout fishing is legendary in the cold, deep lakes and streams of this region, and more and more anglers are making the discovery—particularly as fly-fishing continues to grow in popularity. Skiing, too, is drawing fair numbers of visitors to the Highlands. The rolling mountains and deep forests here have what many westside cross-country-skiing venues lack most: dry snow and profound silence.

Wildlife lovers also find treks to the Okanogan Highlands productive. The woods here are filled with deer, bear, cougar, lynx, and other predators. And lucky visitors might happen upon an even greater rarity, such as a moose, bighorn sheep, or great gray owl.

Choose your reason. Choose your method. But do make the trip. Several days in the Okanogan Highlands are almost enough to restore your faith in the cleansing power of Northwest fresh air.

Getting There

The Okanogan River valley, which begins at the river's confluence with the Columbia near Brewster and runs north to the Canadian border, is best reached from the Seattle area by driving US Highway 2 east to Wenatchee, then US 97 north. The Okanogan Highlands are crossed by driving Hwy 20, the Sherman Pass National Scenic Byway, east from US 97 at Tonasket. An alternate route for visitors of the Columbia Basin and Grand Coulee Dam is Hwy 21, which runs 53 miles north from Keller Ferry east of Coulee Dam to the town of Republic, near Sherman Pass, and continues north to Canada. Allow 4 to 5 hours to make the 225-mile drive from the Seattle area to Omak/Okanogan.

Camping

US 97 area

On the west side of the broad Okanogan Highlands, you'll find a mix of camping pleasures, beginning (for the west-to-east traveler) with a slew of remote, small, primitive Department of Natural Resources campgrounds between the Methow and Okanogan River valleys, along Hwy 20 northeast of Loup Loup summit. Among them are **Sportsman's Camp** (6 sites; no piped water), on Sweat Creek Road; **Rock Creek** (6 sites), on Loup Loup Canyon Road; **Rock Lakes** (8 sites; no piped water), on Rock Lakes Road north of Rock Creek; and **Leader Lake** (16 sites; no piped water), on Leader Lake Road. *North of Hwy 20, east of Loup Loup; (509) 684-7474.*

The largest and most heavily used camping area, however, is around Lake Conconully, a reservoir northwest of Omak. The prime destination is **Conconully State Park,** where broad lawns are shaded by massive willow trees. Don't get too used to your swimming beach, however: waterfront areas for swimming and boating are affected by broad fluctuations in lake levels. The 80-acre campground has 83 sites (10 with water hookups; RVs to 60 feet) divided between a main camping area and a second, more primitive section closer to the lakeshore. Several private resorts ring the lake as well. Conconully is open summers only. Campsites cannot be reserved. *On Conconully Rd 22 miles northwest of Omak (follow signs from Okanogan, Omak, or Tonasket); (509) 826-7408 or (800) 233-0321.*

North of Conconully Lake, along North Fork Salmon Creek Road (Forest Road 38) are four remote Okanogan National Forest campgrounds; all are small, summer-only sites with water but few other facilities (mileages are from Conconully): **Cottonwood** (4 sites), 2 miles; **Oriole** (10 sites), 3 miles; **Kerr** (13 sites), 4 miles; and **Salmon Meadows** (7 sites), 9 miles. Another option in this general area is **Sugarloaf** (4 tent sites; no piped water) on Sinlahekin Road (County Road 4015), about 5 miles northeast of Conconully. For information on all these, call the Tonasket Ranger District; (509) 486-2186.

In the nearby northern Okanogan River drainage to the north lies another set of remote DNR campgrounds. All are small, primitive camps in the Chopaka Mountain/Toats Coulee Creek/Palmer Lake area west of Loomis (which is west of US 97 between Tonasket and Oroville): **Palmer Lake** (6 sites; no piped water), 8.5 miles north of Loomis on Loomis-Oroville Road; **Chopaka Lake** (16 sites), north off Toats Coulee Road; **Toats Coulee** (9 sites; no piped water), on Toats Coulee Road; **North Fork**

Nine Mile (11 sites), north off Toats Coulee Road; and **Cold Springs** (5 sites; no piped water), on Cold Creek Road, south off Toats Coulee Road. Contact the DNR's Northeastern Region office in Colville, (509) 684-7474.

A couple other way-out-there options: A high (6,800 feet), remote Forest Service camp northeast of Winthrop and southeast of Toats Coulee is **Tiffany Springs** (6 sites; no piped water; RVs to 15 feet), a mile from Tiffany Lake off Forest Road 39 (Toats Coulee Road). It's free and open from July through September. Another remote spot, **Crawfish Lake** (19 sites; no hookups; RVs to 31 feet), is a free campgound northeast of Omak, open mid-May to mid-September. *From US 97 at the town of Riverside (north of Omak, south of Tonasket), drive about 20 miles east on County Rd 9320 (it will become Forest Rd 30) to Forest Rd 30-100. Turn right and drive a half mile to the campground.* Contact the Okanogan National Forest's Tonasket Ranger District, (509) 486-2186.

RVers heads might be swimming after all that dinky Forest-Road description. Relax and head for campgrounds close to US 97. **American Legion Park,** a city-run park in Okanogan, is not beautiful, but has 35 open, graveled sites (no hookups). It's on Hwy 215 in Okanogan, on the west side of the river; (509) 422-3600. Another good RV option, albeit a bit out of the way if you're continuing east on Hwy 20, is **Osoyoos Lake State Park** with 87 sites (no hookups; RVs to 45 feet). The park has swimming and boating facilities. It's popular with waterskiers, and open all year. Reservations are available through Reservations Northwest; (800) 452-5687. *1 mile north of Oroville, 4 miles south of the Canadian border on US 97; (509) 476-3321 or (800) 233-0321.*

Wauconda area

Campgrounds get a bit easier to find as one moves east on Hwy 20 from Tonasket. A remote camp, high in the Sanpoil River drainage southeast of Tonasket, is **Lyman Lake** with 4 sites (no piped water); from Hwy 20 take Aeneas Valley Road southeast to Lyman Lake Road, and go a couple miles south to Road 3785. Another string of popular Forest Service campgrounds is found in the Okanogan Highlands on Bonaparte Lake Road (Forest Road 32) north off Hwy 20. The Five Lakes area is home to four campgrounds, all in lakefront areas at about 3,000 feet, with access for swimming, fishing, and boating: **Bonaparte Lake** (25 sites), **Lost Lake** (19 sites)—follow signs northwest off Forest Road 32, **Beaver Lake** (11 sites), and **Beth Lake** (15 sites), just north of Beaver Lake. For information, call the Tonasket Ranger District; (509) 486-2186.

Republic area

Farther east, Hwy 20 in Republic meets Hwy 21, which east of town turns due north and leads up the Kettle River drainage to one of this region's prime camping attractions, **Curlew Lake State Park.** The popular park offers great access to the east shore of Curlew Lake (see Fishing, below), a favorite fishing, boating, and swimming spot. Facilities include a boat launch and large day-use area with a swimming beach. The campground has 87 sites (18 with full hookups, 7 with water only; RVs to 30 feet) spread throughout a hilly, grassy area along the lakeshore. Shade is at a premium here. In the dog days of August, seek a waterfront site to dunk in and keep cool. Sites 73 to 82, in the park's south end beyond the boat launch, fit the bill, but offer little privacy. Sites 28 to 40 in the north end are quieter and grassier, probably better for tents. The campground in general is particularly well suited to tents; 16 sites in the north end are "walk-in" dispersed sites that allow you to spread out and get comfy. Assuming you can be comfy out in the open; there's not much natural vegetation to separate you from your neighbors. You can fly in, as well: the park has five "fly-in" sites with tie-downs for planes landing at nearby Merritt Field (Ferry County Airport). Several private resorts are located nearby. Curlew Lake is open from April through October (depending on snow conditions), although day-use activities such as cross-country skiing and ice fishing are common in the winter. Campsites can be reserved up to 11 months in advance by calling Reservations Northwest; (800) 452-5687. *On Hwy 21, 9 miles north of Republic; (509) 775-3592 or (800) 233-0321.*

Hwy 21 also heads south from Republic, and to the southwest in the Sanpoil River drainage, four lakefront Colville National Forest campgrounds are found. All have pit toilets, piped water, and fishing access, but few other facilities: **Tenmile** (9 sites), 10 miles south of Republic, just east of Hwy 21; **Ferry Lake** (9 sites), 14 miles south of Republic via Hwy 21 and Forest Roads 53 and 5330; **Swan Lake** (25 sites), 15 miles south of Republic via Hwy 21 and Forest Road 53; and **Long Lake** (12 sites), 16.5 miles south of Republic via Hwy 21 and Forest Roads 53 and 400. Contact the Republic Ranger District, (509) 775-3305.

Sherman Pass area

A handful of other Colville National Forest campgrounds are found along Hwy 20 itself. At the summit, **Sherman Pass Overlook** is a tiny, heavily treed camp with 9 sites (no hookups; RVs to 24 feet; no piped water). It's free and open mid-May to late September. On the east side of Sherman Pass, **Canyon Creek** has 12 sites (no hookups; RVs to 30 feet), some short, barrier-free trails, and trout fishing in the creek; *9 miles west of Kettle Falls.* **Trout Lake** has 4 sites and good fishing access; *a couple miles east on Hwy 20 and a few miles north on Trout Lake Rd.* **Ellen Lake** (11 sites) is a bit out of the way, but very private; *south of Hwy 20 on County Rd 412.* Call the Kettle Falls Ranger District; (509) 738-7700.

The remaining public campgrounds in this region are scattered along the west shore of the Columbia River (actually the northern extremes of Franklin D. Roosevelt Lake). **Sherman Creek** (5 sites) and **Haag Cove** (16 sites) on the west lakeshore just south of US 20, are Lake Roosevelt National Recreation Area sites. Contact the office in Kettle Falls for information, (509) 738-6266; www.nps.gov/laro.

Fishing

The Okanogan valley and Highlands provide some of the absolute best **rainbow, brook,** and **lake trout** fishing in Washington State. The first good example is Conconully Lake and Reservoir (see Camping, above), which opens in late April and remains productive through the summer. Both forks of Salmon Creek above the lake also are productive for rainbows, but note these are selective fishery waters: single, barbless hooks only; bait prohibited. Check the state regulations pamphlet. Nearby Blue Lake, a dozen miles north on Sinlahekin Road, also offers good trout fishing. Another Tonasket-area lake worthy of note is Aeneas Lake (just west of Tonasket on Pine Creek Road), a fly-fishing-only water that produces some hefty rainbows every summer. It's a must-visit for state fly-casters.

The Five Lakes area at the end of Bonaparte Road (see Camping, above) is another popular trout-fishing hub. Bonaparte, Beth, Beaver, Little Beaver, and Lost Lakes all provide good fishing for brook and rainbow trout. Bonaparte, in particular, is legendary among the big-fish crowd. The clear, cold lake holds some truly massive **Mackinaw** (lake) trout. A handful of trout over 20 pounds have been horsed into boats here, and legend has it one monster weighing upward of 40 pounds was boated many years ago. At least that's what they say at the Bonaparte Lake Resort, where you can call to argue or get **fish reports;** (509) 486-2828. Bonaparte is open all year, but be warned: we've been here in the winter, and it's c-c-c-cold. (If you put your tongue on your fish bonker, it'll stick.)

Another very hot rainbow fishery is **Curlew Lake** north of Republic (see Camping, above), which receives annual plants supplemented by fish raised here in net pens. It's open all year. On the east side of the region, most of the small streams accessible from Hwy 20 provide fair trout fishing (check the regulations pamphlet for seasons). A particularly good access spot is the trail along Canyon Creek southeast of Sherman Pass (see Hiking/Backpacking, below). Trout Lake (see Camping, above) has good spring trout fishing, as does the Kettle River above the confluence with the Columbia at Kettle Falls (check special regulations and seasons here). The upper portions of Franklin D. Roosevelt Lake are open all year and are particularly known for **walleye** fishing. For details, see the Grand Coulee chapter.

A filling-station owner in Republic sums up the Northwest outdoor experience

Boating/Canoeing

All the notable lakes mentioned in Fishing and Camping, above, are navigable by canoe or small craft. **Curlew Lake,** in particular, is a scenic canoe waterway. Rental boats are available from several Curlew Lake private resorts.

Hiking/Backpacking

There are some easy, family-friendly lakefront and forest paths in this area, and hard-core backpackers won't be disappointed, either. The Five Lakes/Bonaparte Lake area (see Camping, above) is home to a handful of hiking trails that get you up above the rocky peaks and dry forests that dominate this region. Trails fanning out from Sherman Pass, including the deservedly popular 60-mile Kettle Crest route, rank among the finest high-country trekking routes in the state. For more detailed information and a full trail list, contact the ranger stations listed below. Following is a list of favorites.

Five Lakes area

Bonaparte Road, Tonasket Ranger District; (509) 486-2186:

The Strawberry Mountain Trail (moderate; 3.2 miles round trip), which begins near Lost Lake Campground (see Camping, above), is a nice walk with a gentle grade, climbing wild strawberry–dominated slopes to some nice views of Bonaparte and Lost Lakes below and Canadian peaks afar. The crown jewel hike in this region, though, leads to Bonaparte Peak. The South Side Bonaparte Trail (moderate/difficult; 11 miles round trip) begins on Road 100 beyond Lost Lake Campground and climbs steadily to the 7,258-foot tip-top of Bonaparte and a stunning, 360-degree view good enough to merit not one, but two summit fire lookouts. An older leg of the trail begins at Bonaparte Campground and is still hikable, but adds another 1,000 vertical feet to the 1,200-foot ascent. Another good view hike in the area, this one much shorter, is the Pipsissewa Trail (moderate; 2 miles round trip), which climbs at a very agreeable grade (even for early morning) to a nice, flat overlook high above Bonaparte Lake. The trailhead is on Forest Road 100, beyond Lost Lake Campground.

An easy family trail in the Five Lakes area is **Beth Lake** (easy; 3.8 miles round trip), a nearly flat lakeside path along Beaver and Beth Lakes. The trail passes through Beth Lake Campground, but the main trailhead is in Beaver Lake Campground (see Camping, above). Another gem of a trail in the area is the **Big Tree Botanical Loop** (easy; 1.5 miles round trip), which begins on Forest Road 33 and weaves through a truly fantastic old-growth forest of larch and various pine trees, some of which are 500 or more years old. Yet another good family walk is the **Virginia Lilly Old-Growth Trail** (easy; 3-mile loop) off Forest Road 3240. This interpretive trail winds through a rich wildlife area; watch for deer, woodpeckers, and other creatures, and consider a dusk walk to look for magnificent great gray owls, the largest of North American owls.

Sherman Pass area

Hwy 20, Republic Ranger District; (509) 775-3305:

Some of Eastern Washington's premier high, ponderosa-dominated backpacking routes begin at or near Sherman Pass, the state's highest mountain crossing, at 5,575 feet. The star attraction here is the Kettle Crest Trail, which follows the crest of the Kettle Range in two sections north and south of Hwy 20. The **Kettle Crest North Trail** (difficult; 29 miles one way) is best hiked as a one-way through-hike (or a dual-party, swap-keys-in-the-middle hike) between Sherman Pass and a northern trailhead on Boulder Creek Road, west of US 395 just south of Orient. The route climbs high and stays high, following ridge tops over or around Columbia Mountain, Wapaloosie Mountain, Copper Butte, Profanity Peak, and other prominent peaks. Views all along the route are fantastic, and good campsites are ample. The **Kettle Crest South Trail** (difficult; 29 miles round trip), which begins on the south side of Sherman Pass/Hwy 20, is similarly scenic. A highlight is a short side trip to the summit of 7,100-foot Snow Peak. And don't overlook the **Thirteenmile Trail** (moderate; 26 miles round trip), which wanders through a magnificent forest of old-growth ponderosa pine. The grade is moderate to easy, unless you embark on any of a number of side trails to the top of peaks such as Fire Mountain. It's a great route for a 3- to 5-day backpack jaunt, or just a quick day hike on the lower portions. To reach the trailhead, drive 6.5 miles east of Republic on Hwy 20, turn south on Hall Creek Road, proceed 2.5 miles to Road 300, turn east (left), and continue to the road's end.

Sherman Pass has its share of day hikes, too. On the north side, the **Columbia Mountain Trail** (moderate; 4.4 miles round trip) begins on the Kettle Crest North Trail, splitting off to the right about 1.5 miles from the trailhead and climbing to a killer lunch spot, elevation 6,500 feet, views outstanding. Near Kettle Range Campground (see Camping, above), the **Sherman Pass Tie Trail** (easy; 1 mile round trip) is a connector to the Kettle Creek Trail that makes a nice, short day hike on its own.

East of Sherman Pass

Kettle Falls Ranger District; (509) 738-7700:

The **Wapaloosie Trail** (moderate; 5 miles round trip) is another conduit to the Kettle Crest Trail that makes a fine day hike on its own. It's a nice walk through pine forest, with a moderate grade and very good views near the top. You almost have to do it, just so you can repeat the name to friends at the office. The trailhead is off Albion Road, which turns north from US 20 about 5 miles east of Sherman Pass. The **Log Flume Trail** (easy; half-mile round trip) is an educational, though not overly scenic, trail from the south side of Hwy 20 about 5 miles east of Sherman Pass. The old log flume, used to float cut pine trees out of the forest, is an interesting site.

Farther east, in Canyon Creek Campground (see Camping, above), the **Canyon Creek Trail** (easy; 2 miles round trip) is a beautiful, barrier-free trail along the rushing, clear waters of Canyon Creek. This is a great family day hike, with good river access for anglers (see Fishing, above). Another popular view hike is **Barnaby Butte** (moderate; 3.4 miles round trip), which follows an old road from Forest Road 680 to a fine regional viewpoint. Drive 6.5 miles east of Republic, turn south on Hall Creek Road, and continue south until the road turns left and becomes Forest Road 680.

Wildlife Watching

Two of Washington's least-seen but most majestic beasts roam the hillsides in this region. The Okanogan Highlands are **bighorn sheep** country, and one of a small handful of areas in the state where you can reliably see them. Little Vulcan Mountain, in the Kettle River valley between West Kettle River Road and Forest Road 615, northwest of Curlew, is a prime bighorn habitat. The big sheep often are spotted through binoculars and spotting scopes from West Kettle River Road. If you want to get closer, a steep, unmaintained trail runs up the mountain from Forest Road 2114, reached from Hwy 21 near Curlew via Forest Road 615. Your chances improve in spring and fall, when the sheep are more active. You also have a small chance of meeting up with a **moose.** Occasional sightings are made at the Sherman Creek–Growden Heritage Site, about 10 miles west of Kettle Falls, south of Hwy 20. **Deer** and **beaver** are more commonly seen here. But you never know when a Bullwinkle might amble by. Short day-hiking trails begin at the interpretive exhibit here.

Downhill Skiing

It might not be big, glitzy, or even all that organized, but downhill turns can be made at a small day-skiing area in the Okanogan valley. **Sitzmark,** northeast of Tonasket, has two lifts covering about 650 vertical feet. This small ski area is open Thursdays, Saturdays, and Sundays, but schedules vary; call first. All-day adult lift tickets are $18. *From US 97 in Tonasket, take the Havillah Rd northeast 21 miles; (509) 485-3323.*

Also note that **Loup Loup Ski Bowl,** between Twisp and Okanogan on Hwy 20, is a nearby option. See the Methow Valley chapter.

Cross-country Skiing

Sitzmark (see above) also has about 6 kilometers of cross-country trails. A state Sno-Park, **Highlands,** 16.5 miles northeast of Tonasket and 2 miles south of Havillah via Havilla Road and Forest Road 3230, is small

(15-car parking lot) and remote, but the snow can be great, and some of the terrain will test even the most serious free-heelers. Sno-Park trail access also is available at **Sherman Pass** on Hwy 20, where trails aren't groomed or maintained, and at **Deer Creek Summit**, where a 37-kilometer trail system (12.2 kilometers groomed) is found 11 miles east of Curlew/Hwy 21 on Boulder Creek/Deer Creek Road. State **Sno-Park permits,** available at outdoor retailers and ranger stations, are required. For snow and grooming reports, call the Republic Ranger District; (509) 775-3305. **Bonaparte Lake Campground,** 5 miles north of Wauconda, and **Crawfish Lake Campground,** 12 miles east of Riverside, also have ski trails (see Camping, above).

Also note that **Loup Loup Summit,** which has an extensive cross-country trail network, is a nearby option. See the Methow Valley chapter.

Scenic Drives

Sherman Pass on Hwy 20 is a National Scenic Byway, and it's a well-deserved title. This high road across the Okanogan Highlands is a beautiful drive during spring and summer, but it's downright magnificent in the fall, when larch trees turn golden, traffic is even lighter than usual, and local wildlife is active. Keep your eyes peeled for a once-in-your-lifetime lynx spotting. A very pretty **loop trip** off the main highway can be made by driving Hwy 20 east from Tonasket, turning north on Bonaparte Lake Road to the Five Lakes area and Toroda Creek Road to Chesaw, then continuing southwest on Tonasket-Havillah Road past Sitzmark Ski Area and back to Tonasket. Pack a lunch and the hiking boots; this trip can take all day.

Horseback Riding

Experienced riders can go on a **trail ride** or join a **roundup** at K-Diamond-K Ranch, a 35,000-acre, family-owned working cattle ranch; 404 Hwy 21 S; (509) 775-3536.

Acessible Outdoors

Lake Ellen and **Canyon Creek Campgrounds** have barrier-free fishing and trails. **Log Flume Heritage Site,** 11 miles west of Kettle Falls on Hwy 20, has fishing platforms along Canyon Creek and accessible rest rooms and picnic sites. Near Sherman Pass, **Sherman Pass Overlook** has a barrier-free interpretive forest trail with a scenic overlook. The **White Mountain Fire Interpretive Site,** 12 miles east of Republic on Hwy 20, offers a barrier-free vista of an impressive 1988 wildfire, as well as a spectacular view of the Kettle Range.

outside in

Lodgings

The Rodeway Inn   A basic hotel with the distinction of being closest to the Stampede grounds. *$; 122 N Main, Omak; (509) 826-0400 or (888) 700-6625.*

More Information

Colville National Forest Supervisor's Office: *Colville; (509) 684-7000.*

Department of Transportation pass report: *(888) SNO-INFO; http://traffic.wsdot.wa.gov/sno-info/.*

Kettle Falls Ranger District: *(509) 738-7700.*

Okanogan National Forest Supervisor's Office: *Okanogan; (509) 826-3275; www.fs.fed.us/r6/oka.*

Omak Chamber of Commerce: *(509) 826-1880; www.omakchronicle.com/omakchamber.*

Republic Chamber of Commerce: *(509) 775-2704; rchamber@televar.com.*

Republic Ranger District: *(509) 775-3305.*

Tonasket Ranger District: *(509) 486-2186.*

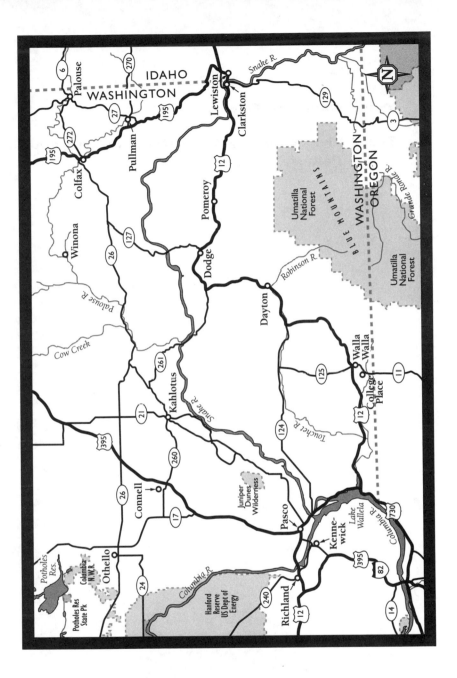

Southeast Washington

Southeast Washington

Tri-Cities

From Benton City east to Kahlotus, north to Othello, and south to the Oregon border, including the towns of Kennewick, Richland, and Pasco; the confluence of the Yakima, Columbia, and Snake Rivers; the Juniper Dunes Wilderness; and Lake Sacajawea and Sacajawea State Park.

You know you're in trouble when you look under the "out-door recreation" section of the local chamber of commerce brochure and it lists "the tallest treeless mountain in the world" as a regional highlight. Such is the case in the Tri-Cities of Kennewick, Richland, and Pasco, where the terrain is just barren enough to make a big, bald hump seem special.

It's not all that bad, actually. What the Tri-Cities lack in vegetation, they make up for in water. Lots of it. The cities sit at the confluence of three mondo river systems: the Yakima, Snake, and Columbia. All that water power, coupled with a nearby Columbia River dam at Umatilla, Oregon, makes a long, broad lake—Lake Wallula—that separates the three municipalities. Tri-Citians take full advantage of it. The region is a water-sports mecca, with waterskiing, Jet-ski riding, fishing, and jet-boat tours leading the way for outdoor recreation. The watery oasis and four large wildlife areas also attract plenty of critters, particularly migratory birds.

The grandest Tri-Cities-area wildlife refuge of all, however, was so designated only recently. The Hanford Reach, a long stretch of the Columbia through the Hanford Nuclear Reservation, was named a national monument in June 2000 by the Clinton administration. It wasn't a universally popular decision in the Tri-Cities, where county commissioners, among others, are still seething over what they see as a loss of "local control" over this last free-flowing stretch of this over-dammed super river. The truth is they've never had it. Sealed off from development for half a century while the Department of Defense fueled the Cold War arms race with Hanford-produced plutonium, the Hanford Reach is a splendid—and unique—example of the Columbia the way it was when explorer David Thompson first set foot here in 1811.

National monument status, long urged by environmentalists, should keep this key wildlife haven free from agribusiness development well into the future, hopefully forever. It's a tiny mitigating measure in the face of the long-term environmental harm the feds have done here by burying tons of highly radioactive waste deep in the sand for the, uh, benefit of future generations. Some of that stuff, ironically or fittingly, depending on one's politics, is likely to continue to seep into the Columbia right in its last seemingly unspoiled section for years to come. But at least the section will remain as it is—wild and unspoiled to the eye. The last tiny slice of a massive river muted by hydropower development is protected, at least for now.

Somehow it makes that tall, treeless mountain seem a lot less seductive.

Getting There

The Tri-Cities are 206 miles east of Seattle via Interstate 90 and I-82. Allow 4 hours. Richland sits between the Yakima and Columbia Rivers; Pasco sits between the Columbia and Snake Rivers; Kennewick is south of the Columbia. Bridges connect the cities via US Highway 12 and Hwy 240. From the Tri-Cities, US 395 runs northeast to I-90 and south into Oregon at McNary Dam; US 12 runs south then east along the east side of the Columbia, eventually to Walla Walla. Hwy 124 runs east along the south shore of Lake Sacajawea; the north end of the lake is reached from US 395 on Hwys 260 and 268.

inside out

Boating

The Tri-Cities area is the boating and water-sports capital of interior Washington. Thanks to the region's always sunny weather and its great access to the broad Columbia (not to mention the absence of much else to do), Tri-Citians take to the water in huge numbers to water-ski, fish, and race their boats. **Lake Wallula,** the 64-mile-long Columbia impoundment behind McNary Dam near Umatilla, Oregon, makes for a broad, smooth boating track. So does **Lake Sacajawea,** the Snake River backup created by the Ice Harbor Dam, 9 miles east of Pasco. You'll find three actual yacht clubs in town, and it's not difficult to find boating supplies and services. Major **public launches** are found at all the waterfront parks listed in Swimming/Picnics, below.

Boatless outdoor lovers searching for the unique heart of this region should consider a **jet-boat tour to Hanford Reach,** the last free-flowing stretch of the Columbia River. This is the upside of the federal government's 50-year experiment with nuclear power on the sprawling Hanford Reservation. Because the river flows through the once heavily protected nuclear reservation, it was locked away from development—and from most human visitation, for that matter—for half a century. Not surprisingly, a wide range of wildlife has taken advantage, making boat or kayak trips through the reach a bird- and animal-watcher's treat. Contact Columbia River Journeys in Richland; (509) 943-0231.

Swimming/Picnics

On the Columbia (aka Lake Wallula), picnicking, swimming, and general lounging sites are available at more than a dozen small parks. The major venue is **Columbia Park,** on Hwy 240 (Columbia Drive) in Kennewick. The sprawling park has boat ramps, hiking/biking trails, picnic grounds, campsites (see Camping, below), and other attractions. **Sacajawea State Park,** east of Pasco at the Columbia/Snake River confluence, has interpretive exhibits describing Lewis and Clark's 1805 stopover, plus a boat ramp, extensive moorage docks, and picnic grounds. Follow signs from US 12. Directly across the Columbia in Kennewick is **Two Rivers County Park,** which has a swimming area, boat launch, and picnic facilities. **Howard Amon Park,** along the bank of the Columbia in Richland, is a great spot for picnics, tennis, golf, jogging, or just ambling. On the lower Snake River (aka Lake Sacajawea), there are picnic and swimming facilities at **Ice Harbor Lock and Dam** and at **Levey Park,** both on the lake's northwest shore, off Pasco-Kahlotus Rd; **and at Charbonneau Park** and **Fishhook Park,** both off Hwy 124 on the southeast side of the lake.

Camping

Many of the waterfront parks listed in Swimming/Picnics, above, also offer camping. **Columbia Park** has 100 sites (18 with full hookups, 26 drive-through) in an open (often hot), grassy area operated by the City of Kennewick. It's open from April to October, and campsites may be reserved. *Off Columbia in Kennewick; (509) 783-3711.*

   Charbonneau Park on Lake Sacajawea is a Corps of Engineers–operated campground with 54 sites (15 full hookups, 39 electric-only hookups) on the lower Snake River near Ice Harbor Dam. The park is open April through September (day-use area all year). Campsites can be reserved; (877) 444-6777; www.reserveusa.com. *On Sun Harbor Rd, off Hwy 124 northeast of Pasco; (509) 547-7781.*

Fishhook Park has 61 sites (41 with hookups, 8 pull-through) on Lake Sacajawea. The park is open April to September. Campsites can be reserved; (877) 444-6777; www.reserveusa.com. *On Fishhook Park Rd, off Hwy 124 northeast of Pasco; (509) 547-7781.*

Hood Park, another Corps of Engineers development, has 69 standard sites on the lower Snake River. There's good river access here for swimming and boating. It's open summers only, and campsites can be reserved; (877) 444-6777; www.reserveusa.com. Note: The Corps says Hood Park might be closed for the 2001 camping season for extensive renovation; call first. *At Hwy 124/US 12, 3 miles south of Pasco; (509) 547-7781.*

Windust Park, another Corps campground with 28 sites (no hookups), is on Sacajawea Lake near Lower Monumental Dam. It's open from April through September. Campsites can be reserved; (877) 444-6777; www.reserveusa.com. *36 miles northeast of Pasco via Pasco-Kahlotus and Burr Canyon Rds; (509) 547-7781.*

The state's McNary Habitat Management Area, next to the McNary National Wildlife Refuge (see Wildlife, below), has a **Fish and Wildlife campground** with 24 primitive sites and no piped water. It's open all year, it's free, and it's not your best choice unless you're a very enthusiastic birder. *Southeast of Pasco, follow signs from US 12; (509) 456-4082.*

To the south, **Crow Butte State Park** is a unique site—it sits on an island in the middle of the Columbia River, called Lake Umatilla here because of the flooded backwater from John Day Dam. The park, which Washington State Parks insists is known as the "Maui of the Columbia," is situated on what once was a high bluff. The campground has 50 sites (full hookups; RVs to 60 feet), a 60-person group camp, a boat launch and moorage, and a swimming area. Short hiking trails lead to the top of 670-foot Crow Butte, which offers views of Mount Hood. The land on the park's eastern border is a portion of the Umatilla National Wildlife Refuge, a significant migratory waterfowl nesting site. Crow Butte is open all year; weekends only October through March. Campsites can be reserved up to 11 months in advance by calling Reservations Northwest; (800) 452-5687. *From Hwy 14, about 15 miles west of Paterson, cross the bridge southwest to the island; (509) 875-2644 or (800) 233-0321.*

Hiking

Hikes in the Tri-Cities area are limited. They're also a study in extremes. On the soft side, the 6.2-mile **trail through Columbia Park** (see Camping, above) is a paved, smooth walkway through the greenest greenery you'll find in this area: watered park lawns. On the harsher side, fans of open, dry country will find plenty of that—and solitude to match—in the 7,140-acre **Juniper Dunes Wilderness** north of Pasco. The wilderness is so wild, it's tough even to get to. There's one unmarked access road, but no marked trailheads or facilities. (In fact, Wilderness managers officially say there's no public access, but hardy souls seem to find it.) Pick up a good map and find the entryway off Peterson Rd, reached by driving US 12 east through Pasco, then north on the Pasco-Kahlotus Highway. Your best bet is to contact the BLM office in Spokane, (509) 536-1200, for directions to the single "trail"—an **old jeep road** that slices through the southern section of the wilderness. Once there, you have to park outside the boundary and bring your own water. You don't need to follow a trail to explore this area. And it is worth the trouble, if you're into unique topography, such as the largest sand dunes—up to 130 feet high and a quarter mile wide—and the largest natural groves of western juniper—some 150 years old—in the state. This pocket of wilderness is all that remains of an ecosystem that once stretched over nearly 400 square miles south to the Snake and Columbia Rivers. The area also is rich with desert wildlife and wildflowers. It's big enough to get lost in, but small enough for you to quickly walk back out. The wilderness is only about 4.5 miles square, so a (fenced) boundary is never more than a couple of hours away. Most of the other maintained trails in the area wind through the four wildlife refuges surrounding the Tri-Cities. See Wildlife, below.

Wildlife

Four wildlife refuges form a bird- and animal-watching square around the Tri-Cities. **Badger Slope,** to the west near Benton City, is a Bureau of Land Management area on an antenna-farm bluff overlooking the Yakima River. Its open grasslands and basalt cliffs are a major feeding/nesting site for raptors, including several **hawk** species, **falcons, turkey vultures,** and **golden eagles. Marmots** also are often seen in the fields. Follow McBee Rd west from I-82 at Kiona.

Right in the center of the Tri-Cities sprawl is Yakima River Delta Wildlife Park, at the confluence of the Yakima and Columbia Rivers. The 300-acre site incorporates Richland's Wye Park and Bateman Island, a Columbia River island connected by a short dike. Trails run north, to the Yakima confluence, and in a loop around Bateman Island. The area is a major waterbird hangout. Watch for **geese, ducks,** and **blue herons.** This is a decent canoeing spot, with some quiet-water shorelines and a boat launch in Wye Park. Off Columbia Drive between Richland and Kennewick; 509-547-7781.

On the far side of the Columbia south of Pasco is the McNary National Wildlife Refuge, a 3,600-acre reserve near the Snake River confluence. This is a major wetland, with acres of swamps, sloughs, and grasslands that attract a wide variety of shorebirds and migratory waterfowl. **Pelicans** also are frequently seen here in the summertime, and **northern harriers** and **burrowing owls** are occasionally seen. A mile-long interpretive trail at the west end of the refuge is open all year, but other areas are closed periodically during nesting seasons. Follow signs from Hwy 12 near Burbank, just south of Pasco; (509) 543-8322; http://nwr.mcnary.wa.us/.

The Wallula Habitat Management Unit is a significant 2,000-acre wetlands farther south on US 12 at the junction with Hwy 730—a good place to view migratory geese, a variety of ducks, some raptor species, and pelicans. There are no maintained trails, but a series of gated access roads skirt three of the area's five ponds. They're open to foot traffic. The area is managed by the Corps of Engineers; (509) 922-3211

Fishing

Here's a shock: a stretch of the Columbia River that you can actually wade out into and fish like a river! The waters around Ringold (north of Richland) in Hanford Reach, the last free-flowing stretch of the Columbia, are notable fall **steelhead** territory, with good success for anglers casting spinning gear from gravel bars. Farther downstream, the deep, slow waters behind McNary Dam also provide good to very good winter steelhead fishing for boat trollers. The river also holds **chinook salmon, whitefish, sturgeon,** and **largemouth** and **smallmouth bass.** Newcomers might be wise to invest in a guide to fish this massive waterway. Fall steelhead action also can be good in the Lower Snake River.

outside in

Restaurants

Atomic Ale Brewpub & Eatery ★   The microbrews are too good for Homer Simpson's taste, but he'd dig their names. *$; 1015 Lee Blvd, Richland; 509/946-5465.*

Casa Chapala ★   Mexican food here is quite filling and includes kid-size and low-fat options. *$; 107 E Columbia Dr, Kennewick; 509/586-4224; 29 E Belfair Pl, Kennewick; 509/783-8080; www.casachapala.com.*

Cedars Pier 1 ★★ A step above "Tri-Cities casual," with cuisine that's high-end surf-and-turf. $$; 355 Clover Island Dr, Kennewick; 509/582-2143.

Chez Chaz Bistro ★ Inside, the decor is tasteful, if whimsical, and the continental cuisine is good. $$; 5011 W Clearwater Ave, Kennewick; 509/735-2138.

The Emerald of Siam ★ Authentic Thai recipes include curries, satays, noodles, and black-rice pudding. $; 1314 Jadwin Ave, Richland; 509/946-9328.

Monterosso's Italian Restaurant ★★ Authentic Italian cuisine in a restored Northern Pacific Pullman dining car. $; 1026 Lee Blvd, Richland; 509/946-4525.

Sundance Grill ★ The casual, business-lunch atmosphere here segues into dinner with live music. $$; 413 N Kellogg St, Ste B, Kennewick; 509/783-6505.

Lodgings

Casablanca B&B ★ A country-style B&B in a desert canyon five minutes east of Kennewick. $$; 94806 E Granada Ct, Kennewick; 888/627-0676; www.casablancabb.com.

Doubletree Hotel ★★ The Tri-Cities' largest hotel, with 279 rooms and convenient to the airport. $$; 2525 N 20th Ave, Pasco; 509/547-0701 or 800/222-8733. &

Red Lion Hanford House ★ Hanford House remains one of the most popular places to stay in the Tri-Cities. $$; 802 George Washington Wy, Richland; 509/946-7611 or 800/733-5466. &

More Information

Sporthaus Northwest (skis, sporting goods, in-line skates): 326 N Columbia Center Blvd, Kennewick; (509) 735-7555.

Tri-Cities Visitors and Convention Bureau: (509) 735-8486 or (800) 666-1929; www.visittri-cities.com.

Walla Walla and the Blue Mountains

From Walla Walla north to Dayton, east to the Idaho border, and west to Touchet, including a section of Umatilla National Forest, the Wenaha-Tucannon Wilderness, Bluewood Ski Area, Chief Joseph Wildlife Area, and Lewis and Clark Trail and Fields Spring State Parks.

The land of the double Walla is the Willie Nelson song of Northwest outdoor venues: high, dry, and lonesome. OK, so scratch the "lonesome" part. Especially these days. Walla Walla represents what writer and social historian Richard Rodriguez notes is an ironic modern twist on the nation's westward-ho mentality: coast dwellers are suddenly heading east in search of the real West—the one of wide-open plains, rugged mountain ranges, awe-inspiring river gorges, and honest, earth-bound people.

Of course, like most Eastern Washington regions in this guide, the Walla Walla area certainly isn't for everybody. Whether you're talking about onions (biggest, sweetest), weather (freezing/boiling), or history (rough and occasionally violent), Walla Walla is a land of extremes. You don't perspire here in summer; you power-sweat. You don't shiver in winter; you turn blue. Then again, you're not likely to ever encounter a traffic jam, either on the road, in the campground, or at the local latte stand. Nor are you likely to see more than a dozen other hikers on the nearest local hiking trail, regardless of the season.

Walla Walla is about as far from Seattle as you can get without lapsing into Idaho, which for many visitors is reason enough to make the trek. Once here, however, they discover that this area is more than just far away. The lands surrounding Walla Walla—which sits on a flat volcanic plateau—are downright impressive, with clear streams; deep, rugged canyons; and wide-open skies.

Impressive gives way to beautiful a short distance to the east, where the lava-forged Blue Mountains rise from the plains of the Snake River flatlands. Here, high, rocky peaks provide stunning territorial views of a half dozen river canyons carved by liquid-crystal rivers. Mountain slopes are roamed by Rocky Mountain elk, trophy-size mule and white-tailed deer, bighorn sheep, and unsettlingly brash black bears and cougars. Most of this wild mountainous area lies within the Umatilla National Forest, which straddles the Washington-Oregon border. The heart of the mountains was protected as federal wilderness in 1978. The Wenaha-Tucannon Wilderness (177,000 acres) is a former game preserve that's still home to some of Washington's healthiest elk, deer, and bighorn sheep herds. More elk set foot inside the wilderness every year than people.

Treks here, whether by automobile, foot, ski, snowshoe, or horse-back, are some of the most scenic—and least crowded—in the state. This Wilderness provides a classic, wide-open Western experience very remi niscent of the best Wyoming or Montana backcountry. And the busy little city of Walla Walla, which manages a degree of unpretentious sophistication that belies its size and location, is a perfect launching point.

As mentioned, weather can be a drawback here; Walla Walla bakes in the summer and gets tongue-sticking cold in the winter. Consider trekking this way during the "shoulder seasons," spring or autumn. A trip to the Blue Mountains in the late spring—when the top layer of snow is gone but the most deadly heat is still on its way—brings pleasant weather, mind-boggling bursts of wildflowers, and very few other people. Likewise, an autumn trip—preferably before mid-October, when hunting season begins in earnest, brings fantastic crisp, clear skies and mountain color.

Whenever you go, you're bound to return convinced there's a lot more to the Walla Walla area than meets the faraway eye. If the weather cooperates and the rattlesnakes stay away, you just might head back West with a set of nature-sparked memories which, like many a local onion, are actually bigger than your own head.

Getting There

It might feel like 400, but the odometer says Walla Walla is a mere 260 miles southeast of Seattle via Interstate 90 to Ellensburg, I-82 to Tri-Cities, then US Highway 12. Give yourself a solid 5 hours. From Walla Walla, US 12 continues northeast to Dayton and Pomeroy, the two gateways into hiking, camping, skiing, and fishing venues in the Umatilla National Forest and Wenaha-Tucannon Wilderness. All the way east to the Snake River–Idaho border, US 12 meets Hwy 129, which heads southwest to the Grande Ronde River and Oregon.

inside out

Camping

Walla Walla's primary public campground, **Fort Walla Walla,** closed in early 2000—the victim of statewide Initiative 695, which slashed state license-tab fees and eliminated funding for many public services, including campgrounds, city officials say. The closure of the 300-acre, 70-site campground leaves a void for campers, especially RVers, visiting the area. Alternative RV campgrounds, all **private,** include Golden West Estates, (509) 526-4659, and Four Seasons RV Resort, (509) 529-6072, both in Walla Walla; Cameron Court in Dayton, (509) 382-4410; Country Estates Mobile Home Park in College Place just west of Walla Walla, (509) 529-5442; and Pierce's Green Valley RV Park and Campground in Touchet, (509) 394-2387.

If you're willing to drive a bit, plenty of quality public camping can be found in the hinterlands. Up US 12 between Waitsburg and Dayton, **Lewis and Clark Trail State Park** (not to be confused with Lewis and Clark State Park in Winlock near I-5) is a small place set in a very pleasant forest of big, straight ponderosa pines with a tinder-dry grassy floor. The park, which fronts on the Tucannon River, is an oasis in this flat, dry area—no doubt one reason the Lewis and Clark Expedition chose it as a stopping point as they returned from their Pacific trek in 1806. The park is split by US 12; day-use areas, playfields, and picnic grounds are on the south side, camping to the north. The two riverside loops contain 34 campsites (no hookups; RVs to 28 feet) and a 100-person group camp. The park also has several hiking trails, including a short interpretive trail from the camping area. Lewis and Clark Trail State Park is open all year, with limited winter camping. Campsites cannot be reserved. *On US 12, about 4.5 miles west of Dayton; (509) 337-6457 or (800) 233-0321.*

For a remote campout—and we're talking really remote here—consider one of several small Umatilla National Forest campgrounds in or near the Wenaha-Tucannon Wilderness. Most of them make excellent jump-off points for wilderness backpacking or fishing treks, and are used most heavily in the fall, when elk and deer hunters flock to the wilderness area. For forest maps and other information on all of these, contact the Pomeroy Ranger District; (509) 843-1891.

Godman is a favorite hiking and horse-packer launching point, with hitching rails and other horse facilities. For campers, there are 8 sites (no hookups; RVs to 15 feet) and few other services. Godman, which lies one creek drainage east of Ski Bluewood, is free, open summers only, and has no piped water. *25 miles southeast of Dayton on Forest Rd 46 (Kendall Skyline Rd; see Scenic Drives/Photography, below).*

Tucannon has 6 sites (no hookups; RVs to 16 feet), a small picnic area, and good access to the Tucannon River, where trout fishing can be excellent (see Fishing, below). It's free, open summers only, and has no piped water. Camp William T. Wooten State Park, an Environmental Learning Center with a group camp but no other camping, is nearby. *20 miles south of Pomeroy on Forest Rd 47, off Hwy 126.*

Alder Thicket has 5 tent sites. The camp, at 5,100 feet in the Blue Mountains and open summers only, is free and has no piped water. *18 miles south of Pomeroy on Forest Rd 40, via Hwy 128.* A short distance to the south as the crow flies, **Big Springs** offers 8 small campsites (no hookups) at a high (5,100 feet), dry location in the Blue Mountains. It's free, open summers only, and has no piped water. *26 miles south of Pomeroy on Forest Rds 42 and 4225, reached via Hwy 128 about 4 miles south of Forest Rd 40.* A bit farther south and a bit more removed is **Teal Spring**, another high-altitude (5,600 feet) campground in the Blue Mountains. Open summers only, Teal Spring has 5 quaint campsites (no hookups; RVs to 15 feet). The campground is popular with off-road vehicle enthusiasts. It's free and has no piped water. The Clearwater Lookout tower (see Scenic Drives/Photography, below) is nearby. *26 miles south of Pomeroy via Sweeney Gulch Rd or Hwy 128, Forest Rd 42, and Forest Rd 40.* The easternmost camp, **Wickiup**, has 5 campsites (no hookups; RVs to 16 feet). The campground is free, open summers only, and has no piped water. *34 miles southeast of Pomeroy via Hwy 128 and Forest Rds 40 and 44.*

Other very small, very remote area Forest Service campgrounds—all free and without piped water, are: **Spruce Springs** (3 sites), 15 miles south of Pomeroy on Forest Rd 40; **Misery Spring** (5 tent sites), 27 miles south of Pomeroy on Forest Rd 4030 (see Scenic Drives/Photography, below); and **Lady Bug** and **Panjab**, 46 miles south of Pomeroy on Forest Rd 4713. Contact the Pomeroy Ranger District, (509) 843-1891.

Western Washington campers frustrated by big crowds and searching for that one state park really, really out there away from the hordes can stop and plant the flag at **Fields Spring State Park.** This park—located 30 miles south of Clarkston, just north of the Grande Ronde River Canyon, and east of . . . well, just about everything—lies in a thicket of trees marking the transition from flat plains lands to the high, dry forests of the Blue Mountains. It's a lovely spot, rich with wildflower blooms on mountain slopes in the spring, and with wildlife all year-round. Don't miss the hiking trail to the grand view atop Puffer Butte (see Hiking/Backpacking, below). The campground has 22 campsites (no hookups; RVs to 30 feet), as well as playfields and other day-use facilities. It's a very popular winter hangout, with lighted sledding and tubing runs near the park's twin Wo-He-Lo and Puffer Butte Environmental Learning Centers, and many marked cross-country ski routes on local fire roads (see Skiing/Snow Play, below). Fields Spring is open all year. Campsites cannot be reserved. *29 miles south of Clarkston on Hwy 129; (509) 256-3332 or (800) 233-0321.*

Hiking/Backpacking

For strolling Walla Walla itself, the city has a nice **walking tour,** outlined on a pamphlet available at the Chamber of Commerce, 29 E Sumach Street. Another option is a **running/jogging/walking path** that stretches from Rooks Park to Eastgate Lions Park in Walla Walla. If you're just looking to get the kids (or yourselves) out of the car for a stretch, Lewis and Clark Trail State Park (see Camping, above) has two nice hiking trails. One is a mile-long **nature loop,** the other a mile-long **bird-watching trail.** Interpretive information is available for both.

Another great day hike is found in Fields Spring State Park (see Camping, above). It's a long haul from the Walla Walla area, but campers at the state park should make the time to climb **to Puffer Butte** (moderate; 2 miles round trip). At the top of this 4,500-foot butte, awesome views loom in all directions: the Grande Ronde River Canyon to the south, the Snake River Canyon to the east, and the Blue Mountains to the southwest. It's one of Eastern Washington's best viewpoints.

Some of the dry side's most inspiring countryside can be reached by trail throughout the 177,000-acre Wenaha-Tucannon Wilderness and the surrounding Umatilla National Forest in the Blue Mountains east of Walla Walla. This is rugged, spectacular country, with high basaltic peaks separated by steep, deep canyons. It's truly wild, a fact reflected in the rich population of large mammals such as elk, deer, bighorn sheep, and black bear. One of the largest Rocky Mountain elk herds in Washington lives here, drawing crowds of winter hunters, who enjoy "grandfathered" status that allows them to continue hunting in this former game reserve. Most hunting takes place from mid-October to mid-November—a good time to stay clear if you're hiking.

Weather can be extreme here, with summer temperatures often in the high 90s and winters brutally cold and often snowy. Most hikes in this wilderness are far from being easy strolls, but backpack trips can be memorable. Wilderness regulations restrict **group size** to 12 and prohibit camping within 75 feet of streams. **Dogs** are allowed, and no permits are required. For road and trailhead updates, maps, and other information, contact the Umatilla National Forest's Pomeroy Ranger District; (509) 843-1891.

The **Tucannon River Trail** (easy; 8.2 miles round trip) is one of the most pleasant hikes in this area, with a gentle grade along the Tucannon River making it a favorite of fly-casters, who come here in pursuit of hefty trout. The Tucannon Trail is a favorite of many Eastern Washington families, who introduce kids to backpacking here. Deer, elk, and bighorn sheep sightings are common, and great campsites are found at Ruchert Camp, about a mile up the trail. The trailhead is reached by driving Tucannon Rd south from US 12 to Forest Rd 4712 and proceeding up the left fork to the end of the road.

Another scenic walk down into the Tucannon River drainage, the **Bear Creek Trail** (moderate; 6 miles round trip) drops south from a ridgetop at Bear Creek trailhead (at Hunter Springs, 28 miles south of Pomeroy via Benjamn Gulch Rd and Mountain Rd/Forest Rd 40) to the Tucannon River Trail. The river is a favorite fly-fishing area, and a good place to wet your whistle before the climb back up to the car. In between are clusters of pine and tamarack that conceal the occasional mule deer or grouse.

Not far from Tucannon Campground (see Camping, above) is the **Panjab Trail** (moderate; 11.2 miles round trip), a popular horseback route that begins on Panjab Rd (Forest Rd 4713) and ends at Indian Corral horse camp. Most of the route maintains a moderate pace along Panjab Creek, then climbs steeply at the end to the camp. From the same trailhead, long-distance backpackers can embark on the **Crooked Creek Trail** (moderate; 22 miles one way), one of several trails that cut through a long portion of the wilderness area. The route follows Panjab Creek to Indian Corral, then drops through the Trout Creek, Third Creek, and Crooked Creek valleys to a southern trailhead at Three Forks, off Forest Rd 4039 near the Oregon border. This is a scenic wilderness traverse, with peaceful, wildlife-rich valleys and plenty of solitude.

Trailheads in the vicinity of Godman Camp on Forest Rd 46 offer some of the best day hiking in the area. A good half-day hike with rich regional views, the **Oregon Butte Trail** (moderate; 6 miles round trip) climbs to a magnificent fire lookout that's still staffed during summer months. Views of the Wallowa and Seven Devil ranges are magnificent from the lookout, which is perched at 6,400 feet. The trail begins at Teepee trailhead at the end of Forest Rd 4608 (from Godman Guard Station, turn left on Rd 4608 and take all right turns for 5 miles to the trailhead). Backpackers needn't turn around at Oregon Butte. For a long, fantastic trip through the wilderness, continue on the same path along the **Smooth Ridge Trail** (difficult; 40 miles round trip), which has good campsites and—a rarity here—plenty of fresh water all along the route. Below, near the Godman Ranger Station, the **West Butte Trail** (moderate; various distances possible) works its way through a number of scenic creek valleys, any one of which makes for a good overnight trip.

In the North Fork Touchet River drainage (the Ski Bluewood resort area), a good day hike can be had on the **Sawtooth Trail** (moderate/difficult; 8 miles round trip). The trail is actually a long, dry traverse to the Wenaha River drainage, but for the first 4 or 5 miles it follows Sawtooth Ridge south, rewarding hikers with grand views of Squaw Peak, Table Rock, and the upper Wenaha River drainage. The trailhead is near Burnt Flat, about 3.5 miles beyond Ski Bluewood on Forest Rd 46.

Farther south, the **Slick Ear Trail,** a popular backcountry angler's route (moderate/difficult; 10.5 miles round trip), drops steeply to a junction with the Wenaha River Trail across the Oregon border. The trailhead is near Twin Buttes, south of Ski Bluewood on Forest Rd 300.

Fishing

The upper Tucannon River, which flows through the Umatilla National Forest, is one of Washington's prettiest trout streams, in the classic, dry-country fly-fishing tradition. The river, which bubbles to life in the Blue Mountains of the Wenaha-Tucannon Wilderness and flows north to join the Snake River near Starbuck on US 12, is accessible from many points along Tucannon Rd, which runs south from US 12 just west of Pomeroy. Much of the challenge of fishing this river is discerning which portions are open when, and with what special regulations. Spend some time with the state fishing pamphlet and a good topographic map when you head out. Some of the river's best, most scenic fishing is in the upper drainage, which holds native and planted **rainbow trout.** See the list of Wenaha-Tucannon Wilderness campgrounds and hiking trails in Camping and Hiking/Backpacking, above, for access information. The lower river, with a decent winter **steelhead** run, is fished from the Snake River confluence upstream to the Tucannon Hatchery, about midway between Pomeroy and the wilderness boundary on Tucannon Rd.

The Touchet River holds **German brown trout** and steelhead, and access is easy at Lewis and Clark Trail State Park (see Camping, above) More fair-to-good rainbow trout action usually can be found on the dozen small lakes and ponds in the W. T. Wooten Wildlife Area along Tucannon Rd (see Wildlife, below). All the lakes are small enough to provide good bank access (indeed, boats are prohibited), and one lake, Big Four, is for fly-fishing only. The lakes are stocked with rainbows, and open March 1, but action often doesn't pick up until later, when the ice melts and the water warms enough for the fish to become active.

In the state's extreme southeast corner, the Grande Ronde River gives up a fair number of winter steelhead every year. Good access is available on Hwy 129, which runs south from Asotin. Finally, if you have a taste for **eels,** head northeast on Hwy 129 to Asotin Creek. Asotin, legend has it, is a native word for "eel creek," and large numbers of the slithery wonders allegedly were harvested from the creek near its confluence with the Snake River. We're not sure if there's a limit on eels, but the creek mouth also is a known rainbow trout producer.

Picnics

Two nicely maintained Walla Walla city parks, **Pioneer** and **Veterans Memorial,** are good picnic spots, as are the grounds of **Whitman Mission Historical Site** west of town south of US 12. For parks outside town, see the listings for Camping, above.

Downhill Skiing

One of Washington's least-known but most-fun ski areas, **Ski Bluewood** is tucked away in the slopes of the Blue Mountains, 21 miles southeast of Dayton. It's a small area, with only three lifts and 1,100 feet of vertical spread over 26 runs. But Bluewood's greatest drawing card—some of the highest, driest snow in the state—continues to lure skiers from afar, who catch on fast to the delights of Walla Walla and Clarkston skiers' secret powder stash. Weather can be extremely erratic here, as the winter of 1995–96 proved in a memorable way. Bluewood, which normally opens in late November or early December, still hadn't opened by mid-January; the resort sent most of its 150 employees home. Then in late January the snow gods let loose and made up for lost time. Bluewood was hammered by more than 7 feet of snow in seven days, creating some of the best ski conditions since Lewis and Clark staggered through here in 1805. Several weeks later, the season ended just as quickly as it began, when record rains and flooding wiped out Bluewood's only access road, closing the area for the season. The lesson: Call the ski report! If conditions are good at Bluewood (which is often the case), it makes a very relaxing weekend ski getaway for wet-side skiers tired of rain and lift lines, and the mountain is rarely, if ever, crowded.

    Bluewood stats: The area serves up 1,125 vertical feet (top elevation, 5,670 feet) with three lifts and 23 major runs spread over 530 acres. The resort is open from 9am to 4pm Tuesdays through Sundays and all holiday Mondays. Adult all-day lift tickets are $27. *From downtown Dayton, drive south on Fourth Avenue, which becomes North Fork Touchet Rd at the city limits and Forest Rd 64 at the forest boundary, and proceed 21 miles to the ski area; mountain information (509) 382-4725, snow phone (509) 382-2877; www.bluewood.com.*

Cross-country Skiing/Snow Play

Ski Bluewood also has 5 kilometers of cross-country/snowmobile trails, as well as access to many miles of backcountry skiing, snowshoeing, and snowmobiling in the Umatilla National Forest. Many of the campgrounds in or around the **Wenaha-Tucannon Wilderness** (see Camping and Hiking/Backpacking, above) are home to backcountry skiers in the winter. Wilderness trails can provide memorable backcountry ski treks, with magnificent surroundings and plentiful wildlife. But be warned that route-finding is tough in the backcountry if you're not familiar with the terrain. Maps and suggestions are available at the Pomeroy Ranger District; (509) 843-1891.

Fields Spring Sno-Park, the winter incarnation of Fields Spring State Park (see Camping, above), provides 12 kilometers of groomed ski trails in loops ranging from an easy 0.2K trail to the 3K Grande Ronde Loop. The snow here usually is dry and cold, the scenery outstanding. State **Sno-Park passes,** available at outdoor stores and ranger district offices, are required to use the groomed trails and to park in the 80-car lot. The grounds of Fields Spring State Park itself also are a favorite winter family getaway, largely because of the diverse offerings here. The park literally offers one-stop winter fun shopping. There's something for everyone here, whether they're standing by the big fire or trekking far into the local hills on snowshoes. Kids are drawn to several excellent sledding/tubing hills, one of which is lighted at night. A nice added touch are picnic shelters heated in the winter for frosty snow revelers. Snow updates: (509) 256-3332.

Snowmobiling is a prolific winter sport on roads throughout the Umatilla National Forest. Contact the Pomeroy Ranger District, (509) 843-1891.

Mountain Biking

We're not sure if anyone makes a water bottle big enough to sustain an average fat-tire sweatmonger in the hills around Walla Walla and Dayton on your average summer day. It's hot, dry, dusty country. If that's your thing, though, the Umatilla National Forest has 100 miles or so of dry forest roads—and a handful of singletrack trails—with your name on them. Popular routes include the **Kendall Skyline Rd 46** (see Scenic Drives/Photography, below) and the **Tucannon River Trail** (see Hiking/Backpacking, above). Contact the Pomeroy Ranger District, (509) 843-1891, for information on other open trails and roads.

Horseback Riding

The **Blue Mountains** are known for their dry, wide-open spaces—ideal terrain for short or extended horse-packing trips. The Umatilla National

Forest, which manages the area, is well suited for equestrians, providing horse ramps, hitching posts, and other facilities throughout the forest and the Wenaha-Tucannon Wilderness. Several local firms offer full-service **horse-packing trips** through this magical area. Call the Pomeroy Ranger District, (509) 843-1891, for outfitter referrals.

Scenic Drives/Photography

For a series of good vistas displaying the volcano- and river-forged wildlands of the Blue Mountains and Wenaha-Tucannon Wilderness, take a drive on **Kendall Skyline Rd.** It's a rough route, probably not suitable for that new Daewoo Leganza. But highlights such as the **Table Rock Lookout** (6,250 feet) make the drive worthwhile for the high-clearance crowd. From Dayton, drive south on Fourth Avenue and turn left on Eckler Mountain Rd (County Rd 9124). Proceed about 28 miles on the road, which turns to Road 46 at the forest boundary, and continue south to Godman guard station and campground, where several good day-hiking trails are found (see Hiking/Backpacking, above).

More sweeping views can be found at the **Ray Ridge Viewpoint,** just south of Misery Spring Campground on Forest Rd 025, off Forest Rds 4030 and 40. Most of the Wenaha-Tucannon Wilderness is visible from here, as well as the **Eaglecap Mountains** in Oregon and the **Seven Devils Peaks** of Idaho. Be sure to look southeast and give a friendly wave to **Mount Horrible.** You'll need a snowmobile to get up here during winter months.

Another popular day trip in the area is the drive to the 100-foot-high **Clearwater Lookout,** which offers a superb view of the wilderness area. Take Benjamin Gulch Rd (Hwy 128) south from Pomeroy and proceed about 25 miles on Forest Rd 40, just before Teal Spring Campground (see Camping, above).

If you're really into natural phenomena, make your way to the **"Big Sink,"** accessible by foot from Forest Rd 63, 2 miles southeast of Jubilee Lake in the Walla Walla Ranger District. It's a vortex of sorts: a big chunk of land mysteriously sank into the earth here, and legend has it compasses will spin and cell phones will start auto-dialing pizza joints in Taiwan. We're kidding about that last part, but not the rest of it; see for yourself.

Wildlife Watching

The William T. Wooten Wildlife Area is a great place to sample the wildlife of the Blue Mountains. **Rocky mountain elk,** big **mule** and **white-tailed deer, bighorn sheep, cougar, turkey,** and **quail** all are abundant in this area. (The Blue Mountains, in fact, are home to one of the state's largest Rocky Mountain elk populations, with more than 20,000 head.) Winter (late December through March) is one of the most productive viewing times; elk, bighorn sheep, and mule deer are commonly seen feeding on the 11,000-acre refuge. Follow Tucannon Rd south from US 12 between Pomeroy and Dayton. A number of lakes in the refuge are popular summertime fishing venues (see Fishing, above). The area is managed by the state Department of Fish and Wildlife; (509) 456-4082.

Even farther afield is Chief Joseph Wildlife Area, a beautiful canyon site along the Grande Ronde River—about as far southeast as you can go in Washington State. This remote canyon, a former winter camp of the Nez Perce, is a wintering area for Blue Mountains mule deer and Rocky Mountain elk. **Raptors,** quail, **partridge,** and **bluebirds** often are spotted on the cliffs in the spring. From Asotin, follow Snake River Rd to Joseph Creek Rd—and just keep going until you run out of state.

The Walla Walla Valley in general is fine bird habitat, with more than 300 species documented. Watch for **yellow warblers** and **spotted towhees** along creeks in the spring, many migratory birds in the summer, and rarities like the **sharp-tailed sandpiper, parasitic jaeger,** and **boreal owl** in the fall. Other rare species spotted in the county include **peregrine falcon** and **cattle egret.**

Nearer to civilization, Whitman Mission National Historic Site, east of Walla Walla, is a designated wildlife site. A trail to the top of Whitman Memorial Hill often affords glimpses of **red-tailed hawks, pheasants,** quail, or **harriers.** Follow signs from US 12 west of Walla Walla. Also within Walla Walla County, birders can do their thing at a number of bird hangouts: Two Rivers Habitat Management Unit, Hod Park, Coppei Creek drainage south of Waitsburg, Rooks Park-Bennington Lake, Fort Walla Walla Museum Natural Area and Park in Walla Walla, and the Touchet/Gardena area.

Accessible Outdoors

Lewis and Clark Trail State Park has an accessible picnic shelter. The William T. Wooten Wildlife Area offers accessible viewing of game birds and deer, elk, and sheep.

outside in

Restaurants

Merchants Ltd. ★★   A mainstay since 1976, Merchants seats 300 and serves healthy meals. *$; 21 E Main St, Walla Walla; 509/525-0900.* &

Paisano's Italian Restaurant & Catering ★☆ Paisano's serves tasty, generous portions in a sophisticated setting. *$$; 26 E Main St, Ste 1, Walla Walla; 509/527-3511.* &

Patit Creek Restaurant ★★★ A small-town restaurant with a highly rated atmosphere and sophisticated food. *$$; 725 E Dayton Ave, Dayton; 509/382-2625.* &

Lodgings

Green Gables Inn ★★ Five rooms celebrate the spirit of the popular Anne of Green Gables books. *$$; 922 Bonsella St, Walla Walla; 888/525-5501; www.greengablesinn.com.*

The Purple House B&B Inn This 1882 house really is purple. The four rooms have modern amenities. *$$–$$$; 415 E Clay St, Dayton; 800/486-2574.* &

The Weinhard Hotel ★ The restored Weinhard is a pleasant surprise: uptown style in tiny Dayton. *$$–$$$; 235 E Main St, Dayton; 509/382-4032; www.weinhard.com.* &

More Information

General Walla Walla region (includes on-line onion ordering in July and early August): *www.wallawallawa.com.*

Pete's Ski and Sports (outdoor gear and rentals): *124 E Main Street, Walla Walla; (509) 529-9804 or (888) 429-9804.*

Umatilla National Forest, Pomeroy Ranger District: *(509) 843-1891.*

Umatilla National Forest, Walla Walla Ranger District: *(509) 522-6290.*

Walla Walla Valley Chamber of Commerce: *(877) WW VISIT or (509) 525-0850; www.wwchamber.com.*

Snake River Country: Clarkston, Pullman, and the Palouse

From Clarkston north to the town of Palouse and west to Kahlotus, including the city of Pullman, the Snake River Canyon, and Palouse Falls, Lyons Ferry, Central Ferry, Steptoe Butte, and Chief Timothy State Parks.

And the wind blows. Man, does it blow. Has for a long, long time, which pretty much explains the great piles of dirt that form the rolling, wheat-growing hills of the Palouse. This loose volcanic dirt—or loess, as it's known to geologists—has been carried by thousands of years of southwesterly winds from the Columbia Plateau to here, the Evergreen State's big brown dumping ground.

In a state known for its greens and blues, that's not much of a recommendation. Yet the Palouse—as the collective hilly area is known (ironically, it's a derivation of the French *pelouse*, which means "short, thick grass")—is beautiful in its own right. The broad, rolling hills are unique, sort of a not-so-badlands. The superbly rich soil grows thousands of annual barge-loads of wheat and legumes. Without the Palouse, we'd all be short on grass seed and lentils in no time. And nobody wants that.

Not surprisingly, most Palouse recreationists are out to beat the heat, and the best refuge is along the water. There's a lot more of it here to go around than there used to be, thanks to a series of dams built on the Snake River between the Tri-Cities and Lewiston, Idaho, from the late 1960s through the 1970s. Lower Granite, Little Goose, Lower Monumental, and Ice Harbor Dams were built to do something that only a creative federal government would have thought possible (or necessary): turn Lewiston, Idaho, into a seaport. In the process, the dams also have largely choked off some of the Northwest's most magnificent steelhead and salmon stocks. These fish once migrated hundreds of miles to the Pacific via the Columbia River, then all the way back, surviving even the gauntlet of dams on the lower Columbia to return and spawn in Idaho streams such as the upper Snake, Clearwater, and Salmon Rivers. The Snake River dams have nearly put an end to that. Snake River chinook salmon now are a federally protected species—probably too late to save them. That fact has finally been recognized in recent years by scientists, who now say breaching the four Snake River dams is perhaps the only chance to save several salmon stocks. But dam supporters—which include a large number of local residents, who rely on them for commerce—argue that it's already too late to save the fish. Stay tuned, but don't get your hopes up for long-term survival of the Snake River salmon, one of the more extraordinary creatures in the Northwest—and perhaps, unfortunately, an indicator species for the lifestyle that grew up around wild Western rivers.

The fish's loss has in some ways been recreation's gain. Not a good tradeoff, perhaps. But the wealth of water behind the dams has been something of a boon to state-parks planners, who have developed a string of waterfront parks and recreation areas in the floodplain. Still, it's fair to say there's not a lot here for the avid outdoorsperson. It's a good area to roll through once, twice, or thrice, just to see it. But once you're done exploring the area's highlight—waterfront parks in the dam-flooded Snake River Canyon—the Palouse becomes just a long stretch of road on the way to somewhere else.

None of which should be construed to mean we don't like the place, which has its own charming shrub-steppe beauty. It's just that we still haven't quite recovered from an initial visit to the Palouse, an occasion on which we drove for what seemed like 4 or 5 days, arrived near Pullman, got out of the car, looked around, and asked: "This is it?"

It was. It is. It ever shall be. Until the really big southwesterly kicks up and moves it all over to Central Idaho.

Getting There

Pullman, the spiritual if not geographical heartland of the Palouse, is 288 miles southwest of Seattle via Interstate 90 and Highway 26 at Vantage. It's a long day's drive that sometimes feels like two. For quick trippers, it's only 76 miles south of Spokane via US Highway 195, where major airlines can get you from Seattle in less than an hour.

inside out

Camping/Picnics/Swimming

You'll see lots of boat trailers and swim fins at **Central Ferry State Park,** which fronts on the Snake River and draws many boaters and water-sports fans: spaces here often are reserved well in advance. The park is built specifically to take advantage of Lake Bryan, the large waterway created by Little Goose Dam on the Snake River. Two basins were dug to protect moored boats from occasionally nasty winds that whip through the river gorge. The campground has 68 sites (60 with full hookups; RVs to 45 feet), supplemented by four boat launches, three moorage floats, sewer dumps for boats and RVs, a bathhouse, a swimming area, and 48—count 'em—waterfront picnic sites, many with protection from sun and wind. There's also a group campsite near the picnic area. The campground will probably be most pleasurable to RVers, especially those who snag sites in loops 2 through 5—those closest to the water. Tents are OK, too, though. Stake 'em down tight, or you might wake up in Washtucna! Central Ferry is open mid-March through mid-November. Campsites can be reserved up to 11 months in advance by calling Reservations Northwest; (800) 452-5687. *On Hwy 127 about 17 miles south of Dusty (on Hwy 26) and 34 miles southwest of downtown Colfax; (509) 549-3551 or (800) 233-0321.*

Similar in character is **Lyons Ferry State Park,** which sits on a point at the confluence of the Palouse and Snake Rivers. As at Central Ferry, the boat that used to cross the wide river here was long ago replaced by a bridge. Unlike Central Ferry, however, the old, current-propelled Lyons Ferry is still here, tied up on shore, where it serves as a fishing pier and historical display. The park bearing its name lies on either side of the north end of the Lyons Ferry Bridge on Hwy 261. On the west side is a plain, poorly landscaped campground with 52 campsites (no hookups). Not exactly a garden spot, but it'd do for an overnight spot, particularly if you're in an RV. In addition to the old ferry, the much nicer day-use area features a long spit of land (a ridge top, before dams flooded the valley) jutting into the lake, providing a wealth of good waterfront picnic spots. Farther south are more picnic grounds, a swimming beach, and a boat launch. At the north end of the day-use area, a trail leads about a mile up on a bluff to a canyon overlook, where you'll find historical information about Marmes Rock Shelter, an ancient Palouse Indian burial cave below here, now flooded by the lake waters. Before the flooding, archaeologists discovered human remains carbon-dated to 10,000 years ago. For a time they were considered the oldest human remains on the continent. Lyons

Ferry is open April through September. Campsites cannot be reserved. *On Hwy 261, 7 miles north of Starbuck, 23 miles southeast of Washtucna (on Hwy 26); (509) 646-3252 or (800) 233-0321.*

Camping facilities are very limited at **Palouse Falls State Park,** but don't let that deter you from visiting. The 200-foot waterfall is one of Washington's most spectacular natural sights, plunging from a half-circle of wall-like columnar basalt into a deep pool. The falls are at their peak in the spring (usually late March), when the Palouse River is at high flow. The prolific spray at the bottom often forms a rainbow, making this a photographer's dream. The falls are believed to have been formed by the same prehistoric floods that carved other Eastern Washington features such as the Grand Coulee. The park does have 10 primitive campsites, but is used most often as a day-use picnic area. Several hiking trails fan out along the cliffs (see Hiking, below). Palouse Falls is open all year. Campsites cannot be reserved. *16 miles northwest of Starbuck via Hwy 261 and Palouse Falls Rd; (509) 549-3551 or (800) 233-0321.*

Chief Timothy State Park west of Clarkston is another "waterworld." It sits on an island in Lower Granite Lake, another Snake River dam-formed impoundment. The proximity of the island to the shore creates a nicely protected waterway—an ideal swimming and water-play area made even better by a broad, flat, sandy beach. The day-use area has shaded picnic sites, playground equipment, a bathhouse, four boat launches, and ample moorage. The campground offers 66 campsites (33 with hookups; RVs of any length) split into three camping loops. The nearby interpretive center tells about Alpowai, an old Nez Perce village here (Timothy was a Nez Perce chief), followed by the old pioneer town of Silcott, which, like many other Snake River historical sites, now lies beneath the lake waters. Chief Timothy State Park is open all year. Campsites can be reserved up to 11 months in advance by calling Reservations Northwest; (800) 452-5687. *On Silcott Rd just off US 12, 8 miles west of Clarkston; (509) 758-9580 or (800) 233-0321.*

In the Clarkston area, alternate camping is available at **Wawawai County Park,** on Lower Granite Lake 30 miles northwest of Clarkston, and at **Blyton Landing** and **Nisqually John Landing,** two Corps of Engineers sites 19 miles and 14 miles northwest of Clarkston, respectively. To reach all of them, cross Red Wolf Bridge at the north end of 15th Street in Clarkston and turn left onto on Rd 9000 (Hwy 193).

Private campgrounds around Pullman include the city's Pullman RV Park, S Street; (509) 334-4555, which has decent RV spots in the summer. **Kamiak Butte County Park** (see Hiking, below), 10 miles north on Hwy 27, also has camping; (509) 397-3791.

Boating/Canoeing/Kayaking

The **Snake River Canyon,** dammed into a series of large, welcoming lakes (see Camping/Picnics/Swimming, above), provides ample waters for boating and paddling. All of the lakes are broad enough for waterskiing. The best access points are the state parks listed above.

For a wilder, truly memorable river trip, don't overlook a boat trip down spectacular, 6,500-foot-deep **Hells Canyon,** which delineates the Oregon-Idaho border south of Clarkston. The canyon isn't technically a canyon at all; it's a river gorge, and the deepest one on the planet. While most of Hells Canyon is not in Washington, Clarkston and nearby Lewiston are the most common departure points for the dozens of outfitters that explore the canyon via single- or multi-day jet-boat, dory, raft, or kayak trips on the Snake River. **Guide services** tend to come and go, so for a list of qualified outfitters, contact the dual Hells Canyon National Recreation Area and Wallowa-Whitman National Forest headquarters in Enterprise, Oregon (503) 426-4978; or contact the Clarkston Chamber of Commerce (see More Information, below).

For canoeists, a popular day trip can be made by launching at Lyons Ferry State Park and paddling upstream several miles to the site of the flooded Marmes Rock Shelter (see Camping/Picnics/Swimming, above), where 10,000-year-old cremated human remains were discovered before the valley was flooded by dams.

Photography

Palouse Falls (see Camping/Picnics/Swimming, above) is a natural feature no serious landscape photographer should miss. The highest water volumes are during the spring melt-off, and the best shooting times for the west-facing falls are in the morning. The **Palouse** itself can be photographed from many roadside vistas, and is particularly impressive in the spring, when sprouting wheat creates multi-level, multi-hued green rolling hills.

The best—and probably only—broad, territorial view is found at **Steptoe Butte State Park,** a day-use park about 30 miles northwest of Pullman, just east of US 195. This big hunk of granite is one of very few to survive the lava flows, floods, and hellacious winds that stripped most of this region clean between 10 million and 20 million years ago. Rocks from the butte are hundreds of millions of years old, suggesting it's the sole survivor of an old mountain range (perhaps all that remains here of the Selkirk Range) predating the relatively new, 15- to 20-million-year-old volcanic basalt that overlays the rest of the area. Today, the 3,600-foot butte stands 1,000 feet taller than anything within sight, providing an amazing 360-degree view of the Palouse, the Blue Mountains to the south, and even the Bitterroots of Idaho. The butte, which also is a popular hang-gliding and kite-flying spot, was named for U.S. Army Colonel E. J. Steptoe, who was defeated in an 1858 battle nearby with a local tribe. Geological trivia department: Thanks to the local tribes' choice of places to defeat Steptoe, the colonel's name lives on not only here, but in geology texts everywhere. "Steptoe" now is an accepted geological term for a remnant rock formation surviving amid a new one.

Hiking

Hiking trails are a relative rarity in Palouse Country, where most locals are too busy farming and most tourists are bound for greener climes to the north near Spokane, or to the south, where the Blue Mountains beckon. Palouse Falls State Park, however, has a small trail system worthy of cautious exploration. An **unmaintained path** skirts around the west side of the massive plunge pool, offering the best views of the 198-foot waterfall and the fascinating, castlelike columnar basalt forming the vertical walls of the splash basin. The trail peters out after about half a mile. Use extreme caution here; the trail skirts to the cliffs very closely, and there's no guardrail. A second reason to watch your step: rattlesnakes are common in the area—sometimes even in the parking lot. Definitely not a good walk for kids, dogs, or adults under the influence of excessive caffeine! Other trails lead down **into the canyon** itself. Prudent—make that even minimally rational—hikers will avoid them.

An interesting trail for natural history lovers is the **Marmes Rock Shelter path** (see Lyons Ferry in Camping/Picnics/Swimming, above). A longer trail (about 2 miles), though unmaintained, follows the river to the upper Marmes site itself. The site is easier to reach via the river, however (see Boating/Canoeing/Kayaking, above).

If you're stuck in—er, have the good fortune to be spending some time in—Pullman, the best trees/view hiking option is 10 miles away on the **Pine Ridge Trail** (moderate; 7 miles round trip), which climbs to the top of 3,360-foot Kamiak Butte, a sister formation to nearby and better-known Steptoe Butte (see Photography, above). The trailhead is within Kamiak Butte County Park, about 10 miles north of Pullman on Hwy 27.

It's not technically part of the Palouse, but the 7-mile, wheelchair-accessible **Clearwater and Snake River National Recreation Trail** (aka **Snake River Bikeway**) from Beachview Park in Clarkston to Chief Looking Glass Park near Asotin has many scenic views, including ancient Swallow's Nest Rock, a basalt cliff that—you guessed it—is a primary swallow nesting ground. The path, which runs along both sides of the river, was built by the Corps of Engineers in 1988—one mitigating effort for the creation of the Lower Granite Dam.

Wildlife Watching

Palouse Falls (see Hiking and Camping/Picnics/Swimming, above) also is a noted wildlife area. **Golden eagles, falcons, hawks,** and other raptors often are seen in the canyon below the falls. All the dams on the Snake River are fitted with fish ladders, and the best viewing area is at Lower Monumental Dam south of Kahlotus. Spring **chinook** pass through here—keep your fingers crossed—in April and May. The fall chinook run peaks in September, and **steelhead** are often seen passing in September and October. The fish-ladder viewing room is open all year, with hours that vary according to the season; (509) 547-7781.

Kamiak Butte County Park (see Hiking, above) is a productive bird-watching site, as is Swallow's Nest Rock south of Clarkston (see Hiking, above). Across the border, the Lewiston Levee ponds, behind the dike along the Clearwater River upstream from its confluence with the Snake, are a welcome stopover for migratory waterfowl and home to resident **Canada geese** and **mallards.** Visit here in the winter to see **pintails, wood ducks, coots, buffleheads,** and others. This area is accessible from the Clearwater and Snake River National Recreation Trail (see Hiking, above.) Also on this side of the river is the Lewiston Wildlife Habitat Area, a 7-acre Idaho Fish and Game wildlife habitat and natural classroom. The self-guided, wheelchair-accessible tour starts behind the Fish and Game office at 16th Street and Warner Avenue; (208) 799-5010. No pets!

Fishing

The Palouse is a dry spot when it comes to almost everything, but it's really a dry spot in the fishing world. The one exception is the Snake River downstream from Clarkston. The deep lakes created by the river's four dams provide decent **bass, perch,** and **crappie** fishing, and many anglers fish at night for **channel catfish.** Trolling for **steelhead** also can be productive, and a few **sturgeon** are caught in the lakes.

Cycling

This is hot, lonely country for cycling, but a relative dearth of traffic on Palouse roads makes it grand touring territory for devoted distance cyclists. A popular 24-mile racing route, the **Tour of the Palouse,** begins at Palouse, follows Hwy 27 south to Clear Creek Rd, then turns right and proceeds to Hwy 272, which can be followed east back to Palouse.

Another route favored by local cyclists is the **Pullman–Snake River**

Loop. The 79-mile tour begins west of Pullman at Wawawai-Pullman Rd at US 195, follows Wawawai-Pullman Rd south and west to the Snake River Canyon, which is followed upstream to the Clearwater Bridge (near the Snake River confluence) and US 12 at Lewiston, Idaho. The route then recrosses the Clearwater, climbs steeply up Lewiston Hill on Old Lewiston Grade, then turns north on US 195 and returns to Pullman. It's a gasser, but the scenery is fine, particularly along the long central Snake River Canyon portion.

In Clarkston, the **Clearwater and Snake River National Recreation Trail** (see Hiking, above) provides a pleasant, low-impact ride along the Snake River. From the boat launch north of the US 12 bridge, the paved path runs 7 miles south to Chief Looking Glass Park in Asotin, passing through Chestnut Street Park and Swallows Park along the way. Or, cross the river and ride the Lewiston portion of the trail, the Lewiston Levee Parkway, which runs from 18th Street to First Street.

Accessible Outdoors

The **Clearwater and Snake River National Recreation Trail** is wheel-chair-accessible. **Chief Timothy State Park** has barrier-free campsites and limited shore access.

outside in

Restaurants

Hilltop Restaurant   This steak house has a romantic vista complemented by attentive service. $$; 920 Olson St, Pullman; 509/334-2555.

Swilly's Cafe & Catering ★★   Casual warmth translates into homemade soups, salads, sandwiches, and burgers. $; 200 NE Kamiaken St, Pullman; 509/334-3395. &

Lodgings

The Churchyard Inn B&B ★   This house was once a parish, later a convent; now it's a three-story B&B. $$–$$$; 206 St. Boniface St, Uniontown; 509/229-3200; pullman-wa.com/housing/chrchbb.htm. &

Paradise Creek Quality Inn   Within walking distance of WSU, this convenient motel has 66 standard rooms. $; 1050 SE Bishop Blvd, Pullman; 800/669-3212; www.qualityinn.com.

More Information

Clarkston Chamber of Commerce: *(509) 758-7712;*
   www.clarkstonchamber.org.

General Lewiston/Clarkston information: *www.lctoday.net.*

Hells Canyon National Recreation Area: *(541) 426-4978;*
   www.fs.fed.us/r6/w-w/hcnra.htm.

Pullman Chamber of Commerce: *(800) 365-6948;*
   www.pullman-wa.com.

Index